STRUCTURAL DESIGN FOR THE STAGE

STRUCTURAL DESIGN FOR THE STAGE

Alys E. Holden
Bronislaw J. Sammler

Focal Press

An Imprint of Elsevier

Boston Oxford Auckland Johannesburg Melbourne New Delhi

Focal Press is an imprint of Elseiver.

A member of the Reed Elsevier group

Recognizing the importance of preserving what has been written, Elsevier prints its books on acid-free paper whenever possible.

GLOBAL ReLeaf Elsevier supports the efforts of American Forests and the Global ReLeaf program in its campaign for the betterment of trees, forests, and our environment.

Library of Congress Cataloging-in-Publication Data
Holden, Alys E. (Alys Elaine), 1971–
    Structural design for the stage / Alys E. Holden, Bronislaw
Sammler.
        p.   cm.
    Includes bibliographical references and index.
      ISBN-13: 978-0-240-80354-8   ISBN-10: 0-240-80354-X (pbk. : alk. paper)
        1. Structural design.   2. Theaters--Stage-setting and scenery-
-Design and construction.   3. Theaters--Design and construction.
    I. Sammler, Bronislaw (Bronislaw Joseph), 1945– .   II. Title.
    TA658.2.H65   1999
    725'.83--dc21   98-53570
                                                                  CIP

British Library Cataloguing-in-Publication Data
A catalogue record for this book is available from the British Library.

The publisher offers special discounts on bulk orders of this book.
For information, please contact:
Manager of Special Sales
Butterworth–Heinemann
225 Wildwood Avenue
Woburn, MA 01801-2041
Tel: 781-904-2500
Fax: 781-904-2620

For information on all Butterworth-Heinemann publications available, contact our World Wide Web home page at: http://www.bh.com

11 10 9 8 7 6

Printed in the United States of America

To

Cosmo & George

———◆———

Laraine

Contents

Preface

This text is intended for theater technicians who are serious about their craft - the art of creating technical solutions for theatrical designs within a collaborative environment. Having said that, it is not our intention to suggest that there is only one appropriate structural solution to each design, and that it can be tabulated on the pages of this text. It is our intention to introduce the reader to the basics of statics and the study of the strength of materials, providing a foundation in structural design for an intuitive understanding of "why sets stand up". This foundation will allow technical designers to explore solutions and employ many materials and construction techniques.

The authors do not have degrees in engineering and have written this text for non-engineers that face small scale structural dilemmas in the course of their work. To that end, the material is presented with a minimum of theory, many scenic examples, and requires only a basic knowledge of algebra, geometry, and trigonometry. When faced with large scale structural problems or life threatening situations that require a professional engineer, the reader will gain the ability to accurately describe the productions' objectives in terms that an engineer will understand.

This text - *Structural Design for the Stage* - and the course for which it was written has evolved over the past twenty-five years at the Yale School of Drama with the help of many former Technical Design and Production alumni. The authors would like to acknowledge those who have contributed to that evolution.

> Tony Straiges, for designing a three story set for *Women Beware Women* in 1973 that posed structural challenges, inspiring research which continued well after the set was struck.

> Rick Silvestro, who did the initial research for *Women Beware Women* and pioneered a course in Structural Design in 1974.

> Bob McClintock contributed to the body of knowledge with his research.

> Bill Buck, without the aid of a computer, produced a much needed structural design workbook which served as the text from 1985 to 1997.

Cosmo Catalano was amongst the first classes to take the course in 1976/77, and read and reread drafts of the current text in 1996 and 1997.

The Yale School of Drama TD&P class of 2000 - the first class to use a draft of this text - for helping to catch innumerable errors.

And, finally, it would be inappropriate if we did not also acknowledge all of the students who asked questions that deserved to be answered.

In the course of the research and compilation of the appendices, many individuals and organizations went out of their way to smooth our path. We would like to thank: Robert Glowinski of the American Forest and Paper Association for his help and advice; Tim Andrassy and the Steel Tube Institute of North America for his enthusiasm and willingness to allow us to reprint entire publications; Marilyn LeMoine, Mary Trodden, and the *APA - The Engineered Wood Association* - not only granted us permission to reprint the plywood design tables, but also sent us their electronic files, saving countless hours of data entry; the Wire Rope Technical Board, the International Conference of Building Officials, W.W. Norton & Company, Broadway Press, and Industrial Press for granting us permission to reproduce various materials.

1

Overview

PURPOSE

Theatrical technical design and carpentry are rooted in a craft-based tradition which places a high value on empirically tested techniques. Consequently, structural engineering techniques are rarely applied to scenery construction, though it may often be desirable. Structural design provides a basis for improving empirical techniques by maximizing efficiency and/or thinness, minimizing weight, etc. In those cases where there is no empirical solution, a technical designer can feel as if he or she is attempting to design in a vacuum, with no foundation from which to work. A firm foundation in structural engineering allows a technical designer to explore viable alternatives as well as providing paradigms for thinking about structural systems.

The best argument for the value of structural engineering is an example of its failure. In *Why Buildings Fall Down*, Matthys Levy and Mario Salvadori describe the "worst structural disaster in the United States." In 1980, at the brand new Hyatt Regency in Kansas City, Missouri, two suspended walkways, one underneath the other, suddenly collapsed, killing 114 people and injuring 200 others (Levy, 224). After extensive investigation, the fundamental cause of the collapse is easy to understand. In the original design, both walkways were suspended from the ceiling by a series of continuous rods. The upper walkway was held up by one nut and one washer at the bottom of its box beams as illustrated in Figure 1.1.

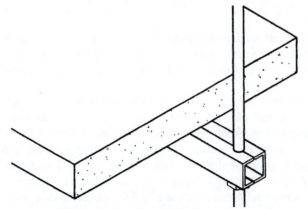

Figure 1.1 Concept of original design, upper walkway

To simplify construction, the contractor suggested that the rod be discontinuous, and the architects and engineers stamped the change as illustrated in Figure 1.2.

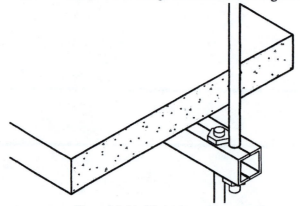

Figure 1.2 Modified design of upper walkway

The modification required that the box beams of the upper walkway, originally designed to support only its pedestrian traffic, also support the lower walkway and its corresponding pedestrian traffic. The failure load, which was, ironically, much lower than the design load for total occupancy, caused the nut and washer to pull through the upper box beam, sending both walkways crashing to the ground. Though the original design was obviously stronger than the modification, subsequent investigations revealed that even it did not meet the design load required by the Kansas City Building Code. Ultimately, in addition to the loss of life and suffering, the accident cost three billion dollars in settlements, and cost the principal engineer and project manager of the engineering firm their licenses. Fortunately, the consequences of most structural failures in theater are not so extreme.

As theatrical designers, two important lessons can be learned from the Hyatt Regency disaster. First it is easy to see how the temptation to reduce "load-in" time prompted the request to use discontinuous rods. The success or failure of a structural system is dependent on its being designed, built, and installed properly. Second, neither the original design nor the modification provided any redundancy. It is always a good idea to design a system which is **single failure proof**, i.e., no single failure should be able to lead to a disastrous series of failures. Accidents may happen, but a firm understanding of structural design can help prevent them.

The goal of modern structural engineering is to develop a mathematical model which can predict the success or failure of a real-life system or member. This is not, however, an inherently mathematical process, which Levy and Salvadori (Levy, 14) express best:

> Structural behavior can be understood by the uninitiated on the basis of physical intuition and without appeal to physics or mathematics simply because whatever the structural system – the steel frame of an office building or the dome of a church – whatever the materials used in construction – steel, wood, reinforced concrete, or stone – and whatever the forces acting on it – caused by gravity, wind, earthquake, temperature changes, or uneven settlements of the soil – the elements of a structure can react to these forces only by being *pulled* or *pushed*.

This text will appear to emphasize mathematics, but we urge you not to lose sight of the forest for the trees. It is more vital to *understand* a structure then it is to analyze it. The end goal of this text is three fold: (1) to provide the basis of an intuitive understanding of "why sets stand up"; (2) to be a reference book for professional technicians who face small scale structural dilemmas; and (3) to enable informed conversations between theatrical technicians and professional engineers. It is rare to find an engineer who also understands theatrical scenery and its requirements. As technical designers, we are responsible for bridging this communication gap.

CONTENTS

This text attempts to introduce the basics of **statics** and the study of the **strength of materials** as they apply to typical theatrical scenarios. To that end, the text is relatively heavy with "how-to" theatrical examples and is relatively light on theory. A large portion is devoted to explicating existing engineering specifications written by various governing agencies. Where appropriate, conservative simplifications are incorporated.

Structural design is fundamentally a process of (1) determining how a system will react to external forces and (2) determining the capacity of the system to resist those forces. The study of statics is the first step of the process and is the study of systems which are stable and are not subject to acceleration. Basic statics is addressed in Chapters 2 and 3. The impact of the cross-sectional characteristics of structural members is discussed in Chapter 4, Geometric Properties. Chapters 5 through 10 incorporate strength of materials for steel and wood with an introduction to beam and column design. Chapter 11 introduces a method for analyzing two-dimensional trusses as well as methods for the structural design of cable systems. The strength characteristics of plywood and the design of plywood structures, including stressed-skin panels, are explored in Chapter 12.

Appendices A through H provide vital data to which the reader will need to refer frequently. Appendix A provides a review of the basics of algebra, geometry, and trigonometry necessary to follow along with the examples. Appendices B and C include formulas which are introduced in Chapters 3 and 4 respectively. These formulas form the foundation for material presented in every chapter thereafter. Appendices D, E, and F contain sawn lumber, steel, and plywood design values and geometric properties needed for the chapters which present design procedures utilizing these materials. Like the examples throughout the text, the data has been limited to smaller structural members which are usually found in theatrical scenery construction. Appendix G contains useful information that applies generally to structural design. Appendix H contains a complete list of all "terms and symbols" with their definitions, which represent the variables throughout the text. Lastly, Appendix I lists the answers to the even numbered problems in the lessons found at the end of each chapter.

Since examples are such an important component of the text, it is important that the reader be able to verify intermediate steps as well as the final solution. Intermediate solutions which may appear to be slightly off have been calculated with the full value of intermediate numbers, though they may be shortened in the text. In short, when performing calculations necessary to solve example problems, do not round off beyond that which your calculator will do automatically.

The original goal of this text was to provide graduate level theatrical technicians with a comprehensive textbook. Consequently, it is designed to be taught linearly, that is, the course begins with Chapter 1 and ends with Chapter 12, and requires two to three semesters of class time. Because the vagaries of academic schedules and individual students may make such an approach inappropriate, it may be helpful to note that the text is composed of six parts. The first part is the study of statics and geometric properties, Chapters 1 through 4, and is a necessary prerequisite to all of the other chapters. Sawn lumber design, Chapters 5 through 7, can be taught independently of steel design, Chapters 8 through 10. Similarly, Chapter 11, cables and trusses, can be taught independently of the sawn lumber and steel sections, but is more complete if taught after them. Finally, Chapter 12, plywood design, is independent of Chapters 5 through 11. A suggested two semester course would include Chapters 1–6, 8, 9, and 11. The third semester would therefore comprise of combined loading for wood and steel members and plywood design, Chapters 7, 10, and 12.

Regardless of the order in which they are taught, each chapter includes a set of lessons at its end. Each lesson lists a page number and a topic(s) indicating the material covered in it. Each lesson is essentially what we judge to be one lecture, assuming that the class time is approximately one hour. As mentioned previously, the answers to the even numbered problems are given in Appendix I, though no intermediate steps are shown.

SCOPE
This text is designed to be a tool for students and qualified professors alike. Though extensive, it does not exhaustively treat the full scope of structural engineering. We do not cover every material choice or manufactured product available. For example, aluminum, manufactured joists, and glue-laminated beams are not discussed. This is not to discourage the use of such materials. Manufactured products are not included because their load capacity is already well-documented by their manufacturers. In addition, we do not discuss connection details because they merit an entire text by themselves. It should be noted that the general structural considerations of connection details are no different from those discussed, but the specific requirements of connection details are quite different.

The basics included in this text can be expanded upon by reading more about structural design, taking advanced courses, and discussing structural issues with other theater professionals. The "concept boxes" which appear throughout the text are meant to highlight interesting issues which merit further thought. Learning the concepts and techniques of structural design is a lifetime endeavor; this course is simply the first step.

2

Forces, Stresses, and Strains

INTRODUCTION

The first step in understanding any science is to learn its language. Like other specializations, technical theater has a unique vocabulary incomprehensible to most lay people. Blank stares and puzzled looks are common reactions when a technician discusses very simple items such as "flats," "keystones," "crosbys," etc. These terms are not hard to understand once they've been defined. Structural design, like technical theater, has its own specialized vocabulary, one which is not especially difficult to understand, and which makes the discussion of ideas easier by assigning names to well-understood concepts. This vocabulary lets structural designers get to the root of a problem without getting lost in trivial details.

This chapter defines many of the basic terms pertaining to structural design. Though at first glance these definitions may seem unrelated, the remaining chapters will provide a framework which shows how they are linked.

FORCES

DEFINITIONS

A **force** is a push or pull. Newton's Second Law states that a net force acting on an object tends to move the object in the direction of the force. This tendency is called **translation**. The **magnitude, line of action, direction**, and **sense** must be specified for a force to be completely defined.

- **Magnitude,** or the quantity of a force, is usually measured in pounds or kips (one kip is 1,000 pounds) in the U.S. and is an absolute value.

- The **line of action** of a force is its straight-line path both before and after it.

- The **direction** of a force is the relationship between its line of action and a reference line, such as a horizontal or vertical line.

- The **sense** of a force is positive or negative and refers to the way in which the force acts along its line of action. Each direction has two possible senses. For example, a horizontal force can act to the right or left. By convention, forces acting up or to the right are positive, and forces acting down or to the left are negative.

Graphically, this text will represent forces as arrows with the following parts: the magnitude of the force is indicated near the arrow; a dashed line before and after the arrow represents its line of action; the direction is indicated by an angle measurement to a vertical or horizontal reference line, and the arrow head indicates its sense (see Figure 2.1). Magnitude can also be indicated by drawing the length of the arrow in scale relative to the other forces and distances in the system.

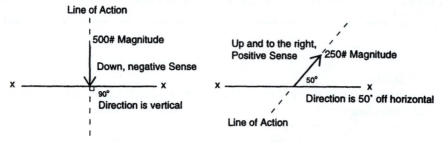

Figure 2.1 Parts of a force

To simplify calculations involving forces, all diagonal forces are resolved into vertical and horizontal component forces using trigonometry. Any diagonal force (or vector) is the resultant of the addition of a vertical and a horizontal force. In calculations, the diagonal force is considered to be the hypotenuse of a right triangle, and the component forces are the two legs. Since one angle is 90° and another is given, the unknown angle can be determined, and the magnitudes of the components can be calculated using the *sine*, *cosine*, or the *tangent* of the angles (see Figure 2.2). For more mathematical review, see Appendix A.

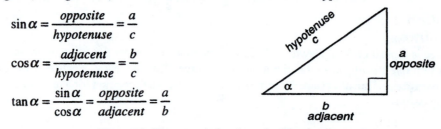

$$\sin \alpha = \frac{opposite}{hypotenuse} = \frac{a}{c}$$

$$\cos \alpha = \frac{adjacent}{hypotenuse} = \frac{b}{c}$$

$$\tan \alpha = \frac{\sin \alpha}{\cos \alpha} = \frac{opposite}{adjacent} = \frac{a}{b}$$

Figure 2.2 Trigonometric functions of a right triangle

For convenience, vertical and horizontal components of a diagonal force are represented with dashed lines which are drawn head to tail to each other. When drawing components, start at the tail of the force and end with a component arrow pointing to the head of the force (see Figure 2.3).

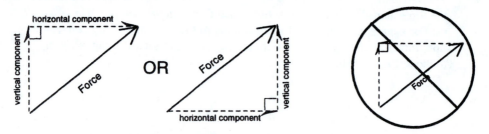

Figure 2.3 Components of a force

Example 1. What are the magnitudes and senses of the vertical and horizontal components of the following force?

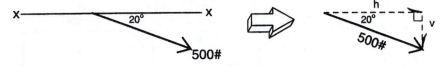

Figure 2.4 Example 1

To find the magnitude of the vertical component, solve for *v*:

$$\sin 20° = \frac{opp}{hyp} = \frac{v}{500\#} \Rightarrow v = (0.3420)500\# = 171\#$$

To find the magnitude of the horizontal component, solve for *h*:

$$\cos 20° = \frac{adj}{hyp} = \frac{h}{500\#} \Rightarrow h = (0.9397)500\# = 470\#$$

CENTER OF GRAVITY

Every object has a point (defined in all three dimensions) around which it will naturally pivot. This point is called its **center of gravity**. The center of gravity of an object is the point where, if a single force acts at that point, only translation (straight line motion) of that object will occur (see Fig. 2.5).

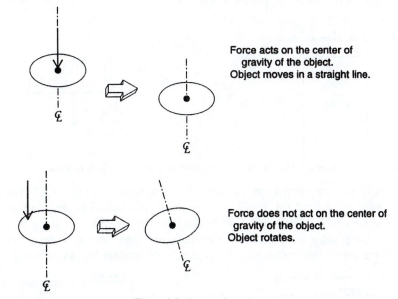

Force acts on the center of gravity of the object. Object moves in a straight line.

Force does not act on the center of gravity of the object. Object rotates.

Figure 2.5 Center of gravity

In structural design, the concept of center of gravity is used to transform distributed loads into point loads. The distributed load is represented by a point load whose line of action passes through its center of gravity. If the load is *evenly* distributed, its center of gravity will be its geometric center (see Figure 2.6).

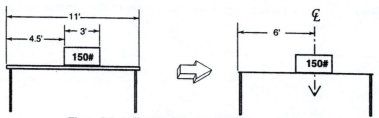

Figure 2.6 A distributed load represented as a point load

A force may be concentrated or widely distributed. For example, a woman standing on a deck is a relatively concentrated force because all of her weight is acting on the deck through the small areas of her feet. If the woman laid down on the deck, the same amount of force would be acting on the deck, but it would be distributed over the length of her body.

FREE BODY DIAGRAMS

The second drawing in Figure 2.6 is the beginning of a **free body diagram**. Since drawing out complete details of a structure every time a simple calculation is required would quickly become tedious, structural designers use a kind of short hand. A free body diagram is a simplified sketch of the structural system under consideration, showing the distances between forces. Typically, the construction and loading details are represented by line drawings so that the relationships between them are easy to see. A free body diagram attempts to isolate the member in question. For example, a standard pipe batten supporting a flat can be diagrammed as shown in Figure 2.7. The upward arrows represent four lift lines and the downward arrows represent the weight of the flat.

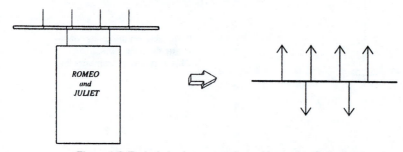

Figure 2.7 Typical pipe batten transformed into a free body diagram

Structural problems are often more complex than that shown in Figure 2.7. For example, consider a platform legged up from the stage floor. The beams in the platform must be designed for the evenly distributed load of the deck itself while the stage floor must be designed for the point loads created by the platform's legs. In this situation, several free body diagrams would need to be drawn to represent the system (see Figure 2.8).

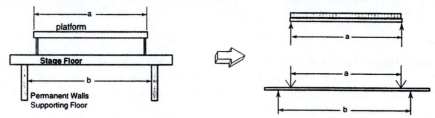

Figure 2.8 A typical deck system transformed into a free body diagram

Example 2. Draw a free body diagram for one of several beams of a platform. The beams of the platform span 8' between legs. Each beam supports an evenly distributed load of 100 plf and a 50 lb boom base 3' from one end.

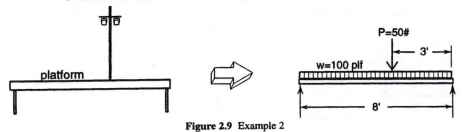

Figure 2.9 Example 2

RIGIDITY

When structural designers draw free body diagrams, they implicitly assume that all members are perfectly rigid or that they possess infinite stiffness. This allows them to be represented as line drawings. In reality, all materials will shrink, stretch, bend, etc. under a load. This deformation changes the problem and greatly complicates the mathematics involved. However, the end results calculated assuming infinite stiffness are very close to what actually happens and, therefore, does not lead to significant error.

MOMENTS

DEFINITIONS

While forces can be adequately described by defining their magnitude, line of action, direction, and sense, the effects of forces cannot be understood without considering their relative locations. The **moment** (*M*) of a force is the effectiveness of a force in producing rotation about an axis. As anyone who has used a wrench has noticed, a longer wrench makes the same amount of force more effective. The magnitude of a moment is defined as the product of a force and its perpendicular distance (moment arm) from its line of action to the axis of rotation (see Figure 2.10).

$$M = Pd$$

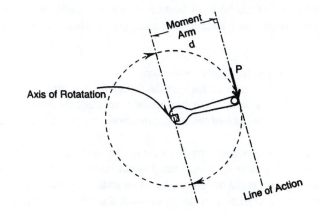

Figure 2.10 Rotation about an axis

MOMENT ARM

The perpendicular distance is the **lever** or **moment arm**. The units of a moment are force (*P*) times distance (*d*), typically expressed as foot-pounds or inch-pounds in the U.S. Like forces, moments also have a positive or negative **sense**. By convention, a moment which would cause clockwise rotation has a positive sense, and a moment which would cause counter-clockwise rotation has a negative sense (see Fig. 2.11).

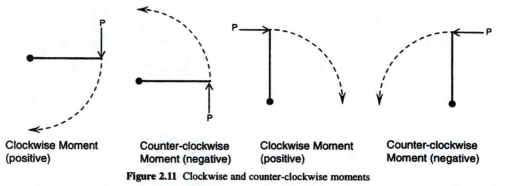

| Clockwise Moment (positive) | Counter-clockwise Moment (negative) | Clockwise Moment (positive) | Counter-clockwise Moment (negative) |

Figure 2.11 Clockwise and counter-clockwise moments

The line of action of the force is tangent to the rotation of the moment. For example, the line of action of a hand pushing a crescent wrench is the direction the hand would move if it slipped off the handle (see Figure 2.10).

> *Example 3.* What is the moment if a technician exerts 20 lbs of force on the bolt of a C-clamp with an eight-inch crescent wrench?
>
> $$M = Pd = (20\#)(8") = 160 \text{ inlb} \Rightarrow 13.3 \text{ ftlb}$$

EQUILIBRIUM

Newton's First Law states that if a body is not moving or accelerating, it must be in **equilibrium**. A body is in equilibrium when all of the forces acting upon it produce no change in the motion of the body. A body is in **static equilibrium** if it is not in motion and all of the forces acting on it cancel each other out. Technically, this is expressed by the following law:

> If a body is in static equilibrium:
> 1. The sum of the vertical forces equals zero $\Sigma V = 0$
> 2. The sum of the horizontal forces equals zero $\Sigma H = 0$
> 3. The sum of the moments about any point equals zero $\Sigma M = 0$

It is easy to understand why the sum of the vertical and horizontal forces must be zero to achieve equilibrium, but condition 3 is not intuitive. Requiring that the sum of the moments be equal to zero is the difference between static equilibrium and **dynamic equilibrium**. It is possible for a system in rotation to meet the first two conditions but not the third. Since unopposed rotation can be as dangerous as unopposed translation in structural systems, condition three is important.

Example 4. Is the following weightless beam in static equilibrium?

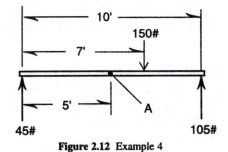

Figure 2.12 Example 4

First, check the sum of the vertical and horizontal forces:

$$\sum V = -150\# + 45\# + 105\# = 0 \quad \checkmark$$

$$\sum H = 0 \quad \text{no horizontal forces present} \quad \checkmark$$

Next, take the sum of the moments around any point (we'll use point A, at the center of the span):

$$\sum M_A = 0 = +(5')(45\#) + (2')(150\#) - (5')(105\#)$$

$$0 = 225 \text{ ftlb} + 300 \text{ ftlb} - 525 \text{ ftlb} \quad \checkmark$$

The system is in equilibrium.

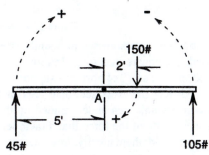

Figure 2.13 Example 4, sense of the moments

STRESSES

DEFINITIONS

By definition, scenery must be in static equilibrium. If a platform was not in static equilibrium, it would be moving, i.e., falling down. Since sets are clearly subjected to many forces, equilibrium can only be maintained if their structural members are somehow exerting their own forces to counter-balance the external ones. These internal forces are called **stresses**. Stresses are internal forces exerted by one part of a body upon other parts of the same body to resist external forces and their effects.

There are two basic kinds of stress, **direct** (or **axial**) stress and **tangential** stress. Direct stresses are responses to external forces which act perpendicular to the cross-sectional plane being stressed. These stresses can be **tensile** in response to a force which pulls on the body, or **compressive** in response to a force which pushes on the body. Tangential stresses are responses to external forces which act perpendicular to the axis of the member. Shear is the most common kind of tangential stress. **Shear** stresses resist the tendency of one part of a body to slide past another part of that body. **Torsional** stress is another kind of tangential stress which resists twisting. Since torsion is not a common problem in scenery construction, it will not be discussed in this text.

DIRECT STRESS

The line of action and direction of a stress will be identical to those of the force causing the stress. To maintain equilibrium, forces and the resulting stresses are equal in magnitude but opposite in sense.

Conventionally, a compression member is represented by arrows which point toward the ends of the member because a compression member is being squeezed from both ends and reacts with internal stresses which push out. Likewise, a tension member is represented by arrows which point away from the ends of the member (see Figure 2.14).

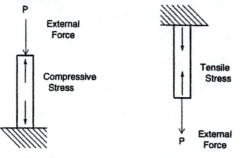

Figure 2.14 Compressive and tensile stresses

While forces are expressed in pounds, stresses are expressed in pounds per unit area, usually pounds per square inch (psi). Intuitively, it is easy to understand that a 4x4 post of the same wood species as a 2x4 post will support more weight. This is because stresses are evenly distributed over the cross-sectional area of the member. The amount of force a member can support per unit area is determined by the type of material of which it is made. Therefore, the magnitude of the force that a member can resist is directly proportional to its cross-sectional area. Mathematically, this relationship is expressed by the **Direct Stress Formula**:

$$f = \frac{P}{A}$$

where f is actual stress, psi
              P is applied external force, lbs
              A is cross-sectional area of the member, in²

The amount of stress a given material can safely withstand is defined as its **allowable stress** and is indicated with an uppercase "F". The allowable stress changes for each type of stress (compressive, tensile, shear, etc.) as well as for each type of material (Eastern White Pine, Douglas Fir-South, A36 steel, 6061 aluminum, etc.). Scientists and engineers determine these allowables empirically and publish them for use by structural designers. All allowables necessary to complete the problems in this book can be found in the various appendices. The subscripts following F and f indicate whether they are the values for compressive, tensile, shear, etc. stresses.

F, allowable stress, can be substituted for f, **actual stress**, so that the Direct Stress Formula can be solved for the maximum allowable external force (P) or the minimum cross-sectional area (A):

$$P = FA \qquad \text{or} \qquad A = \frac{P}{F}$$

TENSILE STRESS

A **tensile force** will have a tendency to lengthen the member on which it is acting. For tensile stress, the Direct Stress Formula is written:

$$f_t = P/A \qquad \text{or} \qquad P = AF_t \qquad \text{or} \qquad A = P/F_t$$

where　　A is the cross-sectional area, in^2
　　　　　P is the applied load, lbs
　　　　　F_t is the allowable tensile stress, psi
　　　　　f_t is the actual tensile stress, psi

F_t, the allowable tensile stress, is a function of the material choice and can be looked up while f_t is dictated by the loading conditions. If f_t is greater than F_t, the member fails for that application. This leaves the structural designer the options of decreasing the load, increasing the cross-sectional area, or choosing a different material.

> ***Example 5.*** A practical light unit is hung from a rod of 1/2" schedule 40 black pipe. The fixture is an elaborate chandelier and weighs approximately 100 lbs. Does this loading condition meet the allowable criteria for this shape? What's the minimum cross-sectional area needed for this load? The F_t of black pipe is 21,000 psi.

First, look up the cross-sectional area of the 1/2" schedule 40 pipe:

From Appendix E, $A = 0.25$ in^2.

Next, use the Direct Stress Formula:

$$f_t = \frac{P}{A} = \frac{100\#}{0.25 \text{ in}^2} = 400 \text{ psi}$$

In order to meet the allowable criteria, f_t, actual stress, must be lower than F_t, allowable stress. Since 400 psi is much less than 21,000 psi, the pipe easily passes.

> To find the minimum cross-sectional area necessary to support the chandelier, solve the Direct Stress Formula for A:

$$A_{min} = \frac{100\#}{21,000 \text{ psi}} = 0.00476 \text{ in}^2$$

Any steel shape with an area greater than 0.00476 in^2 will support the weight of the chandelier. The pipe meets these conditions easily. It is important to note, however, that this calculation does not represent the entire system. Many other details should be examined, including the connections between the hanger and the batten, between the hanger and the chandelier, and within the chandelier itself.

COMPRESSIVE STRESS

Direct **compressive stress** is created by a force which has a tendency to push or shorten a body. Compressive stress analysis, however, is more complex than tensile stress analysis. Unlike tensile stress, the amount of compressive stress a member can resist varies with its length. Basically, a tensile member can fail in only one way – by pulling apart – but a compression member can fail in two ways – crushing and/or **buckling**.

This tendency for compression members to buckle complicates their analysis considerably. The actual stress is calculated using the Direct Stress Formula, but the allowable stress is dependent on the unbraced length of the member and must be calculated for every situation. The design of wood and steel compression members with significant length will be discussed in later chapters. For compressive stress, the Direct Stress Formula is written:

$$f_c = P/A \qquad \text{or} \qquad P = AF_c \qquad \text{or} \qquad A = P/F_c$$

where A is the cross-sectional area, in²
          P is the applied load, lbs
          F_c is the allowable compressive stress, psi
          f_c is the actual compressive stress, psi

If f_c exceeds F_c, then the member fails for that application.

> CONCEPT BOX: The steel industry represents compressive stress as F_a, and the wood industry defines two types of compressive stress, $F_{c\perp}$ and F_c, to differentiate between compressive stress perpendicular and parallel to the grain of the wood member.

Example 6. Consider a platform supported with 4x4 posts which rest on 2x4 bearing plates (Figure 2.15). What is the maximum compressive stress that the 2x4 plate can withstand (no buckling effect) if its allowable compressive stress perpendicular to grain, $F_{c\perp}$, is 625 psi?

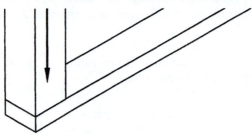

Figure 2.15 Example 6

First, look up the cross-sectional area of a 4x4 in Appendix D or calculate it:

$$A_{4x4} = 12.25 \text{ in}^2 \quad \text{or} \quad bd = 3.5"(3.5") = 12.25 \text{ in}^2$$

Then use the Direct Stress Formula to solve for P:

$$P = AF_{c\perp} = (12.25 \text{ in}^2)(625 \text{ psi}) = 7,656.25\#$$

TANGENTIAL STRESS – SHEAR STRESS

The last type of stress we will discuss is shear stress which acts perpendicular to the axis of the member, or, in other words, parallel to the cross-sectional area of a body. Shear stress is also expressed as force per unit area, usually psi. If the shear stress is extreme, it will slice a body cleanly in two. For example, consider the bolts which attach a hanging iron to a typical hard-framed flat in Figure 2.16. The total cross-sectional area of the bolts resists the weight of the flat.

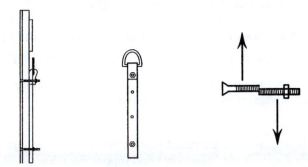

Figure 2.16 Side and rear elevations of a typical hanging iron with bolts in shear

For shear stress, the Direct Stress Formula is written:

$$f_v = P/A \qquad \text{or} \qquad P = AF_v \qquad \text{or} \qquad A = P/F_v$$

where A is the cross-sectional area, in^2
           P is the applied shearing load, lbs
           F_v is the allowable shear stress, psi
           f_v is the actual shear stress, psi

F_v, the allowable shear stress, is determined by the type of material (see Appendices D–F), while f_v, actual shear stress, is determined by the loading condition. If f_v exceeds F_v, then the member fails for that application.

> ***Example 7.*** Consider a flat which is 12'x20', framed with 1x3 pine, skinned with 1/4" lauan, and has two pick points (Figure 2.17). Are two 10-24 stove bolts sufficient for each pick-point? The steel of the bolts has an F_v of 10,000 psi.
>
> First, calculate the loading per bolt:
>
> > 1/4" lauan weighs 18 lbs per sheet
> > Southern Pine No. 2 weighs 37 pcf, or 0.482 plf for 1x3
> > Each sheet of lauan is framed with 36 lf of 1x3.

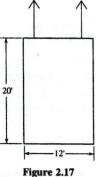

Figure 2.17

$$
\begin{aligned}
\text{Tot. weight} &= W_{ply} + W_{1x3} \\
&= (7.5 \text{ sheets})(18\#) + (7.5 \text{ sheets})[36'(0.482 \text{ plf})] \\
&= 135\# + 130.08\# = 265.08\#
\end{aligned}
$$

For each bolt:

$\text{weight}_{bolt} = (265.08\#/2)/2 = 66.27\#$ per bolt

Next, determine the shear strength of the bolt. The least diameter of a 10-24 (3/16") bolt is 0.145". The area of the shear plane is the area of a circle with a 0.145" diameter.

$$Area = \pi r^2 = \pi \left(\frac{0.145"}{2}\right)^2 = 0.0165 \text{ in}^2$$

Use the direct stress formula to determine the maximum loading on a bolt:

$$P_{all} = F_v A = (10{,}000 \text{ psi})(0.0165 \text{ in}^2) = 165\# > 66.27\#$$

In this case, since the allowable shear stress on one bolt far exceeds the actual shear stress, the 10-24 bolts are adequate.

FLEXURAL STRESS

Thus far, we have discussed the elemental forms of stress – tension, compression, and shear. **Flexural stress** is the result of a horizontal beam supporting a downward load. When a beam bends downward, the top becomes shorter and the bottom becomes longer. Practically, this means that the top half of the beam is in compression and the bottom half is in tension (see Figure 2.18). Thus, flexure is actually a combination of tension and compression. Flexural stress is examined at length in Chapters 4, 5, and 8.

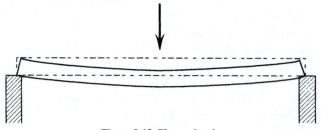

Figure 2.18 Flexure in a beam

ELASTICITY AND STRAIN
STRAIN

External forces on a body cause internal stresses to develop which cause deformations in the body. This deformation is defined as **strain**. As one would expect, tensile stresses cause lengthening deformations and compressive stresses cause shortening deformations. Mathematically, strain is defined as the amount of deformation per inch of the member:

$$s = \frac{e}{l}$$

where s is the strain, inches/inch
          e is the total deformation, in
          l is the length of member, in

Stress cannot be seen, but strain can be seen and measured. A beam will deform when someone walks across it.

HOOKE'S LAW

Intuitively, it seems that the amount of visible strain present in a body is mathematically related to the amount of stress in the body. Robert Hooke, a mathematician and physicist of the seventeenth century, discovered what has become known as Hooke's Law while experimenting with springs. Hooke's Law states that "stress is directly proportional to strain." For example, if twice the stress is applied to a hanger rod, it will lengthen twice as much. In addition, if the stress is removed, the hanger rod will return to its original length.

But this law has a limit. Real materials cannot lengthen indefinitely. For homogeneous materials, Hooke's Law is obeyed to a point called the **elastic limit**. At this point, the relationship between stress and strain is no longer linear – little additional stress leads to great additional strain, and the object is permanently deformed. Eventually, if the stress continues to increase, the object breaks. For example, imagine pulling a piece of taffy apart. At first, it is difficult to lengthen the piece. At some point, the resistance of the taffy to lengthening seems to disappear and the piece breaks. This phenomenon can be represented graphically by plotting stress versus strain (see Figures 2.19, 2.20).

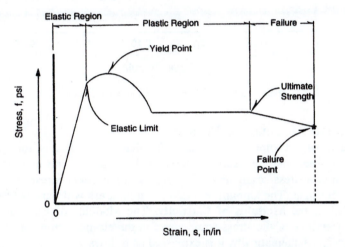

Figure 2.19 Generic stress versus strain diagram

- The **elastic region** is the area of the graph where Hooke's Law applies. If the stress is removed, the object will return to its original shape. The point at which the relationship between stress and strain is no longer linear is called the **elastic limit**.

- The **plastic region** is the area of the graph in which permanent deformation will take place. The **yield point** is the point at which the deformation increases without increasing the load.

- The **ultimate strength** of the material is where the material will finally rupture. Depending on the material, the ultimate strength may occur at a higher or lower stress than the yield point of that material (Parker, 50).

Homogeneous materials such as steel, aluminum, and glass have clearly defined elastic limits, yield points, and ultimate strengths (see Figure 2.20). Heterogeneous materials such as wood and concrete do not have easily defined stress versus strain characteristics. For example, no theory can predict whether a knot will exist in an individual board and cause it to fail at very low stresses. In practice, this means that the allowable stresses for heterogeneous materials are calculated more conservatively than those for homogeneous materials.

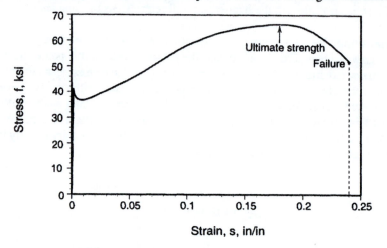

Figure 2.20 Stress versus strain diagram for steel

STIFFNESS AND THE MODULUS OF ELASTICITY

Empirically, we know that some materials are stiffer than others. That is, for a given amount of stress and cross-sectional area, some materials will visibly deform more than others. In the elastic region of a stress/strain curve, the relationship between stress and strain (deformation) will be constant. The amount of strain per unit stress will vary between materials and is quantified as the **Modulus of Elasticity**. The Modulus of Elasticity or Young's Modulus, E, is the slope of the stress-strain curve in the elastic region and is expressed in psi (Fitzgerald, 12). Mathematically, it is expressed as follows:

$$E = \frac{f}{s} = \frac{\text{stress}}{\text{strain}} = \frac{\text{psi}}{\text{in}/\text{in}} = \text{psi}$$

The Modulus of Elasticity, E, defines the *relative* stiffness of a given material.

CONCEPT BOX: Though Young's Modulus is very important to structural design, Thomas Young (1773-1829) did little else in the field. A genius at a young age, he was a medical doctor who made an impression in the field of optics by (correctly) hypothesizing how eyes change their focus. In addition, he hypothesized that light is a wave, though Augustin Fresnel would prove it mathematically. Unfortunately, Young was not a good communicator and many of his ideas were not appreciated at the time. In later years, he concentrated on hieroglyphics and translated the Rosetta Stone in 1814. (Gillispie, 562-569)

ELONGATION

In the elastic region, strain is directly proportional to stress, and the Modulus of Elasticity defines that relationship for a given material. Using this information, it is easy to calculate the actual deformation due to a given load. In tensile systems, the net deformation is called **elongation**. A formula for elongation in the elastic region can be derived from the definition of the Modulus of Elasticity:

$$E = \frac{f}{s} = \frac{P/A}{e/l} = \frac{Pl}{Ae}$$

Rearranged, the above yields:

$$e = \frac{Pl}{AE}$$

where e is the total deformation, in
   P is the applied force, lbs
   A is the cross-sectional area, in^2
   l is the length of member, in
   E is the modulus of elasticity, psi

> **Example 8.** Consider the chandelier problem solved earlier in Example 5. If the 1/2" pipe is 10' long, how much will it elongate under the weight of the 100 lb chandelier? How much will it elongate if it is loaded to its maximum capacity? F_t of black pipe is 21,000 psi, and E is 2.9×10^7 psi.

First, define the four variables (P, l, A, and E).

   $P = 100\#$
   l = length of the member in inches = 10'(12"/ft) = 120"
   $A = 0.25\ in^2$
   $E = 2.9 \times 10^7$ psi

Next, plug in the variables to find the elongation due to the chandelier:

$$e_{100\#} = \frac{Pl}{AE} = \frac{(100\#)(120")}{(0.25\ in^2)(2.9 \times 10^7\ psi)} = 0.00166"$$

To determine the maximum allowable tensile load, use the Direct Stress Formula.

$$P_{all} = F_t A = (21,000\ psi)(0.25\ in^2) = 5,250\#$$

Determine the elongation due to the maximum allowable tensile load:

$$e_{5,250\#} = \frac{Pl}{AE} = \frac{(5,250\#)(120")}{(0.25\ in^2)(2.9 \times 10^7)} = 0.087"$$

ALLOWABLE STRENGTH DESIGN

Many of the allowable stress values are calculated using the stress-strain curve as a guide. Theoretically, a structural engineer could design structures so that each member was stressed to just below the elastic limit. Realistically, however, it would be unsafe to design that way. There would be no margin to account for manufacturing defects, construction errors, engineering errors, material fabrication errors, temporary overloads . . . the list of possible problems can go on and on.

Nonetheless, some engineers use a method of structural design called **ultimate strength design**. These engineers are responsible for their own safety factors, which requires a high degree of structural design sophistication.

This textbook will use a structural design technique called **allowable strength design**. In allowable strength design, safety factors are incorporated into the allowable stress values. Instead of using the ultimate strength of materials, we use an allowable stress designated by various manufacturers' associations and code officials. The testing agencies pick a point in the elastic region to be the maximum allowable stress. This point is different for each material. Heterogeneous materials such as wood have lower allowable stresses than homogeneous materials such as steel.

CHAPTER 2 LESSONS

The format of the numbering system is: chapter.lesson.problem number

LESSON 2.1 FORCES, CENTER OF GRAVITY, FREE BODY DIAGRAMS (PG 5 – 9)

2.1.1   Draw the line of action and indicate the magnitude (lbs), sense, and direction of the force given below.

2.1.2   Draw the line of action and indicate the magnitude, sense, and direction of the force given below.

2.1.3   Draw the line of action and indicate the magnitude, sense, and direction of the force given below.

2.1.4   Determine the magnitude of the vertical and horizontal components of the force given below. Also indicate the sense and direction of the components.

2.1.5   Determine the magnitude of the vertical and horizontal components of the force given below. Also indicate the sense and direction of the components.

2.1.6   Draw a free body diagram for an 8' beam with supports at each end and a 100 plf evenly distributed load.

2.1.7   Draw a free body diagram for a 9' long lineset with two pick-ups set 1' in from each end. A 50# lighting instrument hangs 3' from the left end.

2.1.8   Draw a free body diagram for one of two beams on either side of a 30'x4' catwalk. Each beam is supported by four columns on 10' centers and must hold 250 plf as well as one half of a 400# speaker cluster hung 5' from each end.

2.1.9   Draw a free body diagram for a beam which is 12' long. It has two supports, one at the end of the beam and one set in 2' from the other end. The beam supports a 75 plf load on the overhang and has a 110# point load centered between the two supports.

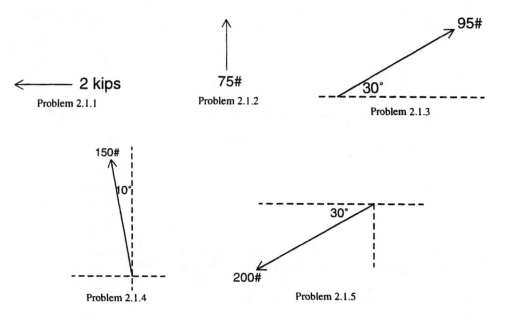

2 kips
Problem 2.1.1

75#
Problem 2.1.2

95#
30°
Problem 2.1.3

150#
10°
Problem 2.1.4

30°
200#
Problem 2.1.5

LESSON 2.2 RIGIDITY, MOMENTS, EQUILIBRIUM, STRESSES (PG 9 – 12)

2.2.1   What is the magnitude and sense of the moment produced by the system given below?

2.2.2   What is the magnitude and sense of the moment produced by the system given below?

2.2.3   What is the magnitude and sense of the moment produced around point A below?

2.2.4   What is the magnitude and sense of the moment produced around point B below?

2.2.5   Is the system below in equilibrium?

2.2.6   Is the system below in equilibrium?

2.2.7   Is the system below in equilibrium? Take the sum of the moments around point A. (Remember that an evenly distributed load can be considered as acting around its center of gravity.)

2.2.8   Is the system below in equilibrium? Take the sum of the moments around point A.

2.2.9   Draw arrows which represent the stress generated in the two members below.

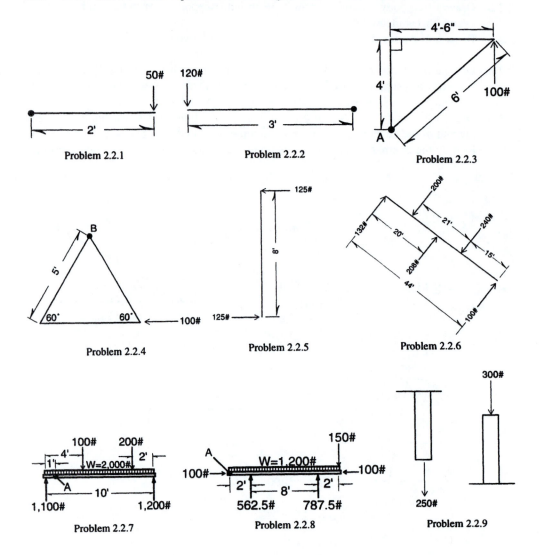

Problem 2.2.1

Problem 2.2.2

Problem 2.2.3

Problem 2.2.4

Problem 2.2.5

Problem 2.2.6

Problem 2.2.7

Problem 2.2.8

Problem 2.2.9

LESSON 2.3 TENSILE, COMPRESSIVE, TANGENTIAL, AND FLEXURAL STRESSES (PG 13 – 16)

2.3.1 What is the maximum tensile load that a 1/2" round rod made from A36 steel can support? The F_t of A36 steel is 21,600 psi.

2.3.2 What is the smallest angle iron shape (non-bar size) which can hold 5,000 lbs in tension? The angle iron is made from A36 steel with an F_t=21,600 psi.

2.3.3 What is the maximum tensile load that a 1/4"x3/4" A36 steel strap can support? The F_t of A36 steel is 21,600 psi.

2.3.4 What is the compressive stress on a 1"x1"x0.109" square mechanical tube if it is used as an extremely short column loaded with 4,000 lbs?

2.3.5 What is the smallest solid round steel shape (to the nearest 1/16") which can hold 2,500 lbs in compression? Assume that the column is very short and use an F_a of 21,500 psi.

2.3.6 What is the smallest size Schedule 40 black pipe which can support 3,000 lbs in compression? Assume that the column is very short and use an F_a of 21,500 psi.

2.3.7 What is the capacity of A36 steel 1/4", 5/16", and 3/8" rods in the shear condition given below? F_v is 14,400 psi.

2.3.8 What is the capacity of A36 steel 1/4", 5/16", and 3/8" rods in the shear condition given below? F_v is 14,400 psi.

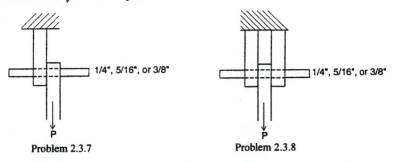

Problem 2.3.7   Problem 2.3.8

LESSON 2.4 ELASTICITY AND STRAIN, ALLOWABLE STRENGTH DESIGN (PG 16 – 20)

2.4.1 Find the Modulus of Elasticity for an 8' long 2x4 which stretches 0.061" with a 4,000 lb tensile load. Round your answer to the nearest 100,000 psi.

2.4.2 Find the Modulus of Elasticity for a 4' long 1/2" square bar of aluminum which stretches 0.0192" with a 1,000 lb tensile load. Round your answer to the nearest 100,000 psi. Approximately how much stiffer is steel compared to aluminum?

2.4.3 How much will a 3' long 3/16" steel round rod elongate due to a 500 lb tensile load? E is 2.9×10^7 psi. Is this a safe loading condition given that F_t is 21,600 psi?

2.4.4 How much will the 10' long piece of 1x1x1/8" angle iron from problem 2.3.2 elongate with the 5,000 lb tensile load? E is 2.9×10^7 psi. Is this a safe loading condition given that F_t is 21,600 psi?

2.4.5 Rearrange the equation for the Modulus of Elasticity to solve for P and then l.

2.4.6 What tensile load will cause a 5' long, 3/4" round bar made of A36 steel to elongate 0.1"? E is 2.9×10^7 psi. Is this a safe loading condition given that F_t is 21,600 psi?

2.4.7 How long is a 1/8"x1" strap made from A36 steel if it elongates 0.01" under a 2,000 lb tensile load? Is this a safe loading condition? E is 2.9×10^7 psi and F_t is 21,600 psi.

2.4.8 What is the strain on a 33" long member which elongates 0.1"?

2.4.9 What is the strain on a 12' long member which elongates 0.25"?

3

Stress Analysis for Beams

INTRODUCTION
BEAM STRESS
Beams are structural members which are subject to tangential loads. Tangential loads act perpendicular to the axis of a member and cause bending (flexure), vertical shear, and horizontal shear stresses to develop in a beam. As discussed in Chapter 2, bending stress is actually a combination of tensile and compressive stresses. However, instead of analyzing the tensile and compressive stresses separately, bending stress is treated as a whole with its own allowable stress design value. Actual bending stress is dependent on the force and/or moment applied and the shape of the member. In this chapter, we will discuss how to calculate the magnitude of the bending and shear stresses generated by tangential loads on beams.

TYPES OF BEAM FAILURE
While columns can also be subject to flexure (referred to as buckling), this chapter is limited to discussing flexural stress in beams. Structural designers must analyze stresses in beams to be sure that they are safe. Beams can fail catastrophically in three ways: bending, horizontal shearing, or vertical shearing.

- When a beam fails due to **bending** stress, the bottom fibers of the beam literally pull apart. A beam is more likely to fail due to bending stress if it has a relatively long span.

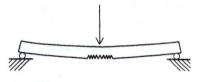

Figure 3.1a Bending stress

  Shape affects a beam's resistance to tangential loads. A 2x4 beam oriented on edge will resist bending better than a 2x4 oriented on flat. This is why 2x4 framed platforms are built with the framing on edge (3.5" high).

- When a beam fails due to **horizontal shear**, the top and bottom fibers slide past each other at the middle of the beam's cross-section. Short beams are more likely to fail due to horizontal shear.

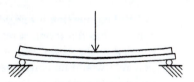

Figure 3.1b Horizontal shear

For solid sections, horizontal shear stress is not dependent on shape, only on cross-sectional area. An indication of failure due to horizontal shear would be a crack in the middle of a wooden beam, often following the grain of the lumber.

- When a beam fails due to **vertical shear**, the fibers of the beam are theoretically "sliced" cleanly on a plane close to a support. For beams, vertical shear failure is very rare; extreme loading conditions must be present for it to occur. A common theatrical example is the crash bar for a counterweight rigging system.

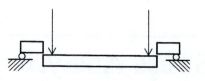

Figure 3.1c Vertical shear

When checking to see if a given loading condition on a beam is safe, each type of stress must be calculated and compared to its respective allowables. However, before beginning to analyze a loading condition, structural designers need to understand how the beam is connected to the structure around it.

TYPES OF BEAM CONNECTIONS

The degree of **fixity** of the ends of a beam effects how it will respond to a load. A beam whose ends are resting on top of a wall will have a different mode of flexure than a comparable beam whose ends cannot move (as if embedded in concrete). These two connections are called pinned and fixed connections, respectively (see Figure 3.2).

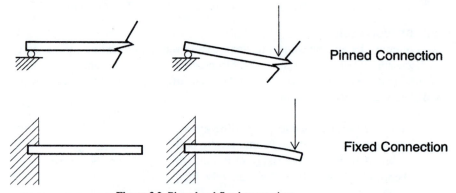

Figure 3.2 Pinned and fixed connections

- A **pinned connection** will resist one force with a known sense and direction. Theoretically, it offers no resistance to rotational movement – the end of the beam is free to rotate around a point.

- A **fixed connection** is one which will support a force of any direction and sense. It has full moment resistance because, unlike a pinned connection, the end of the beam cannot rotate. A beam with both ends anchored in concrete would be considered "fixed." The difference between a pinned and a fixed connection leads to significantly different deflection patterns.

In reality, most connections fall between the two conditions. For example, multiple bolt connections do offer some resistance to rotation, but are not equivalent to fixed connections. Structural designers recognize many intermediate fixity conditions, but to simplify calculations, most connections are analyzed as if they were purely pinned or fixed. Since most theatrical connections are closer to a pure pin connection, this text will treat most connections as such, which will err on the side of safety.

TYPES OF BEAMS

There are five types of beams which are defined by the pattern of the supports and the connections between the beam and its supports. Figure 3.3 shows an example of each type of beam with a load on it and its subsequent deflection pattern, or **elastic curve** (Parker, 77):

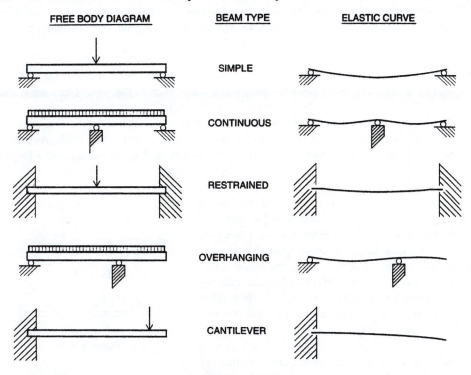

Figure 3.3 Beam types

- A **simple** beam is the most common type. It is supported at both ends by pinned connections which are symbolized by a small circle or a triangle at each support.

- A **continuous** beam is a beam with three or more supports. The connections may be pinned or fixed. A common example of this beam type is a pipe batten with multiple pick-ups.

- A **restrained** beam is supported at both ends with fixed connections. It is unusual to have fixed connections in scenery, but it is common in theaters. For example, loftblock and headblock beams are often restrained beams.

• An **overhanging** beam has one end overhanging a support. A double overhanging beam is a special case in which both ends overhang the supports. Stage extensions are often designed as overhangs.

• A **cantilever** beam has only one fixed support and is distinctly different from an overhanging beam.

Many beam configurations are actually combinations of these five beam types. For example, a pipe batten is usually a continuous beam with a double overhang.

ANALYZING THE LOAD

We have now described various ways that beams can fail, beam connections, and beam types, but, before we can analyze the stresses present in a beam, the loads themselves must be analyzed.

There are two basic types of loads, **live loads** and **dead loads**, both of which can be concentrated or distributed. Dead loads are permanent loads such as the weight of the flooring on a beam. Conversely, live loads are temporary loads such as actors walking across a deck. Loads can be of relatively long duration and still be considered live loads. For example, snow loads that may be on a roof for a day or a month are calculated as live loads. Any member may be subject to dead loads, live loads, or both. The first step in analyzing a loading condition is to identify the types of loads and represent them in a free body diagram.

Point loads are graphically represented as arrows (Figure 3.4a), and distributed loads as hatched rectangles. For most systems, beams will have an evenly distributed load along the entire span of the beam. These loads are due to the weight of the beam itself, the floor above it, a live load rating, and/or a rating applied to the structure (Figure 3.4b). When more than one evenly distributed load is present, the rectangles are stacked (Figure 3.4c).

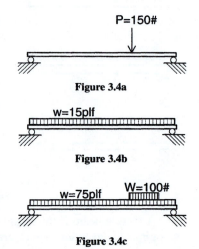

Figure 3.4a

Figure 3.4b

Figure 3.4c

By convention, a lower-case w indicates pounds per linear foot or inch and an uppercase W indicates the total distributed load in pounds. P indicates the magnitude of a point load.

After identifying the types of loads on a structure as live or dead and as point or distributed, the magnitude of each load on the beam must be determined. This seems simple, but actually requires some thought because some loads are shared between members. In these cases, loads are divided up graphically. That is, if a point load lands exactly between two beams, it is assumed that they share the load evenly. If a point load lands one foot away from one beam and three feet from the next, the closer beam will support 75% of the weight. When dealing with evenly distributed loads, it is assumed that each beam supports a **tributary area**, also divided graphically. For example, if floor joists are spaced every four feet, each joist will support two feet of the floor to either side of it, which leads to a total supported area of four square feet per linear foot of beam length. By applying the idea of tributary area, pounds per square foot are converted to pounds per linear foot.

For structural systems, several types of beams are defined. **Joists** are relatively small beams which are used in repetitive systems such as floors. A **rafter** is a special type of joist used in sloping roofs. Joists and rafters are usually used in applications requiring beams at fairly close regular intervals (16" o.c., 24" o.c., etc.). **Girders** are large beams which support smaller beams, such as joists. For a typical flooring system, each joist supports a tributary area of the floor. The joists are in turn supported by girders which are then supported by posts, studwalls, etc. This progression continues until the structure is finally supported by the ground on which it sits.

> **Example 1a.** Consider the following beam-girder system: a 12'x16' deck is constructed of 2x4 framed, 3/4" plywood platforms that are supported by beams on four foot centers. The beams span 16' and are supported at either end by 12' girders. The beams and girders could be wood, steel, or manufactured members. The loading situation is independent of the material choice. What is the loading on each interior beam, B and C, and on each end beam, A and D? Ignore beam weight.

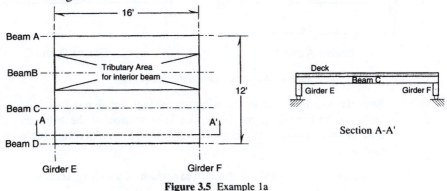

Figure 3.5 Example 1a

- First, calculate the dead load of the deck. Plywood weighs 3.0 psf per inch of thickness. Therefore:

$$\text{weight of 3/4" plywood} = (3.0\ \text{psf} / \text{in})(0.75")(32\ \text{ft}^2) = 72\#$$

The 2x4 framed platforms, with three internal toggles, have a total of 36 linear feet of 2x4 per platform. From the section properties table in Appendix D, if Douglas Fir-South has a density of 35 lb/ft³, it weighs 1.28 plf. Therefore, for one platform:

$$\text{weight of 2x4 framing} = (1.28\ \text{plf})(36') = 46.2\#$$

- To find the dead load of the deck per square foot, divide the total weight of a platform by its area, 32 sf:

$$\text{Dead Load} = \frac{W_{ply} + W_{2x4}}{32 \text{ sf}} = \frac{72\# + 46.2\#}{32} = 3.69 \text{ psf}$$

When analyzing a load, it is reasonable to round up for ease of calculations. We will round up to 4 psf.

• Next, determine the tributary area for the interior beams (B and C) and the exterior beams (A and D).

$$\text{Tributary Area} = (\text{span})(\text{width of supported area})$$
$$\text{T.A. (B\&C)} = 16'(4') = 64 \text{ ft}^2$$
$$\text{T.A. (A\&D)} = 16'(2') = 32 \text{ ft}^2$$

• Finally, calculate the pounds per linear foot that each of the beams supports:

Total weight supported by beams B and C = (4.0 psf)(64 sf) = 256 lbs

Weight per linear foot = 256 lbs/16' = 16 plf

Beams A and D will have a load of 16/2 = 8 plf

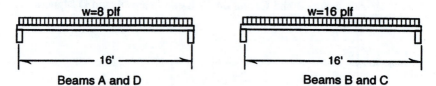

Figure 3.6 Loading solution to Example 1a

• Another way to arrive at the tributary weight per linear foot is to multiply the load (psf) by a one foot long section of the tributary area. In other words, each foot of beam supports an individual tributary area:

Weight per linear foot = (load, psf)(width of a 1' long section)

Beams B and C, plf = (4 psf)(4') = 16 plf

Example 1b. What is the loading on the girders?

• Each girder will support one half of the weight on each beam, which translate into point loads onto the girder.

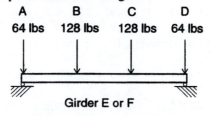

Girder E or F

Figure 3.7 Girder loading solution

Example 1c. What if the set includes a simple wall and two booms on top of the deck as illustrated in Figure 3.8a. The wall is 10' long and weights 25 plf. The booms are 2' from each edge, centered on Beam C, and weigh 150# each. How does this effect the loading on the beams and girders?

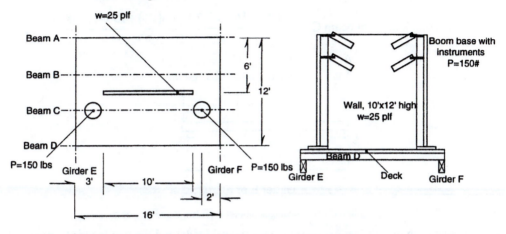

Figure 3.8a Example 1c, plan and front elevation

Beam Loading

*   Beams B and C each support half of the weight of the wall because it is centered between them. Beam C also supports the weight of the two booms which will be considered point loads.

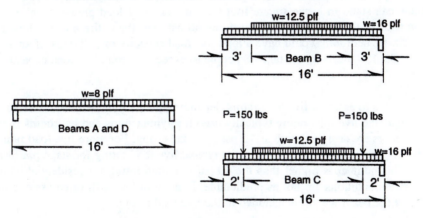

Figure 3.8b Loading solution for beams, Example 1c

Girder Loading

*   The loading on the girders is easy to define since the beams are symmetrically loaded. The girders each support one half of the weight on each beam:

The point loads from beams A and D are $\dfrac{(8\ \text{plf})16'}{2} = 64\#$

The point load from beam B is $\dfrac{(16\ \text{plf})(16') + (12.5\ \text{plf})(10')}{2} = 190.5\#$

The point load from beam C is $\dfrac{(16\ \text{plf})(16') + (12.5\ \text{plf})(10') + 150\# + 150\#}{2} = 340.5\#$

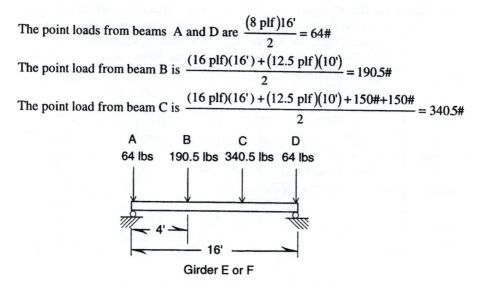

Figure 3.8c Loading solution for girders E and F

In the above example, all loads represented were dead loads, and the live loads of actors and furniture or properties were not taken into account. The analysis of a person walking on a floor would be tedious if structural designers needed to analyze the deck for every possible scenario. To deal with this problem, structural designers designate an evenly distributed load to represent the live loading condition. For the first floor of a residential home, designers typically use 40 psf as the **live load rating**. This may seem counter-intuitive because an average person can stand in a one square foot area and create a load greater than 40 psf. However, the odds of the total live load exceeding 40 psf over the entire area are low. For example, a 12' x 15' bedroom would have a total live load capacity of 7,200 lbs. If an average person weighs 150 lbs, it would take 48 people to exceed the total live load capacity of the bedroom.

Common practice is to assign a live load rating depending on the intended use of the structure. For example, the live load rating typically used for gymnasiums and ballrooms is 100 psf, and stage floors are designed with a 125 psf live load rating. For more live load ratings see Appendix G. This text will use 50 psf as its typical live load rating for stage platforms or structures. This number is higher than the 40 psf live load rating for residential homes because theatrical conditions are not as predictable. In addition, we will often assume that the dead load of the beam weight is included in the live load rating.

If a loading condition is unusual, the live load estimate should be changed to reflect it. For example, if the structural designer knows that a cast of 35 will all stand at the edge of the deck for the curtain call, it should be designed with this loading condition in mind.

> **Example 2.** Reexamine the deck in Example 1c. What is the loading on the beams and girders if a 50 psf live load rating is applied to the entire deck?

For interior beams B and C, Live Load $= \dfrac{(50 \text{ psf})(64 \text{ sf})}{16'} = 200$ plf

For beams A and D, Live Load $\approx \dfrac{(50 \text{ psf})(32 \text{ sf})}{16'} = 100$ plf

Total Load $_{B \text{ and } C}$ = Dead Load + Live Load = 16 plf + 200 plf = 216 plf

Total Load $_{A \text{ and } D}$ = Dead Load + Live Load = 8 plf + 100 plf = 108 plf

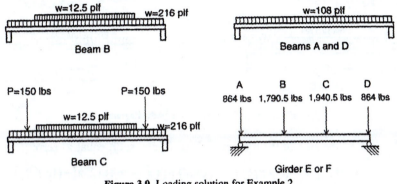

Figure 3.9 Loading solution for Example 2

REACTIONS

Once the loads and a support structure are fully defined, we can begin to design the individual beams in a structure. As always, the laws of equilibrium are applicable: the sums of the vertical forces, the horizontal forces, and the moments in a system must be equal to zero. In order for the sum of the vertical and/or horizontal forces to equal zero, the members supporting the beam must react with forces which are opposite and equal to the loading. Wherever a support interacts with a beam, it translates a reaction that holds the beam in equilibrium. **Reaction** is the technical term for the balancing force that occurs at a support.

A simple beam has two reactions which split the total load depending on the loading distribution. In Examples 1 and 2, the girders provided the reactions for the beams. Since that system was symmetrical, the weight was shared equally by each girder. In asymmetrical systems, we intuitively understand that the reactions may be unequal. The distance a load is from a reaction determines how much of it the reaction supports. Imagine two people holding a 2x12. A man walks slowly from the right to the left end of the plank. At first, the person on the right supports almost all of the man's weight. When the man reaches the center, each person supports half of his weight, and as he reaches the left end, that person supports most of his weight.

But how do we quantify these unequal reactions? For a system to be in equilibrium, the sum of the moments around any point must equal zero. Remember that a moment is defined as a force times distance. We can use this principal to solve for each reaction, in turn, by taking the moments around each of them. Reactions are symbolized by arrows at the supports. Conventionally, R_1 is designated as the reaction farthest to the left. Example 3 demonstrates this technique.

Example 3. Consider beam C in Example 2 with only one boom on the left end. What are the magnitudes of each reaction?

First, draw a free body diagram in which all loads are indicated. For the purposes of moment analysis, we can assume that the weight of an evenly distributed load acts at its center of gravity.

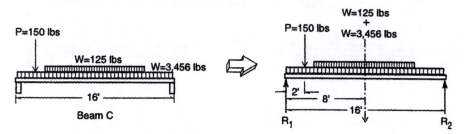

Figure 3.10 Example 3, free body diagram

Next, take the sum of the moments about R_1 and set it equal to zero:

$$\sum M_{R_1} = 0 = (0')(R_1\#) + (2')(150\#) + (8')[3,456\#+125\#] - (16')(R_2)$$
$$0 = 0 + 300 \text{ ftlb} + 28,648 \text{ ftlb} - 16' R_2$$
$$16' R_2 = 28,948 \text{ ftlb}$$
$$R_2 = 1,809.25\#$$

Now, take the sum of the moments around R_2 and set it equal to zero:

$$\sum M_{R_2} = 0 = (0')(R_2\#) - (14')(150\#) - (8')[125\#+3,456\#] + (16')(R_1)$$
$$0 = 0 - 2,100 \text{ ftlb} - 28,648 \text{ ftlb} + 16' R_1$$
$$16' R_1 = 30,748 \text{ ftlb}$$
$$R_1 = 1,921.75\#$$

Notice that R_1 is greater than R_2 because it supports most of the weight of the boom. Finally, check the sum of the vertical forces to confirm that the system is in equilibrium:

$$\sum V = -150\# - 125\# - 3,456\# + 1,809.25\# + 1,921.75\# = 0 \checkmark$$

The system can now be redrawn:

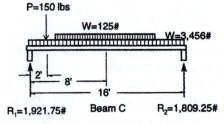

Figure 3. 11 Example 3, solution

SHEAR DIAGRAMS

Once the loads and reactions are determined, we can begin to analyze the magnitude of the stresses within the beam. The first step in this process is to determine the magnitude of the vertical shear acting along the length of the beam and to graphically display the results. The resulting graph is called a **shear diagram** which illustrates the location and magnitude of the maximum vertical shear (V_{max}) as well as where vertical shear equals zero. The maximum bending stress will occur where shear equals zero.

To construct a shear diagram, several definitions must be established:

- V stands for "vertical shear."

- V_{max} stands for the "maximum vertical shear." *For simple beams, V_{max} =* the magnitude of the larger reaction, unless point loads occur directly over the reactions.

- V_x is the vertical shear at x distance along the span of the beam from the left reaction. If x is followed by a superscript "+" or "–", it indicates that the vertical shear is being measured at a point infinitesimally to the right (+) or to the left (–) of that point. In practical terms, x^- indicates that the point load occurring at that location is *not* included in the calculations, and x^+ indicates that the point load is included in the calculations (see Example 4). For distributed loads, a positive or negative following the distance is unnecessary.

To construct a shear diagram, follow these steps:

1. Reduce the system to a free body diagram which represents the distributed loads, point loads, reactions, and connection details in scale. **Do not consider the distributed loads as point loads.**

2. Determine the reactions by taking the sum of the moments around each support. Remember that forces acting up are positive and those acting down are negative. If the sum of the vertical forces (loads and reactions) is not zero, check your work. Remember that distributed loads are considered as acting at their center of gravity, but only for this step in the analysis!

3. Calculate the vertical shear within the beam before and after each reaction, point load, and distributed load. **At any point on the beam, the vertical shear equals the summation of the vertical forces to the left of that point.** For points in the middle of distributed loads, only the portion of the distributed load that is to the left of the point is considered.

    $$V_x = \sum +(\text{reactions to the left of } x) - (\text{loads to the left of } x)$$

4. Plot these values on a graph in which the y-axis represents the magnitude of vertical shear and the x-axis represents the distance along the beam. Connect the dots and shade in the area between the line and the x-axis.

5.   Determine the point(s) where shear crosses through zero ($V_x=0$).

Example 4. Determine the vertical shear diagram for the following beam.

1.   Free body diagram of Example 4.

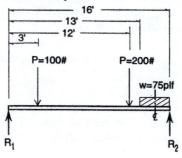

Figure 3.12 Example 4

2.   Find the reactions:

$$\sum M_{R_1} = 0 = (0')(R_1\#) + (3')(100\#) + (12')(200\#) + (14.5')\big[\big((3')(75\text{ plf})\big)\big] - (16')(R_2)$$
$$16'\,R_2 = 5,962.5\text{ ftlb}$$
$$R_2 = 372.66\ \#$$

$$\sum M_{R_2} = 0 = (0')(R_2\#) - (1.5')(225\#) - (4')(200\#) - (13')(100\#) + (16')(R_1)$$
$$16'\,R_1 = 2437.5\text{ ftlb}$$
$$R_1 = 152.34\ \#$$

Check that the sum of the vertical forces equals zero:

$$\sum V = -100\# - 200\# - 225\# + 372.65\# + 152.35\# = 0 \ \checkmark$$

3.   Calculate the vertical shear at various points:

$$V_{0^-} = 0$$
$$V_{0^+} = 152.34\#$$
$$V_{3^-} = 152.34\#$$
$$V_{3^+} = 152.34\# - 100\# = 52.34\#$$
$$V_{12^-} = 152.34\# - 100\# = 52.34\#$$
$$V_{12^+} = 52.34\# - 200\# = -147.66\#$$
$$V_{13} = -147.66\#$$
$$V_{15} = 152.34\# - 100\# - 200\# - (2')(75\text{plf}) = -297.66\#$$
$$V_{16^-} = 152.34\# - 100\# - 200\# - (3')(75\text{plf}) = -372.66\#$$
$$V_{16^+} = -372.66\# + 372.66\# = 0 \ \checkmark$$

$$V_{max} = 372.66\#$$

4 and 5. Construct the shear diagram and determine where shear crosses through zero.

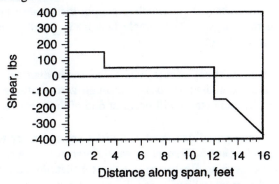

Figure 3.13 Shear diagram for Example 4

V equals zero at 12', therefore M_{max} occurs at 12'.

Notice that point loads cause sharp vertical changes in the shear diagram and distributed loads lead to sloping lines. These changes make sense when considered in light of stress concentration. Point loads cause extreme stress concentrations in the plane of the point load. A distributed load spreads out the stress along the length of the load.

To chart a shear diagram, the vertical shear must be calculated before and after each load. It does not hurt to calculate it more often, but missing a load can radically change the shear diagram.

Example 5. What if a structural designer neglected to calculate the shear at V_{3-} and V_{12-}. How would that change the shear diagram?

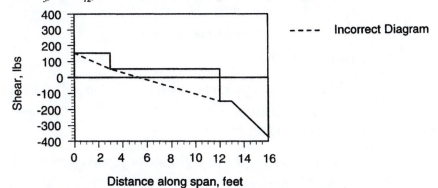

Figure 3.14 Incorrect shear diagram superimposed on correct one

Not calculating V_{3-} and V_{12-} creates a significantly different shear diagram. In addition, the point at which shear passes through zero has changed which leads to an incorrect location and value for the maximum bending stress. A quick check of a shear diagram is to estimate if the area in the positive zone equals the area in the negative zone. If they are not equal (as in the dashed line above), the diagram is incorrect.

A shear diagram imparts two vital pieces of information:

1. The maximum vertical shear, V_{max}, which is simply the greatest absolute value of shear in the diagram. (For simple beams, V_{max} will always be equal to the largest reaction.)

2. The maximum bending stress occurs where the shear diagram passes through zero. If the shear diagram passes through zero multiple times, then the maximum bending stress will occur at one of those points.

If shear passes through zero at a point load, no calculations are necessary to determine the location of the maximum bending stress. If shear passes through zero on a sloped line caused by a distributed load, it is necessary to algebraically solve for that point on the x-axis. If the shear diagram is sketched, the structural designer will know the approximate location of the point and can pin-point the location by using algebra (see Example 6 below).

Example 6. Determine the vertical shear diagram of the following beam.

1. Free body diagram.

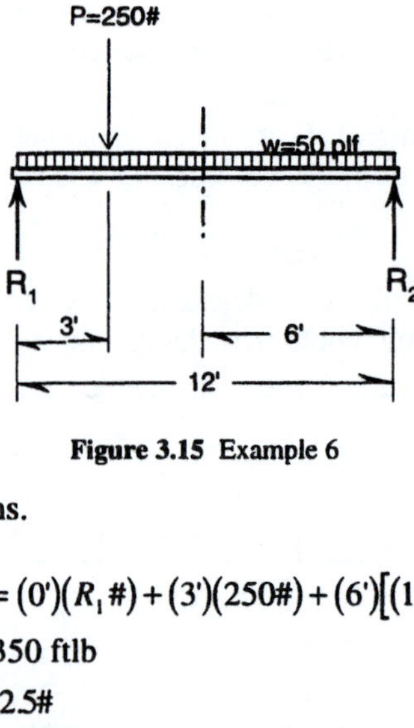

P=250#

w=50 plf

R₁

R₂

3'

6'

12'

Figure 3.15 Example 6

2. Find the reactions.

$$\sum M_{R_1} = 0 = (0')(R_1 \#) + (3')(250\#) + (6')[(12')50 \text{ plf}] - (12')(R_2)$$
$$12' R_2 = 4,350 \text{ ftlb}$$
$$R_2 = 362.5\#$$

$$\sum M_{R_2} = 0 = (0')(R_2 \#) - (6')(600\#) - (9')(250\#) + (12')(R_1)$$
$$12' R_1 = 5,850 \text{ ftlb}$$
$$R_1 = 487.50\#$$

Check that the sum of the vertical forces equals zero:

$$\sum V = -250\# - 600\# + 362.50\# + 487.50\# = 0\# \quad \checkmark$$

3. Calculate the vertical shear at various points.

$$V_{0^-} = 0$$
$$V_{0^+} = 487.50\#$$
$$V_{3^-} = 487.50\#-(3')(50 \text{ plf}) = 337.50\#$$
$$V_{3^+} = 337.50\#-250\# = +87.50\#$$
$$V_6 = 487.50\#-250\#-(6')(50 \text{ plf}) = -62.5\#$$
$$V_{12^-} = 487.50\#-250\#-(12')(50 \text{ plf}) = -362.50\#$$
$$V_{12^+} = -362.50\#+362.50\# = 0 \checkmark$$

V_{max} is 487.5 lbs.

4. Construct a shear diagram.

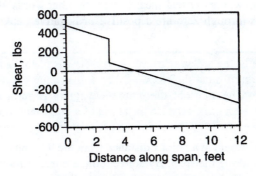

Figure 3.16 Shear diagram for Example 6

5. Determine where shear crosses through zero.

From the calculations and diagram, we know that shear crosses through zero after the 250 lb point load and before the end of the beam (between 3' and 6'). We also know that the sum of the vertical forces will equal zero at that point.

Since vertical shear is the sum of the loads to the left of the point, we know that both R_1 and the point load are included in the equation. If we call the point where V equals zero point x, then the distributed load to the left of x equals x feet multiplied by the pounds per linear foot load rating:

$$V_x = +R_1 - \text{point load(s) to the left of } x - \text{distributed load to left of } x = 0$$
$$V_x = 487.50\#-250\#-x'(50 \text{ plf}) = 0$$
$$50x = 237.50\#$$
$$x = 4.75'$$

HORIZONTAL SHEAR

As illustrated in Figure 3.1b, beams may fail due to **horizontal shear**. Horizontal shear is equal to the vertical shear at any point along the length of the beam. Therefore, the horizontal shear is maximum where vertical shear is maximum (at the ends of a simple beam). Because the maximum horizontal shearing stress is dependent on the shape, the cross-sectional area of the beam, and the magnitude of V_{max}, analyzing horizontal shear stress will not be discussed until Chapter 5.

MOMENT DIAGRAMS

The next step in beam analysis is determining the magnitude of the bending moment at various points along the length of the beam. A **moment diagram** charts the moment (inlb or ftlb) versus distance (in or ft) along the span. The maximum moment of a beam is critical in selecting an appropriate beam.

As mentioned previously, the moment diagram relates to the shear diagram because the maximum moment occurs where vertical shear is zero. In other words, the point(s) at which the shear diagram passes through zero are a positive or negative peak in the moment diagram.

> MATH NOTE: Moment is the integral of vertical shear, or shear is the derivative of moment. The shear diagram plots the slope of the moment diagram at any given point. When shear equals zero, the slope of the moment diagram is zero, indicating that the moment curve has reached a peak because the slope of a horizontal line is zero.

As with shear, M_x is the moment at a point x distance from the left end of the beam, and M_{max} is the maximum moment along the span. By convention, a positive moment indicates that a beam is bending down, and a negative moment indicates that a beam is bending up. M_{max} is the absolute value of the greatest bending moment. If a beam fails due to bending stress, it will fail at the location of M_{max}.

The bending moment at any point, M_x, equals the sum of the moments at and to the left of that point. Remember that moments have positive or negative values for clockwise and counter-clockwise rotation. To determine the sense of a given moment, consider what direction of rotation the force would cause around point x. Figure 3.17 shows which forces to consider and their direction of rotation around point x.

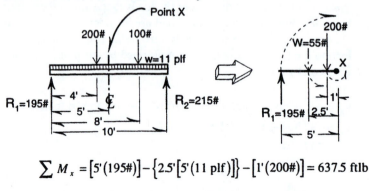

$$\sum M_x = \left[5'(195\#)\right] - \left\{2.5'\left[5'(11\text{ plf})\right]\right\} - \left[1'(200\#)\right] = 637.5 \text{ ftlb}$$

Figure 3.17 An illustration of finding the moment at point x

A moment diagram plots foot- or inch-pounds on the *y*-axis versus distance along the span on the *x*-axis. The number and location of points to take moments around in order to construct a moment diagram varies with the situation. As a rule, moments should always be taken where the shear diagram crosses through zero. Additional points necessary to create an accurate representation of the bending stress in the beam are taken at the structural designer's discretion.

If point *x* falls within a distributed load, then only that portion of the load to the left is considered. The moment is calculated by multiplying the distributed load to the left of point *x* by the distance between its center of gravity and point *x*. See the moment taken at point *x* for the evenly distributed load of 11 plf in Figure 3.17 above.

Example 7. Construct a moment diagram of Example 4.

First, draw a free body diagram.

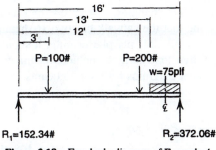

Figure 3.18a Free body diagram of Example 4

Calculate the moments at 0, 3, 12, 13, 15, and 16 feet:

$$M_3 = +\left[3'(152.34\#)\right] = 457.02 \text{ ftlb}$$

$$M_{12} = +\left[12'(152.34\#)\right] - \left[9'(100\#)\right] = 928.08 \text{ ftlb}$$

$$M_{13} = +\left[13'(152.34\#)\right] - \left[10'(100\#)\right] - \left[1'(200\#)\right] = 780.42 \text{ ftlb}$$

$$M_{15} = +\left[15'(152.34\#)\right] - \left[12'(100\#)\right] - \left[3'(200\#)\right] - \left[1'\left[2'(75 \text{ plf})\right]\right] = 335.10 \text{ ftlb}$$

$$M_{16} = +\left[16'(152.34\#)\right] - \left[13'(100\#)\right] - \left[4'(200\#)\right] - \left[1.5'(225\#)\right] + \left[0'(372.66\#)\right] = 0$$

Next, construct a moment diagram:

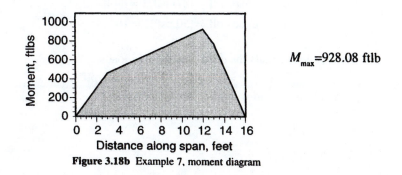

$M_{max} = 928.08 \text{ ftlb}$

Figure 3.18b Example 7, moment diagram

Note the sharp points in the moment diagram which are characteristic of a "weightless" beam. Moment diagrams of beams which have a distributed load along the length of their spans will always have curves which are modified parabolas (as between 13'–16' in Figure 3.18b).

Also note that in order to satisfy the law of equilibrium, moment should always resolve to 0 at both ends of a beam.

For convenience, the shear diagram is usually graphed directly beneath the free body diagram of the beam, and the moment diagram is graphed directly beneath the shear diagram. At a glance, a structural designer can see the relationships between the three and understand the loading condition of the beam.

> ***Example 8.*** A designer specifies a 4' wide, 16' long catwalk with a large bell weighing 400 lbs hanging 6' from one end. For the sake of this problem, assume that the catwalk has two 16' beams which support standard 2x4 framed, 3/4" ply platforming. It should be designed to take a 50 psf live load (which includes beam weight). Construct shear and moment diagrams for the two beams.

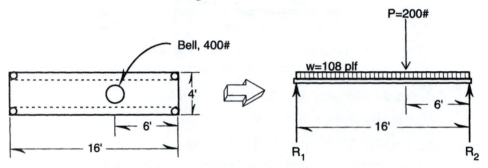

Figure 3.19 Example 8

1. Determine the loading on the beams. Each beam supports a tributary area of 1/2 of the catwalk, or a 2' strip. From Example 5, the dead load due to 2x4 framed platforms is 4 psf. The live load is 50 psf.

    Weight per linear foot = (load, psf)(Area of a 1' long section)

    Dead Load, plf = (4.0 psf)2' = 8 plf

    Live Load, plf = $(50\ \text{psf})2' = 100$ plf

    The total load equals the dead plus the live loads:

    $$w = 8.0\ \text{plf} + 100\ \text{plf} = 108\ \text{plf}$$

    The total distributed weight on the beam equals:

    $$W = (108\ \text{plf})(16') = 1{,}728\#$$

2. Determine the reactions:

$$\sum M_{R_1} = 0 = (0')(R_1\#) + (8')(1,728\#) + (10')(200\#) - (16')(R_2)$$
$$16' R_2 = 15,824 \text{ ftlb}$$
$$R_2 = 989\#$$

$$\sum M_{R_2} = 0 = (0')(R_2\#) - (8')(1,728\#) - (6')(200\#) + (16')(R_1)$$
$$16' R_1 = 15,024 \text{ ftlb}$$
$$R_1 = 939\#$$

Check the sum of the vertical forces:

$$\sum V = +989\# + 939\# - 200\# - 1,728\# = 0\# \checkmark$$

3. Calculate the vertical shear at various points.

$$V_{0^-} = 0$$
$$V_{0^+} = R_1 = 939\#$$
$$V_8 = 939\# - 8'(108 \text{ plf}) = 75\#$$
$$V_{10^-} = 939\# - 10'(108 \text{ plf}) = -141\#$$
$$V_{10^+} = -141\# - 200\# = -341\#$$
$$V_{16^-} = 939\# - 16'(108 \text{ plf}) - 200\# = -989\#$$
$$V_{16^+} = -989\# + 989\# = 0 \checkmark$$

$$V_{max} \text{ is } 989\#$$

4. Calculate where V crosses through zero (the location of M_{max}).

$$V_x = 0 = 939\# - (x')(108 \text{ plf})$$
$$108x = 939\#$$
$$x = 8.694'$$

5. Calculate the moment at various points.

$$M_0 = 0$$
$$M_{8.694} = +8.694'(939\#) - \left(\frac{8.694'}{2}\right)\left[8.694'(108 \text{ plf})\right] = 4,082 \text{ ftlb}$$
$$M_{10} = +10'(939\#) - (5')\left[10'(108 \text{ plf})\right] = 3,990 \text{ ftlb}$$
$$M_{16} = +16'(939\#) - (8')\left[16'(108 \text{ plf})\right] - (6')(200\#) = 0 \text{ ftlb}$$

$$M_{max} \text{ is } 4,082 \text{ ftlbs (the moment taken at 10' was unnecessary).}$$

6. Redraw the free body diagram with *w* and reactions solved, construct shear and moment diagrams, and draw an elastic curve.

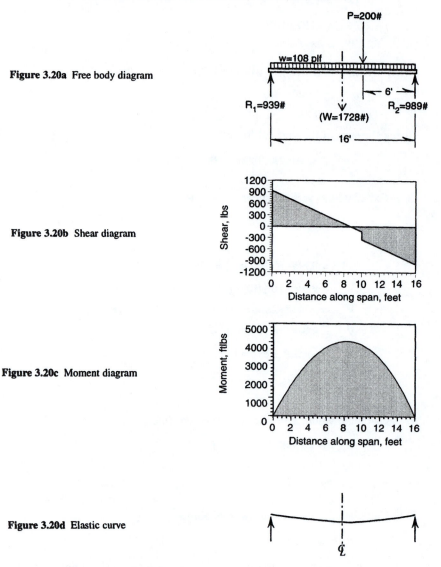

Figure 3.20a Free body diagram

Figure 3.20b Shear diagram

Figure 3.20c Moment diagram

Figure 3.20d Elastic curve

Sometimes it is helpful to draw an elastic curve for the beam. An elastic curve is a representation of the actual flexure (or bending) of the beam. Though an elastic curve does not add any new information, it can help the structural designer understand how the beam will affect other parts of the system.

Shear and moment diagrams have some distinctive patterns that occur frequently. Recognizing them can be useful in structural design:

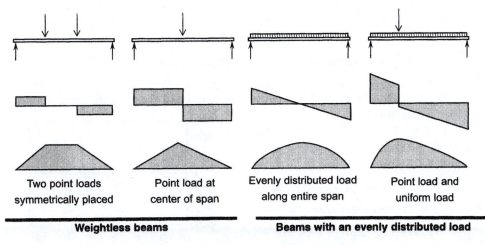

Figure 3.21 Four common beam diagram patterns

Notice that the "weightless" beams are characterized by shear diagrams with vertical drops and moment diagrams with sharp points and straight lines. Distributed loads such as beam weight cause sloped lines in shear diagrams and smooth curves in moment diagrams.

OVERHANGS AND CANTILEVERS

This section presents a series of examples featuring beams other than simple beams. The same analytic techniques are used, but the relationships between forces, moments, etc., are more complicated. Note that V_{max} is not necessarily equal to either reaction, and that shear can cross through zero more than once.

> ***Example 9.*** Construct shear and moment diagrams for the following overhanging beam.

1. Free body diagram.

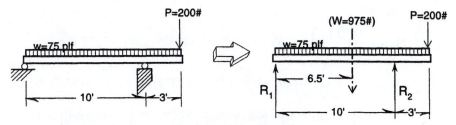

Figure 3.22 Free body diagram for Example 9

2. Determine the reactions:

$$\sum M_{R_1} = 0 = (0')(R_1 \#) + (6.5')\big[(13')(75 \text{ plf})\big] - (10')(R_2) + (13')(200\#)$$
$$10' R_2 = 8,937.5 \text{ ftlb}$$
$$R_2 = 893.75 \#$$

$$\sum M_{R_2} = 0 = (0')(R_2) - (3.5')(975\#) + (10')(R_1) + (3')(200\#)$$
$$10' R_1 = 2,812.5 \text{ ftlb}$$
$$R_1 = 281.25\#$$

Check the sum of the vertical forces:

$$\sum V = +200\# + 975\# - 893.75\# - 281.258\# = 0 \checkmark$$

3. Calculate the vertical shear at various points and construct the shear diagram.

$V_{0^-} = 0$

$V_{0^+} = R_1 = 281.25\#$

$V_{10^-} = 281.25\# - (10')(75 \text{ plf}) = -468.75\#$

$V_{10^+} = -468.75\# + 893.75\# = 425\#$

$V_{13^-} = 281.25\# - (13')(75 \text{ plf}) + 893.75\# = 200\#$

$V_{13^+} = 200\# - 200\# = 0 \checkmark$

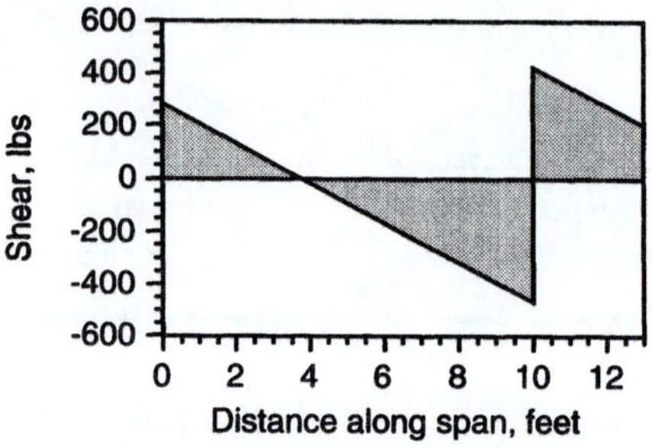

$V_{max} = 468.75\#$

Figure 3.23 Shear diagram for Example 9

4. Calculate distance x where V crosses through zero between the supports.

$$V_x = 0 = 281.25\# - (x')(75 \text{ plf})$$
$$75x = 281.25\#$$
$$x = 3.75'$$

M_{max} will occur at 3.75' or 10'.

5. Calculate the moment at various points, construct the moment diagram, and draw the elastic curve.

$M_0 = 0$

$$M_{3.75} = -\left\{ \left(\frac{3.75'}{2}\right) \left[(3.75')(75 \text{ plf}) \right] \right\} + \left\{ (3.75')281.25\# \right\} = 527.3 \text{ ftlb}$$

$$M_{10} = -\left\{ \left(\frac{10'}{2}\right) \left[(10')(75 \text{ plf}) \right] \right\} + \left\{ 10' (281.25\#) \right\} + 0' R_2 = -937.5 \text{ ftlb}$$

$$M_{13} = +\left\{ 13' (281.25\#) \right\} - \left\{ 6.5' (975\#) \right\} + \left\{ 3' (893.75) \right\} + \left\{ 0' (200\#) \right\} = 0$$

$M_{max} = 937.5$ ftlb and occurs at 10'

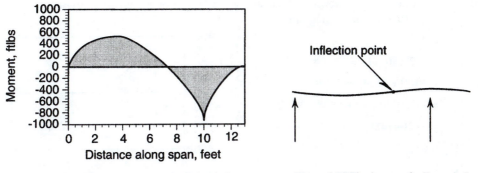

Figure 3.24 Moment diagram for Example 9

Figure 3.25 Elastic curve for Example 9

Notice that the flexure of the beam changes from bending down to bending up when the moment crosses through zero. This point is called the **inflection point** and is rarely crucial for theatrical designs, but is very important in designing buildings and bridges. Remember that bending is a combination of compressive and tensile stresses. When the flexure of the beam inverts, the top of the beam is in tension and the bottom is in compression. To find the inflection point, apply the same technique used to find where shear crosses through zero. Set the moment at M_x equal to zero and solve for distance x.

Notice that overhanging beams will generally have two possible locations of M_{max}. One occurs between the supports and the other at R_2. A handy rule of thumb is that for over-hanging beams, the overhang should be less than one-quarter of the span between supports. The moment between supports will be maximum as long as the overhang is less than 40% of the span between supports.

As illustrated by the following example, **double overhanging** beams have unique shear and moment diagrams.

> **Example 10.** Construct shear and moment diagrams and the elastic curve for the following double overhanging beam.

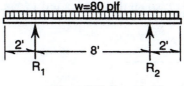

Figure 3.26 Example 10

1. Since the loading is symmetrical, the reactions are equal.

$$R_1 = R_2 = \frac{12'(80\ \text{plf})}{2} = 480\#$$

2.   Calculate the vertical shear along the length of the span, and construct the shear diagram.

$V_0 = 0$

$V_{2^-} = -(2')(80 \text{ plf}) = -160\#$

$V_{2^+} = -160 + 480\# = +320\#$

$V_{10^-} = -(10')(80 \text{ plf}) + 480\# = -320\#$

$V_{10^+} = -320\# + 480\# = +160$

$V_{12} = 0 \checkmark$

$V_{max} = 320\#$

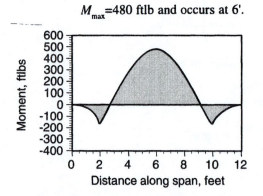

Figure 3.27 Shear diagram for Example 10

3.   Calculate where V crosses through zero between the supports.

$$V_x = 0 = 480\# - (x')(80\text{plf})$$
$$80x = 480\#$$
$$x = 6'$$

M_{max} occurs at 2', 6', or 10'. Note that the above calculation is unnecessary because the loading condition is symmetrical.

4.   Calculate the moment at various points, construct the moment diagram, and draw the elastic curve.

$$M_0 = 0$$
$$M_2 = -\left\{1'\left[2'(80 \text{ plf})\right]\right\} = -160 \text{ ftlb}$$
$$M_6 = -\left\{3'\left[6'(80 \text{ plf})\right]\right\} + \left[4'(480\#)\right] = 480 \text{ ftlb}$$
$$M_{10} = -\left\{5'\left[10'(80 \text{ plf})\right]\right\} + \left\{8'(480\#)\right\} + \left\{0'(480\#)\right\} = -160 \text{ ftlb}$$
$$M_{12} = -\left\{6'\left[12'(80 \text{ plf})\right]\right\} + \left\{10'(480\#)\right\} + \left\{2'(480\#)\right\} = 0 \text{ ftlb}$$

$M_{max} = 480$ ftlb and occurs at 6'.

Figure 3.28 Moment diagram for Example 10

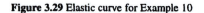

Figure 3.29 Elastic curve for Example 10

CONCEPT BOX: Double overhanging beams can be very useful. For example, the double-overhanging beam in Example 10 would have a lower M_{max} than a simple beam with the same overall 12' length because the primary span has been reduced by 33%:

$$R_{1, simple} = \frac{12'(80 \text{ plf})}{2} = 480\#$$

$$M_6 = M_{max, simple} = +(6')(480\#) - \left\{3'\left[6'(80 \text{ plf})\right]\right\} = +1,440 \text{ ftlb}$$

$$1,440 \text{ ftlb} \gg 480 \text{ ftlb} \ (M_{max} \text{ of Example 10})$$

The more interesting advantage of double overhanging beams is that they result in a lower M_{max} than even simple beams with the same span. For example, the M_{max} for an 8' simple span with the same loading conditions as Example 10 would result in the following moment:

$$R_{1, simple} = \frac{8'(80 \text{ plf})}{2} = 320\#$$

$$M_4 = M_{max, simple} = +\left[4'(320\#)\right] - \left\{2'\left[4'(80 \text{ plf})\right]\right\} = +640 \text{ ftlb}$$

If the moment diagram of the simple beam is superimposed on the moment diagram of the double overhanging beam in Example 10, the following results:

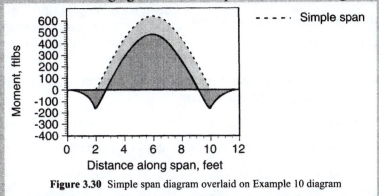

Figure 3.30 Simple span diagram overlaid on Example 10 diagram

The basic moment curves of the two beams are identical along the eight foot span. The overhanging beam decreases M_{max} by shifting the entire curve down. In effect, by changing the location of the reactions and creating a double overhang, a smaller beam could be used for the same load. As a rule of thumb, for an evenly distributed load, the positive and negative moments of a double-overhanging beam will be equal when a/l is 0.354 (where a is the length of the overhang and l is the distance between supports). M_{max} will be the smallest when $a/l=0.354$ and will result in the smallest possible beam relative to bending, though the overhang may deflect too much. If the a/l ratio is greater than 0.354, the moment of the overhang becomes M_{max}. Continuous beams offer the same sort of advantage.

Example 11. Draw shear and moment diagrams for the following cantilever beam:

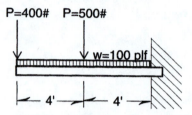

Figure 3.31 Example 11, free body diagram

1. In a cantilever, only one reaction exists; it will have a magnitude
    equal to the total load and will be V_{max}.

$$\sum V = R_1 - \text{load} = R_1 - 8'(100\text{plf}) - 500\# - 400\# = R_1 - 1,700\# \Rightarrow R_1 = 1,700\# = V_{max}$$

2. Calculate the vertical shear along the length of the span and con-
    struct the shear diagram.

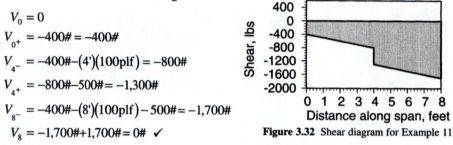

$V_0 = 0$

$V_{0^+} = -400\# = -400\#$

$V_{4^-} = -400\# - (4')(100\text{plf}) = -800\#$

$V_{4^+} = -800\# - 500\# = -1,300\#$

$V_{8^-} = -400\# - (8')(100\text{plf}) - 500\# = -1,700\#$

$V_8 = -1,700\# + 1,700\# = 0\#$ ✓

Figure 3.32 Shear diagram for Example 11

3. Calculate the moment at various points, construct a moment dia-
    gram, and draw the elastic curve.

$$M_0 = 0$$

$$M_2 = -[(2')(400\#)] - \{1'[(2')(100\text{plf})]\} = -1,000 \text{ ftlb}$$

$$M_4 = -[(4')(400\#)] - \{2'[(4')(100\text{plf})]\} = -2,400 \text{ ftlb}$$

$$M_8 = -[(8')(400\#)] - \{4'[(8')(100\text{plf})]\} - \{4'(500\#)\} = -8,400 \text{ ftlb}$$

$M_{max} = 8,400 \text{ ftlb}$

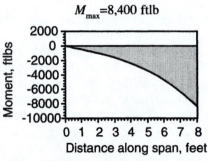

Figure 3.33 Moment diagram for Example 11

Figure 3.34 Elastic curve for Example 11

CASE FORMULAS

Structural designers quickly became tired of constructing shear and moment diagrams for reoccurring loading conditions. In response, they derived **case formulas** which allow you to solve for important variables, such as V_{max} or M_{max}, without constructing a diagram or doing many laborious calculations. Appendix B has the case formulas most frequently used.

Case formulas are unit sensitive. Unit errors can lead to answers that are orders of magnitude off. Typically, we will measure spans in inches and allowable loads in pounds per linear inch (pli). The case formulas do not demand units of inches, but they do require that the units "work out" correctly. For example, if one variable (such as E) is given in pounds per square inch, plugging in length measurements in feet into that formula would yield an incorrect answer. The nomenclature sheet at the front of Appendix B defines all of the variables used in the case formulas.

> ***Example 12.*** Use case formulas to determine R_1, R_2, V_{max}, and M_{max} for the following beam overhanging one support – concentrated load at end of overhang:

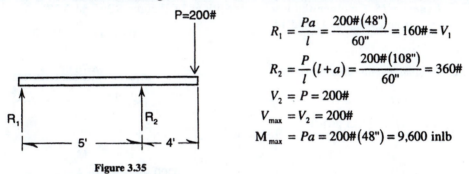

$$R_1 = \frac{Pa}{l} = \frac{200\#(48")}{60"} = 160\# = V_1$$

$$R_2 = \frac{P}{l}(l+a) = \frac{200\#(108")}{60"} = 360\#$$

$$V_2 = P = 200\#$$

$$V_{max} = V_2 = 200\#$$

$$M_{max} = Pa = 200\#(48") = 9{,}600 \text{ inlb}$$

Figure 3.35

> Note that the case formulas ignore sense. In this case, R_1 must be negative for the sum of the vertical forces to equal zero.

> ***Example 13.*** Use case formulas to determine R_1, R_2, V_{max}, and M_{max} for the following simple beam – uniformly distributed load.

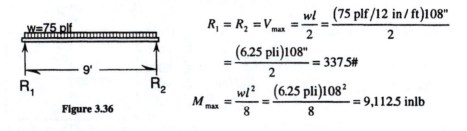

Figure 3.36

$$R_1 = R_2 = V_{max} = \frac{wl}{2} = \frac{(75\ \text{plf}/12\ \text{in}/\text{ft})108"}{2}$$

$$= \frac{(6.25\ \text{pli})108"}{2} = 337.5\#$$

$$M_{max} = \frac{wl^2}{8} = \frac{(6.25\ \text{pli})108^2}{8} = 9{,}112.5 \text{ inlb}$$

Example 14. Use case formulas to determine R_1, R_2, V_{max}, and M_{max} for the following simple beam – two concentrated loads symmetrically placed.

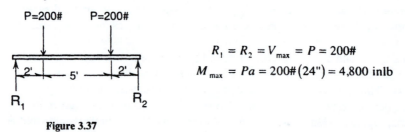

$$R_1 = R_2 = V_{max} = P = 200\#$$
$$M_{max} = Pa = 200\#(24") = 4,800 \text{ inlb}$$

Figure 3.37

We can also combine case formulas to solve problems with more complex loading conditions. If the maximum moment occurs at the same location for both loading conditions, then M_{max} of each loading condition can simply be added together to arrive at the combined M_{max} (see Example 15 below).

Example 15. Combine the loading conditions of Figures 3.36 and 3.37 from Examples 13 and 14.

Simple span, evenly distributed load:

$$V_{max_1} = 337.2\#$$

$$M_{max_1} = \frac{wl^2}{8} = \frac{(6.25 \text{ pli})108^2}{8} = 9,112.5 \text{ inlb}$$

Simple span, two point loads symmetrically placed:

$$V_{max_2} = 200\#$$

$$M_{max_2} = Pa = 200\#(24") = 4,800 \text{ inlb}$$

Combined loading condition:

$$V_{max} = V_{max_1} + V_{max_2} = 337.2\# + 200\# = 537.2\#$$
$$M_{max} = M_{max_1} + M_{max_2} = 9,112.5 \text{ inlb} + 4,800 \text{ inlb}$$
$$M_{max} = 13,912.5 \text{ inlb}$$

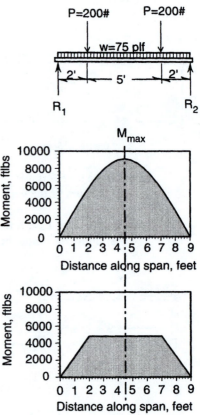

Figure 3.38 Adding case formulas

If the location of M_{max} for two loading conditions is not identical, then adding the case formulas will not yield M_{max}. Therefore, case formulas are not always the solution for complex loading conditions. At times, it is easier to perform the calculations the old-fashioned way.

DERIVATION OF CASE FORMULAS

Case formulas can be derived using the techniques discussed earlier in this chapter. For example, consider the following simple beam with a generic evenly distributed load of w and a generic span of l (Figure 3.39).

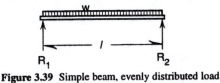

Figure 3.39 Simple beam, evenly distributed load

The load w has units of weight per distance, such as pli or plf. The span l should be in matching units. Since the loading condition is symmetrical, we know that R_1 and R_2 are equal, and that M_{max} will occur in the middle of the span (at $l/2$). With this information, the value of M_{max} is easily derived:

$$R_1 = R_2 = \frac{\text{total load}}{2} = \frac{wl}{2}$$

To find M_{max}, take the moment at $l/2$:

$$M_{1/2} = M_{max} = +\left(\frac{l}{2}\right)R_1 - \left(\frac{l}{4}\right)\left(\frac{wl}{2}\right)$$

Plug in the above value for R_1 and simplify:

$$M_{max} = +\left(\frac{l}{2}\right)\left(\frac{wl}{2}\right) - \left(\frac{l}{4}\right)\left(\frac{wl}{2}\right)$$

$$= \frac{wl^2}{4} - \frac{wl^2}{8} = \frac{2wl^2 - wl^2}{8}$$

$$M_{max} = \frac{wl^2}{8}$$

All of the case formulas for simple beams can be derived using this strategy.

Unit Cancellation

As mentioned previously, case formulas are unit sensitive. For example, while it does not matter if the load on a beam is measured in pounds or kips, matching variables must be used. The unit cancellation method is a useful method for keeping variables matched. Essentially, if all the correct units are plugged into an equation, they should cancel like variables, leaving only the units applicable to the solution of the equation. Constants (pure numbers) are unitless. For example, consider the formula for M_{max} of a simple beam, evenly distributed load (see above). M_{max} can be expressed as ftlbs or inlbs, but not as a combination:

$$M_{max} = \frac{wl^2}{8} = (pli)(in)^2 = \left(\frac{lb}{in}\right)in^2 = inlb$$

$$M_{max} = \frac{wl^2}{8} = (pli)(ft)^2 = \left(\frac{lb}{in}\right)ft^2 = \frac{lbft^2}{in}$$

These techniques can be used with any equation. It is also useful when doing unit conversions within an equation.

CHAPTER 3 LESSONS

The format of the numbering system is chapter.lesson.problem number.

LESSON 3.1 INTRODUCTION TO BEAM STRESS AND LOADING (PG 25 – 33)

3.1.1   Draw a free body diagram for either beam of the 4' wide catwalk illustrated below. The catwalk should be designed to hold a dead load of 10 psf and a live load of 60 psf.

3.1.2   Draw a free body diagram for the loading conditions on a beam which weighs 10 plf and is supported by cables at either end (see below).

3.1.3   Draw free body diagrams of the interior and exterior beams as well as the girders of the system below. The platform should be designed for a live load of 50 psf (which includes the dead weight of the platform). The weight of the girders is estimated at 5 plf.

3.1.4   Draw free body diagrams of the interior and exterior beams and girders for Problem 3.1.3 with the beams on 2' centers. All other loading conditions are identical.

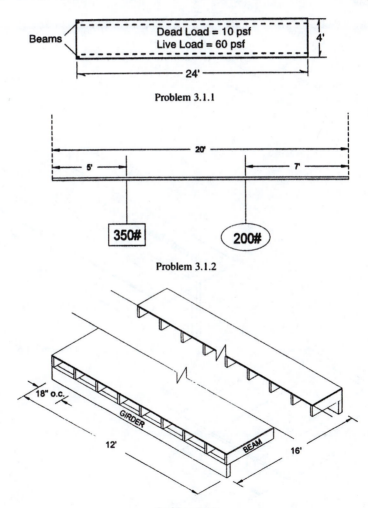

Problem 3.1.1

Problem 3.1.2

Problem 3.1.3

LESSON 3.1 CONTINUED.

3.1.5   Draw a free body diagram for the beam given below. The beam is one of a system which supports a "cut-away" **walkable** rooftop which should be designed for both a live load and a dead load of 10 psf; its tributary area is depicted in the figure.

3.1.6   Draw a free body diagram for the loading conditions on the given overhanging beam (tributary area represented).

3.1.7   Draw a free body diagram for a 6' long cantilever beam with a 200 lb point load at the end of the cantilever. The beam is estimated to weigh 5 plf.

3.1.8   Draw a free body diagram for a 4' long cantilever beam given below. The combined live and dead load is 50 psf.

3.1.9   Draw a free body diagram for a 20' long continuous beam with 5 supports on 5' centers. The beam supports a tributary area of 4 sf per linear foot with combined live and dead loads of 50 psf.

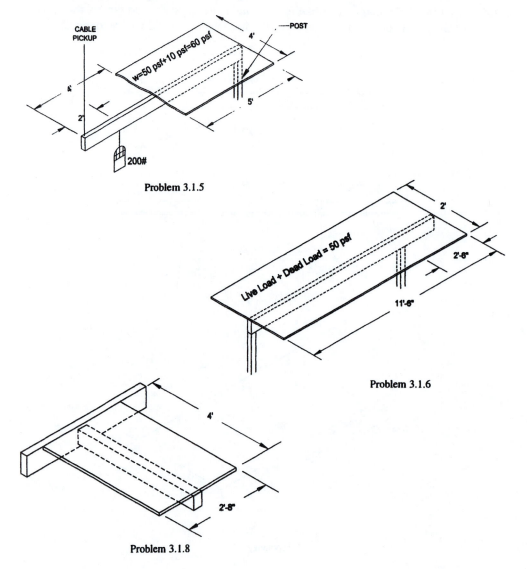

Problem 3.1.5

Problem 3.1.6

Problem 3.1.8

LESSON 3.2 REACTIONS (PG 33 – 34)

3.2.1　Find the reactions for problem 3.1.2.
3.2.2　Find the reactions for problem 3.1.1.
3.2.3　Find the reactions for problem 3.1.4.
3.2.4　Find the reactions for problem 3.1.3.
3.2.5　Find the reactions for beam and loading conditions given below.
3.2.6　Find the reactions for problem 3.1.5.
3.2.7　Find the reactions for beam and loading conditions given below.
3.2.8　Find the reactions for beam and loading conditions given below.

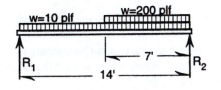

Problem 3.2.5

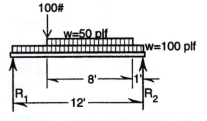

Problem 3.2.7

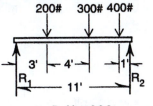

Problem 3.2.8

LESSON 3.3 SHEAR DIAGRAMS (PG 35 – 39)

3.3.1　Construct a shear diagram for problem 3.1.1. Label V_{max} and determine where shear crosses through zero.
3.3.2　Construct a shear diagram for problem 3.1.2. Label V_{max} and determine where shear crosses through zero.
3.3.3　Construct shear diagrams for problem 3.1.3. Label V_{max} and determine where shear crosses through zero for each beam.
3.3.4　Construct shear diagrams for problem 3.1.4. Label V_{max} and determine where shear crosses through zero for each beam.
3.3.5　Construct a shear diagram for problem 3.1.5. Label V_{max} and determine where shear crosses through zero.
3.3.6　Find the reactions and construct a shear diagram for the loading conditions given below. Label V_{max} and determine where shear crosses through zero.
3.3.7　Find the reactions and construct a shear diagram for the loading conditions given below. Label V_{max} and determine where shear crosses through zero.

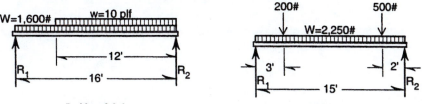

Problem 3.3.6　　　　　　　　　　　　　　　　Problem 3.3.7

LESSON 3.4 MOMENT DIAGRAMS (PG 40 – 45)

3.4.1   Construct a moment diagram for problem 3.1.2. Label M_{max}.
3.4.2   Construct moment diagrams for problem 3.1.3. Label M_{max}.
3.4.3   Construct moment diagrams for problem 3.1.4. Label M_{max}.
3.4.4   Construct a moment diagram for problem 3.1.5. Label M_{max}.
3.4.5   Construct a moment diagram for problem 3.3.6. Label M_{max}.

LESSON 3.5 OVERHANGS AND CANTILEVERS (PG 45 – 50)

3.5.1   Find the reactions and construct shear and moment diagrams for the given over-hanging beam.
3.5.2   Find the reactions and construct shear and moment diagrams for the overhanging beam in problem 3.1.6.
3.5.3   A beam is 12' long, but the designer does not care where the two support points land along its length. Assuming that the load is evenly distributed, where should the beam be supported in order to generate the smallest possible M_{max}?
3.5.4   Find the reaction and construct shear and moment diagrams for the given cantilever beam.
3.5.5   Find the reactions and construct shear and moment diagrams for the given cantilever beam.

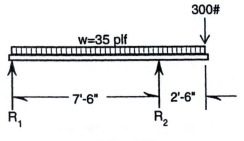

Problem 3.5.1

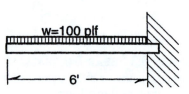

Problem 3.5.4

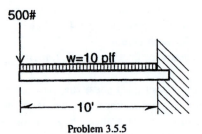

Problem 3.5.5

LESSON 3.6 CASE FORMULAS (PG 51 – 54)

3.6.1 What are R_1, R_2, V_{max}, and M_{max} for a simple beam spanning 11' with one point load of 237# in the center of the span?

3.6.2 What are R_1, R_2, V_{max}, and M_{max} for a simple beam spanning 7'-6" with 2 point loads of 348# 2' from each support?

3.6.3 What are R_1, V_{max}, and M_{max} for a cantilever beam 12' long with an evenly distributed load of 20 plf and a point load of 350# at the free end?

3.6.4 What are R_1, R_2, V_{max}, and M_{max} for an overhanging beam with an overhang of 4' and a span between supports of 8'? It has an evenly distributed load of 100 plf.

3.6.5 What are R_A, R_B, R_C, R_D, V_{max}, and M_{max} for a continuous beam with three spans of 8'? It has an evenly distributed load of 25 plf.

3.6.6 Find R_1, R_2, V_{max}, and M_{max} for the beam given below.

3.6.7 A set design calls for a catwalk which frames the proscenium of the theater. A large gilded decorative frame conceals the catwalk and is estimated to weight 20 plf. The catwalk is 3' wide and is supported on 13' centers with a total length of 39'. Assume the catwalk has two primary beams and that the downstage beam carries the entire load of the decorative frame. Since the show has not been blocked the catwalk should be designed for a live load of 50 psf. The catwalk beams also share the weight of an underhung electric with units hung on 18" centers (25 plf). Find the reactions and construct shear and moment diagrams for the downstage beam. Identify V_{max}, where shear crosses through zero, and M_{max}.

3.6.8 Derive the case formulas for V_{max} and M_{max} for a simple span with a point load at its center. Draw and label the shear and moment diagrams.

3.6.9 Derive the case formulas for V_{max} and M_{max} for a simple span with two symmetrically placed point loads. Draw and label the shear and moment diagrams.

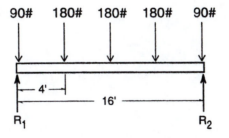

Problem 3.6.6

4

Geometric Properties

INTRODUCTION

To design a beam or column, a structural designer first needs to calculate the actual stresses present, select a shape with the appropriate geometric properties, and identify the material from which the member will be made. In Chapter 3, calculating the stress in beams was discussed, and, in this chapter, quantifying the geometric properties of a shape will be covered. In Chapters 5 through 10, material issues will be considered.

In structural design, "shape" refers to the cross-section of the member and is independent of the material choice. The ability of a shape to resist stresses is quantified by its geometric properties. The geometric properties of primary importance are the *moment of inertia*, *section modulus*, *area* and *radius of gyration*. Other geometric properties include the *centroid*, *neutral axis*, and *extreme fiber distance*. Once the material and shape are selected, a designer uses the section modulus to determine the maximum bending moment that a beam can support; the moment of inertia is used to determine the amount of deflection that a given load will cause; the area determines the total shear stress a member can withstand, and the radius of gyration is used to determine the maximum axial load that a column can support. Likewise, a designer can work backwards and identify the required geometric properties that a beam or column needs to support a given load.

THE NEUTRAL AXIS, CENTROID, AND "c"

Bending causes the top part of the beam to be in compression and the bottom part of the beam to be in tension. Theoretically there is a plane in the "middle" of the cross-section in which there are no compressive or tensile stresses. This plane is perpendicular to the line of action of the load(s) and is called the **neutral axis**, or the plane of bending.

Every beam can have an infinite number of neutral axes, one for every possible loading angle, and every neutral axis of a shape will cross through a point called the **centroid**. The most common neutral axes for any shape are the *x-x* (horizontal) and *y-y* (vertical) axes. Standard shape tables give the location of the centroid by showing the intersection of these two axes. The axis *perpendicular* to the line of action of a load will be the axis which resists that force. Hence, in Figure 4.1a, the *x-x* axis resists the vertical load.

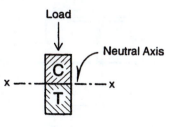

Figure 4.1a Neutral axes

The centroid is the center of gravity of the beam's cross-section (see Figure 4.1b). Instinctively, the centroid of a symmetrical shape is easy to determine – it is at the center of the shape. For asymmetrical sections, it is necessary to calculate the location of the centroid.

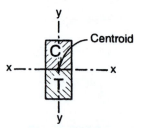

Figure 4.1b Centroid

The **extreme fiber distance, "*c*"** is the perpendicular distance from the neutral axis to the farthest, or extreme, edge of a shape. For symmetrical shapes, *c* is the same distance to either edge. For asymmetrical shapes, it is important to distinguish between the extreme fiber distance and the lesser distance from a neutral axis to the other edge of the shape.

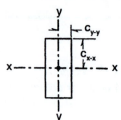

Figure 4.1c *c* for the *x-x*, *y-y* axes

There is a separate extreme fiber distance for each neutral axis of a shape. Conventionally, section properties tables show the *x-x* and *y-y* axes and the corresponding extreme fiber distances c_{x-x} and c_{y-y} (see Figure 4.1c). Typically, the *x-x* axis is defined as the "strong" axis and is the most common orientation of the shape to a load.

Example 1. Find the centroid, c_{x-x} and c_{y-y}, of the following cross-sections.

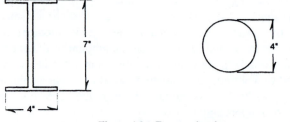

Figure 4.2a Two regular shapes

Both centroids are easy to find because the shapes are symmetrical. For the I-beam, the centroid is located 3.5" from the top or bottom and 2" from the left or right of the shape. For the circle, the centroid is its center, 2" from any point on the circumference.

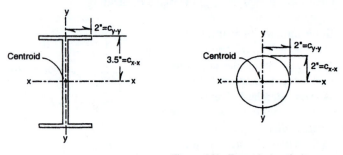

Figure 4.2b Example 1, solution

The concept of **statical moment** is used to find the location of the neutral axes and c for asymmetrical shapes. A statical moment is the perpendicular distance from the centroid of a shape to a reference axis times the area of the shape. It is common practice to use one edge of a shape as the reference axis. The neutral axis occurs where the sum of the statical moments of the component top and bottom areas of a beam are equal. The neutral axis of a shape is *not* necessarily the plane at which the areas of the top and bottom are equal. Mathematically, a statical moment is expressed as follows:

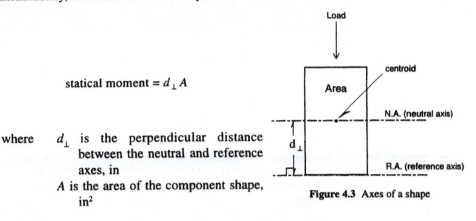

$$\text{statical moment} = d_\perp A$$

where $d_\perp$ is the perpendicular distance between the neutral and reference axes, in

A is the area of the component shape, in^2

Figure 4.3 Axes of a shape

The principal of statical moments states that the sum of the statical moments of components of a shape must be equal to the statical moment of the whole shape.

$$A_{tot} d_{NA} = \sum d_{1_\perp} A_1 + d_{2_\perp} A_2 + d_{3_\perp} A_3 + \ldots d_{\infty_\perp} A_\infty$$

The distance from the neutral axis to the reference axis is d_{NA}, and the distance from the neutral axis to the opposite edge of the shape is d'_{NA}. If the above equation is manipulated to solve for d_{NA}, we can write:

$$d_{NA} = \frac{\sum d_{1_\perp} A_1 + d_{2_\perp} A_2 + d_{3_\perp} A_3 + \ldots d_{\infty_\perp} A_\infty}{A_{tot}}$$

$$d'_{NA} = d_{shape} - d_{NA}$$

$$c = \text{the greater of } d'_{NA} \text{ or } d_{NA}$$

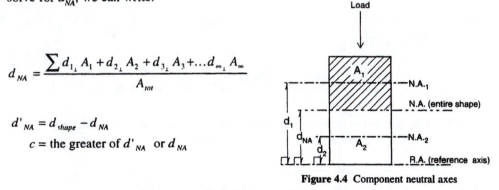

Figure 4.4 Component neutral axes

The extreme fiber distance, c, can be determined once the neutral axis is located. It is the greater of the two distances, d_{NA} or d'_{NA}. The reference axis can be any line which is parallel to the neutral axis in the plane of bending. Though c is a geometric property which is used in calculating other geometric properties, both distances, d_{NA} and d'_{NA}, may be useful in subsequent calculations.

Example 2. Find the neutral axis perpendicular to the load for the following "T" shape and determine $c_{x\text{-}x}$.

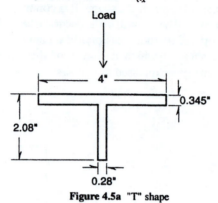

Figure 4.5a "T" shape

First, divide the "T" shape into rectangular components, and then determine the area of each component and the distance between the neutral axis of each component and the reference axis (R.A.) at the bottom of the "T" shape.

$A_B = (bd)_B = 4"(0.345") = 1.38\ \text{in}^2$

$A_C = (bd)_C = (0.28")(2.080" - 0.345")$

$\quad = (0.28")(1.735") = 0.4858\ \text{in}^2$

$d_{\perp B} = \left(2.080" - \dfrac{0.345"}{2}\right) = 1.9075"\ \text{to R.A.}$

$d_{\perp C} = \left(\dfrac{2.080" - 0.345"}{2}\right) = 0.8675"\ \text{to R.A.}$

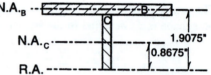

Figure 4.5b Component shapes

$A_{tot} d_{NA} = A_B d_{\perp B} + A_C d_{\perp C}$

$d_{NA} = \dfrac{A_B d_{\perp B} + A_C d_{\perp C}}{A_{tot}}$

$d_{NA} = \dfrac{(1.9075")(1.38\ \text{in}^2) + (0.8675")(0.4858\ \text{in}^2)}{1.38 + 0.4858\ \text{in}^2} = 1.64"\ \text{from R.A.}$

Find the dimension from the top of the shape to the neutral axis and determine the extreme fiber distance for the x-x axis, $c_{x\text{-}x}$:

$$d'_{NA} = d_{shape} - d_{NA}$$
$$d'_{NA} = 2.080" - 1.64" = 0.44"\ \text{from top}$$

since $1.64" > 0.44"$,

$$c_{x-x} = 1.64"$$

Redraw the shape with the neutral axis and $c_{x\text{-}x}$:

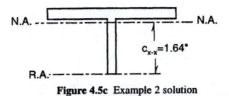

Figure 4.5c Example 2 solution

Example 3. Check the previous calculations by using the top of the shape as the reference axis, and also by using a reference axis which is 1.5" above the top of the shape.

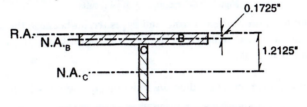

Figure 4.6a Example 3, top as reference axis

$$d_{\perp B} = \frac{0.345}{2} = 0.1725" \text{ to top}$$

$$d_{\perp C} = (0.345" + 0.8675") = 1.2125" \text{ to top}$$

$$d_{NA} = \frac{d_{\perp B} A_B + d_{\perp C} A_C}{A_{tot}} = \frac{(0.1725")(1.38 \text{ in}^2) + (1.2125")(0.4858 \text{ in}^2)}{1.38 \text{ in}^2 + 0.4858 \text{ in}^2} = 0.44" \text{ from top } \checkmark$$

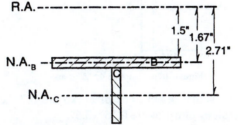

Figure 4.6b Example 3, with R.A. 1.5" above the top of the shape

$$d_{\perp B} = \frac{0.345}{2} + 1.5" = 1.6725" \text{ to reference axis}$$

$$d_{\perp C} = (0.345" + 0.8675" + 1.5") = 2.7125" \text{ to reference axis}$$

$$d_{NA} = \frac{(1.6725")(1.38 \text{ in}^2) + (2.7125")(0.4858 \text{ in}^2)}{1.38 \text{ in}^2 + 0.4858 \text{ in}^2} = 1.94" \text{ to reference axis}$$

Check the dimensions from the bottom and the top and determine c_{x-x}.

$$d_{NA} = (1.5" + 2.080") - 1.94" = 1.64" \text{ from bottom}$$

$$d'_{NA} = 2.080" - 1.64" = 0.44" \text{ from top } \checkmark$$

$$c_{x-x} = 1.64"$$

Now compare the results of the three different calculations:

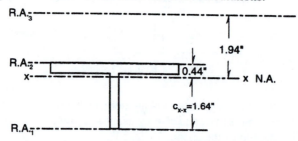

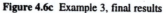

Figure 4.6c Example 3, final results

Finding the location of the centroid and $c_{y\text{-}y}$ is trivial because the shape is symmetrical with respect to the y-y axis, and, therefore, $c_{y\text{-}y}$ is 2" from either edge.

If a shape is loaded against both axes, then we must determine c for both axes.

Example 4. Find the x-x and y-y neutral axes of the following built-up "Z" shape.

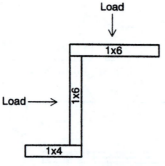

Figure 4.7a Example 4, "Z" shape

First, find $c_{x\text{-}x}$. The actual dimensions of a 1x6 are 0.75"x5.5", and the actual dimensions of a 1x4 are 0.75"x3.5".

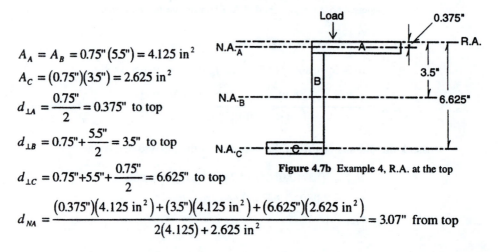

$A_A = A_B = 0.75" (5.5") = 4.125 \text{ in}^2$

$A_C = (0.75")(3.5") = 2.625 \text{ in}^2$

$d_{\perp A} = \dfrac{0.75"}{2} = 0.375" \text{ to top}$

$d_{\perp B} = 0.75" + \dfrac{5.5"}{2} = 3.5" \text{ to top}$

$d_{\perp C} = 0.75" + 5.5" + \dfrac{0.75"}{2} = 6.625" \text{ to top}$

Figure 4.7b Example 4, R.A. at the top

$d_{NA} = \dfrac{(0.375")(4.125 \text{ in}^2) + (3.5")(4.125 \text{ in}^2) + (6.625")(2.625 \text{ in}^2)}{2(4.125) + 2.625 \text{ in}^2} = 3.07" \text{ from top}$

Check the dimension from the bottom and determine c_{x-x}:

$$d'_{NA} = 0.75"+5.5"+0.75"-3.07" = 3.93" \text{ from bottom}$$
$$c_{x-x} = 3.93".$$

Now, find c_{y-y}:

$$d_{\perp A} = 3.5 - 0.75" + \frac{5.5"}{2} = 5.5" \text{ to left}$$

$$d_{\perp B} = 3.5" - \frac{0.75"}{2} = 3.125" \text{ to left}$$

$$d_{\perp C} = \frac{3.5"}{2} = 1.75" \text{ to left}$$

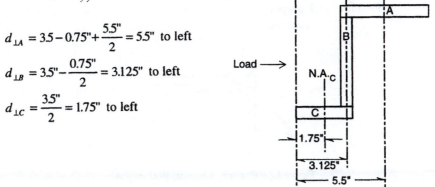

Figure 4.7c Example 4, reference axis at left

$$d_{NA} = \frac{(5.5")(4.125 \text{ in}^2)+(3.125")(4.125 \text{ in}^2)+(1.75")(2.625 \text{ in}^2)}{2(4.125)+2.625 \text{ in}^2} = 3.69" \text{ from left}$$

Check the dimension from the right and determine c_{y-y}:

$$d'_{NA} = 3.5"-0.75"+5.5"-3.69" = 4.56" \text{ from right}$$
$$c_{y-y} = 4.56"$$

Redraw the shape with the x-x and y-y neutral axes:

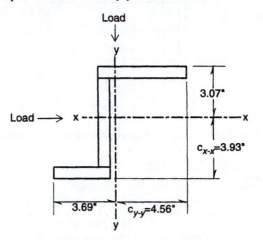

Figure 4.7d Example 4, final solution

For commonly available shapes of wood and steel, the *x-x* and *y-y* neutral axes can be found in Appendices D and E. However, technical designers often build up sections by combining common shapes. In these cases, the neutral axes and *c* must be calculated using the data for the component shapes.

> ***Example 5.*** Determine c_{x-x} and c_{y-y} of the following section built-up from common steel shapes:

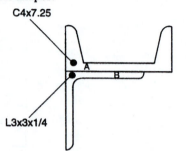

> **Figure 4.8a** Example 5, built-up steel section

> The areas and location of the neutral axis of each component can be found in Appendix E. The area for the angle is 1.44 in²; the area for the channel is 2.13 in². Figure 4.8b illustrates the dimensions found in Appendix E.

The reference axes will be at the bottom and to the left:

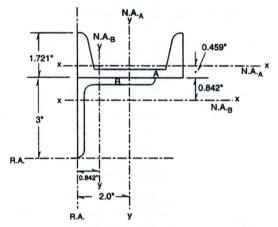

> **Figure 4.8b** Example 5, built-up steel section with dimensions

$$d_{NA_{x-x}} = \frac{d_{\perp A}A_A + d_{\perp B}A_B}{A_{tot}}$$

$$= \frac{(3"+0.459")(2.13 \text{ in}^2) + (3"-0.842")(1.44 \text{ in}^2)}{2.13 \text{ in}^2 + 1.44 \text{ in}^2} = 2.93" \text{ from bottom}$$

$$d'_{NA_{x-x}} = 3"+1.721"-2.93" = 1.79" \text{ from top}$$

$$c_{x-x} = 2.93"$$

$$d_{NA_{y-y}} = \frac{(2")(2.13 \text{ in}^2) + (0.842")(1.44 \text{ in}^2)}{2.13 \text{ in}^2 + 1.44 \text{ in}^2} = 1.533" \text{ from left}$$

$$d'_{NA_{y-y}} = 4" - 1.533" = 2.47" \text{ from right}$$

$$c_{y-y} = 2.47"$$

Redraw the solved section:

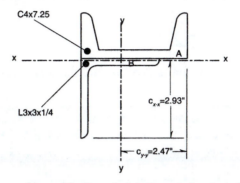

C4x7.25

L3x3x1/4

$c_{x-x} = 2.93"$

$c_{y-y} = 2.47"$

Figure 4.8c Example 5, built-up steel section solved

Example 6. Determine c_{x-x} and c_{y-y} for the following built-up shape.

Since the shape is symmetrical with respect to the y-y axis, we only need to calculate c_{x-x} (c_{y-y} is 3" from either side). The reference axis is at the bottom. From Appendix E, the area of the channel is 3.09 in².

$$d_{NA} = \frac{2(d_{\perp chan} A_{chan}) + (d_{\perp plate} A_{plate})}{2(A_{chan}) + A_{plate}}$$

$$d_{NA} = \frac{2[(3")(3.09 \text{ in}^2)] + (6.125")(1.5 \text{ in}^2)}{2(3.09 \text{ in}^2) + 1.5 \text{ in}^2}$$

$$= 3.61" \text{ from bottom}$$

$$d'_{NA} = 6.25" - 3.61" = 2.64" \text{ from top}$$

$$c_{x-x} = 3.61"$$

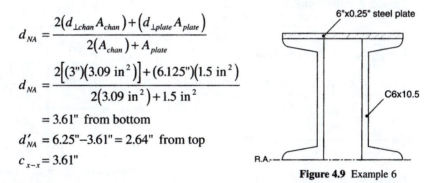

6"x0.25" steel plate

C6x10.5

R.A.

Figure 4.9 Example 6

It is important to note that geometric properties assume that the material choice remains constant for built-up shapes. Determining the section properties of a mixed media beam, such as one which combines plywood and sawn lumber, requires taking into account the different moduli of elasticity of each material.

MOMENT OF INERTIA

Moment of inertia, *I*, is a mathematical concept which quantifies a beam's resistance to deformation, called deflection. For a given loading condition, selecting a beam with a higher *I* value will result in a smaller deflection. Unfortunately, moment of inertia has no simple physical analogy. *I* quantifies a shape's stiffness by relating the area of the cross-section and the distribution of material relative to the neutral axis in the plane of bending.

For an infinitesimally small area (a), the moment of inertia equals the area multiplied by its perpendicular distance (z) from the neutral axis about which it is acting, squared:

$$I_{\infty} = az^2$$

Since area is in inches^2 and the distance is squared, the units of I work out to be inches^4. Conceptually, to find the total I of a shape, the individual I values of all the infinitesimally small areas are summed:

$$I = \sum_{n=1}^{n=\infty} A_n z_n^2$$

The more increments the cross-section is divided into, the more accurate the calculated value of I.

> MATH NOTE: The sigma symbol is mathematical short-hand for "summation." This equation would read, "I equals the sum of the area multiplied by the squared distance of areas 1 through infinity." I is the sum of the I values of a very large number of areas that make up the shape.

Example 7. Calculate the difference between the I value found by dividing this 2x4 into 2 and then 4 equal areas.

Figure 4.10a Example 7

I using 2 equal areas:

$$I = \sum_{n=1}^{n=\infty} A_n z_n^2 = A_A z_A^2 + A_B z_B^2$$

$$I = \left(b\frac{d}{2}\right)\left(\frac{d}{4}\right)^2 + \left(b\frac{d}{2}\right)\left(\frac{d}{4}\right)^2 = 2\left(b\frac{d}{2}\right)\left(\frac{d^2}{16}\right)$$

$$I_{2x4} = \frac{bd^3}{16} = \frac{1.5"(3.5")^3}{16} = 4.0195 \text{ in}^4$$

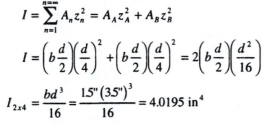

Figure 4.10b Example 7, 2 areas

I using 4 equal areas:

$$I = \sum_{n=1}^{n=\infty} A_n z_n^2 = A_A z_A^2 + A_B z_B^2 + A_C z_C^2 + A_D z_D^2$$

$$I = 2\left[\left(b\frac{d}{4}\right)\left(\frac{d}{8}\right)^2\right] + 2\left[\left(b\frac{d}{4}\right)\left(\frac{3d}{8}\right)^2\right]$$

$$I = \frac{bd^3}{128} + \frac{9bd^3}{128} = \frac{10bd^3}{128} = \frac{5bd^3}{64}$$

$$I_{2x4} = \frac{5(1.5")(3.5")^3}{64} = 5.0244 \text{ in}^4$$

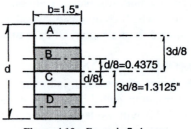

Figure 4.10c Example 7, 4 areas

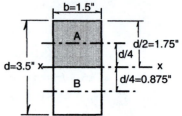

As the areas become smaller, the calculated value for I becomes more accurate. If an infinite number of areas are used, the formula for a rectangle reduces to $I=bd^3/12$, and, for the 2x4, I becomes 5.3594 in⁴. Mathematically, adding the I values of infinitesimally small areas is the same as integrating az^2 along the depth of the section:

$$I_{x-x} = \int z^2 dA = \int_{-d/2}^{+d/2} z^2 b\, dz = b\int_{-d/2}^{+d/2} z^2\, dz$$

$$I_{x-x} = b\frac{z^3}{3}\Big|_{-d/2}^{+d/2} = \frac{b}{3}\left[\left(+\frac{d}{2}\right)^3 - \left(-\frac{d}{2}\right)^3\right] = \frac{bd^3}{12}$$

> **MATH NOTE:** Integration is a shorthand method for summing expressions such as the previous summation of I values. The numbers above and below the integral symbol, indicate the range of values being summed. In this case, d is the depth of the shape. The integral is taken from the center, so it ranges from $+d/2$ to $-d/2$. The next step is the actual integration, which is the calculus method of reiterating what we did in Example 7 an infinite number of times.

Fortunately, structural designers do not need to resort to calculus to do everyday calculations. The formulas to find I values for regular geometric shapes are well known and tabulated (see Appendix C).

Example 8. Find I_{x-x} and I_{y-y} for a 2x4.

$$I_{x-x} = \frac{bd^3}{12} = \frac{1.5''(3.5'')^3}{12} = 5.3594 \text{ in}^4$$

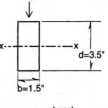

$$I_{y-y} = \frac{bd^3}{12} = \frac{3.5''(1.5'')^3}{12} = 0.984 \text{ in}^4$$

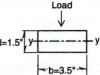

Figure 4.11 Example 8

Example 9. Find I for a circle with a 1.75" diameter.

$$I = \frac{\pi d^4}{64} = \frac{\pi(1.75'')^4}{64} = 0.4604 \text{ in}^4$$

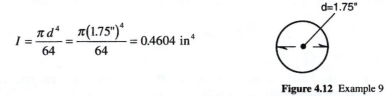

Figure 4.12 Example 9

If shapes share the same neutral axis, their I values can be summed directly.

Example 10. If two 2x4's are laminated together to form a beam as shown below, their I values can be added together.

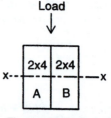

$$I_{tot} = I_A + I_B = 5.3594 \text{ in}^4 + 5.3594 \text{ in}^4 = 10.72 \text{ in}^4$$

Figure 4.13 Example 10

Likewise, the I value of a hollow shape can be determined by subtracting the I value of the inner shape from the I value of the outer shape (some hollow shapes are listed in Appendix C).

Example 11. Find I for a 1-1/2" schedule 40 black pipe.

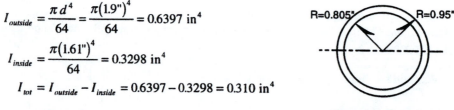

$$I_{outside} = \frac{\pi d^4}{64} = \frac{\pi (1.9")^4}{64} = 0.6397 \text{ in}^4$$

$$I_{inside} = \frac{\pi (1.61")^4}{64} = 0.3298 \text{ in}^4$$

$$I_{tot} = I_{outside} - I_{inside} = 0.6397 - 0.3298 = 0.310 \text{ in}^4$$

Figure 4.14 Example 11

It is important to note that a shape can have an infinite number of I values. Typically, tables will give the x-x, y-y, and sometimes the z-z I values. The orientation of the shape with respect to the load determines which I value is applicable. The I value for the neutral axis *perpendicular* to the load is the one which resists the load. In the case of totally symmetrical shapes such as circles, there is only one I value.

TRANSFERRING MOMENTS OF INERTIA

The I values for standard shapes and sizes of metal and wood are readily available. However, for built-up shapes, I is calculated by transferring the I values of the components to the neutral axis of the whole shape. The I value of a built-up shape equals the sum of the I values of each component, plus the area of the components multiplied by the square of the distance between the neutral axis of each component and the neutral axis of the whole:

$$I_{tot} = \sum_{n=1}^{n=\infty} I_{o_n} + A_n z_n^2$$

where $I_{o(n)}$ is the I value of the component with respect to its neutral axis, in^4

A_n is the area of the component, in^2

z_n is the perpendicular distance between the neutral axis of the component and the neutral axis of the whole shape, in

First, locate the neutral axis of the built-up shape. Next, determine I for each component. Be sure to use the neutral axis for each component that is parallel to the neutral axis of the whole shape.

> **Example 12.** Find I for both axes for the following "T" shape constructed of 2x4's.
>
> First, find c_{x-x}:

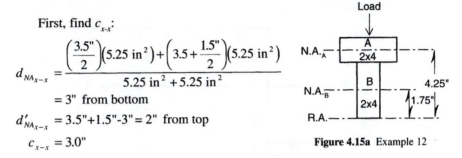

$$d_{NA_{x-x}} = \frac{\left(\frac{3.5"}{2}\right)(5.25 \text{ in}^2) + \left(3.5 + \frac{1.5"}{2}\right)(5.25 \text{ in}^2)}{5.25 \text{ in}^2 + 5.25 \text{ in}^2}$$

$$= 3" \text{ from bottom}$$

$$d'_{NA_{x-x}} = 3.5" + 1.5" - 3" = 2" \text{ from top}$$

$$c_{x-x} = 3.0"$$

Next, calculate I_{x-x} by transferring the I_o values of the individual components:

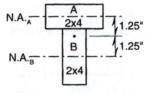

Figure 4.15b Example 12

$$I_{tot_{x-x}} = I_A + I_B$$

$$I_A = I_{o_A} + A_A z_A^2 = \frac{bd^3}{12} + Az^2 = \frac{(3.5")(1.5")^3}{12} + (5.25 \text{ in}^2)(1.25")^2 = 9.1875 \text{ in}^4$$

$$I_B = I_{o_B} + A_B z_B^2 = \frac{bd^3}{12} + Az^2 = \frac{(1.5")(3.5")^3}{12} + (5.25 \text{ in}^2)(1.25")^2 = 13.5625 \text{ in}^4$$

$$I_{tot_{x-x}} = 9.1875 \text{ in}^4 + 13.5625 \text{ in}^4 = 22.75 \text{ in}^4$$

Calculate I_{y-y} by adding the two I values together because the shape is symmetrical with respect to the y-y axis:

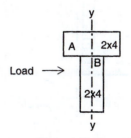

$$I_{tot_{y-y}} = I_{A_{y-y}} + I_{B_{y-y}} = \frac{b_A d_A^3}{12} + \frac{b_B d_B^3}{12}$$

$$= \frac{(1.5")(3.5")^3}{12} + \frac{(3.5")(1.5")^3}{12} = 6.34 \text{ in}^4$$

Figure 4.15c Example 12

Example 13. A built-up shape can be asymmetrical with respect to both axes. Find I_{x-x} and I_{y-y} for the "Z" shape from Example 4.

Remember that the x-x axis was 3.93" from the bottom and 3.07" from the top. Calculate the I value for each component with respect to the x-x axis and sum them to find $I_{tot\,(x-x)}$. See Figure 4.7b for more information.

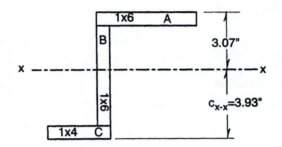

Figure 4.16a Example 13, x-x axis

$$I_{tot_{x-x}} = I_A + I_B + I_C$$

$$I_{A_{x-x}} = I_{oA} + A_A z_A^2 = \frac{bd^3}{12} + Az^2 = \frac{(5.5")(0.75")^3}{12} + (0.75")(5.5")\left(3.07" - \frac{0.75"}{2}\right)^2 = 30.15\ in^4$$

$$I_{B_{x-x}} = I_{oB} + A_B z_B^2 = \frac{bd^3}{12} + Az^2 = \frac{(0.75")(5.5")^3}{12} + \left(4.125\ in^2\right)\left(\frac{5.5"}{2} + 0.75" - 3.07"\right)^2 = 11.16\ in^4$$

$$I_{C_{x-x}} = I_{oC} + A_C z_C^2 = \frac{bd^3}{12} + Az^2 = \frac{(3.5")(0.75")^3}{12} + (0.75")(3.5")\left(3.93" - \frac{0.75"}{2}\right)^2 = 33.30\ in^4$$

$$I_{tot_{x-x}} = 30.15\ in^4 + 11.16\ in^4 + 33.30\ in^4 = 74.61\ in^4$$

I_{y-y} is calculated using the same technique. Figure 4.16b duplicates information found in Figure 4.7c.

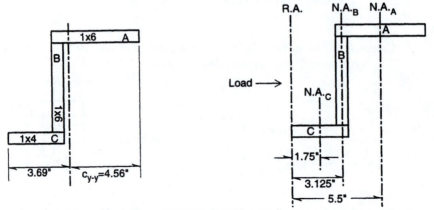

Figure 4.16b Example 13, y-y axis

$$I_{tot_{y-y}} = I_A + I_B + I_C$$

$$I_{A_{y-y}} = I_{o_A} + A_A z_A^2 = \frac{bd^3}{12} + Az^2 = \frac{(0.75")(5.5")^3}{12} + (4.125 \text{ in}^2)(5.5"-3.69")^2 = 23.91 \text{ in}^4$$

$$I_{B_{y-y}} = I_{o_B} + A_B z_B^2 = \frac{bd^3}{12} + Az^2 = \frac{(5.5")(0.75")^3}{12} + (4.125 \text{ in}^2)(3.69"-3.125")^2 = 1.51 \text{ in}^4$$

$$I_{C_{y-y}} = I_{o_C} + A_C z_C^2 = \frac{bd^3}{12} + Az^2 = \frac{(0.75")(3.5")^3}{12} + (2.625 \text{ in}^2)(3.69"-1.75")^2 = 12.56 \text{ in}^4$$

$$I_{tot_{y-y}} = 23.91 \text{ in}^4 + 1.51 \text{ in}^4 + 12.56 \text{ in}^4 = 37.98 \text{ in}^4$$

RADIUS OF GYRATION

The **radius of gyration, r,** is a geometric property which defines the relative resistance of a column to buckling. As mentioned in Chapter 2, slender columns fail due to buckling before they fail due to crushing. Since F_c, the allowable compressive stress, is calculated for crushing failure, structural designers must reduce F_c to account for a column's shape, size, and unbraced length (see Chapters 6 and 9). The radius of gyration is a critical part of that process. The radius of gyration relates the cross-sectional properties of the moment of inertia and area of a column and is mathematically expressed as the following:

$$r = \sqrt{\frac{I}{A}}$$

where I is the moment of inertia of the column, in^4
            A is the cross-sectional area of the column, in^2
            r is the radius of gyration, in

The radius of gyration is measured in inches and has no relationship to an actual radius of any shape. It is tabulated for nominal shapes and sizes (see Appendices C, D, and E).

    Example 14. What is the radius of gyration of a 1-1/2", schedule 40 black pipe?

    From Appendix E, the cross-sectional area of the pipe is 0.799 in^2, and the I value is 0.310 in^4. Calculate the radius of gyration:

$$r = \sqrt{\frac{I}{A}} = \sqrt{\frac{0.310 \text{ in}^4}{0.799 \text{ in}^2}} = 0.623"$$

    Example 15. What is the radius of gyration of any solid circle?

    From Appendix C: $I_{cir} = \frac{\pi d^4}{64}$ $A_{cir} = \frac{\pi d^2}{4}$

$$r_{cir} = \sqrt{\frac{I}{A}} = \sqrt{\frac{\frac{\pi d^4}{64}}{\frac{\pi d^2}{4}}} = \sqrt{\left(\frac{\pi d^4}{64}\right)\left(\frac{4}{\pi d^2}\right)} = \sqrt{\frac{d^2}{16}} = \frac{d}{4}$$

SECTION MODULUS

One more geometric property must be defined before we have all the variables necessary to design a beam. The **section modulus**, S, is a geometric property for beams and is relative to both the size and shape of a section. S predicts a beam's capacity to resist bending forces. Mathematically, the section modulus equals I divided by c and is measured in inches^3. The need for S, like I, is not easy to explain physically, but it is crucial for beam calculations. In broad terms, S determines beam failure, and I determines beam stiffness (deflection). Like I, S is tabulated for standard shapes and sizes. For a rectangular section, S is easily derived:

$$S = \frac{I}{c} \qquad I_{rect} = \frac{bd^3}{12} \qquad c_{rect} = \frac{d}{2}$$

$$S_{rect} = \frac{\frac{bd^3}{12}}{\frac{d}{2}} = \left(\frac{bd^3}{12}\right)\left(\frac{2}{d}\right) = \frac{bd^2}{6}$$

For built-up beams, S is easy to calculate if the values of I and c have already been determined. Remember that c is the greatest distance from the neutral axis to an edge of the section. Like I, S is axis specific.

> *Example 16.* Find $S_{x\text{-}x}$ for the "Z" shape in Examples 4 and 13.

$$I_{x\text{-}x} = 74.61 \text{ in}^4$$
$$c_{x\text{-}x} = 3.93 \text{ in}$$
$$S_{x\text{-}x} = \frac{I_{x\text{-}x}}{c_{x\text{-}x}} = \frac{74.61 \text{ in}^4}{3.93 \text{ in}} = 18.98 \text{ in}^3$$

THE FLEXURE FORMULA

As explained previously, a tangential load on a beam causes bending, which results in a combination of tensile and compressive stresses. The relative ability of a beam to resist a bending force varies with shape, size, and material choice. The **Flexure Formula** quantifies this relationship:

$$M = F_b S$$

where M is the maximum bending moment, inlb
              F_b is the allowable bending stress, psi
              S is the section modulus in the plane of bending, in^3

In words, the Flexure Formula dictates that the amount of moment that a beam can withstand is directly proportional to the allowable bending stress of the material from which the beam is made and the section modulus of the beam in the plane of bending.

The concepts underlying the Flexure Formula are illustrated as follows (Parker, 111):

- Consider a rectangular beam under a point load with a reaction at either end. Now, isolate the end of the beam which includes R_1.

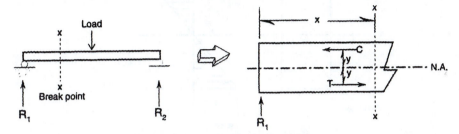

Figure 4.17 Conceptual derivation of the Flexure Formula

- The bending moment at x distance from R_1 is R_1x.

- Since the sum of the moments must always be in equilibrium, the bending moment is resisted by the combination of compressive and tensile stresses. The magnitude of their resistance is equal to the sum of their moments around the neutral axis, $Cy + Ty$.

$$\sum M = 0 = M_{\text{bending}} - M_{\text{resisting}}$$
$$0 = [R_1x] - (Cy + Ty)$$
$$0 = R_1x - (Cy + Ty)$$
$$xR_1 = y(C + T)$$

- Since the bending moment has a much greater lever arm, x, than the resisting moment, y, the combined compressive and tensile forces must be much greater than R_1.

Beams with a greater depth resist bending better than shallow beams because they have a greater distance between the compressive and tensile forces, which gives them a greater lever arm with which to resist the bending moment. Hence, the amount of bending moment a beam can withstand is a product of both the material choice (F_b) and its shape and size (S).

The actual format of the flexure formula can be understood with the following simplified derivation (Parker, 112):

- Consider the following rectangular cross-section and its corresponding stress diagram. Stress increases proportionally from the neutral axis. The farther away a single fiber is from the neutral axis, the more stress it undergoes. Hence, the extreme fibers rupture first when the allowable bending stress of the beam is exceeded. The stress (psi) at the extreme edge is labeled f.

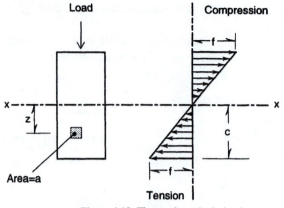

Figure 4.18 Flexure formula derivation

- Tensile and compressive stresses increase linearly through the section as illustrated in Figure 4.18.

- The stress at the extreme fiber distance is equal to f. Remember that the slope of a line is equal to the change in one dimension divided by the change in another. If the centroid of this shape is designated as the origin, the slope of the stress diagram is f/c. To find the stress at any plane of the shape, called the unit stress, we simply multiply the slope times the perpendicular distance from the centroid.

$$\text{unit stress} = \left(\frac{f}{c}\right)z = \frac{fz}{c}$$

where z is the perpendicular distance from the neutral axis to a plane

- The unit stress quantifies the stress at a plane, but it does not tell us the stress at a small area of the shape. For a very small area of the shape, the stress would equal the area, a, times the unit stress:

$$\text{stress} = (\text{unit stress})(\text{area}) = \left(\frac{fz}{c}\right)a$$

where a is a very small area

- The moment of the stress on a fiber is the stress multiplied by its distance from the neutral axis. For each small area, the moment is expressed as:

$$\text{Moment} = (\text{stress})(\text{lever arm}) = \left[\left(\frac{fz}{c}\right)a\right]z$$

where z is still the perpendicular distance of the area from the neutral axis

- The total resisting moment of the beam is equal to the sum of the moments of all of these infinitesimally small areas.

$$M_{resisting} = \sum_{n=1}^{n=\infty}\left[\left(\frac{fz_n}{c}\right)a_n\right]z_n = \sum_{n=1}^{n=\infty}\frac{f}{c}a_n z_n^2$$

- Since f and c do not change from area to area, we can take them outside of the summation (they will be distributed through after the summation):

$$M = \frac{f}{c}\sum_{n=1}^{n=\infty}a_n z_n^2$$

- Remember that:

$$S = \frac{I}{c} \qquad \text{and} \qquad I = \sum_{n=1}^{n=\infty}a_n z_n^2$$

- f is defined as the bending stress at the extreme fiber distance. We can now substitute in F_b, for the allowable bending stress, or simply f_b, the actual bending stress.

$$M = \frac{f}{c}(I) \Rightarrow M = f\left(\frac{I}{c}\right) = F_b S$$

- The Flexure Formula can be rearranged in several ways:

$$M = F_b S \qquad\qquad f_b = \frac{M}{S} \qquad\qquad S = \frac{M}{F_b}$$

where M is the maximum bending moment, inlb
f_b is the actual bending stress, psi
F_b is the allowable bending stress, psi
S is the section modulus of the axis in the plane of bending, in^3

Example 17. What is the resisting moment of a sawn lumber 3x6 beam which has an allowable bending stress of 925 psi with the load acting against the x-x axis?

From Appendix D, $S_{x-x} = 12.604$ in^3. Solve the Flexure Formula for M_R:

$$M_R = F_b S = (925 \text{ psi})(12.604 \text{ in}^3) = 11,658.7 \text{ inlb}$$

CHAPTER 4 LESSONS

The format of the numbering system is: chapter.lesson.problem number.

LESSON 4.1 THE NEUTRAL AXIS, CENTROID, AND "*c*" (PG 61 – 66)

4.1.1   Find the location of the neutral axis perpendicular to the load and the extreme fiber distance of the shape given below.

4.1.2   Find the location of the neutral axis and the extreme fiber distance of 2-1/2" schedule 40 black pipe.

4.1.3   Find the neutral axis perpendicular to the load and the extreme fiber distance of the 5" square tube given below.

4.1.4   Find the location of the neutral axis perpendicular to the load and the extreme fiber distance of the shape given below.

4.1.5   Find the location of the neutral axis perpendicular to the load and the extreme fiber distance of the shape given below.

4.1.6   Find the location of the neutral axis perpendicular to the load and the extreme fiber distance of the shape given below.

4.1.7   Find the location of the neutral axis perpendicular to the load and the extreme fiber distance of the shape given below.

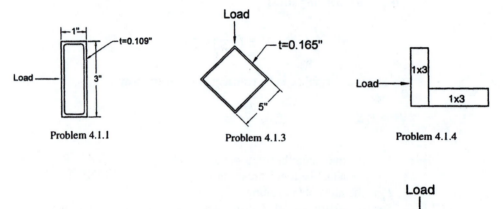

Problem 4.1.1   Problem 4.1.3   Problem 4.1.4

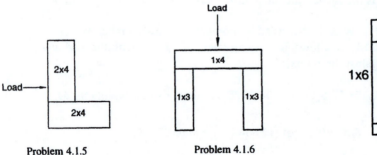

Problem 4.1.5   Problem 4.1.6   Problem 4.1.7

LESSON 4.2 THE NEUTRAL AXIS, CENTROID, AND "c", CONTINUED (PG 66 – 69)

4.2.1 Determine c_{x-x} and c_{y-y} of the shape given below. Indicate the location of the neutral axes.

4.2.2 Determine c_{x-x} and c_{y-y} of the shape given below. Indicate the location of the neutral axes.

4.2.3 Determine c_{x-x} and c_{y-y} of the shape given below. Indicate the location of the neutral axes. The I-beam is symmetrical in both axes, has an area of 2.94 in^2 and a depth of 5".

4.2.4 Determine c_{x-x} and c_{y-y} of the shape given below. Indicate the location of the neutral axes.

4.2.5 Determine c_{x-x} and c_{y-y} of the shape given below. Indicate the location of the neutral axes.

4.2.6 Determine c_{x-x} and c_{y-y} of the shape given below. Indicate the location of the neutral axes.

4.2.7 Determine c_{x-x} and c_{y-y} of the shape given below. Indicate the location of the neutral axes.

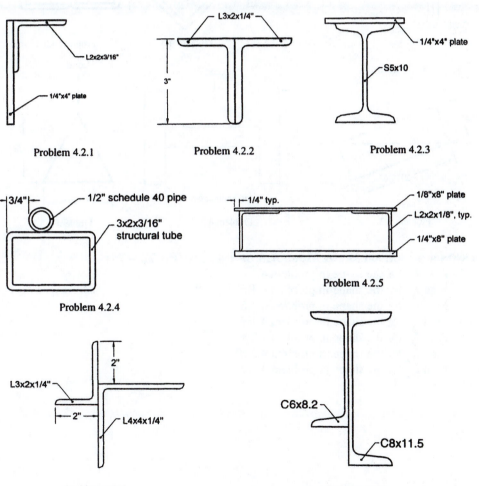

Problem 4.2.1

Problem 4.2.2

Problem 4.2.3

Problem 4.2.4

Problem 4.2.5

Problem 4.2.6

Problem 4.2.7

LESSON 4.3 MOMENT OF INERTIA (PG 69 – 72)

4.3.1   Find I_{x-x} for the built-up shape given below.
4.3.2   Find I_{x-x} for the semicircle of 1-1/4" Schedule 40 black pipe given below.
4.3.3   Find I_{x-x} for the 1-1/2"x1-1/2"x0.134 mechanical tubing given below which is tilted at a 45° angle. Assume that it has square corners.
4.3.4   Find I_{x-x} for the built-up shape of 1"x1"x0.109" square mechanical tubes given below.
4.3.5   Find I_{x-x} for the solid rectangle bar in the configuration given below.
4.3.6   Find I_{x-x} for the built-up shape given below.
4.3.7   Find I_{x-x} for the triangular piece of lumber given below.

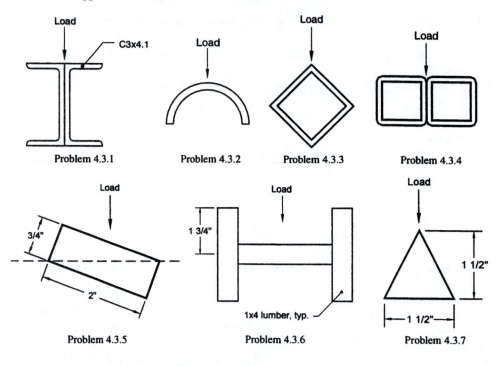

Problem 4.3.1   Problem 4.3.2   Problem 4.3.3   Problem 4.3.4

Problem 4.3.5   Problem 4.3.6   Problem 4.3.7

LESSON 4.4 TRANSFERRING MOMENTS OF INERTIA (PG 72 – 75)

4.4.1   Find I_{y-y} for the shape in problem 4.1.4.
4.4.2   Find I_{y-y} for the shape in problem 4.1.5.
4.4.3   Find I_{x-x} for the shape in problem 4.1.6.
4.4.4   Find I_{x-x} for the shape in problem 4.1.7.
4.4.5   Find I_{x-x} for the shape in problem 4.2.1.
4.4.6   Find I_{x-x} for the shape in problem 4.2.6.
4.4.7   Find I_{x-x} for the shape in problem 4.2.7.

LESSON 4.5 RADIUS OF GYRATION AND SECTION MODULUS (PG 75 – 76)

4.5.1   Find r_{x-x} and S_{x-x} for the shape in problem 4.3.1.
4.5.2   Find r_{x-x} and S_{x-x} for the shape in problem 4.3.2.
4.5.3   Find r_{x-x} and S_{x-x} for the shape in problem 4.3.3.
4.5.4   Find r_{x-x} and S_{x-x} for the shape in problem 4.3.4.
4.5.5   Find r_{x-x} and S_{x-x} for the shape in problem 4.3.5.
4.5.6   Find r_{x-x} and S_{x-x} for the shape in problem 4.3.6.
4.5.7   Find r_{x-x} and S_{x-x} for the shape in problem 4.3.7.

LESSON 4.6 THE FLEXURE FORMULA (PG 76 – 79)

4.6.1   Find c, I, r, and S for the x-x axis of the given built-up shape.
4.6.2   Find c, I, r, and S for both axes of the given shape.
4.6.3   Find c, I, r, and S for the x-x axis of the given shape.
4.6.4   What is the resisting moment of a 2x6 if the lumber from which it is made has an allowable bending stress (F_b) of 1,200 psi, and the load is acting against the x-x axis?
4.6.5   What is the resisting moment of a 1"x3"x0.109" rectangular mechanical tube if the steel from which it is made has an allowable bending stress (F_b) of 19,200 psi, and the load is acting against the y-y axis?

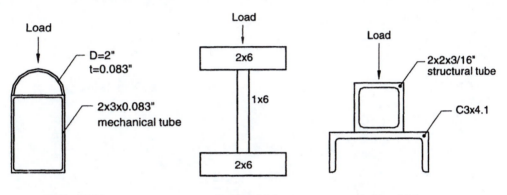

Problem 4.6.1   Problem 4.6.2   Problem 4.6.3

5

Sawn Lumber Beam Design

INTRODUCTION

Beams made of many different materials can be used to support a given loading condition. The choice depends on several factors, including availability, relative cost, workability, and the strength of the material. Selecting a material (wood, steel, aluminum, etc.) is the next step in beam design. Material choice can radically alter the size of the beam as well as affect connection details.

WOOD AND ITS PROPERTIES

Wood is the most commonly used construction material in theatrical scenery. It is inexpensive, versatile, and strong for its weight. Wood comes in a variety of forms, including rough-hewn boards, dressed boards, plywood, chipboard, and engineered wood products such as Oriented-Strand Board and wooden joists. In this chapter, we will deal exclusively with **sawn lumber**, dressed lumber (finished on four sides) that one would find at a lumber yard. Sawn lumber includes boards, dimensional lumber, posts and timbers, beams and stringers, and decking as set forth in Appendix D. Since the analysis of engineered wood products is quite different from that of sawn lumber, plywood will be discussed in Chapter 12.

Wood is a heterogeneous material which reacts differently to external forces depending on which axis is stressed. It also has discontinuities in its fibers such as knots, splits, shakes, and checks. For wood, the axes are defined relative to the grain of the lumber. For example, the allowable compressive stress for a given piece of lumber is different for loads parallel and perpendicular to the grain, and lumber on edge has a lower allowable bending stress than the same piece of lumber on flat. Wooden structural members have a higher probability of sudden, seemingly random, failures than those made of homogeneous materials such as steel. The American Forest & Paper Association (AF&PA) assigns allowable stress values to sawn lumber and accounts for sawn lumber's heterogeneity by using relatively large safety factors. In addition, sawn lumber is sorted into categories based on the quantity and size of knots, splits, shakes, and checks in the member.

Wood is organic, which means that structural traits vary dramatically between species and change with environmental conditions. For example, lumber is weaker in wet conditions than it is in dry conditions. Wood's strength also changes over time as it decays. Consequently, wood design values are calculated assuming a lifespan of 10 years and an adjustment factor is applied if the anticipated lifetime of the structure is shorter or longer.

Specifiers and grading agencies compensate for sawn lumber's heterogeneity and unique organic characteristics by categorizing it by size, species, and grade. Hence, specifying a 2x4 tells a structural designer little about the member. To be complete, a structural designer must note the size, species, and grade of a member, for example, a Douglas-Fir, Select Structural, 2x4. Many lumber yards are not so precise in defining species and grade in the yard or on the bill. However, someone at the lumber yard will know exactly what they are selling; it is the structural designer's responsibility to find out the species and grade of the lumber they are purchasing.

Once a structural designer has identified a member, the base design values can be looked up in various tables published by the AF&PA in the *National Design Specification (NDS) Supplement*®. These same values are also listed in other publications, such as the *Timber Construction Manual*. The tables categorize members by size, species, and grade. For convenience, the information that is necessary for the examples and lessons in this textbook are duplicated in Appendix D. While the tables in Appendix D are abridged versions of the tables found in the *NDS*®, they do include the most commonly encountered sawn lumber species.

CLASSIFYING SAWN LUMBER MEMBERS
Size
Sawn lumber is classified by **nominal size**. Nominal sizes are used by the lumber and construction industries and are not the actual dimensions of the piece of lumber. Typically, the actual dimensions of a piece of lumber are 1/2" less than the nominal dimension. For thicknesses 2x and greater, the actual thickness is always 1/2" less. For widths x2 and wider, the actual width is always 1/2" or 3/4" less. For example, the actual dimensions of a 2x4 are 1.5" x 3.5", a 2x8 is 1.5"x7.25", and an 8x8 is 7.5"x7.5". Boards less than 2" in thickness are exceptions: 1x stock is actually 3/4" thick (a 1x6 is 0.75"x5.5"), and 5/4 stock should be at least 1" thick. The dressed size of lumber can be found in tables listing the section properties of sawn lumber (see Appendix D). In the base design value tables, lumber is listed by nominal size, but the cross-sectional area is calculated using the actual dimensions. For convenience, Appendix D lists sizes up to 6x24, while the *NDS Supplement* includes lumber sizes up to 24x24.

The actual dimensions of nominally sized sawn lumber are very exact; saw mills must meet very specific tolerances. An important exception to this rule is the nominal 1-1/4" or 5/4" size category. The thickness of 5/4" stock should be 1", but the actual size can vary from 1" to 1-3/16" depending on the mill, the species, and the grade. In addition, the 5/4" category is not included in the section properties tables in the *NDS Supplement*. The geometric properties of 5/4 stock listed in Appendix D are calculated assuming a thickness of 1".

The *NDS* divides its allowable base design values for sawn lumber into five broad size categories: **boards** are members that are less than 2" thick. **Dimension lumber** is 2 to 4" thick by at least 2" wide. **Posts and timbers** are approximately square members 5x5" and larger. **Beams and stringers** are members larger than 5x5" which have a width 2" or more greater than the thickness. **Decking** are members that are 2 to 4" thick, tongue and grooved, and meant "for use as a roof, floor, or wall membrane" (*NDS*, 4.1.3.5). All of the above dimension categories were given in nominal sizes. Almost all theatrical applications call for boards or dimension lumber rather than Posts and Timbers or Beams and Stringers (remember, a 4x8 is dimension lumber).

Species

The next classification category of sawn lumber is **species**. A wood's strength characteristics can differ dramatically between species. The species classifications in the *NDS Supplement* are by species group. For example, Hem-Fir is not an individual species of tree; it is a classification made up of a certain proportion of hemlock and fir as defined by the grading agencies. One species of tree may even appear in multiple species groups. The *NDS Supplement* defines base design values for the most commonly used woods in the construc-tion industry and, consequently, concentrates on softwoods.

Most construction industries (except finish carpentry) use soft woods exclusively because they are easy to work, inexpensive, and strong. Theater is no exception. Typical 1x stock is Eastern White Pine, Eastern Softwoods, Spruce-Pine-Fir or Southern Pine. Typical 2x stock is Douglas Fir-South, Hem-Fir or Spruce-Pine-Fir. Species availability will differ according to the region of the country you are in. A species which is cost-prohibitive in one region might be inexpensive in another. The lumber yard should know the species group to which a given piece of lumber belongs. If the lumber yard cannot supply this information, no assumptions about the lumber's structural integrity should be made.

Grade

Finally, sawn lumber is classified by grade. **Grade** is essentially a measure of the structural integrity of the member. Most lumber is "visually graded" which means that the exterior of the piece is inspected to assign it a grade. As the grade increases within one species, the number of visible knots, checks, splits, and shakes decreases, and the strength increases. As the grade increases, the probability of a sudden failure due to heterogeneity decreases.

In general, Select Structural is the highest and most expensive grade of lumber, followed by No. 1, No. 2, and No. 3. After No. 3, Stud, Construction, Standard, and Utility grades are listed. These grades are not necessarily weaker than No. 3, but rather are commonly used categories of that particular species. For example, Studs are not available over 10' in length and are designed to be used in the walls of residential homes. Some species have grades in addition to the basic eight. For example, Hem-Fir has a No. 1 and Btr (better) classification between Select Structural and No. 1.

It is important to note that a grade means nothing without a species classification. No. 1 Hem-Fir bears no resemblance to No. 1 Western Wood. Once again, it is difficult to gener-alize about theaters across the nation, but most theaters probably use No. 2, No. 3, Construction, or Standard grades.

Unfortunately, the most commonly used lumber in theater, 1x board, is not structurally grad-ed. The *NDS Supplement* only provides the base design values for lumber which is at least 2" thick (actual thickness must be 1-1/2" or greater). For example, an Eastern White Pine, No. 2, 1x6 is an appearance graded board. This grade only defines how good the board looks; the structural integrity is not specified. This is also true of 5/4" nominal stock. The structural characteristics of appearance graded boards cannot be discussed.

It is possible to buy **stress-rated boards,** but this is only necessary when 1x is used in a critical structural application. The individual grading agencies for each species defines how that species of stress-rated boards corresponds to the design values found in the *NDS Supplement*. For example, the Southern Pine Inspection Bureau (SPIB) defines stress rated 1" stock as "Industrial 45" or "Industrial 55". Industrial 45 has the same design values as Southern Pine, No. 2 dimension lumber; Industrial 55 has the same values as Southern Pine, No. 1 dimension lumber. This text will consider only stress-graded lumber in examples and problems. The theater industry uses appearance graded 1x and 5/4x boards because most applications for which they are used are non-structural. For example, flats only have to hold their own weight, and molding is strictly decorative.

Conclusion
Since wood is a natural product, its characteristics are not easily defined. This brief discussion barely skims the surface of the subject. The rules and specifications of the AF&PA (via the *NDS*) have been simplified to include only those issues of interest to the theatrical technician.

Many theatrical applications of wood are decorative, and, thus, structural issues are moot. For these applications, technical directors can safely buy the most inexpensive lumber which they know, empirically, will do the job. However, in those situations where life safety is in question, i.e., in second story sets or bridges, the structural strength of the wood is critical. In these cases, the technical designer must determine the size, species, and grade of the wood members they intend to use and develop the structure accordingly.

BASIC BEAM DESIGN TESTS AND THEIR SPECIFICATIONS
OVERVIEW
Once the loading conditions are analyzed and a species and grade of sawn lumber are selected, a designer can begin to design a beam. Greatly simplified, the process of structural design is to compare actual stresses to allowable stresses. If the actual stress is less than the allowable stress, then the member is acceptable. Likewise, the allowable stresses of an existing system may be calculated to find out how large the actual load can be. In Chapter 2, simple tension and compression members were tested to see if they were acceptable by applying the direct stress formula. Beam design, however, requires three tests: a beam must pass tests to confirm that it is strong enough to withstand both flexural and shear stresses, as well as passing an empirical criteria for deflection.

Design Standards
Obtaining an allowable stress sounds easy: just flip to a table and look it up. Alas, it is not so simple. The American Forest & Paper Association periodically publishes a strict set of rules for structural designers to follow when calculating allowable stresses. These rules are termed "recommended practices" and are published in the *National Design Specification for Wood Construction (NDS)*. As mentioned before, the *NDS* publishes the **base design values** and their adjustment factors in *Design Values for Wood Construction*, also known as the *NDS Supplement*. In addition, the *NDS* outlines how a structural designer should use those allowables. The base design values and recommended practices found in the *Timber Construction Manual* are identical.

The *NDS* defines practices for bending, compression, tension, and combined loading members. This chapter is limited to discussing bending members which have to meet criteria for flexural stress, shear stress, and deflection. It is important to realize that the use of multiple adjustment factors is a relatively new specification, not found in the *NDS* until 1991 and not used until the fourth edition of the *TCM*. The design values found in earlier versions of those works should not be used with these adjustment factors, because the resultant allowable design values would be too high.

Be aware that the *NDS* is not law unless it is adopted as law by an individual state. Most states, in fact, adopt a more elaborate and detailed code. An example of this is the *Uniform Building Code*™, published by the International Conference of Building Officials. In general, the provisions for wood structural design are much the same as the *NDS*, but some codes have stricter rules. For example, building codes in California are stricter than in the Northeast because of the higher probability of earthquakes. In the Midwest, the codes might be designed with floods, tornadoes, or snow loads in mind. This text will teach the recommended practices found in the *NDS* because they are nationally recognized as sound engineering practice. In addition, interpreting building codes to apply to set construction would be tricky at best. If a structural designer is concerned about meeting legal code, he or she should find out what code has been adopted by the state in which he or she is working.

BENDING TEST

A bending, or flexure, test is the first test that must be applied to a beam to find out if it is appropriate for the application. This test determines whether or not failure will occur due to bending stress caused by the loading conditions on the beam. The Flexure Formula, $M=F_bS$, is the foundation for determining actual or allowable bending stress. We already know that M is determined by the loading conditions and that S, the Section Modulus, is a geometric property of the cross-section of a given beam. The allowable bending stress, F_b, is tabulated by the *NDS*. In order to find a base allowable design value, the species, grade, and size range of a member must be known. For example, the base F_b for Eastern White Pine, No. 2, 2-4" thick and 2" and wider, is 575 psi. Once the base design value is found, the *NDS* requires that a series of adjustment factors be applied to find the allowable bending stress. This allowable bending stress is notated as F_b' (read as "F prime of b"). Adding a prime to a variable is the standard way of indicating that the base design value has been adjusted.

The Adjustment Factors

The *NDS* lists eight adjustment factors that apply to the base allowable bending design values of sawn dimension lumber. They are the load duration, wet service, temperature, beam stability, size, flat use, repetitive member, and form factors (*NDS*, Table 2.3.1). Fortunately, theatrical structural designers do not need to apply all eight on a regular basis. This text will only discuss those factors and issues likely to be encountered in theatrical design. For further discussion of the temperature (C_t), wet service (C_M), and form factors (C_f), see the *NDS*, sections 2.3.3, 2.3.4, and 2.3.8, respectively.

- **Load Duration Factor, C_D (*NDS*, 2.3.2)**
  As mentioned previously, wood's strength changes over time. The load duration factor, C_D, accounts for this characteristic. Ten years is defined as the "normal" life span of a member, and, therefore, the C_D for a life span of ten years is 1.0.

If the load duration is permanent (greater than 10 years) the adjustment factor is 0.9. If the load duration is less than 10 years, the factor varies from 1.0 to 2.0 as per the table below (*NDS*, Table 2.3.2):

Load Duration	C_D
permanent (>10 yrs)	0.9
ten years (normal)	1.0
two months	1.15
seven days	1.25
ten minutes	1.6
impact	2.0

For most regional or academic theater scenery applications, we can apply a C_D of 1.15, increasing the base allowable design value by 15%, because the lifetime of a set is often two months or less.

The load duration factor is also applicable to the tension, shear, compression (parallel to grain), and bearing (parallel to grain) base design values.

- **Beam Stability Factor, C_L** (*NDS*, 2.3.7, 3.3.1, and 4.4.1)
  The beam stability factor is intended to ensure that a member is adequately braced to prevent the compression side of the member from buckling. In general, the "thinner" a shape is, the more unstable it is laterally. Shapes closer to square require less bracing. The *NDS* defines a set of bracing conditions which must be met to achieve a C_L of 1.0:

"4.4.1.2. . . . If the depth to breadth, d/b, based on nominal dimensions is:
(a) d/b ≤ 2; no lateral support shall be required.
(b) 2 < d/b ≤ 4; the ends shall be held in position, as by full depth solid blocking, bridging, hangers, nailing or bolting to other framing members, or other acceptable means.
(c) 4 < d/b ≤ 5; the compression edge of the member shall be held in line for its entire length to prevent lateral displacement, as by adequate sheathing or subflooring, and ends at point of bearing shall be held in position to prevent rotation and/or lateral displacement.
(d) 5 < d/b ≤ 6; bridging, full depth solid blocking or diagonal cross bracing shall be installed at intervals not exceeding 8 feet, the compression edge of the member shall be held in line as by adequate sheathing or subflooring, and the ends at points of bearing shall be held in position to prevent rotation and/or lateral displacement.
(e) 6 < d/b ≤ 7; both edges shall be held in line for their entire length and ends at point of bearing shall be held in position to prevent rotation and/or lateral displacement."

The *NDS* also defines a method for mathematically determining C_L (see section 3.3.3 of *NDS*). Unfortunately, this method is complex and impractical for daily use. It is much simpler to decide that we will always meet the bracing conditions required for C_L to equal 1.0.

- **Size Factor, C_F** (*NDS*, 4.3.2)

  The size factor is the single most important adjustment factor for our purposes. The value of the factor varies by size and type of stress and can be found in the tables adjacent to the base design values in Appendix D. A size factor is applied to the bending, tension, and compression (parallel) allowables, but note that the size factor is different for each type of stress. For example, a piece of visually graded dimension lumber of any species except Southern Pine, No. 2, 5" wide and 3" thick, has a C_F for bending of 1.4; C_F for tension is 1.4; and C_F for compression is 1.1. Thickness refers to the breadth (the dimension perpendicular to the load) of the beam, and width refers to the depth (the dimension parallel to the load). If a 2x4 is oriented "on edge" the 2" nominal dimension is its thickness and the 4" nominal dimension is its width. For visually graded dimension lumber with a thickness 5" or greater and a width greater than 12", the size factor must be calculated. See section 4.3.2.2 of the *NDS* for more information.

  The base design values for visually graded Southern Pine dimension lumber already have the size factors incorporated into them. Southern Pine dimension lumber larger than a 4x8 will have a size factor that is explained in a table adjacent to the base design values in the *NDS Supplement*.

- **Flat Use Factor, C_{fu}** (*NDS*, 4.3.3)

  Wood actually has a larger F_b if the load is applied to the wide face of the member due to grain characteristics. But remember that the S_{y-y} will be weaker than the S_{x-x} because the extreme fiber distance is less. The flat use factor is applicable only to F_b and is listed by size in tables adjacent to the base design value tables.

  The flat use factor could be used when analyzing built-up shapes. For example, a built-up box beam will be made of two on edge and two on flat members. Technically, two values of F_b should be used. Practically, this makes the calculations more complex, and it is easier to neglect the flat use factor and use the F_b of the on edge members for all of the component pieces.

- **Repetitive Member Factor, C_r** (*NDS*, 4.3.4)

  If a member is part of a repetitive system, the chances that the system will fail due to the failure of an individual member go down. The repetitive member factor can be used when "joists, truss chords, rafters, studs, planks, decking or similar members . . . are in contact or spaced not more than 24" on centers." (*NDS*, 4.3.4) This factor only applies to dimension lumber 2 to 4" thick. In addition, there must be at least three members in the system and they must be connected by a floor, roof, deck, etc. The floor or deck must be a system which can support its design load without unreasonable deflection or structural weaknesses (*NDS*, 4.3.4). In other words, the sheathing material over the repetitive system must be rated to carry its design load. For example, typical 3/4" plywood sheathing is rated for spans of 24". The joist system must then be on 24" or less centers. If C_r is applicable, it is equal to 1.15.

The *NDS* lists base design values for sawn lumber which is specifically graded as Decking. The base bending design values for Decking already incorporate a repetitive member factor and a flat-use factor.

It may now seem that determining the F_b' for sawn lumber is a hopeless morass of adjustment factors:

$$F_b' = \left(C_D C_L C_F C_{fu} C_r\right)F_b$$

Fortunately, for most applications, simplifications can be made: the lateral bracing requirements should always be met such that $C_L=1.0$; the flat use factor is very specialized and, if ignored, the beam will be oversized, not undersized. This leaves, for normal theatrical purposes, three adjustment factors that need to be applied to the base design value for bending: the load duration (C_D), size (C_F), and repetitive member (C_r) factors. Therefore, the adjusted allowable bending stress, F_b', can be reduced as follows:

$$F_b' = \left(C_D C_F C_r\right)F_b$$

SHEAR TEST
Shear is the next test in the beam design process. As mentioned in Chapter 3, shear failure occurs when one plane slides past an adjacent plane of the member. Shear failure can occur vertically, horizontally, or diagonally relative to the length of the member. Because of its horizontal grain, wood is most vulnerable to horizontal shear forces and will almost always fail due to horizontal shear before it fails due to vertical shear. Only in extreme circumstances would wood fail vertically. Thus, the critical shear test for wood beams is the horizontal shear test.

Derivation of the Shear Formula
The magnitude of horizontal shear is related to the magnitude of the maximum vertical shear along the length of the beam. Remember that V_{max} is determined by generating a shear diagram or using case formulas. The following formula defines the relationship between the two:

$$f_v = \frac{VQ}{Ib}$$

where f_v is the actual horizontal shearing stress, psi
           V is the actual vertical shear, usually V_{max}, lb
           Q is the statical moment of area above or below the plane at which
              the horizontal shear is being computed, in³
           I is the Moment of Inertia in the plane of bending, in⁴
           b is the width of the shear plane, i.e., the width of the cross-section
              at the plane under consideration, in

This is the general formula for computing horizontal shear stress. It is true for all materials and all shapes and sizes of beams and is valid for any plane in the cross-section of a beam. Though the maximum horizontal shear of any shape will always occur at the neutral axis, a structural designer might want to check the shearing stress in other critical planes, such as the joint(s) of a built-up shape.

To calculate the horizontal shear stress at a specific plane of a shape, the **statical moment of area**, Q, must be found for the area above or below that plane. Q **is the area above the shear plane multiplied by the distance between the neutral axis of that area and the neutral axis of the entire shape.** Q will have the same magnitude above or below the plane in question because it is taken with respect to the neutral axis. For convenience, Q should be calculated for whichever area (above or below the neutral axis) that is the least complex mathematically.

If the area for which Q must be found is a simple shape, calculating Q is easy. If, however, the area for which Q must be found is made of two or more shapes, the structural designer can either: (1) find the statical moment of area of each component of the total area and add them together to find Q or (2) first find the neutral axis of the complex area and then find the statical moment of area for the entire shape. The first method is usually easier because it eliminates the extra step of calculating another neutral axis. Mathematically, then, Q can be expressed as the following:

$$Q = d_A A_A + d_B A_B + d_C A_C + \ldots$$

where d is the perpendicular distance between neutral axes, in
                 A is the area of the component, in^2
                 Q is a statical moment of area, in^3

Example 1. Prove that the statical moments of the area above and below the plane between the two 2x4's are equal for the following T-shape.

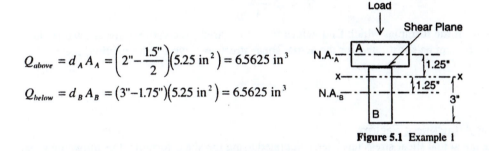

$$Q_{above} = d_A A_A = \left(2" - \frac{1.5"}{2}\right)\left(5.25 \text{ in}^2\right) = 6.5625 \text{ in}^3$$

$$Q_{below} = d_B A_B = \left(3" - 1.75"\right)\left(5.25 \text{ in}^2\right) = 6.5625 \text{ in}^3$$

Figure 5.1 Example 1

We can derive a simpler formula for calculating the maximum horizontal shear of solid, rectangular shapes. For a generic rectangular beam, the following figure can be drawn:

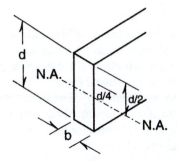

Figure 5.2 Definition of N.A., b, and d for a rectangle

We know that I for a solid rectangle is $bd^3/12$. Q for a solid rectangle can be calculated as follows:

$$Q = d_{\perp} A_{half}$$

$$A_{half} = \frac{1}{2}bd = \frac{bd}{2}$$

$$d_{\perp rect} = \frac{d}{4}$$

$$Q_{rect} = \frac{d}{4}\left(\frac{bd}{2}\right) = \frac{bd^2}{8}$$

The formula for a rectangular beam can be derived by plugging I and Q into the general formula for horizontal shear stress:

$$f_v = \frac{VQ}{Ib} = \frac{V_{max}\left(bd^2/8\right)}{\left(\dfrac{bd^3}{12}\right)b} = V_{max}\left(\frac{bd^2}{8}\right)\left(\frac{12}{b^2d^3}\right) = V_{max}\left(\frac{3}{2bd}\right) = \frac{3}{2}\frac{V_{max}}{bd}$$

$$f_v = 1.5\frac{V_{max}}{bd} \qquad \text{for rectangular, solid sections}$$

Since bd is actually the cross-sectional area of any rectangular section, the maximum horizontal shear formula for a solid rectangle can be written:

$$f_v = 1.5\frac{V_{max}}{A}$$

Like all of the formulas which find values for actual stress, the variable for allowable shear stress, F_v, can be substituted for the actual shear stress to solve for the required area:

$$A_{req'd} = 1.5\frac{V_{max}}{F_v}$$

Shear Adjustment Factors

Once the actual shear stress has been calculated using the shear formula, the allowable shear stress must be determined. In the *NDS* tables, horizontal shear, F_v, is referred to as "shear parallel to grain." Like F_b, F_v is found in the *NDS* tables for a specific species, grade, and size of lumber. For example, the base F_v for Eastern White Pine, No. 2, 2-4" thick and 2" and wider, is 70 psi.

There are four adjustment factors which can possible apply to F_v: load duration (C_D), wet service (C_M), temperature (C_t), and shear stress (C_H) factors. As for F_b, the temperature and wet service factors can be ignored for traditional theatrical applications. The C_D factor is described in the preceding section on adjustment factors for bending stress. The shear stress factor is the only factor unique to determining F_v'. For simplicity, we will assume, conservatively, that the shear stress factor is 1.0. See the Shear Stress Factor table adjacent to the base design value tables in the *NDS Supplement* for more details. It is important to note that there is no size factor for shear stress calculations.

For normal theatrical applications, finding the allowable shear stress is simple. The load duration factor, C_D, is the only applicable adjustment factor. Remember that C_D is usually 1.0 (10 years) or 1.15 (two months). The adjusted allowable design value is notated F_v':

$$F_v' = (C_D C_M C_t C_H)F_v \Rightarrow F_v' = (C_D)F_v$$

It is also important to note that the above techniques are applicable to solid sawn lumber sections only. The design of notched and built-up sections differs significantly and will be discussed later in this chapter.

DEFLECTION TEST

The final test in beam design is deflection. Unlike the bending and shear tests, the deflection test is not a test of failure. Structural designers have established a set of empirical criteria to guide the amount of deflection that a beam should be allowed for a given application. Deflection is expressed as the amount of sag per unit of span length. Mathematically, the three most commonly used criteria are expressed as the following:

$$\Delta_{max} \le \frac{l}{360} \qquad \Delta_{max} \le \frac{l}{240} \qquad \Delta_{max} \le \frac{l}{180}$$

where Δ_{max} is the allowable maximum deflection, in
     l is the length of the span, in

The criteria of $l/360$ was determined empirically to be the maximum allowable deflection for a live load such that a plaster ceiling would not crack over time. This amount of deflection is not visible to the naked eye. The criteria of $l/240$ is often applied to beams that do not support a plaster ceiling – a trained observer would notice the deflection. The criteria of $l/180$ is the least restrictive criteria and is not often used. An average person would notice the deflection visually and would feel that the beam is uncomfortably springy. The structure might be safe, but it would not *feel* safe.

Depending on the application, a deflection criteria may be applied to a live load or to the total combined dead and live loads. We will typically use the criteria of $l/240$ and apply it to the total loading condition. The above criteria are commonly used, but the permissible deflection of a beam is at the discretion of the structural designer. For example, a mirrored wall which would visibly amplify the slightest deflections may call for a live load deflection criteria of $l/1000$ while the design of another unit may incorporate a visible sag and call for a criteria less than $l/180$.

The actual deflection of a beam will depend on its loading conditions, the stiffness of the material of which it is made (E), and its cross-sectional geometry (I). Calculating the actual deflection is done using case formulas. Typically, the case formulas for a given loading condition will list an equation for finding the deflection anywhere along the span (Δ_x) and an equation for finding the maximum deflection (Δ_{max}) of the beam. We are generally only concerned with the maximum deflection. All deflection formulas will have variables representing the load and the span in the numerator and will have the E value of the material and the I value of the axis in the plane of bending in the denominator. This implies two simple concepts:

- As load or span increases, deflection increases.

- As the strength of the beam increases due to its material or section properties, the deflection decreases proportionally.

The following deflection formulas demonstrate these general principles for a simple beam.

Simple beam with a concentrated load at its center:

$$\Delta_{max} = \frac{Pl^3}{48EI}$$

Continuous beam with two equal spans uniformly loaded:

$$\Delta_{max} = \frac{wl^4}{185EI}$$

However, there are many atypical loading conditions for which there are no case formulas; how then do we find the deflection? To find the deflection of an atypical loading condition, use the following procedures:

1) The actual M_{max} for that loading condition is calculated, and then that value is plugged into the equation used to find the maximum moment of a simply supported, evenly distributed load.

$$M_{max} = \frac{wl^2}{8}$$

2) Since M_{max} and l are known, we can solve for w, the **equivalent evenly distributed load** that will generate the same actual M_{max}.

$$w_{equiv} = \frac{8M_{max}}{l^2}$$

3) Then plug the known values of w, l, E, and I into the deflection formula for an evenly distributed load. The maximum deflection that results is the approximate deflection of the original loading condition.

$$\Delta_{\approx} = \frac{5w_{equiv}l^4}{384EI}$$

where $\Delta_{\approx}$ is the approximate deflection, in
w_{equiv} is the equivalent evenly distributed load, pli
l is the length of the span, in
E is the modulus of elasticity of the material, psi
I is the Moment of Inertia of the beam, in^4

This technique generates an approximate deflection that is usually greater than the actual deflection due to the atypical loading condition.

Example 2. Approximate the maximum deflection of a Spruce-Pine-Fir Construction grade 2x4 with the following loading conditions.

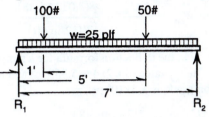

Figure 5.3 Example 2, free body diagram

A. Determine the loading conditions; calculate R_1 and R_2:

$$\Sigma M_{R_1} = 0 = (0')(R_1\#) + (1')(100\#) + (3.5')[(25 \text{ plf})(7')] + (5')(50\#) - (7')(R_2)$$
$$7' R_2 = 962.5 \text{ ftlb}$$
$$R_2 = 137.5\#$$
$$\Sigma M_{R_2} = 0 = (0')(R_2\#) - (2')(50\#) - (3.5')(175\#) - (6')(100\#) + (7')(R_1)$$
$$7' R_1 = 1,312.5 \text{ ftlb}$$
$$R_1 = 187.5\#$$

B. Determine V_{max} and M_{max} using case formulas or by generating shear and moment diagrams:

$$V_{0^-} = 0$$
$$V_{0^+} = 187.5\#$$
$$V_{1^-} = 187.5\# - 1'(25 \text{ plf}) = 162.5\#$$
$$V_{1^+} = 162.5\# - 100\# = 62.5\#$$
$$V_{5^-} = 187.5\# - 5'(25 \text{ plf}) - 100\# = -37.5\#$$
$$V_{5^+} = -37.5\# - 50\# = -87.5$$
$$V_{7^-} = 187.5\# - 7'(25 \text{ plf}) - 100\# - 50\# = -137.5\#$$
$$V_{7^+} = -137.5\# + 137.5\# = 0 \checkmark$$

Find where shear crosses through zero, between 1' and 5':

$$V_x = 0 = 187.5\# - x'(25 \text{ plf}) - 100\#$$
$$25x = 87.5\#$$
$$x = 3.5'$$

Calculate M_{max} (at 3.5'):

$$M_{max} = M_{3.5} = +(3.5')(187.5\#) - \left(\frac{3.5'}{2}\right)[(3.5')(25 \text{ plf})] - (2.5')(100\#)$$
$$= 253.125 \text{ ftlb} \Rightarrow 3,037.5 \text{ inlb}$$

C. Solve for an equivalent evenly distributed load, w, for a 7' simple span.

$$M_{max} = \frac{wl^2}{8} \Rightarrow w_{equiv} = \frac{8M_{max}}{l^2} = \frac{8(3,037.5 \text{ inlb})}{[7'(12 \text{ in}/\text{ft})]^2} = 3.44 \text{ pli}$$

D. We can now use this w in the deflection formula for a simple span with an evenly distributed load. The I_{x-x} value of a 2x4 is 5.359 in^4 and the E value of Spruce-Pine-Fir construction grade is 1.3x10^6 psi.

$$\Delta_{max} = \frac{5w_{equiv}l^4}{384EI} = \frac{5(3.44 \text{ pli})(84")^4}{384(1.3x10^6 \text{ psi})(5.359 \text{ in}^4)} = 0.32"$$

This 2x4 will deflect approximately 5/16" over 7'. A deflection criteria of $l/240$ limits the permissible deflection to 0.35", so this deflection condition is acceptable. Bending and shear tests must be performed to determine if this loading condition is safe.

The calculated results of any deflection test may or may not resemble the actual amount that the beam will deflect, primarily because the actual construction details do not exhibit "pure" behavior. For example, a plywood floor increases the relative stiffness of the beams. In addition, connections we define as pure pin often have some fixity to them. The deflection test is obviously an area in which the structural designer should exercise discretion.

Due to its material characteristics, wood beams that pass the bending and shear tests will generally pass the applicable deflection criteria. However, one should note that the longer the span or overhang, the more likely it is that the deflection criteria will be the determining factor in the design process.

BEAM DESIGN
STEPS IN BEAM DESIGN
We now have all the tools necessary to design a solid, sawn lumber beam from start to finish. The outline of the process is as follows:

A. Draw a beam diagram, indicating all loads and reactions (calculate the reactions if necessary).
B. Determine V_{max} and M_{max} using case formulas or by generating shear and moment diagrams.
C. Pick a species and grade of sawn lumber and identify the base design values F_b and F_v and E.
D. Bending test.
    1.   Calculate F_b':
        a. C_D, load duration factor (two months = 1.15; ten years = 1.0)
        b. C_F, size factor, must be estimated. A good rule of thumb to start with is that every foot of span requires 1 inch of depth in a 2x member.
        c. C_r, repetitive member factor (1.0 or 1.15)
        d. $F_b' = (C_D C_F C_r)F_b$

2. Using F_b' and M_{max}, solve the Flexure Formula for the minimum required S.

$$S_{req'd} = \frac{M_{max}}{F_b'}$$

3. Using the section properties tables, find a beam which satisfies the minimum S requirement for bending. Make sure that the construction techniques used meet the requirements that allow us to use a beam stability factor, C_L, of 1.0.

4. Now that the actual beam weight is known, M_{max}, $S_{req'd}$, and F_b' may need to be recalculated. Beam weights are found in the section properties table in Appendix D.

5. Select beams which meet the S requirement.

E. Shear test
   1. Calculate F_v'
      a. C_D, load duration factor, is the same value used for bending.
      b. $F_v' = C_D F_v$
   2. Solve the rectangular shear formula for the required cross-sectional area:

$$A_{req'd} = 1.5 \frac{V_{max}}{F_v'}$$

   3. Check that the beam(s) selected for bending have the required area. If it does not, shear is the ruling factor for this loading condition, and a larger beam which meets both the A and S requirements should be selected.

F. Deflection
   1. Choose a deflection criteria appropriate for the application, and calculate the maximum allowable deflection, Δ_{all}.

$$\Delta_{all} = \frac{1}{360}; \quad \frac{1}{240} \quad \text{or} \quad \frac{1}{180}$$

   2. Look up the deflection formula for the applicable loading condition in Appendix B and solve for the minimum required I. If this loading condition is atypical, use the deflection approximation technique discussed previously (see Example 2).

G. Selecting a beam
   1. Select beams which meet $S_{req'd}$, $A_{req'd}$, and $I_{req'd}$ simultaneously. Be sure to use the I and S values for the correct axis.
   2. If the beams are not in the size range estimated, recalculate $S_{req'd}$.
   3. Choose the most appropriate beam for the application. This could be the lightest, the least deep, the cheapest, etc. Be careful when choosing beams that are much deeper than they are thick due to lateral bracing requirements.

BEAM DESIGN EXAMPLES

> *Example 3.* In Chapter 3, Examples 1 and 2, a deck system of 4x8 platforms supported by beams on 4' centers was analyzed. One beam had an evenly distributed dead and live load of 108 plf over its 16' span. Design a sawn lumber beam for a load duration of two months that meets a deflection criteria of $l/240$. Use a species and grade of Douglas Fir-South, No. 2.

A. Free Body Diagram:

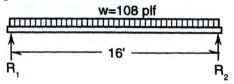

w=108 plf

16'

R_1 R_2

Figure 5.4 Free body diagram of Example 3

B. Analyze the loading condition using case formulas:

$$R_1 = R_2 = V_{max} = \frac{wl}{2} = \frac{(108 \text{ plf})(16 \text{ ft})}{2} = 864\#$$

$$M_{max} = \frac{wl^2}{8} = \frac{(108 \text{ plf})(16 \text{ ft})^2}{8} = 3,456 \text{ ftlb} \Rightarrow 41,472 \text{ inlb}$$

C. Identify the base design values:

$F_v = 90$ psi; $F_b = 850$ psi; $E = 1.2 \times 10^6$ psi

D. Apply the bending test.

1. Calculate F_b':
   a. C_D (load duration) = 1.15 for two months.
   b. C_F, size factor.
      By our rule of thumb, we need a 2x beam with a 16" depth. A 2x16 does not meet the lateral bracing requirements, so we'll test a 4x8 which has the same cross-sectional area as a 2x16 and a much better b:d ratio. A 4x8 has a size factor of 1.3.
   c. C_r (repetitive member) = 1.0 because the on center spacing is greater than 2'.
   d. Calculate F_b':

   $$F_b' = (C_D C_F C_r)F_b$$
   $$F_b' = 1.15(1.3)(1.0)(850 \text{ psi}) = 1,270.75 \text{ psi}$$

2. Solve the Flexure Formula for the minimum required value of S.

$$S_{req'd} = \frac{M_{max}}{F_b'} = \frac{41,472 \text{ inlb}}{1,270.75 \text{ psi}} = 32.64 \text{ in}^3$$

3. Select a beam.
    A single 2x14, 3x10, 4x10, or doubling up two 2x10's would satisfy the S requirement. A 2x14 would be the lightest beam, but its b to d ratio is 1:7, which would require "both edges to be held in line for their entire length." A 3x10 would be a logical choice to test because it combines a decent b to d ratio and is lightweight. But, laminating 2x10s together may be easier than finding a 3x10 or 4x10 to purchase. We will put the actual beam weight and size factor for the laminated 2x10s through the calculations again.

4. Recalculate M_{max}, F_b', and $S_{req'd}$ for two 2x10s.
    a. For one 2x10:

    $S_{x-x} = 21.39$ in^3; $A = 13.88$ in^2; $I_{x-x} = 98.93$ in^4;
    $wt = 3.372$ plf (using a density of 35 pcf)

    For two laminated 2x10s:

    $S_{x-x} = 42.78$ in^3; $A = 27.76$ in^2; $I_{x-x} = 197.86$ in^4; $wt = 6.744$ plf

    c. Recalculate F_b'. C_F for a 2x10 = 1.1.

    $$F_b' = (C_D C_F C_r) F_b$$
    $$F_b' = 1.15(1.1)(1.0)(850 \text{ psi}) = 1,075.25 \text{ psi}$$

    d. Recalculate the minimum required S:

    $$S_{req'd} = \frac{M_{max}}{F_b'} = \frac{41,472 \text{ inlb}}{1,075.25 \text{ psi}} = 38.6 \text{ in}^3$$

5. Select possible beam choices.
    Since $42.78 > 38.6$ in^3, the laminated 2x10's pass the bending test. Note that a 3x10, with a S of 35.65 in^3 and the same size factor as a 2x10, would have failed for this loading condition. A 4x10, with a S of 49.91 in^3 and a larger size factor, would pass easily.

E. Apply the shear test.

1. Calculate F_v'. $C_D = 1.15$.

    $$F_v' = C_D F_v = 1.15(90 \text{ psi}) = 103.5 \text{ psi}$$

2. Find the minimal cross-sectional area of the beam required for shear:

    $$A_{req'd} = 1.5 \frac{V_{max}}{F_v'} = 1.5 \left(\frac{864 \#}{103.5 \text{ psi}} \right) = 8.35 \text{ in}^2$$

3. From the geometric properties table, a single 2x8, 3x4, or 4x4 all have an area greater than 8.35 in^2. Shear is therefore not the ruling factor for this loading condition.

F. Apply the deflection test.

1. Determine the maximum allowable deflection, Δ_{all}, based on a criteria of $l/240$:

$$\Delta_{all} = \frac{l}{240} = \frac{(16')(12 \text{ in}/\text{ft})}{240} = 0.8"$$

2. From the case formulas for a simple span, evenly distributed load:

$$\Delta_{max} = \frac{5wl^4}{384EI}$$

$$I_{req'd} = \frac{5wl^4}{384E\Delta_{max}} = \frac{5\left(114.744 \text{ plf}\Big/12 \text{ in}/\text{ft}\right)\left[(16')(12 \text{ in}/\text{ft})\right]^4}{384\left(1.2x10^6 \text{ psi}\right)(0.8")}$$

$$I_{req'd} = \frac{5(9.562 \text{ pli})(192")^4}{384\left(1.2x10^6 \text{ psi}\right)(0.8")} = 176.3 \text{ in}^4$$

G. Selecting a beam.

1. With a combined I of 197.86 in^4, the two 2x10's meet the deflection criteria as well as meeting the bending and shear requirements.
2. No recalculations are necessary.
3. Two laminated 2x10's are an appropriate choice for this loading condition.

Example 4. Design the beams for a 6' custom deck extension with a 3' overhang (see Figure 5.5a). The set designer would like the thickness of the deck to be as thin as possible. We will assume that the extension will be built with 6' long stringers every 2' on center and will have a dead weight of 10 psf. The director has indicated that actors may be sitting on the downstage edge of the overhang. If the actors are approximately 2' apart when seated and weigh approximately 175 lbs each, then each beam will support a 175 lb point load at the end of the overhang. Since the edge of the deck is so visible to the audience, a deflection criteria of $l/360$ will be used. Design for a load duration of two months. Since making the deck as thin as possible is a priority, use Southern Pine, No. 1, Dense, a high quality, high cost lumber.

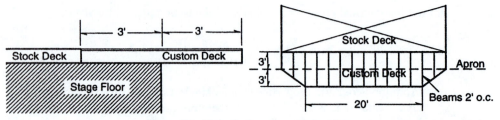

Figure 5.5a Example 4, section and plan views

A. Determine the loading conditions and sketch a free body diagram.

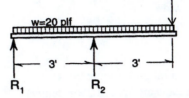

Figure 5.5b Example 4, free body diagram

Convert the dead weight (psf) to pounds per linear foot on the beam:

$$w, \text{ plf} = (\text{tributary width of a 1' section, ft})(w, \text{ psf})$$
$$= (2 \text{ ft})(10 \text{ psf}) = 20 \text{ plf}$$

Calculate R_1 and R_2:

$$\Sigma M_{R_1} = 0 = (0')(R_1 \#) + (3')\left[(20 \text{ plf})(6')\right] + (6')(175\#) - (3')(R_2)$$
$$3' R_2 = 1{,}410 \text{ ftlb}$$
$$R_2 = 470 \#$$
$$\Sigma M_{R_2} = 0 = (0')(R_2 \#) + (0)(120\#) + (3')(175\#) + (3')(R_1)$$
$$3' R_1 = 525 \text{ ftlb}$$
$$R_1 = -175 \#$$

Notice that R_1 is negative – this means that the connection detail at R_1 must also be designed for tension.

B. Determine V_{max} and M_{max} using case formulas or by generating shear and moment diagrams. The case formulas could be added together at several points to find the maximum values of shear and moment. In this case, however, it is easier to simply generate our own values for V_{max} and M_{max}.

$$V_{0^-} = 0$$
$$V_{0^+} = -175\#$$
$$V_{3^-} = -175\# - 3'(20 \text{ plf}) = -235\#$$
$$V_{3^+} = -235\# + 470\# = +235\#$$
$$V_{6^-} = -175\# - 6'(20 \text{ plf}) + 470\# = +175\#$$
$$V_{6^+} = +175\# - 175\# = 0 \checkmark$$

$$M_0 = 0$$
$$M_3 = -\left[3'(175\#)\right] - \left\{1.5'\left[3'(20 \text{ plf})\right]\right\} = 615 \text{ ftlb} = 7{,}380 \text{ inlb}$$

$$V_{max} = 235 \text{ lbs} \qquad\qquad M_{max} = 7{,}380 \text{ inlb}$$

C. Identify the base design values for Southern Pine, No. 1, Dense. Since this is Southern Pine, we must estimate a size range to find the base design values. Use 2"-4" thick to 5"-6" wide.

$$F_b = 1,750 \text{ psi}; \quad F_v = 90 \text{ psi}; \quad E = 1.8 \times 10^6 \text{ psi}$$

D. Apply the bending test.

1. $C_D = 1.15$ (load duration is two months).
   $C_r = 1.15$ (the beams are spaced 2' on center).

   $$F_b' = (C_D C_r)F_b = 1.15(1.15)(1,750 \text{ psi}) = 2,314.375 \text{ psi}$$

2. Solve the Flexure Formula for the minimum required S.

   $$S_{req'd} = \frac{M_{max}}{F_b'} = \frac{7,380 \text{ inlb}}{2,314.375 \text{ psi}} = 3.19 \text{ in}^3$$

3. Select a beam.
   A 2x5 is the lightest beam which meets the criteria, but a 3x4 also meets the criteria and has less depth. If 3x4's are hard to find, two laminated 2x4's would work as well. Since the beam selected is within our specified size range, there is no need to recalculate F_b'.

E. Apply the shear test.

1. Calculate F_v'. $C_D = 1.15$ (load duration is two months).

   $$F_v' = C_D F_v = 1.15(90 \text{ psi}) = 103.5 \text{ psi}$$

2. Find the minimal cross-sectional area of the beam required for shear.

   $$A_{req'd} = 1.5 \frac{V_{max}}{F_v'} = 1.5\left(\frac{235\#}{103.5 \text{ psi}}\right) = 3.41 \text{ in}^2$$

3. Any member with an area larger than a 2x3 satisfies this requirement. Remember that this grade is not available in 1x or 5/4x thicknesses.

F. Apply the deflection test.

1. The deflection criteria is $l/360$. Since the span and the overhang are the same length, they have the same maximum permissible deflection:

   $$\Delta_{max_{all}} = \Delta_{max_{span}} = \Delta_{max_{overhang}} = \frac{l}{360} = \frac{(3')(12 \text{ in / ft})}{360} = 0.1"$$

2. Normally, the deflection for both the span and the overhang should be calculated. However, in this example, it is only necessary to check the deflection in the overhang because it is so large compared to the span, and because it is more visible to the audience. For the overhang, the deflection caused by the evenly distributed load must be added to the deflection caused by the point load.

For the uniformly distributed load, the deflection at the end of the overhang, when $x_l = a$, equals the following (Appendix B):

$$\Delta_{max_{overhang}} = \frac{wa}{24EI}\left(4a^2l - l^3 + 3a^3\right)$$

For the point load at the end of the overhang:

$$\Delta_{max_{overhang}} = \frac{Pa^2}{3EI}\left(l + a\right)$$

Combine the uniformly distributed load and point load formulas:

$$\Delta_{max_{overhang},\,tot} = \frac{wa}{24EI}\left(4a^2l - l^3 + 3a^3\right) + \frac{Pa^2}{3EI}\left(l + a\right)$$

At the end of the overhang, $l = a$, so we can simplify the above equation:

$$\Delta_{max_{overhang},\,tot} = \frac{wa}{24EI}\left(4a^2a - a^3 + 3a^3\right) + \frac{Pa^2}{3EI}\left(a + a\right)$$

$$= \frac{wa}{24EI}\left(6a^3\right) + \frac{Pa^2}{3EI}\left(2a\right) = \frac{wa^4}{4EI} + \frac{2Pa^3}{3EI}$$

Solve for the minimum value of I required:

$$\Delta_{max_{overhang},\,tot} = \frac{wa^4}{4EI} + \frac{2Pa^3}{3EI} = \frac{1}{EI}\left[\frac{wa^4}{4} + \frac{2Pa^3}{3}\right]$$

$$I_{req'd} = \frac{1}{E\Delta_{max_{overhang},\,tot}}\left[\frac{wa^4}{4} + \frac{2Pa^3}{3}\right]$$

$$I_{req'd} = \frac{1}{\left(1.8x10^6 \text{ psi}\right)\left(0.1"\right)}\left[\frac{\left(\frac{20 \text{ plf}}{12 \text{ in / ft}}\right)\left(36"\right)^4}{4} + \frac{2\left(175\#\right)\left(36"\right)^3}{3}\right] = 34.13 \text{ in}^4$$

3. The smallest members which meet this requirement are a 3x6 or a 4x6. Two 2x6's laminated together are also sufficient. In this example, the deflection test is the most restrictive criteria – the above choices also satisfy the bending and shear requirements. Regardless of the final choice, the thickness of the downstage edge of the deck can be reduced by tapering the overhanging beams, being sure to maintain the full cross-section at the support where the maximum bending moment occurs.

Another approach to this problem would be to estimate the loading condition with the recommended 50 psf live and dead load rating without the 175 lb point load. In this case, M_{max} and $I_{req'd}$ can be calculated using case formulas:

$$w = (\text{tributary width of a 1' section, ft})(w, \text{psf}) = (2 \text{ ft})(50 \text{ psf}) = 100 \text{ plf} = 8.33 \text{ pli}$$

$$M_2 = \frac{wa^2}{2} = \frac{(8.33 \text{ pli})(36\text{"})^2}{2} = 5{,}400 \text{ inlb}$$

$$\Delta_{max_{overhang}} = \frac{wa}{24EI_{req'd}}\left(4a^2l - l^3 + 3a^3\right)$$

$$I_{req'd} = \frac{wa}{24E\Delta_{all}}\left(4a^2l - l^3 + 3a^3\right)$$

$$= \left[\frac{(8.33 \text{ pli})(36\text{"})}{24\left(1.8x10^6 \text{ lb}/\text{in}\right)(0.1\text{"})}\right]\left[4(36\text{"})^2(36\text{"}) - (36\text{"})^3 + 3(36\text{"})^3\right] = 19.44 \text{ in}^4$$

As the numbers demonstrate, the worst case scenario for a long overhang relative to the span would be point loading at the end of the span. If R_2 is moved so that the overhang is 2' and the span is 4', the point load scenario is still the worst case, but if R_2 is moved so that the overhang is 1' and the span is 5', the 50 psf rating becomes the worst case scenario.

NOTCHING SAWN LUMBER BEAMS

It is a common practice to notch wooden beams in order to make a connection detail practical. Unfortunately, notching reduces the integrity of a beam with respect to shear and bending, especially if the notch is on the tension side of the beam (usually the bottom). The *NDS* recommends avoiding notching whenever possible, but concedes that the **flexural** properties of a beam will be unaffected if the following conditions are met (*NDS*, 3.2.3.1):

- No notches are permitted in the middle third of the span.
- No notch length can be longer than 1/3 of the actual beam depth.
- For notches in the end-thirds, the notch depth cannot be longer than 1/6 of the actual beam depth except those directly bearing over a support at the end of the beam (which can be up to 1/4 of the beam depth).

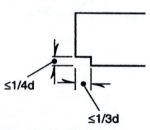

Figure 5.6 End notch requirements

Since shear stress is greatest at the ends of a beam or a support, reducing the material at these locations will increase the actual shear stress of the beam. The actual shear stress (parallel to the grain) for a member notched at the ends can be calculated using the following equation (*NDS*, 3.4.4.1):

$$f_v = \left(\frac{3V}{2bd_n}\right)\left(\frac{d}{d_n}\right)$$

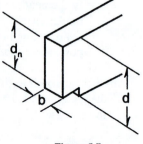

Figure 5.7

where f_v is the actual shear stress, psi
          b is the width of the member, in
          d is the depth of the member, in
          d_n is the depth of the member less the notch depth, in
          V is the vertical shear at the support in question, lbs

Notice that the actual shear stress present in a notched beam is larger than it would be for an unnotched beam with a depth equal to d_n. This is due to stress concentrations and inherent grain weaknesses of wood beams. The *NDS* notes that the effects of stress concentration can be lessened by sloping a notch instead of leaving it square (*NDS*, 3.4.4.4). Reinforcing a notch with glued plywood plates will also reduce the stress concentrations, and placing a wood cleat below the notch will effectively restore the beam to its original strength because the notched section no longer supports the weight (see Figure 5.8 below).

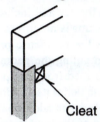

Cleat

Figure 5.8 Cleat supporting a notch

Example 5. What is the V_{max} that the beam shown in Figure 5.9 can withstand? Assume a normal load duration, a species and grade of Eastern Softwoods, No. 2, and that the notch bears directly over a support.

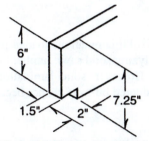

6"

1.5"   2"   7.25"

Figure 5.9 Example 5; notched 2x8

Check that the notch meets the *NDS* requirements:

$$\text{length}_{all} = \frac{7.25"}{3} = 2.42" \Rightarrow 2" < 2.42" \;\checkmark$$

$$\text{depth}_{all} = \frac{7.25"}{4} = 1.8125" \Rightarrow 1.25" < 1.8125" \;\checkmark$$

Since $C_D = 1.0$:

$$F_v' = C_D F_V = 1.0(70 \text{ psi}) = 70 \text{ psi}$$

Substitute F_v' into the shear equation and solve for V_{max}:

$$f_v = \left(\frac{3V}{2bd_n}\right)\left(\frac{d}{d_n}\right) \Rightarrow F_v' = \left(\frac{3V_{max}}{2bd_n}\right)\left(\frac{d}{d_n}\right)$$

$$V_{max} = \frac{2bd_n^2 F_v'}{3d} = \frac{2(1.5")(6")^2(70 \text{ psi})}{3(7.25")} = 347.6\#$$

Therefore, this beam can withstand any loading condition that creates a V_{max} of 347.6 lbs or less.

BUILT-UP BEAMS

INTRODUCTION

Built-up beams are quite common in theater and include solid laminations, hollow boxes, hogtroughs, etc. Analyzing built-up beams is no different than analyzing solid sawn lumber beams, except that we must calculate the geometric properties for the built-up shape and apply an additional safety factor. Computing the geometric properties of a built-up shape implicitly assumes that the shape is formed from one piece – that the joints between members are as strong or stronger than the material itself. Unfortunately, most shops do not have a wood welder, so we recommend applying an additional **Built Up Shape (BUS)** adjustment factor of 0.75 to the allowable stresses of the lumber from which the built-up shape is constructed. In addition, it is assumed that all the joints are nail-glued and that the edges of the components are resurfaced to provide a larger and rougher glue surface.

It is important to note that the analysis of built-up wooden sections discussed in this chapter is not covered by the *NDS* nor endorsed by any official organization of professional engineers.

SOLID LAMINATIONS

The beam design procedures for solid laminations loaded parallel to the edges of the laminations are no different than analyzing solid sawn lumber beams because the *I* and *S* values can be added together directly. However, solid laminations loaded perpendicular to the edges of the laminations are considered built-up shapes because their extreme fiber distance changes (see Figure 5.10).

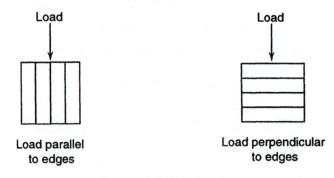

Figure 5.10 Solid laminated beams

Example 6. What is the maximum point load, at the center of an 8' span, that three 2x4's laminated as drawn can support? Assume that the grade and species of lumber is Hem-Fir No. 2, the load duration is two months, and the applicable deflection criteria is *l*/240. (In this case, it is unnecessary to resurface the 2x4's because the wide face provides plenty of glue surface).

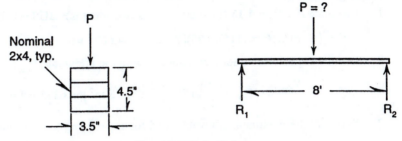

Figure 5.11 Example 6

A. Determine the base design values and geometric properties.
1. From the design tables in Appendix D:

$$A_{2x4} = 5.25 \text{ in}^2; \quad wt = 1.276 \text{ plf or } 0.106 \text{ pli at } 35 \text{ lb/ft}^3$$

$$F_b = 850 \text{ psi}; \quad F_v = 75 \text{ psi}; \quad E = 1.3 \times 10^6 \text{ psi}$$

2. Calculate S_{x-x}, I_{x-x}, and A_{tot} for the section:

$$S_{x-x} = \frac{bd^2}{6} = \frac{3.5''(4.5'')^2}{6} = 11.8125 \text{ in}^3$$

$$I_{x-x} = \frac{bd^3}{12} = \frac{3.5''(4.5'')^3}{12} = 26.578 \text{ in}^4$$

$$A_{tot} = 3(5.25 \text{ in}^2) = 15.75 \text{ in}^2$$

The maximum point load allowed by each test must be calculated. The lowest value of *P* found will be the ruling condition.

B. Apply the bending test.
1. Calculate F_b'. $C_D = 1.15$ (load duration is two months); $C_F = 1.5$ (size factor for a 2x4); BUS = 0.75.

$$F_b' = (C_D C_F BUS)F_b = 1.15(1.5)(0.75)(850 \text{ psi}) = 1,100 \text{ psi}$$

2. Use the Flexure Formula to find the allowable M_{max}:

$$M_{max} = SF_b' = (11.8125 \text{ in}^3)(1,100 \text{ psi}) = 12,993.75 \text{ inlb}$$

3. Solve for the maximum allowable load for bending using the case formulas:

$$M_{max} = M_{point\ load} + M_{distributed\ load}$$

$$M_{max} = \frac{Pl}{4} + \frac{wl^2}{8}$$

$$P_{all} = \frac{4}{l}\left(M_{max} - \frac{wl^2}{8}\right) = \frac{4}{96"}\left(12{,}993.75 \text{ inlb} - \frac{[3(0.106 \text{ pli})](96")^2}{8}\right)$$

$$P_{all} = 526.1\#$$

C. Apply the shear test.
  1. Calculate F_v'. $C_D = 1.15$ (load duration is two months); BUS = 0.75.

$$F_v' = (C_D BUS)F_v = (1.15)(0.75)(75 \text{ psi}) = 64.6875 \text{ psi}$$

  2. Use the shear formula for a rectangle to find the allowable V_{max}:

$$F_v' = \left(\frac{3}{2}\right)\frac{V_{max}}{A} \Rightarrow V_{max} = \left(\frac{2}{3}\right)AF_v' = \left(\frac{2}{3}\right)(15.75 \text{ in}^2)64.6875 \text{ psi} = 679.22\#$$

  3. Solve for the maximum allowable load for shear using the case formulas:

$$V_{max} = V_{point\ load} + V_{distributed\ load}$$

$$V_{max} = \frac{P}{2} + \frac{wl}{2}$$

$$P_{all} = 2\left(V_{max} - \frac{wl}{2}\right) = 2\left(679.22\# - \frac{[3(0.106 \text{ pli})]96"}{2}\right) = 1{,}328\#$$

D. Apply the deflection test with an $l/240$ criteria.
  1. Solve for Δ_{all}:

$$\Delta_{all} = \frac{l}{240} = \frac{96"}{240} = 0.4"$$

  2. Solve for the maximum allowable load for deflection using the case formulas:

$$\Delta_{all} = \Delta_{all,\ point\ load} + \Delta_{all,\ distributed\ load}$$

$$\Delta_{all} = \frac{Pl^3}{48EI} + \frac{5wl^4}{384EI} =$$

$$P_{all} = \frac{48EI}{l^3}\left(\Delta_{all} - \frac{5wl^4}{384EI}\right)$$

$$= \left[\frac{48(1.3x10^6 \text{ psi})(26.578 \text{ in}^4)}{(96")^3}\right]\left[0.4" - \frac{5[3(0.106 \text{ pli})](96")^4}{384(1.3x10^6 \text{ psi})(26.578 \text{ in}^4)}\right]$$

$$P_{all} = 730.7\#$$

In this example, bending failure is the ruling criteria, so the maximum allowable point load in the center of the span is 526 lbs. Note that the deflection test does not include the BUS factor because deflection is not a failure mode.

NON-SOLID LAMINATIONS

Example 7. What is the greatest uniformly distributed load on a 12' simple span that a hollow box beam constructed of resurfaced 2x6's can support? Assume that the grade and species of the lumber is Western Woods Select Structural, the load duration is two months, and the applicable deflection criteria is $l/240$.

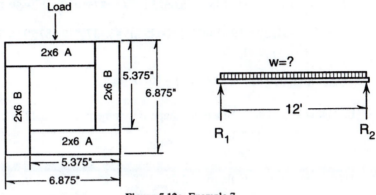

Figure 5.12a Example 7

A. Determine the base design values and geometric properties.
1. From the design tables in Appendix D:

$$F_b=900 \text{ psi}; \quad F_v=70 \text{ psi}; \quad E=1.2 \times 10^6 \text{ psi}$$

2. Since the 2x6's are resurfaced, the geometric properties must be calculated:

$$A_{2x6} = bd = 1.5''(5.375'') = 8.0625 \text{ in}^2$$

$$S_{x-x} = \frac{bd^2}{6} = \frac{1.5''(5.375'')^2}{6} = 7.22 \text{ in}^3$$

$$I_{x-x} = \frac{bd^3}{12} = \frac{1.5''(5.375'')^3}{12} = 19.41 \text{ in}^4$$

$$S_{y-y} = \frac{5.375''(1.5'')^2}{6} = 2.01 \text{ in}^3$$

$$I_{y-y} = \frac{5.375''(1.5'')^3}{12} = 1.51 \text{ in}^4$$

3. The weight of the hollow box beam must be calculated. We will approximate the weight by assuming it is four full 2x6's:

$$wt_{box} = 4\left(\frac{2.01 \text{ plf}}{12 \text{ in}/\text{ft}}\right) = 4(0.1675 \text{ pli}) = 0.67 \text{ pli}$$

B. Bending
1. Calculate F_b'. $C_D = 1.15$ (two month duration); $C_F = 1.3$ (size factor for a 2x6); BUS = 0.75.

$$F_b' = (C_D C_F BUS)F_b = 1.15(1.3)(0.75)(900 \text{ psi}) = 1,009.125 \text{ psi}$$

2. Find S for the built-up box beam.
    a. First, find I by transferring and adding moments of inertia. The transferred I of the top and bottom 2x6's will be identical, as will the transferred I of the two side 2x6's.

$$I_A = I_o + Az^2$$

$$I_A = I_{y-y} + A_A z_A^2 = 1.51 \text{ in}^4 + \left(8.0625 \text{ in}^2\right)\left(3.4375" - 1.5"\!\big/\!_2\right)^2 = 59.74 \text{ in}^4$$

$$I_B = I_{x-x} + A_B z_B^2 = 19.41 \text{ in}^4 + \left(8.0625 \text{ in}^2\right)\left(3.4375" - 2.6875"\right)^2 = 23.95 \text{ in}^4$$

$$I_{tot} = 2I_A + 2I_B$$

$$I_{tot} = 2\left(59.74 \text{ in}^4\right) + 2\left(23.95 \text{ in}^4\right) = 167.38 \text{ in}^4$$

    b. Now, calculate S. Since the shape is symmetrical, $c = 3.4375"$.

$$S = \frac{I}{c} = \frac{167.38 \text{ in}^4}{3.4375"} = 48.69 \text{ in}^3$$

3. Use the Flexure Formula to find M_{max}:

$$M_{max} = SF_b' = \left(48.69 \text{ in}^3\right)\left(1,009.125 \text{ psi}\right) = 49,134.3 \text{ inlb}$$

4. Solve for the maximum allowable load for bending:

$$M_{max} = \frac{wl^2}{8} \Rightarrow w_{all} = \frac{8M_{max}}{l^2} = \frac{8\left(49,134.3 \text{ inlb}\right)}{\left(144"\right)^2} = 18.96 \text{ pli}$$

5. Subtract the approximate beam weight to get a working load:

$$w = 18.96 \text{ pli} - 0.67 \text{ pli} = 18.29 \text{ pli}$$

C. Shear
    1. Calculate F_v'. $C_D = 1.15$; BUS $= 0.75$.

$$F_v' = \left(C_D BUS\right)F_v = 1.15(0.75)(70 \text{ psi}) = 60.375 \text{ psi}$$

    2. Find Q:

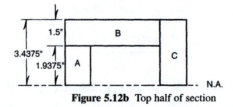

Figure 5.12b Top half of section

$$d_A A_A = \left(\frac{1.9375"}{2}\right)\left[\left(1.9375"\right)\left(1.5"\right)\right] = 2.815 \text{ in}^3$$

$$d_B A_B = \left(3.4375" - 0.75"\right)\left(8.0625 \text{ in}^2\right) = 21.668 \text{ in}^3$$

$$d_C A_C = \left(\frac{3.4375"}{2}\right)\left[\left(3.4375"\right)\left(1.5"\right)\right] = 8.862 \text{ in}^3$$

$$Q = d_A A_A + d_B A_B + d_C A_C = 2.815 \text{ in}^3 + 21.668 \text{ in}^3 + 8.862 \text{ in}^3 = 33.345 \text{ in}^3$$

3. Solve the general shear formula for V_{max}:

$$f_v = \frac{V_{max}Q}{Ib}$$

$$V_{max} = \frac{F_v'Ib}{Q} = \frac{(60.375 \text{ psi})(167.38 \text{ in}^4)(3")}{33.345 \text{ in}^3} = 909.2\#$$

4. Solve for the maximum allowable load for shear by using the case formulas:

$$V_{max} = \frac{wl}{2} \Rightarrow w_{all} = \frac{2V_{max}}{l} = \frac{2(909.2\#)}{144"} = 12.6 \text{ pli}$$

5. Subtract the approximate beam weight to get a working load:

$$w = 12.6 \text{ pli} - 0.67 \text{ pli} = 11.93 \text{ pli}$$

D. Apply a deflection criteria of $l/240$.
   1. Solve for Δ_{all}:

$$\Delta_{all} = \frac{l}{240} = \frac{144"}{240} = 0.6"$$

   2. Solve for the maximum allowable load for deflection by using the case formulas:

$$\Delta_{max} = \frac{5wl^4}{384EI}$$

$$w_{all} = \frac{384EI\Delta_{max}}{5l^4} = \frac{384(1.2\text{x}10^6)(167.38 \text{ in}^4)(0.6")}{5(144")^4} = 21.5 \text{ pli}$$

   3. Subtract the approximate beam weight to get a working load:

$$w = 21.5 \text{ pli} - 0.67 \text{ pli} = 20.83 \text{ pli}$$

So, the ruling test is shear, with a w_{all} of 11.93 pli (143 plf or a total load, W, of 1,718 lbs). The M_{max} caused by this evenly distributed load is the equivalent of the M_{max} caused by a point load of 859 lbs in the center of the span. Once again, note that we did not apply the BUS factor to the deflection test because deflection is not a failure mode.

Example 8. L-shaped beams made of 1x3 have many names in the theater industry: hogstrough, L-braces, battens, or strong-backs to name a few. Regardless of what they are called, hogstroughs are widely used to make scenery stiffer. But how strong are they? Analyze the L-brace pictured in Figure 5.13a made of Southern Pine Industrial 45 (equivalent to Southern Pine No. 2). Determine the maximum evenly distributed load it can support over a 14' span with a normal load duration and a deflection criteria of $l/240$. Since 1x3's are normally ripped from 1x6 boards, no additional resurfacing is required.

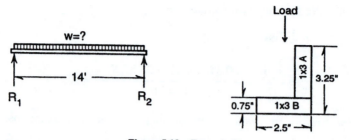

Figure 5.13a Example 8

A. Determine the base design values and geometric properties.

1. From the design tables in Appendix D (Southern Pine No. 2, 2-4" thick and 5-6" wide):

$$F_b = 1,250 \text{ psi}; \; F_v = 90 \text{ psi}; \; E = 1.6 \times 10^6 \text{ psi}$$

2. Geometric properties for a 1x3:

$$A = 1.875 \text{ in}^2; \; S_{x-x} = 0.781 \text{ in}^3; \; I_{x-x} = 0.977 \text{ in}^4; \; S_{y-y} = 0.234 \text{ in}^3; \; I_{y-y} = 0.088 \text{ in}^4$$

3. Estimated weight of the beam at a density of 35 lb/ft³:

$$wt = 2(1x3) \approx 1x6 = 0.0833 \text{ pli}$$

B. Apply the bending test.

1. Calculate F_b'. $C_D = 1.0$; no size factor for Southern Pine; BUS = 0.75.

$$F_b' = (C_D BUS)F_b = 1.0(0.75)1,250 \text{ psi} = 937.5 \text{ psi}$$

2. Find S for the built-up beam.

   a. First, calculate c_{x-x} because the shape is not symmetrical.

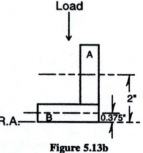

$$d_{NA} = \frac{2"(1.875 \text{ in}^2) + 0.375"(1.875 \text{ in}^2)}{2(1.875 \text{ in}^2)} = 1.1875" \text{ from bottom}$$

$$d_{NA}' = (3.25") - 1.1875" = 2.0625" \text{ from top}$$

$$c_{x-x} = 2.0625"$$

Figure 5.13b

   b. Find I by transferring and adding the moments of inertia:

$$I_A = I_{x-x} + A_A z_A^2 = 0.977 \text{ in}^4 + (1.875 \text{ in}^2)(2" - 1.1875")^2 = 2.215 \text{ in}^4$$

$$I_B = I_{y-y} + A_B z_B^2 = 0.088 \text{ in}^4 + (1.875 \text{ in}^2)(1.1875" - 0.375")^2 = 1.326 \text{ in}^4$$

$$I_{tot, x-x} = I_A + I_B = 2.215 \text{ in}^4 + 1.326 \text{ in}^4 = 3.54 \text{ in}^4$$

   c. Now, calculate S_{x-x}:

$$S_{x-x} = \frac{I_{tot}}{c_{x-x}} = \frac{3.54 \text{ in}^4}{2.0625"} = 1.717 \text{ in}^3$$

3. Use the Flexure Formula to find M_{max}:

$$M_{max} = S_{x-x}F_b' = (1.717 \text{ in}^3)(937.5 \text{ psi}) = 1,609.7 \text{ inlb}$$

4. Using the case formula, solve for w:

$$w_{all} = \frac{8M_{max}}{l^2} = \frac{8(1,609.7 \text{ inlb})}{\left[14'(12 \text{ in}/\text{ft})\right]^2} = 0.456 \text{ pli}$$

5. Subtract the approximate beam weight to get a working load:

$$w = 0.456 \text{ pli} - 0.0833 \text{ pli} = 0.373 \text{ pli}$$

C. Apply the shear test.
   1. Calculate F_v'. $C_D = 1.0$; BUS = 0.75.

$$F_v' = (C_D BUS)F_v = 1.0(0.75)(90 \text{ psi}) = 67.5 \text{ psi}$$

   2. Find Q for the top half (the top is an easier shape to analyze):

$$Q = d_{\text{top half}} A_{\text{top half}}$$

$$Q = \left(\frac{2.0625"}{2}\right)\left[2.0625"(0.75")\right] = 1.595 \text{ in}^3$$

   3. Solve the general shear formula for V_{max}:

$$V_{max} = \frac{F_v' I b}{Q} = \frac{(67.5 \text{ psi})(3.54 \text{ in}^4)(0.75")}{1.595 \text{ in}^3} = 112.4\#$$

   4. Solve for the maximum allowable load for shear by using the case formula:

$$w_{all} = \frac{2V_{max}}{l} = \frac{2(112.4\#)}{168"} = 1.34 \text{ pli}$$

   5. Subtract the approximate beam weight to get a working load:

$$w = 1.34 \text{ pli} - 0.0833 \text{ pli} = 1.26 \text{ pli}$$

D. Apply the deflection test.
   1. Solve for Δ_{all}:

$$\Delta_{all} = \frac{l}{240} = \frac{14'(12 \text{ in}/\text{ft})}{240} = \frac{168"}{240} = 0.7"$$

   2. Solve for the maximum allowable load for deflection by using the case formulas:

$$w_{all} = \frac{384 EI\Delta_{max}}{5l^4} = \frac{384(1.6x10^6)(3.54 \text{ in}^4)(0.7")}{5(168")^4} = 0.382 \text{ pli}$$

   3. Subtract the approximate beam weight to get a working load:

$$w = 0.382 \text{ pli} - 0.0833 \text{ pli} = 0.299 \text{ pli}$$

So, the ruling test is deflection, with an allowable w of 0.299 pli or 3.58 plf or a total W of 50.2 lbs. Since deflection is not failure, we may choose to use the maximum load found with respect to bending, $w = 0.373$ pli (4.48 plf or a total W of 62.7 lbs). This evenly distributed load is the equivalent of a 31.3 lb point load in the center of the span. The L-brace is not a very strong beam for a 14' span. Remember, however, that they often have multiple attachment points, so the spans are often very short.

Remember that stress-rated boards are not commonly used and that the values obtained in the above examples cannot be applied to hollow box shapes or L-braces made from appearance grade lumber. In addition, all joints between the component members of the beams must be brush glued and allowed to dry before use.

DESIGNING BACKWARDS

In the preceding examples of built-up shapes, we determined the capacity of a given beam for a given loading condition. Therefore, the beam design steps outlined earlier in the chapter are not directly applicable. The following outline summarizes the technique used for designing the built-up shapes.

A. Gather information. Draw a beam diagram and cross-section of the member.
   1. Look up the base design values of the selected species and grade.
   2. Determine the geometric properties (I and S for the relevant axis) of a solid member or of the component pieces of a built-up shape.
B. Bending.
   1. Look up the relevant adjustment factors and calculate F_b'. Remember to include the BUS factor of 0.75.
   2. Find S (for solid sections, skip to step 3).
      a. Transfer the moments of inertia.
      b. Determine c and calculate S:

$$S = \frac{I_{tot}}{c}$$

   3. Use the Flexure Formula to find the allowable M_{max}:

$$M_{max} = SF_b'$$

   4. Solve for the maximum allowable load for bending with the appropriate case formula(s).
C. Shear.
   1. Look up the relevant adjustment factors and calculate F_v'. Remember to include the BUS factor of 0.75.
   2. Find Q (see Chapter 4). If designing a solid section, skip to step 3.
   3. If designing a solid section, solve the shear formula of a rectangle for the maximum allowable shear stress:

$$V_{max} = \left(\frac{2}{3}\right)AF_v'$$

If designing a hollow shape or an open shape, solve the general shear formula for the maximum allowable shear stress:

$$V_{max} = \frac{F_v'Ib}{Q}$$

4. Solve for the maximum allowable load for shear with the appropriate case formula(s).

D. Deflection.
1. Choose a deflection criteria, and calculate the maximum allowable deflection, Δ_{max}.
2. Solve for the maximum allowable load for deflection with the appropriate case formula(s).

E. Compare the allowable loads.

The lowest allowable load of the three tests is the allowable load for the member. Remember that any allowable load is inclusive of the beam weight, i.e., for a working allowable load, the beam weight must be subtracted from the allowable load determined.

CHAPTER 5 LESSONS

The format of the numbering system is: chapter.lesson.problem number.
Assume normal adjustment factors and a deflection criteria of $l/240$ unless otherwise noted.

LESSON 5.1 WOOD AND ITS PROPERTIES, BASIC BEAM TESTS (PG 85 – 92)

5.1.1   Find F_b' for a Hem-Fir Construction grade 2x4. It will have a lifetime of six weeks and is part of a deck with framing on 1' centers.

5.1.2   Find F_b' for a Douglas-Fir South No. 2 2x4. It will have a lifetime of one year and will be used to frame either side of a 3' wide platform.

5.1.3   Find F_b' for a Western Woods No. 1 3x10. It will have a lifetime of 20 years and will be used to support either side of a 12' wide deck.

5.1.4   Find F_b' for an Eastern White Pine 2x6 Stud with a lifetime of four weeks which is used as framing on 16" centers.

5.1.5   Find F_b' for an Eastern Softwoods Select Structural 4x12. It will have a lifetime of 1 year and is part of a repetitive member system with framing on 2' centers.

5.1.6   Find F_b' for a Spruce-Pine-Fir No. 1 3x20 used to support a permanent trapped stage. The 3x20 beams are spaced 3' on center.

5.1.7   Find F_b' for a Hem-Fir No. 2 2x12 used as the tread for a staircase with a lifetime of 2 months.

5.1.8   Find F_b' for a Douglas-Fir South No. 1 2x6 used as the surface of a platform with a lifetime of 4 weeks.

LESSON 5.2 SHEAR TEST (PG 92 – 95)

5.2.1   Find F_v' for the member in problem 5.1.1.

5.2.2   Find F_v' for the member in problem 5.1.2.

5.2.3   Find F_v' for the member in problem 5.1.3.

5.2.4   Find F_v' for the member in problem 5.1.4.

5.2.5   What is the statical moment of area, Q, above the shear plane indicated for the I-shape given below?

5.2.6   What is the statical moment of area, Q, above the shear plane indicated for the box shape given below?

5.2.7   What is the statical moment of area, Q, above the shear plane indicated for the T-shape given below?

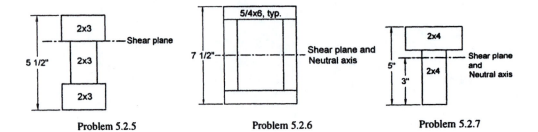

Problem 5.2.5   Problem 5.2.6   Problem 5.2.7

LESSON 5.3 DEFLECTION TEST (PG 95 – 98)

5.3.1   Find Δ_{max} for a simple beam with a span of 8' with two symmetrically placed point loads of 250 lbs 2'-8" from each end. The beam is a Hem-Fir No. 2 4x8. Does it pass a deflection criteria of $l/240$?

5.3.2   Find Δ_{max} for the beam in Problem 5.3.1 with a 400 plf evenly distributed load added to the full length of the beam. Does it pass a deflection criteria of $l/240$?

5.3.3   Find Δ_{max} for the overhang of a beam with a span between supports of 6' and an overhang of 2'. The beam has an evenly distributed load of 200 plf along its full length, and is a Western Woods No. 1 3x6. Does it pass a deflection criteria of $l/360$ on the overhang?

5.3.4   Find Δ_{max} for the span between supports at M_1 for problem 5.3.3. Does it pass a deflection criteria of $l/360$?

5.3.5   Find Δ_{max} for the 12' simple beam given below. It is a Spruce-Pine-Fir No. 2 4x12. Does it pass a deflection criteria of $l/240$?

5.3.6   The M_{max} of a 16' beam with a complex loading condition has been determined to be 5,100 ftlbs. Approximate Δ_{max} assuming that the beam is a Douglas Fir-South No. 3 4x16. Does it pass a deflection criteria of $l/240$?

5.3.7   The M_{max} of a 12' beam with a complex loading condition has been determined to be 40,800 inlbs. Approximate Δ_{max} assuming that the beam is a Southern Pine No. 2 2x10. Does it pass a deflection criteria of $l/240$?

LESSON 5.4 BEAM DESIGN (PG 98 – 102)

5.4.1   Choose an appropriate 2x sawn lumber member with a species category of Douglas Fir-South No. 1 with a lifetime of six weeks for the loading condition given below.

5.4.2   Choose an appropriate 3x sawn lumber member with a species category of Eastern White Pine No. 1 with a lifetime of 5 years for the loading condition given below. It is part of a deck framed 18" on center. Assume that the weight of the beam is included in the evenly distributed load.

5.4.3   Choose an appropriate 2x sawn lumber member with a species category of Hem-Fir No. 1 for the loading condition given below. It is part of a deck framed 2' on center and has a lifetime of 5 weeks. Assume that the weight of the beam is included in the evenly distributed load.

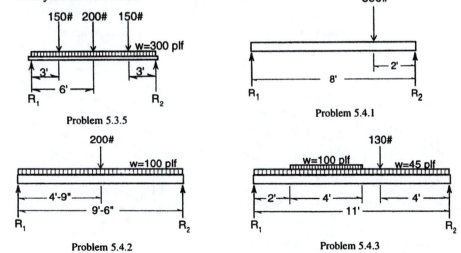

Problem 5.3.5

Problem 5.4.1

Problem 5.4.2

Problem 5.4.3

LESSON 5.5 BEAM DESIGN, CONTINUED WITH EXAMPLE 4 (PG 102 – 106)

5.5.1 Choose an appropriate 2x sawn lumber member with a species category of Southern Pine No. 1 for the loading condition given below. Assume a lifetime of 2 months and that the beam is part of a deck system with framing on 2' centers. The weight of the beam is included in the evenly distributed load.

5.5.2 Choose an appropriate 2x sawn lumber member with a species category of Douglas Fir-South No. 1 for the loading condition given below. The weight of the beam is included in the evenly distributed load. Assume a lifetime of 1 year, and that the beam is part of a deck with framing on 2' centers. Use an $l/360$ deflection criteria.

LESSON 5.6 NOTCHING SAWN LUMBER BEAMS (PG 106 – 108)

5.6.1 What is the V_{max} that the beam given below can withstand? Use a species category of Hem-Fir No. 3, and assume that the notch bears directly over a support.

5.6.2 What is the V_{max} that the beam given below can withstand? Use a species category of Western Woods No. 1. Assume that the beam has a 2 month load duration and that the notch bears directly over a support.

5.6.3 What is f_v for a 2x10 with a 2" deep by 3" long end-notch and a V_{max} of 500 lb?

5.6.4 What is f_v for a 4x8 with a 2" deep by 2" long end-notch and a V_{max} of 1,500 lb?

5.6.5 If the beam selected in Problem 5.4.1 has an end-notch with a depth 1/4 of its actual depth, does the beam selection change?

5.6.6 If the beam selected in Problem 5.4.3 has an end-notch with a depth 1/4 of its actual depth, does the beam selection change?

5.6.7 What is the maximum evenly distributed load that the beam given below with a species category of Douglas Fir-South No. 1 can withstand? The load duration is two months, and the beam is part of a deck with framing on 16" centers.

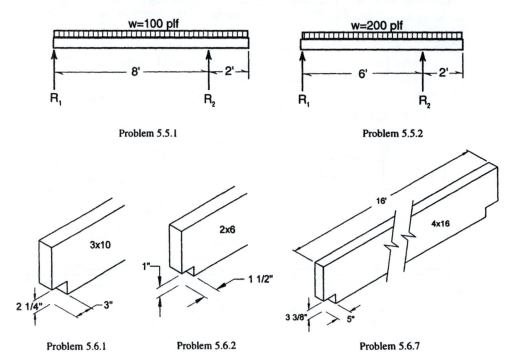

Problem 5.5.1   Problem 5.5.2

Problem 5.6.1   Problem 5.6.2   Problem 5.6.7

LESSON 5.7 BUILT-UP BEAMS (PG 108 – 117)

5.7.1 What is the maximum point load that the I-shaped beam in Problem 5.2.5 can support as a 10' simple span? Use a species category of Eastern White Pine No. 2. The beams are part of a deck system and are spaced on 3' centers. Assume a six week load duration and that 2x4 members have been resurfaced to the actual dimensions of 2x3's. Ignore beam weight.

5.7.2 What is the maximum evenly distributed load that the box beam in Problem 5.2.6 can support as a 14' simple span? Use a species category of Southern Pine Industrial 45 (Southern Pine No. 2). The beams are part of a deck system and are spaced on 4' centers. Assume a lifetime of 1 year, and use 35 lb/ft³ as the density of the wood. The 5/4x6 members are ripped from 5/4x12's and, thus, have actual dimensions of 1"x5.5". Note: use the base design values for a 12" deep member.

5.7.3 What is maximum evenly distributed load that the hogstrough analyzed in Example 8 can support with a 4' span?

6

Wood Column Analysis and Design

INTRODUCTION
The basic process of column design is similar to beam design: actual stresses are computed and compared to allowable stresses until a column that exceeds or meets the requirements is found.

Columns are generally considered to be vertical members which support downward loads. However, the techniques described in this chapter apply to any structural member which resists axial, compressive loads. In some applications, columns also resist bending moments. The procedures for analyzing these combined loading conditions will be discussed in Chapter 7.

In Chapter 2, the design of compression members was introduced using the direct stress formula with the assumption that the member in question would fail by crushing. In reality, columns can fail by crushing, buckling, or a combination of the two. This complex failure mode combines with material characteristics to form unique techniques of column analysis. This chapter will address the specifics of sawn lumber column design for members subject to axial compressive stress.

Imagine a yardstick held between two hands: If pressure is applied to the ends, the yardstick bows out. This is an example of a column buckling. If the yardstick is cut in half, more pressure must be applied before the now 18" stick begins to buckle. The shorter the yardstick, the more force is required to make it buckle. When the yardstick is extremely short, a very heavy load would have to be applied, and it would fail by crushing instead of buckling. Additionally, a thicker yardstick would have a greater resistance to buckling.

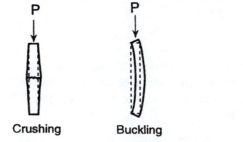

Figure 6.1 Crushing versus. buckling of a wood column

The trends illustrated by the yardstick example are true for any column: the longer or thinner the column, the easier it is to cause the column to fail by buckling. The shorter or thicker the column, the more likely it is to fail by crushing. Most columns fall somewhere between the two extremes and fail due to a combination of buckling and crushing. F_c, the base allowable design value for compressive stress, represents only the crushing strength of a material. It must be adjusted for the unbraced length of the column relative to its weakest axis. Structural engineers have spent many years attempting to formulate equations which accurately correlate material and section properties to column failure.

EULER'S EQUATION

Leonard Euler (pronounced "oiler") first described buckling failure in 1757, when he developed an equation for long columns which determines their critical buckling load, or ultimate failure load (Fitzgerald, 276). **Euler's equation** was derived using calculus and assumed that the column was homogeneous and behaved elastically. The general formula is as follows:

$$P_{cr} = \frac{n^2 \pi^2 EI}{l^2}$$

where P_{cr} is the critical buckling load, lbs
              n is the buckling mode, 1, 2, 3, . . .
              E is the modulus of elasticity, psi
              I is the moment of inertia, in⁴
              l is the unbraced length, in

Each integer, n, is a product of the mathematical derivation and represents a different mode of buckling (a different pattern of flexing) by which the column could fail. Theoretically, there are an infinite number of Euler buckling modes. The "first mode of buckling" occurs when n equals 1; the second mode occurs when n equals 2 and so on.

In general, only the first mode of buckling is important because the column will fail before loads sufficient to cause the second or subsequent modes of failure are reached. Figure 6.2 illustrates the first three Euler modes of buckling. When Euler's equation is used today, n is set to 1, so it can be written as follows:

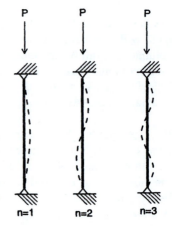

$$P_{cr} = \frac{\pi^2 EI}{l^2}$$

Figure 6.2 Euler buckling modes (Fitzgerald, 259)

In addition to setting n equal to 1, Euler's equation is commonly transformed to solve for the maximum allowable compressive stress, F_{cr}, by the following substitutions and rearrangement of variables:

- Define I in terms of the radius of gyration and area.

$$r = \sqrt{\frac{I}{A}} \Rightarrow r^2 = \frac{I}{A} \Rightarrow I = Ar^2$$

- Substitute Ar^2 for I.

$$P_{cr} = \frac{\pi^2 E A r^2}{l^2}$$

- Divide both sides by area.

$$\frac{P_{cr}}{A} = \frac{\pi^2 E r^2}{l^2}$$

- Substitute F_{cr} for P_{cr}/A.

$$F_{cr} = \frac{\pi^2 E r^2}{l^2}$$

- Algebraically, multiplying by a quantity is the same as dividing by its inverse, so this equation can be rearranged:

$$F_{cr} = \frac{\pi^2 E r^2}{l^2} = \pi^2 E \left(\frac{r}{l}\right)^2 = \frac{\pi^2 E}{\left(l/r\right)^2}$$

where F_{cr} is the maximum allowable compressive stress, psi
           E is the modulus of elasticity, psi
           l is the unbraced length of the column, in
           r is the radius of gyration, in

The above formula is a common form of Euler's equation. The ratio l/r is called the **slenderness ratio**, and it quantifies the strength of a column by simultaneously evaluating both its geometry and unbraced length. Regardless of all other tests, every material has a designated maximum slenderness ratio beyond which columns made from it are considered unstable. **The maximum l/r for wood is 173.**

To this point, the above form of Euler's equation is true for all materials. The following section will show how the general form of the equation is modified to apply to solid sawn lumber columns. The first step is to include a safety factor of 2.74 for sawn lumber:

$$F_{cr} = \frac{\pi^2 E}{\left(l/r\right)^2} \Rightarrow F_{cr} = \frac{\left(\pi^2/2.74\right)E}{\left(l/r\right)^2} \approx \frac{3.6E}{\left(l/r\right)^2}$$

The next step in transforming Euler's equation into a convenient form for solid sawn lumber columns is to express the slenderness ratio as l/d instead of l/r, where d is the least cross-sectional dimension. **Standard engineering practice and the *NDS* stipulate that the maximum allowable slenderness ratio, l/d, for wood is 50.** An l/d of 50 is mathematically equivalent to an l/r of 173. Euler's equation can be expressed in terms of l/d for solid rectangular columns by substituting known variables of I and A for solid, rectangular sections into the formula for the radius of gyration:

- Solve for r in terms of d:

$$r = \sqrt{\frac{I}{A}} = \sqrt{\frac{bd^3/12}{bd}} = \sqrt{\frac{bd^3}{12bd}} = \sqrt{\frac{d^2}{12}} = \frac{d}{\sqrt{12}}$$

- Substituting into Euler's equation and multiplying out the π term yields:

$$F_{cr} = \frac{3.6E}{\left(l/r\right)^2} \Rightarrow \frac{3.6E}{\dfrac{l^2}{\left(d/\sqrt{12}\right)^2}} = \frac{3.6E}{\dfrac{l^2}{\left(d^2/12\right)}} = \frac{3.6E}{12\left(l^2/d^2\right)} = \frac{0.3E}{\left(l/d\right)^2}$$

It is important to note that l/d is determined by the greatest slenderness ratio of the two primary axes of a column. When a column buckles, the axis with the smallest I value will fail. For solid rectangular columns with no cross-bracing, the weakest axis will have the least thickness of material resisting the load. For rectangular columns with one or both axes braced, the greatest slenderness ratio is determined by comparing the two.

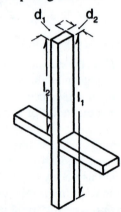

$$ratio_1 = \frac{l_1}{d_1}$$

$$ratio_2 = \frac{l_2}{d_2}$$

Figure 6.3 Simple column with bracing on one axis

The *National Design Specifications* use the Euler equation as one step in its column design process, and has very specific definitions for each variable. The *NDS* expresses Euler's equation as the following (*NDS*, 3.7.1.5):

$$F_{cr} = \frac{0.3E}{\left(l/d\right)^2} \Rightarrow F_{cE} = \frac{K_{cE}E'}{\left(\dfrac{l_e}{d}\right)^2}$$

where F_{cE} is the critical buckling design value and replaces F_{cr}, the maximum allowable compressive stress.

               E' is the allowable modulus of elasticity which is simply the E of the wood under consideration multiplied by the wet service, C_M, and temperature, C_t, factors. As discussed in Chapter 5, for most theatrical applications, C_M and C_t are 1.0, so E' is simply E.

K_{cE} is the Euler buckling coefficient for columns, 0.3 for sawn lumber (NDS, 3.7.1.5).

l_e is the **effective buckling length** and is the actual unbraced length, l, adjusted by K_e, the buckling length coefficient:

$$l_e = K_e l$$

The effective buckling length is critical to understanding the everyday use of Euler's equation. The original derivation of Euler's equation assumed that the end connections of the column were pinned. Much like beams, the elastic curve of a column will change with the degree of fixity of the end connections: fixed ends decrease buckling, and free ends increase buckling. K_e accounts for different types of end fixity found in the physical world. Figure 6.4 shows the different types of end fixity conditions and their associated values of K_e (NDS, Appendix. G):

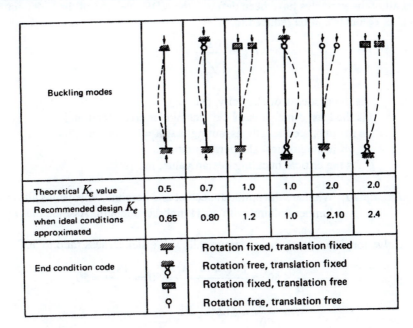

Buckling modes						
Theoretical K_e value	0.5	0.7	1.0	1.0	2.0	2.0
Recommended design K_e when ideal conditions approximated	0.65	0.80	1.2	1.0	2.10	2.4
End condition code		Rotation fixed, translation fixed				
		Rotation free, translation fixed				
		Rotation fixed, translation free				
		Rotation free, translation free				

Figure 6.4 Buckling length coefficients. Reprinted courtesy of the American Forest & Paper Association, Washinton D.C.

For most theatrical applications, we assume that our connections are pure pinned connections, so $K_e=1.0$. This is a safe assumption since a pure pinned connection is the worst possible end condition except for "flagpole" type conditions where K_e is 2 or more. Conveniently, then, unless designing a flagpole type column, l_e equals l, the unbraced length of the column.

It is important to insure that a given structure meets the fixity conditions described above. Imagine a hollywood frame for a typical flat before it is hard-covered. If the frame is stapled or nailed together, it is very easy to "accordion" it, to make it collapse by applying horizontal pressure. In this case, K_e does not equal 1.0 because the top connections are free to translate. The end fixity of the toggles is inadequate.

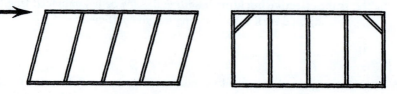

Figure 6.5 End fixity conditions

Studwalls and typical legging schemes have the same type of weakness. Crossbracing within the frame or structure which locks the top of the deck in place allows us to set K_e equal to 1.0.

Now that all of the variables have been defined, the *NDS*'s version of the Euler equation for sawn lumber columns can be reduced to:

$$F_{cE} = \frac{0.3E}{\left(\frac{l}{d}\right)^2}$$

where E is the modulus of elasticity, psi
           d is the least dimension of the rectangular cross-section, in
           l is the unbraced length, assuming that K_e=1.0, in, and that
               l/d is the greatest slenderness ratio
           F_{cE} is the critical buckling design value, psi

> **Example 1.** What are the minimum actual and nominal dimensions allowed for a sawn lumber column with an 11' unbraced length. Assume that K_e=1.0.

Solve for d by setting the maximum allowable slenderness ratio to 50:

$$\frac{l}{d} \leq 50 \Rightarrow \frac{11'(12 \text{ in / ft})}{d} = 50 \Rightarrow \frac{132"}{d} = 50$$

$$d = \frac{132"}{50} = 2.64"$$

Since 2.64" is the minimum actual dimension allowed, 4x stock, with an actual width of 3.5", is the minimum nominal dimension allowed.

> **Example 2a.** Find the F_{cE} for a nominal 3x5 column made from Eastern White Pine No. 1 with an unbraced length of 10'. Assume K_e=1.0.

Draw a free body diagram for the loading condition:

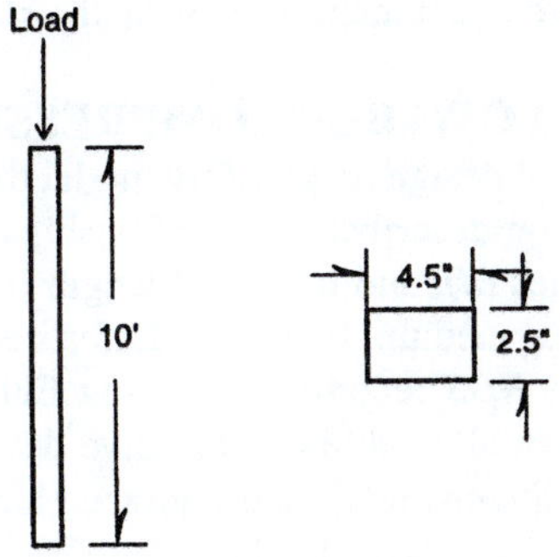

Figure 6.6 Example 2a

Calculate the slenderness ratio:

$$\frac{l}{d} = \frac{10'(12 \text{ in} / \text{ft})}{2.5"} = 48 \Rightarrow 48 \le 50 \checkmark$$

Use the Euler equation to calculate F_{cE}. E is 1.1×10^6 psi for Eastern White Pine No. 1 (Appendix D).

$$F_{cE} = \frac{0.3E}{\left(\frac{l}{d}\right)^2} = \frac{0.3\left(1.1 \times 10^6 \text{ psi}\right)}{(48)^2} = 143.2 \text{ psi}$$

Example 2b. Find F_{cE} for the column in Example 2a using the Euler equation with the slenderness ratio expressed in terms of the radius of gyration (r).

Calculate I_{x-x}, I_{y-y}, and A for a 3x5:

$$I_{x-x} = \frac{bd^3}{12} = \frac{2.5"(4.5")^3}{12} = 18.98 \text{ in}^4$$

$$I_{y-y} = \frac{bd^3}{12} = \frac{4.5"(2.5")^3}{12} = 5.86 \text{ in}^4$$

$$A = bd = (2.5")(4.5") = 11.25 \text{ in}^2$$

Calculate the least radius of gyration and its corresponding slenderness ratio:

$$r_{y-y} = \sqrt{\frac{I}{A}} = \sqrt{\frac{5.86 \text{ in}^4}{11.25 \text{ in}^2}} = 0.722"$$

$$\frac{l}{r} = \frac{120"}{0.722"} = 166.3 \Rightarrow 166.3 \le 173 \checkmark$$

Calculate F_{cE} using the appropriate form of the Euler equation:

$$F_{cE} = \frac{3.6E}{\left(\frac{l}{r}\right)^2} = \frac{3.6\left(1.1 \times 10^6 \text{ psi}\right)}{(166.3)^2} = 143.2 \text{ psi}$$

F_{cE} will be the same regardless of which version of the Euler equation is used. For solid sawn lumber columns, it is more convenient to express the slenderness ratio in terms of d.

CALCULATING THE ALLOWABLE COMPRESSIVE STRESS

Euler's equation allows structural designers to safely model the behavior of long columns in the real world. This one equation describes the relationships between the material characteristics (E), geometric properties (d), and unbraced length (l) of a column. However, most columns are relatively short or of medium length, so Euler's equation can not be used alone. This section describes how the *NDS* recommends using Euler's equation, in combination with other formulas, to derive an allowable compressive design value for a column with a given species and grade, least dimension(s), and unbraced length(s).

DEFINITIONS

The *NDS* describes how to calculate the allowable compressive stress, F_c', for solid, rectangular columns in sections 3.6 to 3.7. Like bending and shear stress, determining the allowable compressive stress involves identifying a series of adjustment factors by which the base compressive design value must be multiplied. In order for the following discussion to be clear, four design values must be defined:

- F_c is the base allowable compressive design value parallel to grain given by the *NDS Supplement* for a given species and grade.

- F_{cE} is the critical buckling design value as discussed above.

- F_c^* is an intermediate base allowable compressive design value (described below).

- F_c' is the allowable compressive design value for a given column. F_c' is derived from the three design variables above.

DETERMINING F_c'

The definition of F_c' is deceptively simple:

$$F_c' = C_p F_c^*$$

where $\quad$ F_c' is the adjusted allowable compressive design value, psi
$\quad\quad\quad\quad$ C_p is the column stability factor
$\quad\quad\quad\quad$ F_c^* is an intermediate base allowable compressive design value, psi

Determining C_p, the column stability factor, is the most complex part of the process, and requires that we first calculate F_c^* and F_{cE}.

- The first step is to find F_c^*:

$$F_c^* = \left(C_D C_F C_M C_t\right)F_c$$

where $\quad$ F_c is the base compressive design value parallel to grain, psi
$\quad\quad\quad\quad$ C_D is the load duration factor
$\quad\quad\quad\quad$ C_F is the size factor for F_c
$\quad\quad\quad\quad$ C_M is the wet service factor
$\quad\quad\quad\quad$ C_t is the temperature factor

These adjustment factors are the same factors applied to F_b, the allowable bending stress. The wet service and temperature factors are 1.0 for normal indoor scenery applications. The load duration factor will be 1.15 for a two month load duration or 1.0 for a normal load duration. The size factor is dependent on the size of the column chosen and is tabulated adjacent to the base design value tables. For typical theatrical applications, the above equation can be rewritten:

$$F_c^* = (C_D C_F) F_c$$

- The next step is to find F_{cE}, the critical buckling design value (Euler equation).

$$F_{cE} = \frac{0.3E}{\left(\frac{l}{d}\right)^2}$$

Remember to check the slenderness ratio of both axes and that the maximum allowable l/d is less than or equal to 50.

- The third step in finding F_c' is to solve for C_p, the column stability factor, defined by the NDS for sawn lumber in the following equation (NDS, 3.7.1.5):

$$C_p = \frac{1 + \left(F_{cE}/F_c^*\right)}{1.6} - \sqrt{\left[\frac{1 + \left(F_{cE}/F_c^*\right)}{1.6}\right]^2 - \frac{\left(F_{cE}/F_c^*\right)}{0.8}}$$

If we replace F_{cE}/F_c^* with the word "ratio," then the equation can be rewritten:

$$C_p = \frac{1 + ratio}{1.6} - \sqrt{\left[\frac{1 + ratio}{1.6}\right]^2 - \frac{ratio}{0.8}}$$

- The last step is to calculate F_c', the allowable compressive stress:

$$F_c' = C_p F_c^*$$

Finding F_c' may seem complex at first; however, breaking it down into a series of small steps will help. Setting up automatic formulas via a spreadsheet or other computer programs will also reduce the possibility of math errors and save time.

STEPS IN COLUMN DESIGN

We now have all the tools necessary to design a solid, rectangular sawn lumber column. In some cases, the column is already known and only its capacity needs to be calculated; in others, the load and unbraced length are known, and an appropriate column needs to be identified.

FINDING THE CAPACITY OF A SOLID, RECTILINEAR COLUMN FOR A GIVEN LENGTH:

1. Draw a free body diagram of the column, indicating its unbraced lengths, and a plan view, indicating its dimensions.
2. Calculate the slenderness ratio(s), l/d. If $l/d > 50$, the column is not appropriate.

3. Identify F_c and E based on the species and grade given.
4. Determine the appropriate load duration factor, C_D, and the size range factor, C_F, of the given column in order to calculate F_c*.

$$F_c* = (C_D C_F)F_c$$

5. Calculate F_{cE} using the Euler equation:

$$F_{cE} = \frac{0.3E}{\left(\dfrac{l}{d}\right)^2}$$

6. Determine C_p.
   a. Calculate the ratio of F_{cE}/F_c*.
   b. Calculate C_p:

$$C_p = \frac{1 + ratio}{1.6} - \sqrt{\left[\frac{1 + ratio}{1.6}\right]^2 - \frac{ratio}{0.8}}$$

7. Calculate F_c':

$$F_c' = C_p F_c*$$

8. Calculate the capacity, P, of the column:

$$P = AF_c'$$

FINDING A SOLID RECTILINEAR COLUMN FOR A GIVEN LOAD AND UNBRACED LENGTH:

1. Draw a free body diagram, indicating all loads, bracing, and unbraced lengths.
2. Determine P, the total compressive load.
3. Determine the minimum d required for an $l/d = 50$. Select an appropriate nominal width and calculate the actual l/d.
4. Select a species and grade of sawn lumber; identify F_c and E.
5. Select a size range (using dxd as the minimum size) and an appropriate load duration, and calculate F_c*.

$$F_c* = (C_D C_F)F_c$$

6. Calculate F_{cE} using the Euler equation:

$$F_{cE} = \frac{0.3E}{\left(\dfrac{l}{d}\right)^2}$$

7. Determine C_p.
   a. Calculate the ratio of F_{cE}/F_c*.
   b. Calculate C_p:

$$C_p = \frac{1 + ratio}{1.6} - \sqrt{\left[\frac{1 + ratio}{1.6}\right]^2 - \frac{ratio}{0.8}}$$

8. Calculate F_c':
$$F_c' = C_p F_c *$$

9. Calculate the required cross-sectional area:
$$A_{req'd} = \frac{P}{F_c'}$$

10. Calculate the least dimension of the other axis, b:
$$A_{req'd} = db \Rightarrow b = \frac{A_{req'd}}{d} \quad \text{where } b \geq d_{min}$$

11. Select an appropriate column with a minimum d which meets the area requirement.

> ***Example 3.*** What is the maximum load that a 2x4, Spruce-Pine-Fir No. 3, column can support with unbraced lengths of 7', 6', and 3'? Assume normal load durations.

1. Free body diagrams of all three columns:

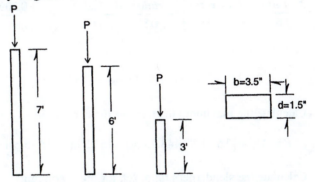

Figure 6.7 Example 3, free body diagrams and plan view

2. Identify the base design values and the applicable adjustment factors for all three cases:

F_c=650 psi; E=1.2x10⁶ psi; C_D=1.0; C_F=1.15

a. Calculate the slenderness ratio, l/d, for the 7' column:
$$\frac{l}{d} = \frac{84"}{1.5"} = 56$$

7' exceeds the maximum allowable slenderness ratio for an unbraced 2x4 column:
$$\frac{l}{d} = 50 \Rightarrow l = 50(1.5") = 75" \Rightarrow 6'-3"$$

Therefore, the maximum unbraced length for a 2x column is 6'-3".

b.   Calculate the slenderness ratio, l/d, for the 6' column:

$$\frac{l}{d} = \frac{72"}{1.5"} = 48$$

Calculate F_c*:

$$F_c* = (C_D C_F)F_c = 1.0(1.15)(650 \text{ psi}) = 747.5 \text{ psi}$$

Calculate F_{cE}:

$$F_{cE} = \frac{0.3E}{\left(\dfrac{l}{d}\right)^2} = \frac{(0.3)1.2 x 10^6 \text{ psi}}{(48)^2} = 156.25 \text{ psi}$$

Calculate the ratio of F_{cE}/F_c*:

$$ratio = \frac{F_{cE}}{F_c^*} = \frac{156.25 \text{ psi}}{747.5 \text{ psi}} = 0.209$$

Calculate C_p:

$$C_p = \frac{1 + ratio}{1.6} - \sqrt{\left[\frac{1 + ratio}{1.6}\right]^2 - \frac{ratio}{0.8}} = \frac{1 + 0.209}{1.6} - \sqrt{\left[\frac{1 + 0.209}{1.6}\right]^2 - \frac{0.209}{0.8}} = 0.199$$

Calculate F_c':

$$F_c' = C_p F_c^* = (0.199)747.5 \text{ psi} = 148.75 \text{ psi}$$

Calculate the maximum load, P, for the 6' column:

$$P = AF_c' = \left[3.5"(1.5")\right]148.75 \text{ psi} = \left(5.25 \text{ in}^2\right)148.75 \text{ psi} = 780.9\# \Rightarrow 780\#$$

c.   Calculate the slenderness ratio, l/d, for the 3' column:

$$\frac{l}{d} = \frac{36"}{1.5"} = 24$$

Calculate F_c*. F_c* equals 747.5 psi, the same value as the 6' column.

Calculate F_{cE}:

$$F_{cE} = \frac{0.3E}{\left(\dfrac{l}{d}\right)^2} = \frac{(0.3)1.2 x 10^6 \text{ psi}}{24^2} = 625 \text{ psi}$$

Calculate the ratio of F_{cE}/F_c*:

$$ratio = \frac{F_{cE}}{F_c^*} = \frac{625 \text{ psi}}{747.5 \text{ psi}} = 0.836$$

Calculate C_p:

$$C_p = \frac{1+ratio}{1.6} - \sqrt{\left[\frac{1+ratio}{1.6}\right]^2 - \frac{ratio}{0.8}} = \frac{1+0.836}{1.6} - \sqrt{\left[\frac{1+0.836}{1.6}\right]^2 - \frac{0.836}{0.8}} = 0.626$$

Calculate F_c':

$$F_c' = C_p F_c^* = (0.626)747.5 \text{ psi} = 468 \text{ psi}$$

Calculate the maximum load, P, for the 3' column:

$$P = AF_c' = (5.25 \text{ in}^2)468 \text{ psi} = 2,457\#$$

The above example illustrates the advantage of bracing columns; reducing the unbraced length by half more than tripled the allowable load on the 2x4 column.

> ***Example 4.*** A set design calls for a picturesque wooden footbridge between two areas of the stage. The bridge spans 15', is 5' wide and 11' high. In total, the bridge has eight columns on 5' centers (see Figure 6.8). The designer has specified that the bridge appear rustic and worn. The director and designer are not sure how many people may be on the bridge at once; the total cast is 15. Design a typical interior column using Western Woods No. 1 and assume that the load duration is two months. Also assume that the bridge is locked in place by two towers, which prevents the translation of the top of the bridge. There is no interior cross-bracing.

1. Plan view and free body diagram.

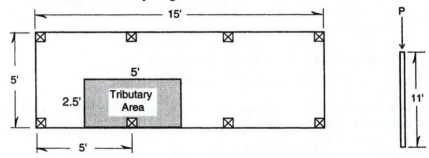

Figure 6.8 Example 4, plan view and free body diagram

2. Determine P:

The tributary area (T.A.) of an interior column is:

$$\text{T.A.} = 5'(2.5') = 12.5 \text{ ft}^2$$

To calculate the dead weight, we have to estimate a construction technique. Assume that the bridge is planked with 1" thick lumber. If the lumber weighs 40 pcf, then a 1"x1'x1' square will weigh:

$$w_{planks} = \frac{40\#}{\text{ft}^3}\left(\frac{1}{12} \text{ ft}\right) = 3.33 \text{ psf}$$

For a 12.5 ft² area:

$$P_{planks} = (12.5 \text{ ft}^2)(3.33 \text{ psf}) = 41.7\#$$

Since all the spans between columns are 5', assume that the planking will rest on 2x6 beams on 1' centers. We'll need about 12.5 linear feet of 2x6.

$$w_{beam} = \frac{40\#}{\text{ft}^3}\left(\frac{1.5}{12} \text{ ft}\right)\left(\frac{5.5}{12} \text{ ft}\right) = 2.29 \text{ plf}$$

$$P_{beam} = (12.5 \text{ ft})(2.29 \text{ plf}) = 28.6\#$$

So, the total estimated dead weight is:

$$P_{dead} = 41.7\# + 28.6\# = 70.3\#$$

For ease of calculations and to account for hardware, paint, etc., we'll use **75# as the dead weight** on each interior column.

For the live load, we will approximate a worst case scenario of a curtain call with all 15 actors on the downstage half of the bridge at once. If we assume that their weight will be evenly distributed across the downstage half of the bridge and that the average weight per person is 175#, then the live load can be calculated as follows:

$$P = (15 \text{ actors})(175\#) = 2,625\#$$

$$w_{live} = \frac{P_{actor}}{A_{\text{DS bridge}}} = \frac{2,625\#}{2.5'(15')} = 70 \text{ psf}$$

The live load on one column will be:

$$P_{live} = w_{live}(T.A.) = (70 \text{ psf})(12.5 \text{ ft}^2) = 875\#$$

The total load on one interior column will be:

$$P_{tot} = P_{dead} + P_{live} = 75\# + 875\# = 950\#$$

3. Determine the minimum d required, select an appropriate nominal width, and calculate its slenderness ratio.
   a. Calculate d_{min}:

   $$d_{min} = \frac{l}{50} = \frac{11'(12 \text{ in}/\text{ft})}{50} = 2.64"$$

   b. The least nominal d is a 4x, or 3.5", so the slenderness ratio is calculated for that condition:

   $$\frac{l}{d} = \frac{132"}{3.5"} = 37.7$$

With the current bracing conditions, the smallest column allowed is a 4x4, regardless of the loading conditions.

4. Look up the base design values for Western Woods No. 1:

$$F_c = 950 \text{ psi}; \quad E = 1.1 \times 10^6 \text{ psi}$$

5. Calculate F_c^* for a 4x4 with a two month load duration, $C_D = 1.15$ and the size factor, C_F, for a 4x4 is 1.15. Therefore:

$$F_c^* = (C_D C_F) F_c = 1.15(1.15)950 \text{ psi} \Rightarrow F_c^* = 1,256.375 \text{ psi}$$

6. Calculate F_{cE}:

$$F_{cE} = \frac{0.3E}{\left(\frac{l}{d}\right)^2} = \frac{(0.3)1.1 \times 10^6 \text{ psi}}{37.7^2} = 232 \text{ psi}$$

7. Calculate C_p.
   First, calculate the ratio F_{cE}/F_c^*:

$$ratio = \frac{F_{cE}}{F_c^*} = \frac{232 \text{ psi}}{1,256.375 \text{ psi}} = 0.1847$$

$$C_p = \frac{1+ratio}{1.6} - \sqrt{\left[\frac{1+ratio}{1.6}\right]^2 - \frac{ratio}{0.8}} = \frac{1+0.1847}{1.6} - \sqrt{\left[\frac{1+0.1847}{1.6}\right]^2 - \frac{0.1847}{0.8}} = 0.1771$$

8. Calculate F_c':

$$F_c' = C_p F_c^* = (0.1771)(1,256.375 \text{ psi}) = 222.5 \text{ psi}$$

9. Calculate the required cross-sectional area.

$$A_{req'd} = \frac{P}{F_c'} = \frac{950\#}{222.5 \text{ psi}} = 4.27 \text{ in}^2$$

10. Calculate the least dimension of the other axis, b:

$$b = \frac{A_{req'd}}{d} = \frac{4.27 \text{ in}^2}{3.5"} = 1.22"$$

11. Select an appropriate column.
    By the above calculations, it may be tempting to select a 4x2 column. However, a 4x4 is the minimum column size allowed given an unbraced length of 11'.

ODD-SHAPED COLUMNS

The analysis of odd-shaped columns differs from that of rectangular, solid columns because the slenderness ratio cannot be expressed in terms of l/d. There are many varieties of odd-shaped columns: round, tapered, spaced, and built-up columns are common. The *NDS* has specifications for the design of round, tapered, and spaced columns, but does not state an explicit methodology for the design of built-up columns.

The *NDS* makes the analysis of round columns very simple. To design a round column, do the design calculations for a square column having the same cross-sectional area (*NDS*, 3.7.3). If specifically using round timber piles, see *NDS* Section 3.7.1.5.

The *NDS* also states a technique for the design of tapered columns (*NDS*, 3.7.2). When analyzing tapered rectilinear tension members, the structural designer must use the smallest cross-sectional area that occurs in the member. When analyzing compression members, the cross-sectional area is considered a complex average between the greatest and least areas. For simplicity and safety, we recommend simply using the least area that occurs in the column. If designing a *round*, tapered column, design a square column with the same cross-sectional area as the least area of the round column.

Spaced columns are made by sandwiching spacer blocks between two identical wood members. By definition, the spacer blocks must be made of the same material as the columns. This technique can be useful in some specialized applications, such as wooden trusses. The *NDS* outlines a series of requirements which allow structural designers to violate the traditional slenderness ratio requirement (*NDS*, 15.2). Once again, for simplicity of calculations, we recommend that calculations be based on the load that two independent identical members can support.

The *NDS* does not recommend a specific technique for the design of columns with a built-up cross-section, such as a "T" or hollow box, though it does mention solid, rectilinear built-up sections. The capacity of hollow and open built-up shapes can be estimated by calculating their I value and their cross-sectional area. The radius of gyration, r, can then be computed and the version of the Euler equation expressed in terms of l/r is used:

$$F_{cE} = \frac{3.6E}{\left(\frac{l}{r}\right)^2} \qquad \text{where } \frac{l}{r} \le 173$$

Once the slenderness ratio is determined, the same column design procedures outlined earlier are used to calculate F_c^*, C_p, and F_c'. It is important to note that this method assumes perfect joints between the individual members of the built-up shape. As mentioned in Chapter 5, we recommend applying an additional built up shape (BUS) adjustment factor of 0.75. In this case, the BUS factor is applied after C_p is calculated (it is not used to calculate F_c^*). Remember that it is assumed that all the joints are nail-glued and that the edges of the components are resurfaced to provide a larger and rougher glue surface.

> ***Example 5.*** What is the maximum allowable load for a round column with a 3" diameter and an unbraced length of 8'? Use Western Woods No. 2, assume a normal load duration, and that K_e equals 1.0.

1. Plan view and free body diagram.

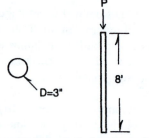

Figure 6.9 Example 5, plan view and free body diagram

2. Calculate d for an equivalent square column:

$$A_{circle} = A_{square}$$

$$\pi r^2 = d^2$$

$$d = \sqrt{\pi r^2} = r\sqrt{\pi} = 1.772r = 1.772(1.5") = 2.66"$$

where r is the radius of the circle, in
          d is the length of one side of an equivalent square, in

3. Using 2.66" as the least dimension of an equivalent square column, calculate l/d:

$$\frac{l}{d} = \frac{96"}{2.66"} = 36.1 \Rightarrow 36.1 < 50 \checkmark$$

4. Calculate F_c^*, using the F_c of a 3x3 size category. $C_D = 1.0$; $C_F = 1.15$.

$$F_c^* = (C_D C_F)F_c = 1.0(1.15)(900 \text{ psi}) = 1,035 \text{ psi}$$

5. Calculate F_{cE}:

$$F_{cE} = \frac{0.3E}{\left(\frac{l}{d}\right)^2} = \frac{0.3(1.0 \times 10^6 \text{ psi})}{(36.1)^2} = 230.1 \text{ psi}$$

6. Calculate C_p.
First, find the ratio of F_{cE}/F_c^*:

$$ratio = \frac{F_{cE}}{F_c^*} = \frac{230.1 \text{ psi}}{1,035 \text{ psi}} = 0.222$$

$$C_p = \frac{1+ratio}{1.6} - \sqrt{\left[\frac{1+ratio}{1.6}\right]^2 - \frac{ratio}{0.8}} = \frac{1+0.222}{1.6} - \sqrt{\left[\frac{1+0.222}{1.6}\right]^2 - \frac{0.222}{0.8}} \approx 0.211$$

7. Calculate F_c':

$$F_c' = C_p F_c^* = 0.211(1,035 \text{ psi}) = 218.4 \text{ psi}$$

8. Calculate the maximum allowable load by using the direct stress formula.

$$A = A_{square} = d^2 = (2.66")^2 = 7.07 \text{ in}^2$$

$$P = AF_c' = (7.07 \text{ in}^2)(218.4 \text{ psi}) = 1,544.1\#$$

The capacity of a round column can also be determined by using the version of the Euler equation expressed in terms of r. For the 8' round column in Example 5, this method would yield a maximum allowable load of 1,477 lbs.

Example 6. Consider the following "T" shape made of two 2x6's ripped down to actual dimensions of 1.5"x5". What is the maximum load it can support with an unbraced length of 12'? Use Eastern White Pine No. 2, and assume a normal load duration.

1. Free body diagram.

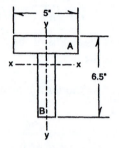

Figure 6.10 Example 6

2. Identify the allowable design values and the applicable adjustment factors for a 2x6, Eastern White Pine No. 2:

$$F_c = 825 \text{ psi}; \quad E = 1.1 \times 10^6 \text{ psi}; \quad C_D = 1.0; \quad C_F = 1.1$$

3. Calculate the area, I_{x-x}, and I_{y-y} for the component pieces:

$$A = bd = 1.5"(5") = 7.5 \text{ in}^2$$

$$I_{x-x} = \frac{bd^3}{12} = \frac{1.5"(5")^3}{12} = 15.625 \text{ in}^4$$

$$I_{y-y} = \frac{bd^3}{12} = \frac{5"(1.5")^3}{12} = 1.406 \text{ in}^4$$

4. Locate the neutral axis by finding c_{x-x} and c_{y-y}:

$$d_{NA} = \frac{d_A A_A + d_B A_B}{A_A + A_B} = \frac{(5.0"+0.75")(7.5 \text{ in}^2) + \left(5.0"\!\!\big/\!2\right)(7.5 \text{ in}^2)}{15 \text{ in}^2} =$$

$$d_{NA} = c_{x-x} = 4.125" \text{ from bottom}$$

$$d'_{NA} = 6.5" - 4.125" = 2.375" \text{ from top}$$

$$c_{y-y} = \frac{5"}{2} = 2.5" \text{ from left or right}$$

5. Calculate I_{x-x} and I_{y-y} for the built-up shape:

$$I_{x-x} = \left[I_{o_A} + A_A z_A^2\right] + \left[I_{o_B} + A_B z_B^2\right]$$

$$= \left[1.406 \text{ in}^4 + (7.5 \text{ in}^2)(2.375"-0.75")^2\right] + \left[15.625 \text{ in}^4 + (7.5 \text{ in}^2)(4.125"-2.5")^2\right]$$

$$= 21.21 \text{ in}^4 + 35.43 \text{ in}^4 = 56.64 \text{ in}^4$$

$$I_{y-y} = I_{o_A} + I_{o_B} = 15.625 \text{ in}^4 + 1.406 \text{ in}^4 = 17.03 \text{ in}^4$$

6. Calculate $r_{x\text{-}x}$ and $r_{y\text{-}y}$, the radii of gyration for the built-up shape:

$$r_{x\text{-}x} = \sqrt{\frac{I}{A}} = \sqrt{\frac{56.64 \text{ in}^4}{15 \text{ in}^2}} = 1.943" \qquad r_{y\text{-}y} = \sqrt{\frac{I}{A}} = \sqrt{\frac{17.03 \text{ in}^4}{15 \text{ in}^2}} = 1.0655"$$

7. Calculate l/r, the slenderness ratio:

$$\frac{l}{r_{y\text{-}y}} = \frac{144"}{1.0655"} = 135.1 \Rightarrow 135.1 < 173 \checkmark$$

8. Calculate F_c^*:

$$F_c^* = (C_D C_F) F_c = 1.0(1.1)(825 \text{ psi})$$
$$F_c^* = 907.625 \text{ psi}$$

9. Calculate F_{cE}:

$$F_{cE} = \frac{3.6E}{\left(\frac{l}{r}\right)^2} = \frac{(3.6)1.1 \times 10^6 \text{ psi}}{(135.1)^2} = 216.8 \text{ psi}$$

10. Calculate C_p.
First, calculate the ratio of F_{ce}/F_c^*:

$$ratio = \frac{F_{cE}}{F_c^*} = \frac{216.8 \text{ psi}}{907.625 \text{ psi}} = 0.239$$

$$C_p = \frac{1 + ratio}{1.6} - \sqrt{\left[\frac{1 + ratio}{1.6}\right]^2 - \frac{ratio}{0.8}} = \frac{1 + 0.239}{1.6} - \sqrt{\left[\frac{1 + 0.239}{1.6}\right]^2 - \frac{0.239}{0.8}} = 0.2257$$

11. Calculate F_c' and apply the BUS factor of 0.75:

$$F_c' = (\text{BUS})(C_p) F_c^* = 0.75(0.2257)(907.625 \text{ psi}) = 153.65 \text{ psi}$$

12. Calculate the maximum allowable load by using the direct stress formula:

$$P_{all} = A F_c' = (15 \text{ in}^2)(153.65 \text{ psi}) = 2,304.8\#$$

CHAPTER 6 LESSONS

The format of the numbering system is: chapter.lesson.problem number.
Unless otherwise noted, assume a normal load duration and $K_e = 1.0$.

LESSON 6.1 INTRODUCTION TO COLUMN DESIGN, EULER'S EQUATION (PG 123 – 130)

6.1.1   What are the minimum actual and nominal dimensions allowed for a sawn lumber column with a 9' unbraced length?

6.1.2   What are the minimum actual and nominal dimensions allowed for a sawn lumber column with a 16' unbraced length?

6.1.3   What are the minimum actual and nominal dimensions allowed for a sawn lumber flagpole type column with a 3' unbraced length?

6.1.4   (a) Find the F_{cE} for a 12' high 4x6 column with a species and grade of Southern Pine No. 2. (b) Find the F_{cr} for the same column using the slenderness ratio expressed in terms of the radius of gyration.

6.1.5   Find F_{cE} for an 8' high 3x4 column with a species and grade of Hem-Fir Construction grade.

6.1.6   Find F_{cE} for a 12' high 4x4 column with a species and grade of Western Woods No. 2.

6.1.7   (a) Find F_{cE} for the column given below with a species and grade of Eastern Softwoods No. 3. (b) What would F_{cE} be if the bracing were on the other axis?

6.1.8   Find F_{cE} for the column given below with a species and grade of Douglas Fir-South No. 1.

LESSON 6.2 ALLOWABLE COMPRESSIVE STRESS, STEPS IN COLUMN DESIGN (PG 130 – 135)

6.2.1   What is the maximum load that a 2x2, Douglas Fir-South No. 1, column can support with unbraced lengths of 6' and 4'?

6.2.2   What is the maximum load that a 4x4, Spruce-Pine-Fir No. 2, column can support with unbraced lengths of 7' and 14'?

6.2.3   What is the maximum load that a 2x6, Southern Pine Stud, column can support if it is braced as given below? Assume a two month load duration.

6.2.4   What is the maximum load that a 2x6, Eastern White Pine Select Structural, column can support with an unbraced length of 8'? Assume a two month load duration.

6.2.5   What is the maximum load that a 3x6, Western Woods No. 2, column can support if it is braced as given below?

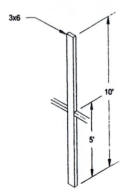

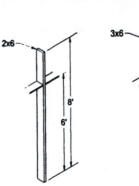
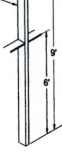

Problem 6.1.7   Problem 6.1.8   Problem 6.2.3   Problem 6.2.5

LESSON 6.3 COLUMN DESIGN, CONTINUED WITH EXAMPLE 4 (PG 135 – 137)

6.3.1 Choose an appropriate nominal size column with a species and grade category of Eastern White Pine No. 1 with the loading condition given below. The columns are 10'-3" high and are unbraced. They will have a load duration of 6 weeks.

6.3.2 Choose an appropriate nominal size square column with a species and grade category of Douglas Fir-South No. 3 with the loading conditions given below.

6.3.3 Choose an appropriate nominal size column with a species and grade category of Western Woods No. 2 with the loading conditions given below.

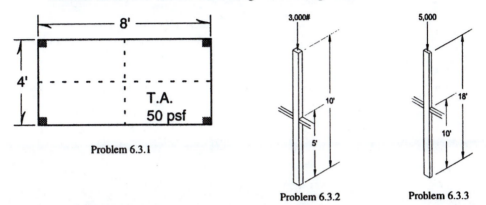

Problem 6.3.1

Problem 6.3.2

Problem 6.3.3

LESSON 6.4 ODD-SHAPED COLUMNS (PG 137 – 141)

6.4.1 A 30" high table is built with decorative round, tapered legs. The minimum diameter of the legs is 2", and they have a species and grade category of Southern Pine No. 2. What is the capacity of each leg?

6.4.2 Calculate the maximum capacity of the table legs in problem 6.4.1 using the slenderness ratio expressed in terms of the radius of gyration.

6.4.3 What is the maximum capacity of the "L" shape given below if it has an unbraced length of 9' and a species and grade category of Hem-Fir Construction?

6.4.4 Consider the following hollow box built with Industrial 45 Southern Pine (Southern Pine No. 2) 1x8 boards ripped as shown. What is its maximum unbraced length and maximum capacity at that length? Assume a two month load duration.

6.4.5 What is the maximum load that an "I" shaped column as drawn below can support with an unbraced length of 12'. The "I" shape is built-up using Industrial 45 Southern Pine (Southern Pine No. 2) 5/4x4 boards ripped to the dimensions given below. Assume a two month load duration.

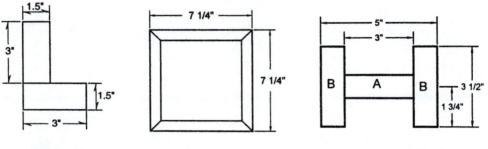

Problem 6.4.3

Problem 6.4.4

Problem 6.4.5

7

Combined Loading for Wood Members

INTRODUCTION

Thus far, we have discussed structural members subject to bending stress against one axis or pure axial stress (tension or compression). Oftentimes, however, structural members must be designed to resist a combined loading condition. For example, the load on a column may be off-center, causing both an axial stress and a bending moment. This chapter includes discussions of the following types of combined loading: single axis bending and axial tension, single axis bending and axial compression, eccentric loads on columns, and biaxial bending. Figure 7.1 illustrates these loading conditions.

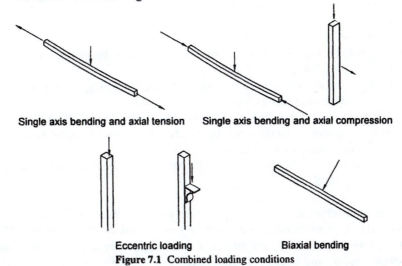

Single axis bending and axial tension   Single axis bending and axial compression

Eccentric loading   Biaxial bending

Figure 7.1 Combined loading conditions

The basic concept of combined-loading design is straightforward: any structural member can only resist a given amount of total stress, regardless of the type. The trick in combined-loading analysis is to ascertain, for each type of stress, the proportion of total stress that each "uses up." When a member is at its maximum capacity, the total actual stress is 100% of the total allowable stress. For example, if the allowable compressive stress of a member is 900 psi and the actual compressive stress is 900 psi, than 100% of the total available stress is being used. In decimal form, f_c divided by F_c' is 1.0. If this idea is expanded to include all possible types of stress, the total must still be less than or equal to 1.0 and can be expressed as the following interaction equation:

$$\frac{f_t}{F_t'} + \frac{f_c}{F_c'} + \frac{f_{bx}}{F_{bx}'} + \frac{f_{by}}{F_{by}'} \leq 1.0$$

where f_t is the actual tensile stress, psi

             f_c is the actual compressive stress parallel to the grain, psi

             f_{bx} is the actual bending stress in the x-x axis, psi

             f_{by} is the actual bending stress in the y-y axis, psi

             F_t' is the allowable tensile stress, psi

             F_c' is the allowable compressive stress parallel to grain, psi

             F_{bx}' is the allowable bending stress in the x-x axis, psi

             F_{by}' is the allowable bending stress in the y-y axis, psi

The above equation is conceptual; the formulas actually used for calculating the total stress on a member are complicated by the addition of buckling and lateral stability factors and equations.

SINGLE AXIS BENDING AND AXIAL TENSION

The analysis of members subject to single axis bending and axial tension closely resembles the conceptual formula for combined loading because buckling and lateral stability are not critical for tension members. *Sawn lumber* members subject to single axis bending and axial tension must meet the following equation (*NDS*, 3.9.1):

$$\frac{f_t}{F_t'} + \frac{f_b}{F_b'} \leq 1.0$$

where f_t is the actual tensile stress, calculated using the direct stress formula, $f_t = P/A$, psi.

             F_t' is the allowable tensile design value multiplied by all applicable adjustment factors, psi

             F_b' is the allowable bending design value multiplied by all applicable adjustment factors, psi. Remember that a set of lateral bracing requirements must be met for $C_L=1.0$.

             f_b is the actual bending stress, calculated using the Flexure Formula, $f_b = M/S$, psi

Calculating the allowable tensile stress (F_t') has not been discussed previously. F_t' equals the base design value for tension parallel to grain (F_t) multiplied by the wet service (C_M), temperature (C_t), load duration (C_D), and size (C_F), factors. Once again, for normal indoor theatrical applications, C_M and C_t are 1.0, and therefore:

$$F_t' = (C_D C_F) F_t$$

The allowable bending design stress, F_b', is calculated using the techniques described in Chapter 5. For normal indoor theatrical applications for sawn lumber in which the lateral bracing requirements are met:

$$F_b' = (C_D C_F) F_b$$

Example 1. Design the 6' long bottom chord of a truss with a 4,375 lb tensile load and a 250 lb midspan point load (see Figure 7.2). Use Hem Fir No. 2 and assume a normal load duration.

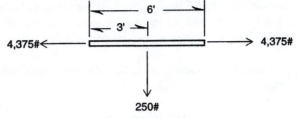

Figure 7.2 Example 1

1. Determine a minimum cross-sectional area based on the tensile load only. F_t of Hem-Fir No. 2 is 525 psi.

$$A_{min} = \frac{P}{F_t} = \frac{4,375\#}{525 \text{ psi}} = 8.33 \text{ in}^2$$

The bottom chord will require a 2x8 or 3x6 to resist the tensile load only. We will try a 3x6 with the *x-x* axis resisting the bending load.

2. Determine F_t' and F_b' for a 3x6. C_D is 1.0 and C_F is 1.3. F_b for Hem-Fir No. 2 is 850 psi.

$$F_t' = (C_D C_F) F_t = 1.0(1.3)(525 \text{ psi}) = 682.5 \text{ psi}$$

$$F_b' = (C_D C_F) F_b = 1.0(1.3)(850 \text{ psi}) = 1,105 \text{ psi}$$

3. Determine f_t for the 3x6, which has an area of 13.75 in².

$$f_t = \frac{P}{A} = \frac{4,375\#}{13.75 \text{ in}^2} = 318 \text{ psi}$$

4. Determine f_b for the 3x6, which has an S_{x-x} of 12.604 in³.

$$M_{max} = \frac{Pl}{4} = \frac{250\#(72")}{4} = 4,500 \text{ inlb}$$

$$f_b = \frac{M_{max}}{S_{x-x}} = \frac{4,500 \text{ inlb}}{12.604 \text{ in}^3} = 357 \text{ psi}$$

5. Plug the variables into the interaction equation.

$$\frac{f_t}{F_t'} + \frac{f_b}{F_b'} \le 1.0 \Rightarrow \frac{318 \text{ psi}}{682.5 \text{ psi}} + \frac{357 \text{ psi}}{1,105 \text{ psi}} = 0.789 \Rightarrow 0.789 < 1.0 \checkmark$$

The 3x6 is an appropriate choice for this application. Note that if the 3x6 were turned 90° so that the weak axis resisted the bending load, the S_{y-y} of 5.729 in³ would not be adequate for this loading condition.

SINGLE AXIS BENDING AND AXIAL COMPRESSION

The analysis of columns subject to both bending and axial compression utilizes the basic interaction formula with an additional adjustment factor that reduces the F_b' value to account for potential lateral buckling due to the bending load. It is even possible to analyze a member subject to bending in two axes with a compressive load, however we will limit our presentation to single axis bending combined with axial compression.

The *NDS* interaction formula can be expressed as the following when reduced to single axis bending and axial compression (*NDS*, 3.9.2):

$$\left(\frac{f_c}{F_c'}\right)^2 + \frac{f_b}{F_b'\left[1-\left(f_c\big/F_{cE}\right)\right]} \le 1.0$$

where f_c is the actual axial compressive stress, psi
F_c' is the adjusted allowable compressive stress, psi
f_b is the actual bending stress in the plane of bending, psi
F_b' is the adjusted allowable bending stress in the plane of bending, psi
F_{cE} is the critical buckling design value for compression, psi

For the second term of the above equation, the adjusted allowable bending stress, F_b', and the critical buckling design value, F_{cE}, should both be calculated for the axis subject to bending, which is not necessarily the most slender axis. The *NDS* has slightly more stringent lateral bracing requirements for members subject to bending and axial compression loads. The depth to breadth ratio can be as much as 5:1 if one entire edge is held in line (*NDS*, 4.4.1.3). The normal maximum ratio of 7:1 is not applicable.

We have discussed how to calculate the value for every variable in the interaction equation in Chapters 5 and 6. Now, it is simply a matter of combining them into one equation. Finding an appropriate choice for a given combined loading situation is a trial-and-error process. Consequently, it is well worth the time to enter the above equation and its intermediate equations into a computer program. Problems done by hand are labor-intensive and subject to frustrating "math errors."

> *Example 2.* Design a column to support both a deck and a winch frame as illustrated below. It must support a 4'x8' tributary area with combined live and dead loads of 50 psf and a 250 lb pull from the winch assembly. Assume a normal load duration and use Spruce-Pine-Fir No. 2.
>
> 1.   Free body diagram.

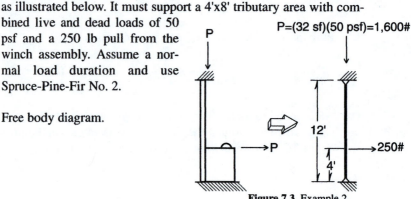

Figure 7.3 Example 2

2. Determine the minimum d required due to the slenderness ratio requirement.

$$\frac{l}{d} = 50 \Rightarrow d_{min} = \frac{144"}{50} = 2.88"$$

The smallest allowable nominal size for the column is a 4x4.

3. Look up the base design values and the geometric properties for a Spruce-Pine Fir No. 2 4x4.

F_b=875 psi; F_c=1,150 psi; E=1.4x10^6 psi; S=7.146 in^3; A=12.25 in^2

4. Bending Stress.
a. Calculate the bending moment caused by the 250 lb pull from the winch using the applicable case formula.

$$M_{max} = \frac{Pab}{l} = \frac{250\#(4')(8')}{12'} = 666.67 \text{ ftlb} \Rightarrow 8,000 \text{ inlb}$$

b. Calculate the actual bending stress using the Flexure Formula.

$$f_b = \frac{M}{S} = \frac{8,000 \text{ inlb}}{7.146 \text{ in}^3} = 1,119.5 \text{ psi}$$

c. Calculate the allowable bending stress, F_b'. Since the $b{:}d$ ratio of a 4x4 is 1:1, no lateral bracing is required (C_L=1.0), C_D is 1.0, and C_F is 1.5.

$$F_b'=C_F F_b=1.5(875 \text{ psi})=1,312.5 \text{ psi}$$

5. Compressive Stress.
a. Calculate F_c^*. C_D is 1.0 and C_F is 1.15 for a 4x4.

$$F_c^*=C_F F_c=1.15(1,150 \text{ psi})=1,322.5 \text{ psi}$$

b. Calculate F_{cE}:

$$F_{cE} = \frac{0.3E}{\left(\frac{l}{d}\right)^2} = \frac{0.3(1.4x10^6 \text{ psi})}{\left(\frac{144"}{3.5"}\right)^2} = 248.1 \text{ psi}$$

c. Calculate the ratio of F_{cE}/F_c^*:

$$ratio = \frac{F_{cE}}{F_c^*} = \frac{248.1 \text{ psi}}{1,322.5 \text{ psi}} = 0.1876$$

d. Calculate C_p:

$$C_p = \frac{1+ratio}{1.6} - \sqrt{\left[\frac{1+ratio}{1.6}\right]^2 - \frac{ratio}{0.8}} = \frac{1+0.1876}{1.6} - \sqrt{\left[\frac{1+0.1876}{1.6}\right]^2 - \frac{0.1876}{0.8}} = 0.180$$

e. Calculate F_c':

$$F_c' = C_p F_c^* = 0.180(1,322.5 \text{ psi}) = 237.7 \text{ psi}$$

f.   Calculate f_c using the Direct Stress Formula.

$$f_c = \frac{P}{A} = \frac{1,600\#}{12.25 \text{ in}^2} = 130.6 \text{ psi}$$

6.   Plug the variables into the interaction formula:

$$\left(\frac{f_c}{F_c'}\right)^2 + \frac{f_b}{F_b'\left[1-\left(\frac{f_c}{F_{cE}}\right)\right]} \leq 1.0$$

$$= \left(\frac{130.6 \text{ psi}}{237.7 \text{ psi}}\right)^2 + \frac{1,119.5 \text{ psi}}{(1,312.5 \text{ psi})\left[1-\left(\frac{130.6 \text{ psi}}{248.1 \text{ psi}}\right)\right]}$$

$$= 0.302 + 1.801 = 2.103 \Rightarrow 2.103 \geq 1.0 \; \texttt{✗}$$

A 4x4 is inadequate for this loading condition. Since the bending load is obviously causing the majority of the stress, we should increase the depth of the beam in the axis that resists the bending load. We will now test a 4x6 with the x-x axis resisting the bending load (see Figure 7.4).

A 4x6 still requires no lateral bracing (C_L=1.0), but the size factor for bending, C_F, changes to 1.3. The actual bending moment remains the same at 8,000 inlb. The section modulus, S_{x-x}, of a 4x6 is 17.65 in³, and its area is 19.25 in².

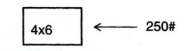

Figure 7.4 Plan view of 4x6 column

1.   Bending Stress.
a.   Calculate the actual bending stress using the Flexure Formula.

$$f_b = \frac{M}{S_{x-x}} = \frac{8,000 \text{ inlb}}{17.65 \text{ in}^3} = 453.3 \text{ psi}$$

b.   Calculate the allowable bending stress (F_b').

$$F_b' = C_F F_b = 1.3(875 \text{ psi}) = 1,137.5 \text{ psi}$$

c. F_{cE} must be calculated for bending in the x-x axis:

$$F_{cE} = \frac{0.3E}{\left(\frac{l}{d}\right)^2} = \frac{0.3(1.4x10^6 \text{ psi})}{\left(\frac{144"}{5.5"}\right)^2} = 612.7 \text{ psi}$$

2.   Compressive Stress.
a.   The F_c', F_{cE}, C_p, and F_c^* found for the 4x4 are still valid for the first term of the interaction equation.

b.   Calculate f_c using the Direct Stress Formula:

$$f_c = \frac{P}{A} = \frac{1,600\#}{19.25 \text{ in}^2} = 83.1 \text{ psi}$$

3. Plug the variables into the interaction equation:

$$\left(\frac{f_c}{F_c'}\right)^2 + \frac{f_b}{F_b'\left[1-\left(f_c/F_{cE}\right)\right]} \le 1.0$$

$$= \left(\frac{83.1\text{ psi}}{237.7\text{ psi}}\right)^2 + \frac{453.3\text{ psi}}{(1{,}137.5\text{ psi})\left[1-\left(83.1\text{ psi}/612.7\text{ psi}\right)\right]}$$

$$= 0.1222 + 0.461 \Rightarrow 0.583 \le 1.0 \;\checkmark$$

A 4x6 passes when oriented with the strong axis resisting the load imposed by the winch assembly.

ECCENTRIC LOADING

An **eccentric load** can be the result of an off-center load at the top of a compression member or a load acting on a side bracket of a compression member. Eccentric loads induce both a compressive load and a bending moment in the member, producing a defacto combined loading condition. The more off-center the load, the greater the applied moment. Therefore, in structural design, eccentric loads are avoided whenever possible.

A little eccentricity can make a big difference due to a phenomena called the "P-delta" effect. An eccentric load causes a member to bend, which causes the load to be a tiny bit more eccentric, which makes the moment greater. This greater moment causes the member to bend even more, which causes the eccentricity to increase . . . and so forth. This effect obviously does not continue infinitely or else every eccentrically loaded column would collapse, but it is significant. Including provisions for the P-Δ effect has made the *NDS* interaction equation for members subject to eccentric loads complex (*NDS*, 15.4.1).

Consequently, this text will use a simpler, more conservative technique which treats an eccentric load as two loads, one axial compressive load and one equivalent bending load acting at the middle of the column. The bending load is designated P_s and causes a bending moment with a magnitude equivalent to that of the eccentric load. The following equation is used to calculate P_s (*NDS*, 15.4.2):

$$P_s = \frac{3Pal_p}{l^2}$$

where P is the actual load on the bracket, lbs
P_s is the equivalent side load acting at the center of the column, lbs
a is the horizontal distance from the load to the neutral axis of the column (the eccentricity of the load), in
l is the length of the column, in
l_p is the vertical distance from the bracket to the farthest end of the column, $l=l_p$ for eccentric loads at the top of the column, in

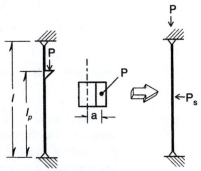

Figure 7.5 Eccentric load

The eccentric load, P, is assumed to act axially in addition to P_s, a side load acting at the middle of the column. If a column is subject to both an eccentric load and an additional axial load, than the two loads are added together when calculating the actual compressive stress (using the Direct Stress Formula). The bending moment due to the side load is calculated using the case formula for a simple span, concentrated load in the center:

$$M_{max} = \frac{P_s l}{4}$$

Once the bending moment is calculated, the bending stress can be determined by using the Flexure Formula where the S used is the one for the axis resisting the load.

$$f_b = \frac{M_{max}}{S}$$

When the stresses are defined, the single axis bending and axial compression interaction equation is used:

$$\left(\frac{f_c}{F_c'}\right)^2 + \frac{f_b}{F_b'\left[1-\left(\frac{f_c}{F_{cE}}\right)\right]} \leq 1.0$$

Example 3. Consider the following bracket load. Find the smallest allowable column which can support the loading condition. Assume a two month load duration, and use Eastern White Pine No. 2.

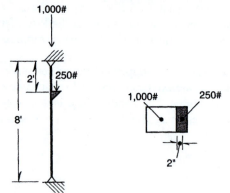

Figure 7.6 Example 3

1. Determine the least dimension required due to the slenderness ratio.

$$d_{min} = \frac{96"}{50} = 1.92"$$

Therefore, the smallest allowable nominal size of the column is a 3x3, and the smallest readily available size is a 3x4, which we will test with the *x-x* axis resisting the bending force.

2. Look up the base design values and the geometric properties for an Eastern White Pine No. 2 3x4.

F_b=575 psi $\qquad$ S_{x-x}=5.104 in³

F_c=825 psi $\qquad$ S_{y-y}=3.646 in³

E=1.1x10⁶ psi; $\qquad$ A=8.75 in²

3. Calculate the loads:

$$P_s = \frac{3Pal_p}{l^2} = \frac{3(250\#)\left(\frac{3.5"}{2}+2"\right)(72")}{(96")^2} = 21.97\#$$

$P_{axial} = 1{,}000\# + 250\# = 1{,}250\#$

4. Calculate the variables necessary for the bending portion of the interaction equation.

a. Calculate the moment due to the equivalent side load:

$$M_{max} = \frac{P_s l}{4} = \frac{21.97\#(96")}{4} = 527.3 \text{ inlb}$$

b. Calculate the actual bending stress using the Flexure Formula.

$$f_b = \frac{M}{S_{x-x}} = \frac{527.3 \text{ inlb}}{5.104 \text{ in}^3} = 103.3 \text{ psi}$$

c. Calculate the allowable bending stress (F_b'). Since the $b{:}d$ ratio of a 3x4 is less than 2:1, no lateral bracing is required (C_L=1.0). C_D is 1.15, and C_F=1.5.

$F_b' = C_D C_F F_b = 1.15(1.5)(575 \text{ psi}) = 991.9 \text{ psi}$

d. Calculate F_{cE} for the bending axis:

$$F_{cE_{x-x}} = \frac{0.3E}{\left(\frac{l}{d}\right)^2} = \frac{0.3\left(1.1x10^6 \text{ psi}\right)}{\left(\frac{96"}{3.5"}\right)^2} = 438.6 \text{ psi}$$

5. Calculate the variables necessary for the compressive portion of the interaction equation.

a. Calculate F_c^*. C_D is 1.15, and C_F is 1.15.

$F_c^* = C_D C_F F_c = 1.15(1.15)(825 \text{ psi}) = 1{,}091.06 \text{ psi}$

b. Calculate F_{cE}:

$$F_{cE} = \frac{0.3E}{\left(\frac{l}{d}\right)^2} = \frac{0.3\left(1.1x10^6 \text{ psi}\right)}{\left(\frac{96"}{2.5"}\right)^2} = 223.8 \text{ psi}$$

c.   Calculate the ratio of $F_{cE}/F_c{}^*$:

$$ratio = \frac{F_{cE}}{F_c^*} = \frac{223.8 \text{ psi}}{1{,}091.06 \text{ psi}} = 0.205$$

d.   Calculate C_p:

$$C_p = \frac{1 + ratio}{1.6} - \sqrt{\left[\frac{1 + ratio}{1.6}\right]^2 - \frac{ratio}{0.8}} = \frac{1 + 0.205}{1.6} - \sqrt{\left[\frac{1 + 0.205}{1.6}\right]^2 - \frac{0.205}{0.8}} = 0.196$$

e.   Calculate F_c':

$$F_c' = C_p F_c^* = 0.196(1{,}091.06 \text{ psi}) = 213.4 \text{ psi}$$

f.   Calculate f_c using the Direct Stress Formula.

$$f_c = \frac{P}{A} = \frac{1{,}250\#}{8.75 \text{ in}^2} = 142.9 \text{ psi}$$

6.   Plug the variables into the interaction equation:

$$\left(\frac{f_c}{F_c'}\right)^2 + \frac{f_b}{F_b'\left[1 - \left(f_c \big/ F_{cE}\right)\right]} \leq 1.0$$

$$= \left(\frac{142.9 \text{ psi}}{213.4 \text{ psi}}\right)^2 + \frac{103.3 \text{ psi}}{(991.9 \text{ psi})\left[1 - \left(142.9 \text{ psi} \big/ 438.6 \text{ psi}\right)\right]}$$

$$= 0.449 + 0.154 = 0.603 \Rightarrow 0.603 \leq 1.0 \;\checkmark$$

A 3x4 is adequate to support this loading condition in this orientation (strong axis resisting the bracket load).

Example 4. Compare two slightly different loading conditions on a 2x4 leg which is 5' long. Each leg has the same axial load of 950 lbs, but one is carrying the load with a 1" eccentricity. Are both columns safe? Use Hem-Fir No. 3 and assume a normal load duration.

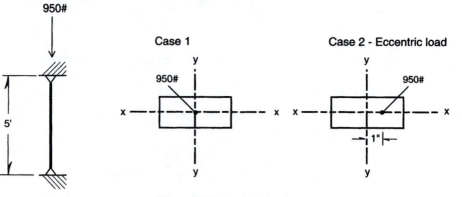

Figure 7.7 Example 4

Case #1 – Axial Load

1. Look up the base allowable design values for Hem-Fir No. 3 and the geometric properties for a 2x4.

F_b=500 psi S_{x-x}=3.063 in^3
F_c=725 psi S_{y-y}=1.313 in^3
E=1.2x10^6 psi A=5.25 in^2

2. Calculate F_c*. C_F is 1.15.

$$F_c^*=C_F F_c=1.15(725 \text{ psi})=833.75 \text{ psi}$$

a. Calculate F_{cE}:

$$F_{cE} = \frac{0.3E}{\left(l/d\right)^2} = \frac{(0.3)\left(1.2x10^6 \text{ psi}\right)}{\left(60''/1.5''\right)^2} = 225 \text{ psi}$$

b. Calculate the ratio of F_{cE}/F_c*:

$$ratio = \frac{F_{cE}}{F_c^*} = \frac{225 \text{ psi}}{833.75 \text{ psi}} = 0.2699$$

c. Calculate C_p:

$$C_p = \frac{1+ratio}{1.6} - \sqrt{\left[\frac{1+ratio}{1.6}\right]^2 - \frac{ratio}{0.8}} = \frac{1+0.2699}{1.6} - \sqrt{\left[\frac{1+0.2699}{1.6}\right]^2 - \frac{0.2699}{0.8}} = 0.253$$

d. Calculate F_c':

$$F_c' = C_p F_c^* = 0.253(833.75 \text{ psi}) = 210.9 \text{ psi}$$

e. Calculate f_c using the Direct Stress Formula:

$$f_c = \frac{P}{A} = \frac{950\#}{5.25 \text{ in}^2} = 180.95 \text{ psi}$$
$$180.95 < 210.9 \ \checkmark$$

Since $f_c < F_c'$, the 2x4 is loaded within its tolerances.

Case #2 – Eccentricity

1. Calculate the loads:

$$P_s = \frac{3Pal_p}{l^2} = \frac{3(950\#)(1'')(60'')}{(60'')^2} = 47.5\#$$
$$P_{axial} = 950\#$$

2. Calculate the variables necessary for the bending portion of the inter-
    action equation.

a. Calculate the moment:

$$M_{max} = \frac{P_s l}{4} = \frac{47.5\#(60")}{4} = 712.5 \text{ inlb}$$

b. Calculate the actual bending stress using the Flexure Formula:

$$f_b = \frac{M_{max}}{S_{x-x}} = \frac{712.5 \text{ inlb}}{3.063 \text{ in}^3} = 232.6 \text{ psi}$$

c. Calculate the allowable bending stress (F_b'). Since the b:d ratio of a
    2x4 is 1:2, no lateral bracing is required ($C_L=1.0$). C_F is 1.5.

    $$F_b' = C_F F_b = 1.5(500 \text{ psi}) = 750 \text{ psi}$$

d. Calculate F_{cE} for the bending term of the interaction equation:

$$F_{cE} = \frac{0.3E}{\left(\frac{l}{d}\right)^2} = \frac{(0.3)(1.2x10^6 \text{ psi})}{\left(\frac{60"}{3.5"}\right)^2} = 1,225 \text{ psi}$$

3. The compressive stress answers found in Case #1 are still valid, so
    we can go directly to the interaction equation:

$$\left(\frac{f_c}{F_c'}\right)^2 + \frac{f_b}{F_b\left[1-\left(\frac{f_c}{F_{cE}}\right)\right]} \leq 1.0$$

$$= \left(\frac{180.95 \text{ psi}}{210.9 \text{ psi}}\right)^2 + \frac{232.6 \text{ psi}}{(750 \text{ psi})\left[1-\left(\frac{180.95 \text{ psi}}{1,225 \text{ psi}}\right)\right]}$$

$$= 0.736 + 0.364 \Rightarrow 1.100 \geq 1.0 \ \times$$

The 2x4 fails for this loading condition.

A mere 1" of eccentricity caused an adequate 2x4 column to be stressed beyond its allowable limits. This example serves as a caution for carpenters. Fortunately, most sets are overbuilt, and the formulas we use assume that the connections are pinned and allow rotation.
Most theatrical connections, such as a 2x4 leg which butts into the lid of a platform (and is
connected to the framing) allow limited rotation because of their square corners and multiple connections. In other words, our average end fixity is better than a pure pin connection,
and that compensates for some eccentric loading conditions. In any case, avoid eccentric
loading whenever possible.

BIAXIAL BENDING

Biaxial bending occurs when a beam is subject to bending loads against both axes. *NDS* Interaction Equation 3.9-3 can be expressed as the following for biaxial bending (*TCM*, 5-167):

$$\frac{f_{bx}}{F'_{bx}} + \frac{f_{by}}{F'_{by}\left[1-\left(f_{bx}/F_{bE}\right)\right]^2} \leq 1.0$$

where f_{bx} is the actual bending stress in the x-x axis, psi
f_{by} is the actual bending stress in the y-y axis, psi
F_{bx}' is the allowable bending stress in the x-x axis, psi
F_{by}' is the allowable bending stress in the y-y axis, psi
F_{bE} is the critical buckling design value for bending, psi

Most of the variables in the equation above are familiar from Chapter 5. F_{bE}, the critical buckling design value for bending members, is new. In the same way that F_{cE} is a step in finding C_p, F_{bE} is a step in finding C_L, the beam lateral stability factor.

Since the compression and tension edges of a beam with biaxial bending are hard to define, the usual rules which we use to set $C_L=1.0$ are not readily applicable. If the *d/b* ratio is 2:1 or less, then no lateral bracing is required and C_L is 1.0. If the *d/b* ratio is greater than 2:1, C_L must be determined. C_L for beams is analogous to C_p for columns. Calculating C_L is a multi-step process which begins with the following equation:

$$C_L = \frac{1+F_{bE}/F_b^*}{1.9} - \sqrt{\left[\frac{1+F_{bE}/F_b^*}{1.9}\right]^2 - \frac{F_{bE}/F_b^*}{0.95}} = \frac{1+ratio}{1.9} - \sqrt{\left[\frac{1+ratio}{1.9}\right]^2 - \frac{ratio}{0.95}}$$

where C_L is the beam lateral stability factor
F_{bE} is the critical buckling design value for bending, psi
F_b^* is F_b multiplied by all applicable adjustment factors except C_L and C_{fu}, psi.
ratio is F_{bE}/F_b^*

- Once C_L is determined, F_b' can be calculated by multiplying F_b^* by C_L.
- F_{bE} is calculated as follows (*TCM*, 5-129):

$$F_{bE} = \frac{K_{bE}E'}{R_B^2} \Rightarrow \frac{0.438E}{R_B^2}$$

where K_{bE} is the Euler buckling coefficient for beams and is equal to 0.438 for sawn lumber.
E' is the allowable modulus of elasticity adjusted by C_t and C_M, usually E, because the factors equal 1.0 for theatrical use, psi.
R_B is the slenderness ratio, and is calculated as follows:

$$R_B = \sqrt{\frac{l_e/d}{b^2}}$$

where l_e is the effective length (see below), in
d is the depth, in
b is the width or breadth, in

• The effective length of a member, l_e, can be determined from the following chart (*NDS*, Table 3.3.3) which is based on l_u, the unbraced length of the beam.

Simple Span	$l_u/d<7$	$l_u/d\geq7$
uniformly distributed load	$l_e=2.06l_u$	$l_e=1.63l_u+3d$
concentrated load at center with no intermediate lateral support	$l_e=1.80l_u$	$l_e=1.37l_u+3d$
concentrated load at center with lateral support at center	$l_e=1.11l_u$	$l_e=1.11l_u$

For other loading conditions:

$l_e=2.06l_u$ when $l_u/d<7$
$l_e=1.63l_u+3d$ when $7\leq l_u/d\leq14.3$
$l_e=1.84l_u$ when $l_u/d>14.3$

• Calculating l_e is only necessary for finding R_b.

Doing the calculations for a biaxial bending member may seem overwhelming at first glance. Several observations help to simplify the process. First, many biaxial members will have a d/b ratio of 2:1 or less which means that $C_L=1.0$, and l_e, R_B, and F_{bE} do not have to be calculated. If C_L must be calculated, it only needs to be calculated for one axis because if the d/b ratio of one axis is greater than 2, the d/b ratio of the other axis is the inverse (by definition, less than 1). R_B, l_e, and F_{bE} only have to be calculated for the x-x axis, the axis with the greatest depth. Examples 5 and 6 will make these observations clearer.

The most common example of biaxial bending is a beam in which the bending load is not perpendicular to either the x-x or the y-y axis. The very first step in this type of biaxial bending problem is to find the perpendicular components of the applied load, P. This is easily done using trigonometry (see Example 5).

Example 5. Is a Southern Pine, No. 2 Dense 3x6 adequate to support the following loading condition? Assume that the end connections are adequately restrained and that the load duration is normal.

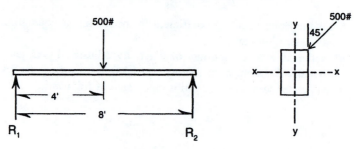

Figure 7.8 Example 5

1. Gather the base design allowables and geometric properties of the 3x6:

   F_b=1,450 psi; S_{x-x}=12.604 in³; S_{y-y}=5.729 in³

2. Find the perpendicular components of the diagonal load.

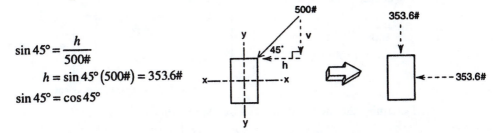

$$\sin 45° = \frac{h}{500\#}$$

$$h = \sin 45° (500\#) = 353.6\#$$

$$\sin 45° = \cos 45°$$

Figure 7.9 Example 5, components

3. Due to the 45° angle, the moment in both axes is identical:

$$M_{max} = \frac{Pl}{4} \Rightarrow M_{x-x} = \frac{vl}{4} = \frac{(353.6\#)(96")}{4} = 8,485.3 \text{ inlb}$$

$$M_{x-x} = M_{y-y}$$

4. Determine F_b'. In this case, the d/b ratio is 2, and C_L is therefore 1.0. Since Southern Pine incorporates a size factor into the base design tables, and all other adjustment factors are normal, $F_b'=F_b$=1,450 psi.

5. Determine the minimum required value of S and compare it to S_{x-x} and S_{y-y} of the 3x6.

$$S_{req'd} = \frac{M_{max}}{F_b'} = \frac{8,485.3 \text{ inlb}}{1,450 \text{ psi}} = 5.85 \text{ in}^3$$

$$S_{y-y} = 5.729 \text{ in}^3 \Rightarrow 5.85 > 5.729 \text{ in}^3 \text{ ✗}$$

A 3x6 will not support this loading condition.

Example 6. Consider the following loading condition in which the end connections are adequately restrained. Find a beam to support the load as drawn. Use Spruce-Pine-Fir No. 1 and assume a normal load duration.

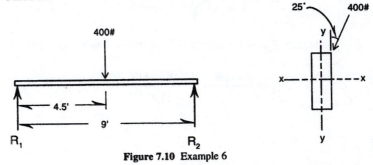

Figure 7.10 Example 6

1.   Find the perpendicular components of the diagonal load.

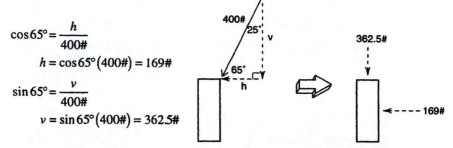

$$\cos 65° = \frac{h}{400\#}$$

$$h = \cos 65°(400\#) = 169\#$$

$$\sin 65° = \frac{v}{400\#}$$

$$v = \sin 65°(400\#) = 362.5\#$$

Figure 7.11 Example 6, components

2.   Determine the moments induced by the two loads.

$$M_{max} = \frac{Pl}{4} \Rightarrow M_{x-x} = \frac{vl}{4} = \frac{362.5\#(108")}{4} = 9{,}788 \text{ inlb}$$

$$M_{max} = \frac{Pl}{4} \Rightarrow M_{y-y} = \frac{hl}{4} = \frac{169\#(108")}{4} = 4{,}564 \text{ inlb}$$

3.   Determine a minimum S based on the larger of the two loads. Use the base design value of F_b for Spruce-Pine-Fir No. 1.

$$S_{min} = \frac{M_{max}}{F_b} = \frac{9{,}788 \text{ inlb}}{875 \text{ psi}} = 11.2 \text{ in}^3$$

The beam will require at least a 2x8 or a 3x6 to resist the bending moment acting against the x-x axis. Therefore, we will test a 3x8 with the x-x axis resisting the larger bending moment.

4.   Determine l_e. A 3x8 has a d of 7.25" and a b of 2.5".

$$\frac{l_u}{d} = \frac{108"}{7.25"} = 14.9$$

Since 14.9>7, the effective length must be:

$$l_e = 1.37l_u + 3d = 1.37(108") + 3(7.25") = 169.7"$$

5.   Calculate R_B:

$$R_B = \sqrt{\frac{l_e/d}{b^2}} = \sqrt{\frac{169.7"/7.25"}{(2.5")^2}} = 1.935$$

6.   Calculate F_{bE}. E for Spruce-Pine-Fir No. 1 is 1.4x10⁶ psi.

$$F_{bE} = \frac{0.438E}{R_B^2} = \frac{0.438(1.4x10^6 \text{ psi})}{(1.935)^2} = 163{,}724 \text{ psi}$$

7. Determine C_L.
   a. Calculate F_b^*. C_F is 1.2, and all other adjustment factors are 1.0.

   $$F_b^* = C_F F_b = 1.2(875 \text{ psi}) = 1,050 \text{ psi}$$

   b. Calculate ratio:

   $$ratio = \frac{F_{bE}}{F_b^*} = \frac{163,724 \text{ psi}}{1,050 \text{ psi}} = 155.9$$

   c. Calculate C_L:

   $$C_L = \frac{1 + F_{bE}/F_b^*}{1.9} - \sqrt{\left[\frac{1 + F_{bE}/F_b^*}{1.9}\right]^2 - \frac{F_{bE}/F_b^*}{0.95}} = \frac{1 + 155.9}{1.9} - \sqrt{\left[\frac{1 + 155.9}{1.9}\right]^2 - \frac{155.9}{0.95}} = 0.9997$$

8. Calculate the allowable bending values:

   $$F_{bx}' = C_L F_b^* = 0.9997(1,050 \text{ psi}) = 1,049.7 \text{ psi}$$

   For F_{by}', $C_L = 1.0$, $C_F = 1.2$ and $C_{fu} = 1.15$.

   $$F_{by}' = C_L C_F C_{fu} F_b = 1.0(1.2)(1.15)(875 \text{ psi}) = 1,207.5 \text{ psi}$$

9. Determine the actual bending stresses.

   $$f_{bx} = \frac{M_{max}}{S_{x-x}} = \frac{9,788 \text{ inlb}}{21.9 \text{ in}^3} = 446.9 \text{ psi}$$

   $$f_{by} = \frac{M_{max}}{S_{y-y}} = \frac{4,564 \text{ inlb}}{7.552 \text{ in}^3} = 604.4 \text{ psi}$$

10. Plug the variables into the interaction equation.

   $$\frac{f_{bx}}{F_{bx}'} + \frac{f_{by}}{F_{by}'\left[1 - \left(f_{bx}/F_{bE}\right)\right]^2} \leq 1.0$$

   $$= \frac{446.9 \text{ psi}}{1,049.7 \text{ psi}} + \frac{604.4 \text{ psi}}{(1,207.5 \text{ psi})\left[1 - \left(446.9 \text{ psi}/163,724 \text{ psi}\right)\right]^2}$$

   $$= 0.426 + 0.503 \Rightarrow 0.929 \leq 1.0 \checkmark$$

   A 3x8 will support this loading condition.

CHAPTER 7 LESSONS

The format of the numbering system is: chapter.lesson.problem number.
Assume a normal load duration, and neglect beam weight unless otherwise noted.

LESSON 7.1 SINGLE AXIS BENDING AND AXIAL TENSION (PG 145 – 147)

7.1.1   Design the lightest 2x sawn lumber member which will support the loading condition given below. Use Western Woods No. 1 and assume a 2 month load duration.

7.1.2   Design the lightest 3x sawn lumber member which will support the loading condition given below. Use Southern Pine No. 1.

7.1.3   Design the lightest 2x sawn lumber member which will support the loading condition given below. Use Southern Pine No. 2 and assume a 2 month load duration.

7.1.4   Design the lightest 2x sawn lumber member which will support the loading condition given below. Use Hem-Fir No. 2.

7.1.5   Design the lightest pair of 1x sawn lumber members which will support the loading condition given below. Use Industrial 45 Southern Pine (Southern Pine No. 2).

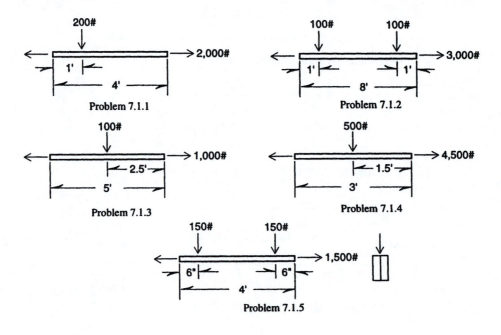

Problem 7.1.1

Problem 7.1.2

Problem 7.1.3

Problem 7.1.4

Problem 7.1.5

LESSON 7.2 SINGLE AXIS BENDING AND AXIAL COMPRESSION (PG 148 – 151)

7.2.1   Design the lightest sawn lumber member which will support the loading condition given below. Use Douglas Fir-South No. 1 and assume a 2 month load duration.

7.2.2   Design the lightest 2x sawn lumber member which will support the loading condition given below. Use Hem-Fir No. 1.

7.2.3   Design the lightest 2x sawn lumber member which will support the loading condition given below. Use Southern Pine No. 1, and assume a 2 month load duration.

LESSON 7.3 ECCENTRIC LOADING (PG 151 – 156)

7.3.1   Design the lightest sawn lumber member which will support the loading condition given below. Use Hem-Fir No. 2 and assume a 2 month load duration.

7.3.2   Will a Southern Pine No. 2 2x4 support the loading condition given below? The column is laterally braced against the weak axis at its midpoint.

7.3.3   Design the lightest sawn lumber member which will support the loading condition given below. Use Douglas Fir-South No. 1 and assume a 2 month load duration. The column is braced in both directions at the bracket.

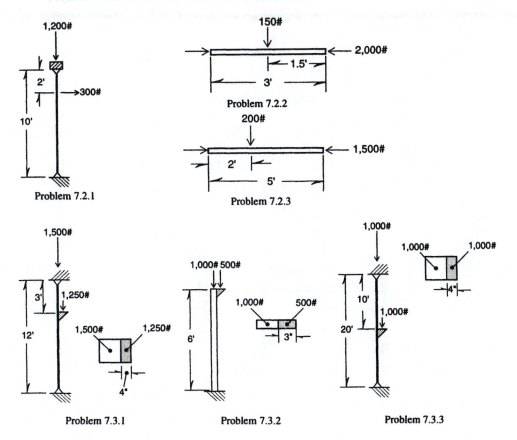

Problem 7.2.1

Problem 7.2.2

Problem 7.2.3

Problem 7.3.1

Problem 7.3.2

Problem 7.3.3

LESSON 7.4 BIAXIAL BENDING (PG 157 – 161)

7.4.1   Will a Hem-Fir No. 1 4x8 beam support the loading condition given below? Assume
a 2 month load duration. Use 5 plf as an estimated beam weight.

7.4.2   Design the lightest 3x sawn lumber member which will support the loading condition given below. Use Southern Pine No. 1. Use 5 plf as an estimated beam weight.

7.4.3   Design the lightest 2x sawn lumber member which will support the loading condition given below. Use Hem-Fir No. 2 and assume a 2 month load duration.

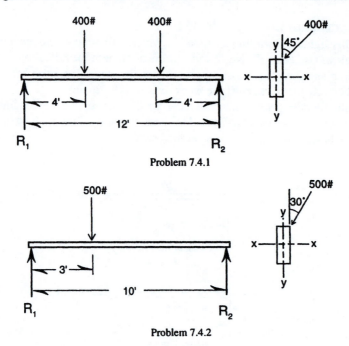

Problem 7.4.1

Problem 7.4.2

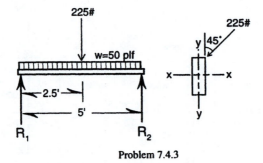

Problem 7.4.3

8

Steel Beam Design

INTRODUCTION
Chapters 2, 3, and 4 described how to determine the stresses in a beam due to its loading conditions. Chapter 5 described how to design beams with sawn lumber, this chapter will explore procedures for designing steel beams.

STEEL AND ITS PROPERTIES
The primary source for information regarding steel, steel shapes, and steel structural design procedures is the *Manual of Steel Construction, Allowable Stress Design*, published by the American Institute of Steel Construction, AISC. For ease of reference the manual will be referred to as the *Steel Construction Manual (SCM)*. The *SCM* is to steel design what the *Timber Construction Manual* is to wood design. This text will use the techniques, section properties, and allowables recommended in the first revised printing of the ninth edition of the *SCM*, published in 1989. The basic tenets of structural design remain constant regardless of material, but steel structural design has its own unique language. For example, the *SCM* uses **kips** and **ksi**, not pounds and psi, as the basic units for loads and stresses. A kip is defined as 1,000 pounds, and ksi is therefore 1,000 pounds per square inch.

Structural design was revolutionized when consistently high quality steel became available. Structures that were formerly impossible to build, such as cantilevered balconies in theater houses, suddenly became feasible due to the strength characteristics of steel. Most common steels have a Modulus of Elasticity of 2.9×10^7 psi. Remember that an average sawn lumber species has a Modulus of Elasticity of 1.2×10^6 psi, which is an average stiffness difference between steel and wood of 24 times.

The other important characteristic of steel is its homogeneity. Unlike heterogeneous materials such as wood, steel is not subject to the limitations of knots, splits, and moisture and temperature effects. This is reflected in smaller safety factors and a design process unhindered by complex grading systems and many adjustment factors. The behavior of steel can be predicted so accurately that some schools of engineering design use the ultimate strength of steel, adding safety factors depending on the application.

Steel's homogeneity also allows it to be readily manufactured into a wide variety of shapes such as hollow rectangular and circular tubes, pipes, angles, channels, I-beams, and plates. Each of these categories has unique geometric properties making them more suitable for certain applications. The geometric properties of shapes which are considered "structural" are listed in the *Steel Construction Manual*. Structural shapes are those which are used as primary members in buildings and bridges. Consequently, the geometric properties of some small steel shapes useful in scenery construction must be found in other sources.

In addition to the variety of shapes, steel is available in many grades. The strength of each grade varies with its carbon content. As the strength of a steel changes, so do other properties, such as brittleness and ductility. The American Society for Testing and Materials, ASTM, assigns each grade of steel a code which lets structural designers look up its strength properties. It is a structural designers responsibility to choose a steel that is appropriate for the application.

In theater, a structural designer is likely to encounter several distinct grades of steel. ASTM A36 is the single most common grade of steel used in building construction in the U.S. (*SCM*, pg. 1-5). The 36 in A36 refers to its yield point of 36 ksi or 36,000 psi. The I-beams, channels, angles, tees, and plates listed in the *SCM* are all available in A36 steel. Other shapes such as pipe and tubing are of steels with various yield strengths and are discussed at length later in this chapter.

The fundamental variables for stress in steel are as follows:

F_a	allowable axial compressive stress, ksi or psi
f_a	actual axial compressive stress, ksi or psi
F_b	allowable bending stress, ksi or psi
f_b	actual bending stress, ksi or psi
F_t	allowable axial tensile stress, ksi or psi
f_t	actual axial tensile stress, ksi or psi
F_y	minimum yield stress, ksi or psi
F_u	ultimate stress, ksi or psi

The **minimum yield stress**, F_y, is the point at which further stress would create permanent deformation. It is the dividing line between the elastic and plastic regions of the stress versus strain diagram for steel (see Chapter 2, Figure 2.20). The **ultimate stress**, F_u, is the point at which rupture occurs when the steel is tested in tension. For A36 steel, F_u has a range of 58 to 80 ksi. For the purposes of calculation, it is always safest to use the lower number.

The *SCM* lists F_u and F_y for various grades of steel. The allowable stresses are expressed as percentages of F_y and F_u, regardless of the grade of steel. Hence, F_b is usually between 60% and 66% of F_y, and F_t is 60% of F_y or 50% of F_u. F_a is dependent on the slenderness ratio of the column under consideration. See the table *Yield Strengths of Commonly Used Steels* in Appendix E for values of F_b, F_y, and F_t for various steel grades.

STEEL SHAPES

Steel is fabricated into many shapes. This text will discuss six general categories: tube, pipe, angles, channel, I-beams, and plates and bars. Appendix E has extensive geometric property charts for most of these shapes.

TUBE

In general, tube is a very efficient structural shape because it offers both large I and S values relative to weight by concentrating material at the extreme edges of the shape. Rectangular tube is particularly efficient when used as a beam, and square and round tube is particularly efficient when used as a column. In general, tubes are lightweight, easy to cut, and fairly easy to bend into "designer shapes."

Mechanical Tube

Mechanical tube (or tubing) can be hollow square, rectangular, or round and is **not** listed in the *Steel Construction Manual* because it is considered "decorative" by the AISC. It is, however, manufactured and specified for structural uses by its producers and is available in an ideal size range for theater. Mechanical tube may be the most commonly used steel shape in theatrical applications because it is used to frame flats and platforms and to build many mechanical effects.

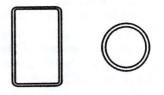

Figure 8.1 Typical mechanical tube

Round mechanical tube is specified by its actual diameter and wall thickness and has a smooth surface finish. Round tube is available in sizes from 1/8"x0.022" to 16"x1-1/2". Square mechanical tube is available in sizes ranging from 3/8"x0.035" to 6"x1/4". Rectangular mechanical tube is available in sizes from 3/8"x5/8"x0.035" to 4"x8"x1/4". The geometric properties listed in this textbook were obtained from the *Handbook of Welded Carbon Steel Mechanical Tubing* published by the Steel Tube Institute of North America.

Mechanical tube is categorized by the methods used to create it. Commonly referenced types include "cold drawn seamless," "hot finished seamless," "drawn-over-mandrel" (DOM), "butt-weld," and "electrical resistance welded" (ERW). This text will only discuss mechanical tubing defined by ASTM A513, designated as MT1010, MT1020, etc. For the purposes of simplicity, this text will assume that all mechanical tube is the ERW type, that it is "as-welded" from hot rolled steel, and that it is MT1010 grade with a F_y of 32 ksi. For reference, we have also included charts for MT1020 with a F_y of 38 ksi. This is a conservative assumption; much stronger types and grades of mechanical tubing (such as DOM) are readily available. It is the structural designers responsibility to determine the specifications of the tubing obtained from a distributor. Mechanical tubing is generally sold in 20' or 24' lengths.

Structural Tube

Structural tube (or tubing) can also be hollow square, rectangular, or round. Structural tube tends to have larger dimensions and wall thicknesses than mechanical tube. Rectilinear tubing has rounded corners and is specified by the outside dimensions and wall thickness.

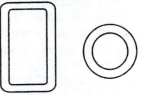

Structural square tube is available in sizes ranging from 1-1/2"x1-1/2"x3/16" to 30"x30"x5/8". Structural rectangular tube is available in sizes ranging from 3"x2"x 1/8" to 30"x24"x1/2". Round structural tube is available in sizes ranging from 2-3/8"x1/8" to 20"x1/2". The *SCM* lists the geometric properties of structural tube in Section 1 and lists allowable column loads

Figure 8.2 Structural tube

in Section 3. Unlike the *SCM*, the structural tube itemized by the Steel Tube Institute of North America (STINA) is listed by nominal wall thicknesses which do not match the actual wall thickness of the tubes. The geometric properties listed in this textbook were obtained from *Structural Steel Tubing* published by STINA. The structural tube commonly sold conforms to ASTM specification A500, Grade B, and has an F_y of 46 ksi. It is usually sold in 20' or 40' lengths.

PIPE

Pipe has a hollow, circular cross-section and is often called "black pipe" because of its imperfect surface finish caused by scale left from the fabricating process. Schedule 40 pipe is the standard wall thickness of black pipe. Schedule 80, also known as Extra Strong, has thicker walls. ASTM specification A53 lists thicknesses from Schedule 10 to Schedule 160.

Figure 8.3 Typical Pipe

It is important to understand that pipe is specified by a nominal dimension and its relative wall thickness (schedule). The outer diameter, O.D., of any nominal size pipe is always the same; the inner diameter, I.D., is different for each schedule. This insures that pipes with the same nominal diameter but different schedules can share the same threaded connectors. For example, 2" black pipe, be it Schedule 10, 40, or 80, has an O.D. of 2.375". The wall thickness of 2" Schedule 40 pipe is 0.154" while the corresponding 2" Schedule 80 pipe has a wall thickness of 0.218", and the 2" Schedule 120 pipe has a wall thickness of 0.436". The *SCM* lists the dimensions, weight, and geometric properties of Standard (Schedule 40), Extra-Strong (Schedule 80), and Double-Extra Strong pipes in Section 1 as well as allowable load tables for pipe columns in Section 3.

> CONCEPT BOX: 1-1/4" and 1-1/2" standard weight pipes are the two most common sizes used in technical theater because they are often used as battens in counterweight rigging systems. Ironically, beams with round cross-sections are very poor at resisting deflection. Why are they the most common beam in theater? (Perhaps because they are compatible with C-clamps.)

Anyone working in technical theater should be familiar with the actual diameter of 1-1/4" and 1-1/2" pipe. A 1-1/2" Schedule 40 pipe has an O.D. of 1.9", and a 1-1/4" Schedule 40 pipe has an O.D. of 1.66". By paying attention to the actual dimensions of nominal pipe sizes listed in the *SCM*, a structural designer can sleeve pipes into each other to achieve rotation effects. For example, 1-1/2" Schedule 40 pipe fits snugly inside 2" Schedule 80 pipe (unless an internal weld seam or other defect interferes). In addition to the sizes listed in the *SCM*, Schedule 40 pipe is available in 1/8", 1/4", and 3/8" nominal diameters.

Common black pipe conforms to ASTM Specification A53. A53 defines several different types and grades of pipe. In general, pipe is manufactured for transporting steam, water, gas, and air; it is not intended for structural use. When in doubt, it is conservative to assume that any black pipe encountered in a theater is Type F, Grade A, with a F_y of 30 ksi (ASTM A53, Table 2). Black pipe is also available as Type E, Grade B, and Type S, Grade B, both with a F_y of 35 ksi (*SCM*, 1-92). Pipe is generally sold in 21' lengths and can be bought with threaded or unthreaded ends.

ANGLES

Angles are L-shaped sections that have equal or unequal legs and are available in several thicknesses. Angles are designated by an "L," followed by the length of one flange, the length of the other flange, and then its thickness. For example, an L4x3x1/4 is an angle with one leg of 4", one leg of 3", and a thickness of 1/4". The smallest angle listed in the *SCM* is an L1x1x1/8. Smaller angles are available, but their geometric properties are not published. For convenience, the size and weight of these "bar size" angles are listed with the structural angles in Appendix E.

Figure 8.4 Typ. angle

Angles are typically used to frame flats and platforms or in mechanical projects. The inside corner and both edges are rounded which prevents rectilinear shapes from butting cleanly into the inside corner. However, bar size angles do have square corners. Angles are usually sold in 20' or 40' lengths and are priced by the pound.

CHANNEL

Channels are C-shaped sections which resemble I-beams cut in half along the *y*-axis. Channels are designated as follows: a C, followed by the actual depth and weight per lineal foot. A C5x9 is a channel that is 5" deep and weighs 9 plf. The smallest channel listed in the *SCM* is a C3x4.1. Like angle, smaller channels are available, but their geometric properties are not published. The *SCM* lists allowable load tables for channels used as beams when oriented as shown in Figure 8.5. Two types of channels are listed in the *SCM*, American Standard (C) and Miscellaneous (MC) channels. This text will not discuss MC channels. Like angle, small "bar size" channels are available commercially. The size and weight of these channels are listed with the structural channels in Appendix E.

Figure 8.5 Channel

The two flanges and web of a channel provide the same structural advantages as I-beams (see below) while the flat surface on one side can make connection details easier. Channels are commonly used as the walkable surface of grids and as beams or columns in sets. They can also be a useful shape for mechanical projects such as frames or tracks. Channels are usually sold in 20', 40' or 60' lengths and are priced by the pound.

I-BEAMS

I-beams are commonly used as girders, joists, and columns in building construction. The "I" shape is ideal for beams because it concentrates material at its extreme edges in the **flanges**, while the middle **web** is sufficient to resist shear. I shaped beams are available as W, M, S, or HP shapes. Each I-beam category has the same general proportions and a tremendous size range. For example, W-shapes range in depth from 4" to 44" and in weight from 9 pounds to 848 pounds per foot.

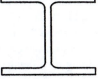

Figure 8.6 I-beam

S-shapes are popular beams for theatrical applications because they are available in relatively small sizes down to 3" in depth and 5.7 pounds per foot. However, S-shapes have tapered flanges, which makes connection details more challenging.

I-beams are designated by shape, nominal depth, and weight per lineal foot. Hence, a W8x15 is a W-shape beam 8.11" deep which weighs 15 plf. Note that the depth dimension of I-beams is nominal, not actual. The *SCM* lists the dimensions and geometric properties of every I-beam shape in Section 1. It also lists allowable beam load tables in Section 2 and allowable column load tables in Section 3. When using the allowable load tables in the *SCM*, be sure that you are using the appropriate loading conditions and steel grade.

Theatrical applications of I-beams are rare in regional theater, and when they are used, we tend to use the lightest I-beams available. A theatrical structural designer is more likely to encounter I-beams in permanent structures such as headblock beams or the beams supporting a trapped stage floor. I-beams are usually sold in 20', 40', or 60' lengths and are priced by the pound.

PLATES AND BARS

Plates and bars are solid rectilinear or round shapes. Plates, also called flat stock, are rectangles which are usually wider than they are thick, and are designated by their width and thickness. Bars are solid square or round shapes. Square bars are designated by the length of a side, and round shapes are designated by their diameter. The cross-sectional area and weight of plates and bars are listed in the *SCM*.

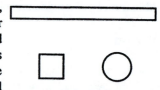

Figure 8.7 Typical plate and bars

This text will not include any specific discussion of beam or column design using plates and bars because they are usually used in specialty hardware, mechanical components, and connection details such as hanging irons. For example, cold-rolled round stock is often used for shafts because cold-rolled steel is manufactured to strict dimensional tolerances. Cold-rolled and hot-rolled plates and bars are available in a variety of sizes and lengths.

STEEL BEAM DESIGN

INTRODUCTION

Steel beam design follows the same pattern as wood beam design: every beam must pass bending, shear, and deflection tests. However, the specifics of the bending and shear tests vary depending on the steel shape being tested. Steel beam design does differ from wood beam design in that the order in which the tests will most likely govern will be deflection, bending, and then shear.

Steel tends to fail the deflection criteria because, ironically, it is so strong. It is strong enough to hold loads without bending failure but is not correspondingly stiff enough to eliminate "springiness." Shear is rarely the ruling test for steel beam design because the loading conditions to produce shear failure call for a very heavy load on a very short span. It is difficult to imagine a theatrical scenario extreme enough to cause shear failure in a steel beam.

Since deflection is not a failure test, the procedures do not change by shape category. The deflection test methods are the same as those used for wood beam design. Therefore, this section will first discuss general steel beam design issues, including deflection, and then will discuss the specifics of the bending and shear failure tests for each shape category.

Compact Shapes

Each shape category of steel has unique advantages and/or disadvantages when being considered as a beam. Quantitatively, these shape characteristics translate into different safety factors for calculating F_b and F_v.

Qualitatively, these differences are caused by the degree to which shapes are open or closed. **Closed shapes**, such as solid or hollow circles, squares, and rectangles, have no unsupported flanges. **Open shapes** are characterized by flanges or gaps and include I-beams, tees, channels, and angles. In general, closed shapes are stronger than open shapes because open shapes are susceptible to stress concentrations and flange failure.

> CONCEPT BOX: The concept of open and closed shapes is applicable to more than just structural steel shapes. For example, Unistrut and traveler track are both open shapes commonly found onstage. Neither are rated for carrying people because point loads can cause the flanges to fail before the unit would fail as a beam.
>
> In addition, whole systems can be thought of as open or closed. Intuitively, open shapes look like they can be "cracked open." For example, a flat with a door in it is an open shape unless a bottom threshold is added. Any carpenter can describe what happens to an "open" flat during load-in.

The vulnerability of a shape to this type of failure is quantified by a compactness criteria. A **compact** shape is one in which overall failure will occur before local failures, and the compactness criteria encompasses geometric properties, F_y, and unbraced length (Parker, 272). Some closed shapes are non-compact. For example, consider a typical aluminum can. It is a very strong column, but the slightest lateral force can cause it to catastrophically fail. In order to create a stronger column, it is necessary to increase the thickness of the skin of the can or to laterally brace it. Since the lateral bracing can change the compactness of a shape, if a shape is defined as compact, it is assumed that its bracing requirements are met. Each shape category has a different compactness criteria which is applicable to the bending and shear tests.

DEFLECTION TEST

The deflection test procedures for steel shapes is the same as those described for wood beam design because no allowable stresses are involved in the calculations. The general strategy is to find a required value of I using the appropriate case formulas and deflection criteria.

The rules for choosing a deflection criteria of $l/360$, $l/240$, or $l/180$ are also the same as those described for wood beam design. We will continue to limit the deflection to $l/240$ and apply it to the total loading condition (all dead and live loads). The deflection test involves solving the appropriate deflection formula for I. The Modulus of Elasticity, E, of the steel we use is almost always $2.9x10^7$ psi. If we commit to a $l/240$ criteria and plug in an E of $2.9x10^7$ psi, some of the most common deflection formulas can be reduced to the following:

- Simply supported, evenly distributed load:

$$I_{req'd} = \frac{5wl^4}{384E\Delta_{all}} = \frac{5wl^4}{384\left(2.9x10^7\,\text{psi}\right)\left(\frac{l}{240}\right)} = \frac{wl^3}{\left(9.28x10^6\,\text{psi}\right)}$$

- Simply supported, concentrated load at center:

$$I_{req'd} = \frac{Pl^3}{48E\Delta_{all}} = \frac{Pl^3}{48\left(2.9x10^7\,psi\right)\left(\frac{l}{240}\right)} = \frac{Pl^2}{\left(5.80x10^6\,psi\right)}$$

- Simply supported, two equal concentrated loads symmetrically placed:

$$I_{req'd} = \frac{Pa\left(3l^2 - 4a^2\right)}{24E\Delta_{all}} = \frac{Pa\left(3l^2 - 4a^2\right)}{24\left(2.9x10^7\,psi\right)\left(\frac{l}{240}\right)} = \frac{Pa\left(3l^2 - 4a^2\right)}{\left(2.9x10^6\,psi\right)l}$$

- Cantilever beam, uniformly distributed load:

$$I_{req'd} = \frac{wl^4}{8E\Delta_{all}} = \frac{wl^4}{8\left(2.9x10^7\,psi\right)\left(\frac{l}{240}\right)} = \frac{wl^3}{\left(9.67x10^5\,psi\right)}$$

- Beam overhanging one support, uniformly distributed load.
  Δ at the end of the overhang:

$$I_{req'd} = \frac{wa\left(4a^2l - l^3 + 3a^3\right)}{24E\Delta_{all}} = \frac{wa\left(4a^2l - l^3 + 3a^3\right)}{24\left(2.9x10^7\,psi\right)\left(\frac{a}{240}\right)} = \frac{w\left(4a^2l - l^3 + 3a^3\right)}{\left(2.9x10^6\,psi\right)}$$

  Δ between supports:

$$I_{req'd} = \frac{wx\left(l^4 - 2l^2x^2 + lx^3 - 2a^2l^2 + 2a^2x^2\right)}{24EI\Delta_{all}} = \frac{wx\left(l^4 - 2l^2x^2 + lx^3 - 2a^2l^2 + 2a^2x^2\right)}{24\left(2.9x10^7\,psi\right)l\left(\frac{l}{240}\right)}$$

$$= \frac{wx\left(l^4 - 2l^2x^2 + lx^3 - 2a^2l^2 + 2a^2x^2\right)}{l^2\left(2.9x10^6\,psi\right)} \qquad \text{where} \qquad x = \frac{l}{2}\left[1 - \frac{a^2}{l^2}\right]$$

As with wood, the most complicated deflection test is approximating deflection for loading conditions that are **not** covered by case formulas. The method described in Chapter 5 can be utilized: (1) the M_{max} of the actual loading condition is determined, (2) that M_{max} is used to solve for an equivalent evenly distributed load, w_{equiv}, which would create the same M_{max} on a simple beam; and (3) w_{equiv} is used to calculate an approximate deflection using the deflection formula for a simple span with an evenly distributed load.

> *Example 1.* What is the maximum point load based on a deflection criteria of $l/240$ that a C4x5.4 piece of grid steel can support at the center of its 4'-6" span? The channel is loaded against the weak axis as shown below.

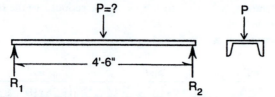

Figure 8.8a Example 1, free body diagram and cross-section orientation

From the section properties tables in Appendix E, $I_{y\text{-}y}$ of a C4x5.4 is 0.319 in^4. Since deflection is limited by $l/240$, we can use the simplified case formulas provided previously and solve for P.

$$I_{req'd} = \frac{Pl^2}{\left(5.80x10^6\,\text{psi}\right)} \Rightarrow P_{max} = \frac{I\left(5.80x10^6\,\text{psi}\right)}{l^2} = \frac{\left(0.319\text{ in}^4\right)\left(5.80x10^6\,\text{psi}\right)}{\left(54"\right)^2} = 634.5\#$$

What would be the maximum allowable load based on deflection if the load were oriented against the channel's strong axis? $I_{x\text{-}x}$ of a C4x5.4 is 0.385 in^4.

$$P_{max} = \frac{I\left(5.80x10^6\,\text{psi}\right)}{l^2} = \frac{\left(3.85\text{ in}^4\right)\left(5.80x10^6\,\text{psi}\right)}{\left(54"\right)^2} = 7,657.75\#$$

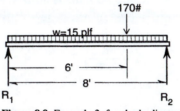

P=?

Figure 8.8b Channel orientation

Example 2. What is the minimum required I value for the following loading condition based on deflection?

170#

w=15 plf

6'

8'

R_1 R_2

Figure 8.9 Example 2, free body diagram

First, determine the reactions:

$$\sum M_{R_1} = 0 = \left(0'\right)\left(R_1\right) + \left(4'\right)\left[\left(15\text{ plf}\right)\left(8'\right)\right] + \left(6'\right)\left(170\#\right) - \left(8'\right)\left(R_2\right)$$
$$R_2 = 187.5\#$$
$$\sum M_{R_2} = 0 = \left(0'\right)\left(R_2\right) - \left(4'\right)\left[\left(15\text{ plf}\right)\left(8'\right)\right] - \left(2'\right)\left(170\#\right) + \left(8'\right)\left(R_1\right)$$
$$R_1 = 102.5\#$$

Check the sum of the vertical forces:

$$\sum V = 187.5\# + 102.5\# - 170\# - 8'\left(15\text{ plf}\right) = 0 \checkmark$$

Calculate the shear at various points to determine where shear crosses through zero and where M_{max} occurs:

$$V_{0^-} = 0$$
$$V_{0^+} = +102.5\#$$
$$V_{6^-} = +102.5\# - 6'\left(15\text{ plf}\right) = 12.50\#$$
$$V_{6^+} = 12.50\# - 170\# = -157.5\# \quad \text{Shear crosses through zero at 6'}$$

Calculate M_{max} at 6':

$$M_{max} = M_{6'} = -\left\{3'\left[\left(6'\right)\left(15\text{ plf}\right)\right]\right\} + \left[6'\left(102.5\#\right)\right] = 345\text{ ftlb} \Rightarrow 4,148\text{ inlb}$$

Calculate an equivalent w which generates the same M_{max}:

$$M_{evenly\ dist.} = \frac{wl^2}{8} \Rightarrow w_{equiv} = \frac{8M_{max}}{l^2} = \frac{8(4,148\ inlb)}{(96")^2} = 3.59\ pli$$

Calculate the minimum $I_{req'd}$ using the equivalent w:

$$I_{req'd} = \frac{wl^3}{9.28x10^6\ psi} = \frac{(3.59\ pli)(96")^3}{9.28x10^6\ psi} = 0.343\ in^4$$

BENDING AND SHEAR TESTS BY SHAPE
Introduction
Although deflection is often the ruling criteria, one must be sure to test a steel beam for bending and shear failure. Exceeding a deflection criteria is merely a matter of aesthetics or comfort; exceeding the maximum allowable bending or shear stress could lead to failure. Remember that, for bending, the Flexure Formula is utilized and expressed in one of these three ways:

$$M_{max} = F_b S \qquad \text{or} \qquad f_b = \frac{M_{max}}{S} \qquad \text{or} \qquad S_{req'd} = \frac{M_{max}}{F_b}$$

When a structural designer is looking for a beam with the best fit for a given loading condition, the third equation is most useful. F_b is determined and the actual M_{max} is calculated in order to solve for the minimum required value of S.

The shear test is usually superfluous for steel beams unless the beam span is very short but should be checked to finalize a beam selection. Since steel shapes are usually not solid rectangles, the general shear stress equation is adapted for the various shapes and is used to find the actual shear stress:

$$f_v = \frac{VQ}{Ib}$$

where f_v is the actual unit shearing stress, psi
       V is the actual vertical shear, usually V_{max}, lb
       Q is the statical moment of area above or below the plane at which
          the horizontal shear is being computed, in^3
       I is the Moment of Inertia, in^4
       b is the width of the shear plane, in

Rectilinear Hollow Shapes
Bending Test
All rectilinear hollow shapes are closed, symmetrical shapes. Consequently, the vast majority of these shapes are compact, simplifying the calculations of F_b. All rectilinear hollow shapes must meet the following minimum compactness criteria to be considered as a valid beam choice (SCM, 5-36):

$$\frac{b}{t} \leq \frac{238}{\sqrt{F_y}}$$

where b is the inside clear distance of the longest side, in
          t is the wall thickness of the tube, in
          F_y is the yield strength of the steel, ksi

For convenience, we will take b as the total length of the longest side instead of the inside clear distance. For the two common grades of tube, the maximum width to thickness ratios are as follows:

Type	Steel Grade (F_y)	maximum b/t
Tubing, mechanical, MT1010	32 ksi	42.1
Tubing, structural, A500	46 ksi	35.1

The full value of F_b, $0.66F_y$, can be used if the beam is both compact and adequately braced or if the shape is square (*SCM*, Sect. B5, 5-48). Unfortunately, the bracing requirements change with every loading condition. However, there is no lateral bracing requirement if F_b is taken as $0.6F_y$ and the section's depth is less than 6 times its width (*SCM*, 5-48). For convenience, unless the beam under consideration is continuously braced or square, we will use an F_b of $0.6F_y$. In most cases, deflection will govern our choice regardless of the value of F_b, so this simplification will not lead to overbuilt scenery. Appendix E lists both the F_y and the width to thickness ratios for the types of steel shapes discussed in this text.

Shear Test
The allowable shear stress, F_v, of all rectilinear hollow shapes which pass the compactness criteria (b/t limit) is $0.4F_y$. The actual shear stress is approximated by dividing the maximum vertical shear by the area of the webs:

$$f_v = \frac{V}{d(2t_w)}$$

where f_v is actual shear stress, psi
          V is the maximum vertical shear, lbs
          d is the total depth of the beam, in
          t_w is the web thickness, in

Note that the wall thickness of tubing must be doubled to find the thickness of the shear plane.

> **Example 3.** What is the lightest rectangular or square tubing beam that can span 12' with an evenly distributed load of 90 plf? Use mechanical tubing (MT1010, F_y = 32 ksi) and a deflection criteria of $l/240$.

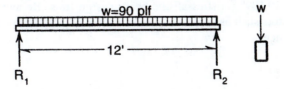

Figure 8.10 Example 3, free body diagram

Use the deflection case formula to find $I_{req'd}$:

$$I_{req'd} = \frac{wl^3}{9.28x10^6\,psi} = \frac{\left(90\,plf\Big/12"\right)(144")^3}{9.28x10^6\,psi} = \frac{(7.5\,pli)(144")^3}{9.28x10^6\,psi} = 2.41\,in^4$$

Use the Flexure Formula and the case formulas to find $S_{req'd}$:

$$F_b = 0.6F_y = 0.6(32,000\,psi) = 19,200\,psi$$

$$M_{max} = \frac{wl^2}{8} = \frac{(7.5\,pli)(144")^2}{8} = 19,440\,inlb$$

$$S_{req'd} = \frac{M_{max}}{F_b} = \frac{19,440\,inlb}{19,200\,psi} = 1.0125\,in^3$$

Here are some of the most likely choices (Appendix E):

Section	Weight, plf	S_{x-x} (in³)	I_{x-x} (in⁴)	b/t
1.5"x4"x0.134"	4.65	1.2651	2.5302	29.8✔
2"x3.5"x0.165"	5.52	1.4121	2.4712	21.2✔
2"x4"x0.109"	4.22	1.2776	2.5553	36.7✔
2"x5"x0.065"	3.02	1.1192	2.7980	76.9✖
3.5"x3.5"x0.109"	4.90	1.5580	2.7265	32.1✔

The lightest beam choice would be the 2"x5"x0.065", but it exceeds the permissible b/t ratio of 42.1. It is inappropriate for use as a beam because its wall thickness is so thin that it would be prone to local failure. The next lightest choice which passes the compactness criteria is a 2"x4"x0.109".

The last step in the process is to check for shear failure. Since the 2"x4"x0.109" passes the b/t compactness criteria, the allowable shear stress can be taken as $0.4F_y$, or 12.8 ksi for MT1010 tubing.

Since this beam is symmetrically loaded, the maximum vertical shear, V_{max}, is half the total load on the beam. Calculate the actual shear stress:

$$V_{max} = \frac{W}{2} = \frac{wl}{2} = \frac{(90\,plf)12'}{2} = 540\#$$

$$f_v = \frac{V_{max}}{d(2t_w)} = \frac{540\#}{(4")[2(0.109")]} = 619\,psi \Rightarrow 619\,psi \ll 12,800\,psi \checkmark$$

A 2"x4"x0.109" satisfies all the beam design tests. Be aware that other factors such as depth and availability may factor into the final beam choice.

Example 4. Imagine a suspended catwalk 14' long which has two speaker clusters hanging underneath it. The catwalk is 4' wide and the weight of the speakers can be considered to be 1' from each end and centered in the 4' direction. The proposed construction details call for one 4x14' platform with structural steel tube framing on 2' centers and a 3/4" plywood skin. The director has agreed to limit the number of people on the catwalk so a live load rating of 30 psf can be used. Each speaker cluster weighs 235 lbs. The catwalk is suspended and is braced from side to side. Design the interior framing member which spans 14' and has a tributary area of two square feet per linear foot of beam.

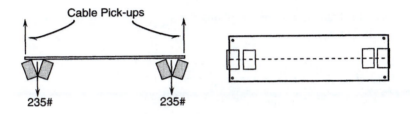

Figure 8.11 Example 4

First, determine the loading conditions and draw a free body diagram.

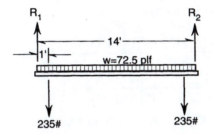

Figure 8.12 Example 4, free body diagram

Live load estimate:

live load = Area • Load Rating = $(2 \text{ ft}^2)(30 \text{ psf}) = 60$ plf

Dead load estimate:

3/4" plywood	(2.25 psf)(2 ft)	=4.5 plf
est beam weight		=8.0 plf
total dead load		=12.5 plf

Total load per foot on beam = 60 plf + 12.5 plf = **72.5 plf = 6.04 pli**

Next, use case formulas to solve for a minimum required value of *I* since both loading conditions are symmetrical.

$$I_{req'd} = \frac{wl^3}{9.28x10^6 \text{ psi}} + \frac{Pa(3l^2 - 4a^2)}{(2.9x10^6 \text{ psi})l}$$

$$I_{req'd} = \frac{(6.04 \text{ pli})(168")^3}{9.28x10^6 \text{ psi}} + \frac{235\#(12")\left[3(168")^2 - 4(12")^2\right]}{(2.9x10^6 \text{ psi})168"}$$

$$= 3.087 \text{ in}^4 + 0.487 \text{ in}^4 = 3.574 \text{ in}^4$$

Select possible choices from Appendix E:

	wt (plf)	act. t	I_{x-x} (in⁴)	S_{x-x} (in³)	b/t
3.5"x3.5"x3/16"	8.15	0.174"	4.05	2.31	20.1
4"x4"x1/8"	6.46	0.116"	4.40	2.20	34.5
4"x2"x3/16"	6.90	0.174"	3.66	1.83	23.0

Check for bending failure by solving for $S_{req'd}$. The F_b for structural tube is 27.6 ksi.

$$M_{max} = \frac{wl^2}{8} + Pa = \frac{(6.04 \text{ pli})(168")^2}{8} + (235\#)12"$$

$$= 24{,}129 \text{ inlb}$$

$$S_{req'd} = \frac{M_{max}}{F_b} = \frac{24{,}129 \text{ pli}}{27{,}600 \text{ psi}} = 0.874 \text{ in}^3$$

Check for shear failure (check the thinnest tube, 4"x4"x1/8"). The F_v for structural tube is 18.4 ksi.

$$V_{max} = \frac{W}{2} = \frac{(72.5 \text{ plf})14'+2(235\#)}{2} = 742.5\#$$

$$f_v = \frac{V_{max}}{d(2t_w)} = \frac{742.5\#}{(4")\left[2(0.116")\right]}$$

$$= 800 \text{ psi} \Rightarrow 800 \text{ psi} << 18.4 \text{ ksi } \checkmark$$

All of the possible choices easily meet the bending and shear requirements. If the weight is critical the 4"x4"x1/8" tube is a good choice; if the depth is critical, the 3.5" square tube also works but adds a lot of weight. Note that the most challenging aspect of this problem would be to design a safe connection between the bridge and the suspension points and between the beams and the "header" pieces at each end of the span.

Round Hollow Shapes

Bending Test

Like the rectilinear shapes discussed previously, round hollow shapes are all closed, symmetrical shapes. Consequently, the vast majority of them are compact. In order to simplify the calculations, all round hollow shapes must meet the following minimum compactness criteria to be considered as a valid beam choice (SCM, 5-36):

$$\frac{D}{t} \le \frac{3,300}{F_y}$$

where D is the diameter of the tube, in
                t is the wall thickness of the tube, in
                F_y is the yield strength, kips

For the common types of round tubes, the limiting ratios are as follows:

Type	Steel Grade (F_y)	D/t
Black pipe, Type F, Grade A (plumbing)	30 ksi	110
Black pipe, Type E&S, Grade B	35 ksi	94
Tubing, mechanical, MT1010	32 ksi	103.1
Tubing, structural, A500	46 ksi	71.1

These values for the limiting width to thickness ratios are repeated in a table at the beginning of Appendix E. For round shapes which meet the above criteria, the allowable bending stress, F_b, is $0.66F_y$. The actual bending stress, f_b, is calculated using the Flexure formula.

Shear Test

The allowable shear stress for hollow, round sections can be taken as $0.4F_y$. The actual stress is calculated using the general form of the shear equation:

$$f_v = \frac{VQ}{Ib}$$

where f_v is the actual unit shearing stress, psi
                V is the actual vertical shear, usually V_{max}, lb
                Q is the statical moment of area above or below the plane at which
                     the horizontal shear is being computed, in^3
                I is the Moment of Inertia, in^4
                b is the width of the shear plane, in

V_{max} is dependent on the loading conditions, b is double the wall thickness, and Appendix C lists the geometric properties (I and Q) for hollow circles and half circles. The following series of equations illustrates how to combine the geometric properties into one Q/I factor:

$$A_{hollow\ semicircle} = \frac{\pi(R^2 - r^2)}{2} \qquad Z_{hollow\ semicircle} = \frac{4(R^3 - r^3)}{3\pi(R^2 - r^2)}$$

$$Q_{hollow\ semicircle} = Az = \left[\frac{\pi(R^2 - r^2)}{2}\right]\left[\frac{4(R^3 - r^3)}{3\pi(R^2 - r^2)}\right] = \frac{2}{3}(R^3 - r^3)$$

$$I_{hollow\ circle} = \frac{\pi(D^4 - d^4)}{64} = \frac{\pi}{4}(R^4 - r^4)$$

$$\frac{Q}{I} = \frac{\frac{2}{3}(R^3 - r^3)}{\frac{\pi}{4}(R^4 - r^4)} = \left(\frac{8}{3\pi}\right)\left(\frac{R^3 - r^3}{R^4 - r^4}\right)$$

where R is the radius of the outside circle, in
         r is the radius of the inside circle, in
         A is the area of a hollow semicircle, in^2
         z is the distance from the neutral axis of the hollow circle to the neutral axis of the hollow semicircle, in
         D is the diameter of the outside circle, in
         d is the diameter of the inside circle, in

Therefore, for a hollow, round shape:

$$f_v = \frac{VQ}{Ib} = \frac{V}{b}\left[\left(\frac{8}{3\pi}\right)\frac{\left(R^3 - r^3\right)}{\left(R^4 - r^4\right)}\right]$$

Example 5. What is the maximum allowable load that a 1-1/2" Schedule 40 black pipe batten spanning 10' can support? Assume that the pipe is Type E, Grade B, and use a deflection criteria of $l/240$.

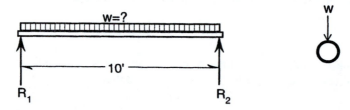

Figure 8.13 Example 5, free body diagram and cross-section orientation

First, collect the geometric properties. For a 1-1/2" Schedule 40 pipe:

$$I = 0.310 \text{ in}^4 \qquad S = 0.326 \text{ in}^3 \qquad wt = 2.72 \text{ plf}$$

Next, calculate the allowable load for deflection:

$$I_{req'd} = \frac{wl^3}{\left(9.28x10^6\,\text{psi}\right)}$$

$$w = \frac{I\left(9.28x10^6\,\text{psi}\right)}{l^3} = \frac{\left(0.310 \text{ in}^4\right)\left(9.28x10^6\,\text{psi}\right)}{\left(120"\right)^3} = 1.665 \text{ pli} \Rightarrow 19.97 \text{ plf}$$

Calculate the allowable load for bending. Since this is a Type E, Grade B batten, F_y is 35 ksi, and F_b is 23,100 psi.

$$M_{max} = F_b S = \frac{wl^2}{8}$$

$$w = \frac{8F_b S}{l^2} = \frac{8\left(23,100 \text{ psi}\right)\left(0.326 \text{ in}^3\right)}{\left(120"\right)^2} = 4.184 \text{ pli} \Rightarrow 50.2 \text{ plf}$$

Calculate the allowable load for shear. F_v for black pipe is 14 ksi.

$$f_v = \frac{V}{b}\left[\left(\frac{8}{3\pi}\right)\frac{\left(R^3 - r^3\right)}{\left(R^4 - r^4\right)}\right]$$

$$V_{all} = \frac{F_v b\left[3\pi\left(R^4 - r^4\right)\right]}{8\left(R^3 - r^3\right)} = \frac{(14{,}000 \text{ psi})\left[2(0.145")\right]\left[3\pi\left(0.95"^4 - 0.805"^4\right)\right]}{8\left(0.95"^3 - 0.805"^3\right)} = 5{,}621.6\#$$

$$W = 2V = 2(5{,}621.6\#) = 11{,}243.2\#$$

$$w = \frac{11{,}243.2\#}{10'} = 1{,}124 \text{ plf}$$

The 10' long, 1-1/2" batten can support an evenly distributed load of 50.2 plf without failure and a load of 19.97 plf based on a $l/240$ deflection criteria. To arrive at an allowable live load, the beam weight of 2.72 plf must be subtracted from the total allowable load. Therefore, a 1-1/2" 10' long batten can support a live load of 47.5 plf without failure and a 17.25 plf load based on a $l/240$ deflection criteria.

Several notes should be made about this example:

- Pipe battens are actually continuous beams. As discussed in Chapter 3, considering a batten to be a series of discrete 10' simple spans is a conservative approximation. An allowable load for a continuous beam can be calculated using the case formulas in Appendix B. For example, if the batten is taken as having three continuous spans, the allowable load for bending would be 62.8 plf.

- We ignored several potential weak links in the problem. For example, pipe battens often overhang at each end. If the overhang is loaded, the stresses in the batten change; there are no convenient rules of thumb for these situations – each case should be analyzed separately. In addition, we ignored the presence of joints between segments of the batten. The strength of the joint changes depending on the connection detail. A threaded pipe coupling is substantially weaker than a fully spliced joint. In general, pipe connections should be made near pick-up points if possible.

- An average leko (or ellipsoidal) instrument weighs between 12 and 20 lbs. After cabling, color, etc., an average weight of 25 to 30 lbs per linear foot on a batten is a reasonable estimate for design purposes. Hence, a batten loaded 18" on center would not exceed the bending allowable if it is supported every 10', but may exceed the deflection criteria depending upon the actual weight of the lighting units.

- Black pipe resists shear very effectively for the same reason that it is an inefficient beam: the majority of its material is concentrated around the shear plane (the neutral axis). Example 5 illustrates this with an allowable load based on shear stress of 1,124 plf.

Angles

Bending Test

Angle iron is perhaps the hardest category of steel shape to analyze for bending. The extremely open nature of the shape guarantees that all angles are non-compact. Consequently, the AISC includes a separate specification for angle iron entitled "Specification for Allowable Stress Design of Single-Angle Members" in Section 5 of the *SCM*.

Analyzing single-angle bending members is difficult because they are subject to failure by "lateral-torsional buckling" which complicates the process of determining F_b. The *SCM* provides a lengthy technique for calculating whether an angle iron beam will fail due to bending or lateral-torsional buckling. Instead of repeating the lengthy and complex specifications found in the *SCM* (5-311), the allowable bending stress, F_b, of each size of angle is listed in Appendix E. F_b was calculated using an F_y of 36 ksi because angles are usually made from A36 steel. The values of F_b listed in Appendix E also assume that the angle is adequately braced, which means that the compression flange of the angle is continuously supported. This would be the case when angle is used to frame flats or platforms with a skin or lid. Once F_b is determined, the Flexure Formula is used to test the beam for bending failure. It is important to note that the tabulated values of F_b were calculated using the techniques described in the *SCM*, but are not endorsed by any official or professional organization of engineers.

Shear Test

The shear test has also been simplified by listing a maximum allowable vertical shear for each angle shape in Appendix E. Since the general shear stress formula is dependent on section properties (I, Q, and b), the allowable maximum shear is different for the x-x and y-y axes of angles with unequal legs. With the help of the angle table, the shear test is a simple matter of comparing the actual shear, V_{max}, to the allowable vertical shear, V_{all}, listed.

> **Example 6.** Determine the allowable uniform load that a 2"x2"x1/8" angle iron beam spanning 8' can support. The beam is continuously supported as would be the case if it were a framing member for an 8' platform. Assume a deflection criteria of $l/240$.

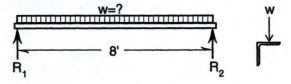

Figure 8.14 Example 6, free body diagram and orientation

From Appendix E:

$I = 0.19$ in⁴; $S = 0.131$ in³; $F_b = 19.68$ ksi; $V_{all} = 2.59$ kips; $wt=1.65$ plf

Calculate the allowable load for deflection:

$$\Delta_{max} = \frac{5wl^4}{384EI} \Rightarrow w_{all} = \frac{384EI\Delta_{all}}{5l^4}$$

$$w_{all} = \frac{384(2.9x10^7\ \text{psi})(0.19\ \text{in}^4)\left(\frac{96"}{240}\right)}{5(96")^4} = 1.99\ \text{pli} \Rightarrow 23.9\ \text{plf}$$

Calculate the allowable load for bending using the Flexure Formula:

$$M_{max} = F_b S = (19{,}680 \text{ psi})(0.131 \text{ in}^2) = 2{,}578 \text{ inlb}$$

$$w_{all} = \frac{8M_{max}}{l^2} = \frac{8(2{,}578 \text{ inlb})}{(96")^2} = 2.24 \text{ pli} \Rightarrow 26.9 \text{ plf}$$

Calculate the allowable load for shear:

$$V_{max} = \frac{wl}{2} \Rightarrow w_{all} = \frac{2V_{all}}{l} = \frac{2(2{,}590\#)}{8'} = 647.5 \text{ plf}$$

In this case, deflection is the ruling criteria, yielding an allowable load (including beam weight) of 23.9 plf or an allowable live load of 22.3 plf.

Example 7. Design an angle iron beam to meet the following loading conditions. Assume the angle iron is being used to support a platform which is continuously attached to the compression flange.

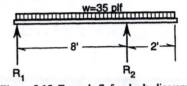

Figure 8.15 Example 7, free body diagram

First, calculate M_{max} using the case formula for a uniformly distributed load on a beam overhanging one support (Appendix B). Remember that two moments must be calculated to determine which is M_{max}.

$$M_1 = \frac{w}{8l^2}(l+a)^2(l-a)^2 = \frac{35 \text{ plf}}{8(8')^2}(10')^2(6')^2 = 246.09 \text{ ftlbs} \Rightarrow 2{,}953.12 \text{ inlbs}$$

$$M_2 = \frac{wa^2}{2} = \frac{(35 \text{ plf})(2')^2}{2} = 70 \text{ ftlbs} \Rightarrow 840 \text{ inlbs}$$

$$M_1 = M_{max} = 2{,}953.12 \text{ inlbs}$$

Next, calculate $I_{req'd}$ for deflection on the overhang and for the span.
Overhang:

$$I_{req'd} = \frac{w(4a^2l - l^3 + 3a^3)}{(2.9x10^6 \text{ psi})} = \frac{\left(\frac{35 \text{ plf}}{12}\right)\left[4(24")^2(96") - (96")^3 + 3(24")^3\right]}{(2.9x10^6 \text{ psi})} = -0.626 \text{ in}^4$$

Span:

$$x = \frac{l}{2}\left[1 - \frac{a^2}{l^2}\right] = \frac{96"}{2}\left[1 - \frac{(24")^2}{(96")^2}\right] = 45" \qquad I_{req'd} = \frac{wx(l^4 - 2l^2x^2 + lx^3 - 2a^2l^2 + 2a^2x^2)}{l^2(2.9x10^6 \text{ psi})}$$

$$= \frac{(2.92 \text{ pli})(45")\left[(96")^4 - 2(96")^2(45")^2 + (96")(45")^3 - 2(24")^2(96")^2 + 2(24")^2(45")^2\right]}{(96")^2(2.9x10^6 \text{ psi})}$$

$$= 0.236 \text{ in}^4$$

Select a section based on the $I_{req'd}$ for the overhang (because it is greater, though negative):

	I_{x-x} (in⁴)	S_{x-x} (in³)	F_b (psi)	$V_{all, x-x}$ (kips)	wt (plf)
2-1/2"x2"x1/4"	0.654	0.381	23.76	6.42	3.62
3"x2"x3/16"	0.842	0.415	19.68	5.88	3.07
3"x2-1/2"x3/16"	0.907	0.430	19.68	5.86	3.39

Confirm that the lightest angle iron, the 3"x2"x3/16", passes for bending and shear:

$$M_{max_{allow}} = F_b S = (19{,}680 \text{ psi})(0.415 \text{ in}^3) = 8{,}167.2 \text{ inlb} \Rightarrow 2{,}953.12 \text{ inlb} < 8{,}167.2 \text{ inlb} \checkmark$$

$$V_1 = \frac{w}{2l}(l^2 - a^2) = \frac{35 \text{ plf}}{2(8')}(8'^2 - 2'^2) = 131.25\# \quad V_2 = wa = (35 \text{ plf})2' = 70\#$$

$$V_{max} = V_3 = \frac{w}{2l}(l^2 + a^2) = \frac{35 \text{ plf}}{2(8')}(8'^2 + 2'^2) = 148.75\# \Rightarrow 148.75\# << 5{,}880\# \checkmark$$

Channels

Channels are open shapes, so lateral bracing is an important design criteria. An abridged version of the *SCM* dimension and properties tables for channels are listed in Appendix E. These tables have an unfamiliar variable, L_u. L_u is the maximum unbraced length, in feet, of the compression flange for which the allowable bending stress of the channel may be taken as $0.6F_y$. While it is possible to calculate the allowable bending stress for channels used in noncompact conditions, it is beyond the scope of this text. For our purposes, it is simplest to assume that the bracing requirement will always be met. If the bracing requirement is met, there is no limiting width to thickness ratio requirement.

Channel design can be done "by hand," using the techniques of finding an $I_{req'd}$ and an $S_{req'd}$ for a given loading condition. In these cases, $F_b = 0.6F_y$, and F_y for channels is 36 ksi (A36 steel).

The allowable shear, F_v, is $0.4F_y$. The actual shear is calculated by dividing the maximum vertical shear by the area of the web:

$$f_v = \frac{V}{A_{web}} = \frac{V}{dt_w}$$

where V is the maximum vertical shear, lbs
          d is the total depth of the beam, in
          t_w is the web thickness, in

The above techniques are valid as long as the beam is braced at L_u intervals.

Using the Allowable Load Tables

In Section 2, the *SCM* provides tables labeled *Channels, Allowable uniform loads in kips for beams laterally supported*. This table lists the channel size across the top and provides a maximum allowable evenly distributed load for a variety of spans. The loads are given in kips, and the spans and L_u are given in feet. Running parallel to the allowable loads is an actual deflection for that condition. The allowable load listed above the heavy line is ruled by the shear requirements, and is the same for all spans above the heavy line. Note that these tables are only applicable to evenly (or uniformly) distributed loads and that the load given is the total load, not the load per foot. All other loading conditions will require the "old-fashioned" techniques discussed previously.

> ***Example 8.*** Determine the maximum allowable point load for bending and shear of the C4x5.4 tested for deflection in Example 1. Remember that it is loaded against the weak axis.

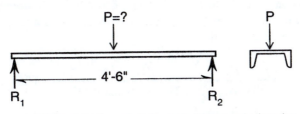

Figure 8.16 Example 8, free body diagram and orientation

Bending test: the span, l, is 54" and, from the charts in Appendix E, $S_{y\text{-}y} = 0.283$ in^3.

$$F_b = 0.6F_y = 0.6(36,000 \text{ psi}) = 21,600 \text{ psi}$$

$$M_{all} = F_b S = (21,600 \text{ psi})(0.283 \text{ in}^3) = 6,112.8 \text{ inlb}$$

For a point load,

$$M_{max} = \frac{Pl}{4} \Rightarrow P_{all} = \frac{4M_{max}}{l} = \frac{4(6,112.8 \text{ inlb})}{54"} = 452.8\#$$

Shear test: from the charts in Appendix E, we know that the average flange thickness, t_f, is 0.296". Unlike a channel oriented with the x-x axis resisting the load, the shear area of a channel oriented on its y-y axis is simply twice the flange thickness.

$$F_v = 0.4F_y = 0.4(36,000 \text{ psi}) = 14,400 \text{ psi}$$

$$f_v = \frac{V}{A} = \frac{V}{b_f 2t_f} \Rightarrow V_{all} = F_v(b_f 2t_f)$$

$$V_{all} = (14,400 \text{ psi})(4")(2)(0.296") = 34,099.2\#$$

Since the section is oriented with its y-y axis resisting the load, the lateral bracing requirement is met. The allowable load for deflection was 634.5 lbs as compared to the allowable load for bending of 452.8 lbs. Therefore, the bending test governs this example, which is unusual in steel beam design. Bending failure governs this loading condition because the span is relatively short and the channel is loaded against its weak axis. As usual, the allowable shear load is orders of magnitude more than the allowable bending and deflection loads.

Example 9. What is the lightest standard channel which can span 10' with an evenly distributed load of 0.5 kips/foot? Use a deflection criteria of $l/360$, and assume that the channel is braced continuously.

The total load on this beam is 5 kips, and the allowable deflection is 0.333". Using the *SCM*, we know that a C5x9 can support a total load of 5.1 kips, but it has a deflection of 0.45" at that load, so it is unacceptable.

Since deflection is likely to rule this loading condition, it would have been quicker to solve for an $I_{req'd}$ using the case formula for a simple span, uniformly distributed load:

$$I_{req'd} = \frac{5wl^4}{384E\Delta_{all}} = \frac{5\left(500 \text{ plf}\big/12 \text{ in}/\text{ft}\right)(120")^4}{384\left(2.9x10^7\text{psi}\right)0.333"} = 11.64 \text{ in}^4$$

A C6x8.2 can support 6.3 kips over 10' with a deflection 0.37", but that is for the full load of 6.3 kips, not 5 kips. Since it has an I_{x-x} of 13.1 in⁴, it meets the deflection criteria.

I-beams
Bending Test
I-beams must be designed in concert with the *SCM*. The AISC does most of the calculations necessary for the bending test for I-beams. In addition to the standard dimensions and properties charts, the *SCM* includes several styles of charts that allow the structural designer to simply "look-up" the appropriate beam. The calculations used to determine the allowable loads for I-beams are not complex; the charts simply save rote repetition. Like channels, it is possible to design I-beams "by hand" by determining $I_{req'd}$ and $S_{req'd}$. Also like channels, I-beams have flanges which make them susceptible to local buckling if they are not adequately braced.

A table in Section 2 of the *SCM* titled *Allowable uniform loads in kips for beams laterally supported, W, M, or S Shapes* defines the bracing requirements for I-beams. It is in the same format as the table which lists allowable loads for channels: the top of each page lists the shape(s) and depth designation(s), such as W44. Directly below this area, the beam designation, weight per foot, flange width, and allowable unbraced lengths are listed in rows. The rest of the table lists the span (ft), total allowable load (kips), and subsequent deflection (in) in columnar form. The following are important details to know when interpreting this and other tables:

- The tables assume that the shapes are oriented with the strong axis (*x-x*) resisting the load.
- L_c is the maximum unbraced length, in feet, of the compression flange at which the allowable bending stress may be taken at $0.66F_y$.

$l < L_c$	$F_b = 0.66F_y$
$L_c < l < L_u$	$F_b = 0.60F_y$
$l = L_u$	$F_b = 0.60F_y$

Figure 8.17 Values of F_b

- L_u is the maximum unbraced length, in feet, of the compression flange for which the allowable bending stress may be taken at $0.60F_y$.

- The allowable load is the total distributed load in kips on the beam and will be represented as W in the example problems.
- The tables assume that the span is simply supported.
- The allowable loads given are calculated assuming that the lateral bracing meets the L_c requirement. (If the bracing does not meet L_c, F_b must be recalculated.)
- Do not confuse the span with the unbraced length. The span is the total length of the beam from reaction to reaction, and the unbraced length is the distance between lateral supports.
- The first allowable load for every shape is above a "heavy line." As noted at the bottom of the table, the "load above heavy line is limited by maximum allowable web shear." Since shear stress is limited by cross-sectional area, not span, the allowable load is the same for all spans above the heavy line.
- Tables of steel shapes with an F_y of 50 ksi are indicated by pages marked in gray as well as a small box at the top of each table.

The bracing requirements expressed as L_c and L_u are very restrictive. Since theatrical conditions usually do not load I-beams to their full capacity, meeting the bracing requirements can lead to a beam which is grossly oversized. Fortunately, the AISC provides tables for the design of beams "with unbraced lengths greater than L_u" in Section 2 (*SCM*, 2-146). Explaining this table in depth would be repetitive, because the *SCM* provides a general notes section with all the necessary information. Example 11 demonstrates the use of this table.

The *SCM* lists many other charts that are worth exploring when performing extensive work with I-beams. Two handy tables are the *Allowable Stress Design Selection Table* which lists W, M and S shapes in order of section modulus (S_{x-x}) and the *Moment of Inertia Selection Table* which lists W and M shapes in order of both I_{x-x} and I_{y-y} (*SCM*, 2-13, 2-27).

Shear Test
The shear test for I-beams is much the same as that described for channels. In order for the allowable shear, F_v, to equal $0.4F_y$, the following must be true:

$$\frac{h}{t_w} \leq \frac{380}{\sqrt{F_y}} \Rightarrow \frac{h}{t_w} = \frac{380}{\sqrt{36 \text{ ksi}}} = 63$$

where h is the clear distance between flanges, in
             t_w is the thickness of the web, in
             F_y is the yield stress, ksi

All W, S, and HP flange beams meet this criteria. Some M shapes will not; for details on their design, see the *SCM*, Part 5, Section F4. If the shear load is less than 50% of 14,400 psi ($0.4F_y$) for a shape which does not meet this criteria, the additional steps described in Part 5, Section F4, of the *SCM* are probably unnecessary.

Once it is determined that the shape qualifies for an F_v of 14,400 psi, the actual shear stress is calculated using the same equation as that used for channels:

$$f_v = \frac{V_{max}}{A_{web}} = \frac{V_{max}}{dt_w}$$

where V_{max} is the maximum vertical shear, lbs
           d is the total depth of the beam, in
           t_w is the web thickness, in

Example 10. Design an S-shape beam to meet the following loading conditions. Assume that the lateral support will meet the L_u requirements for the selected beam.

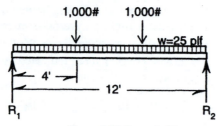

Figure 8.18 Example 10

The loading conditions are symmetrical. Therefore:

$$R_1 = R_2 = V_{max} = \frac{wl}{2} + P = \frac{(25 \text{ plf})12'}{2} + 1,000\# = 1,150\#$$

Bending test:
    Calculate M_{max} using the appropriate case formulas:

$$M_{max} = \frac{wl^2}{8} + Pa = \frac{(25 \text{ plf})(12')^2}{8} + 1,000\#(4') = 4,450 \text{ ftlb} \Rightarrow 53,400 \text{ inlb}$$

Calculate $S_{req'd}$ using the Flexure Formula. The F_b for A36 steel is 21.6 ksi.

$$S_{req'd} = \frac{M_{max}}{F_b} = \frac{53,400 \text{ inlb}}{21,600 \text{ psi}} = 2.47 \text{ in}^3$$

Deflection test:
    Use M_{max} to calculate an equivalent evenly distributed load, w:

$$w_{equiv} = \frac{8 M_{max}}{l^2} = \frac{8(53,400 \text{ inlb})}{(144")^2} = 20.6 \text{ pli}$$

Use w_{equiv} to solve for a minimum required I value:

$$I_{req'd} = \frac{wl^3}{9.28x10^6 \text{ psi}} = \frac{(20.6 \text{ pli})(144")^3}{9.28x10^6 \text{ psi}} = 6.628 \text{ in}^4$$

Select a beam which satisfies both $S_{req'd}$ and $I_{req'd}$.

S4x9.5: I_{x-x}=6.79 in⁴; S_{x-x}=3.39 in³; d=4"; t_w=0.326"; L_u=9.5'

Check to make sure that the choice passes for shear:

$$f_v = \frac{V_{max}}{dt_w} = \frac{1{,}150\#}{4"(0.326")} = 881.9 \text{ psi} \Rightarrow 881.9 \text{ psi} \ll 14{,}400 \text{ psi } \checkmark$$

Example 11. Design a W or M flange beam support structure for a trapped stage. Each trap is 3'x7' (see Figure 8.19 for a plan view). The primary beams span 12' (upstage to downstage) and are supported by columns at their ends. The secondary beams span 7' and need to be removable.

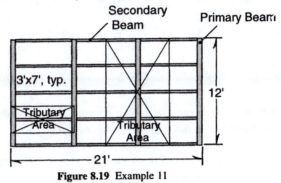

Figure 8.19 Example 11

Start with the secondary members.

7' span (secondary member):

First, determine the live and dead loads. Use a live load rating for the permanent stage floor of 150 psf. For every foot of beam, an internal secondary beam supports a 3' wide tributary area. Therefore:

The dead load has to be estimated:

live load = Area • Load Rating = (3 sf)(150 psf) = 450 plf

Traps	(3 ft)(6 psf)	= 18 plf
estimated weight of secondary beams		= 10 plf
	Total Dead Load	= 28 plf

Total load per foot on primary beams = 450 plf + 28 plf = 478 plf
Calculate the minimum required value of I:

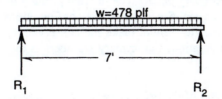

Figure 8.20 Example 11, free body diagram, secondary beam

Calculate the minimum required value of I:

$$w = 478 \text{ plf} \Rightarrow 39.83 \text{ pli}$$

$$I_{req'd} = \frac{wl^3}{9.28x10^6 \text{ psi}} = \frac{(39.83 \text{ pli})(84")^3}{9.28x10^6 \text{ psi}} = 2.54 \text{ in}^4$$

Select possible choices from the *Moment of Inertia Selection Table* (*SCM,* 2-27), determine L_u (for reference) from the *Allowable uniform loads* table (*SCM,* 2-72, 73, 75), and list a maximum moment for an unbraced length of 7' from the *Allowable Moments in Beams* table (*SCM,* 2-175).

	I (in^4)	L_u (ft)	M_{max} (kip-ft)
M6x4.4	7.20	2.4	N.A.
W4x13	11.3	15.6	10
W6x9	16.4	6.7	9.5
M8x6.5	18.5	2.5	NA
W6x12	22.1	8.6	13.25

The two M shapes are not applicable because the *Allowable Moments in Beams* table does not extend their load curve to 7'.

In order to determine if the remaining W shapes are good choices, the actual maximum moment is calculated and compared to the allowable (listed above):

$$M_{max_{actual}} = \frac{wl^2}{8} = \frac{(39.83 \text{ pli})(84")^2}{8} = 35,130 \text{ inlb} \Rightarrow 2.93 \text{ kip-ft}$$

Any of the W shapes listed above can satisfy both the deflection and bending requirements. A final choice informed by connection details will be made after a primary beam is selected. A shear test is unnecessary in this case because the full capacity of the beam is not being utilized.

12' span (primary beam):

The primary beams support the secondary beams. Therefore, at each connection, the internal primary beams are subject to a point load which equals the load on one of the secondary beams (or twice the reaction from each secondary beam). The internal primary beams will be the worst case scenario. Since the future configurations of the trapped stage are unknown, we will make the conservative assumption that the unbraced length of the primary members is the full span of 12' (not 3').

The loads at each end of the primary beams are disregarded for bending, so the internal primary beams have three point loads symmetrically placed as well as an evenly distributed load due to its own weight.

The loads generated by the end reactions of the secondary beams are also adjusted to reflect the actual weight of a W4x13, the heaviest of our secondary beam options:

$$W = (\text{tributary length, ft})(\text{weight on secondary beams, plf})$$

$$R_1 = R_2 = \frac{W}{2} = \frac{(7')(478 \text{ plf} + 3 \text{ plf})}{2} = 1,683.5\#$$

$$P = 2(1,683.5\#) = 3,367\# \text{ (each internal primary beam supports two reactions)}$$

The primary beam can be represented as follows:

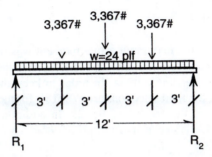

Figure 8.21 Example 11, free body diagram, primary member

Calculate the minimum required value of I. To do this, the actual M_{max} is calculated and an equivalent evenly distributed load is determined so that an $I_{req'd}$ for the entire loading condition can be calculated. Combine the moments for the three case formula conditions (M_{max} occurs in the center of the span for all three):

$$M_{max_{point}} = \frac{Pl}{4} = \frac{3,367\#(144")}{4} = 121,212 \text{ inlb}$$

$$M_{max_{sym}} = Pa = 3,367\#(36") = 121,212 \text{ inlb}$$

$$M_{max_{beam}} = \frac{wl^2}{8} = \frac{(2 \text{ pli})(144")^2}{8} = 5,184 \text{ inlb}$$

$$M_{max_{total}} = 2(121,212 \text{ inlb}) + 5,184 \text{ inlb} = 247,608 \text{ inlb} \Rightarrow 20.63 \text{ kip-ft}$$

Calculate an equivalent w:

$$w_{equiv} = \frac{8 M_{max}}{l^2} = \frac{8(247,608 \text{ inlb})}{(144")^2} = 95.5 \text{ pli}$$

Calculate $I_{req'd}$:

$$I_{req'd} = \frac{wl^3}{9.28x10^6 \text{ psi}} = \frac{(95.5 \text{ pli})(144")^3}{9.28x10^6 \text{ psi}} = 30.74 \text{ in}^4$$

Select possible choices from the *Moment of Inertia Selection Table*, determine L_u (for reference) from the *Allowable uniform loads* table, and list a maximum moment for an unbraced length of 12' from the *Allowable Moments in Beams* table.

	I (in⁴)	L_u(ft)	M_{max} (kip-ft)
W6x16	32.1	12.0	18.75
M10x7.5	32.8	2.7	NA
M10x9	38.8	2.7	NA
W6x20	41.4	16.4	24.5
W8x15	48.0	7.2	12.75
W8x18	61.9	9.9	22.5

In order to find $I_{req'd}$, the maximum actual moment was determined to be 20.63 kip-ft. Therefore, the W8x18 and W6x20 shapes both meet the deflection and bending criteria. In order to keep the weight of the system down, the final selections are W8x18's for the primary beams and W6x9's for the secondary beams. In addition, the secondary beams will nicely sleeve into the primary beams (see Figure 8.22 below).

As a final check, the shear failure of the primary beam (W8x18) should be tested:

$$F_v = 0.4 F_y = 0.4(36,000 \text{ psi}) = 14,400 \text{ psi}$$

$$V_{max} = \frac{W}{2} = \frac{3(3,367\#) + 12'(18 \text{ plf})}{2} = 5,158.5\#$$

$$f_v = \frac{V_{max}}{dt_w} = \frac{5,158.5\#}{8.14''(0.230)} = 2,755 \text{ psi} \Rightarrow 2,755 \text{ psi} \ll 14,400 \text{ psi} \checkmark$$

The connection details between I-beams are very important (see the *SCM*). The following picture illustrates a possible connection detail for this trap room:

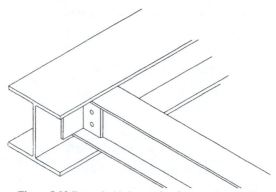

Figure 8.22 Example 11, isometric of connection detail

STEPS IN STEEL BEAM DESIGN

The following flow chart summarizes the beam design process for all steel shapes.

Analyze the loading conditions and determine V_{max}, M_{max}, Δ_{max} ($l/240$), and $I_{req'd}$.

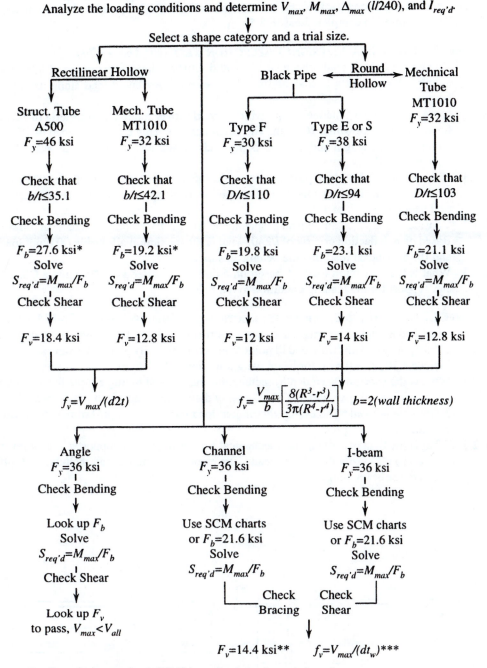

* F_b can be increased to $0.66F_y$ if the section is continuously braced or square.

**   Some M shapes will have a lower F_v value.

***   For channels loaded against the y-y axis, $f_v = b_f 2t_f$

Figure 8.23 Steel beam design flow chart

CHAPTER 8 LESSONS

The format of the numbering system is: chapter.lesson.problem number.
Assume normal adjustment factors and a deflection criteria of $l/240$ unless otherwise noted.
The *SCM* is required to complete Lesson 8.5.

LESSON 8.1 STEEL BEAM DESIGN: DEFLECTION TEST (PG 165 – 174)

8.1.1   Choose the lightest angle shape which would satisfy a deflection criteria of $l/240$ for a simple beam with a 6' span and a 110 plf evenly distributed load along its entire length.

8.1.2   Choose the lightest channel shape which would satisfy a deflection criteria of $l/240$ for a simple beam with a 20' span. The beam has an evenly distributed load of 75 plf along its entire length and has two point loads of 400 lbs, symmetrically placed, 5' from each end.

8.1.3   Choose the lightest black pipe which would satisfy a deflection criteria of $l/240$ for a beam with the loading condition given below. Hint: approximate the actual deflection using a span, l, of 10'.

8.1.4   Consider a simple beam with an 8' span made from 1"x3"x0.083" mechanical tubing. Based on a deflection criteria of $l/240$, what is the maximum allowable (a) point load and (b) distributed load that the beam can support?

8.1.5   What is the maximum load, P, based on a deflection criteria of $l/240$ that a C3x4.1 can support for the loading condition given below?

LESSON 8.2 BENDING AND SHEAR TESTS: RECTILINEAR HOLLOW SHAPES (PG 174 – 178)

8.2.1   What is the lightest rectangular or square structural tubing beam that can support a 15' simple span with two 1,000 lb point loads symmetrically placed 5' from each end? Include a 10 plf estimate for beam weight in your calculations.

8.2.2   What is the shortest (least depth) rectangular mechanical tubing simple beam which can support a 12' span with a 210 plf evenly distributed load and a 250 lb point load 3' from the left end? The evenly distributed load includes a 10 plf estimate for beam weight.

8.2.3   What is the lightest rectangular mechanical tubing which can support a 4' cantilever with a 110 plf evenly distributed load? The evenly distributed load includes a 10 plf estimate for beam weight.

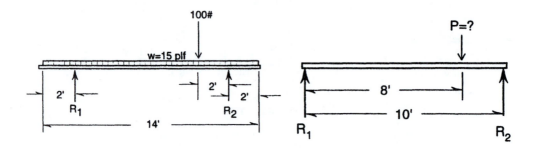

Problem 8.1.3   Problem 8.1.5

LESSON 8.3 BENDING AND SHEAR TESTS: ROUND HOLLOW SHAPES (PG 178 – 181)

8.3.1   What is the least diameter black pipe (Type E, Grade B) and mechanical tube (MT1010) that can support a 12' simple span with a 24 plf evenly distributed load? The evenly distributed load includes a 4 plf estimate for beam weight.

8.3.2   What is the lightest round mechanical tube which can support an 8' simple span with two 300 lb point loads symmetrically placed 1' from each end? Include a 5 plf estimate for beam weight.

8.3.3   What is the lightest black pipe (Type F, Grade A) which can support a 14' simple span with a 500 lb point load in the center of the span? Include a 10 plf estimate for beam weight.

LESSON 8.4 BENDING AND SHEAR TESTS: ANGLES, CHANNELS (PG 182 – 186)

8.4.1   What is the lightest angle iron which can support a 14' simple span with a 110 plf evenly distributed load and a 200 lb point load 4' from the right end? A 10 plf estimate for beam weight is included in the evenly distributed load.

8.4.2   What is the lightest angle iron beam which can support a 4' simple span with a 205 plf evenly distributed load and a 150 lb point load in the center of the span?

8.4.3   What is the lightest standard channel beam which can support the loading conditions given below? Assume that the channel is braced to meet the L_u requirement.

LESSON 8.5 BENDING AND SHEAR TESTS: I-BEAMS (PG 186 – 193)

8.5.1   What is the lightest W shape beam which can support the loading condition given below? A 24 plf beam weight estimate is included in the loading conditions. Assume that the beam is braced to meet the L_u requirement.

8.5.2   What is the lightest S shape beam which can support a 6' cantilever with a 15 plf evenly distributed load and a 200 lb point load at the cantilevered end of the beam? Assume that the beam is braced to meet the L_u requirement.

8.5.3   Design a W shape beam support structure for a trapped stage with a live load rating of 150 psf. Each trap is 4'x8' and rests on secondary beams which are in turn supported by 16' primary beams. The primary beams are supported by the walls of the traproom. All of the beams are removable. Use 8 psf as the weight of the traps, a 15 plf estimated weight for the secondary beams, and a 30 plf estimated weight for the primary beams. See the illustration below.

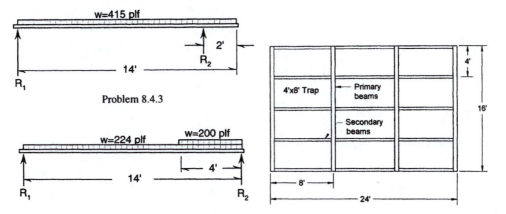

Problem 8.4.3

Problem 8.5.1

Problem 8.5.3

9

Steel Column Analysis and Design

INTRODUCTION

The fundamental theories of column design were discussed in the introduction to Chapter 6, Wood Column Analysis and Design. Regardless of the material from which a column is made, the actual compressive stress must be less than the allowable compressive stress. Unlike steel beam design, the basic approach to column design remains constant for most shapes. The exception is single-angle members, whose allowable compressive stress must be reduced to account for "local buckling" characteristics. This chapter will therefore describe the essentials of column design, and then the design of single-angle columns.

SLENDERNESS RATIO CRITERIA FOR STEEL COLUMNS

Although columns are usually vertical, the following techniques apply to any member which resists axial compressive loads only. A column can fail due to crushing and/or buckling depending on the slenderness ratio between its unbraced length and its least radius of gyration. For steel, the slenderness ratio is expressed as the following:

$$\text{slenderness ratio} = \frac{Kl}{r} \leq 200$$

where K is the effective length factor (see Chapter 6)
l is the unbraced length, in
r is the radius of gyration, in

The AISC applies the same general guidelines for determining K as those covered in Chapter 6. For most of our applications, a K value of 1 is used, which assumes that the column has simple pin connections at both ends. As the fixity of the end connections increases, K decreases. As the fixity of the end connections decreases, K increases, culminating in a value of 2.4 for flagpole type applications.

The AISC recommends that "the slenderness ratio, Kl/r preferably should not exceed 200." (*SCM*, 5-37) This Kl/r criteria is slightly higher than the limit of 173 endorsed in the *NDS* for wood. The homogeneity and, therefore, the predictability of steel columns enables the AISC to allow the use of more slender columns.

DETERMINING ALLOWABLE COMPRESSIVE STRESS, F_a

ALLOWABLE STRESS EQUATIONS

If the empirical data on steel column stress versus slenderness ratio were plotted, the result would be the bold curve in Figure 9.1. The lower curve describes the allowable steel column stress as mandated by the AISC. The curve of allowable stress mirrors but stays proportionally below the curve for empirical failure.

The curve, or function, for column failure cannot be adequately described by a single equation. Consequently, the AISC uses two equations to calculate the allowable stress curve. These equations are expressed as the following (*SCM*, 5-42):

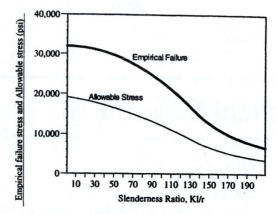

Figure 9.1 Empirical and allowable stress curves, F_y=32 ksi

When Kl/r is less than C_c, the allowable compressive stress is calculated using the first equation.

$$\text{Equation 1} \qquad F_a = \frac{\left[1 - \dfrac{(Kl/r)^2}{2C_c^2}\right]F_y}{\dfrac{5}{3} + \dfrac{3(Kl/r)}{8C_c} - \dfrac{(Kl/r)^3}{8C_c^3}}$$

$$\text{where} \qquad C_c = \sqrt{\frac{2\pi^2 E}{F_y}}$$

When Kl/r exceeds C_c, the allowable compressive stress is calculated using the second equation.

$$\text{Equation 2} \qquad F_a = \frac{12\pi^2 E}{23(Kl/r)^2}$$

The numerator of Equation 1 represents the empirical behavior of steel columns. The denominator is a variable safety factor which equals 1.67 for a Kl/r of 1 to 1.92 for a Kl/r of C_c or higher (Fitzgerald, 282). Equation 2 is the classic Euler buckling equation with a safety factor of 23/12 (or 1.92) in the denominator. C_c represents the intersection of the two functions. Figure 9.2 shows how the allowable curve is formed by the first and second equations.

The need for two distinct equations is made obvious by the extremely high values for the Euler buckling equation when the slenderness ratio is less than C_c. For a Kl/r of 1, the allowable Euler buckling stress would be about 150 million psi. In other words, the column would crush well before it would fail by buckling.

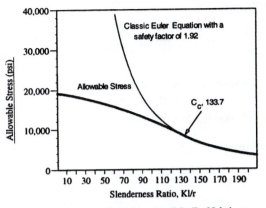

Figure 9.2 Equations 1 and 2, F_y=32 ksi

The C_c values for the most common grades of steel are as follows:

$$C_c = \sqrt{\frac{2\pi^2 E}{F_y}} = \sqrt{\frac{2\pi^2 \left(2.9 \times 10^7 \text{ psi}\right)}{30,000 \text{ psi}}} = 138.1 \text{ for } F_y \text{ of 30 ksi}$$

$C_c = 133.7$ for F_y of 32 ksi

$C_c = 126.1$ for F_y of 36 ksi

$C_c = 111.6$ for F_y of 46 ksi

In sum, columns with a slenderness ratio less than C_c fail due to crushing or a combination of crushing and buckling, and the allowable stress is calculated using the first equation. Columns with a slenderness ratio greater than C_c fail due to buckling and the allowable stress is calculated using Euler's equation.

It is important to remember that a column can have more than one slenderness ratio. Any shape may have one to three distinct radii of gyration, $r_{x\text{-}x}$, $r_{y\text{-}y}$, and $r_{z\text{-}z}$, each with unique unbraced lengths. The largest effective slenderness ratio (Kl/r) for a given section is used to determine the allowable compressive stress.

NON-SLENDER CRITERIA

In addition to the unbraced length of the column, the allowable compressive stress of a column, F_a, is also dependent on whether its cross-sectional shape is considered **slender** or **non-slender**. If a shape is considered slender, the allowable compressive stress is reduced. This criteria is identical to the compactness requirements for steel beams, and should not be confused with the slenderness ratio (Kl/r). Fortunately, the majority of steel sections used in theatrical column design are non-slender, including all black pipes and all structural tubes 6"x6" or smaller. If a shape is slender, it is simplest to choose another section. This text will not include the design of slender shapes used as columns, but the procedures can be found in Appendix B of Section 5 in the *SCM*.

The criteria for determining if a shape is slender or non-slender are expressed as "limiting width-thickness ratios" and are listed in Table B5.1 in the *SCM* (*SCM*, 5-36). To use the full value of F_a for a given slenderness ratio (Kl/r), the following criteria must be met:

- Rectilinear hollow sections:

$$\frac{b}{t} < \frac{238}{\sqrt{F_y}}$$

where b is the length of the longest side, in
         t is the wall thickness, in
         F_y is the yield stress, ksi

- Round hollow sections:

$$\frac{D}{t} < \frac{3,300}{F_y}$$

where D is the diameter, in
         t is the wall thickness, in
         F_y is the yield stress, ksi

- For channels, the web and flanges must meet separate criteria:

Web   Flanges

$$\frac{b}{t} < \frac{253}{\sqrt{F_y}} \qquad\qquad \frac{b}{t} < \frac{95}{\sqrt{F_y/k_c}}$$

where b is the height of the web or the depth of the flanges, in
         t is the thickness of the web or the flanges, in
         $k_c = 1$ for theatrical applications (*SCM*, 5-36)
         F_y is the yield stress, ksi

The above requirements may seem bewildering at first, but they have been resolved into the chart labeled "Limiting Width-Thickness Ratios for Beams and Columns" in Appendix E. All I-beams are non-slender, and thus have no criteria for use as columns. The ratio listed for I-beams in Appendix E is applicable for beams, not columns. Angles are not included because they require an entirely separate analysis (see single angle columns in this chapter).

FINDING F_a

The *SCM* provides a table in Section 3 listing the F_a values for slenderness ratios between 1 and 200 for steel with a F_y of 36 ksi that is titled *Table C-36, Allowable Stress For Compression Members of 36-ksi Specified Yield Stress Steel*. For convenience, we have provided tables listing F_a for the most common steel grades with F_y's of 30, 32, 36, 38, and 46 ksi in Appendix E. These tables are not sanctioned by any official organization. Both our tables and the *SCM* tables assume that the section being analyzed qualifies as non-slender. Though black pipe, Type E or S, has an F_y of 35 ksi, the AISC recommends that the F_a values from the table for A36 steel be used (*SCM*, 3-35). When in doubt about the grade of a pipe, assume the weaker Type F pipe with an F_y of 30 ksi.

Slenderness ratios are usually decimal numbers which should be rounded up to the next integer for both safety and convenience. For example, a column with a Kl/r value of 121.2

should be analyzed using the F_a for a slenderness ratio of 122, not 121. Remember that the allowable F_a increases as the slenderness ratio decreases.

The *SCM* also lists allowable column load tables for I-beams, tees, double-angles, and hollow shapes in Section 3. These tables are handy for repetitive structural design work.

> ***Example 1.*** What is the maximum unbraced length for a column made from a 4"x0.109" square mechanical tube (MT1010)? Assume $K=1.0$.

First, gather data for the 4"x0.109" tube:

$$F_y = 32 \text{ ksi}; \quad r = 1.5793"; \quad b/t = 36.7 \checkmark$$

Next, calculate the maximum allowable unbraced length:

$$\frac{Kl}{r} \leq 200 \Rightarrow l_{max} = \frac{200r}{K} = \frac{200(1.5793")}{1} = 315.86" \Rightarrow 26.3'$$

> ***Example 2.*** What is the allowable compressive stress, F_a, for a 4"x0.109" square mechanical tube (MT1010) with an unbraced length of 20'? Assume $K=1.0$.

Determine the slenderness ratio and look up the appropriate value of F_a in Appendix E.

$$\frac{Kl}{r} = \frac{1(12 \text{ in / ft})(20')}{1.5793"} = 151.97 \Rightarrow 152$$

$$F_{a_{152}} = 6{,}460 \text{ psi}$$

DETERMINING THE ALLOWABLE LOAD, P_{all}

The allowable compressive load, P_{all}, for steel columns is calculated using the Direct Stress Formula.

$$P_{all} = F_a A$$

where P_{all} is the allowable compressive load, lb
            F_a is the allowable compressive stress, psi
            A is the cross-sectional area of the column, in²

The allowable load is then compared to the actual. If the allowable load is larger, the chosen section is an acceptable column for the given loading condition.

STEPS IN STEEL COLUMN DESIGN

The typical steps in the design of steel columns are as follows:

> A.   Determine the loading conditions, P, and the unbraced length(s), l, for each axis.

B.   Calculate the minimum required radius of gyration to meet the slenderness ratio criteria of 200.

C.   Choose a section to test which meets both the slenderness ratio requirement and the non-slender criteria.

D.   Determine F_a, based on the slenderness ratio for the chosen section in Step C.

E.   Calculate the allowable load, P_{all}, with the direct stress formula and compare it to the actual load. If P_{all} is greater, the chosen section is an adequate column.

Example 3.   A set designer has designed a platform with stairs on either side which is framed with steel and surfaced with metal grating (see Figure 9.3). The designer wants to know the minimum possible dimension of the four black pipe columns which support the 5'x7' platform. Use Schedule 40 Type E or S pipe.

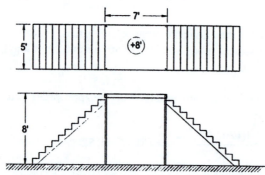

Figure 9.3a Front elevation and plan views of Example 3

First, determine the loading conditions. We will estimate the dead weight of the center platform and each stair unit to be 800 lbs. One half of the weight of each stair unit (400 lbs) will be supported by the stage floor. Therefore, each leg must support 400 lbs of dead weight:

$$P_{dead} = \frac{P_{platform} + 2(P_{stairs})}{4 \text{ columns}} = \frac{800\# + 2(400\#)}{4} = 400\#$$

The dead weight of the platform and stair units should be examined more closely after actual construction choices are made. If the actual dead load exceeds the estimates, the design process should be reviewed.

The director hasn't blocked the show yet, but we know that it is a musical with a cast of 15. For what we believe to be a worst case scenario, we will assume that all fifteen actors will be dancing on the unit at once. A believable scenario could have 5 actors on the center platform, and 5 on each stair unit. Of the ten actors on the two stair units, 5 will be directly supported by the stage floor. Therefore, each pipe column supports 1/4 of the weight of 10 actors. We will estimate that the actors average a heavy 200 pounds each, and, since they are dancing, we will double their weight to account for the dynamic loading condition. Therefore, each column supports 1,000 lbs of live load.

$$P_{live} = \frac{2[10(200\#)]}{4} = 1,000\#$$

$$P_{tot} = P_{live} + P_{dead} = 1,000\# + 400\# = 1,400\#$$

Figure 9.3b Example 3

Next, calculate the minimum required r to meet the slenderness ratio criteria of 200. There is no intermediate bracing, so l is 8' or 96", and we will assume that K is 1.0.

$$\frac{Kl}{r} = 200 \Rightarrow r_{min} = \frac{Kl}{200} = \frac{1(96")}{200} = 0.48"$$

1-1/4" Schedule 40 black pipe, with an r value of 0.54", is the smallest diameter which meets r_{min}.

Remember that all black pipe qualifies as non-slender, so no check is necessary. Determine the allowable compressive stress for a 1-1/4" pipe using the F_a chart for an F_y of 36 ksi.

$$\frac{Kl}{r} = \frac{1(96")}{0.54"} = 177.78 \Rightarrow 178$$
$$F_{a_{178}} = 4.71 \text{ ksi} = 4,710 \text{ psi}$$

Finally, calculate the total allowable load.

$$P_{all} = AF_a = (0.669 \text{ in}^2)(4,710 \text{ psi}) = 3,151\# \Rightarrow 3,151\# > 1,400\#$$

The given loading condition is obviously well within the range of the 1-1/4" pipe. In scenery applications, the slenderness ratio requirement is often the governing factor.

The design process is different when one is simply determining the capacity of a given column. Example 4 illustrates this technique.

Example 4. What is the maximum allowable compressive load, P_{all}, on a 1-1/2"x3-1/2"x0.109" mechanical tube (MT1010) with an unbraced length of 6' for both axes? Assume $K = 1.0$.

Look up the geometric properties in Appendix E:

$$r_{x-x} = 1.2207"; \quad r_{y-y} = 0.6262"; \quad A = 1.022 \text{ in}^2; \quad b/t = 32.1 \checkmark$$

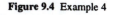

Figure 9.4 Example 4

The section qualifies as non-slender because its b/t is less than 42.1.

Determine the slenderness ratio and look-up the appropriate value of F_a in
Appendix E.

$$\frac{Kl}{r_{y-y}} = \frac{1(72")}{0.6262"} = 114.98 \Rightarrow 115$$

$$F_{a_{115}} = 10,560 \text{ psi}$$

Use the Direct Stress Formula to find the allowable compressive load.

$$P_{all} = AF_a = (1.022 \text{ in}^2)(10,560 \text{ psi}) \Rightarrow 10,792\#$$

This mechanical tube steel column has the same actual dimensions as a
nominal wood 2x4. It is informative to compare this answer to the
allowable compressive load calculated for the 6' tall 2x4 wood column in Example 1 of Chapter 6.

	2x4, wood	1-1/2"x3-1/2"x0.109"
Area	5.25 in²	1.022 in²
Weight	1.28 plf	3.4743 plf
P_{all}	779.7 lb	10,795 lb

SINGLE ANGLE COLUMNS

The calculations for determining the allowable axial stress for single angle columns are
based upon Equations 1 and 2 given at the beginning of this chapter. An additional reduction factor, Q, is applied to equation 1 and the C_c equation. The value of Q depends upon the
degree of compactness of the angle iron (SCM, 5-510):

when $\quad Kl/r < C_c'$

$$F_a = \frac{Q\left[1 - \frac{(Kl/r)^2}{2C_c'^2}\right]F_y}{\frac{5}{3} + \frac{3(Kl/r)}{8C_c'} - \frac{(Kl/r)^3}{8C_c'^3}}$$

where $\quad C_c' = \sqrt{\frac{2\pi^2 E}{QF_y}}$

when $\quad Kl/r > C_c' \quad F_a = \frac{12\pi^2 E}{23(Kl/r)^2}$

For convenience, we have calculated Q and C_c' for every structural angle iron shape of A36
steel and tabulated them in the tables for angles in Appendix E.

Obviously, the calculations for determining F_a for single angle columns is laborious, but many steps are often unnecessary: if the slenderness ratio is greater than C_c', then the original tables for F_a can be used. In addition, if Q equals 1, the original tables for F_a can be used for all slenderness ratios.

1,000#

Example 5. Select the smallest angle iron section which can support a 1,000 lb load with an unbraced length of 4'. Limit your selection to angles with a Kl/r value over C_c' or a Q factor of 1.

First, calculate the minimum required r:

$$r_{min} = \frac{Kl}{200} = \frac{1(48")}{200} = 0.24"$$

Figure 9.5 Example 5

Choose a trial section. Remember that $r_{z\text{-}z}$ will always be the least r value for angle iron. A 1-1/4"x1-1/4"x3/16"angle iron with a $r_{z\text{-}z}=0.244"$ is the smallest section which exceeds r_{min}, and its Q equals 1.

Next, determine F_a:

$$\frac{Kl}{r} = \frac{1(48")}{0.244"} = 196.72 \Rightarrow 197$$
$$F_{a_{197}} = 3.85 \text{ ksi} = 3,850 \text{ psi}$$

Finally, calculate P_{all}:

$$P_{all} = AF_a = (0.434 \text{ in}^2)(3,850 \text{ psi}) = 1,670.9\# \Rightarrow 1,670.9\# > 1,000\# \checkmark$$

Therefore, a 1-1/4"x1-1/4"x3/16" angle iron is adequate for this loading condition. Once again, the slenderness ratio criteria governed this loading condition.

Example 6. What is the maximum load that a 2"x2"x1/8" angle iron can support with an unbraced length of 4'-3"? Assume K is 1.0.

P

Look up the geometric properties for a 2"x2"x1/8" angle iron.

$$r_{z\text{-}z}=0.398"; \quad Q=0.911; \quad C_c'=132.12; \quad A=0.484 \text{ in}^2$$

Calculate the slenderness ratio:

$$\frac{Kl}{r} = \frac{1(51")}{0.398"} = 128.1$$

4'-3"

Figure 9.6 Example 6

Calculate F_a. Since 128.1<132.12 (C_c'), the first equation is used.

$$F_a = \frac{Q\left[1 - \dfrac{(Kl/r)^2}{2C_c'^2}\right]F_y}{\dfrac{5}{3} + \dfrac{3(Kl/r)}{8C_c'} - \dfrac{(Kl/r)^3}{8C_c'^3}} = \frac{0.911\left[1 - \dfrac{(128.1)^2}{2(132.12)^2}\right]36,000 \text{ psi}}{\dfrac{5}{3} + \dfrac{3(128.1)}{8(132.12)} - \dfrac{(128.1)^3}{8(132.12)^3}}$$

$$F_a = \frac{17,370.9}{1.916} = 9,064.7 \text{ psi}$$

Finally, calculate the allowable compressive load:

$$P_{all} = AF_a = \left(0.484 \text{ in}^2\right)(9,065 \text{ psi}) = 4,387.3\#$$

- It should be noted that the allowable compressive load is only about 50 pounds less than the allowable load for a non-slender column with a Kl/r of 128. It may be useful to use the full value of F_a to find a section which is in the right ballpark. Once a choice has been made, the reduced value of F_a for that angle iron can be calculated and used to find the allowable load.

- Remember that this problem assumes that the load is perfectly axial. Most loading conditions on angle iron columns are not centered directly over the axis of the column. In actual construction details, it seems unlikely that a 2"x2"x1/8" angle should be chosen to support over 2 tons.

- Having pinned connections at the top and bottom of a column allows us to assume that K equals 1.0. It should be noted that the legs of platforms or decks are often not anchored to the floor. In this case, the assumption that K equals 1.0 would be incorrect.

CHAPTER 9 LESSONS

The format of the numbering system is: chapter.lesson.problem number.
Assume $K=1.0$ unless otherwise noted.

LESSON 9.1 SLENDERNESS RATIO, DETERMINING F_a (PG 197 – 201)

9.1.1   What is the maximum allowable unbraced length of a column made from 1-1/2"
schedule 40 black pipe (Type E, Grade B)?

9.1.2   What is the maximum allowable unbraced length of a column made from
1.0"x3.0"x0.165" mechanical tube (MT1010)?

9.1.3   What is the maximum allowable unbraced length of a C3x4.1 column?

9.1.4   What is the maximum allowable unbraced length of a column made from a 5"x0.049"
round mechanical tube (MT1010)?

9.1.5   What is the allowable compressive stress, F_a, for a 1.5"x0.065" round mechanical
tube (MT1010) column with an unbraced length of 8'?

9.1.6   What is F_a for a 2"x3/16" square structural tube column with an unbraced length of
4'?

9.1.7   What is F_a for a W6x9 column with an unbraced length of 12'?

9.1.8   What is F_a for a C4x7.25 column with an unbraced length of 10'?

LESSON 9.2 DETERMINING P_{all}, STEEL COLUMN DESIGN (PG 201 – 204)

9.2.1   What is the maximum allowable capacity that a 5"x0.065" round mechanical tube
(MT 1010) can support with an unbraced length of 24'?

9.2.2   What is the maximum allowable capacity that a 1-1/2" schedule 40 black pipe (Type
E, Grade B) can support with an unbraced length of 10'?

9.2.3   Compare the maximum allowable capacities of a C4x7.25 and a C4x5.4 used as
columns with an unbraced length of 7'.

9.2.4   What is the maximum allowable capacity that a W4x13 can support with an unbraced
length of 14'?

9.2.5   A 1"x3"x0.083" mechanical tube (MT1010) column has an unbraced length of 7' and
a load of 2,500 lbs. Is this an appropriate choice?

9.2.6   Choose the smallest structural tube appropriate for the loading conditions given
below.

9.2.7   Choose the lightest channel appropriate for the loading conditions given below.

9.2.8   Choose the lightest round mechanical tube (MT 1010) column which can support a
load of 600 lbs with an unbraced length of 3'.

9.2.9   A column with an unbraced length of 9' supports a tributary area of 32 sf which is
loaded at 50 psf. Choose an appropriate square mechanical tube (MT1010) member.

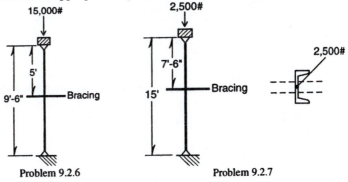

Problem 9.2.6   Problem 9.2.7

LESSON 9.3 SINGLE ANGLE COLUMNS (PG 204 – 206)

9.3.1   What is the maximum allowable capacity that an L3x2x1/4" column can support with an unbraced length of 7'?

9.3.2   What is the maximum allowable capacity that an L4x4x1/4" column can support with an unbraced length of 15'?

9.3.3   What is the maximum allowable capacity that an L1x1x1/8" column can support with an unbraced length of 3'?

9.3.4   Choose the lightest angle iron column which can support 1,000 lbs with an unbraced length of 12'.

9.3.5   Choose the lightest angle iron column which can support 2,000 lbs with an unbraced length of 10'.

9.3.6   Choose the lightest angle iron column which can support 750 lbs with an unbraced length of 8'.

9.3.7   Choose the lightest angle iron column which can support 500 lbs with an unbraced length of 6'.

10

Combined Loading for Steel Members

INTRODUCTION

As discussed in Chapter 7, beams and columns may be subject to combined loading conditions. A given loading condition may cause bending, compression, or tension or any combination of the three. In these cases, the AISC recommends various interaction equations which are based on exactly the same precepts as the equations recommended by the *NDS* for sawn lumber members; the sum of the ratios of actual to allowable stress for each type of stress must be less than or equal to 1.0 to insure that the total capacity of the beam is not exceeded:

$$\frac{f_a}{F_a} + \frac{f_{bx}}{F_{bx}} + \frac{f_{by}}{F_{by}} + \frac{f_t}{F_t} \leq 1.0$$

For the sake of simplicity, we will not discuss every possible permutation of combined loading, but instead will limit our examination to common situations. Therefore, five types of combined loading conditions will be discussed: single axis bending and axial tension, single axis bending and axial compression, eccentric loading, biaxial bending, and biaxial bending and axial compression. The techniques described "pertain to doubly and singly symmetrical members only" (*SCM*, 5-54). This caveat excludes single-angle members used in combined loading conditions, the design of which is beyond the scope of this text. However, every other shape category introduced in Chapter 8 meets this criteria.

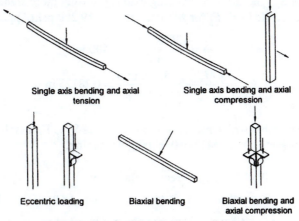

Figure 10.1 Combined loading conditions

SINGLE AXIS BENDING AND AXIAL TENSION

Members subject to both axial tension and bending in one axis must satisfy the following equation (*SCM*, 5-55):

$$\frac{f_a}{F_t} + \frac{f_b}{F_b} \leq 1.0$$

where f_a is the actual axial tensile stress, psi
         F_t is the allowable tensile stress, psi
         f_b is the actual bending stress, psi
         F_b is the allowable bending stress, psi

Do not be confused by the use of "f_a" for tensile stress; the AISC considers tension and compression different sides of the same coin – remember that "*a*" stands for axial. F_t can be considered 60% of the yield stress of the steel grade under consideration (*SCM*, 5-40). For the F_t values of various steel grades, see Appendix E.

Actual tensile stress, f_a, is calculated using the direct stress formula. Deciding where to start testing sections for combined axial tension and bending problems depends on the loading conditions. If the bending force is significant, calculate the minimum S required to resist the bending moment. If the tensile force is significant, calculate the minimum A required to resist the tensile load. The AISC recommends that the slenderness ratio, l/r, of a tensile member should not exceed 300 (*SCM*, 5-37).

> **Example 1.** Design a rectilinear tubing member to support the following loading conditions. The tensile load is axial. Use MT1010 tubing (F_y=32,000 psi).

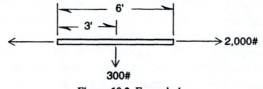

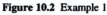

Figure 10.2 Example 1

> Solve for $S_{req'd}$ because the bending load is probably more significant than the tensile load. F_b for MT1010 steel is 19,200 psi (Appendix E).
>
> $$M_{max} = \frac{Pl}{4} = \frac{(300\#)72"}{4} = 5,400 \text{ inlb}$$
>
> $$S_{req'd} = \frac{M_{max}}{F_b} = \frac{5,400 \text{ inlb}}{19,200 \text{ psi}} = 0.28125 \text{ in}^3$$

> Select a member which has a S value larger than $S_{req'd}$. Remember to check that $b/t \leq 42.1$ for MT1010 rectangular tubing.

> Try a 1.0"x3.0"x0.065" rectangular tube:
>
> S_{x-x}=0.3488 in^3 A=0.4971 in^2 wt=1.69 plf b/t=46.2✗
>
> Since 46.2>42.1, this tube is a slender member and is unacceptable.

To pass the *b/t* criteria, a 1.0"x3.0"x0.083" tube is required.

$$S_{x-x}=0.4331 \text{ in}^3 \quad A=0.6279 \text{ in}^2 \quad wt=2.13 \text{ plf} \quad b/t=36.1 ✓$$

Calculate the actual tensile stress:

$$f_a = \frac{P}{A} = \frac{2,000\#}{0.6279 \text{ in}^2} = 3,185.2 \text{ psi}$$

Calculate the ratio of actual to allowable bending stress when oriented as shown in Figure 10.3.

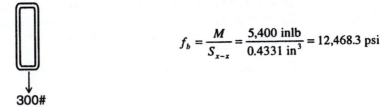

$$f_b = \frac{M}{S_{x-x}} = \frac{5,400 \text{ inlb}}{0.4331 \text{ in}^3} = 12,468.3 \text{ psi}$$

300#
Figure 10.3 Orientation of section

Plug the variables into the interaction equation.

$$\frac{f_a}{F_t} + \frac{f_b}{F_b} = \frac{3,185.2 \text{ psi}}{19,200 \text{ psi}} + \frac{12,468.3 \text{ psi}}{19,200 \text{ psi}} = 0.166 + 0.649 = 0.815 \le 1.0 ✓$$

Therefore, the 1.0"x3.0"x0.083" tube is an appropriate choice for this loading condition when oriented as shown in Figure 10.3.

SINGLE AXIS BENDING AND AXIAL COMPRESSION

The straightforward process implied by the general interaction equation becomes muddled when safety and adjustment factors are added to it. Fortunately, the design of steel members does not require as many factors as wood design. Primarily, the AISC is concerned with the P-Δ (P-delta) effect described in Chapter 7 which causes a synergistic reaction when members are subject to both axial compression and bending forces (see Figure 10.1). For single axis bending and axial compression, the AISC mandates that the following requirements be met (*SCM*, 5-54):

when $f_a/F_a > 0.15$, Equations 1 and 2 must be satisfied:

Equation 1 $$\frac{f_a}{F_a} + \frac{C_m f_b}{\left(1 - \frac{f_a}{F_e'}\right)F_b} \le 1.0$$

Equation 2 $$\frac{f_a}{0.6F_y} + \frac{f_b}{F_b} \le 1.0$$

when $f_a/F_a \le 0.15$, Equation 3 must be satisfied:

Equation 3 $$\frac{f_a}{F_a} + \frac{f_b}{F_b} \le 1.0$$

The added factor in the denominator of the first equation is called the amplification factor and accounts for the P-delta effect. For beam-columns with a ratio of actual to allowable compressive stress of under 15%, the P-delta effect is considered negligible and Equation 3 can be used. Many theatrical applications, however, will have ratios over 15% and Equations 1 and 2 must be simultaneously satisfied.

Fortunately, the entire process can be simplified by assuming that C_m will always equal 1.0. C_m allows the actual bending stress to be reduced if the connection details satisfy certain conditions (SCM, 5-55), and a value of 1.0 is its worst case condition. Obviously, setting C_m to 1.0 simplifies Equation 1. In addition, the solution of Equation 1 will always be greater than the solution to Equation 2, making Equation 2 redundant. This leaves the following interaction equations for single axis bending and axial compression:

when $f_a/F_a > 0.15$, Equation 1 must be satisfied:

Equation 1
$$\frac{f_a}{F_a} + \frac{f_b}{\left(1 - \frac{f_a}{F_e'}\right)F_b} \leq 1.0$$

when $f_a/F_a \leq 0.15$, Equation 3 must be satisfied:

Equation 3
$$\frac{f_a}{F_a} + \frac{f_b}{F_b} \leq 1.0$$

where
f_a is the actual axial compressive stress, psi
F_a is the allowable compressive stress, psi
f_b is the actual bending stress for the axis in the plane of bending, psi
F_b is the allowable bending stress for the same axis, psi
F_e' is the Euler buckling stress for the axis in the plane of bending for the corresponding Kl/r, psi:

$$F_e' = \frac{12\pi^2 E}{23\left(\frac{Kl_b}{r_b}\right)^2}$$

Each actual and allowable variable is calculated as if the member were subject to only that one type of stress. F_e' is calculated for the unbraced length in the plane of bending, as indicated by the subscript b. F_e' will have the same value as F_a if the plane of bending is acting against the weak axis and the slenderness ratio is greater than C_c. For convenience, we have tabulated the values of F_e' for the full range of slenderness ratios in Appendix E. Note that F_e' is the same for all grades of steel with an E of 2.9×10^7 psi.

Designing a member subject to single axis bending and axial compression adds only two unfamiliar steps to the design process, that of looking up F_e' and plugging the variables into the interaction equation. F_a and F_b are both calculated using the techniques described in Chapters 8 and 9, respectively. The actual compressive stress, f_a, is equal to P/A, and the actual bending stress, f_b, is equal to M/S. Deflection is usually ignored for two reasons: the amplification factor in the first interaction equation ensures adequate stiffness, and actual deflection can only be calculated via computer modeling due to the P-Δ effect. However, if Equation 3 is applicable and deflection is important, deflection can be assessed using the appropriate case formula for the bending load only. This should be regarded as an estimate only; there are no deflection formulas for combined loading conditions.

As in column design, solving combined loading situations is a trial and error process; it is impossible to solve for section modulus, radius of gyration, and area values which simultaneously satisfy all of the stress requirements. However, any of these variables can be solved for to establish a starting point for the problem. In addition, square or round sections are usually inefficient compared to a rectangular section which has a strong axis to resist the bending load. Be sure to pick a trial section which exceeds the minimum S, r, or A requirement. A section which barely meets one of them will probably fail for the combined loading condition.

Example 2. Determine an appropriate rectangular mechanical tubing member to satisfy the given loading conditions. Use MT1010 tubing (F_y=32,000 psi) and assume K is 1.0.

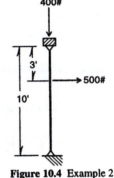

Figure 10.4 Example 2

First, calculate the minimum required r value:

$$\frac{Kl}{r} = 200 \Rightarrow r_{min} = \frac{Kl}{200} = \frac{1(120")}{200} = 0.6"$$

Next, calculate the M_{max} induced by the bending load. Use the case formula for a simple beam, concentrated load at any point.

$$M_{max} = \frac{Pab}{l} = \frac{(500\#)(3')(7')}{10'} = 1,050 \text{ ftlb} \Rightarrow 12,600 \text{ inlb}$$

Calculate $S_{req'd}$. Remember that F_b for mechanical tubing is taken as 19.2 ksi.

$$S_{req'd} = \frac{M}{F_b} = \frac{12,600 \text{ inlb}}{19,200 \text{ psi}} = 0.65625 \text{ in}^3$$

Now, select a trial section which exceeds both the S and r requirements, and remember that a rectangular section will probably be the most efficient. In addition, in order to meet the compact section requirements, the b/t ratio must be less than or equal to 42.1

Try a 1.5"x3.0"x0.134" tube:

S_{x-x}=0.8055 in^3	r_{x-x}=1.0484"	A=1.0993 in^2
S_{y-y}=0.5401 in^3	r_{y-y}=0.6071"	wt=3.74 plf b/t=22.4✓

Calculate the ratio of actual to allowable axial stress in order to determine if an amplification factor is necessary.

$$f_a = \frac{P}{A} = \frac{400\#}{1.0993\ in^2} = 363.9\ psi$$

$$\frac{Kl}{r} \Rightarrow \frac{l}{r_{y-y}} = \frac{120"}{0.6071"} = 197.7 \Rightarrow 198$$

$$F_{a_{198}} = 3,810\ psi$$

$$\frac{f_a}{F_a} = \frac{363.9\ psi}{3,810\ psi} = 0.0955$$

Since 0.095<0.15, no amplification factor is necessary.

Calculate the bending stress when oriented as Figure 10.5.

$$f_b = \frac{M}{S_{x-x}} = \frac{12,600\ inlb}{0.8055\ in^3} = 15,642.46\ psi$$

Figure 10.5 orientation of section

Plug all the variables into the interaction equation:

$$\frac{f_a}{F_a} + \frac{f_b}{F_b} = \frac{363.9\ psi}{3,810\ psi} + \frac{15,642.6\ psi}{19,200\ psi} = 0.0955 + 0.815 = 0.911 < 1.0$$

The 1.5"x3.0"x0.134" tube is acceptable when oriented as indicated in Figure 10.5. Note that this section would fail if it were oriented with the y-y axis in the plane of bending. Also remember that lateral bracing is not required for hollow tubes with b:d ratios of 6:1 or less if F_b is taken as $0.6F_y$.

Some of the most common examples of combined axial compression and bending in theater are not obvious at first glance. For example, imagine any rigging situation which requires that the load be bridled, such as dead-hanging or rigging with chain hoists, cranes, and block-and-falls. The bridle induces a compressive force into the structure by attempting to "squeeze" the two bridle points together. The magnitude of the compressive force is dependent on the angle at which the bridle is rigged. The less distance between the primary pickup point and the unit, i.e., the more shallow the bridle angle, the greater the compressive force generated.

Bridling that is meant to be used for the run of a show is usually thought through, but bridling used during load-in to raise heavy scenery into its permanent hanging position is often a different matter. The temporary bridling can induce a compressive force in a member which may not have been designed for that purpose. Ignoring the implications of bridling can and has caused accidents.

Example 3. The design of a production requires that a 12'x21' pipe grid be hung 18' above stage level (see Figure 10.6 for grid layout). For convenience in construction and hanging lighting instruments, 1-

1/2" Schedule 40 pipe is used. The master electrician has requested that the grid be built, hung and cabled on the ground, and then flown as a unit. The pipe grid will eventually be dead hung on nine picks as indicated by the circles in the plan view. In order to fly the grid during load-in, a chain hoist will be bridled to each end of the grid as shown on the isometric view. The bridling points are indicated by squares. Unfortunately, this theater does not have a traditional fly house, so there's very little room between the pipe grid and the ceiling of the stage house, i.e., the bridle needs to be shallow. Will the 1-1/2" pipe be sufficient for the load-in stresses caused by a 30° bridle angle? Use Type E, Grade B pipe.

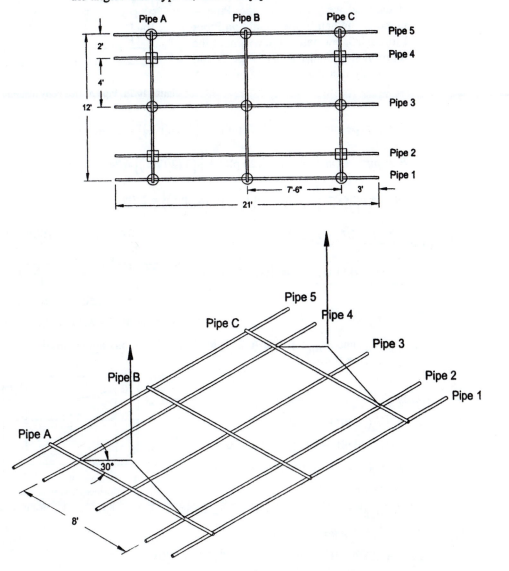

Figure 10.6 Example 3, plan and isometric views

First, the loading conditions on Pipe A must be estimated. Assume that every pipe is hung with lighting instruments on 18" centers and that each instrument and its cable weigh an average of 25 lbs. The pipe weighs 2.72 plf. Therefore:

$$w_{pipe A} = \text{lights and cable} + \text{pipe weight} = \frac{25\#}{15'} + 2.72 \text{ plf} = 19.4 \text{ plf} \Rightarrow 20 \text{ plf}$$

The weight on each pipe is transferred to pipe A at each joint such that pipe A supports one half of the grid. Since the loading is symmetrical, the reactions are one half of the total weight on the pipe. Pipe A supports one half of the weight on Pipes 1 through 5, one half of the weight of the appropriate tributary area of Pipe B, and the evenly distributed weight of Pipe A itself.

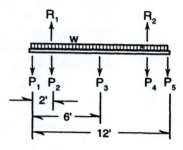

Figure 10.7a Pipe A, free body diagram

$$P_1 = P_5 = pipe_1 + pipe_B = \frac{1}{2}(21')(20 \text{ plf}) + \frac{1}{2}\left[1'(20 \text{ plf})\right] = 220\#$$

$$P_2 = P_4 = pipe_2 + pipe_B = \frac{1}{2}(21')(20 \text{ plf}) + \frac{1}{2}\left[3'(20 \text{ plf})\right] = 240\#$$

$$P_3 = pipe_3 + pipe_B = \frac{1}{2}(21')(20 \text{ plf}) + \frac{1}{2}\left[4'(20 \text{ plf})\right] = 250\#$$

$$R_1 = R_2 = \frac{2P_1 + 2P_2 + P_3 + P_A}{2}$$

$$= \frac{2(220\#) + 2(240\#) + 250\# + \left[(12')(20 \text{ plf})\right]}{2}$$

$$= 705\#$$

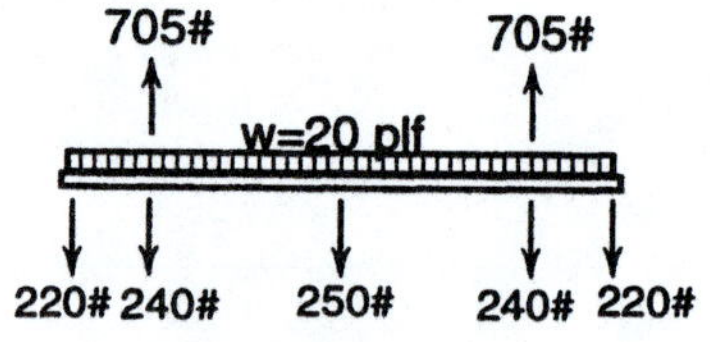

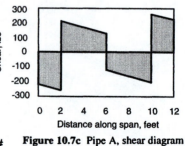

Figure 10.7b Pipe A, free body diagram

Next, find V_{max} and M_{max} for Pipe A. This loading condition is not covered by any case formula.

$$V_{0^-} = 0$$

$$V_{0^+} = -220\#$$

$$V_{2^-} = -220\# - (2')(20 \text{ plf}) = -260\#$$

$$V_{2^+} = -220\# - (2')(20 \text{ plf}) - 240\# + 705\# = +205\#$$

$$V_{6^-} = -220\# - (6')(20 \text{ plf}) - 240\# + 705\# = +125\#$$

$$V_{6^+} = +125\# - 250\# = -125\#$$

$$V_{10^-} = -220\# - (10')(20 \text{ plf}) - 240\# + 705\# - 250\# = -205\#$$

$$V_{10^+} = -205\# + 705\# - 240\# = +260\#$$

$$V_{12^-} = -220\# - (12')(20 \text{ plf}) - 240\# + 705\# - 250\# + 705\# - 240\# = +220\#$$

$$V_{12^+} = -220\# + 220\# = 0$$

Figure 10.7c Pipe A, shear diagram

Shear crosses through zero at 2', 6', and 10', so the moment at each of these three points must be calculated to find M_{max}.

$$M_{2'} = M_{10'} = -2'(220\#) - 1'[(2')(20 \text{ plf})] = -480 \text{ ftlb} \Rightarrow 5,760 \text{ inlb}$$

$$M_{6'} = -6'(220\#) + 4'(705\#) - 4'(240\#) - 3'[(6')(20 \text{ plf})] = +180 \text{ ftlb} \Rightarrow 2,160 \text{ inlb}$$

Next, resolve the forces to determine the axial compression on the pipe.

$$\tan \theta = \frac{opp}{adj}$$

$$\tan 30° = \frac{R_1}{h}$$

$$h = \frac{R_1}{\tan 30°} = \frac{705\#}{0.5774} = 1,221.1\#$$

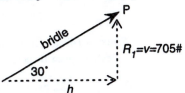

Figure 10.8 Resolution of bridle forces

The geometric properties of Schedule 40, 1-1/2" pipe are:

$$S = 0.326 \text{ in}^3 \qquad r = 0.623" \qquad A = 0.799 \text{ in}^2$$

Now, calculate the ratio of actual to allowable compressive stress in order to determine if an amplification factor is necessary. The maximum unbraced length, l, is 8' because the pipe has no restraints to keep it from buckling up or down between the bridle points.

$$f_a = \frac{P}{A} = \frac{1,221.1\#}{0.799 \text{ in}^2} = 1,528.3 \text{ psi}$$

$$\frac{Kl}{r} = \frac{1(96")}{0.623} = 154.09 \Rightarrow 155$$

$$F_{a_{155}} = 6,220 \text{ psi}$$

$$\frac{f_a}{F_a} = \frac{1,528.3 \text{ psi}}{6,220 \text{ psi}} = 0.246$$

Since 0.246>0.15, an amplification factor is required.

Calculate the actual bending stress:

$$f_b = \frac{M}{S} = \frac{5,760 \text{ inlb}}{0.326 \text{ in}^3} = 17,669 \text{ psi}$$

In this case, $F_e' = F_a$ because there is only one r value and the slenderness ratio is greater than C_c. From Appendix E, the F_b of Type E or S pipe is 23.1 ksi. The variables can now be plugged into interaction Equation 1.

$$\frac{f_a}{F_a} + \frac{f_b}{\left(1 - \frac{f_a}{F_e'}\right)F_b} = 0.246 + \frac{17,669 \text{ psi}}{(1 - 0.246)(23,100 \text{ psi})}$$

$$= 0.246 + 1.014 \Rightarrow 1.26 > 1.0 \quad \times$$

The 1-1/2" pipe fails for a 30° bridle. Try a 45° bridle.

Recalculate f_a and the ratio of f_a/F_a:

$$h = \frac{v}{\tan 45°} = \frac{705\#}{1} = 705\#$$

$$f_a = \frac{705\#}{0.799 \text{ in}^2} = 882 \text{ psi}$$

$$\frac{f_a}{F_a} = \frac{882 \text{ psi}}{6,220 \text{ psi}} = 0.142$$

Since 0.142<0.15, no amplification factor is needed and the variables can plug directly into interaction Equation 3.

$$\frac{f_a}{F_a} + \frac{f_b}{F_b} = \frac{882 \text{ psi}}{6,220 \text{ psi}} + \frac{17,669 \text{ psi}}{(23,100 \text{ psi})} = 0.142 + 0.765 = 0.907 \Rightarrow 0.907 < 1.0 \checkmark$$

The 1-1/2" Schedule 40 pipe is adequate if a bridling angle of 45° or greater is employed.

We now know that our bridling member is sufficient, but what about the span of pipes 1 through 5 between the two bridles? No spans will exceed 7'-6" when the dead picks are attached, but a temporary 15' span occurs between the bridles under the current load-in plan. The loading conditions on pipe 3 are represented by Figure 10.9. The point load in the center is generated by the loading on the appropriate tributary area from Pipe B.

$$R_1 = R_2 = \frac{21'(20 \text{ plf}) + 80\#}{2} = 250\#$$

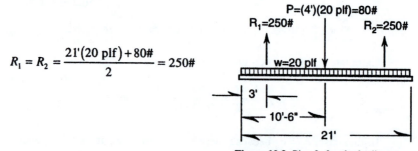

Figure 10.9 Pipe 3, free body diagram

This is not a combined loading situation, so we only need to calculate the actual bending stress. The loading is symmetrical, so M_{max} will occur at the center of the span.

$$M_{max} = M_{10.5'} = +7.5'(250\#) - 5'\left[10.5'(20 \text{ plf})\right] = 825 \text{ ftlb} \Rightarrow 9,900 \text{ inlb}$$

$$f_b = \frac{M}{S} = \frac{9,900 \text{ inlb}}{0.326 \text{ in}^3} = 30,368 \text{ psi}$$

Since 30,368 psi>>23,100 psi, the pipe fails for the load-in loading condition. Possible solutions include adding a third bridle, reconfiguring the grid layout to decrease the span, leaving some of the instruments off until the grid is dead hung, etc.

Several notes should be made about this problem:

- We made no allowances for the acceleration/deceleration or jerkiness of the chain hoists. In addition, our analysis assumed that the chain hoists would move at the same rate. It they do not, one chain hoist and its corresponding pipe would take more than half the weight.

- We assumed an absolutely uniform load. Once the actual loading conditions are more defined, the estimate should be reviewed.

- The weakest link in a system can cause failure. In addition to pipe size and unbraced spans, the size of the bridle lines, the capacity of the chain hoists, and the connection details must be considered. The pick points must be capable of resisting a 1,221 lb sideways force, and the hanging point for each chain hoist must be capable of supporting one half the total weight (1,410 lbs) of the grid.

- The relationship between the generated compressive force and bridle angle is exponential. For example, if the vertical component of the force is considered P, an axial load of 2.83P is generated by a 10° angle, at 5°, the axial load is 5.7P, and at 1°, the axial load is 28.6P.

- It is a good idea to design systems which are "single-failure proof," i.e., no single failure can lead to a disastrous series of failures. If one of the permanent cables snapped, could the remaining cables support the load?

ECCENTRIC LOADING

Eccentric loading is a sub-category of combined single axis bending and axial compression. An eccentric load is one which does not act at the geometric center of a column; it is offset from one or both axes. Eccentric loads can be caused by an off-center joint at the top of the column or by a bracket connection somewhere along the length of the column. An eccentric or bracket load will induce a bending moment as well as compressive stress. See Figure 10.1 for a typical bracket loading condition.

The moment induced by a bracket load becomes smaller as the bracket is placed closer to the middle of the unbraced length of the column. Imagine how easy it is to bend a yardstick by torquing it at the top. Analyzing the moment induced by a bracket load is complex, so we will use the convenient and conservative assumption of considering all bracket loads as acting at the top of the column.

The same interaction equations used for single axis bending and axial compression apply to an eccentric loading condition.

when $f_a/F_a > 0.15$, Equation 1 must be satisfied:

Equation 1
$$\frac{f_a}{F_a} + \frac{f_b}{\left(1 - \frac{f_a}{F_e'}\right)F_b} \leq 1.0$$

when $f_a/F_a \leq 0.15$, Equation 3 must be satisfied:

Equation 3 $\qquad \dfrac{f_a}{F_a} + \dfrac{f_b}{F_b} \leq 1.0$

For a column subject to an eccentric load, the P used to find f_a is the magnitude of the down-ward load. The M used to find f_b is calculated by multiplying the load, P, by e, the amount of eccentricity (see Figure 10.10).

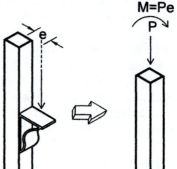

$$f_a = \frac{P_{all}}{A}$$

$$f_b = \frac{M}{S} = \frac{Pe}{S_b}$$

Figure 10.10 Resolution of an eccentric load

where S_b is the section modulus in the plane of bending, in³
           e is the perpendicular distance from the load to the neutral axis of the
              column, in

When a column is subject to both an eccentric load and an additional axial load, the magni-tudes of both loads are used to calculate f_a, while only the magnitude of the eccentric load is used to calculate M.

Once again, the design procedure is a trial and error process, and the easiest approach is to start by selecting sections which can support the axial load(s) and/or meet the slenderness ratio requirement.

Example 4. Design an appropriate rectilinear mechanical tubing member to satisfy the following loading condition. A column supports a beam which overlaps exactly half of the top of a column. The beam load therefore always acts at 1/4 of the column depth from the neu-tral axis (see Figure 10.11). Note that the actual eccentric distance varies with the column choice. Use MT1010 tubing and assume K is 1.0.

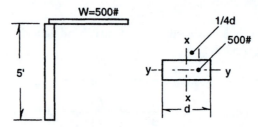

Figure 10.11 Example 4

First, calculate the minimum value of r and the A required to support the axial load at a Kl/r of 200.

$$r_{min} = \frac{Kl}{200} = \frac{1(60")}{200} = 0.3"$$

$$F_{a_{200}} = 3,730 \text{ psi}$$

$$A_{req'd} = \frac{P}{F_a} = \frac{500\#}{3,730 \text{ psi}} = 0.134 \text{ in}^2$$

Now, select a section which exceeds the r and A requirements. Remember that a rectangular section with the strong axis in the plane of bending will probably be an efficient choice. In addition, in order to meet the compact section requirements, the b/t ratio must be less than or equal to 42.1.

Try a 0.75"x1.25"x0.049" mechanical tube:

$S_{x-x}=0.0606 \text{ in}^3$ $\quad r_{x-x}=0.4546"$ $\quad A=0.1832 \text{ in}^2$
$S_{y-y}=0.0454 \text{ in}^3$ $\quad r_{y-y}=0.3049"$ $\quad wt=0.63 \text{ plf}$ $\quad b/t=22.5\checkmark$

Calculate the ratio of actual to allowable axial stress to determine if an amplification factor is necessary.

$$f_a = \frac{P}{A} = \frac{500\#}{0.1832 \text{ in}^2} = 2,729 \text{ psi}$$

$$\frac{Kl}{r} \Rightarrow \frac{l}{r_{y-y}} = \frac{60"}{0.3049"} = 196.8 \Rightarrow 197$$

$$F_{a_{197}} = 3,850 \text{ psi}$$

$$\frac{f_a}{F_a} = \frac{2,729 \text{ psi}}{3,850 \text{ psi}} = 0.71$$

0.71>0.15, so Equation 1 with the amplification factor must be used.

Next, calculate the ratio of actual to allowable bending stress, assuming that the section is oriented so that the strong axis resists the eccentric load (see Figure 10.12).

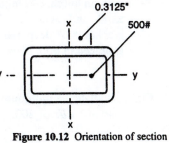

Figure 10.12 Orientation of section

Calculate e:

$$e = \frac{d}{4} = \frac{1.25"}{4} = 0.3125"$$

Calculate f_b:

$$M = Pe = (500\#)(0.3125") = 156.25 \text{ inlb}$$

$$f_b = \frac{M}{S_{x-x}} = \frac{156.25 \text{ inlb}}{0.0606 \text{ in}^3} = 2,578.38 \text{ psi}$$

Calculate F_e' and the amplification factor:

$$\frac{Kl}{r} = \frac{l}{r_{x-x}} = \frac{60"}{0.4546"} = 131.98 \Rightarrow 132$$

$$F_{e_{132}}' = 8{,}570 \text{ psi}$$

$$1 - \frac{f_a}{F_e'} = 1 - \frac{2{,}729 \text{ psi}}{8{,}570 \text{ psi}} = 0.682$$

Determine the bending ratio:

$$\frac{f_b}{\left(1 - \dfrac{f_a}{F_e'}\right) F_b} = \frac{2{,}578.38 \text{ psi}}{0.682(19{,}200 \text{ psi})} = 0.197$$

Plug all of the variables into interaction Equation 1:

$$\frac{f_a}{F_a} + \frac{f_b}{\left(1 - \dfrac{f_a}{F_e'}\right) F_b} = 0.710 + 0.197 = 0.907 \Rightarrow 0.907 \leq 1.0 \quad \checkmark$$

Therefore, the 0.75"x1.25"x0.049" mechanical tube is an appropriate choice when oriented with the x-x axis in the plane of bending.

Example 5. Select the lightest possible structural tube which can meet the following loading conditions. This example represents a loading condition typical of a multi-story set. The loading conditions on the lower half of the column are the worst case scenario, i.e., a column with an unbraced length of 9' with axial and eccentric loads. The bracket is 6" deep and the column is braced in both planes at a height of 9'.

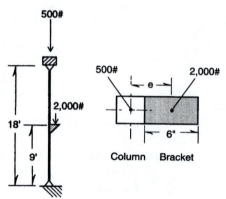

Figure 10.13 Example 5

First, calculate the minimum value of r and A required to support the axial load at a Kl/r of 200.

$$r_{min} = \frac{Kl}{200} = \frac{1(108")}{200} = 0.54"$$

$$F_{a_{200}} = 3{,}730 \text{ psi}$$

$$A_{req'd} = \frac{P_{ax} + P_{ecc}}{F_a} = \frac{500\#+2{,}000\#}{3{,}730 \text{ psi}} = 0.67 \text{ in}^2$$

Now, select a trial section which exceeds the r and A requirements. Usually, we would pick a rectangular section. In this case, however, the smallest square section more than meets the preliminary estimates. In addition, in order to meet the compact section requirements, the b/t ratio must be less than or equal to 35.1.

Try a 2.0"x2.0"x3/16" structural tube:

$$S=0.640 \text{ in}^3; \quad r=0.732"; \quad A=1.19 \text{ in}^2; \quad wt=4.32 \text{ plf}; \quad b/t=11.5\checkmark$$

Calculate the ratio of actual to allowable axial stress to determine if an amplification factor is necessary.

$$f_a = \frac{P}{A} = \frac{2{,}500\#}{1.19 \text{ in}^2} = 2{,}100.8 \text{ psi}$$

$$\frac{Kl}{r} = \frac{108"}{0.732"} = 147.54 \Rightarrow 148$$

$$F_{a_{148}} = 6{,}820 \text{ psi}$$

$$\frac{f_a}{F_a} = \frac{2{,}100.8 \text{ psi}}{6{,}820 \text{ psi}} = 0.308$$

0.308>0.15, so the amplification factor is required.

Next, calculate the bending moment, the actual bending stress, the amplification factor, and the bending ratio (see Figure 10.14). The allowable bending stress is $0.66F_y$ or 30.4 ksi for square tube sections. Since the section is square, and Kl/r is greater than C_c (111.6 for steels with F_y=46,000 psi), F_e' equals F_a.

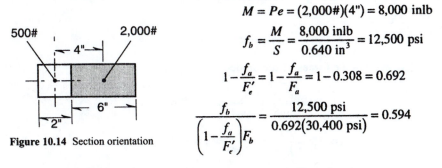

$$M = Pe = (2{,}000\#)(4") = 8{,}000 \text{ inlb}$$

$$f_b = \frac{M}{S} = \frac{8{,}000 \text{ inlb}}{0.640 \text{ in}^3} = 12{,}500 \text{ psi}$$

$$1 - \frac{f_a}{F_e'} = 1 - \frac{f_a}{F_a} = 1 - 0.308 = 0.692$$

$$\frac{f_b}{\left(1 - \frac{f_a}{F_e'}\right)F_b} = \frac{12{,}500 \text{ psi}}{0.692(30{,}400 \text{ psi})} = 0.594$$

500# 2,000#

4"

6"

2"

Figure 10.14 Section orientation

Finally, plug all of the variables into interaction Equation 1:

$$\frac{f_a}{F_a} + \frac{f_b}{\left(1 - \frac{f_a}{F_e'}\right)F_b} = 0.308 + 0.594 = 0.902 \Rightarrow 0.902 \leq 1.0 \checkmark$$

Therefore, the 2"x2"x3/16" structural tube is an appropriate choice for this loading condition. Note that the bending load could be reduced by decreasing the length of the bracket.

BIAXIAL BENDING

Members subject to bending in both axes must satisfy the following equation (*SCM*, 5-55):

$$\frac{f_{bx}}{F_{bx}} + \frac{f_{by}}{F_{by}} \leq 1.0$$

Each actual and allowable bending stress is calculated using the techniques previously discussed. Any steel shape which is not square or round will have two distinct section moduli and a corresponding f_b value. Be sure that the bracing requirements of the shape category are met.

The most common instance of biaxial bending is a beam which supports one or more sheaves which change the angle of a tension line. When a beam is subject to an angled load; that is, a load which is not perpendicular to either axis, the angled load is algebraically resolved into its vertical and horizontal component forces. The beam is then analyzed as if it had a discrete load acting against each axis.

> **Example 6.** The following beam is part of a deck system and is subject to an angled point load as well as the live and dead loads on the deck (see Figure 10.15). The total of the live and dead loads is 25 plf. Determine an appropriate structural tubing beam (F_y=46,000 psi).

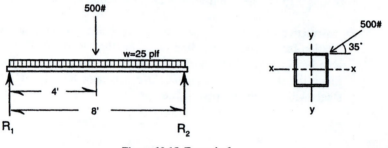

Figure 10.15 Example 6

First, resolve the forces of the angled point load.

$$\sin 35° = \frac{opp}{hyp} = \frac{v}{500\#} \Rightarrow v = 286.8\#$$

$$\cos 35° = \frac{adj}{hyp} = \frac{h}{500\#} \Rightarrow h = 409.6\#$$

Find M_{max} for both axes.

$$M_{max_{x-x}} = \text{distributed load} + \text{point load}$$

$$= \frac{wl^2}{8} + \frac{vl}{4} = \frac{\left(25\,plf/_{12}\right)(96'')^2}{8} + \frac{(286.8\#)(96'')}{4} = 9,282.9 \text{ inlb}$$

$$M_{max_{y-y}} = \text{point load} = \frac{hl}{4} = \frac{(409.6\#)(96'')}{4} = 9,829.8 \text{ inlb}$$

Solve for $S_{req'd}$ for each axis.

$$S_{req'd} = \frac{M_{max}}{F_b}$$

$$S_{req'd_{x-x}} = \frac{M_{max_{x-x}}}{F_b} = \frac{9{,}282.9 \text{ inlb}}{27{,}600 \text{ psi}} = 0.336 \text{ in}^3$$

$$S_{req'd_{y-y}} = \frac{M_{max_{y-y}}}{F_b} = \frac{9{,}829.8 \text{ inlb}}{27{,}600 \text{ psi}} = 0.356 \text{ in}^3$$

Since the $S_{req'd}$'s are almost identical, a relatively square section should be the first choice. A square section has only one value for S and does not require lateral bracing. In addition, F_b can be taken as $0.66F_y$ (30.4 ksi) instead of $0.6F_y$.

Try a 2"x2"x3/16" structural tube:

$$S = 0.640 \text{ in}^3 \quad wt = 4.32 \text{ plf} \quad I = 0.640 \text{ in}^4 \quad b/t = 11.5 \checkmark$$

Solve for the actual bending stress against each axis.

$$f_b = \frac{M_{max}}{S}$$

$$f_{bx} = \frac{9{,}282.9 \text{ inlb}}{0.640 \text{ in}^3} = 14{,}504.5 \text{ psi}$$

$$f_{by} = \frac{9{,}829.8 \text{ inlb}}{0.640 \text{ in}^3} = 15{,}359.1 \text{ psi}$$

Plug all of the variables into the interaction equation.

$$\frac{f_{bx}}{F_{bx}} + \frac{f_{by}}{F_{by}} = \frac{14{,}504.5 \text{ psi}}{30{,}400 \text{ psi}} + \frac{15{,}359.1 \text{ psi}}{30{,}400 \text{ psi}} = 0.477 + 0.505 = 0.982 \Rightarrow 0.982 \leq 1.0$$

The 2"x2"x3/16" structural tube just passes.

Since this is a framing member of a deck, we should check deflection (for the x-x axis only). Use case formulas to solve for $I_{req'd}$ for the deflection due to the evenly distributed load and the vertical point load of 286.8 lbs using a deflection criteria of $l/240$:

$$I_{req'd} = \frac{wl^3}{9.28x10^6 \text{ psi}} + \frac{Pl^2}{5.8x10^6 \text{ psi}}$$

$$= \frac{(2.083 \text{ pli})(96")^3}{9.28x10^6 \text{ psi}} + \frac{286.8\#(96")^2}{5.8x10^6 \text{ psi}} = 0.654 \text{ in}^4 \Rightarrow 0.654 > 0.640 \; \times$$

The 2"x2"x3/16" structural tube barely fails the deflection criteria. A slightly larger member, such as a 2"x2"x1/4" tube, may be a better choice for this loading condition.

BIAXIAL BENDING AND AXIAL COMPRESSION

Members subject to both biaxial bending and axial compression must satisfy the following equations (*SCM*, 5-54):

when $f_a/F_a > 0.15$, Equation 1 must be satisfied:

Equation 1
$$\frac{f_a}{F_a} + \frac{f_{bx}}{\left(1 - \frac{f_a}{F'_{ex}}\right)F_{bx}} + \frac{f_{by}}{\left(1 - \frac{f_a}{F'_{ey}}\right)F_{by}} \leq 1.0$$

when $f_a/F_a \leq 0.15$, Equation 3 must be satisfied:

Equation 3
$$\frac{f_a}{F_a} + \frac{f_{bx}}{F_{bx}} + \frac{f_{by}}{F_{by}} \leq 1.0$$

The above interaction equations are logical extensions of the equations used for combined axial compression and single axis bending and biaxial bending. The variables are calculated using exactly the same techniques described previously.

Biaxial bending and axial compression conditions are commonly generated by eccentric loads which are offset in both axes. For example, the column described in Example 4 would meet these conditions if the first floor beams had rested on two brackets at 90° to each other as shown in Figure 10.1 previously.

CHAPTER 10 LESSONS

The format of the numbering system is: chapter.lesson.problem number.

LESSON 10.1 SINGLE AXIS BENDING AND AXIAL TENSION (PG 209 – 211)

10.1.1 Choose the lightest rectangular mechanical tube (MT1010) which can support the loading conditions given below. Disregard beam weight.

10.1.2 Choose the least diameter black pipe (Type E, Grade B) which can support the loading conditions given below. Include beam weight.

10.1.3 Choose the least diameter round mechanical tube (MT1010) which can support the loading conditions given below. Disregard beam weight.

LESSON 10.2 SINGLE AXIS BENDING AND AXIAL COMPRESSION (PG 211 – 219)

10.2.1 Choose the lightest rectangular mechanical tube (MT1010) which can support the loading conditions given below.

10.2.2 Choose the least diameter round mechanical tube (MT1010) which can support the loading conditions given below.

10.2.3 Choose the least diameter black pipe (Type F, Grade A) which can support the loading conditions given below.

10.2.4 Choose the lightest W flange beam which can support the loading conditions given below. The beam is laterally braced at 6' intervals as shown below. Include beam weight.

10.2.5 Choose the smallest (least outside dimension) square structural tube which can support the loading conditions given below. Include beam weight.

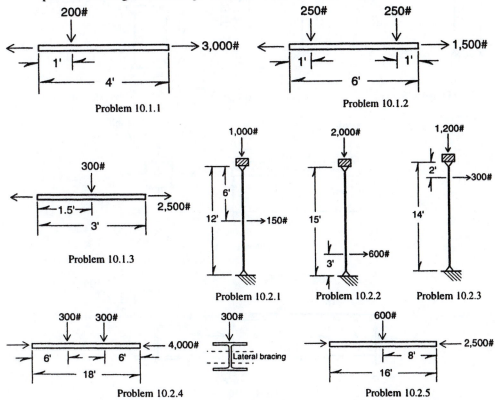

Problem 10.1.1

Problem 10.1.2

Problem 10.1.3

Problem 10.2.1

Problem 10.2.2

Problem 10.2.3

Problem 10.2.4

Problem 10.2.5

LESSON 10.3 ECCENTRIC LOADING (PG 219 – 223)

10.3.1 Choose the least diameter round mechanical tube (MT1010) which can support the loading conditions given below.

10.3.2 Choose the lightest square structural tube which can support the loading conditions given below.

10.3.3 Choose the lightest rectangular mechanical tube (MT1010) which can support the loading conditions given below. The *y-y* axis is braced at the height of the bracket.

LESSON 10.4 BIAXIAL BENDING (PG 224 - 226)

10.4.1 Choose the lightest rectangular mechanical tube (MT1010) which can support the loading conditions given below. Include beam weight.

10.4.2 Choose the lightest square mechanical tube (MT1010) which can support the loading conditions in Example 6 in the text.

10.4.3 Choose the lightest W flange beam which can support the loading conditions given below. Lateral bracing will be added to meet the L_u requirements. Include beam weight.

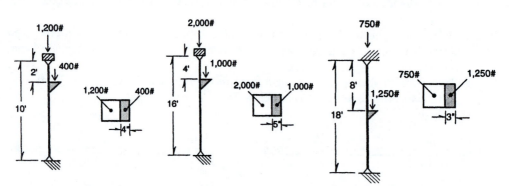

Problem 10.3.1   Problem 10.3.2   Problem 10.3.3

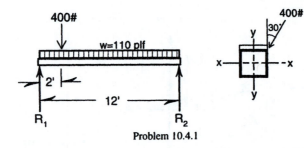

Problem 10.4.1

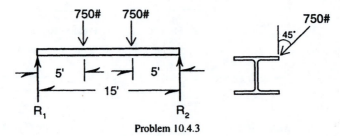

Problem 10.4.3

11

Trusses and Cables

INTRODUCTION

Trusses and cables are common methods of efficiently supporting weight. Both are designed to maximize the loading per unit of material, which has obvious advantages in theatrical situations. Quite frequently, the concepts behind truss and cable design are shrouded in mystery, implying that genius-level intelligence is required to understand them. In reality, the analysis of both is based on the rules of static equilibrium and basic trigonometry.

Simply stated, "A **truss** is a structure composed of slender members joined together at their end points" (Hibbeler, 81). A truss can range from a simple three-member triangle to a complicated repeating pattern which spans hundreds of feet. In this chapter, we will focus on a limited range of trusses which are useful for scenery applications.

Cables are commonly used to hang, suspend, or support scenery. Quite frequently, the cable hangs straight down, which makes determining the load on the cable a trivial problem. But, if the cable is not hanging straight down, the resultant cable tension must be calculated. In this chapter two techniques for calculating cable tension will be discussed, one for the sharp angles generated by point loads and one for the curves produced by evenly distributed loads. In either case, the behavior of the cable needs to be modeled so that the set designer can make informed decisions.

TRUSSES
INTRODUCTION

Entire books have been written on the topic of "trusses." Of necessity, we will limit our discussion to the analysis of planar, or two-dimensional trusses (see Figure 11.1).

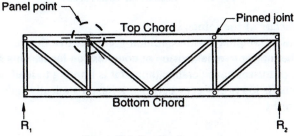

Figure 11.1 Sample planar truss

In addition, we will only discuss **statically determinate** trusses because they can be analyzed using trigonometry and the laws of equilibrium. A **statically indeterminate** truss is one in which the magnitude of the stresses are unsolvable using simple math because the load on a single member cannot be considered independently of the rest of the system. Statically indeterminate and three-dimensional trusses can be analyzed with the aid of computer programs and/or a professional engineer.

In order to ensure that the trusses are statically determinate, three conditions must be met (Hibbeler, 86, 90):

1. All connections are pin connections.
2. All loads occur at the joints.
3. Stability criteria are satisfied.

1. **All connections are pin connections.**
   Assuming that each member is connected to the others via a pin connection allows us to disregard moments induced at the joints in the calculations. Theoretically, if the joint is more rigid than a pin connection, the distribution of the moment through the other members at that joint is unknown, and the truss is statically indeterminate. In reality, most joints are more rigid than a pin connection. However, the induced moments are so small that they are insignificant. In other words, we deliberately make an assumption which we know does not accurately reflect the reality of the construction.

   For all the connections to be considered pin connections, the line of action of all the joint members must intersect at one panel point (see Figure 11.2). If they do not, a statically indeterminate moment is produced and the actual capacity of the truss will be lower than the calculated capacity.

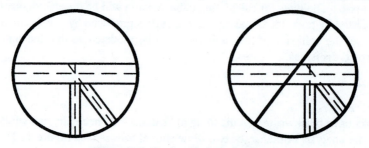

Figure 11.2 Good and bad panel points

2. **All loads occur at the joints.**
   This condition, combined with condition 1, ensures that the truss members will only be subject to axial tension or compression loads. This simplifies the design of trusses considerably, though it is limiting to load only at the panel points. If loads do occur between joints, a statically indeterminate truss is formed.

3. **Stability criteria are satisfied.**
   Trusses must meet this specification (Ambrose, 101):

   $$m = 2j - 3$$

   where   *m* is the number of members of the truss
              j is the total number of joints

If $m > 2j-3$, then the truss has too many members and is statically indeterminate (see Figure 11.3).

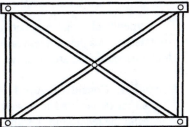

$$m = 2j - 3$$
$$m = 8$$
$$j = 5$$
$$m = 2(5) - 3 = 7 \; ✗$$

Figure 11.3 Indeterminate truss

If $m < 2j-3$, then the truss has too few members and will collapse (see Figure 11.4).

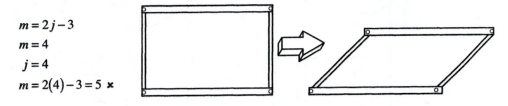

$$m = 2j - 3$$
$$m = 4$$
$$j = 4$$
$$m = 2(4) - 3 = 5 \; ✗$$

Figure 11.4 Unstable truss

THREE-MEMBER TRUSSES

A three-member truss is simply a triangle, which we know instinctively is a stable shape. In scenery construction, we incorporate triangles by adding diagonals to flats or by cross-bracing the legs of a deck system. When homemade brackets are built to hang speakers or props, a closed triangular shape is preferable over an open "L" shape. In order to decide what size and shape members are best for a particular three-member truss, the stresses in each member must first be determined. Before proceeding, it may be helpful to review the techniques used to resolve a diagonal force into two component forces, one vertical and one horizontal, discussed in Chapter 2 and Appendix A.

Once a three-member system is defined by its geometry and one force is determined, static equilibrium allows for only one unique solution. In the analysis, trigonometry is used to resolve each angled force into its component forces, and then algebra is used to apply the conditions of static equilibrium:

1.	The sum of the vertical forces equals zero	$\Sigma V = 0$
2.	The sum of the horizontal forces equals zero	$\Sigma H = 0$
3.	The sum of the moments about any point equals zero	$\Sigma M = 0$

Remember to apply the sense conventions established in Chapter 2 throughout the analysis:

1.   Forces up or to the right are positive and forces down or to the left are negative.

2.   Compressive members are indicated by arrows which point toward the joints, and tensile members are indicated by arrows which point away from the joints.

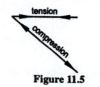

Figure 11.5

3.   The perpendicular distance between the line of action of the force and the pivot point determines the moment arm. Clockwise moments are positive, and counter-clockwise moments are negative.

> *Example 1.* Consider Figure 11.6. The weight of a speaker hanging from a bracket secured to a wall and the angle of the bracket are given. Find the tension in AB and the compression in BC.

Draw a free body diagram which incorporates the forces and the component forces acting at point B:

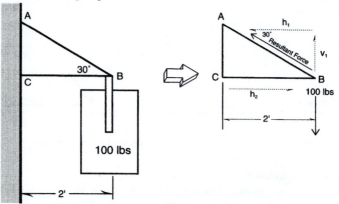

Figure 11.6 Example 1 with free body diagram

Next, determine the values of the unknown forces using the rules of equilibrium. Since the angled member of the bracket is the only member of the system which can have a vertical component, v_1 is determined by setting the sum of the vertical forces equal to zero and solving for v_1.

$$\Sigma V = 0 = v_1 + (-100\#)$$
$$v_1 = 100\# \text{ (up)}$$

Note that the direction of a force or component of a force is established by the sense which is assigned to it in the original equation. Since both sides of the final equation have the same sign, that indicates that the original assumption that v_1 has a positive sense is correct and that it is acting up.

Use the tangent of the angle to determine h_1:

$$\tan 30° = \frac{opp}{adj} = \frac{v_1}{h_1}$$

$$0.5774 = \frac{100\#}{h_1} \Rightarrow h_1 = 173\# \text{ (left)}$$

Solve for the sum of the horizontal forces to determine h_2:

$$\Sigma H = 0 = h_1 + h_2 = -173\# + h_2$$
$$h_2 = +173\# \text{ (right)}$$

Use the Pythagorean theorem to determine the resultant tension in member AB.

$$\text{Tension in AB} = h_1^2 + v_1^2 = \sqrt{(173\#)^2 + (100\#)^2} = 199.8\#$$

Redraw the system with all forces solved, and check that the sum of the moments equals zero to confirm the solution:

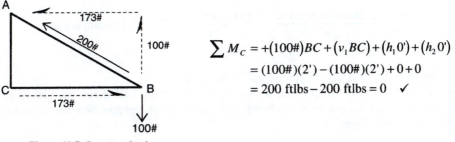

$$\Sigma M_C = +(100\#)BC + (v_1 BC) + (h_1 0') + (h_2 0')$$
$$= (100\#)(2') - (100\#)(2') + 0 + 0$$
$$= 200 \text{ ftlbs} - 200 \text{ ftlbs} = 0 \quad \checkmark$$

Figure 11.7 System solved

Example 2. Consider Figure 11.8. The weight of a speaker hanging from a bracket secured to a wall and the bracket dimensions are given. Find the tension in AB and the compression in BC.

First, draw a free body diagram which incorporates the forces and their components acting at B.

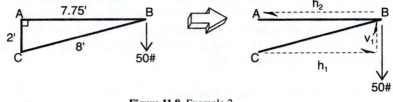

Figure 11.8 Example 2

Next, determine the values of the unknown forces using the rules of equilibrium. Determine v_1:

$$\Sigma V = 0 = v_1 + (-50\#)$$
$$v_1 = 50\# \text{ (up)}$$

Determine the relationship of the two horizontal forces:

$$\Sigma H = 0 = h_1 - h_2$$
$$h_2 = h_1$$

Next, draw similar triangles which represent the lengths of the bracket members and their respective forces acting at point B:

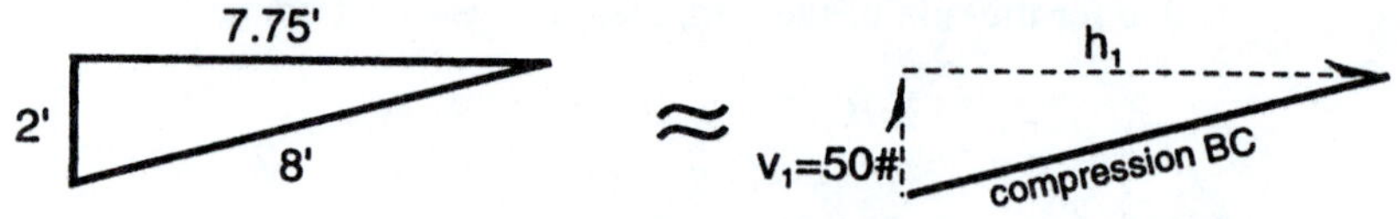

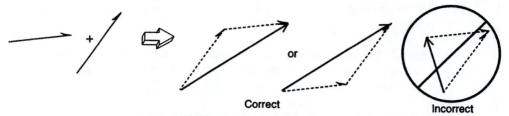

Figure 11.9 Similar triangles

Solve for the unknown forces by comparing the ratios of the sides of the two triangles:

$$\frac{v_1}{2'} = \frac{h_1}{7.75'} \Rightarrow \frac{50\#}{2'} = \frac{h_1}{7.75'} \Rightarrow h_1 = 193.75\# \text{ (right)}$$
$$h_2 = \text{tension in AB} = 193.75\# \text{ (left)}$$
$$\frac{v_1}{2'} = \frac{\text{compression in BC}}{8'} \Rightarrow \frac{50\#}{2'} = \frac{BC}{8'} \Rightarrow BC = 200\# \text{ (compression)}$$

Analyzing Non-Rectilinear Three Member Systems

The principles of a closed triangle can be applied to any system with 3 non-parallel co-planar forces which intersect at a common point. The force vectors can then be arranged to form a closed triangle (see Figure 11.10).

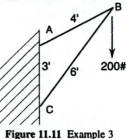

Figure 11.10 Addition of vectors

The magnitudes of the forces can then be determined with trigonometry. If the vectors are drawn to scale, the unknown forces are also scalable. The concept of similar triangles can also be used to solve for unknowns by drawing two triangles: one which represents the length of the forces in the system and a second which represents the magnitudes of the forces. Example 3 illustrates this technique.

Example 3. Find the magnitude and type of stresses present in the bracket shown in Figure 11.11.

Figure 11.11 Example 3

First, draw similar, closed, triangles which represent the lengths of the members and their respective forces acting at point B.

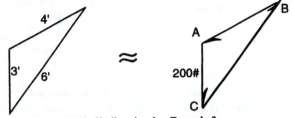

Figure 11.12 Similar triangles, Example 3

Next, solve for the forces:

$$\frac{3'}{4'} = \frac{200\#}{AB}$$

$$(3')AB = 4'(200\#)$$

$$AB = \frac{4'(200\#)}{3'} = 267\#$$

$$\frac{3'}{6'} = \frac{200\#}{BC}$$

$$(3')BC = 6'(200\#)$$

$$BC = \frac{6'(200\#)}{3'} = 400\#$$

When choosing appropriate members for this application, the type of stress is important. In this case, the force in BC is acting toward joint B and is therefore in compression. The force in AB is acting away from joint B and is therefore in tension.

Example 4. Find the magnitude and type of stresses present in the system given below.

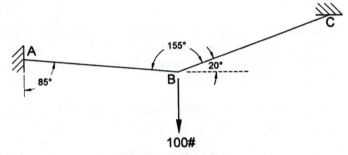

Figure 11.13 Example 4

Draw a closed triangle which represents the forces which act at point B. Start by drawing a vertical line which represents the 100 lb load. The scaled length of this line will be one unit, or 100 lbs. At the tail of the arrow, draw a line with the same angle (relative to horizontal) of member AB. At the head of the arrow, draw a line with the same angle as member BC. The AB line and BC line will intersect (see Figure 11.14). The lengths of these lines to the intersection represent the magnitude of the stresses in the respective members:

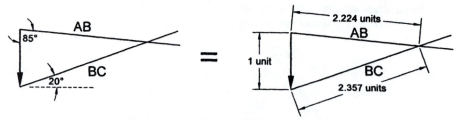

Figure 11.14 Vector addition of Example 4

To find the forces in members AB and BC, simply multiply their length by 100 lbs:

$$\text{tension } AB = (2.224 \text{ units})(100 \text{ \#/unit}) = 222.4\#$$

$$\text{tension } BC = (2.357 \text{ units})(100 \text{ \#/unit}) = 235.7\#$$

This problem can also be solved by using the law of sines instead of scaling the vectors (see Appendix A):

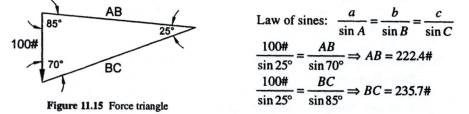

Figure 11.15 Force triangle

Law of sines: $\dfrac{a}{\sin A} = \dfrac{b}{\sin B} = \dfrac{c}{\sin C}$

$$\frac{100\#}{\sin 25°} = \frac{AB}{\sin 70°} \Rightarrow AB = 222.4\#$$

$$\frac{100\#}{\sin 25°} = \frac{BC}{\sin 85°} \Rightarrow BC = 235.7\#$$

This example illustrates how a non-parallel co-planar system can be solved without resolving each force into its vertical and horizontal components.

At first glance, this method of scaling lines to find the forces may seem old-fashioned and even inaccurate because the precision depends on the skill of the draftsperson. However, with modern computer-aided drafting programs, the scaled vector method is once again viable – it is both easy and highly accurate.

> ***Example 5.*** Analyze the stresses present in the speaker bracket shown in Figure 11.16. Assume that all joints are pin connections.

Draw a free body diagram which incorporates the forces and their components:

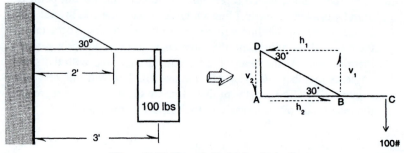

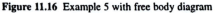

Figure 11.16 Example 5 with free body diagram

Second, take the sum of the moments around A and B and set them to zero:

$$\sum M_A = 0 = (0')v_2 - (2')v_1 + (3')(100\#) \qquad \sum M_B = 0 = (0')v_1 - (2')v_2 + (1')(100\#)$$

$$2v_1 = 300 \qquad\qquad\qquad\qquad 2v_2 = 100$$

$$v_1 = 150\# \text{ (up)} \qquad\qquad\qquad v_2 = 50\# \text{(down)}$$

Note that the sense of the moments requires an understanding of the directions of v_1 and v_2. Confirm these calculations by checking that the sum of the vertical forces equals zero:

$$\sum V = v_1 - v_2 - 100\# = 150\# - 50\# - 100\# = 0 \checkmark$$

Next, using trigonometry, determine the horizontal forces present in the system:

$$\tan 30° = \frac{opp}{adj} = \frac{v_1}{h_1} = \frac{150\#}{h_1}$$

$$0.57735 = \frac{150\#}{h_1} \Rightarrow h_1 = 259.8\# \text{ (left)}$$

Set the sum of the horizontal forces equal to zero to determine h_2:

$$\sum H = 0 = -h_1 + h_2 = -259.8\# + h_2$$

$$h_2 = 259.8\# \text{ (right)}$$

The tension in member BD can be calculated using the Pythagorean theorem:

$$T_{BD} = \sqrt{v_1^2 + h_1^2} = \sqrt{(150\#)^2 + (259.8\#)^2} = 300\#$$

The compression in AB is equal to h_2, or 259.8 lbs. Member AC must be designed as a combined loading condition: an overhanging beam with a compressive load. From the case formulas, we know that the moment induced by the point load is Pa or 1,200 inlbs.

Redraw the system with all the stresses and forces:

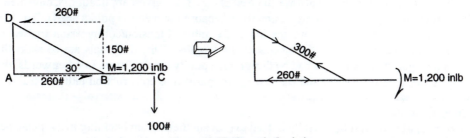

Figure 11.17 Example 5 solution

When members are selected and construction details are determined for this bracket, member AC at Joint B will be subject to a large moment. If the bracket load changes frequently, fatigue failure from frequent flexing could be an issue at that joint. Finally, the connection to the wall at point D must be able to withstand a pull-out force.

TRADITIONAL TRUSSES
Types of Traditional Trusses

Trusses, like beams, are a means of supporting transverse loads which span between two points. Unlike solid beams, *the individual members of a truss are assumed to undergo only axial stress; no flexural stresses are present.* Efficient beams, such as I-beams, concentrate material at the extreme edges of the shape and make the center as light as possible; trusses follow this same pattern. Like flexural members over a simple span, the top edge is subject to compression, and the bottom edge is subject to tension. Unlike flexural members, the middle truss members are in tension or compression caused by the differences in elongation between the top and bottom chords. The general direction of the diagonals, i.e., whether the bottom ends point toward or away from the center of the truss, determines whether they are in tension or compression. In general, two-dimensional trusses can be categorized as tension, compression, or combined tension/compression trusses as illustrated in Figure 11.18 (Ambrose, 120).

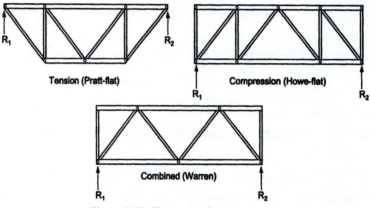

Figure 11.18 Three general truss patterns

As a rule, tension trusses are lighter and more efficient than compression trusses because the allowable tensile stress of most members is higher than their allowable compressive stress. This is especially true for trusses which have long diagonals with high slenderness ratios. However, a tension truss is not always the best choice for a given application. Convenience of construction may require a compression truss because the reaction points need to be along the bottom chord. Homemade compression and combined tension/compression trusses are often seen in theatrical applications because the lengths of the diagonals are so short that there is no significant gain to be had by designing a purely tension truss. In other words, theatrical trusses tend to be short and shallow in comparison to construction industry trusses.

Lateral Bracing

Like beams, trusses must be laterally braced to prevent them from buckling in the plane perpendicular to the plane of bending. In fact, this problem is exacerbated in trusses because the b:d ratio is generally high. Imagine a typical prefabricated wooden roofing truss with a total thickness (*b*) of nominal 4x with a height (*d*) of 8 feet. Compare this ratio of approximately 1:27 to the maximum ratio of 1:7 mandated by the *NDS* for solid beams. Unfortunately, the actual bracing requirements of a truss cannot be computed without the aid of a computer modeling program. Despite this limitation, lateral support for trusses can be designed manually if good judgment is employed:

- Individual compression members should be selected so that there is no need for intermediate bracing between joints. This is simply a matter of not exceeding the maximum unbraced length of the applicable *kl/r* requirement between joints.

- A continuous compression chord (usually the top) of the truss should also be braced so as not to exceed the *kl/r* requirement. This is often a moot point because the chord is usually braced at every joint by the floor or deck that the truss is supporting.

- The tension chord should also be braced periodically as good engineering practice dictates. We recommend a minimum scheme of laterally bracing the middle and ends of any truss up to 16' long. For trusses over 16' long, we recommend adding lateral braces on 8' centers as well as the ends. For a more complete discussion of this topic, see *Design of Building Trusses* by James Ambrose.

Lateral bracing is very important and should not be approached cavalierly. It is particularly important to identify every potential compression member because if one member buckles, the geometry of the truss changes and can cause a runaway collapse. Trusses, like any beam, can be designed as cantilevers, single overhangs, and double-overhangs. When a truss overhangs a reaction, the compression and tension sides of the truss can reverse, i.e., the bottom chord is in compression and the top is in tension on the overhang. A lack of adequate bracing in the outer members of an overhung space frame was partially responsible for the collapse of the Hartford Arena roof in 1978 (Levy, 68-75). In this incident, the entire roof collapsed a mere six hours after the stadium was packed with 5,000 hockey fans.

In addition, for an overhanging truss, variable loading conditions will effect where the compression/tension chord reversal occurs. For example, a truss with a slight overhang and a continuous evenly distributed load may not cause the compression and tension stresses to shift. But if that same truss had a heavy load on the overhang and little or no load over the span (imagine a curtain call), the stresses in the chords and the diagonals could reverse. Thus, a truss which supports one loading condition could fail due to a smaller unanticipated loading condition. It should be noted that the mistakes made in engineering the Hartford Arena, and most structural disasters, were made by qualified, competent engineers.

TRUSS ANALYSIS: METHOD OF JOINTS

Trusses can be analyzed using a variety of methods. This text will discuss the **method of joints** which is a step by step process by which the equilibrium conditions of each joint are calculated. As always, it is assumed that the truss is in static equilibrium, all connections are pin connections, and all loads occur at the joints.

The first step of the analysis is to take the sum of the moments around the two reaction points and set them to zero. After the value of each reaction is determined, it is possible to solve for equilibrium at one of those two joints. The type of stress (compression or tension) and its magnitude at one joint are transferred to adjacent joints. For a statically determinate truss, this provides enough information to solve for the equilibrium conditions at each joint in turn.

Conventionally, a compression member is represented by arrows which point toward the joints at either end of the member; a tension member is represented by arrows pointing away from the joints (see Figure 11.5). The convention is easily explained: a compression member is being squeezed from both ends, and it responds with internal stresses which push out, toward the joints. Likewise, a tension member responds with stresses which pull in, away from the joints.

Stress analysis in trusses can be greatly simplified if the redundant members with no stresses are identified early in the process. These **zero-force members** are usually ones which are horizontal or vertical. Zero force members can be determined by observation prior to any calculations.

The method of joints is a logical extension of the technique used to analyze three member trusses. The following examples illustrate the technique.

Example 6. Analyze the stress in each member of the following truss and design a general scheme for its construction using steel. This tension truss follows the Pratt-flat truss pattern. For clarity, the magnitude of the stresses will be rounded when represented as vectors, but the more precise numbers will be used in the calculations.

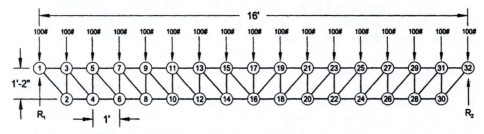

Figure 11.19a Truss and loading conditions for Example 6

The joints are numbered for convenience. The first step in truss analysis is to determine if the truss is statically determinate and to identify any zero-force members:

$$m = 61 \text{ and } j = 32$$
$$m = 2j - 3 \Rightarrow m = 2(32) - 3 = 61 \checkmark$$

The truss is statically determinate. In this loading condition, there are no zero-force members.

Next, the reactions must be calculated. Since this truss is symmetrically loaded each reaction is simply one half of the total weight. Note that the weight of the truss has been neglected.

$$R_1 = R_2 = \frac{W}{2} = \frac{1,700\#}{2} = 850\#$$

Finally, the forces at each joint are analyzed. Picking a starting place can be intimidating, but there is usually little choice. Only an extreme end or a reaction point will have few enough variables to solve for the unknown stresses. For example, the analysis can not begin at joint 3 because it would be impossible to determine how the vertical and diagonal members would split the downward load (see Figure 11.19f for joint 3).

In this case, **joint 1** is a good place to start because the vertical component of the diagonal member is the only unknown vertical force acting at joint 1. First, draw the joint with solid lines representing the physical members and dashed lines representing unknown components and forces (Figure 11.19b).

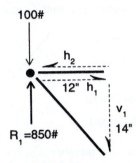

$$\sum V = 0 = -100\# + 850 - v_1$$
$$v_1 = 750\# \text{ (down)}$$

Figure 11.19b Joint 1 unknowns

Now the horizontal component of the diagonal can be calculated using the rigid geometry of the truss.

$$\frac{14"}{12"} = \frac{750\#}{h_1}$$

$$h_1 = \frac{12"}{14"}(750\#) = 0.8571(750\#) = 642.9\# \text{ (right)}$$

The resultant tensile stress in the member can be calculated using the Pythagorean theorem.

$$f_t = \sqrt{v_1^2 + h_1^2} = \sqrt{(750\#)^2 + (642.9\#)^2} = 987.8\#$$

The horizontal component force pulling away from the joint must be resisted by an equal and opposite horizontal force in order to preserve equilibrium. Thus, the top chord member is in compression because it is pushing toward the joint.

$$\sum H = 0 = +h_1 - h_2$$
$$0 = 642.9\# - h_2$$
$$h_2 = 642.9\# \text{ (left)}$$

The last step is to notate the magnitude and type of stress for each member on a line drawing of the truss (see Figure 11.19c). This process is repeated for every joint.

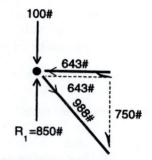

Figure 11.19c Joint 1 solution

Next, proceed to **joint 2**. First, draw the joint with solid lines representing the members and dashed lines representing the components and unknown forces. We know that the diagonal member is in tension and is acting away from the joint. (This becomes confusing if two joints are analyzed simultaneously because it appears that the same force changes its sense from joint to joint.) We also know the magnitude of the vertical and horizontal components of the diagonal. In this case, it is easy to solve for equilibrium because there is only one unknown vertical force and one unknown horizontal force.

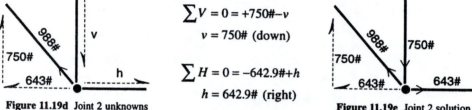

$$\sum V = 0 = +750\# - v$$
$$v = 750\# \text{ (down)}$$

$$\sum H = 0 = -642.9\# + h$$
$$h = 642.9\# \text{ (right)}$$

Figure 11.19d Joint 2 unknowns   **Figure 11.19e** Joint 2 solution

Since v is down, toward the joint, the vertical member is in compression. Since h is to the right, away from the joint, the horizontal member is in tension.

Next, proceed to **joint 3**. We already know the forces in one horizontal and in the only vertical member. The vertical component of the diagonal member is the only unknown vertical force. Once this vertical is determined, the horizontal component can be calculated using similar triangles. The horizontal force in the other top chord can be solved for by applying the law of equilibrium.

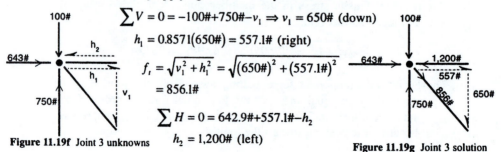

$$\sum V = 0 = -100\# + 750\# - v_1 \Rightarrow v_1 = 650\# \text{ (down)}$$
$$h_1 = 0.8571(650\#) = 557.1\# \text{ (right)}$$
$$f_t = \sqrt{v_1^2 + h_1^2} = \sqrt{(650\#)^2 + (557.1\#)^2}$$
$$= 856.1\#$$
$$\sum H = 0 = 642.9\# + 557.1\# - h_2$$
$$h_2 = 1{,}200\# \text{ (left)}$$

Figure 11.19f Joint 3 unknowns   **Figure 11.19g** Joint 3 solution

The horizontal force in the top chord points to the left, toward the joint, which indicates that it is in compression.

This method of analysis continues until all stresses in the truss are known. If a calculation error is made, then it will be impossible to achieve equilibrium at the last joint. We will show the calculations and line drawings for the rest of the joints, but will not describe the process.

joint 4:

$$\sum V = 0 = 650\#-v$$
$$v = 650\# \text{ (down)}$$

$$\sum H = 0 = -642.9\#-557.1\#+h$$
$$h = 1,200\# \text{ (right)}$$

joint 5:

$$\sum V = 0 = -100\#+650\#-v_1$$
$$v_1 = 550\# \text{ (down)}$$

$$h_1 = 0.8571(550\#) = 471.4\# \text{ (right)}$$
$$f_1 = \sqrt{v_1^2 + h_1^2}$$
$$= \sqrt{(550\#)^2 + (471.4\#)^2} = 724.4\#$$

$$\sum H = 0 = 1,200\#+471.4\#-h_2$$
$$h_2 = 1,671.4\# \text{ (left)}$$

joint 6:

$$\sum V = 0 = 550\#-v$$
$$v = 550\# \text{ (down)}$$

$$\sum H = 0 = -1,200\#-471.4\#+h$$
$$h = 1,671.4\# \text{ (right)}$$

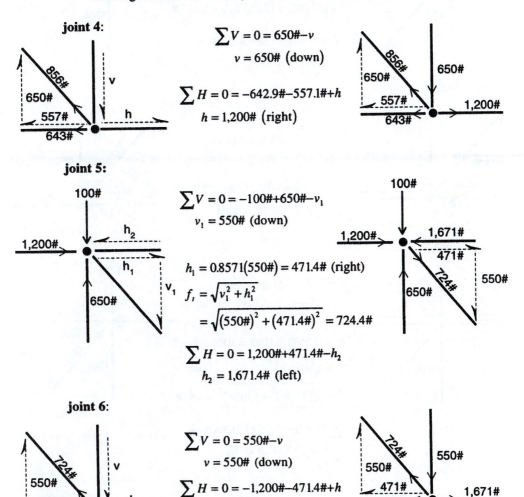

joint 7:

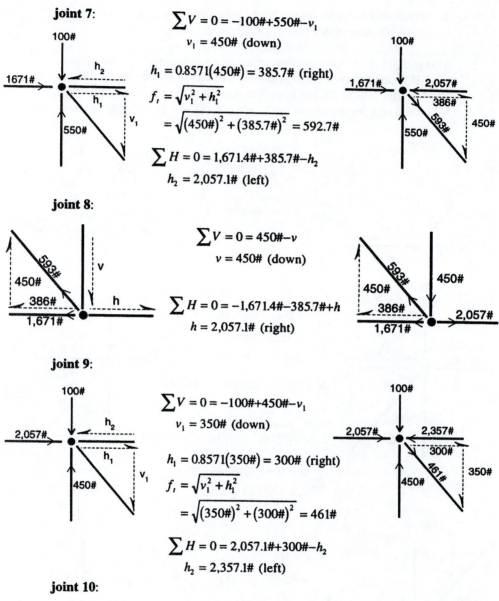

$$\sum V = 0 = -100\# + 550\# - v_1$$
$$v_1 = 450\# \text{ (down)}$$

$$h_1 = 0.8571(450\#) = 385.7\# \text{ (right)}$$
$$f_t = \sqrt{v_1^2 + h_1^2}$$
$$= \sqrt{(450\#)^2 + (385.7\#)^2} = 592.7\#$$

$$\sum H = 0 = 1,671.4\# + 385.7\# - h_2$$
$$h_2 = 2,057.1\# \text{ (left)}$$

joint 8:

$$\sum V = 0 = 450\# - v$$
$$v = 450\# \text{ (down)}$$

$$\sum H = 0 = -1,671.4\# - 385.7\# + h$$
$$h = 2,057.1\# \text{ (right)}$$

joint 9:

$$\sum V = 0 = -100\# + 450\# - v_1$$
$$v_1 = 350\# \text{ (down)}$$

$$h_1 = 0.8571(350\#) = 300\# \text{ (right)}$$
$$f_t = \sqrt{v_1^2 + h_1^2}$$
$$= \sqrt{(350\#)^2 + (300\#)^2} = 461\#$$

$$\sum H = 0 = 2,057.1\# + 300\# - h_2$$
$$h_2 = 2,357.1\# \text{ (left)}$$

joint 10:

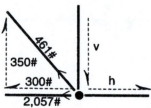

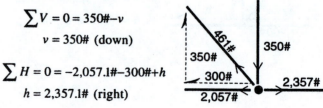

$$\sum V = 0 = 350\# - v$$
$$v = 350\# \text{ (down)}$$

$$\sum H = 0 = -2,057.1\# - 300\# + h$$
$$h = 2,357.1\# \text{ (right)}$$

joint 11:

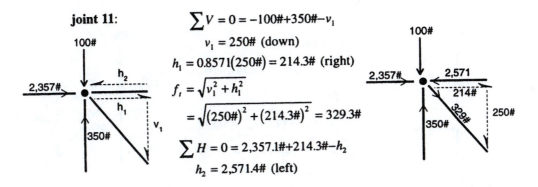

$$\sum V = 0 = -100\# + 350\# - v_1$$

$$v_1 = 250\# \ (\text{down})$$

$$h_1 = 0.8571(250\#) = 214.3\# \ (\text{right})$$

$$f_t = \sqrt{v_1^2 + h_1^2}$$

$$= \sqrt{(250\#)^2 + (214.3\#)^2} = 329.3\#$$

$$\sum H = 0 = 2{,}357.1\# + 214.3\# - h_2$$

$$h_2 = 2{,}571.4\# \ (\text{left})$$

joint 12:

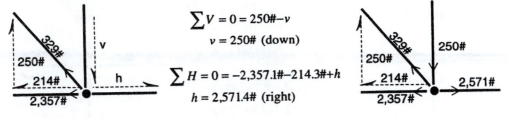

$$\sum V = 0 = 250\# - v$$

$$v = 250\# \ (\text{down})$$

$$\sum H = 0 = -2{,}357.1\# - 214.3\# + h$$

$$h = 2{,}571.4\# \ (\text{right})$$

joint 13:

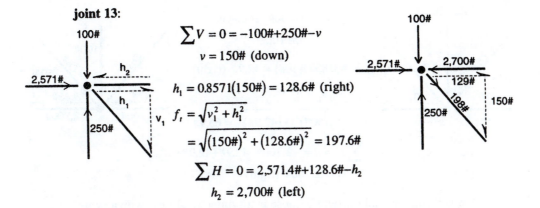

$$\sum V = 0 = -100\# + 250\# - v$$

$$v = 150\# \ (\text{down})$$

$$h_1 = 0.8571(150\#) = 128.6\# \ (\text{right})$$

$$f_t = \sqrt{v_1^2 + h_1^2}$$

$$= \sqrt{(150\#)^2 + (128.6\#)^2} = 197.6\#$$

$$\sum H = 0 = 2{,}571.4\# + 128.6\# - h_2$$

$$h_2 = 2{,}700\# \ (\text{left})$$

joint 14:

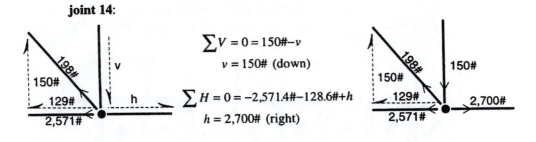

$$\sum V = 0 = 150\# - v$$

$$v = 150\# \ (\text{down})$$

$$\sum H = 0 = -2{,}571.4\# - 128.6\# + h$$

$$h = 2{,}700\# \ (\text{right})$$

joint 15:

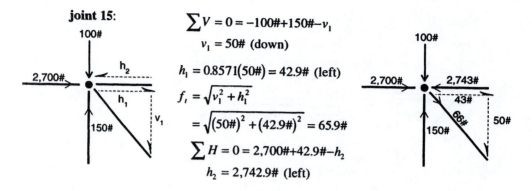

$$\sum V = 0 = -100\# + 150\# - v_1$$
$$v_1 = 50\# \text{ (down)}$$

$$h_1 = 0.8571(50\#) = 42.9\# \text{ (left)}$$
$$f_t = \sqrt{v_1^2 + h_1^2}$$
$$= \sqrt{(50\#)^2 + (42.9\#)^2} = 65.9\#$$
$$\sum H = 0 = 2,700\# + 42.9\# - h_2$$
$$h_2 = 2,742.9\# \text{ (left)}$$

joint 17: Note that joint 16 cannot be solved before joint 17.

$$\sum V = 0 = -100\# + v$$
$$v = 100\# \text{ (up)}$$

$$\sum H = 0 = 2,742.9\# - h$$
$$h = 2,742.9\# \text{ (left)}$$

joint 16:

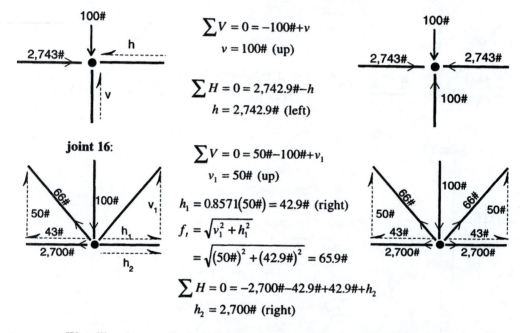

$$\sum V = 0 = 50\# - 100\# + v_1$$
$$v_1 = 50\# \text{ (up)}$$

$$h_1 = 0.8571(50\#) = 42.9\# \text{ (right)}$$
$$f_t = \sqrt{v_1^2 + h_1^2}$$
$$= \sqrt{(50\#)^2 + (42.9\#)^2} = 65.9\#$$

$$\sum H = 0 = -2,700\# - 42.9\# + 42.9\# + h_2$$
$$h_2 = 2,700\# \text{ (right)}$$

We will end our analysis here because in a symmetrical truss with a symmetrical loading condition, it is not necessary to analyze the entire
truss. The stresses in the other half will be a reverse and repeat of the
first. Analyzing the entire truss, however, is a good method for
catching math errors.

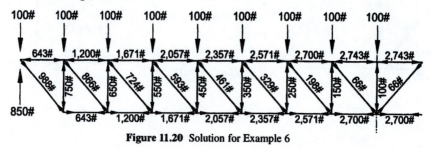

Figure 11.20 Solution for Example 6

This truss problem shows how the stresses form definite patterns. Consider the stresses in the vertical members, which are all under compression and decrease by the amount of the load at each joint. Also, the stresses in the interior "web" members decrease toward the center while the stresses in the top and bottom chords increase toward the center. From beam analysis, this is the general trend we would expect. Notice that the magnitude of the stresses in the top and bottom chords are identical, except that the bottom chord stresses are offset from the top and, therefore, reach a lower maximum stress.

Example 7. Analyze the stress in each member of the following truss. This compression truss follows the Howe-flat truss pattern.

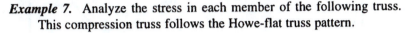

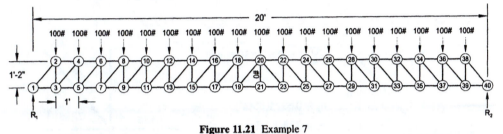

Figure 11.21 Example 7

Determine if the truss is statically determinate, and identify any zero-force members:

$$m = 77 \text{ and } j = 40$$

$$m = 2j - 3 \Rightarrow m = 2(40) - 3 = 77 \checkmark$$

The truss is statically determinate. In this loading condition, the center vertical must be a zero-force member, which is obvious because at joint 21 there is no member or force to balance a force in the vertical member. In effect, the truss could be manufactured without that vertical.

Since this truss is symmetrically loaded each reaction is simply one half of the total weight. Once again, the weight of the truss is neglected.

$$R_1 = R_2 = \frac{W}{2} = \frac{1,900\#}{2} = 950\#$$

The method-of-joints analysis is identical to Example 6. Begin with the left-most joint and proceed to the right.

joint 1:

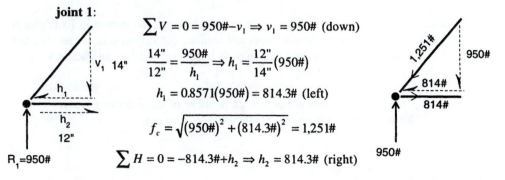

$$\sum V = 0 = 950\# - v_1 \Rightarrow v_1 = 950\# \text{ (down)}$$

$$\frac{14"}{12"} = \frac{950\#}{h_1} \Rightarrow h_1 = \frac{12"}{14"}(950\#)$$

$$h_1 = 0.8571(950\#) = 814.3\# \text{ (left)}$$

$$f_c = \sqrt{(950\#)^2 + (814.3\#)^2} = 1,251\#$$

$$\sum H = 0 = -814.3\# + h_2 \Rightarrow h_2 = 814.3\# \text{ (right)}$$

joint 2:

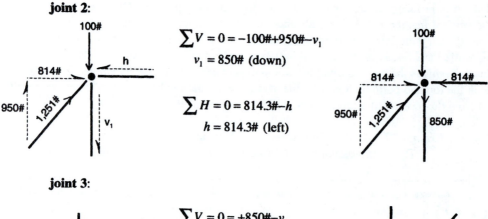

$$\sum V = 0 = -100\# + 950\# - v_1$$
$$v_1 = 850\# \text{ (down)}$$

$$\sum H = 0 = 814.3\# - h$$
$$h = 814.3\# \text{ (left)}$$

joint 3:

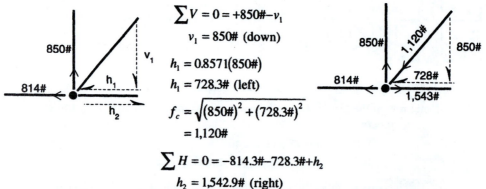

$$\sum V = 0 = +850\# - v_1$$
$$v_1 = 850\# \text{ (down)}$$
$$h_1 = 0.8571(850\#)$$
$$h_1 = 728.3\# \text{ (left)}$$
$$f_c = \sqrt{(850\#)^2 + (728.3\#)^2}$$
$$= 1,120\#$$

$$\sum H = 0 = -814.3\# - 728.3\# + h_2$$
$$h_2 = 1,542.9\# \text{ (right)}$$

The analysis continues until the centerline is reached to result in the following stresses:

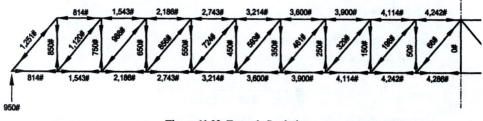

Figure 11.22 Example 7 solution

Take a moment and consider the differences in stresses between the trusses in Examples 6 and 7. Note that the stresses in the diagonals are similar, but opposite in sense, that the stresses in the verticals are similar, and that stresses in the top and bottom chords are also similar, but have the reverse pattern.

> *Example 8a.* Analyze the stress in each member of the following truss.
> This compression truss follows the Warren truss pattern.

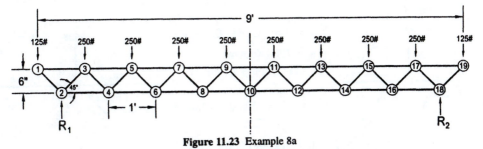

Figure 11.23 Example 8a

Determine if the truss is statically determinate and identify any zero-force members.

$$m = 35 \text{ and } j = 19$$
$$m = 2j - 3 \Rightarrow m = 2(19) - 3 = 35 \checkmark$$

The truss is statically determinate. There are no obvious zero force members.

Since this truss is symmetrically loaded each reaction is simply one half of the total weight. Once again, the weight of the truss is neglected.

$$R_1 = R_2 = \frac{W}{2} = \frac{2,250\#}{2} = 1,125\#$$

The method-of-joints analysis is simplified by the 45° triangle pattern. The horizontal and vertical components of every diagonal have a 1:1 ratio.

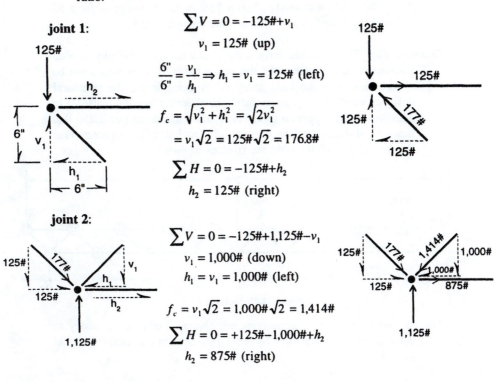

joint 1:

$$\sum V = 0 = -125\# + v_1$$
$$v_1 = 125\# \text{ (up)}$$

$$\frac{6"}{6"} = \frac{v_1}{h_1} \Rightarrow h_1 = v_1 = 125\# \text{ (left)}$$

$$f_c = \sqrt{v_1^2 + h_1^2} = \sqrt{2v_1^2}$$
$$= v_1\sqrt{2} = 125\#\sqrt{2} = 176.8\#$$

$$\sum H = 0 = -125\# + h_2$$
$$h_2 = 125\# \text{ (right)}$$

joint 2:

$$\sum V = 0 = -125\# + 1,125\# - v_1$$
$$v_1 = 1,000\# \text{ (down)}$$
$$h_1 = v_1 = 1,000\# \text{ (left)}$$

$$f_c = v_1\sqrt{2} = 1,000\#\sqrt{2} = 1,414\#$$

$$\sum H = 0 = +125\# - 1,000\# + h_2$$
$$h_2 = 875\# \text{ (right)}$$

joint 3:

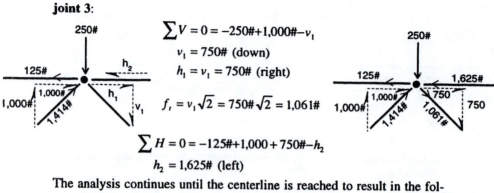

$$\sum V = 0 = -250\# + 1{,}000\# - v_1$$
$$v_1 = 750\# \text{ (down)}$$
$$h_1 = v_1 = 750\# \text{ (right)}$$
$$f_1 = v_1 \sqrt{2} = 750\# \sqrt{2} = 1{,}061\#$$

$$\sum H = 0 = -125\# + 1{,}000 + 750\# - h_2$$
$$h_2 = 1{,}625\# \text{ (left)}$$

The analysis continues until the centerline is reached to result in the following stresses:

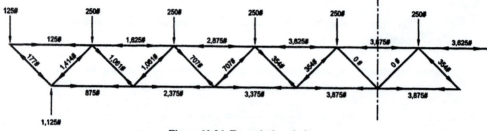

Figure 11.24 Example 8a solution

The stress patterns for this type of truss are very clear. Especially note the flip-flop of tension and compression in adjacent diagonals. The loading on this truss was modeled on a 5'x9' platform designed for a 50 psf load supported by two trusses, one on each 9' side.

Example 8b. Thus far, we have only explored symmetrically loaded trusses. But quite frequently, the actual loads on a truss may not be symmetrical. For the truss analyzed in example 8a, the structural designer would feel quite confident in claiming that the platform in question could support a total evenly distributed load of 2,250 lbs. But what if the entire load was on only one half of the structure (see Figure 11.25). What would the stresses be then?

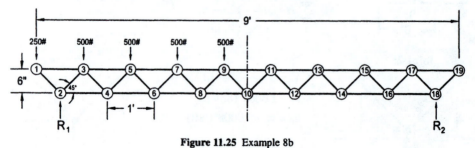

Figure 11.25 Example 8b

The method-of-joints technique does not change, but it is necessary to solve for the two reactions by setting the sum of the moments equal to zero:

$$\sum M_{R_1} = 0 = -(0.5')(250\#) + (0.5')(500\#) + (1.5')(500\#) + (2.5')(500\#) + (3.5')(500\#) - (8')R_2$$
$$8R_2 = 3,875 \text{ ftlb}$$
$$R_2 = 484.375\#$$
$$\sum M_{R_2} = 0 = -(8.5')(250\#) + (8')R_1 - (7.5')(500\#) - (6.5')(500\#) - (5.5')(500\#) - (4.5')(500\#)$$
$$8R_1 = 14,125 \text{ ftlb}$$
$$R_1 = 1,765.625\#$$

$$R_1 + R_2 = 1,765.625\# + 484.375\# = 2,252\# \checkmark$$

Now, analyze the truss beginning at joint 1:

joint 1:

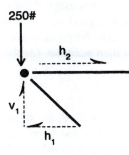

$$\sum V = 0 = -250\# + v_1$$
$$v_1 = 250\# \text{ (up)}$$
$$h_1 = v_1 = 250\# \text{ (left)}$$
$$\sum H = 0 = -250 + h_2$$
$$h_2 = 250\# \text{ (right)}$$

$$f_c = v\sqrt{2} = 250\#\sqrt{2} = 354\#$$

joint 2:

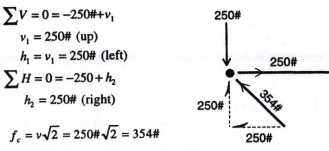

$$\sum V = 0 = -250\# + 1,765.625\# - v$$
$$v_1 = 1,515.625\# \text{ (down)}$$
$$h_1 = v_1 = 1,515.625\# \text{ (left)}$$

$$f_c = 1,515.625\#\sqrt{2} = 2,143\#$$

$$\sum H = 0 = +250\# - 1,515.625\# + h_2$$
$$h_2 = 1,265.625\# \text{ (right)}$$

joint 3:

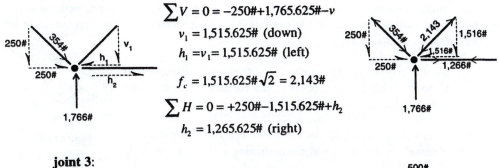

$$\sum V = 0 = -500\# + 1,515.625\# - v_1$$
$$v_1 = 1,015.625\# \text{ (down)}$$
$$h_1 = v_1 = 1,015.625\# \text{ (right)}$$

$$f_t = 1,015.625\#\sqrt{2} = 1,436\#$$

$$\sum H = 0 = -250\# + 1,515.625\# + 1,015.625\# - h_2$$
$$h_2 = 2,281.25\# \text{ (left)}$$

If the analysis continues, it results in the following stress pattern:

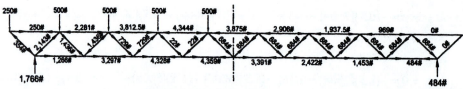

Figure 11.26 Example 8b solution

The overall order of magnitude of the stresses for the above example is similar to that found for the symmetrically loaded truss in Example 8a. However, there are some substantial differences in the stresses of individual members. For example, the two center diagonals had no stress in the symmetrical loading condition, but have 684 lbs of tension or compression with the unsymmetrical loading condition. This example highlights the need to define a worst case loading condition. It also makes a strong argument for designing all members to withstand the greatest stress in their category. In Example 8b, all diagonals should be designed for a 2,143 lb compressive load; the top chord members should be designed for a 4,344 lb compressive load, and the bottom chord members should be designed for a 4,356 lb tensile load. Note that since the unsymmetrical loading condition leads to the greatest load concentration in individual members, this design would also be more than adequate for the loading condition in Example 8a.

TRUSS CONSTRUCTION

After the magnitude of the stresses present in each member has been quantified, the minimum sizes and shapes of those members must be determined. Tension members are designed using the direct stress formula and compression members are designed using column design procedures appropriate to the material from which the truss is to be fabricated.

After the minimum sizes and shapes of individual members have been determined, the structural designer must look at the truss as a whole. Many decisions in truss design are made for construction considerations:

- Similar cross-sections are often used to simplify construction or to maintain a single plane at the expense of over-sizing some members (see Figure 11.27).

- It is also common to double miter diagonal members to achieve a panel point while maintaining a single plane (see Figure 11.28).

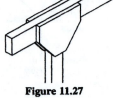

Figure 11.27

- Common joint details for wooden trusses include plywood or steel gusset plates (plywood shown in Figure 11.27). Steel trusses commonly use welded joints. Both wooden and steel trusses also use bolted connections.

Figure 11.28

- Often either the chords or the diagonals are made as two members with a gap between them to facilitate the connection details as shown in Figures 11.29 and 11.30. Figure 11.30 also shows a

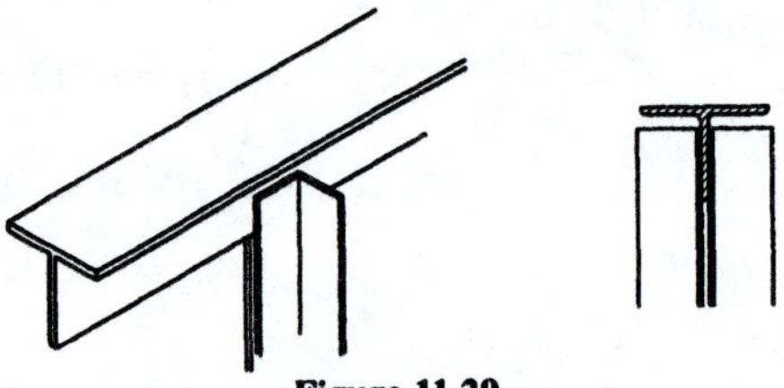

Figure 11.29

detail of how a nailing plate is bolted through the gap between a double-angle iron top chord. The nailing plate makes attaching a wooden deck to the steel truss quick and easy, but can be removed or replaced for convenience. In addition to the steel spaced members, wooden spaced members are often used as chords or diagonals for the same reasons.

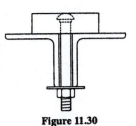

Figure 11.30

• Trusses are often built to support an evenly distributed load such as a floor, deck, or ceiling. In order to concentrate the loads at the joints as required by Condition 2, structural designers often use floor joists to span between trusses (see Figure 11.31).

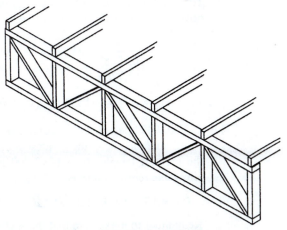

Figure 11.31 Panel point loading

• When designing joints, it is also necessary to pay attention to the type of stresses present in the members being joined as well as their magnitude. When using bolts, be sure that they are adequately sized for the connection. A gusset plate joint between compressive members should have plates on both sides of the joint. A gusset plate joint between tensile members should be adequately sized to maintain the tensile strength of the members. A good rule of thumb for tensile plywood gusset plates is that the total area of the plate(s) should be at least twice the required area of the solid wood members they are joining.

Example 9. Design a general construction scheme for the truss analyzed in Example 6.

Construction details are highly dependent on the unique use planned for a truss. A simple idea would be to plan to use steel tubing and make the truss as light as possible. Remember that square and round shapes make the most efficient compression members, and that the most highly stressed members should be used as the design criteria.

Therefore, we will start with the compression chord, which has the greatest stresses in the exact center of the span, between joints 15 and 17 and 17 and 18. They are subject to a compressive load of 2,743 lbs and have an unbraced length of 12". Assume that the tubing grade is MT1010 (F_y=32 ksi).

First, try a 3/8"x3/8"x0.035" (the lightest tubing available).

$$\frac{Kl}{r} = \frac{1(12")}{0.1378"} = 87.08 \Rightarrow 88$$

$$F_{a_{88}} = 13,350 \text{ psi}$$

$$P_{all} = AF_a = (0.0458 \text{ in}^2)(13,350 \text{ psi}) = 611\# \Rightarrow 611\# < 2,743\# \quad \times$$

Though the size is within the slenderness ratio requirements, it is obviously too small, so we will go to a 1"x1"x0.049" member.

$$\frac{Kl}{r} = \frac{1(12")}{0.3868"} = 31.02 \Rightarrow 32$$

$$F_{a_{32}} = 17,720 \text{ psi}$$

$$P_{all} = AF_a = (0.1832 \text{ in}^2)(17,720 \text{ psi}) = 3,246\# \Rightarrow 3,246\# > 2,743\# \quad \checkmark$$

The 1"x1"x0.049" passes with a comfortable margin for the compression chord members with the greatest stress. It should also easily support the greatest tensile stress (f_t=2,700 lbs) in the bottom chord. The allowable tensile stress is 19.2 ksi (see Appendix E).

$$P_{all} = AF_t = (0.1832 \text{ in}^2)(19,200 \text{ psi}) = 3,517\# \Rightarrow 3,517\# > 2,700\# \quad \checkmark$$

Remember to make sure that the section meets the compactness criteria discussed in Chapters 8 and 9 (see Limiting Width-Thickness Ratios, Appendix E).

$$b/t = 20.4 \Rightarrow b/t < 42.1 \quad \checkmark$$

Next, the verticals and diagonals need to be designed. Though the diagonals are longer, the verticals are in compression, so they will probably need to be larger. It is certainly acceptable to design the interior members as 1"x1" tube to simplify construction, but that would overbuild the truss. In order to reduce weight but also keep the layout uncomplicated, 3/8"x1" members will be tested. The advantages would be the elimination of double bevels and keeping the same overall thickness (see Figure 11.32) while reducing the weight.

Try a 3/8"x1"x0.049" for the compression verticals.

$$\frac{Kl}{r_{y-y}} = \frac{1(14")}{0.1511"} = 92.65 \Rightarrow 93$$

$$F_{a_{93}} = 12,870 \text{ psi}$$

$$P_{all} = AF_a = (0.1219 \text{ in}^2)(12,870 \text{ psi}) = 1,569\# \Rightarrow 1,569\# > 950\# \quad \checkmark$$

Now, try it for the tension diagonals.

$$P_{all} = AF_t = (0.1219 \text{ in}^2)(19,200 \text{ psi}) = 2,340.5\# \Rightarrow 2,340.5 > 1,120\# \quad \checkmark$$

The 3/8"x1"x0.049 tube also passes the compactness criteria.

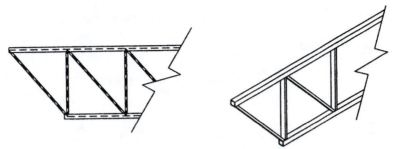

Figure 11.32 Joint details of Example 9

The 3/8"x1"x0.049" tube will work for the interior members of the truss. It may be tempting to reduce the wall thicknesses to 0.035. However, 0.035" may prove to be too thin to be successfully welded. In general, 0.065" or thicker tubing is recommended when welding joints.

When the truss is actually used, it is important to make sure that it is laterally braced at appropriate intervals as determined by the compression chord and good engineering practice.

$$\frac{Kl}{r} = 200$$

$$l_{max} = 200r = 200(0.3868") = 77.36" \approx 6'-5"$$

Therefore, the compression chord should be braced at every 6th joint or at the third points of the truss. It is probably advisable to brace the tension chord at those intervals as well.

Example 10. What is the minimum diameter A36 rod which could be used for the diagonals in Examples 8a and 8b?

The greatest compressive stress present is in the member between joints 2 and 3 in Example 8b. It is approximately 8.5" long and has a compressive stress of 2,143 lbs.

First, try a 3/8" rod. From Chapter 4, remember that the radius of gyration, r, of any solid circle is equal to one half the radius:

$$r = \frac{radius}{2} = \frac{0.1875"}{2} = 0.09375"$$

Using the calculated value of the radius of gyration, the allowable load is determined:

$$\frac{Kl}{r} = \frac{1(8.5")}{0.09375"} = 90.67 \Rightarrow 91$$

$$F_{a_{91}} = 14.09 \text{ ksi} = 14,090 \text{ psi}$$

$$P_{all} = AF_a = (\pi r^2)F_a = \left[\pi(0.1875")^2\right]14,090 \text{ psi} = 1,555.5\#$$

Since 1,555#<2,143#, 3/8" rod is an inappropriate choice.

Next, try 7/16" rod:

$$r = \frac{radius}{2} = \frac{0.21875"}{2} = \frac{7"}{64} = 0.109375"$$

$$\frac{Kl}{r} = \frac{1(8.5")}{0.109375"} = 77.7$$

$$F_{a_n} = 15.58 \text{ ksi} = 15,580 \text{ psi}$$

$$P_{all} = AF_a = (\pi r^2)F_a = \left[\pi(0.21875")^2\right]15,580 \text{ psi} = 2,342.1\# \Rightarrow 2,342.1\# > 2,143\#$$

7/16" rod would be adequate for both loading conditions on the truss.

CABLES

In this section, techniques for analyzing cables with point loads and evenly distributed loads will be discussed, but first we need background information on cable. The term **cable** is applicable to any flexible tensile member regardless of material. Hence, a cable problem can involve natural fiber, synthetic fiber, or wire rope. We will concentrate on wire rope issues, but the discussions of safety factors and stress analysis are equally pertinent to natural or synthetic fiber ropes.

CABLE STRENGTH AND SAFETY FACTORS

Comprehensively discussing the many issues involving cable use in theater is beyond the scope of this text, so we recommend the *Wire Rope Users Manual* (*WRUM*) published by the Wire Rope Technical Board. The *WRUM* is to wire rope what the *SCM* is to steel. This section will explicate how to determine an allowable load for a given cable in typical theatrical applications.

First, what kind of cable do we use in theater? Ask a technician, and the answer will usually be, "aircraft cable." Technically speaking, the 1/16"-1/4" cable commonly found in temporary scenery applications is defined as 7x7 or 7x19, Seal, preformed, galvanized, EIPS, IWRC, right regular lay (Carter, 100). Knowing this information, makes it possible to look up the strength of the wire rope (*WRUM*, 107). A more complete table is available in Appendix G:

Nominal diameter (in)	Nominal Strength (lbs), Galvanized	
	7x7	7x19
1/16	480	480
1/8	1,700	2,000
3/16	3,700	4,200
1/4	6,100	7,000

The strength of other types of wire rope, such as rotation resistant rope, can also be found in the *Wire Rope Users Manual*. It should be noted that cable strength is measured in pounds, not pounds-per-square inch. Hence, it is not technically proper to discuss stress in cables, only cable load or strength.

The **nominal strength** (N.S.) of wire rope is an industry accepted value which should be used in design calculations as if it were the ultimate breaking strength (*WRUM*, 139). Unlike the steel and wood industries, the wire rope industry does not establish elaborate procedures in order to calculate the allowable load on a cable. Instead, the industry relies on the good sense of individual engineers to determine the acceptable **working load** on a cable.

It is generally accepted that cables should not be loaded to their nominal strength for two reasons: (1) a temporary dynamic loading condition could easily overstrain the cable, and (2) the service life of the cable will be drastically reduced.

Given that the working load on a cable should be less than the nominal strength, what standards should be applied?

- In general, cables unlikely to receive severe shock loads and whose failure would not produce a life-threatening condition should be designed with a **safety factor** (S.F.) of 5.

- Cables used in critical situations should be designed with a safety factor of ten. These cables include those used in overhead rigging, those likely to experience shock loads, and those whose failure could result in injury or loss-of-life. Examples are cables used in linesets, elevators, or flying rigs.

- If the planned service life is long or if the cable will be subjected to hard use (heavy loads with sharp turns), a higher design factor is appropriate.

The **end fitting** or **termination** of the wire rope also affects its working load. The *WRUM* lists an approximate **efficiency** (EFF) of 95% for end loops formed with a thimble and a mechanical spliced sleeve (also called a "nicopress" or swage) for wire ropes with a diameter of 1" or less. The efficiency for end terminations using wire rope clips is 80% (*WRUM*, 35). These ratings assume that the end terminations meet the manufacturers specifications. This is especially true for wire rope clips, where "saddling a dead horse" can decrease rope life significantly by crimping the live side of the cable.

> ***Example 11.*** What is the safe working load of a 7x19 1/8" wire rope being used in a critical situation if it has a mechanical spliced sleeve at one end and a wire rope clip at the other? Assume that both terminations are made to the manufacturer's specifications.
>
> Adjusted Nominal Strength = (Efficiency)(Nominal Strength)
> $$= (EFF)(N.S.) = 0.8(2,000\#)$$
> $$= 1,600\#$$
> Working Strength = (Adjusted Nominal Strength)/ (Safety Factor)
> $$= 1,600\# / 10 = 160 \text{ lbs}$$
>
> Note that the strength of the wire rope system is determined by its "weakest link," the wire rope clip termination.

ANALYZING CABLE SYSTEMS

As in any structural design problem, the actual loads on a cable must be calculated before selecting a cable. In this section, techniques for finding cable tension generated by a single point load or by an evenly distributed load will be discussed.

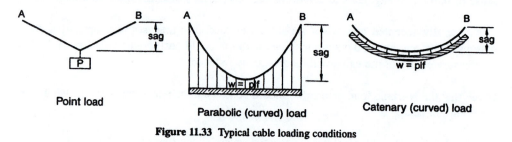

| Point load | Parabolic (curved) load | Catenary (curved) load |

Figure 11.33 Typical cable loading conditions

All cable problems are analyzed by applying the rules of equilibrium. Like a beam, the two connection points at each end of the cable are reaction points. If a cable system suspended by two points is in equilibrium, several observations can be made:

- The only horizontal forces are those developed at the reaction points. Therefore, the horizontal forces of the two reaction points must be equal and opposite:

$$H_A = H_B$$

- The vertical components of the reactions together must be equal and opposite to the downward loading on the cable:

$$V_A + V_B = Load$$

- Once either the horizontal or vertical components are known, the geometry of the cable system will determine the rest of the unknowns. Figure 11.34 shows how the resultant tension in a cable can be resolved into horizontal and vertical components. (For a more detailed discussion, see Appendix A.)

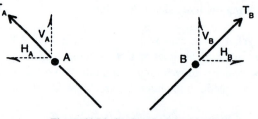

Figure 11.34 Components of cable tension

CONCEPT BOX: As seen in the method of joints, the component force triangles are similar triangles to the actual physical geometry of the cable problem. In other words, the ratios between the vertical, horizontal, and resultant forces must be identical to the ratios between the vertical distance, horizontal distance, and the "hypotenuse" distance of the cable. For the system to maintain equilibrium, the component forces of the tension must be equal and opposite to the component forces at the connection or reaction points.

POINT LOAD CABLE SYSTEMS

When a point load is hung along the span of a cable, the tension on either side of the load and the forces acting at the reaction points can be analyzed. The basic strategy for solving cable problems is the same as the method of joints for truss analysis. For a typical problem, one should first take the sum of the moments around the two reactions where the cable is anchored. By setting the sum of the moments to zero (an equilibrium condition), some variables can be eliminated. Once again, an example is worth a thousand words.

> ***Example 12.*** What is the tension in the cable on either side of the point load in Figure 11.35a? Choose an appropriate diameter of 7x19 galvanized cable assuming that this is an overhead rigging situation.

First, break up the system into component forces and similar triangles (see Figure 11.35a).

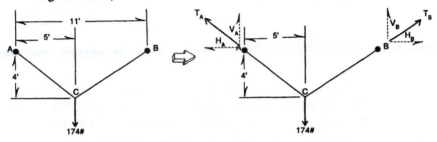

Figure 11.35a Example 12 transformed into system components

Take the sum of the moments about A and B and set them equal to zero.

$$\Sigma M_A = 0 = +(5')(174\#) - (11')V_B - (0')H_B - (0')V_A - (0')H_A$$
$$V_B = 79.09\#$$
$$\Sigma M_B = 0 = -(6')(174\#) + (11')V_A - (0')H_A - (0')V_B - (0')H_B$$
$$V_A = 94.91\#$$

Check that the sum of the vertical and horizontal forces equal zero. Remember that the only load is vertical, and therefore, any horizontal forces will be generated by the tension in the cables at the reaction points.

Check the sum of the vertical forces:

$$\Sigma V = -P + V_A + V_B$$
$$\Sigma V = -174\# + 94.91\# + 79.09\# = 0 \checkmark$$

Determine the relationship between the horizontal forces by setting the sum the horizontal forces equal to zero:

$$\Sigma H = 0 = -H_A + H_B$$
$$H_A = H_B$$

Solve for the horizontal forces by using similar triangles:

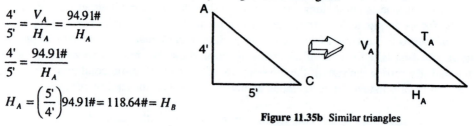

$$\frac{4'}{5'} = \frac{V_A}{H_A} = \frac{94.91\#}{H_A}$$

$$\frac{4'}{5'} = \frac{94.91\#}{H_A}$$

$$H_A = \left(\frac{5'}{4'}\right)94.91\# = 118.64\# = H_B$$

Figure 11.35b Similar triangles

The horizontal forces can also be determined using trigonometry:

$$\tan\theta = \frac{opp}{adj} = \frac{4'}{5'} = 0.8$$

$$0.8 = \frac{V_A}{H_A} = \frac{94.91\#}{H_A}$$

$$H_A = \frac{94.91\#}{0.8} = 118.64\# = H_B$$

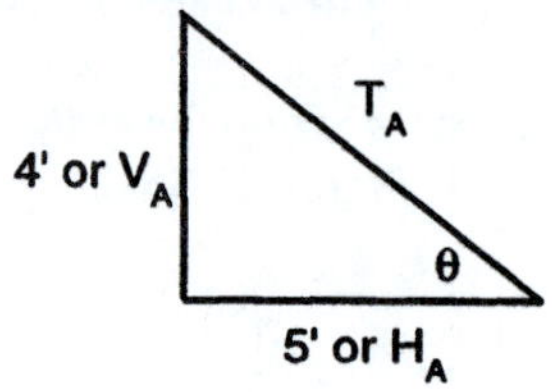

Figure 11.35c Trigonometry

In this case, there is essentially no difference between the trigonometric and similar triangles methods. In other situations, where only the angles are known, trigonometry may be the easier approach.

Finally, the tension on each side of the cable is calculated using the Pythagorean theorem.

$$a^2 = b^2 + c^2$$

$$T_{AC} = \sqrt{H_A^2 + V_A^2} = \sqrt{(118.64\#)^2 + (94.61\#)^2} = 151.9\#$$

$$T_{BC} = \sqrt{H_B^2 + V_B^2} = \sqrt{(118.64\#)^2 + (79.09\#)^2} = 142.6\#$$

As example 11 demonstrated, an 1/8" cable (7x19 galvanized), with a safe working load of 160 lbs, is acceptable for this loading condition.

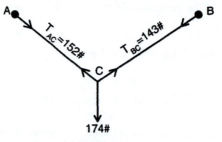

Figure 11.35d Example 12 solution

Several notes should be made about this example:

- It is wise to double-check a problem to see if it makes sense by taking a step back and looking at the overall solution. For example, the cable which is closest to vertical will always take more of the vertical load.

- If the connections at points A and B are not in line with the cable, they must be designed to take both a 118 lb pull-out force and a shear force of up to 95 lbs.

- As the cable becomes closer to horizontal, the horizontal force increases exponentially. The **sag** of a system is the vertical distance between reactions and the lowest point of the cable. In this case, if the sag is reduced to 1", the pull-out force increases to 5,695 lbs!

- It is implicitly assumed that this cable problem is actually the analysis of two physically discrete cables. If the cable was continuous, the 174 lb weight would simply slide down the cable until it settled into the center of the span.

> *Example 13.* Find the tension present on either side of the point load in Figure 11.36a, and choose an appropriate diameter cable for an overhead rigging situation. Assume that the end terminations are made with swaged sleeves.

First, break up the system into component forces and similar triangles.

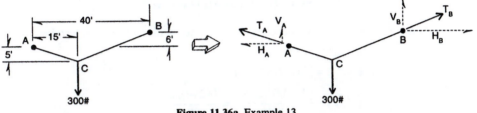

Figure 11.36a Example 13

Second, take the sum of the moments about A and B and set them to zero.

$$\Sigma M_A = 0 = (15')(300\#) - (40')V_B + (6')H_B + (0')V_A + (0')H_A$$
$$-4{,}500 \text{ ftlb} = -40'V_B + 6'H_B$$
$$\Sigma M_B = 0 = -(25')(300\#) + (40')V_A + (6')H_A + (0')V_B + (0')H_B$$
$$7{,}500 \text{ ftlb} = 40'V_A + 6'H_A$$

Next, use the geometric relationship between the vertical and horizontal forces to solve the moment equations for one variable.

$$\frac{V_A}{H_A} = \frac{5'}{15'} \quad \Rightarrow \quad \begin{array}{c} 7{,}500 \text{ ftlb} = 40'V_A + 6'(3V_A) \\ 58V_A = 7{,}500 \text{ ftlb} \end{array} \quad \Rightarrow \quad H_A = 3V_A = 3(129.3\#) = 387.9\#$$
$$3V_A = H_A \qquad\qquad V_A = 129.3\#$$

For equilibrium to be achieved, the horizontal forces must be equal and opposite,

$$H_A = H_B = 387.9\#$$

Now V_B can be solved for by using its geometric relationship to H_B:

$$\frac{V_B}{H_B} = \frac{11'}{25'}$$

$$V_B = \left(\frac{11}{25}\right)H_B = \left(\frac{11}{25}\right)387.9\# = 170.7\#$$

The tension on each side of the cable is calculated using the Pythagorean theorem.

$$T_{AC} = \sqrt{H_A^2 + V_A^2} = \sqrt{(387.9\#)^2 + (129.3\#)^2} = 408.9\# \Rightarrow 409\#$$

$$T_{BC} = \sqrt{H_B^2 + V_B^2} = \sqrt{(387.9\#)^2 + (170.7\#)^2} = 423.8\# \Rightarrow 424\#$$

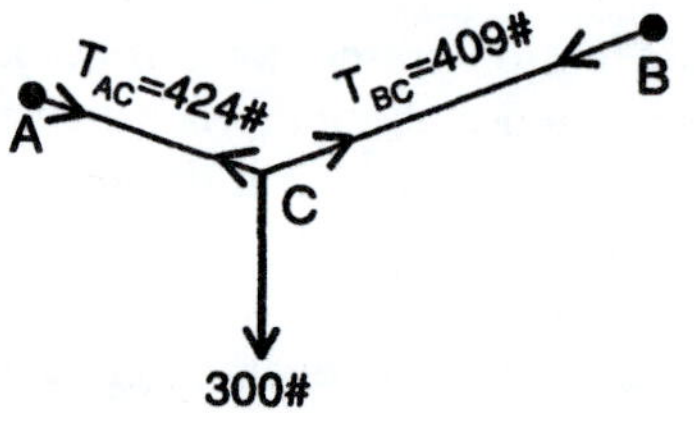

Figure 11.36b Example 13 solution

Select a cable for an overhead rigging situation with nicopressed terminations:

$$(EFF)(N.S.) = (LOAD)(S.F.)$$

$$(N.S.) = \frac{(LOAD)(S.F.)}{(EFF)} = \frac{(424\#)10}{0.95}$$

$$= 4{,}463.16\# \Rightarrow 4{,}464\# = \text{required nominal strength}$$

A 7/32" or larger 7x7 or 7x19 cable (nominal strength of 4,800 lbs and 5,600 lbs, respectively) will be adequate.

CURVED CABLE SYSTEMS

Occasionally, a set designer calls for an effect which creates a curved arc in a cable span. Imagine a "shower curtain" in which a painted fabric curtain is pulled across a wire. When the curtain is fully stretched across the stage, a curve is created. There are two common techniques for modeling this behavior: **parabolic cables**, which have an evenly distributed load with respect to their span, and **catenary cables**, which have an evenly distributed load with respect to their length (see previous Figure 11.33).

The curve of a theatrical shower curtain is neither a pure parabolic nor a catenary. We will model it as a parabolic cable because that technique is less cumbersome and there is no significant difference between the answers generated by the two techniques for typical theatrical loading conditions. An important note is that the worst case scenario for a curtain effect could actually occur when the curtain is bunched up in the middle of the span. In these cases, the tension in the cable can be determined using the single point load technique.

PARABOLIC CABLES

For a true parabolic curve to be formed, the horizontal distance between each pick point supporting the load must be equal, and the load must be uniform with respect to the span. The cable must also be one continuous length. As in a cable with a single point load, the vertical components at the reactions must sum to be equal and opposite to the downward load. The cable tension is greatest at each reaction if the two points are at the same height, and greater at the higher reaction if they are not. Notice that the point of lowest cable sag is always closer to the lower support point.

To analyze the tension in the system, we split the cable into two systems at the point of lowest sag. Essentially, all of the weight to the left of the low point is supported at A, and all of the weight to the right of the low point is supported at B. When the sum of the moments is taken at point A or B the weight is considered to act from the center of gravity of that part of the cable (see Figure 11.37).

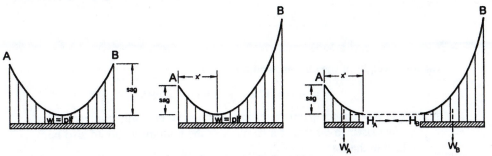

Figure 11.37 Parabolic curves

At the point of lowest sag, the slope of a line tangent to the curve is zero. Remember that slope is the change in vertical distance divided by the change in horizontal distance ($\Delta y/\Delta x$) of a given curve. A slope of 0 implies that there is no vertical component to the curve. As discussed previously, the only horizontal forces present in the system are those generated at the reaction points, therefore the horizontal forces H_A and H_B must be equal and opposite. If the horizontal forces are identical, then the maximum tension will occur on the side which has the greatest vertical component – the highest support point.

The maximum tension of a parabolic system is found by using the logic expressed above and the laws of equilibrium. The only information necessary is the length of the span, the vertical relationships between points A and B, and the cable sag. Examples 14 and 15 illustrate the technique.

> ***Example 14.*** A designer has requested that a painted drop be manually drawn across the stage via rings strung onto an aircraft cable. The drop is 12' high and 30' wide. The designer has requested that the total sag be limited to 6". What is the tension in the cable and the pull-out force at the connection points?

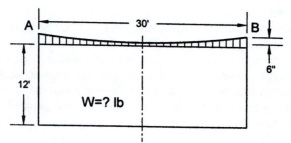

Figure 11.38a Example 14

First, model the loading conditions. If the fabric weighs 12 oz per square yard of fabric, the weight of the curtain in psf would be:

$$w = \frac{12 \text{ oz}}{9 \text{ ft}^2} = 1.33 \text{ oz}/\text{ft}^2$$

$$w = \frac{1.33 \text{ oz}/\text{ft}^2}{16} = 0.083 \text{ psf}$$

The total weight of the curtain would then be:

$$W = Aw = \left[12'(30')\right]0.083 \text{ psf} = 29.9\#$$

In order to account for paint, webbing, grommets, etc., this number will be increased to 50 lbs. If a chain is in the bottom, it should also be added to the total.

Now the tension in the cable can be calculated. Since the loading condition is symmetrical, each reaction will support one half of the load. The vertical component, V_A, of the reaction is one half of W, or 25 lbs. The horizontal component, H_A, of the load can be calculated by taking the sum of the moments about one reaction and setting it equal to zero.

Remember only one half of the cable is considered at a time (see Figure 11.38b), and, in this example, the two halves are identical.

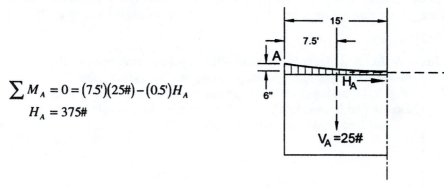

$$\sum M_A = 0 = (7.5')(25\#) - (0.5')H_A$$
$$H_A = 375\#$$

Figure 11.38b Example 14

The tension is calculated using the Pythagorean theorem:

$$T_{max} = \sqrt{V_A^2 + H_A^2} = \sqrt{25\#^2 + 375\#^2} = 375.8\#$$

The worst case scenario for this situation is actually the tension created if the entire curtain is bunched up in the center of the span. This changes the parabolic cable problem into a point-load problem.

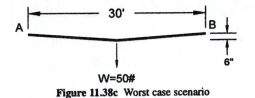

W=50#

Figure 11.38c Worst case scenario

Once again, the vertical component of the tension is 25 lbs, but the horizontal component must be calculated using the geometric relationship between the two.

$$\frac{V_A}{H_A} = \frac{0.5'}{15'}$$

$$H_A = 30V_A = 30(25\#) = 750\#$$

The tension is calculated as always:

$$T_{max} = \sqrt{V_A^2 + H_A^2} = \sqrt{25\#^2 + 750\#^2} = 750.4\#$$

The resultant tension from the point load is almost exactly twice the tension due to a parabolic loading condition.

Example 15. Determine the point of greatest sag and the maximum tension in the following parabolic loading condition.

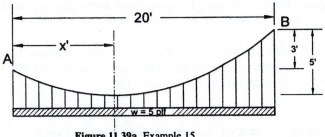

Figure 11.39a Example 15

First, take the sum of the moments about points A and B and set them to zero. Remember that each half of the system is considered independently. Also remember that H_A and H_B must be equal and opposite in order for the sum of the horizontal forces to be zero.

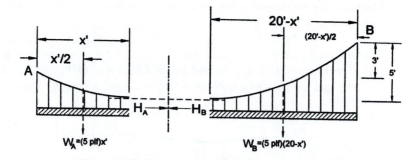

Figure 11.39b Example 15 system components

$$\sum M_A = 0 = \left\{\left[x'(5 \text{ plf})\right]\frac{x'}{2}\right\} - (2')H \qquad \sum M_B = 0 = -\left\{\left[(20-x')(5 \text{ plf})\right]\left(\frac{20-x'}{2}\right)\right\} + (5')H$$

$$0 = 2.5x^2 - 2H$$

$$H = 1.25x^2 \qquad\qquad\qquad 0 = -\left[(100-5x)\left(10-\frac{x}{2}\right)\right] + 5H$$

$$H_A = H_B \qquad\qquad\qquad 5H = 1,000 - 100x + 2.5x^2$$

Plug in the previously determined value of H:

$$5(1.25x^2) = 1,000 - 100x + 2.5x^2$$

$$0 = -3.75x^2 - 100x + 1,000$$

Now, use the quadratic formula to solve for x, the location of greatest sag.

$$x = \frac{-b \pm \sqrt{b^2 - 4ac}}{2a} \qquad x = \frac{-(-100) + \sqrt{(-100)^2 - 4(-3.75)(1,000)}}{2(-3.75)} = -34.415'$$

$$a = -3.75$$
$$b = -100$$
$$c = +1,000 \qquad\qquad x = \frac{-(-100) - \sqrt{(-100)^2 - 4(-3.75)(1,000)}}{2(-3.75)} = 7.75'$$

Since a negative number makes no sense in the physical world, the location of greatest sag is 7.75' from point A.

The B side of the system will have the maximum tension because it supports most of the weight. The vertical component will be equal to 20–x multiplied by the load of 5 plf:

$$V_B = (20'-x')w = (12.25')(5 \text{ plf}) = 61.25\#$$

H_B is calculated using the previously determined formula:

$$H_B = 1.25x^2 = 1.25(7.75)^2 = 75.08\#$$

The tension is calculated using the Pythagorean theorem:

$$T_{\max} = \sqrt{V_B^2 + H_B^2} = \sqrt{61.25\#^2 + 75.08\#^2} = 96.9\#$$

For all cable problems, the less sag, the greater the tension present in the cable. Example 16 illustrates the exponential change in cable tension when the sag is restricted to 1".

> *Example 16.* What would be the tension present if the cable sag in Example 14 were 1"?

Calculate the new horizontal force using 0.0833' instead of 0.5':

$$\sum M_A = +(7.5')(25\#) - 0.0833' H$$

$$H = 2{,}250\#$$

The tension is calculated using the Pythagorean theorem:

$$T_{max} = \sqrt{V^2 + H^2} = \sqrt{25\#^2 + 2{,}250\#^2} = 2{,}250.1\#$$

> The original tension was 375 lbs. If the curtain were bunched in the center and the sag remained 1", 4,500 lbs of tension would be created.

Tension in cables is determined by the cable sag and the magnitude of the load. As the cable sag decreases, the cable tension and, hence, pull-out force on fasteners radically increases. This is exactly the same principle which encourages bridles with generous angles. It is also important to identify the weight of your curtain. Traditional velour curtains can be very heavy, and the weight of the paint on painted drops can be significant, especially if it is painted more than once.

CHAPTER 11 LESSONS

The format of the numbering system is: chapter.lesson.problem number.
Assume normal loading conditions and adequate lateral support unless otherwise noted.

LESSON 11.1 INTRODUCTION TO TRUSSES (PG 229 – 234)

11.1.1 Analyze the stresses in the system given below.
11.1.2 Analyze the stresses in the system given below.
11.1.3 Analyze the stresses in the system given below.
11.1.4 Analyze the stresses in the system given below.
11.1.5 Analyze the stresses in the system given below.
11.1.6 Analyze the stresses in the system given below.

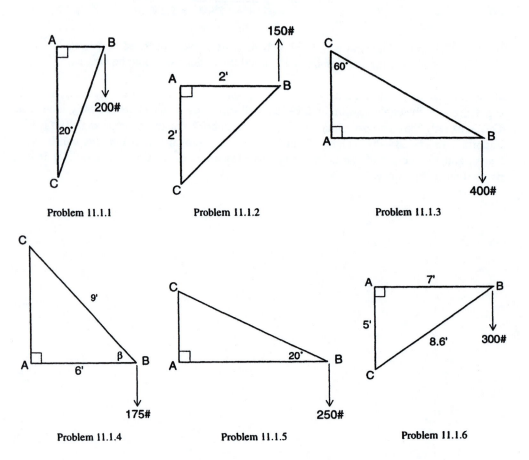

Problem 11.1.1   Problem 11.1.2   Problem 11.1.3

Problem 11.1.4   Problem 11.1.5   Problem 11.1.6

LESSON 11.2 ANALYZING THREE MEMBER TRUSSES (PG 234 – 238)

11.2.1 Analyze the stresses in the system given below.
11.2.2 Analyze the stresses in the system given below.
11.2.3 Analyze the stresses in the system given below.
11.2.4 Analyze the stresses in the system given below.
11.2.5 Analyze the stresses in the system given below.
11.2.6 Analyze the stresses in the system given below.
11.2.7 Analyze the stresses in the system given below.

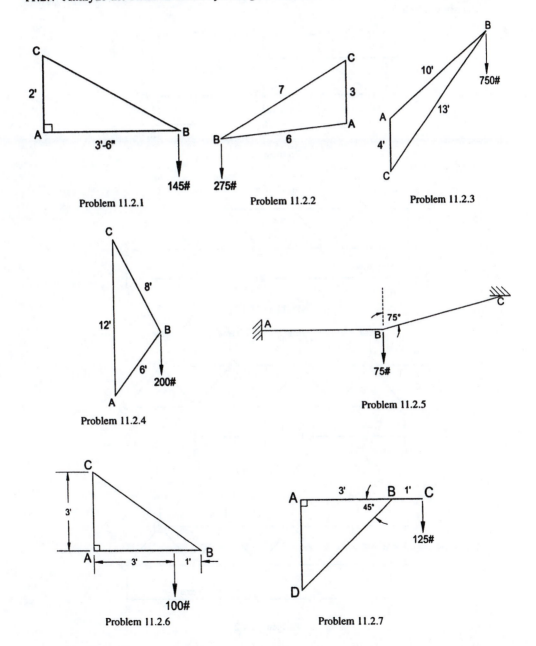

Problem 11.2.1

Problem 11.2.2

Problem 11.2.3

Problem 11.2.4

Problem 11.2.5

Problem 11.2.6

Problem 11.2.7

LESSON 11.3 TRUSS ANALYSIS: METHOD OF JOINTS (PG 238 – 247)

11.3.1 Analyze the stresses in the truss given below.

11.3.2 Analyze the stresses in the truss given below.

LESSON 11.4 TRUSS ANALYSIS: CONTINUED WITH EXAMPLE 7 (PG 247 – 252)

11.4.1 Analyze the stresses in the truss given in problem 11.3.2 with R_2 located as shown below.

11.4.2 Analyze the stresses in the truss given in problem 11.3.2 with the added point load as shown below.

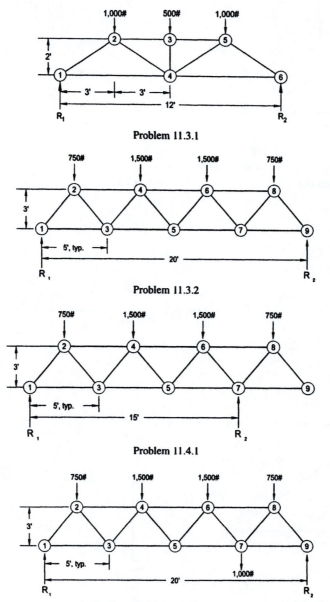

Problem 11.3.1

Problem 11.3.2

Problem 11.4.1

Problem 11.4.2

LESSON 11.5 TRUSS CONSTRUCTION (PG 252 – 256)

11.5.1 Design a general construction scheme for the truss analyzed in 11.3.1. Use 2x stock made from Douglas Fir-South No. 2. List the minimum nominal size stock required for each member.

11.5.2 Design a general planar construction scheme for the truss analyzed in problem 11.3.1. List the minimum square tube size required for each member. Use MT1010 mechanical tube with a wall thickness of 0.065".

11.5.3 Design a general planar construction scheme which can satisfy the maximum requirements for the truss analyzed in problems 11.3.2, 11.4.1, and 11.4.2. Use the smallest square MT1010 mechanical tube with a wall thickness of 0.065".

LESSON 11.6 CABLES, POINT LOAD CABLE SYSTEMS (PG 256 – 262)

11.6.1 Determine the maximum tension and pick a cable size for the overhead rigging system given below. Assume that the end terminations are made with wire rope clips.

11.6.2 Determine the maximum tension and pick a cable size for the overhead rigging system given below. Assume that the end terminations are made with nicopress sleeves.

11.6.3 Determine the maximum tension and pick a cable size for the overhead rigging system given below. Assume that the end terminations are made with nicopress sleeves.

11.6.4 Determine the maximum tension and pick a cable size for the overhead rigging system given below. Assume that the end terminations are made with wire rope clips.

11.6.5 Determine the maximum tension and pick a cable size for the overhead rigging system given on the following page. Assume that the end terminations are made with nicopress sleeves.

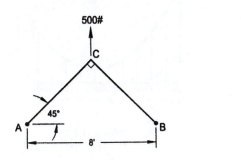

Problem 11.6.1

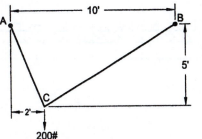

Problem 11.6.2

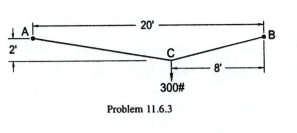

Problem 11.6.3

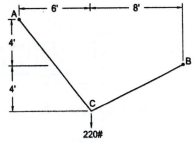

Problem 11.6.4

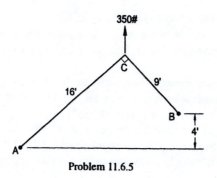

Problem 11.6.5

LESSON 11.7 CURVED CABLE SYSTEMS (PG 262 – 267)

11.7.1 Determine the maximum tension and pick a cable size for the rigging system given below. Assume that the end terminations are made with wire rope clips.

11.7.2 Determine the maximum tension and pick a cable size for the overhead rigging system given below. Assume that the end terminations are made with nicopress sleeves.

11.7.3 Determine the maximum tension and pick a cable size for the overhead rigging system given below. Assume that the end terminations are made with wire rope clips.

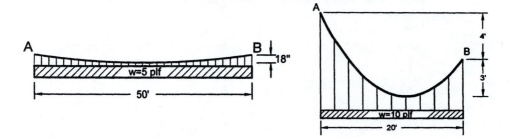

Problem 11.7.1   Problem 11.7.2

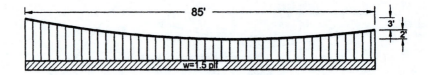

Problem 11.7.3

12

Plywood Design

INTRODUCTION

Modern technology has made it possible to manufacture a wide array of engineered wood products. These include oriented strand board, glued laminated timbers, and I-shaped wooden joists. These engineered products have load capacities clearly defined by their manufacturers and will therefore not be further discussed. There are also innumerable sheet goods made from wood such as masonite, medite, lauan, and hardwood plywoods. The structural integrity of these products is undefined. They are not intended for weight bearing applications and will not be further discussed. This text will focus exclusively on the design techniques regarding structural **plywood**.

Before the development of plywood, the construction industry built all walkable surfaces with planking. Now plywood can be found in almost every aspect of building construction, from walls and floors to finished cabinet work. In scenery construction, plywood is found in decks, flats, and finished props. Understanding how to design with plywood is, therefore, of utmost importance to the theatrical structural designer.

As its name implies, plywood is made from overlapping plies, or **veneers** (see Figure 12.1). In the manufacturing process, veneers are rotary peeled off logs with a huge lathe (*PDS*, 1.2). When the veneers are glued together, the direction of the grain is alternated so that the grains of adjacent layers are perpendicular to each other (see Figure 12.1 below). All plywoods have an odd number of layers so that the grain of the top and bottom (face and back) layers are parallel. Though, as Figure 12.1 illustrates, some plywoods have an even number of veneers with two parallel veneers glued together to form one layer. The thinnest plywood is made with 3-layers and 3 veneers.

The manufacturing process and the perpendicular orientation of the layers make it possible to produce large sheets of rated material with good dimensional stability. Structurally rated plywood products are usually sold as 4'x8' panels from 1/4" to 1-1/8" thick, but can be special ordered in larger sheets in 5' widths and lengths of 10' and 12'.

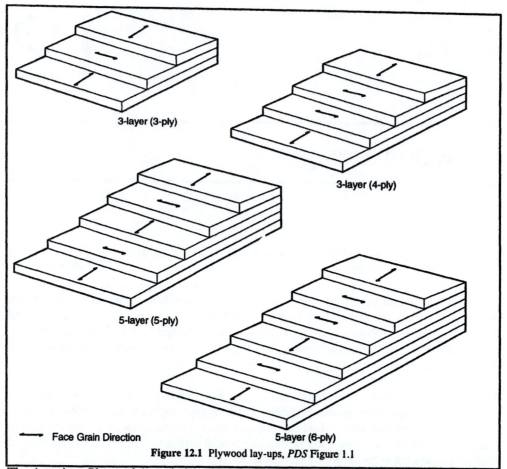

3-layer (3-ply)

3-layer (4-ply)

5-layer (5-ply)

5-layer (6-ply)

→ Face Grain Direction

Figure 12.1 Plywood lay-ups, *PDS* Figure 1.1

The American Plywood Association, **APA** – *The Engineered Wood Association*, is the governing agency for plywood. It is not a government body, but publishes voluntary standards for plywood manufacturers, design values for rated plywood, and guidelines for plywood design. The APA's *Plywood Design Specification (PDS)* is to plywood what the *NDS for Wood Construction* is to sawn lumber. Since the manufacturing standards are voluntary, a sheet of plywood must be stamped with an APA stamp in order for the published design values to be applicable.

DESIGN VALUES
SECTION PROPERTIES
Like sawn lumber, plywood has geometric properties such as area, moment of inertia, and section modulus (see Appendix F). Unlike sawn lumber, these properties are adjusted to reflect the alternating perpendicular layers. In any one stress condition, only the odd or even layers of the plywood effectively resist the load. Hence, the thickness for some calculations is actually the effective thickness for shear, t_s. The section modulus is actually the effective section modulus, KS, and cannot be calculated as I/c. The area and moment of inertia are also adjusted. Note that all the properties are given per foot of width. For example, I is listed as in^4/ft, not in^4. Therefore, a 4' wide x 5/16" thick unsanded panel would have an I value of 0.022 in^4/ft multiplied by 4' or 0.088 in^4.

Notice also that two values for every property are listed because plywood has a strong and a weak orientation. It is strongest when the direction of the grain runs perpendicular to the supports (see Figure 12.2). The *PDS* calls this "Stress Applied Parallel to Face Grain." When the supports run parallel to the face grain, the set of properties listed under "Stress Applied Perpendicular to Face Grain", is applicable. Although the *PDS* labels seem counterintuitive, they make sense. When the grain of the plywood spans between the supports, the load is resisted by the plies which are *parallel* to the face grain, and the cross-plies contribute little strength. Hence, the stress is developed, or applied, parallel to the face grain.

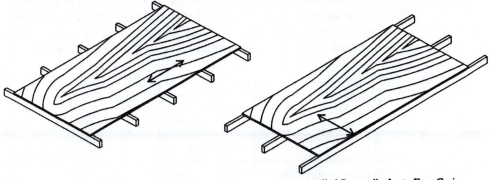

Stress Applied Parallel to Face Grain   Stress Applied Perpendicular to Face Grain

Figure 12.2 Plywood orientation

The **effective geometric properties** are further divided by both thickness and finish (unsanded, sanded, or touch-sanded) because the finish of the face and back plies affects their relative thickness compared to the other layers. As a quick examination of the chart will show, the changes due to finish do not form regular patterns.

Rolling shear, F_s, is a special type of stress relating to potential delamination between alternating layers of plywood. Imagine the tension and compression stresses developed in the top and bottom plies of a 3-layer (3 ply) sheet. These stresses tend to form a couple which attempts to rotate, or roll, the middle ply (see Figure 12.3).

Figure 12.3 Rolling shear

A panel's geometric resistance to rolling shear is quantified in the rolling shear constant, Ib/Q, and changes with the orientation of the sheet.

ALLOWABLE STRESSES

Most of the allowable stress variables for plywood are familiar from sawn lumber design, with the exception of F_s and G. F_s, the allowable rolling shear stress, is explained above. G, the **modulus of rigidity**, is not used in most plywood design equations. The allowable stresses for plywood are listed in Appendix F.

To find the allowable stresses for a panel, the **Species Group, Grade Stress-Level**, and moisture conditions must be cross-referenced. The APA defines wet conditions as "when the equilibrium moisture content will be 16% or greater . . ." (*PDS*, 3.2.2). Grade Stress Level and species will be explained in the following section on grading and selection.

Load duration and panel width effect the allowable stresses for a given member. Like sawn lumber, the normal load duration assumed for a plywood structure is 10 years. The allowable F_b, F_t, F_c, F_v, and F_s stresses may be increased 15% for applications with a two month duration and 25% for applications with a seven day duration (*PDS*, 3.3.1.1). The allowable F_b, F_t, and F_c stresses listed assume a panel width of 24" or more. In addition to a visual inspection for obvious defects, it is recommended that the allowable stresses of strips 8" or less in width be reduced 50%. The allowable stresses of strips between 8" and 24" are reduced proportionally (see Figure 12.4).

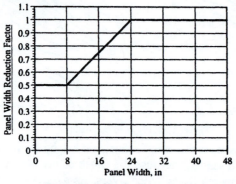

Figure 12.4 Panel width reduction factor

GRADING/SELECTION
VARIABLES

Determining the grade of a given sheet is confusing because the building industry has a plethora of common names for plywood products which have no relationship to the official terminology. For example, while a TD may order 3/4" CDX or 3/4" A/C plywood from a lumber yard, these names do not fully describe an actual APA grade.

As implied by the manufacturing process, three primary factors effect the strength of plywood: the species of the veneers, the quality and finish of the veneers, and the type of glue used in the laminating process.

All plywood veneers are classified as **Species Group** 1, 2, 3, 4, or 5. Each group contains many different species (see Appendix F for details) with Group 1 being the strongest and Group 5 being the weakest. Species is perhaps the most important variable in determining the strength characteristics of plywood. For example, it is possible to buy 1/2" plywood made from a Group 1 species which is as strong as 5/8" plywood made from a Group 4 species (see Appendix F). The applicable species group of a sheet of plywood is determined from the face and back plies only.

The quality of a veneer can be thought of as the general appearance of the layers. In decreasing order of quality, the APA classifies plywood as **N, A, B, C-plugged, C,** or **D grade**. As the grade decreases, the number of seams, knots, plugs, patches, roughness of finish, etc. increase. The N grade is not always available and is intended for natural finish uses while the A grade is intended for applications in which the surface is painted (*PDS*, 1.4.2). Though, in general, as the appearance quality of the veneer increases, the strength increases, veneer grade does not always correspond to strength design values. For example, though C-plugged veneers look better than C veneers, they are weaker because the plugging, patching, and sanding process violates their structural integrity (*PDS*, 3.1.2).

Plywood sheets are also classified as **sanded, touch-sanded,** or **unsanded.** In general, appearance graded sheets are sanded; underlayment, C-D plugged sheets, and Sturd-I-Floor are touch-sanded; and rated sheathing is unsanded. To determine the finish of a sheet, consult Appendix F.

Finally, the type of glue used in the manufacturing process effects the strength of the panel. Essentially, like wristwatches, the glue in plywood can be fully waterproof, somewhat waterproof, or water resistant. Subsequently, plywood has four exposure categories: **Exterior, Exposure 1, IMG** or **Exposure 2,** and **Interior.** Exterior panels are made with fully waterproof glue and have only C-grade or better veneers. Exposure 1 panels have fully waterproof glue but may include D-grade veneers. IMG or Exposure 2 panels are made with an intermediate (IMG) glue. Interior panels are made with "moderately moisture resistant interior glue" (*PDS*, 1.3). It is important to realize that the use of "exterior" glue does not necessarily classify a sheet as an Exterior panel. For most theatrical situations, the exposure classification is not critical, but it is necessary to know a panel's exposure classification so that the appropriate allowable stresses can be found.

The combination of glue and veneer choices determines the Grade Stress Level of a panel. Grade Stress Levels are best defined by the APA (*PDS*, 3.1.2):

> Plywood with exterior glue, and with face and back plies containing only N, A, or C veneers, shall use level one (S-1) stresses. Plywood with exterior glue, and with B, C-plugged or D veneers in either face or back, shall use level two (S-2) stresses. All grades with interior or intermediate glue (IMG or Exposure 2) shall use level three (S-3) stresses.

APA STAMPS
In order to enforce its standards, panels which meet APA voluntary standards are stamped such that their species group, veneer grade, and exposure classification can be identified (see Figure 12.5). In addition to information on the stamp, the sheet thickness must be specified. Once all this information is determined, the design values for the sheet can be found.

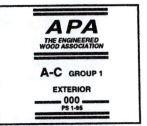

Figure 12.5 APA stamp

> *Example 1.* Determine the allowable stresses and geometric properties for a sheet of 3/4" A/C-plugged plywood, exposure 1 ("exterior"), group 1 and compare it to a sheet of 3/4" A/C, interior, group 4. Assume dry conditions and a normal load duration.

The *Guide to Use of Allowable Stress and Section Properties Table* in Appendix F indicates that the 3/4" A/C, Exposure 1, Group 1, Exterior sheet is sanded and has a Grade Stress Level of S-2 (it would have a Grade Stress Level of S-1 if the C side were natural, not repaired). The 3/4" A/C, Group 4, Interior sheet is sanded and has a Grade Stress Level of S-3.

The material properties of the sheets are as follows (Appendix F):

	Exterior Group 1	Interior Group 4
F_t, F_b	1,650 psi	1,110 psi
F_c	1,540 psi	950 psi
F_v	190 psi	115 psi
F_s	53 psi	48 psi
$F_{c\perp}$	340 psi	160 psi
E	1.8×10^6 psi	1.0×10^6 psi

The geometric properties of both sheets are identical (Appendix F):

	Stress Parallel	Stress Perpendicular
A	2.884 in²/ft	2.081 in²/ft
I	0.197 in⁴/ft	0.063 in⁴/ft
KS	0.412 in³/ft	0.285 in³/ft
Ib/Q	6.792 in²/ft	4.079 in²/ft

$t_s = 0.568$ in

As one can imagine, contractors would have little patience for performing the structural calculations and then specifying sheet goods with four different variables. They are only interested in sheet materials which meet the building code in their area. In response to this need, the APA developed a **Span Rating** system to shortcut the above process. Span rated plywood, such as Sturd-I-Floor or Rated Sheathing includes three extra numbers on the stamp (see Figure 12.6).

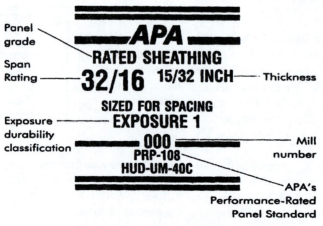

Figure 12.6 APA Rated Sheathing stamp

The numbers separated by a slash are the "on center" spacing requirements when the framing is perpendicular to the face grain of the plywood. The number on the left of the slash indicates the spacing requirements for roofs (30 psf live load); the number on the right of the slash indicates the spacing requirement for floor supports with "average residential loading." The *PDS* indicates that the average residential loading for span rated panels can be considered, at the minimum, 160 psf (*PDS*, 1.4.1). The fractional thickness is included for the convenience of the customer in ordering matching material. The 160 psf load capacity of span-rated panels is meant to account for point loads created by pianos, refrigerators, etc. The actual capacity of the floor will be determined by the framing scheme which is usually 40 psf for residential loading conditions.

The Sturd-I-Floor stamp includes only one span because it is manufactured specifically as a flooring material (Figure 12.7). The number followed by "oc" indicates the maximum spacing of supports under average residential loading. Sturd-I-Floor has good dimensional stability, a touch-sanded finish, and a high resistance to point and impact loads. Though it is not a theater industry standard, it should be considered as an option more frequently. Sturd-I-Floor is available through most lumber yards.

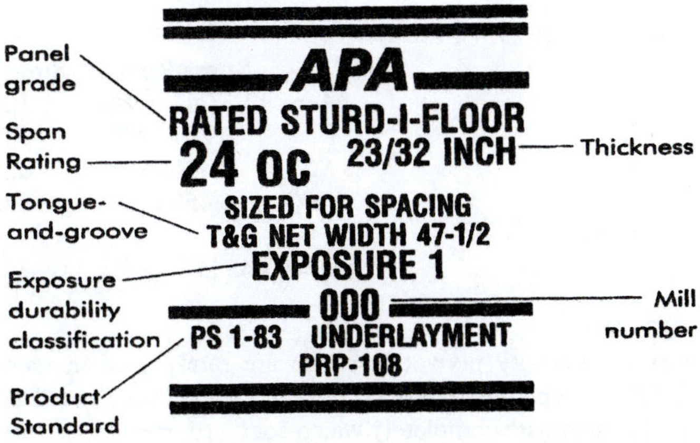

Figure 12.7 APA Rated Sturd-I-Floor stamp

In order to find the allowable stresses of span-rated panels, it is necessary to work backwards from the stamp using Appendix F. First, use the *Key to Span Rating and Species Group* table to define a species group for the Rated Sheathing or Sturd-I-Floor plywood. Next, use the *Guide to Use of Allowable Stress and Section Properties Table* to find the finish and the Grade-Stress Level. Finally, the allowable stresses are determined using the Grade-Stress Level and the species group. Example 2 explicates this process.

> ***Example 2.*** Determine the allowable stresses and geometric properties for a 19/32" APA Rated Sturd-I-Floor, 20 o.c., Exposure 1 plywood panel.
>
> From Appendix F, the finish is touch-sanded, the Grade Stress Level is S-2 (see footnote at the bottom of the table), and the Species Group is 1.

From Appendix F:

			Stress Parallel	Stress Perpendicular
F_t, F_b	1,650 psi	A	2.358 in²/ft	1.555 in²/ft
F_c	1,540 psi	I	0.123 in⁴/ft	0.016 in⁴/ft
F_v	190 psi	KS	0.327 in³/ft	0.135 in³/ft
F_s	53 psi	Ib/Q	5.346 in²/ft	3.220 in²/ft
E	1.8x10⁶ psi			

$$t_s = 0.408 \text{ in}$$

Example 3. CDX is one of the most commonly ordered plywoods, yet it is not listed on any APA stamps. The APA writes that CDX is actually All-veneer APA Rated Sheathing Exposure 1. What are the allowable stresses and geometric properties of a 3/4" CDX panel? Assume a span rating of 40/20.

From Appendix F, the panel is unsanded, has a Grade Stress Level of S-2, and is made from Species Group 4.

From Appendix F:

			Stress Parallel	Stress Perpendicular
F_t, F_b	1,110 psi	A	3.247 in²/ft	1.563 in²/ft
F_c	950 psi	I	0.234 in⁴/ft	0.036 in⁴/ft
F_v	130 psi	KS	0.496 in³/ft	0.232 in³/ft
F_s	53 psi	Ib/Q	6.455 in²/ft	3.613 in²/ft
E	1.0x10⁶ psi			

$$t_s = 0.445 \text{ in}$$

SPECIALTY PLYWOOD

There are numerous specialty plywoods which are rarely used in scenery construction. **Structural I** and **Marine** plywood have all plies of Group I species (*PDS*, 1.5), and marine plywood is manufactured with completely waterproof glue. Their design values are listed in Appendix F. Plywood is also available with a variety of overlays. For example, Medium-Density Overlay (MDO) is an "exterior plywood with an opaque resin-treated fiber overlay" which is paint-ready (*Panel Handbook*, 20). It is available as an APA rated siding and is, in general, a very good quality plywood (see Figure 12.8) which can be considered to have a sanded finish. In short, the number and variety of rated plywood products is tremendous. When confused about the best choice for a given application, ask your lumber salesperson. S/he may know of a product of which you've never heard.

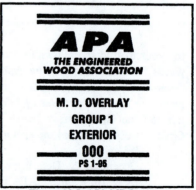

Figure 12.8 APA MDO stamp

DESIGNING FOR UNIFORM LOADS

The basic strategy of plywood design is like column design in that it is a trial and error process. Like sawn lumber, plywood should be tested for bending, shear, and deflection. An allowable uniform load is determined for each test with the lowest value determining the allowable uniform load on the panel. This design process tests the strength of the plywood between framing members. The framing is analyzed separately, i.e., do not confuse plywood strength with platform strength.

Before finding the allowable load due to bending, shear, or deflection, a **span condition** must be determined (*PDS*, 4.1):

- When a 4'x8' sheet of plywood is oriented with the face grain perpendicular to the supports (strong orientation), the three-span condition is used if the framing is 32" or less on center; the two-span condition is used for spacing greater than 32" (see Figure 12.9).

- When a 4'x8' sheet of plywood is oriented with the face grain parallel to the supports (weak orientation), the three-span condition is used if the framing is 16" or less on center; the two-span condition is used if the spacing is greater than 16" and up to 24" on center; and the single span condition is used if the spacing is greater than 24" on center.

- In either orientation and regardless of the length of the span, a panel that is only supported by two framing members uses the single span condition.

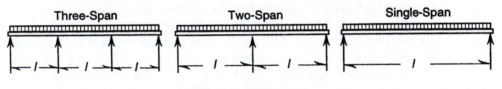

Figure 12.9 Span conditions

The *PDS* notes that the equations used to design plywood beams "assume one-way "beam" action, rather than two-way "slab" action" (*PDS*, 4.1). This implies that if a sheet is framed on all four sides, two of those framing members are ignored, i.e., only one span is designed for (though both should be investigated). In addition, the supports perpendicular to the design span must be the full width of the sheet. If a sheet of plywood is supported only at the four corners, it will be subject to bending both parallel and perpendicular to the grain, i.e., slab action.

UNIFORM LOADS BASED ON BENDING STRESS (*PDS*, 4.1.1)

The *PDS* requires the use of the following equations to calculate the allowable load due to the bending stress of the plywood for each span condition:

single and two-span: $w_b = \dfrac{96 F_b (KS)}{l^2}$

three-span: $w_b = \dfrac{120 F_b (KS)}{l^2}$

where w_b is the allowable load based on bending stress, psf
F_b is the allowable bending stress, psi
KS is the effective section modulus, in³/ft
l is the center to center distance between supports, in

UNIFORM LOADS BASED ON SHEAR STRESS (PDS, 4.1.2)

The *PDS* requires the use of the following equations to calculate the allowable load due to shear stress of the plywood for each span condition:

single span: $$w_s = \frac{24 F_s (Ib/Q)}{l}$$

two span: $$w_s = \frac{19.2 F_s (Ib/Q)}{l}$$

three-span: $$w_s = \frac{20 F_s (Ib/Q)}{l}$$

where w_s is the allowable load based on shear stress, psf
F_s is the allowable rolling shear stress, psi
Ib/Q is the rolling shear constant, in²/ft
l is the center to center distance between supports, in

Note: The APA allows l to be considered the clear span between supports, but we recommend the conservative assumption of the center to center distance to simplify the process.

UNIFORM LOADS BASED ON BENDING DEFLECTION (PDS, 4.1.3.1)

Plywood will deflect due to both bending and shear stresses. In most cases, when the spans (l) are 30 to 50 times the thickness (t) of the plywood, the shear deflection is negligible and left out of the calculations. If the l/t ratio is between 15 to 20, the APA recommends that shear deflection be calculated separately. Such short spans (15" and less for 3/4" plywood) are rare in theatrical applications, and, therefore, we will only examine bending deflection. Refer to *PDS* section 4.1.3 for details on shear deflection if necessary. As will always be the case, an allowable deflection criteria of $l/240$ for combined dead and live loads is recommended.

The APA mandates the following deflection equations (*PDS*, 4.1.3.1):

single span: $$\Delta_b = \frac{wl^4}{921.6EI} \Rightarrow w_\Delta = \frac{921.6EI\Delta_{all}}{l^4}$$

two span: $$\Delta_b = \frac{wl^4}{2,220EI} \Rightarrow w_\Delta = \frac{2,220EI\Delta_{all}}{l^4}$$

three-span: $$\Delta_b = \frac{wl^4}{1,743EI} \Rightarrow w_\Delta = \frac{1,743EI\Delta_{all}}{l^4}$$

where Δ_b is the actual bending deflection , in
Δ_{all} is the allowable deflection, in
w_Δ is the allowable load based on deflection, psf

E is the modulus of elasticity, psi

I is the effective moment of inertia, in⁴/ft

l is the center to center distance between supports, in

Note: Once again, the APA allows a slightly less conservative value of l (*PDS*, 4.1.3.1), but we recommend using the center to center distance for all three tests.

DERIVATION OF THE PLYWOOD DESIGN FORMULAS

The plywood equations are easily derived from the case formula equations for an evenly distributed load on a simple span (McClintock, 3-22). The case formulas are solved for w and adjusted for the unique units of plywood design.

For example, the case formula for the maximum bending moment (M_{max}) of an evenly distributed load on a simple span is:

$$M_{max} = \frac{wl^2}{8}$$

From the Flexure Formula, the maximum moment can also be expressed as:

$$M_{max} = F_b S$$

If these two equations are set equal to each other and w is isolated, the fundamental form of the plywood design formula for bending emerges:

$$\frac{wl^2}{8} = F_b S \Rightarrow w = \frac{8F_b S}{l^2}$$

Since KS is in units of in³ per foot of panel width, and w is expressed in psf, the formula is multiplied by 1/12 and 144 respectively, resulting in the plywood design formula for bending:

$$w = \frac{8F_b S}{l^2} \Rightarrow w = \frac{8F_b KS}{l^2}\left(\frac{1}{12}\right)144 = \frac{96F_b KS}{l^2}$$

The derivation of the single-span plywood design formula for shear is similar:

The formula for maximum vertical shear (V_{max}) for an evenly distributed load on a simple span is:

$$V_{max} = \frac{wl}{2}$$

The formula for determining shear stress is:

$$F_v = \frac{V_{max}Q}{Ib}$$

If the definition of V_{max} is plugged into the formula for shear stress, and w is isolated, the fundamental form of the plywood design formula for shear emerges.

Note that the subscript for rolling shear stress (horizontal shear in plywood) is "s" instead of "v."

$$F_s = \frac{\left(w l/2\right)Q}{Ib} = \frac{wl}{2}\left(\frac{Q}{Ib}\right) \Rightarrow wl = 2F_s\left(\frac{Ib}{Q}\right) \Rightarrow w = \frac{2F_s\left(Ib/Q\right)}{l}$$

Again, because Ib/Q is in units of in^2 per foot of panel width and w is in units of psf, the shear formula is multiplied by 1/12 and 144, respectively, resulting in the plywood design formula for shear:

$$w = \frac{2F_s\left(Ib/Q\right)}{l}\left(\frac{1}{12}\right)(144) \Rightarrow w = \frac{24F_s\left(Ib/Q\right)}{l}$$

The single-span plywood deflection formula can also be derived from the case formula for an evenly distributed load on a simple span:

$$\Delta = \frac{5wl^4}{384EI} = \frac{5\left(w/144\right)l^4}{384E\left(I/12\right)} = \frac{5\left(12/144\right)wl^4}{384EI} = \frac{wl^4}{921.6EI} \Rightarrow w_\Delta = \frac{921.6EI\Delta_{all}}{l^4}$$

The plywood design formulas for all other loading conditions, including the two and three span conditions, can be derived using the above techniques.

EXAMPLES

Example 4a. Determine the maximum allowable load for a sheet of 3/4" A/C-plugged plywood, Interior, Group 4 (see Example 1 for the allowables) with supports running perpendicular to the grain at 24", 32", and 48" on-center. Assume a normal load duration.

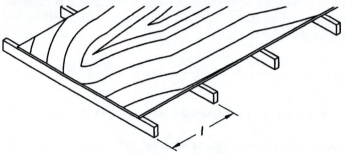

Figure 12.10 Example 4a

24" on center. Since 24"<32", the three span condition is used:

$$w_b = \frac{120F_b\left(KS\right)}{l^2} = \frac{120(1{,}110\ \text{psi})(0.412\ \text{in}^3\,/\,\text{ft})}{(24")^2} = 95\ \text{psf}$$

$$w_s = \frac{20F_s\left(Ib/Q\right)}{l} = \frac{20(48\ \text{psi})(6.792\ \text{in}^2\,/\,\text{ft})}{24"} = 272\ \text{psf}$$

$$\Delta_{all} = \frac{l}{240} = \frac{24"}{240} = 0.1"$$

$$w_\Delta = \frac{1{,}743 EI\Delta_{all}}{l^4} = \frac{1{,}743(1.0x10^6 \text{ psi})(0.197 \text{ in}^4 / \text{ft})(0.1")}{(24")^4} = 103 \text{ psf}$$

In this case, bending is the ruling factor, and 95 psf is the maximum allowable load for a 24" span.

32" on center. Since 32"=32", the three span condition is used.

$$w_b = \frac{120 F_b(KS)}{l^2} = \frac{120(1{,}110 \text{ psi})(0.412 \text{ in}^3 / \text{ft})}{(32")^2} = 54 \text{ psf}$$

$$w_s = \frac{20 F_s(Ib/Q)}{l} = \frac{20(48 \text{ psi})(6.792 \text{ in}^2 / \text{ft})}{32"} = 204 \text{ psf}$$

$$\Delta_{all} = \frac{l}{240} = \frac{32"}{240} = 0.133"$$

$$w_\Delta = \frac{1{,}743 EI\Delta_{all}}{l^4} = \frac{1{,}743(1.0x10^6 \text{ psi})(0.197 \text{ in}^4 / \text{ft})(0.133")}{(32")^4} = 44 \text{ psf}$$

In this case, deflection is the ruling factor, and 44 psf is the maximum allowable load for a 32" span.

48" on center. Since 48">32", the two span condition is used.

$$w_b = \frac{96 F_b(KS)}{l^2} = \frac{96(1{,}110 \text{ psi})(0.412 \text{ in}^3 / \text{ft})}{(48")^2} = 19 \text{ psf}$$

$$w_s = \frac{19.2 F_s(Ib/Q)}{l} = \frac{19.2(48 \text{ psi})(6.792 \text{ in}^2 / \text{ft})}{48"} = 130 \text{ psf}$$

$$\Delta_{all} = \frac{l}{240} = \frac{48"}{240} = 0.2"$$

$$w_\Delta = \frac{2{,}220 EI\Delta_{all}}{l^4} = \frac{2{,}220(1.0x10^6 \text{ psi})(0.197 \text{ in}^4 / \text{ft})(0.2")}{(48")^4} = 16 \text{ psf}$$

Deflection is again the ruling factor, and 16 psf is the maximum allowable load for a 48" span.

Example 4b. Determine the maximum allowable load for the same sheet of 3/4" plywood in Example 4a, if the supports run parallel to the grain and are 16", 24", and 48" on center.

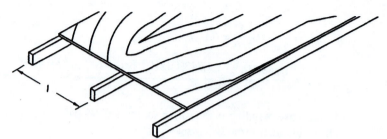

Figure 12.11 Example 4b

16" on center. Since 16"=16", the three span condition is used.

$$w_b = \frac{120F_b(KS)}{l^2} = \frac{120(1{,}110 \text{ psi})(0.285 \text{ in}^3/\text{ft})}{(16")^2} = 148 \text{ psf}$$

$$w_s = \frac{20F_s(Ib/Q)}{l} = \frac{20(48 \text{ psi})(4.079 \text{ in}^2/\text{ft})}{16"} = 245 \text{ psf}$$

$$\Delta_{all} = \frac{l}{240} = \frac{16"}{240} = 0.0667"$$

$$w_\Delta = \frac{1{,}743EI\Delta_{all}}{l^4} = \frac{1{,}743(1.0x10^6 \text{ psi})(0.063 \text{ in}^4/\text{ft})(0.0667")}{(16")^4} = 112 \text{ psf}$$

In this case, deflection is the ruling factor, and 112 psf is the maximum allowable load for the 16" span.

24" on center. Since 24"=24", the two span condition is used.

$$w_b = \frac{96F_b(KS)}{l^2} = \frac{96(1{,}110 \text{ psi})(0.285 \text{ in}^3/\text{ft})}{(24")^2} = 53 \text{ psf}$$

$$w_s = \frac{19.2F_s(Ib/Q)}{l} = \frac{19.2(48 \text{ psi})(4.079 \text{ in}^2/\text{ft})}{24"} = 157 \text{ psf}$$

$$\Delta_{all} = \frac{l}{240} = \frac{24"}{240} = 0.1"$$

$$w_\Delta = \frac{2{,}220EI\Delta_{all}}{l^4} = \frac{2{,}220(1.0x10^6 \text{ psi})(0.063 \text{ in}^4/\text{ft})(0.1")}{(24")^4} = 42 \text{ psf}$$

In this case, deflection is the ruling factor, and 42 psf is the maximum allowable load for a 24" span.

48" on center. Since 48">24", this is a single span condition.

$$w_b = \frac{96F_b(KS)}{l^2} = \frac{96(1{,}110 \text{ psi})(0.285 \text{ in}^3/\text{ft})}{(48")^2} = 13 \text{ psf}$$

$$w_s = \frac{24F_s(Ib/Q)}{l} = \frac{24(48 \text{ psi})(4.079 \text{ in}^2/\text{ft})}{48"} = 98 \text{ psf}$$

$$\Delta_{all} = \frac{l}{240} = \frac{48"}{240} = 0.2"$$

$$w_{\Delta} = \frac{921.6EI\Delta_{all}}{l^4} = \frac{921.6\left(1.0x10^6 \text{ psi}\right)\left(0.063 \text{ in}^4 / \text{ft}\right)\left(0.2"\right)}{\left(48"\right)^4} = 2 \text{ psf}$$

In this case, deflection is still the ruling factor, and 2 psf is the maximum allowable load for a 48" span.

Examples 4a and 4b shed light on the spacing of interior framing members in traditional 4'x8', 2x4 framed, platforms. Often, a 4'x8' platform will be framed at 32" on center to save one toggle per unit. Example 4a demonstrates that this reduces the allowable load on the plywood lid to 50% of the allowable load on a sheet framed on 2' centers. The consequences of providing only one interior toggle (48" spacing) are also illustrated. Example 4b demonstrates why platforms are framed with the supports perpendicular to the face grain. With the same on center spacing of 24", the plywood lid of a platform with toggles perpendicular to the face grain is twice as strong as one framed with stringers parallel to the face grain.

STRESSED-SKIN PANELS

Stressed-skin panels are a very specific type of platform construction. The APA's *Supplement 3* to the *PDS*, *Design and Fabrication of Plywood Stressed-Skin Panels*, details requirements of stressed skin design and construction.

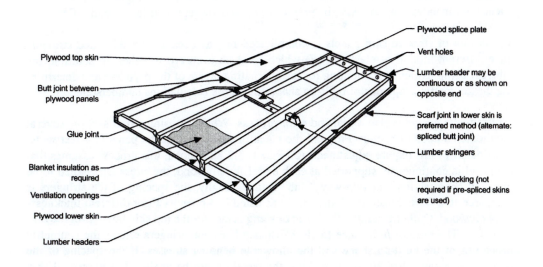

Figure 12.12 Typical stressed-skin panel construction, *PDS Supplement 3*, Figure 1

In most stressed-skin construction, the framing runs parallel to the face grain of the plywood and the panel is double-sided. Neither of these are requirements, but they are the focus of this text. For details on other types of stressed-skin construction, see the APA's *Supplement 3*. A double-sided stressed-skin panel with framing parallel to the grain requires blocking at each end and at all plywood butt joints (as in Figure 12.12). Notice that the stringers run the full length of the panel so that, unlike traditionally framed platforms, the end caps are not necessarily continuous.

The driving force behind stressed-skin design is that the whole is greater than the sum of the parts. That is, the strength of a panel is not simply the strength of the framing or the strength of the plywood. When the skin and frame are glued together the panel acts like a series of I-beams, with the stringers acting as the webs and the skin acting as the top and (or) bottom flanges. Like a truss, the top skin is subject to compressive stresses, the bottom skin to tensile stresses, and the stringers to shear stresses.

For panels longer than 8', it is necessary to include splice plates and additional blocking at the plywood butt joint(s). The location of the splice plate is important; locate the splices away from the center of the span (where the stresses are greatest) if possible. Splicing will effect the strength of the panel as shown in Example 5.

The glue joint between the lumber stringers and plywood skins is critical to the ability of the stressed-skin panel to behave as a unit. Consequently, the APA mandates that the sawn lumber stringers be resurfaced to provide a larger, squarer, and rougher glue surface (*S3 Part 2*, 3.2.2). If double-sided MDO or HDO skins are being used, the finish veneer must be sanded at the glue joints.

Specific construction techniques such as splice plate thickness and length and nailing frequency are mandated by the APA in *Supplement 3* and are reprinted in Appendix F.

The design of stressed-skin panels is complicated in part because the skins and stringers have different moduli of elasticity (E) which must be averaged together. In addition, the inherent complexities of accounting for the alternating layers of the plywood and determining the geometric properties of built-up shapes make the calculations cumbersome.

Stressed-skin design is also a trial and error process. When choosing a trial section, several requirements need to be met. First, all the equations assume that the panel is 4 feet wide; other panel widths require adjustments (*S3 Part 1*, 3.2.1). Second, this process assumes that the panel is continuously supported at each end. Like plywood, the stress is assumed to be one-way beam action, not two-way "slab" action. Finally, the spacing of the stringers is compared to a Basic Spacing ("*b*-distance") as listed in Appendix F for different thicknesses of plywood. Quite frequently, the Basic Spacing is met for the top skin but not for the bottom skin. The ratio of *b*-distance to clear distance between stringers effects the geometric properties of the built-up shape and the allowable bending stresses. If the spacing of the stringers is greater than 2*b* for both skins, the panel cannot be analyzed as a stressed-skin panel (*S3 Part 1*, 3.2.2).

STEPS IN STRESSED-SKIN PANEL DESIGN

The calculations in stressed-skin design result in seven allowable loads based on: overall panel deflection, deflection in the top skin, bending in the top skin, bending in the bottom skin, tension in the splice plate, rolling shear, and horizontal shear. The lowest of these defines the maximum allowable load of the panel. The actual equations are best illustrated in the context of an example. The following is a simple list of the steps involved in the process:

A. Choose a trial section.
    1. Sketch the loading conditions and construction details.
    2. Specify the stringers and plywood.
    3. Find the geometric properties and allowables of each component of the panel, Appendices D and F.
    4. Look up b-distances for the top and bottom skins, Appendix F.
    5. Determine the clear distance between stringers.
    6. Determine the total splice plate width (if necessary).

B. Determine the allowable load due to overall panel deflection, w_Δ.
    1. Locate the neutral axis for deflection ($S3$, 3.4.2).
    2. Calculate $E_L I_g$, the gross stiffness factor, ($S3$, 3.4.3).
    3. Calculate the allowable load, w_Δ ($S3$, 3.4.4).

C. Determine the allowable load due to top-skin deflection between stringers, $w_{\Delta(ts)}$ ($S3$, 3.4.5).

D. Determine the allowable load due to bending in the top skin, w_{bt}, and in the bottom skin w_{bb}.
    1. Locate the neutral axis for bending ($S3$, 3.5.2) (use the adjusted value of E and calculate the effective width of the bottom skin).
    2. Calculate $E_L I_n$, the net stiffness factor ($S3$, 3.5.3).
    3. Calculate the allowable loads, ($S3$, 3.5.4).
        a. for the top skin, w_{bt}
        b. for the bottom skin, w_{bb}.

E. Determine the allowable load due to the tensile stress in the splice plate, w_p, ($S3$, 3.5.6).

F. Determine the allowable load due to rolling shear stress, w_s.
    1. Calculate Q_s ($S3$, 3.6.3).
    2. Calculate the allowable capacity ($S3$, 3.6.4).
    3. Calculate the allowable load, w_s ($S3$, 3.6.5).

G. Determine the allowable load due to horizontal shear stress, w_v.
    1. Calculate the statical moment for horizontal shear, Q_v ($S3$, 3.7.1).
    2. Calculate the allowable load, w_v ($S3$, 3.7.3).

H. Compare the allowable loads and select the most restrictive as the overall allowable load.

The calculations for stressed-skin analysis are tedious and repetitive, with a high probability of simple math errors. A simple spread sheet program can be set up to do many of the calculations. The time spent doing so is probably the equivalent of manually doing the calculations for two stressed-skin panels. It is also valuable to first analyze a few stressed-skin panels manually to achieve a firm understanding of the concepts involved.

>   ***Example 5a.*** What is the maximum allowable load that a 4'x12' double-sided stressed-skin panel with the following components can support?
>
>>   Top skin of 5/8" underlayment, Group 1, Exposure 1
>>   Bottom skin of 1/4" A/C, Group 1, Exposure 1
>>   4-2x6 stringers of Southern Pine No. 2
>
>   The panel spans 12' and is continuously supported on the 4' ends. Assume that it will be used indoors, in a dry, protected environment and will have a normal load duration.
>
>   A.   Choose a trial section.
>   1.   Sketch the loading conditions and the construction details.

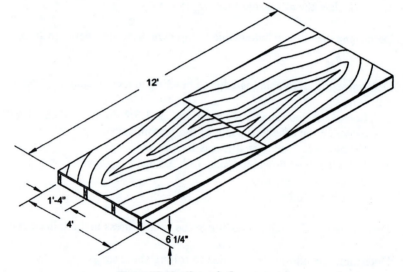

Figure 12.13a Example 5a

>   2 and 3. Specify the geometric properties and allowable stresses of the components of the stressed-skin panel.
>
>   a.   top skin of 5/8" underlayment, Group 1, Exposure 1
>   From Appendix F:
>   Grade Stress Level is S-2 (see footnote)
>   touch-sanded

Section Properties

A	2.354 in²/ft
I	0.123 in⁴/ft
$I_\perp$	0.016 in⁴/ft

Allowable Stresses

F_t, F_b	1,650 psi
F_c	1,540 psi
F_s	53 psi
E	1,800,000 psi

b.   bottom skin of 1/4" A/C, Group 1, Exposure 1
From Appendix F:
Grade Stress Level is S-2 (see footnote)
sanded

Section Properties

A	0.996 in²/ft
I	0.008 in⁴/ft
$I_\perp$	0.001 in⁴/ft

Allowable Stresses

F_t, F_b	1,650 psi
F_c	1,540 psi
F_s	53 psi
E	1,800,000 psi

c.   stringers of 2x6 Southern Pine No. 2.
Remember to shave 1/16" off of each side of the 2x6 for a good glue surface. The section properties are based on the actual dimensions of 1.5"x5.375".

Section Properties

$A_{x\text{-}x}$	8.0625 in²
$I_{x\text{-}x}$	19.4 in⁴

From Appendix D, Allowable Stresses

F_v	90 psi
E	1,600,000 psi

4.   Basic Spacing.
From Appendix F, the b-distance for the top skin is 26" and the b-distance for the bottom skin is 9".

5.   Determine the clear distance between stringers.

$$\text{clear distance} = \frac{\text{panel width} - (\text{\# of stringers})(\text{stringer width})}{\text{number of spans}} = \frac{48"-4(1.5")}{3} = 14"$$

6.   Determine the total splice plate width (if necessary). The APA recommends leaving 1/4" of clearance on each side of each splice plate.

$$\text{total splice plate width} = 3(14"-0.5") = 40.5"$$

B.   Calculate the allowable load for deflection, w_Δ.

1.   Locate the neutral axis for deflection.

a.   Calculate the adjusted modulus of elasticity, E_L, values.
The E values listed for plywood and lumber are conservative because shear deflection is left out of normal beam design procedures. Since the APA includes a separate shear deflection component, the listed E value for plywood is increased by 10% and the listed E value for the stringers is increased by 3%.

$$E_{L_{ply}} = 1.1E = 1.1(1,800,000 \text{ psi}) = 1,980,000 \text{ psi}$$

$$E_{L_{str}} = 1.03E = 1.03(1,600,000 \text{ psi}) = 1,648,000 \text{ psi}$$

where E is the listed modulus of elasticity, psi
          E_L is the adjusted modulus of elasticity, psi

b.   Sketch an end view of the panel showing the location of the neutral
      axes of the component pieces relative to the bottom of the panel:

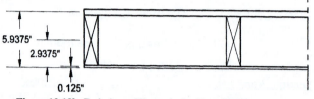

Figure 12.13b End view of Example 5 with y distances

c.   Calculate the location of the neutral axis for deflection.
      If the stressed-skin panel is symmetrical, the neutral axis is located at the geo-
      metric center. If the stressed-skin panel is not symmetrical, the concept of sta-
      tical moment is used to find the location of the neutral axis. The calculations
      for finding the A of each component are included below.

	A, in^2	E_L, psi	AE_L	y, in	$AE_L y$
top	4'(2.354 in^2/ft)= 9.42	1,980,000	18,643,680	5.9375	110,696,850
stringers	4(8.0625 in^2)= 32.3	1,648,000	53,148,000	2.9375	156,122,250
bottom	4'(0.996 in^2/ft)= 3.98	1,980,000	7,888,320	0.125	986,040
totals			79,680,000		267,805,140

$$\bar{y} = \frac{\sum AE_L y}{\sum AE_L} = \frac{267,805,140}{79,680,000} = 3.361\text{" from the bottom}$$

2.   Determine the gross stiffness factor ($E_L I_g$).
      In order to calculate the moment of inertia for the gross section,
      transfer the moments of each individual member to the neutral axis
      of the entire section.

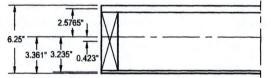

Figure 12.13c End view with neutral axis and d distances

	I_o, in^4	A, in^2	d, in	$I_g = I_o + Ad^2$	E_L, psi	$E_L I_g$
top	4'(0.123 in^4/ft)= 0.492	9.416	2.5765	63.0 in^4	1,980,000	1.247x10^8
stringers	4(19.4 in^4)= 77.6	32.25	0.423	83.4 in^4	1,648,000	1.374x10^8
bottom	4'(0.008 in^4/ft)= 0.032	3.984	3.236	41.8 in^4	1,980,000	8.276x10^7
total						3.45x10^8

$$E_L I_g = EI_{top} + EI_{str} + EI_{bot} = 3.45\text{x}10^8 \text{ psi per 4' width}$$

3. Determine the allowable load due to deflection, w_Δ (*S3*, 3.4.4).
a. Calculate G, modulus of rigidity, for the **stringers**:

$$G = 0.06\left(E_{L_{STR}}\right) = 0.06\left(1.65x10^6 \text{ psi}\right) = 98,880 \text{ psi}$$

b. Calculate the allowable load, w_Δ:

$$w_\Delta = \cfrac{1}{CL\left[\cfrac{7.5L^2}{E_L I_g} + \cfrac{0.6}{AG}\right]}$$

where w_Δ is the allowable load due to deflection, psf
        C is the deflection criteria (240 or 360)
        L is the span length, ft
        $E_L I_g$ is the gross stiffness factor, psi per 4' width
        A is the total cross-sectional area of the stringers, in^2
        G is the modulus of rigidity of the stringers, psi

$$w_\Delta = \cfrac{1}{CL\left[\cfrac{7.5L^2}{E_L I_g} + \cfrac{0.6}{AG}\right]} = \cfrac{1}{240(12')\left[\cfrac{7.5(12')^2}{3.45x10^8 \text{ psi}} + \cfrac{0.6}{\left(32.25 \text{ in}^2\right)\left(98,880 \text{ psi}\right)}\right]} = 105 \text{ psf}$$

C. Determine the allowable load due to top-skin deflection, $w_{\Delta(ts)}$.
    1. As a rule of thumb, if 1/2" or thicker plywood is used on 16" or less centers, it will pass the deflection criteria for a 50 psf load.

    2. The deflection in the top skin is calculated using the following equations (*S3*, 3.4.5):

$$\Delta_{ts} = \frac{wl^4}{384EI_\perp 12} \Rightarrow w_{\Delta(ts)} = \frac{384EI_\perp 12\Delta_{all}}{l^4}$$

where Δ_{ts} is the actual deflection of the top skin, in
        Δ_{all} is the allowable deflection ($l/240$), in
        w is the evenly distributed load, psf
        $w_{\Delta(ts)}$ is the allowable load due to top skin deflection, psf
        l is the clear span between stringers, in
        E is the listed modulus of elasticity of the top skin, psi
        $I_\perp$ is the moment of inertia (stress applied perpendicular to face grain) of
            a 1-ft width of the top skin from Appendix F, in^4

The actual deflection must be less than the allowable deflection of $l/240$. The above deflection equation is based on the deflection equation of a fixed beam, evenly distributed load (hence, the constant of 1/384) and is adjusted for the units of w and I (hence, the factor of 12 in the denominator).

For the 5/8" touch-sanded plywood with a 14" clear-span:

$$w_{\Delta(ts)} = \frac{384 EI_{\perp} 12\Delta_{all}}{l^4} = \frac{384(1.8 \times 10^6 \text{ psi})(0.016 \text{ in}^4)12\left(\dfrac{14"}{240}\right)}{(14")^4} = 201.5 \text{ psf}$$

D.   Determine the allowable load due to bending, w_{bt} and w_{bb}, in the top and bottom skins, respectively.

If the clear distance between stringers exceeds the b-distance of the top and/or bottom skin, the effective width(s) must be calculated and a new neutral axis must be found. This new neutral axis is used to calculate $E_L I_n$, the net stiffness factor for bending.

1.   Determine the location of the neutral axis for bending.
Supplement 3 explains how to determine the effective width of the skins ($S3$, 3.5.1):

"If the clear distance is greater than b, the effective width of the skins must be reduced. It equals the sum of the widths of the stringers plus a portion of the skin extending a distance equal to $0.5b$ on each side of each stringer (except, of course, for outside stringers . . .)"

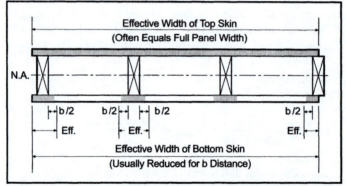

Figure 12.13d   Effective width, *PDS Supplement 3*, Figure 3.5.1

The effective width can also be determined using the following equation:

eff. width = panel width − (# of spans)(clear distance − b-spacing)

For this stressed-skin panel, the clear distance of both skins is 14". Therefore, the effective width of the top skin is the entire panel width because its b-spacing is 26", and the effective width of the bottom skin must be calculated because its b-spacing is 9".

$$\text{eff. width} = 48" - 3(14" - 9") = 33"$$

This effective width proportionally reduces both the area and the moment of inertia of the bottom skin.

$$A_{bending} = (A)\frac{\text{effective width}}{\text{panel width}}$$

$$= (3.984 \text{ in}^2)\frac{33"}{48"} = 2.74 \text{ in}^2 \text{ per 4' width}$$

$$I_{o_{bending}} = (I_o)\frac{\text{effective width}}{\text{panel width}}$$

$$= (0.032 \text{ in}^4)\frac{33"}{48"} = 0.022 \text{ in}^4 \text{ per 4' width}$$

In this case, when calculating the neutral axis for bending, only the values for the bottom skin change (in bold type).

	A, in^2	E_L, psi	AE_L	y, in	$AE_L y$
top	9.416	1,980,000	18,643,680	5.9375	110,696,850
stringers	32.25	1,648,000	53,148,000	2.9375	156,122,250
bottom	2.739	1,980,000	**5,423,220**	0.125	**677,903**
totals			77,214,900		267,497,003

$$\bar{y} = \frac{\sum AE_L y}{\sum AE_L} = \frac{267,497,003}{77,214,900} = 3.464" \text{ from the bottom}$$

2.   Calculate $E_L I_n$.
     The net stiffness factor must be calculated to account for the effective width of the bottom skin and the location of the neutral axis for bending. New values are printed in bold type.

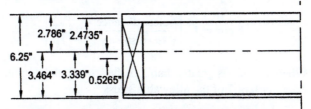

Figure 12.13e Neutral axis for bending and d distances

	I_o in^4	A, in^2	d, in	$I_n = I_o + Ad^2$	E_L, psi	$E_L I_n$
top	0.492	9.416	2.4735	58.1 in^4	1,980,000	1.15x10^8
stringers	77.6	32.25	0.5265	86.5 in^4	1,648,000	1.43x10^8
bottom	**0.022**	2.74	3.339	30.6 in^4	1,980,000	6.05x10^7
					total	3.19x10^8

$$E_L I_n = EI_{top} + EI_{str} + EI_{bot} = 3.19 \times 10^8 \text{ psi per 4' width}$$

3.   Allowable stress.
     The allowable bending stress is expressed as an allowable compressive stress in the top skin and an allowable tensile stress in the bottom skin. These stresses are also adjusted relative to the b-spacing of each plywood skin. If the clear distance between stringers is less

than one-half of the b-distance, the allowable stress is the full value listed in Appendix F. If the clear distance is greater than one-half of the b-distance for that skin, then the allowable stress must be reduced as depicted in Figure 12.13f.

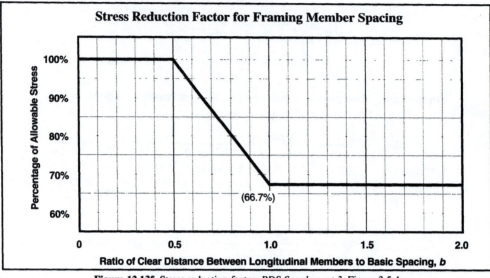

Figure 12.13f Stress reduction factor, *PDS Supplement 3*, Figure 3.5.4

Mathematically, the allowable stress reduction factor when the clear-distance to b-spacing ratio is between 0.5 and 1.0 can be determined as follows:

$$\text{factor} = 1 - \left[\left(\frac{\text{clear distance}}{b \text{-distance}} - 0.5 \right) \frac{2}{3} \right]$$

When the ratio is greater than 1.0, the stress reduction factor is taken as 2/3 or 0.667 of the allowable stress.

a. Top skin.

$$\frac{\text{clear distance}}{b \text{-distance}} = \frac{14"}{26"} = 0.538 > 0.5$$

$$\text{factor} = 1 - \left[\left(\frac{\text{clear distance}}{b \text{-distance}} - 0.5 \right) \frac{2}{3} \right] = 1 - \left[(0.538 - 0.5) \frac{2}{3} \right] = 0.974$$

$$F_c' = (\text{factor}) F_c = (0.974)(1{,}540 \text{ psi}) = 1{,}500 \text{ psi}$$

b. Bottom skin.

$$\frac{\text{clear distance}}{b \text{-distance}} = \frac{14"}{9"} = 1.55 > 1.0$$

$$F_t' = (\text{factor}) F_t = (0.667)(1{,}650 \text{ psi}) = 1{,}100 \text{ psi}$$

4. Calculate the allowable load due to bending (both skins).
The allowable loads due to bending are calculated as follows:

$$w_{bt} = \frac{8F_c'(E_L I_n)}{48cL^2 E_L} \qquad\qquad w_{bb} = \frac{8F_t'(E_L I_n)}{48cL^2 E_L}$$

where w_{bt} is the allowable load due to top skin bending, psf
w_{bb} is the allowable load due to bottom skin bending, psf
F_t' is the adjusted allowable tensile stress of the bottom skin, psi
F_c' is the adjusted allowable compressive stress of the top skin, psi
$E_L I_n$ is the net stiffness factor, psi per 4' width
c is the distance from the neutral axis to the extreme tension or compression
fiber, in
L is the span length, ft
E_L is the adjusted modulus of elasticity for the top or bottom skin, psi

a. Top skin.

$$w_{bt} = \frac{8F_c'(E_L I_n)}{48cL^2 E_L} = \frac{8(1{,}500.5 \text{ psi})(3.19x10^8 \text{ psi})}{48(2.786")(12')^2(1.98x10^6 \text{ psi})} = 100 \text{ psf}$$

b. Bottom skin.

$$w_{bb} = \frac{8F_t'(E_L I_n)}{48cL^2 E_L} = \frac{8(1{,}100 \text{ psi})(3.19x10^8 \text{ psi})}{48(3.464")(12')^2(1.98x10^6 \text{ psi})} = 59 \text{ psf}$$

E. Allowable load due to tension in the splice plate, w_p.
The tension splice plate is often the weak link of a stressed-skin
panel. Appendix F lists allowable splice plate stress, F, by plywood
thickness and species group. The allowable load on the tension
splice plate (usually the bottom skin) is calculated using the following equation:

$$w_p = \frac{8F\left(\dfrac{\text{total splice plate width}}{\text{bottom skin width}}\right)(E_L I_g)}{48cL^2 E_L}$$

where w_p is the allowable load due to tension in the splice plate, psf
F is the allowable tensile stress for the tension splice plate, psi
$E_L I_g$ is the gross stiffness factor, psi per 4' width
c is the distance from the neutral axis (calculated for deflection) to the
extreme tension fiber, in
L is the span length, ft
E_L is the adjusted modulus of elasticity for the bottom skin, psi

Paragraph 3.1.2 in Part 2 of *Supplement 3*, states that "splice plates
shall be at least equal in thickness to the skin, except that minimum

thickness shall be 15/32" if nail glued." Furthermore, the minimum length of a 15/32" joint is 6 inches. As previously calculated, the total width of the splice plate is 40.5". The maximum splice plate stress is 1,200 psi (*PDS*, Table 5.6.1.2 – see Appendix F). Note that the maximum splice plate stress is found for the plywood skin, not the splice plate.

$$w_p = \dfrac{8F\left(\dfrac{\text{total splice plate width}}{\text{bottom skin width}}\right)\left(E_L I_g\right)}{48cL^2 E_L} = \dfrac{8\left[(1{,}200 \text{ psi})\dfrac{40.5"}{48"}\right]\left(3.45 \times 10^8 \text{ lb-in}^2\right)}{48(3.36")(12')^2\left(1.98 \times 10^6 \text{ psi}\right)} = 61 \text{ psf}$$

F. Determine the allowable load due to rolling shear stress, w_s.

1. Calculate Q_s.

The critical plane for rolling shear occurs between the bottom two plies of the top (or thicker) skin when the stringers are parallel to the face grain of the plywood. See *Supplement 3*, 3.6.2, for details on calculating rolling shear when the stringers are perpendicular to the face grain of the plywood. To simplify calculations, the APA provides the table in Appendix F, which lists the effective area, A, outside of the critical shear plane and the center of the effective area, y'. The statical moment for rolling shear, Q_s, is calculated as follows:

$$d_s = c - y'$$
$$Q_s = A d_s$$

where d_s is the distance from the neutral axis to the center of the effective area outside of the critical plane, in.

 c is the appropriate extreme fiber distance (usually from the top) to the neutral axis for deflection, in

 y' is the distance from the edge of the plywood to the center of the effective area, in

 Q_s is the statical moment for rolling shear, in³ per 4' panel

 A is the area of the parallel plies outside of the critical rolling shear plane, in² per 4' panel

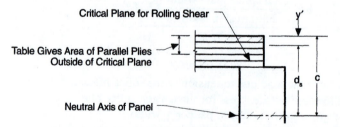

Figure 12.13g Critical plane for rolling shear, *PDS Supplement 3*, Figure 3.6.2

From Appendix F, y' is 0.0685" and A is 4.38 in² for a 5/8" touch-sanded panel. Also see Figure 12.13c.

$$c = 6.25" - 3.36" = 2.89" \Rightarrow d_s = c - y' = 2.89" - 0.0685" = 2.82"$$

$$Q_s = A d_s = \left(4.38 \text{ in}^2\right)(2.82") = 12.35 \text{ in}^3 \text{ per 4' panel}$$

2. Calculate allowable capacity.

The allowable rolling shear capacity is equal to the allowable rolling shear stress, F_s, multiplied by the total "glue width," i.e., the total width of the stringers. However, for the exterior stringers, the allowable rolling shear stress is taken as $0.5F_s$ due to stress concentrations at the edges of the panel.

$$\sum F_s t = \left[\left(\frac{F_s}{2}\right)(\text{\# of ext. stringers})t\right] + \left[(F_s)(\text{\# of interior stringers})t\right]$$

where F_s is the allowable rolling shear stress, psi
         t is the thickness of the stringers, in

For the example panel:

$$\sum F_s t = \left[\frac{53 \text{ psi}}{2}(2)(1.5")\right] + \left[(53 \text{ psi})(2)(1.5")\right] = 238.5 \text{ inlb}$$

3. Calculate the allowable load due to rolling shear stress, w_s.

The allowable load due to rolling shear stress is calculated using the following equation (*PDS*, 3.6.5):

$$w_s = \frac{2(E_L I_g)\sum F_s t}{4Q_s L E_L}$$

where w_s is the allowable load based on rolling shear stress, psf
         $E_L I_g$ is the gross stiffness factor, psi per 4' width
         $\sum F_s t$ is the sum of the glue widths multiplied by the applicable rolling shear stress, inlb
         Q_s the statical moment of rolling shear, computed for the thicker skin, in³ per 4' panel
         L is the span length, ft
         E_L is the adjusted modulus of elasticity of the thicker skin, psi

For the example panel:

$$w_s = \frac{2(E_L I_g)\sum F_s t}{4Q_s L E_L} = \frac{2(3.45x10^8 \text{ lb-in}^2)(238.5 \text{ lb-in})}{4(12.35 \text{ in}^3)(12')(1.98x10^6 \text{ psi})} = 140 \text{ psf}$$

G. Determine the allowable load due to horizontal shear stress, w_v.

1. Calculate the statical moment for horizontal shear stress, Q_v (*S3*, 3.7.1).

To calculate the allowable load due to horizontal shear stress, a statical moment, Q_v, which includes the area of the parallel plies and the stringers above the neutral axis for deflection, must be calculated. Again, the differences in E of the skin and stringers must be accounted for.

$$Q_v = (\text{\# of stringers})(Q_{stringer}) + \left(\frac{E_{L_{skin}}}{E_{L_{stringers}}}\right)(Q_{skin})$$

where Q_v is the statical moment for horizontal shear, in³ per 4' width

For the example panel:

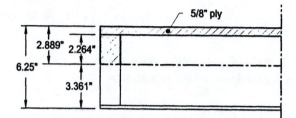

Figure 12.13h Distances for determining statical moment

Therefore,

$$A_{str} \text{ above N.A.} = bd = (1.5")(6.25"-3.361"-0.625") = (1.5")(2.264") = 3.396 \text{ in}^2$$

$$Q_{str} = Ad = \left[3.396 \text{ in}^2\right]\left(\frac{2.264"}{2}\right) = 3.84 \text{ in}^3$$

$$Q_{skin} = Ad = \left[4'(2.354 \text{ in}^2/ft)\right]\left(2.889" - \frac{0.625"}{2}\right) = 24.26 \text{ in}^3$$

$$Q_v = (\text{\# of stringers})(Q_{stringer}) + \left(\frac{E_{L_{skin}}}{E_{L_{stringers}}}\right)(Q_{skin})$$

$$= 4(3.84 \text{ in}^3) + \left(\frac{1.98x10^6 \text{ psi}}{1.648x10^6 \text{ psi}}\right)(24.26 \text{ in}^3) = 44.5 \text{ in}^3$$

2.   Calculate the allowable load due to horizontal shear stress, w_v.
     The allowable load for horizontal shear stress is calculated using the
     following equation (*PDS*, 3.7.3):

$$w_v = \frac{2(E_L I_g)F_v t}{4Q_v LE_{L_{str}}}$$

where w_v is the allowable load due to horizontal shear stress, psf
           F_v is the allowable horizontal shear stress for the stringers, psi
           t is the sum of the stringer widths, in
           L is the span length, ft
           E_L is the adjusted modulus of elasticity of the stringers, psi
           Q_v is the statical moment for horizontal shear, in³ per 4' width
           $E_L I_g$ is the gross stiffness factor, psi per 4' width

For the example panel:

$$w_v = \frac{2(E_L I_g)F_v t}{4Q_v LE_{L_{ar}}} = \frac{2(3.45x10^8 \text{ psi})(90 \text{ psi})[4(1.5")]}{4(44.5 \text{ in}^3)(12')(1.648x10^6 \text{ psi})} = 106 \text{ psf}$$

H. Compare the allowable loads.

$w_\Delta =$	105 psf
$w_{\Delta(ts)} =$	202 psf
$w_{bt} =$	100 psf
$w_{bb} =$	59 psf
$w_p =$	61 psf
$w_s =$	140 psf
$w_v =$	106 psf

In this case, the allowable load due to bending in the bottom skin, w_{bb}, is the limiting condition. The panel is therefore rated for a load of 59 psf or 2,832 total pounds.

Though the splice plate is not the limiting condition in this example, it is important to understand how to calculate the allowable load due to tension in a splice plate that is not in the middle of a span. Since the bending moment is greatest at the center of a span, it makes sense to move the splice plate(s) away from the center. The allowable load due to tension in the splice plate can be calculated for locations other than the center of the span with the following equation (McClintock, 5-17):

$$w_p = \frac{2F\left(\frac{\text{total splice plate width}}{\text{bottom skin width}}\right)(E_L I_g)}{48cX(L-X)E_L}$$

where X is the distance from the splice to the nearest end of the panel, ft
All other variables are as defined previously.

Example 5b. What would be the allowable load due to tension in the splice plate for Example 5a if it had two symmetrically spaced splices 2' from each end of the panel?

$$w_p = \frac{2F\left(\frac{\text{total splice plate width}}{\text{bottom skin width}}\right)(E_L I_g)}{48cX(L-X)E_L} = \frac{2\left[(1,200 \text{ psi})\frac{40.5"}{48"}\right](3.45x10^8 \text{ psi})}{48(3.36")(2')(12'-2')(1.98x10^6 \text{ psi})} = 109 \text{ psf}$$

In general, the 1/4" skin is not a good choice for panels spanning over 8' because the panel strength will almost always be governed by that skin. If the panel were built using a 3/8" sanded bottom skin (splice in the center of the span), the following allowable loads would result:

$w_\Delta =$	113 psf
$w_{bt} =$	109 psf
$w_{bb} =$	89 psf

$$w_p = \quad 65 \text{ psf}$$
$$w_s = \quad 147 \text{ psf}$$
$$w_v = \quad 108 \text{ psf}$$

Bending in the bottom skin, w_{bb}, is no longer the limiting condition. Although the splice plate is now the limiting factor, as shown in Example 5b, moving them to two feet from each end would increase w_p substantially (to at least 109 psf). Therefore, by merely increasing the thickness of the bottom skin 1/8", the allowable load of the 12' stressed-skin panel would increase from 59 psf to 89 psf because w_{bb} would be the ruling factor.

The above analysis may seem fearfully complex. As the following example demonstrates, stressed-skin analysis is considerably simpler for symmetrical panels without splice plates.

> ***Example 6.*** What is the maximum capacity of a 4'x8' double-sided stressed-skin panel with top and bottom skins of 1/2" APA Rated Sheathing, 32/16, Exposure 1, and 5/4x3.25" framing of Southern Pine Industrial 55 (Southern Pine No. 1) on 1' centers? The platform will be continuously supported on the 4' ends and spans 8'. Assume indoor use in a dry, protected environment and a normal load duration.

A.   Choose a trial section.
  1.   Sketch the loading conditions and the construction details:

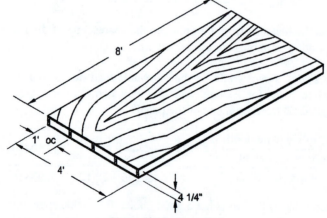

8'

1' oc

4'

4 1/4"

Figure 12.14a Example 6

2 and 3. Specify the geometric properties and allowable stresses for the components of the stressed-skin panel.

a.   1/2" APA Rated Sheathing, 32/16, Exposure 1
         From Appendix F:
                    Grade Stress Level is S-2 (see footnote)
                    unsanded

From the *Key to Span Rating* table:
Species Group is 1

<u>Section Properties</u>

A 2.292 in²/ft
I 0.067 in⁴/ft
$I_\perp$ 0.004 in⁴/ft

<u>Allowable Stresses</u>

F_t, F_b 1,650 psi
F_c 1,540 psi
F_s 53 psi
E 1,800,000 psi

b. 5/4x4 Southern Pine Industrial 55 (Southern Pine No. 1).
The section properties are calculated for the actual dimensions of
1"x3.25".

<u>Section Properties</u>

$A_{x\text{-}x}$ 3.25 in²
$I_{x\text{-}x}$ 2.8607 in⁴

<u>From Appendix D, Allowable Stresses</u>

F_v 100 psi
E 1,700,000 psi

4. Basic Spacing.
From Appendix F, the *b*-distance is 18" for both the top and bottom
skins.

5. Determine the clear distance between stringers.

$$\text{clear distance} = \frac{\text{panel width} - \text{total stringer width}}{\text{number of spans}} = \frac{48" - 5(1")}{4} = 10.75"$$

6. Determine the total splice plate width (if necessary). In this case,
there is no need for a splice plate.

B. Calculate the allowable load due to deflection, w_Δ.
1. Locate the neutral axis for deflection.
a. Calculate adjusted values of E.

$$E_{L_{ply}} = 1.1E = 1.1(1,800,000 \text{ psi}) = 1,980,000 \text{ psi}$$

$$E_{L_{str}} = 1.03E = 1.03(1,700,000 \text{ psi}) = 1,751,000 \text{ psi}$$

b. Sketch an end view of the panel.

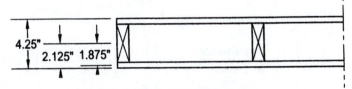

Figure 12.14b End view of Example 6

c. Calculate the location of the neutral axis for deflection.
Because the stressed-skin panel is symmetrical, the neutral axis is at
the center of the section, or 2.125".

2.   Determine the gross stiffness factor ($E_L I_g$):

	I_o, in^4	A, in^2	d, in	$I_g = I_o + Ad^2$	E_L, psi	$E_L I_g$
top	4'(0.067 in^4/ft)= 0.27	4'(2.292 in^2/ft)= 9.17	1.875	32.5 in^4	1,980,000	6.435x10^7
str	5(2.86 in^4)= 14.3	5(3.25 in^2)= 32.3	0	14.3 in^4	1,751,000	2.505x10^7
bot	4'(0.067 in^4/ft)= 0.27	4'(2.292 in^2/ft)= 3.98	1.88	32.5 in^4	1,980,000	6.435x10^7
total						1.537x10^8

$$E_L I_g = EI_{top} + EI_{str} + EI_{bot} = 1.537 \times 10^8 \text{ psi per 4' width}$$

3.   Determine the allowable load due to deflection, w_Δ.
      a. Calculate G, modulus of rigidity, for the **stringers**:

$$G = 0.06(E_L) = 0.06(1.75 \times 10^6 \text{ psi}) = 105,060 \text{ psi}$$

      b. Calculate the allowable load due to deflection:

$$w_\Delta = \cfrac{1}{CL\left[\cfrac{7.5L^2}{E_L I_g} + \cfrac{0.6}{AG}\right]} = \cfrac{1}{240(8')\left[\cfrac{7.5(8')^2}{1537 \times 10^8 \text{ psi}} + \cfrac{0.6}{(16.25 \text{ in}^2)(105,060 \text{ psi})}\right]} = 150 \text{ psf}$$

C.   Determine the allowable load due to top-skin deflection, $w_{\Delta(ts)}$.

$$w_{\Delta(ts)} = \frac{384 EI_\perp 12\Delta_{all}}{l^4} = \frac{384(1.8 \times 10^6 \text{ psi})(0.004 \text{ in}^4)12\left(\frac{10.75"}{240}\right)}{(10.75")^4} = 111 \text{ psf}$$

D.   Determine the allowable load due to bending, w_{bt} and w_{bb}.
      1 and 2. Determine the location of the neutral axis for bending and cal-
                culate $E_L I_g$.
                Since the clear distance between stringers is not greater than the b-
                spacing of the top and bottom skins, the effective widths of the top
                and bottom skins are the entire width of the panel. Therefore, the
                neutral axis for bending is the same as the neutral axis for deflection:

$$E_L I_g = E_L I_n$$

      3. Allowable stress.
      a. Top skin.

$$\text{factor} = 1 - \left[\left(\frac{\text{clear distance}}{b\text{-distance}} - 0.5\right)\frac{2}{3}\right] = 1 - \left[\left(\frac{10.75"}{18"} - 0.5\right)\frac{2}{3}\right] = 0.935 > 0.5$$

$$F_c' = (\text{factor})F_c = (0.935)(1,540 \text{ psi}) = 1,440 \text{ psi}$$

      b. Bottom skin.

$$\text{factor} = 0.935 \Rightarrow F_t' = (\text{factor})F_t = (0.935)(1,650 \text{ psi}) = 1,543 \text{ psi}$$

4. Calculate the allowable load due to bending.
a. Top skin.

$$w_{bt} = \frac{8F_c(E_L I_n)}{48cL^2 E_L} = \frac{8(1{,}440 \text{ psi})(1.537 x 10^8 \text{ psi})}{48(2.125")(8')^2(1.98 x 10^6 \text{ psi})} = 137 \text{ psf}$$

b. Bottom skin.

$$w_{bb} = \frac{8F_t(E_L I_n)}{48cL^2 E_L} = \frac{8(1{,}543 \text{ psi})(1.537 x 10^8 \text{ psi})}{48(2.125")(8')^2(1.98 x 10^6 \text{ psi})} = 146.8 \text{ psf}$$

E. Determine the allowable load due to tension in the splice plate, w_p.
There are no splices in this panel.

F. Determine the allowable load due to rolling shear stress, w_s.
1. Calculate Q_s:

$$d_s = c - y' = 2.125" - 0.0575" = 2.0675"$$

$$Q_s = Ad_s = (4.60 \text{ in}^2)(2.0675") = 9.5105 \text{ in}^3 \text{ per 4' panel}$$

2. Calculate the allowable capacity:

$$\sum F_s t = \left[\frac{53 \text{ psi}}{2}(2)(1") \right] + (53 \text{ psi})[(3)(1")] = 212 \text{ inlb}$$

3. Calculate the allowable load, w_s:

$$w_s = \frac{2(E_L I_g)\sum F_s t}{4Q_s L E_L} = \frac{2(1.537 x 10^8 \text{ psi})(212 \text{ inlb})}{4(9.5105 \text{ in}^3)(8')(1.98 x 10^6 \text{ psi})} = 108 \text{ psf}$$

G. Determine the allowable load due to horizontal shear stress, w_v.
1. Calculate the statical moment for horizontal shear, Q_v:

$$Q_{stringer} = Ad = \left[\left(\frac{3.25"}{2} \right) 1" \right](0.8125") = 6.602 \text{ in}^3$$

$$Q_{skin} = Ad = \left[(2.292 \text{ in}^2 / \text{ft})4' \right](1.875") = 19.4 \text{ in}^3$$

$$Q_v = (\# \text{ of stringers})(Q_{stringer}) + \left(\frac{E_{L_{skin}}}{E_{L_{stringers}}} \right)(Q_{skin})$$

$$= 5(6.602 \text{ in}^3) + \left(\frac{1.98 x 10^6 \text{ psi}}{1.75 x 10^6 \text{ psi}} \right)(19.4 \text{ in}^3) = 26.04 \text{ in}^3 \text{ per 4' width}$$

2. Calculate the allowable load due to horizontal shear stress, w_v:

$$w_v = \frac{2(E_L I_g)F_v t}{4Q_v L E_{L_{str}}} = \frac{2(1.537 x 10^8 \text{ psi})(100 \text{ psi})[5(1")]}{4(26.04 \text{ in}^3)(8')(1.75 x 10^6 \text{ psi})} = 105 \text{ psf}$$

H.   Compare the allowable loads:

$w_\Delta =$ 150 psf
$w_{\Delta(ts)} =$ 111 psf
$w_{bt} =$ 137 psf
$w_{bb} =$ 147 psf
$w_p =$ NA
$w_s =$ 108 psf
$w_v =$ 105 psf

In this case, the allowable load due to horizontal shear stress, w_v, is the limiting condition, and the panel is rated for a load of 105 psf or 3,360 total pounds.

For convenience, Appendix F includes a table of several stressed-skin panel designs and their allowable loads. Be sure to meet the splice plate and glue and nail requirements when building the panels.

Plywood can be used in a myriad of ways. In the construction industry, plywood is used edgewise as shear walls or diaphragms in buildings. In addition, the APA has written specifications which cover All-Plywood Beams, Plywood-Lumber Beams, Plywood Curved Panels, and Plywood Sandwich Panels. All of these construction techniques are occasionally useful in theatrical applications. For the sake of brevity, they will not be discussed in this text.

CHAPTER 12 LESSONS

The format of the numbering system is: chapter.lesson.problem number.

Assume dry conditions and a normal load duration unless otherwise noted.

LESSON 12.1 INTRODUCTION, DESIGN VALUES, GRADING SELECTION (PG 273–281)

12.1.1 What are the allowable stresses and geometric properties of a sheet of 1/4" A/D, exposure 1, group 1 plywood?

12.1.2 What are the allowable stresses and geometric properties of a sheet of 5/8" C/D plugged, group 2, interior plywood? Assume a two month load duration.

12.1.3 What are the allowable stresses and geometric properties of a sheet of 19/32" underlayment, group 4, interior plywood?

12.1.4 What are the allowable stresses and geometric properties of a sheet of 3/8" Structural I rated sheathing, exposure 1 plywood?

12.1.5 What are the allowable stresses and geometric properties of a sheet of 1-1/8" Sturd-I-Floor, 48" o.c., exposure 1 plywood? Assume a two month load duration.

LESSON 12.2 DESIGNING FOR UNIFORM LOADS, EXAMPLES (PG 281 – 287)

12.2.1 Using the same plywood from Examples 4a and 4b, determine the maximum allowable load for simple spans of 24", 32", and 48" with only two supports running **perpendicular** to the grain. Use $l/240$ as the deflection criteria.

12.2.2 Using the same plywood from Examples 4a and 4b, determine the maximum allowable load for simple spans of 16", 24", and 48" with only two supports running **parallel** to the grain. Use $l/240$ as the deflection criteria.

12.2.3 Using the same plywood from Example 2, determine the maximum allowable load for the sheet of plywood with supports running **perpendicular** to the face grain at 32" o.c. Use $l/240$ as the deflection criteria and assume a two month load duration.

12.2.4 Using the same plywood from Example 2, determine the maximum allowable load for the sheet of plywood with supports running **parallel** to the face grain at 24" o.c. Use $l/240$ as the deflection criteria and assume a two month load duration.

LESSON 12.3 STRESSED-SKIN PANELS: EXAMPLE 5a THROUGH STEP C (PG 287–294)

12.3.1 Calculate the maximum allowable load due to deflection (w_Δ) that a 4'x14' double sided stressed-skin panel with the following components can support. Use a deflection criteria of $l/240$.

        Top skin is 3/4" APA rated Sturd-I-Floor, 24" o.c., exposure 1
        Bottom skin is 1/2" underlayment, group 1, exposure 1
        4-2x6 stringers are Doug Fir-South No. 1 (actual depth is 5.375")

12.3.2 Calculate the maximum allowable load due to deflection between stringers of the top skin ($w_{\Delta(ts)}$) for the stressed-skin panel in Problem 12.3.1.

LESSON 12.4 STRESSED-SKIN PANELS: EXAMPLE 5a, STEPS D AND E (PG 294 – 298)

12.4.1 Calculate the maximum allowable load due to bending in the top skin (w_{bt}), bending in the bottom skin (w_{bb}), and tension in the splice plate (w_p) that the stressed-skin panel in Problem 12.3.1 can support.

LESSON 12.5 STRESSED-SKIN PANELS: EXAMPLE 5a, TO THE END (PG 298 – 301)

12.5.1 Calculate the maximum allowable load due to rolling shear (w_s) and horizontal shear (w_v) that the stressed-skin panel in Problem 12.3.1 can support. What is the maximum allowable load that the 4'x14' panel can support?

LESSON 12.6 STRESSED-SKIN PANELS: EXAMPLES 5b AND 6 (PG 301 – 306)

12.6.1 Calculate the maximum allowable load due to tension in the splice plate that the stressed-skin panel in Problem 12.3.1 can support if the splice is 6' from one end.

12.6.2 Calculate the maximum allowable load due to tension in the splice plate that the stressed-skin panel in Problem 12.3.1 can support if there are two splice plates 3' from each end.

12.6.3 Calculate the maximum allowable load that a 4'x8' double sided stressed-skin panel with the following components can support. Use a deflection criteria of $l/240$.

>> Top skin is 1/2" A/C, interior, group 1
>> Bottom skin is 1/2" A/C, interior, group 1
>> 4-2x3 stringers are Southern Pine No. 2 ripped to a depth of 2"

A

Appendix A: Math Review

CONTENTS:

NOMENCLATURE

+	Plus (sign of addition) or positive
−	Minus (sign of subtraction) or negative
±	Plus or minus
( )( ),×, •	Multiplied by (multiplication sign)
÷, /	Divided by (division sign)
=	Equals
≠	Is not equal to
≈, ≅	Approximately equals
≡	Is identical to
>	Greater than
>>	Much greater than
<	Less than
<<	Much less than
≥	Greater than or equal to
≤	Less than or equal to
√	Square root
∴	Therefore
α, β, θ, φ	alpha, beta, theta, phi – used to denote angles
π	pi (3.1416)
Σ	sigma (sign of summation)
sin	Sine
cos	Cosine
tan	Tangent
arcsin$a$ or asin$a$	Arc (angle) the sine of which is a (also expressed as $\sin^{-1}a$)
Δ	delta (change in)
⊥	Perpendicular to
‖	Parallel to
°	Degree (angle or temperature)
'	Feet
"	Inches
( )	Parenthesis
[ ]	Brackets
{ }	Braces
| |	Absolute value

The techniques used in this text assume a fundamental understanding of algebra, geometry, and trigonometry. The following math review is a quick refresher which hits the highlights pertinent to this text.

NUMBERS

POSITIVE AND NEGATIVE NUMBERS

Numbers can be positive or negative. The **absolute value** of a number is its "distance" from zero and is, therefore, always positive.

$$|-4| = 4$$
$$|4| = 4$$

Addition and subtraction of negative numbers are self-explanatory, but the multiplication and division of them requires a few rules:

- Multiplying or dividing two positive numbers results in a positive number:

$$(+)(+) = +$$

- Multiplying or dividing two negative numbers results in a positive number:

$$(-)(-) = +$$

- Multiplying or dividing a positive number and a negative number results in a negative number:

$$(+)(-) = -$$

Remember that any quantity multiplied by zero is zero and any quantity divided by zero is undefined.

FRACTIONS AND DECIMALS

Numbers are frequently expressed as fractions or decimals and can be written in a variety of styles.

$$\frac{3}{4} = {}^{3}\!/_{4} = 3/4 \qquad 0.75 = 7.5x10^{-1}$$

$$\underbrace{\hphantom{\frac{3}{4} = {}^{3}\!/_{4} = 3/4}}_{\text{fractions}} \qquad \underbrace{\hphantom{0.75 = 7.5x10^{-1}}}_{\text{decimals}}$$

A **fraction** has two parts, the **numerator** (top value) and **denominator** (bottom value). Fractions can be used to express any real number which is not an integer (whole number), and are used as shorthand for expressing division. In the example above, 3/4 is actually 3 divided by 4, or 0.75. An **improper fraction** is one in which the numerator is greater than the denominator. The improper equivalent of a proper fraction is found by multiplying the whole number component by the denominator and adding that number to the numerator:

$$5\frac{1}{2} = \frac{(5 \times 2) + 1}{2} = \frac{10 + 1}{2} = 11\!/_{2}$$

Improper fractions can be reduced to proper fractions by dividing the numerator by the denominator.

$$^{167}\!/_{16} = 10\frac{7}{16}$$

The reciprocal of a whole number or fraction is its inverse. Thus, the reciprocal of 5/4 is 4/5. Since whole numbers can be considered fractions which have denominators of 1, the reciprocal of a whole number is simply the number divided by one:

$$\text{The reciprocal of } \frac{x}{y} \text{ is } \frac{y}{x} \qquad\qquad 3 = \frac{3}{1}, \ \therefore \text{ the reciprocal is } \frac{1}{3}$$

The reciprocal of a quantity has the same sign as the original quantity. Any number multiplied by its reciprocal is equal to one:

$$\left(\frac{x}{y}\right) \times \left(\frac{y}{x}\right) = 1 \qquad\qquad \left(\frac{3}{1}\right) \times \left(\frac{1}{3}\right) = 1$$

The reciprocal of zero, 1/0, is undefined.

Any improper fraction or fraction less than 1 can be reduced to a **decimal** by simply dividing the numerator by the denominator:

$$39\!/_4 \Rightarrow 4\overline{)39.00} \quad\begin{array}{r} 9.75 \\ \underline{36} \\ 30 \\ \underline{28} \\ 20 \end{array} \qquad\qquad \frac{1}{5} \Rightarrow 5\overline{)1.00} \quad\begin{array}{r} 0.20 \\ \underline{0} \\ 10 \end{array}$$

The decimal system represents parts of a whole in terms of powers of ten. The first place to the right of the decimal represents 10^1 or 10; the second place represents 10^2 or 100; the third place represents 10^3 or 1,000, and so on. Therefore, 0.7 represents 7/10, 0.85 represents 85/100, 0.955 represents 955/1,000, etc.

PERCENTAGES
Percentages are a special type of decimal. To calculate the decimal equivalent of a percentage, divide it by 100. For example, when calculating 80% of a quantity, the quantity is multiplied by 80/100 or 0.8.

SCIENTIFIC NOTATION
Decimals are sometimes expressed in **scientific notation**. Scientific notation is used when a number is extraordinarily large or small. For example, twenty nine million can be expressed as follows:

$$29,000,000 = 2.9 \, x \, 10^7$$

The above notation represents twenty-nine million as 2.9 multiplied by $1x10^7$, or 10,000,000. Notice that the exponent is the number of places to the left that the decimal has been moved. Scientific notation can also express numbers that are less than 1 by using a negative exponent:

$$0.0000562 = 5.62x10^{-5}$$

Notice that the exponent is the number of places to the right that the decimal has been moved. Numbers can be entered in scientific notation on most calculators. Simply enter the first component of the number, press "E" or "exp," and enter the positive or negative exponent of ten. Scientific notation has several advantages. First, it reduces the chance of math errors due to entering one too many or one too few zeros. Second, it clarifies rounding issues and maintains a set of **significant figures**.

For the purposes of this text, significant figures will represent the degree of accuracy and precision of our numbers. For example, suppose the allowable deflection of a beam is determined to be one-two hundred fortieth of it's span (1/240th). If the beam is 8'-10" long, the amount of allowable movement is easily calculated:

$$\left(\frac{1}{240}\right) \times 106" = 0.4441666667"$$

The variables and constants used in structural design are not accurate to the 10th decimal place and are usually rounded to 2 or 3 significant figures. Thus, it is reasonable to consider the allowable movement to be 0.444" or $4.44x10^{-1}$ inches. If this number is then multiplied or divided to arrive at other numbers, those numbers cannot have an accuracy greater than 3 significant figures.

ROUNDING

When and how to round numbers is largely a matter of opinion, and we advocate the following rules: (1) choose a number of significant figures and round all numbers to have that many digits; (2) round up or down to the next nearest digit. If this is ambiguous because the last digit is exactly 5, then round up.

The second rule must be leavened with common sense. For example, if we calculated that we needed a minimum area of 3.4 in^2 to support a load, it would be inappropriate to round down to 3 in^2. On the other hand, if the calculations resulted in a required area of 3.415 in^2, it would be acceptable to round up to 3.5 in^2 because the difference results in a safer condition. In either case, the conservative, and safe, approach would be to round up values which are requirements and to round down allowable values. For example, if a member has an allowable load of 35.5 lbs per in^2, it is conservative to round down to 35 psi; rounding up to 36 psi would overload the member.

PROPERTIES OF ADDITION AND MULTIPLICATION

Remember that addition and subtraction are not truly different. Subtraction is simply adding a negative number. Likewise, multiplication and division are not truly different because division is simply multiplication by the reciprocal of the divisor. 3/4 can be expressed as "3 divided by 4" or "3 multiplied by 1/4." This review will concentrate on addition and multiplication – the rules of addition are applicable to subtraction and the rules of multiplication are applicable to division.

If two numbers are written side by side with one or both in a parenthesis, it is assumed that they are to be multiplied. **Variables** are letters which represent numbers in equations. They are typically used if an expression is true for all numbers, or they are used to represent an unknown number. If two variables are written side by side, it is also assumed that they are multiplied:

$$-10(4) = -(10)(4) = (-10)4 = -10 \times 4$$
$$ab = a \times b$$

Many equations have more than two numbers or variables. When solving and manipulating these equations, it is important to understand the Associative and Commutative Laws of Addition and Multiplication.

Communicative Law of Addition and Multiplication:

$$a + b = b + a$$
$$a \times b = b \times a$$

$$5 + 4 = 4 + 5 = 9$$
$$(5)4 = 4(5) = 20$$

Associative Law of Addition and Multiplication:

$$(a + b) + c = a + (b + c)$$
$$(a \times b) \times c = a \times (b \times c)$$

$$(10 + 12) + 3 = 10 + (12 + 3) = 25$$
$$(10 \times 12)3 = 10(12 \times 3) = 360$$

If an expression only involves addition or multiplication, the order in which the numbers are added or multiplied does not effect the answer.

EQUATIONS

An equation is an equal sign with expressions on each side of it. An equation is true if the expressions on each side are equal (an equation is useless if they are not). Equations can be manipulated in many ways which are based on the idea that what is done to one side of the equation must be done to the other. The concept can be specified as follows (Sperling, 79):

1. A term may be transposed from one side of an equation to the other if its sign is changed from + or −, or from − to +.

$$a = b$$
$$a - b = b - b$$
$$a - b = 0$$

2. The same number may be added to both sides of an equation.

$$a = b$$
$$a + 7 = b + 7$$

3. Both sides of an equation may be multiplied by the same number.

$$a = b$$
$$3a = 3b$$

4. A factor, or multiplier, may be removed from one side of an equation by making it a divisor in the other and vice-versa.

$$5(a+2) = b$$

$$\frac{5(a+2)}{5} = \frac{b}{5}$$

$$a+2 = \frac{b}{5}$$

This property is applied in a common technique called cross-multiplication:

$$\frac{a}{b} = \frac{c}{d}$$

$$ad = bc$$

When a set of terms in parenthesis is multiplied by a number or variable, the parenthesis is eliminated by **distributing** the multiplier:

$$5(a+2) = b$$

$$5a + 5(2) = b$$

$$5a + 10 = b$$

If two terms are multiplied together, each individual part of each term must be multiplied and added to the others in turn:

$$(x+1)(x-4) = 0$$

$$xx - 4x + 1x - 4 = 0$$

$$x^2 - 3x - 4 = 0$$

ORDER OF OPERATIONS

If an expression or equation mixes operations, then they must be solved in a particular order, called the **order of operations**:

1. Perform operations inside parenthesis. If there are several levels of brackets, work from the inside out.
2. Perform multiplications (this includes powers and roots).
3. Perform additions.

Essentially, parenthesis and "pluses and minuses" separate an expression into discrete terms. Ideally, a complicated equation is reduced to a series of terms which are added together.

Example 1. Reduce the following expression.

$$10\{(5+3) - [7 + 3(2)] + 4\}$$

$$10\{8 - [7+6] + 4\} = 10\{8 - 13 + 4\} = 10(-1) = -10$$

ADDING AND MULTIPLYING FRACTIONS

Fractions can be added or subtracted directly if they have the same denominator by adding or subtracting the numerators and leaving the denominator the same:

$$\frac{1}{5}+\frac{3}{5}=\frac{4}{5} \qquad \frac{2}{3}-\frac{1}{3}=\frac{1}{3}$$

In multiplication and division, the numerators and denominators of each term are multiplied:

$$\left(\frac{1}{5}\right)\left(\frac{3}{5}\right)=\frac{3}{25} \qquad \left(\frac{2}{3}\right)(-3)=-\frac{6}{3}=-2 \qquad \frac{\frac{3}{4}}{\frac{1}{5}}=\left(\frac{3}{4}\right)\left(\frac{5}{1}\right)=\frac{15}{4}$$

Fractions with different denominators can be added together if they are transformed to fractions with the same denominator. A **common denominator** can always be found by multiplying the different denominators. While this is not always the least common denominator (LCD), it always works. In the example below, a common denominator is 35. Thus, the first fraction is multiplied by 7/7 and the second is multiplied by 5/5:

$$\frac{2}{5}+\frac{3}{7}=\left(\frac{7}{7}\right)\left(\frac{2}{5}\right)+\left(\frac{5}{5}\right)\left(\frac{3}{7}\right)=\frac{14}{35}+\frac{15}{35}=\frac{29}{35}$$

This technique is also applicable to fractions with variables:

$$\frac{a}{x}+\frac{b}{y}=\frac{y}{y}\left(\frac{a}{x}\right)+\frac{x}{x}\left(\frac{b}{y}\right)=\frac{ay}{xy}+\frac{bx}{xy}=\frac{ay+bx}{xy}$$

This process does not change the fraction because it is the equivalent to multiplying each fraction by 1.

EXPONENTS

Exponents are superscripts which appear to the right of a number or variable. They are a shorthand representation of how many times that number or variable is multiplied by itself:

$$x^2 = xx$$
$$10^6 = 10\times10\times10\times10\times10\times10$$
$$(x+1)^3 = (x+1)(x+1)(x+1)$$

A negative exponent indicates that the quantity is a reciprocal:

$$x^{-2} = \frac{1}{x^2} = \frac{1}{xx}$$
$$10^{-6} = \frac{1}{10^6} = \frac{1}{10\times10\times10\times10\times10\times10}$$
$$(x+1)^{-3} = \frac{1}{(x+1)^3} = \frac{1}{(x+1)(x+1)(x+1)}$$
$$\frac{1}{b^{-4}} = \frac{1}{\frac{1}{b^4}} = \left(\frac{1}{1}\right)\left(\frac{b^4}{1}\right) = b^4 = bbbb$$

Exponents can be fractions. For example, **square roots** are indicated by an exponent of 1/2. "The square root of a number is one of two equal factors which, if multiplied together, produce the number" (Sperling, 85). Likewise, the cube root of a number is indicated by an exponent of 1/3 and so on. **Roots** can be represented by fractional exponents or **radicals**. Fractional exponents follow the general form:

$$x^{a/n} = \sqrt[n]{x^a} \qquad x^{1/2} = \sqrt{x} \qquad x^{2/3} = \sqrt[3]{x^2} \qquad (a+b)^{4/5} = \sqrt[5]{(a+b)^4}$$

Any quantity with an exponent of 0 equals 1.

$$5^0 = 1$$
$$x^0 = 1$$
$$(ab + c^2 - xy)^0 = 1$$

To add and multiply quantities with exponents, the following rules apply (Buck, A-3):

1. $x^n x^m = x^{n+m}$

   $x^2 x^4 = x^{2+4} = x^6$

   $x^2 x^4 = (xx)(xxxx) = xxxxxx = x^6$

2. $\dfrac{x^n}{x^m} = x^{n-m}$

   $\dfrac{x^2}{x^3} = x^{2-3} = x^{-1} = \dfrac{1}{x}$

   $\dfrac{x^2}{x^3} = \dfrac{xx}{xxx} = \dfrac{1}{x}$

3. $(x^n)^m = x^{n \times m}$

   $(x^2)^4 = x^{2(4)} = x^8$

   $(x^2)^4 = (x^2)(x^2)(x^2)(x^2) = (xx)(xx)(xx)(xx) = xxxxxxxx = x^8$

4. $(xy)^n = (x^n)(y^n)$

   $(xy)^3 = x^3 y^3$

   $(xy)^3 = (xy)(xy)(xy) = (xxx)(yyy) = x^3 y^3$

   $(xy)^n \neq xy^n$

5.   if $y \neq 0$,

$$\left(\frac{x}{y}\right)^n = \frac{x^n}{y^n}$$

$$\left(\frac{x}{y}\right)^5 = \frac{x^5}{y^5}$$

$$\left(\frac{x}{y}\right)^5 = \left(\frac{x}{y}\right)\left(\frac{x}{y}\right)\left(\frac{x}{y}\right)\left(\frac{x}{y}\right)\left(\frac{x}{y}\right) = \frac{xxxxx}{yyyyy} = \frac{x^5}{y^5}$$

QUADRATIC EQUATION

The quadratic equation is applicable for any equation which can be expressed in the following form:

$$ax^2 + bx + c = 0$$

where x is a variable
           a, b, and c are constants

If a, b, and c are known quantities, x can be solved for by using the quadratic equation:

$$x = \frac{-b \pm \sqrt{b^2 - 4ac}}{2a}$$

The quadratic equation will yield two solutions for x. When solving problems which have a physical reality, one of the two answers will usually be inapplicable. If the solution requires the square root of a negative number, then that solution is not the answer (physical reality does not correspond to imaginary numbers).

Example 2.   Solve for x for the following equation: $15x^2 - 20.5x - 17 = 0$

$a = 15;\ b = -20.5;\ c = -17$

$$x = \frac{-b + \sqrt{b^2 - 4ac}}{2a} = \frac{-(-20.5) + \sqrt{(-20.5)^2 - 4(15)(-17)}}{2(15)} = \frac{20.5 + \sqrt{420.25 + 1,020}}{30} = 1.94$$

$$x = \frac{-b - \sqrt{b^2 - 4ac}}{2a} = \frac{-(-20.5) - \sqrt{(-20.5)^2 - 4(15)(-17)}}{2(15)} = \frac{20.5 - \sqrt{420.25 + 1,020}}{30} = -0.58$$

x is 1.94 or −0.58

SIMULTANEOUS LINEAR EQUATIONS

Some equations have two unknown variables. If only one equation with two unknowns is given, the unknowns cannot be found. If, however, a pair of equations relate the same two unknowns, both unknowns can be solved for. For example, consider the following pair of simultaneous equations:

$$2x + 7y = 3$$
$$3x - 5y = 51$$

The unknowns x and y can be solved for by either of the following two methods. The first method solves one equation for one unknown and substitutes the solution into the second equation:

$$2x + 7y = 3$$
$$2x = 3 - 7y$$
$$x = \frac{3 - 7y}{2} = 1.5 - \frac{7}{2}y$$

Substitute into the second equation:

$$3x - 5y = 51$$
$$-5y = 51 - 3x$$
$$-5y = 51 - 3\left(1.5 - \frac{7}{2}y\right) = 51 - \left(4.5 - \frac{21}{2}y\right)$$
$$-5y = 51 - 4.5 + \frac{21}{2}y$$
$$-5y - \frac{21}{2}y = 46.5$$
$$y(-5 - 10.5) = 46.5$$
$$-15.5y = 46.5$$
$$y = -\frac{46.5}{-15.5} = -3$$

Solve for x:

$$x = 1.5 - \frac{7}{2}y = 1.5 - \left(\frac{7}{2}\right)(-3) = 1.5 + \frac{21}{2} = 1.5 + 10.5 = 12$$

$$x = 12 \qquad y = -3$$

The unknowns can also be solved for by adding the two equations together. Before doing so, it is important to manipulate them so that one unknown will cancel out when they are added together. For the same two equations solved above, the first equation can be multiplied by −3 and the second equation by 2. As long as both sides of each equation are treated the same, the equations are still true.

$$2x + 7y = 3$$
$$3x - 5y = 51$$

$\Rightarrow$

$$-3(2x + 7y) = (3)(-3)$$
$$2(3x - 5y) = (51)2$$

$\Rightarrow$

$$-6x - 21y = -9$$
$$6x - 10y = 102$$

Add the equations:

$$-6x - 21y = -9$$
$$\underline{6x - 10y = 102}$$
$$0 - 31y = 93 \quad \Rightarrow \quad y = \frac{93}{-31} = -3$$

solve for x:

$$2x + 7y = 3$$
$$2x = 3 - 7y$$
$$2x = 3 - 7(-3) = 3 + 21$$
$$2x = 24$$
$$x = 12$$

$$x = 12 \qquad y = -3$$

GEOMETRY

CARTESIAN COORDINATES

The Cartesian System divides two-dimensional space into four quadrants using an **x-axis** and **y-axis** (see Figure A.1).

The center of the system where the two axes cross is the (0,0) point or the **origin**. The location of any point in the plane is described by specifying an **x-value** and a **y-value**. Conventionally, the x and y-values are enclosed in parentheses and separated by a comma; the x-value is listed first, (x, y). The x and y values can be positive or negative. Thus, the four quadrants form the distinct patterns shown in Figure A.1.

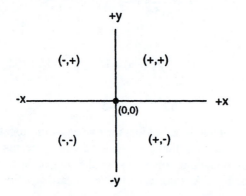

Figure A.1 Cartesian coordinate system

Any straight line can be described with the following general formula.

$$y = mx + b$$

where y is the y-value at point x
         m is the slope
         b is the y-intercept

The **slope** of a line, m, is a measurement of its steepness and is defined as the change in y divided by the change in x:

$$slope = m = \frac{\Delta y}{\Delta x} = \frac{y_2 - y_1}{x_2 - x_1} = \frac{rise}{run}$$

The **y-intercept** of a line, b, is the point at which the line will cross through the y-axis.

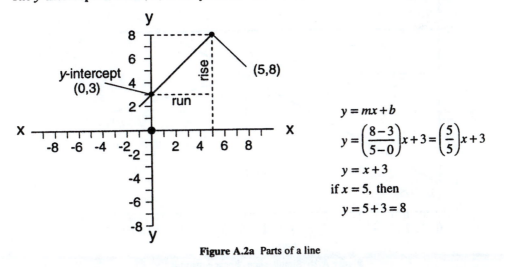

$$y = mx + b$$

$$y = \left(\frac{8-3}{5-0}\right)x + 3 = \left(\frac{5}{5}\right)x + 3$$

$$y = x + 3$$

if $x = 5$, then

$$y = 5 + 3 = 8$$

Figure A.2a Parts of a line

The slope of a horizontal line is 0 because the numerator, the change in y, Δy, is 0. The slope of a vertical line is undefined because the denominator, the change in x, Δx, is 0.

The two simultaneous equations analyzed previously represented lines. Hence, the name simultaneous *linear* equations. They are simultaneous at their point of intersection which is the solution found for x and y. We can graph them to show the point of intersection. The first step is to rearrange the equations so that they follow the form for a line:

$$2x + 7y = 3 \qquad\qquad 3x - 5y = 51$$

$$7y = 3 - 2x \qquad\qquad -5y = 51 - 3x$$

$$y = \frac{3 - 2x}{7} = \frac{3}{7} - \frac{2}{7}x \qquad\qquad y = \frac{51 - 3x}{-5} = -\frac{51}{5} + \frac{3}{5}x$$

$$y = -\frac{2}{7}x + \frac{3}{7} \qquad\qquad y = \frac{3}{5}x - \frac{51}{5}$$

To graph the line, we need two points (any two points make a line). The y-intercept will be one of those points. For the first equation, the first point is $(0, 3/7)$. To graph the line we can either use the slope or calculate a second point by plugging a value for x into the linear equation and connecting the two points. In this case, we'll use $x=19$. For the second equation, the first point is $(0, -51/5)$, and we will find y at $x=20$.

$$y = -\frac{2}{7}x + \frac{3}{7} \qquad\qquad y = \frac{3}{5}x - \frac{51}{5}$$

$$y = -\frac{2}{7}(19) + \frac{3}{7} = -\frac{38}{7} + \frac{3}{7} = -\frac{35}{7} = -5 \qquad\qquad y = \frac{3}{5}(20) - \frac{51}{5} = \frac{60}{5} - \frac{51}{5} = \frac{9}{5}$$

When plotted, the two lines intersect at $(12, -3)$, as predicted by the previous solution. Notice that the slope of one equation is negative while the other is positive, giving the lines opposite senses.

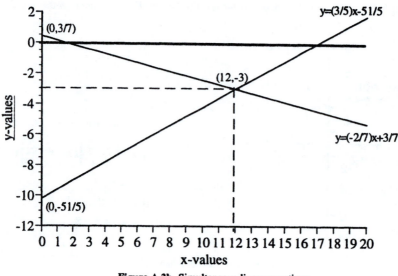

Figure A.2b Simultaneous linear equations

DEGREES AND RADIANS

Another way of describing a line or point in space is to specify an angle. A complete revolution around the origin is 360°. Each quadrant describes 90° (see Figure A.3). A degree can be further divided into 60 minutes and a minute can be divided into 60 seconds. The Greek letters alpha, beta, theta, and phi (α, β, θ, and ϕ) are commonly used to represent unknown angles.

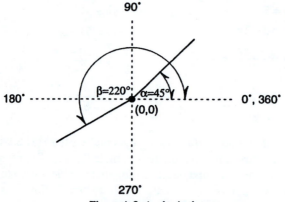

Figure A.3 Angles in degrees

While the "degree" system is commonly used and is probably more familiar, angles are also described in terms of radians or pi (π, 3.1415926 . . .). Figure A.4 shows the same coordinate system illustrated in Figure A.3 in terms of radians. One radian is approximately 57.3°. Note that 180° is equal to π radians, and 360° is equal to 2π radians.

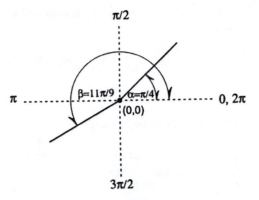

Figure A.4 Angles in radians

Therefore, to convert degrees to radians, the following formula can be used:

$$\theta_{radians} = \left(\frac{\theta^\circ}{180^\circ} \right) \pi$$

Example 3. What are 45° and 353° in radians?

$$\left(\frac{45^\circ}{180^\circ} \right) \pi = \frac{\pi}{4} \text{ radians} \qquad\qquad \left(\frac{353^\circ}{180^\circ} \right) \pi = 1.961\pi \text{ radians}$$

SHAPES

Polygons

A **polygon** is any shape which has three or more straight sides. A regular polygon is one in which all the internal angles are equal, such as an equilateral triangle. Quadrilaterals are polygons with four sides. Figure A.5 shows several examples of quadrilaterals and triangles. Right angles (90°) are represented by a square in the corner.

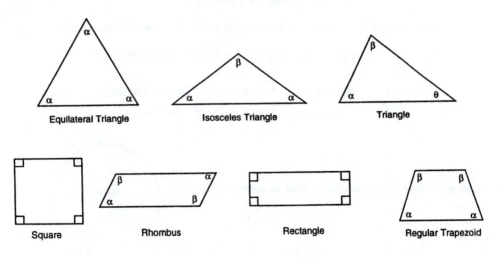

Figure A.5 Various triangles and quadrilaterals

The sum of the internal angles of any polygon (including irregular polygons) can be calculated using the following equation:

$$\sum angles = (180°)(n-2) \qquad \text{or} \qquad \sum angles = (\pi)(n-2)$$

where n is the total number of interior angles

Thus, the following conclusions can be reached:

Shape	# of sides	total of interior angles	interior angle for a regular shape
triangle	3	180°	60°
square	4	360°	90°
decagon	5	540°	108°
hexagon	6	720°	120°
heptagon	7	900°	128°34'17"
octagon	8	1,080°	135°

Example 4. What is the missing angle in the following polygon?

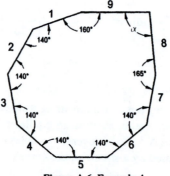

Figure A.6 Example 4

First, determine the sum of the internal angles for a 9-sided polygon:

$$\sum angles = (180°)(n-2) = (180°)(9-2) = 1,260°$$

Calculate the missing angle by subtracting the known angles from the total:

$$\alpha = 1,260° - 6(140°) - 160° - 165° = 95°$$

Circles

The parts of a circle can be labeled as shown in Figure A.7.

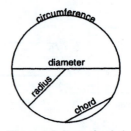

Figure A.7 Parts of a circle

The constant pi, π, is found by dividing the circumference of a circle by its diameter (Sperling, 137). It has the same value for all circles. The circumference of a circle is therefore:

$$\pi = \frac{C}{d} \Rightarrow C = \pi d = 2\pi r$$

where C is the circumference
        d is the diameter
        r is the radius

The area of a circle is:

$$A = \pi r^2$$

The basic properties of common geometric shapes are listed at the end of this appendix and in Appendix C.

TRIGONOMETRY

ANGULAR RELATIONSHIPS

By definition, any angle has complementary and supplementary angles. A complementary angle is the angle necessary to complete 90°; a supplementary angle is the angle necessary to complete 180° (see Figure A.8).

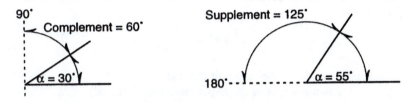

Figure A.8 Complementary and supplementary angles

Complements and supplements are useful in analyzing many systems, especially right triangles.

It is important to recognize two common patterns formed by intersecting lines as described in Figure A.9. Identical angles are represented by the same Greek letter.

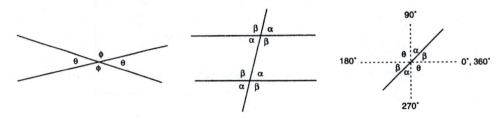

Figure A.9 Congruent angles in systems

RIGHT TRIANGLES

Trigonometry is basically the study of triangles, especially right triangles. A right triangle is any triangle which has a square (90°) corner as shown in Figure A.10. Once an angle other than the 90° angle between two sides of a right triangle has been defined, the proportional relationship betweeen the sides is known. That is, for a given angle, the ratio of the two sides will be constant, regardless of their length. The length of one leg of a triangle divided by the other will always be identical.

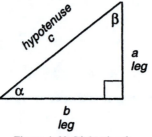

Figure A.10 Right triangle

Since the sum of the internal angles of any triangle is 180° and one angle of a right triangle, by definition, is 90°, the sum of the two remaining angles must be 90°, and are therefore complements.

The **Pythagorean Theorem** describes the relationship between the hypotenuse and the legs of a right triangle:

$$a^2 + b^2 = c^2$$

where a and b are the length of the legs
            c is the length of the hypotenuse (the diagonal)

The Pythagorean Theorem is often used by carpenters to establish a square corner. Any 3-4-5 triangle will yield a 90° angle. That is, any triangle with legs of 3 and 4 and a hypotenuse of 5 (or multiples thereof) fits the Pythagorean Theorem:

$$a^2 + b^2 = c^2$$
$$3^2 + 4^2 = 5^2$$
$$9 + 16 = 25 \checkmark$$

$$a^2 + b^2 = c^2$$
$$6^2 + 8^2 = 10^2$$
$$36 + 64 = 100 \checkmark$$

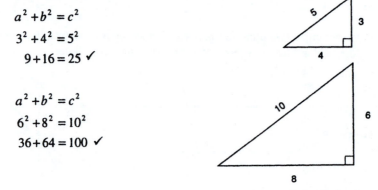

Figure A.11 3-4-5 triangles

Other useful right triangles include 5-12-13 and 8-15-17 triangles.

The trigonometric functions of sine, cosine, and tangent are names for the ratios between two sides of any right triangle. As discussed previously, these ratios are constant for a given angle. The values of the trigonometric functions are relative to the angle.

$$\sin \alpha = \frac{opposite}{hypotenuse} = \frac{opp}{hyp} = \frac{a}{c}$$

$$\cos \alpha = \frac{adjacent}{hypotenuse} = \frac{adj}{hyp} = \frac{b}{c}$$

$$\tan \alpha = \frac{\sin \alpha}{\cos \alpha} = \frac{opposite}{adjacent} = \frac{opp}{adj} = \frac{a}{b}$$

$$\sin \beta = \frac{b}{c}$$

$$\cos \beta = \frac{a}{c}$$

$$\tan \beta = \frac{b}{a}$$

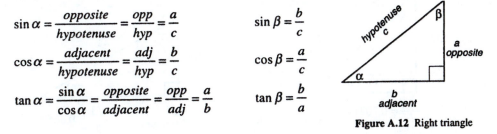

Figure A.12 Right triangle

Notice that $\sin\alpha = \cos\beta$, as is always the case for complementary angles. Also notice that values for sine and cosine must always be less than 1 because the length of the hypotenuse is always larger than either of the two sides.

When the ratio of the sides has been determined by finding the sine, cosine, or tangent, the corresponding angle is found by cross-referencing a trigonometric chart or using the "asin," "acos," or "atan" key or the 2nd function feature with the "sin," "cos," or "tan" key on a calculator. When trigonometric values for sine, cosine, or tangent are expressed, at least four decimal places are necessary to accurately define an angle.

Example 5. Find the sine, cosine, and tangent for both non-90° angles in the following triangle.

$$\sin \alpha = \sin 50° = 0.7660$$

$$\cos \alpha = \cos 50° = 0.6428$$

$$\tan \alpha = \tan 50° = 1.1918$$

$$\alpha + \beta = 90° \Rightarrow \beta = 90° - 50° = 40°$$

$$\sin \beta = \sin 40° = 0.6428$$

$$\cos \beta = \cos 40° = 0.7660$$

$$\tan \beta = \tan 40° = 0.8391$$

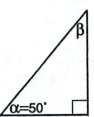

Figure A.13a Example 5

Example 6. Find α and β.

$$\sin \alpha = \frac{opp}{hyp} = \frac{9}{15} = 0.6$$

$$\alpha = \sin^{-1}(0.6) = 36.9°$$

$$\sin \beta = \frac{opp}{hyp} = \frac{12}{15} = 0.8$$

$$\beta = \sin^{-1}(0.8) = 53.1°$$

$$\alpha + \beta = 36.9° + 53.1° = 90° \checkmark$$

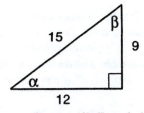

Figure A.13b Example 6

Two common right triangles are 45° triangles and 30°-60°-90° triangles. If the hypotenuse equals 1, the sides will equal the following:

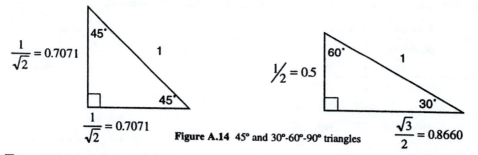

Figure A.14 45° and 30°-60°-90° triangles

TRIANGLES

Like right triangles, any triangle is fully defined if three of its six parts are known and one of them is a side (2 sides and 1 angle, 2 angles and 1 side, or 3 sides) because the other three can then be calculated. The length of the sides of all triangles relate to their opposite angle, so any unknown quantities can be determined using the Law of Sines and/or the Law of Cosines:

Law of Sines

$$\frac{a}{\sin A} = \frac{b}{\sin B} = \frac{c}{\sin C}$$

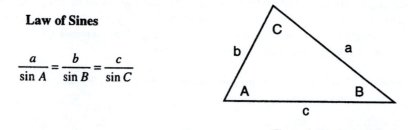

Figure A.15a Law of Sines

The Law of Sines can be proven if we drawn a line from intersection C perpedicular to side c. If this line is labeled d, we can use it to compare the sines for angles A and B:

$$\sin A = \frac{opp}{hyp} = \frac{d}{b} \Rightarrow \frac{a}{\sin A} = \frac{a}{d/b} = \frac{ab}{d}$$

$$\sin B = \frac{opp}{hyp} = \frac{d}{a} \Rightarrow \frac{b}{\sin B} = \frac{b}{d/a} = \frac{ab}{d}$$

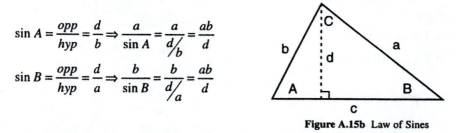

Figure A.15b Law of Sines

In this fashion, the relationship between any two sides is easily defined. If a line is drawn perpendicular to sides a or b, it can be proven that $c/\sin C$ is equal to $a/\sin A$ or $b/\sin B$, and since the above equation proves that $a/\sin A$ and $b/\sin B$ are equal, all the expressions are equal to each other and the Law of Sines can be written as it is above. This expression can be rearranged to solve for any variable, such as:

$$\frac{a}{\sin A} = \frac{c}{\sin C} \Rightarrow a = c\frac{\sin A}{\sin C}$$

Law of Cosines

$$a^2 = b^2 + c^2 - 2bc(\cos A)$$
$$b^2 = a^2 + c^2 - 2ac(\cos B)$$
$$c^2 = a^2 + b^2 - 2ab(\cos C)$$

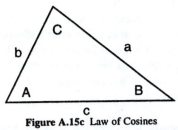

Figure A.15c Law of Cosines

For a right triangle, the cosine of 90° is zero and the law of cosines reduces to the Pythagorean Theorem. This expression is applicable to any angle in the triangle as long as the angle and side in question are opposite to each other.

SIMILAR TRIANGLES

The concept of similar triangles allows us to solve an unknown triangle if one of its sides and a similar triangle are known. Similar triangles are ones in which the proportions, or ratios, between the sides are identical, but the lengths are not. For example, a 3-4-5 triangle is similar to a 6-8-10 triangle or a 9-12-15 triangle, etc. Essentially, similar triangles are multiplies of each other. By definition, they have the same angles.

Example 7. Solve for sides a and b of the second triangle, and solve for angle α.

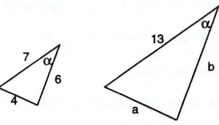

Figure A.16 Example 7

The sides are solved for by comparing the ratios of the sides of the similar triangles:

$$\frac{7}{6} = \frac{13}{b}$$
$$7b = 6(13) = 78$$
$$b = \frac{78}{7} = 11.14$$

$$\frac{7}{4} = \frac{13}{a}$$
$$7a = 4(13) = 52$$
$$a = \frac{52}{7} = 7.43$$

The angle is calculated using the law of cosines:

$$a^2 = b^2 + c^2 - 2bc(\cos \alpha)$$
$$4^2 = 6^2 + 7^2 - 2(6)(7)(\cos \alpha)$$
$$16 = 36 + 49 - 84(\cos \alpha)$$
$$84(\cos \alpha) = 85 - 16 = 69$$
$$\cos \alpha = \frac{69}{84} = 0.8214 \Rightarrow \alpha = 34.8°$$

VECTOR ADDITION

Often the triangles in question in structural design are actually force triangles formed by vectors. A vector is a line with a direction (indicated by an arrowhead). Frequently, vectors are used to represent forces which will have a tendency to move objects in a certain direction. If more than one force is acting on an object, the object will move in the direction of the resultant of the two vectors. If the vectors are equal and opposite, the object would be stationary.

Graphically, if vectors are drawn to scale, they can be added together by placing them head to tail. A new vector is drawn from the tail of one to the head of the other (pointing in the direction of the head):

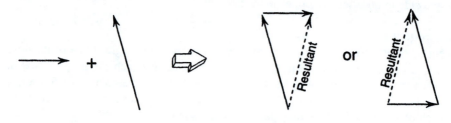

Figure A.17 Vector addition

Most frequently, vectors are not drawn to scale, but their magnitude and direction are known. The resultant magnitude and direction can then be calculated using the techniques for triangles discussed above.

At times, it is convenient to draw all three vectors as originating from one point:

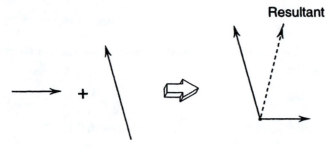

Figure A.18 Alternate vector addition

This representation does not change the magnitude or direction of the vectors in any way.

AREAS AND VOLUMES

A=area
V=volume

Square	$A = s^2$ $A = \dfrac{1}{2}d^2$
Rectangle	$A = ab$ $d = \sqrt{a^2 + b^2}$
Parallelogram	$A = ab$
Right triangle	$A = \dfrac{bc}{2}$ $a^2 = b^2 + c^2$
Circle	$A = \pi\ r^2$ $C = 2\pi\ r = \pi\ d$
Ellipse	$P =$ perimeter or circumference $A = \pi\ ab$ approximate perimeter: $P = \pi\ \sqrt{2\left(a^2 + b^2\right)}$
Regular polygon	$n =$ number of sides $\alpha = \dfrac{360°}{n}$ $\beta = 180° - \alpha$ $A = \dfrac{nsr}{2} = \dfrac{ns}{c}\sqrt{R^2 - \dfrac{s^2}{4}}$

AREAS AND VOLUMES

A=area
V=volume

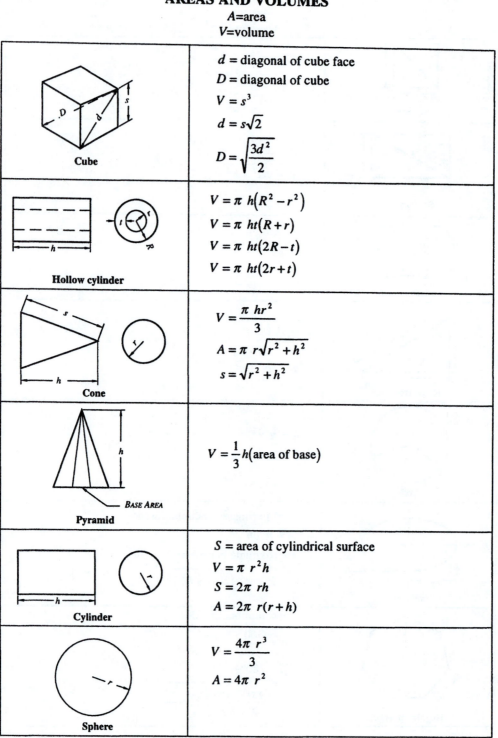

Cube	d = diagonal of cube face D = diagonal of cube $V = s^3$ $d = s\sqrt{2}$ $D = \sqrt{\dfrac{3d^2}{2}}$
Hollow cylinder	$V = \pi\, h\left(R^2 - r^2\right)$ $V = \pi\, ht(R + r)$ $V = \pi\, ht(2R - t)$ $V = \pi\, ht(2r + t)$
Cone	$V = \dfrac{\pi\, hr^2}{3}$ $A = \pi\, r\sqrt{r^2 + h^2}$ $s = \sqrt{r^2 + h^2}$
Pyramid	$V = \dfrac{1}{3}h(\text{area of base})$
Cylinder	S = area of cylindrical surface $V = \pi\, r^2 h$ $S = 2\pi\, rh$ $A = 2\pi\, r(r + h)$
Sphere	$V = \dfrac{4\pi\, r^3}{3}$ $A = 4\pi\, r^2$

B

Appendix B: Case Formulas

TERMS AND SYMBOLS:

a is a measured distance along the beam, in or ft

b is another measured distance along the beam, in or ft

E is the modulus of elasticity, psi or ksi

I is the moment of inertia of the beam, in^4

l is the length of the beam between reaction points, in or ft

M_{max} is the maximum moment, inlb, ftlbs, kip ft, or kip in

M_1 is the maximum moment in the left section of the beam

M_2 is the maximum moment in the right section of the beam

M_x is the moment at distance x from the left end of the beam

P is a point load, lbs or kips

P_1 is the point load nearest the left reaction

P_2 is the point load nearest the right reaction and is not equal to P_1

R is the end beam reaction of any condition of symmetrical loading, lbs or kips

R_1 is the left end beam reaction

R_2 is the right end beam reaction

V_{max} is the maximum vertical shear for any symmetrical loading condition, lbs or kips

V_1 is the maximum vertical shear in the left section of the beam, kips

V_2 is the maximum vertical shear at the right reaction point, or to the left of the intermediate reaction point of the beam

V_3 is the vertical shear at the right reaction point, or to the right of the intermediate reaction point of the beam

V_x is the vertical shear at distance x from the left end of the beam

W is a total uniformly distributed load on a beam, lbs or kips

w is a uniformly distributed load per unit of length, pli, plf, kips/in, or kips/ft

x is any distance measured along the beam from the left reaction, in or ft

x_1 is any distance measured along the overhang section from the nearest reaction point, in or ft

Δ_{max} is the maximum deflection, in

Δ_a is the deflection at the point of load, in

Δ_x is the deflection at any point x distance from the left reaction, in

Δ_{x1} is the deflection of the overhanging section at any point x_1 measured from R_2, in

BEAM DIAGRAMS AND FORMULAS, continued
for various static loading conditions

---

1. SIMPLE BEAM, uniformly distributed load

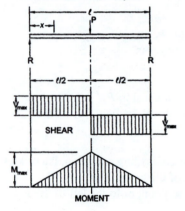

$$R = V_{max} \qquad = \frac{wl}{2}$$

$$M_{max} \qquad = \frac{wl^2}{8}$$

$$\Delta_{max} \text{ (at center)} \qquad = \frac{5wl^4}{384EI}$$

$$V_x \qquad = w\left(\frac{l}{2} - x\right)$$

$$M_x \qquad = \frac{wx}{2}(l - x)$$

$$\Delta_x \qquad = \frac{wx}{24EI}\left(l^3 - 2lx^2 + x^3\right)$$

---

2. SIMPLE BEAM, concentrated load at center

$$R = V_{max} \qquad = \frac{P}{2}$$

$$M_{max} \text{ (at center)} \qquad = \frac{Pl}{4}$$

$$\Delta_{max} \text{ (at center)} \qquad = \frac{Pl^3}{48EI}$$

$$M_x \left(\text{when } x < \frac{l}{2}\right) \qquad = \frac{Px}{2}$$

$$\Delta_x \left(\text{when } x < \frac{l}{2}\right) \qquad = \frac{Px}{48EI}\left(3l^2 - 4x^2\right)$$

BEAM DIAGRAMS AND FORMULAS, continued
for various static loading conditions

---

3. *SIMPLE BEAM, concentrated load at any point*

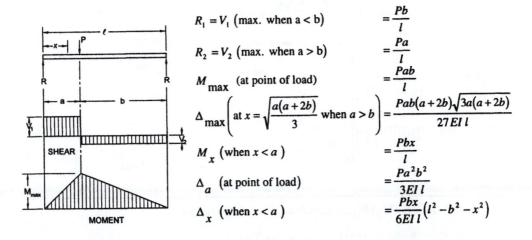

$$R_1 = V_1 \ (\text{max. when a} < \text{b}) \qquad = \frac{Pb}{l}$$

$$R_2 = V_2 \ (\text{max. when a} > \text{b}) \qquad = \frac{Pa}{l}$$

$$M_{max} \ (\text{at point of load}) \qquad = \frac{Pab}{l}$$

$$\Delta_{max}\left(\text{at } x = \sqrt{\frac{a(a+2b)}{3}} \ \text{ when } a > b \right) = \frac{Pab(a+2b)\sqrt{3a(a+2b)}}{27 EI \, l}$$

$$M_x \ (\text{when } x < a) \qquad = \frac{Pbx}{l}$$

$$\Delta_a \ (\text{at point of load}) \qquad = \frac{Pa^2 b^2}{3 EI \, l}$$

$$\Delta_x \ (\text{when } x < a) \qquad = \frac{Pbx}{6 EI \, l}\left(l^2 - b^2 - x^2\right)$$

---

4. *SIMPLE BEAM, two equal concentrated loads symmetrically placed*

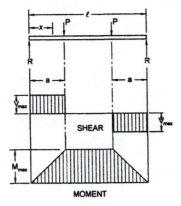

$$R = V_{max} \qquad\qquad\qquad = P$$

$$M_{max} \ (\text{between loads}) \qquad = Pa$$

$$\Delta_{max} \ (\text{at center}) \qquad = \frac{Pa}{24 EI}\left(3l^2 - 4a^2\right)$$

$$M_x \ (\text{when } x < a) \qquad = Px$$

$$\Delta_x \ (\text{when } x < a) \qquad = \frac{Px}{6 EI}\left(3la - 3a^2 - x^2\right)$$

$$\Delta_x \ \left(\text{when } x > a \text{ and } < (l-a)\right) = \frac{Pa}{6 EI}\left(3lx - 3x^2 - a^2\right)$$

BEAM DIAGRAMS AND FORMULAS, continued
for various static loading conditions

5. *CANTILEVER BEAM, uniformly distributed load*

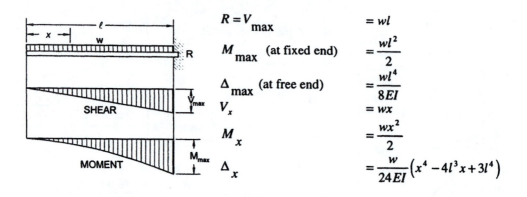

$$R = V_{max} \qquad\qquad = wl$$

$$M_{max} \text{ (at fixed end)} \quad = \frac{wl^2}{2}$$

$$\Delta_{max} \text{ (at free end)} \quad = \frac{wl^4}{8EI}$$

$$V_x \qquad\qquad = wx$$

$$M_x \qquad\qquad = \frac{wx^2}{2}$$

$$\Delta_x \qquad\qquad = \frac{w}{24EI}\left(x^4 - 4l^3x + 3l^4\right)$$

6. *CANTILEVER BEAM, concentrated load at free end*

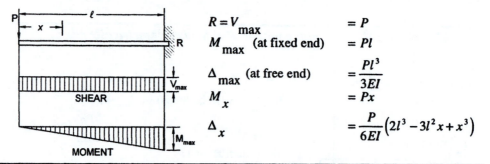

$$R = V_{max} \qquad\qquad = P$$

$$M_{max} \text{ (at fixed end)} \quad = Pl$$

$$\Delta_{max} \text{ (at free end)} \quad = \frac{Pl^3}{3EI}$$

$$M_x \qquad\qquad = Px$$

$$\Delta_x \qquad\qquad = \frac{P}{6EI}\left(2l^3 - 3l^2x + x^3\right)$$

7. *CANTILEVER BEAM, concentrated load at any point*

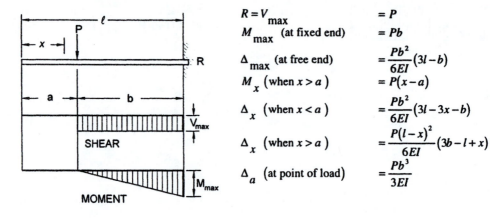

$$R = V_{max} \qquad\qquad = P$$

$$M_{max} \text{ (at fixed end)} \quad = Pb$$

$$\Delta_{max} \text{ (at free end)} \quad = \frac{Pb^2}{6EI}(3l - b)$$

$$M_x \text{ (when } x > a) \quad = P(x - a)$$

$$\Delta_x \text{ (when } x < a) \quad = \frac{Pb^2}{6EI}(3l - 3x - b)$$

$$\Delta_x \text{ (when } x > a) \quad = \frac{P(l-x)^2}{6EI}(3b - l + x)$$

$$\Delta_a \text{ (at point of load)} \quad = \frac{Pb^3}{3EI}$$

BEAM DIAGRAMS AND FORMULAS, continued
for various static loading conditions

8. BEAM OVERHANGING ONE SUPPORT, *uniformly distributed load*

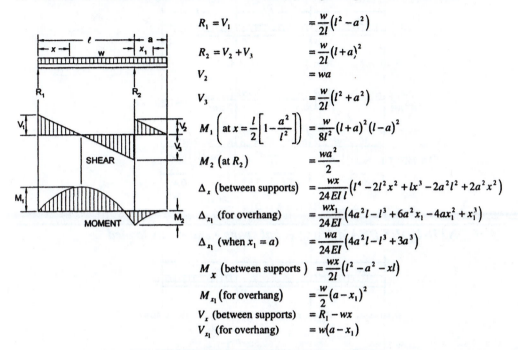

$$R_1 = V_1 \qquad = \frac{w}{2l}\left(l^2 - a^2\right)$$

$$R_2 = V_2 + V_3 \qquad = \frac{w}{2l}\left(l + a\right)^2$$

$$V_2 \qquad = wa$$

$$V_3 \qquad = \frac{w}{2l}\left(l^2 + a^2\right)$$

$$M_1 \left(\text{at } x = \frac{l}{2}\left[1 - \frac{a^2}{l^2}\right]\right) = \frac{w}{8l^2}\left(l + a\right)^2\left(l - a\right)^2$$

$$M_2 \left(\text{at } R_2\right) \qquad = \frac{wa^2}{2}$$

$$\Delta_x \text{ (between supports)} = \frac{wx}{24EI\,l}\left(l^4 - 2l^2 x^2 + lx^3 - 2a^2 l^2 + 2a^2 x^2\right)$$

$$\Delta_{x_1} \text{ (for overhang)} = \frac{wx_1}{24EI}\left(4a^2 l - l^3 + 6a^2 x_1 - 4ax_1^2 + x_1^3\right)$$

$$\Delta_{x_1} \text{ (when } x_1 = a) = \frac{wa}{24EI}\left(4a^2 l - l^3 + 3a^3\right)$$

$$M_x \text{ (between supports)} = \frac{wx}{2l}\left(l^2 - a^2 - xl\right)$$

$$M_{x_1} \text{ (for overhang)} = \frac{w}{2}\left(a - x_1\right)^2$$

$$V_x \text{ (between supports)} = R_1 - wx$$

$$V_{x_1} \text{ (for overhang)} = w\left(a - x_1\right)$$

9. BEAM OVERHANGING ONE SUPPORT, *concentrated load at end of overhang*

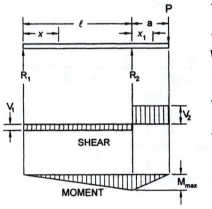

$$R_1 = V_1 \qquad = \frac{Pa}{l}$$

$$R_2 = V_1 + V_2 \qquad = \frac{P}{l}\left(l + a\right)$$

$$V_2 \qquad = P$$

$$M_{max} \left(\text{at } R_2\right) \qquad = Pa$$

$$\Delta_{max} \left(\text{between supports at } x = \frac{l}{\sqrt{3}}\right) = 0.06415\frac{Pal^2}{EI}$$

$$\Delta_{max} \text{ (for overhang at } x_1 = a) = \frac{Pa^2}{3EI}\left(l + a\right)$$

$$M_x \text{ (between supports)} = \frac{Pax}{l}$$

$$M_{x_1} \text{ (for overhang)} = P\left(a - x_1\right)$$

$$\Delta_x \text{ (between supports)} = \frac{Pax}{6EI\,l}\left(l^2 - x^2\right)$$

$$\Delta_{x_1} \text{ (for overhang)} = \frac{Px_1}{6EI}\left(2al + 3ax_1 - x_1^2\right)$$

BEAM DIAGRAMS AND FORMULAS, continued
for various static loading conditions

10. *CONTINUOUS BEAM, three equal spans - all spans loaded*

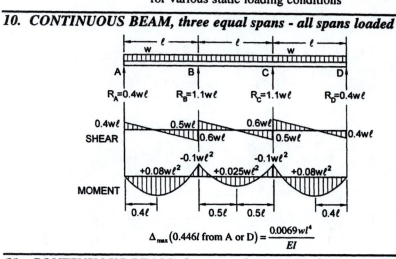

$$\Delta_{max}\left(0.446l \text{ from A or D}\right) = \frac{0.0069wl^4}{EI}$$

11. *CONTINUOUS BEAM, three equal spans - end spans loaded*

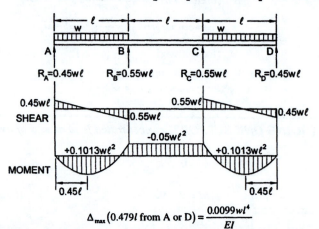

$$\Delta_{max}\left(0.479l \text{ from A or D}\right) = \frac{0.0099wl^4}{EI}$$

12. *CONTINUOUS BEAM, three equal spans - one end span unloaded*

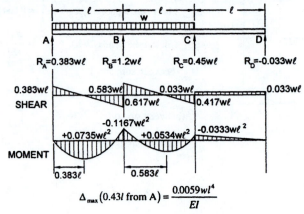

$$\Delta_{max}\left(0.43l \text{ from A}\right) = \frac{0.0059wl^4}{EI}$$

C

Appendix C: Geometric Properties

The following tables are reprinted from the *Machinery's Handbook*, 25th Edition, courtesy of Industrial Press.

Moments of Inertia, Section Moduli, etc., of Sections

Section A = area y = distance from axis to extreme fiber	Moment of Inertia I	Section Modulus $Z = \dfrac{I}{y}$	Radius of Gyration $k = \sqrt{\dfrac{I}{A}}$
$A = a^2; \quad y = \frac{1}{2}a$	$\dfrac{a^4}{12}$	$\dfrac{a^3}{6}$	$\dfrac{a}{\sqrt{12}} = 0.289\,a$
$A = a^2; \quad y = a$	$\dfrac{a^4}{3}$	$\dfrac{a^3}{3}$	$\dfrac{a}{\sqrt{3}} = 0.577\,a$
$A = a^2$ $y = \dfrac{a}{\sqrt{2}} = 0.707\,a$	$\dfrac{a^4}{12}$	$\dfrac{a^3}{6\sqrt{2}} = 0.118\,a^3$	$\dfrac{a}{\sqrt{12}} = 0.289\,a$
$A = a^2 - b^2; \quad y = \frac{1}{2}a$	$\dfrac{a^4 - b^4}{12}$	$\dfrac{a^4 - b^4}{6a}$	$\sqrt{\dfrac{a^2 + b^2}{12}}$ $= 0.289\sqrt{a^2 + b^2}$
$A = a^2 - b^2$ $y = \dfrac{a}{\sqrt{2}} = 0.707\,a$	$\dfrac{a^4 - b^4}{12}$	$\dfrac{\sqrt{2}\,(a^4 - b^4)}{12a}$ $= 0.118\,\dfrac{a^4 - b^4}{a}$	$\sqrt{\dfrac{a^2 + b^2}{12}}$ $= 0.289\sqrt{a^2 + b^2}$
$A = bd; \quad y = \frac{1}{2}d$	$\dfrac{bd^3}{12}$	$\dfrac{bd^2}{6}$	$\dfrac{d}{\sqrt{12}} = 0.289\,d$

Moments of Inertia, Section Moduli, etc., of Sections

A = area y = distance from axis to extreme fiber	Moment of Inertia I	Section Modulus $Z = \dfrac{I}{y}$	Radius of Gyration $k = \sqrt{\dfrac{I}{A}}$
 $A = bd;\quad y = d$	$\dfrac{bd^3}{3}$	$\dfrac{bd^2}{3}$	$\dfrac{d}{\sqrt{3}} = 0.577\,d$
 $A = bd - hk$ $y = \frac{1}{2}\,d$	$\dfrac{bd^3 - hk^3}{12}$	$\dfrac{bd^3 - hk^3}{6d}$	$\sqrt{\dfrac{bd^3 - hk^3}{12(bd - hk)}}$ $= 0.289\sqrt{\dfrac{bd^3 - hk^3}{bd - hk}}$
 $A = bd$ $y = \dfrac{bd}{\sqrt{b^2 + d^2}}$	$\dfrac{b^3 d^3}{6(b^2 + d^2)}$	$\dfrac{b^2 d^2}{6\sqrt{b^2 + d^2}}$	$\dfrac{bd}{\sqrt{6(b^2 + d^2)}}$ $= 0.408\,\dfrac{bd}{\sqrt{b^2 + d^2}}$
 $A = bd$ $y = \frac{1}{2}(d\cos\alpha + b\sin\alpha)$	$\dfrac{bd}{12}(d^2\cos^2\alpha + b^2\sin^2\alpha)$	$\dfrac{bd}{6} \times$ $\left(\dfrac{d^2\cos^2\alpha + b^2\sin^2\alpha}{d\cos\alpha + b\sin\alpha}\right)$	$\sqrt{\dfrac{d^2\cos^2\alpha + b^2\sin^2\alpha}{12}}$ $= 0.289 \times$ $\sqrt{d^2\cos^2\alpha + b^2\sin^2\alpha}$
 $A = \frac{1}{2}\,bd;\quad y = \frac{2}{3}\,d$	$\dfrac{bd^3}{36}$	$\dfrac{bd^2}{24}$	$\dfrac{d}{\sqrt{18}} = 0.236\,d$
 $A = \frac{1}{2}\,bd;\quad y = d$	$\dfrac{bd^3}{12}$	$\dfrac{bd^2}{12}$	$\dfrac{d}{\sqrt{6}} = 0.408\,d$

Moments of Inertia, Section Moduli, etc. of Sections

Section	Area of Section, A	Extreme fiber distance, y	Moment of Inertia, I	Section Modulus, Z	Radius of gyration, k
	$\dfrac{\pi d^2}{4}$	$\dfrac{d}{2}$	$\dfrac{\pi d^4}{64}$	$\dfrac{\pi d^3}{32}$	$\dfrac{d}{4}$
	$\dfrac{\pi\left(D^2-d^2\right)}{4}$	$\dfrac{D}{2}$	$\dfrac{\pi\left(D^4-d^4\right)}{64}$	$\dfrac{\pi\left(D^4-d^4\right)}{32D}$	$\dfrac{\sqrt{D^2+d^2}}{4}$
	$\pi\,ab$	a	$\dfrac{\pi\,a^3b}{4}$	$\dfrac{\pi\,a^2b}{4}$	$\dfrac{a}{2}$
	$t(2a-t)$	$a-\dfrac{a^2+at-t^2}{2(2a-t)}$	$\dfrac{1}{3}\left[\begin{array}{c}ty^3+a(a-y)^3\\-(a-t)(a-y-t)^3\end{array}\right]$	$\dfrac{I}{y}$	$\sqrt{\dfrac{I}{A}}$
	$t(2a-t)$	$\dfrac{a^2+at-t^2}{2(2a-t)\cos 45^\circ}$	$\dfrac{A}{12}\left[\begin{array}{c}7\left(a^2+b^2\right)-12y^2\\-2ab^2(a-b)\end{array}\right]$ in which $b=a-t$	$\dfrac{I}{y}$	$\sqrt{\dfrac{I}{A}}$
	$\dfrac{\pi d^2}{8}$	$\dfrac{(3\pi-4)d}{6\pi}$	$\dfrac{\left(9\pi^2-64\right)d^4}{1152\pi}$	$\dfrac{\left(9\pi^2-64\right)d^3}{192(3\pi-4)}$	$\dfrac{\sqrt{\left(9\pi^2-64\right)d^2}}{12\pi}$
	$\dfrac{\pi\left(R^2-r^2\right)}{2}$	$\dfrac{4\left(R^3-r^3\right)}{3\pi\left(R^2-r^2\right)}$	$0.1098\left(R^4-r^4\right)$ $-\dfrac{0.283R^2r^2(R-r)}{R+r}$	$\dfrac{I}{y}$	$\sqrt{\dfrac{I}{A}}$

D

Appendix D: Sawn Lumber Reference Values

The following tables are provided courtesy of The American Forest & Paper Association, Washington, D.C., and are excerpted from the *National Design Specifications Supplement* (*Design Values for Wood Construction*).

*Abridged from the *NDS* table to limit the size range and 5/4 boards added.

SECTION PROPERTIES OF STANDARD DRESSED SAWN LUMBER

| nominal size | Std Dressed size | | | | x-x Axis | | y-y Axis | | Approximate weight in plf of piece | | |
| bxd | b | x | d | Area | S_{x-x} | I_{x-x} | S_{y-y} | I_{y-y} | when density of wood equals: | | |
	inches	x	inches	in^2	in^3	in^4	in^3	in^4	30 lb/ft^3	35 lb/ft^3	40 lb/ft^3
1x3	0.75	x	2.5	1.875	0.781	0.977	0.234	0.088	0.39	0.46	0.52
1x4	0.75	x	3.5	2.625	1.531	2.680	0.328	0.123	0.55	0.64	0.73
1x6	0.75	x	5.5	4.125	3.781	10.40	0.516	0.193	0.86	1.00	1.15
1x8	0.75	x	7.25	5.438	6.570	23.82	0.680	0.255	1.13	1.32	1.51
1x10	0.75	x	9.25	6.938	10.695	49.47	0.867	0.325	1.45	1.69	1.93
1x12	0.75	x	11.25	8.438	15.820	88.99	1.055	0.396	1.76	2.05	2.34
5/4x3	1	x	2.5	2.50	1.042	1.302	0.417	0.208	0.52	0.61	0.69
5/4x4	1	x	3.5	3.50	2.042	3.573	0.583	0.292	0.73	0.85	0.97
5/4x6	1	x	5.5	5.50	5.042	13.86	0.917	0.458	1.15	1.34	1.53
5/4x8	1	x	7.25	7.25	8.760	31.76	1.208	0.604	1.51	1.76	2.01
5/4x10	1	x	9.25	9.25	14.260	65.95	1.542	0.771	1.93	2.25	2.57
5/4x12	1	x	11.25	11.25	21.094	118.65	1.875	0.938	2.34	2.73	3.13
2x2*	1.5	x	1.5	2.25	0.563	0.422	0.563	0.422	0.47	0.55	0.63
2x3	1.5	x	2.5	3.75	1.563	1.953	0.938	0.703	0.78	0.91	1.04
2x4	1.5	x	3.5	5.25	3.063	5.359	1.313	0.984	1.09	1.28	1.46
2x6	1.5	x	5.5	8.25	7.563	20.80	2.063	1.547	1.72	2.01	2.29
2x8	1.5	x	7.25	10.875	13.141	47.63	2.719	2.039	2.27	2.64	3.02
2x10	1.5	x	9.25	13.875	21.391	98.93	3.469	2.602	2.89	3.37	3.85
2x12	1.5	x	11.25	16.875	31.641	177.98	4.219	3.164	3.52	4.10	4.69
2x14	1.5	x	13.25	19.875	43.891	290.78	4.969	3.727	4.14	4.83	5.52
3x3*	2.5	x	2.5	6.25	2.604	3.255	2.604	3.255	1.30	1.52	1.74
3x4	2.5	x	3.5	8.75	5.104	8.932	3.646	4.557	1.82	2.13	2.43
3x6	2.5	x	5.5	13.75	12.604	34.66	5.729	7.161	2.86	3.34	3.82
3x8	2.5	x	7.25	18.125	21.901	79.39	7.552	9.440	3.78	4.41	5.03
3x10	2.5	x	9.25	23.125	35.651	164.89	9.635	12.044	4.82	5.62	6.42
3x12	2.5	x	11.25	28.125	52.734	296.63	11.719	14.648	5.86	6.84	7.81
3x14	2.5	x	13.25	33.125	73.151	484.63	13.802	17.253	6.90	8.05	9.20
3x16	2.5	x	15.25	38.125	96.901	738.87	15.885	19.857	7.94	9.27	10.59
4x4	3.5	x	3.5	12.25	7.146	12.51	7.146	12.505	2.55	2.98	3.40
4x5	3.5	x	4.5	15.75	11.813	26.58	9.188	16.078	3.28	3.83	4.38
4x6	3.5	x	5.5	19.25	17.646	48.53	11.229	19.651	4.01	4.68	5.35
4x8	3.5	x	7.25	25.375	30.661	111.15	14.802	25.904	5.29	6.17	7.05
4x10	3.5	x	9.25	32.375	49.911	230.84	18.885	33.049	6.74	7.87	8.99
4x12	3.5	x	11.25	39.375	73.828	415.28	22.969	40.195	8.20	9.57	10.94
4x14	3.5	x	13.25	46.375	102.41	678.48	27.052	47.341	9.66	11.27	12.88
4x16	3.5	x	15.25	53.375	135.66	1,034	31.135	54.487	11.12	12.97	14.83
5x5	4.5	x	4.5	20.25	15.188	34.17	15.188	34.172	4.22	4.92	5.63
6x6	5.5	x	5.5	30.25	27.729	76.26	27.729	76.255	6.30	7.35	8.40
6x8	5.5	x	7.5	41.25	51.563	193.36	37.813	103.98	8.59	10.03	11.46
6x10	5.5	x	9.5	52.25	82.729	392.96	47.896	131.71	10.89	12.70	14.51
6x12	5.5	x	11.5	63.25	121.23	697.07	57.979	159.44	13.18	15.37	17.57
6x14	5.5	x	13.5	74.25	167.06	1,128	68.063	187.17	15.47	18.05	20.63
6x16	5.5	x	15.5	85.25	220.23	1,707	78.146	214.90	17.76	20.72	23.68
6x18	5.5	x	17.5	96.25	280.73	2,456	88.229	242.63	20.05	23.39	26.74
6x20	5.5	x	19.5	107.25	348.56	3,398	98.313	270.36	22.34	26.07	29.79
6x22	5.5	x	21.5	118.25	423.73	4,555	108.40	298.09	24.64	28.74	32.85
6x24	5.5	x	23.5	129.25	506.23	5,948	118.48	325.82	26.93	31.41	35.90

*Included for convenience. Not available commercially.

TABLE 4A ADJUSTMENT FACTORS

Flat Use Factor, C_{fu}

Bending design values adjusted by size factors are based on edgewise use (load applied to narrow face). When dimension lumber is used flatwise (load applied to wide face), the bending design value, F_b, shall also be multiplied by the adjacent flat use factors.

Flat Use Factors, C_{fu}

Width	Thickness (breadth)	
(depth)	2" & 3"	4"
2" & 3"	1.0	--
4"	1.1	1.0
5"	1.1	1.05
6"	1.15	1.05
8"	1.15	1.05
10" & wider	1.2	1.1

SIZE FACTOR, C_F

Tabulated bending, tension, and compression parallel to grain design values for dimension lumber 2" to 4" thick shall be multiplied by the following size factors:

Size Factors, C_F

Grades	Width (depth)	F_b Thickness (breadth) 2" & 3"	4"	F_t	F_c
	2", 3" & 4"	1.5	1.5	1.5	1.15
Select	5"	1.4	1.4	1.4	1.1
Structural	6"	1.3	1.3	1.3	1.1
No. 1 & Btr	8"	1.2	1.3	1.2	1.05
No. 1, No. 2,	10"	1.1	1.2	1.1	1.0
No. 3	12"	1.0	1.1	1.0	1.0
	14" & wider	0.9	1.0	0.9	0.9
	2", 3" & 4"	1.1	1.1	1.1	1.05
Stud	5" & 6"	1.0	1.0	1.0	1.0
	8" & wider	Use No. 3 Grade tabulated design values and size factors			
Construction & Standard	2", 3" & 4"	1.0	1.0	1.0	1.0
Utility	4"	1.0	1.0	1.0	1.0
	2" & 3"	0.4	---	0.4	0.6

NOTE:

The Construction, Standard, and Utility grade design values are based on a 4" nominal width, the Stud grade design values are based on a 6" nominal width, and the Select Structural, No. 1 & Btr, No. 1, No. 2, and No. 3 grade design values are based on a 12" nominal width.

Table 4A   Base Design Values for Visually Graded Dimension Lumber
(Tabulated design values are for normal load duration and dry service conditions.
See *NDS* 2.3 for comprehensive description of design value adjustment factors.)

USE WITH TABLE 4A ADJUSTMENT FACTORS

Species and commerical grade	Size classification	Design values in psi					
		Bending F_b	Tension parallel to grain F_t	Shear parallel to grain F_v	Compression perpendicular to grain $F_{c\perp}$	Compression parallel to grain F_c	Modulus of Elasticity E
DOUGLAS FIR-SOUTH							
Select Structural	2"-4" thick	1,350	900	90	520	1,600	1,400,000
No. 1		925	600	90	520	1,450	1,300,000
No. 2	2" & wider	850	525	90	520	1,350	1,200,000
No. 3		500	300	90	520	775	1,100,000
Stud		675	425	90	520	850	1,100,000
Construction	2"-4" thick	975	600	90	520	1,650	1,200,000
Standard		550	350	90	520	1,400	1,100,000
Utility	2"-4" wide	250	150	90	520	900	1,000,000
EASTERN SOFTWOODS							
Select Structural	2"-4" thick	1,250	575	70	335	1,200	1,200,000
No. 1		775	350	70	335	1,000	1,100,000
No. 2	2" & wider	575	275	70	335	825	1,100,000
No. 3		350	150	70	335	475	900,000
Stud		450	200	70	335	525	900,000
Construction	2"-4" thick	675	300	70	335	1,050	1,000,000
Standard		375	175	70	335	850	900,000
Utility	2"-4" wide	175	75	70	335	550	800,000
EASTERN WHITE PINE							
Select Structural	2"-4" thick	1,250	575	70	350	1,200	1,200,000
No. 1		775	350	70	350	1,000	1,100,000
No. 2	2" & wider	575	275	70	350	825	1,100,000
No. 3		350	150	70	350	475	900,000
Stud		450	200	70	350	525	900,000
Construction	2"-4" thick	675	300	70	350	1,050	1,000,000
Standard		375	175	70	350	850	900,000
Utility	2"-4" wide	175	75	70	350	550	800,000
HEM-FIR							
Select Structural		1,400	925	75	405	1,500	1,600,000
No. 1 & Btr	2"-4" thick	1,100	725	75	405	1,350	1,500,000
No. 1		975	625	75	405	1,350	1,500,000
No. 2	2" & wider	850	525	75	405	1,300	1,300,000
No. 3		500	300	75	405	725	1,200,000
Stud		675	400	75	405	800	1,200,000
Construction	2"-4" thick	975	600	75	405	1,550	1,300,000
Standard		550	325	75	405	1,300	1,200,000
Utility	2"-4" wide	250	150	75	405	850	1,100,000
SPRUCE-PINE-FIR							
Select Structural	2"-4" thick	1,250	700	70	425	1,400	1,500,000
No. 1/No. 2		875	450	70	425	1,150	1,400,000
No. 3	2" & wider	500	250	70	425	650	1,200,000
Stud		675	350	70	425	725	1,200,000
Construction	2"-4" thick	1,000	500	70	425	1,400	1,300,000
Standard		550	275	70	425	1,150	1,200,000
Utility	2"-4" wide	275	125	70	425	750	1,100,000
WESTERN WOODS							
Select Structural	2"-4" thick	900	400	70	335	1,050	1,200,000
No. 1		675	300	70	335	950	1,100,000
No. 2	2" & wider	675	300	70	335	900	1,000,000
No. 3		375	175	70	335	525	900,000
Stud		525	225	70	335	575	900,000
Construction	2"-4" thick	775	350	70	335	1,100	1,000,000
Standard		425	200	70	335	925	900,000
Utility	2"-4" wide	200	100	70	335	600	800,000

TABLE 4B ADJUSTMENT FACTORS

Flat Use Factor, C_{fu}

Bending design values adjusted by size factors are based on edgewise use (load applied to narrow face). When dimension lumber is used flatwise (load applied to wide face), the bending design value, F_b, shall also be multiplied by the adjacent flat use factors.

Flat Use Factors, C_{fu}

Width	Thickness (breadth)	
(depth)	2" & 3"	4"
2" & 3"	1.0	--
4"	1.1	1.0
5"	1.1	1.05
6"	1.15	1.05
8"	1.15	1.05
10" & wider	1.2	1.1

Table 4B Base Design Values for Visually Graded Southern Pine Dimension Lumber
(Tabulated design values are for normal load duration and dry service conditions. See *NDS* 2.3 for comprehensive description of design value adjustment factors.)

USE WITH TABLE 4B ADJUSTMENT FACTORS

Species and commerical grade	Size classification	Bending F_b	Tension parallel to grain F_t	Shear parallel to grain F_v	Compression perpendicular to grain $F_{c\perp}$	Compression parallel to grain F_c	Modulus of Elasticity E
SOUTHERN PINE							
Dense Select Structural		3,050	1,650	100	660	2,250	1,900,000
Select Structural		2,850	1,600	100	565	2,100	1,800,000
Non-Dense Select Structural		2,650	1,350	100	480	1,950	1,700,000
No. 1 Dense		2,000	1,100	100	660	2,000	1,800,000
No. 1	2"-4" thick	1,850	1,050	100	565	1,850	1,700,000
No. 1 Non-Dense		1,700	900	100	480	1,700	1,600,000
No. 2 Dense	2"-4" wide	1,700	875	90	660	1,850	1,700,000
No. 2		1,500	825	90	565	1,650	1,600,000
No. 2 Non-Dense		1,350	775	90	480	1,600	1,400,000
No. 3 and Stud		850	475	90	565	975	1,400,000
Construction	2"-4" thick	1,100	625	100	565	1,800	1,500,000
Standard		625	350	90	565	1,500	1,300,000
Utility	2"-4" wide	300	175	90	565	975	1,300,000
Dense Select Structural		2,700	1,500	90	660	2,150	1,900,000
Select Structural		2,550	1,400	90	565	2,000	1,800,000
Non-Dense Select Structural		2,350	1,200	90	480	1,850	1,700,000
No. 1 Dense		1,750	950	90	660	1,900	1,800,000
No. 1	2"-4" thick	1,650	900	90	565	1,750	1,700,000
No. 1 Non-Dense		1,500	800	90	480	1,600	1,600,000
No. 2 Dense	5"-6" wide	1,450	775	90	660	1,750	1,700,000
No. 2		1,250	725	90	565	1,600	1,600,000
No. 2 Non-Dense		1,150	675	90	480	1,500	1,400,000
No. 3 and Stud		750	425	90	565	925	1,400,000
Dense Select Structural		2,450	1,350	90	660	2,050	1,900,000
Select Structural		2,300	1,300	90	565	1,900	1,800,000
Non-Dense Select Structural		2,100	1,100	90	480	1,750	1,700,000
No. 1 Dense		1,650	875	90	660	1,800	1,800,000
No. 1	2"-4" thick	1,500	825	90	565	1,650	1,700,000
No. 1 Non-Dense		1,350	725	90	480	1,550	1,600,000
No. 2 Dense	8" wide	1,400	675	90	660	1,700	1,700,000
No. 2		1,200	650	90	565	1,550	1,600,000
No. 2 Non-Dense		1,100	600	90	480	1,450	1,400,000
No. 3 and Stud		700	400	90	565	875	1,400,000

Table 4B Base Design Values for Visually Graded Southern Pine Dimension Lumber, Cont.
(Tabulated design values are for normal load duration and dry service conditions.
See *NDS* 2.3 for comprehensive description of design value adjustment factors.)

USE WITH TABLE 4B ADJUSTMENT FACTORS

Species and commerical grade	Size classification	Design values in psi					
		Bending F_b	Tension parallel to grain F_t	Shear parallel to grain F_v	Compression perpendicular to grain $F_{c\perp}$	Compression parallel to grain F_c	Modulus of Elasticity E
SOUTHERN PINE, CONT.							
Dense Select Structural		2,150	1,200	90	660	2,000	1,900,000
Select Structural		2,050	1,100	90	565	1,850	1,800,000
Non-Dense Select Structural		1,850	950	90	480	1,750	1,700,000
No. 1 Dense		1,450	775	90	660	1,750	1,800,000
No. 1	2"-4" thick	1,300	725	90	565	1,600	1,700,000
No. 1 Non-Dense		1,200	650	90	480	1,500	1,600,000
No. 2 Dense	10" wide	1,200	625	90	660	1,650	1,700,000
No. 2		1,050	575	90	565	1,500	1,600,000
No. 2 Non-Dense		950	550	90	480	1,400	1,400,000
No. 3 and Stud		600	325	90	565	850	1,400,000
Dense Select Structural		2,050	1,100	90	660	1,950	1,900,000
Select Structural		1,900	1,050	90	565	1,800	1,800,000
Non-Dense Select Structural		1,750	900	90	480	1,700	1,700,000
No. 1 Dense		1,350	725	90	660	1,700	1,800,000
No. 1	2"-4" thick	1,250	675	90	565	1,600	1,700,000
No. 1 Non-Dense		1,150	600	90	480	1,500	1,600,000
No. 2 Dense	12" wide	1,150	575	90	660	1,600	1,700,000
No. 2		975	550	90	565	1,450	1,600,000
No. 2 Non-Dense		900	525	90	480	1,350	1,400,000
No. 3 and Stud		575	325	90	565	825	1,400,000
MIXED SOUTHERN PINE							
Select Structural		2,050	1,200	100	565	1,800	1,600,000
No. 1	2"-4" thick	1,450	875	100	565	1,650	1,500,000
No. 2		1,300	775	90	565	1,650	1,400,000
No. 3 and Stud	2"-4" wide	750	450	90	565	950	1,200,000
Construction	2"-4" thick	1,000	600	100	565	1,700	1,300,000
Standard		550	325	90	565	1,450	1,200,000
Utility	4" wide	275	150	90	565	950	1,100,000
Select Structural		1,850	1,100	90	565	1,700	1,600,000
No. 1	2"-4" thick	1,300	750	90	565	1,550	1,500,000
No. 2		1,150	675	90	565	1,550	1,400,000
No. 3 and Stud	5"-6" wide	675	400	90	565	875	1,200,000
Select Structural		1,750	1,000	90	565	1,600	1,600,000
No. 1	2"-4" thick	1,200	700	90	565	1,450	1,500,000
No. 2		1,050	625	90	565	1,450	1,400,000
No. 3 and Stud	8" wide	625	375	90	565	850	1,200,000
Select Structural		1,500	875	90	565	1,600	1,600,000
No. 1	2"-4" thick	1,050	600	90	565	1,450	1,500,000
No. 2		925	550	90	565	1,450	1,400,000
No. 3 and Stud	10" wide	525	325	90	565	825	1,200,000
Select Structural		1,400	825	90	565	1,550	1,600,000
No. 1	2"-4" thick	975	575	90	565	1,400	1,500,000
No. 2		875	525	90	565	1,400	1,400,000
No. 3 and Stud	12" wide	500	300	90	565	800	1,200,000

E

Appendix E: Steel Reference Values

This Appendix contains the following tables:

The following organizations generously allowed us to reprint the above information:

The *Manual of Steel Construction* (*SCM*), 9th Edition published by the American Institute of Steel Construction.

The *Handbook of Welded Carbon Steel Mechanical Tubing* (*HMT*), published by the Steel Tube Institute of North America.

The handbook of *Hollow Structural Sections* (*HSS*), also published by the STINA.

YIELD STRENGTHS OF COMMONLY USED STEELS

Shape category	Grade	E (ksi)	F_y (ksi)	F_b $0.6F_y$	$0.66F_y$	F_v $0.4F_y$	F_t $0.6F_y$	F_a
Tube, mech "as-welded"	MT1010	29,000	32	19 2 ksi	21 1 ksi	12 8 ksi	19 2 ksi	depends on Kl/r
	MT1020	29,000	38	22 8 ksi	25 ksi	15 2 ksi	22 8 ksi	depends on Kl/l
Tube, struc	A500, Grade B	29,000	46	27 6 ksi	30 4 ksi	18 4 ksi	27 6 ksi	depends on Kl/l
Pipe, black (plumbing)	A53, Type F Grade A	29,000	30	NA	19 8 ksi	12 ksi	18 ksi	depends on Kl/r
Pipe, black Structural	A53, Types E&S Grade B	29,000	35	NA	23 1 ksi	14 ksi	21 ksi	Use Kl/l chart for A36 steel
Angle	A36	29,000	36	varies	NA	varies	21 6 ksi	depends on Kl/r
Channel	A36	29,000	36	21 6 ksi	NA	14 4 ksi	21 6 ksi	depends on Kl/l
I beam	A36	29,000	36	21 6 ksi	24 ksi	14 4 ksi	21 6 ksi	depends on Kl/l

LIMITING WIDTH-THICKNESS RATIOS FOR BEAMS AND COLUMNS

Shape	ruling ratio	ratio limit for a given F_y, ksi					
		30	32	35	36	38	46
rectilinear tube	b/t	NA	42 1	NA	NA	38 6	35 1
round tube	D/t	NA	103 1	NA	NA	86 8	71 7
Pipe, Type F (plumbing)	D/t	110*	NA	NA	NA	NA	NA
Pipe, Type E&S (structural)	D/t	NA	NA	94*	NA	NA	NA
channels, web	h/t_w	NA	NA	NA	42 2	NA	NA
channel, flange	b/t	NA	NA	NA	15 8	NA	NA
I-beams	h/t_w	NA	NA	NA	63	NA	NA

* all schedule 40, 80, and double extra strong pipes pass

ALLOWABLE AXIAL STRESS
For Compression Members with F_y=30 ksi (black pipe, Type F)

F_y=30 ksi		F_y=30 ksi		F_y=30 ksi		F_y=30 ksi	
Kl/r	F_a, ksi	Kl/r	F_a, ksi	Kl/r	F_a, ksi	Kl/r	F_a, ksi
1	17.97	51	15.54	101	11.62	151	6.55
2	17.94	52	15.48	102	11.53	152	6.46
3	17.91	53	15.41	103	11.43	153	6.38
4	17.88	54	15.34	104	11.34	154	6.30
5	17.84	55	15.28	105	11.25	155	6.22
6	17.81	56	15.21	106	11.15	156	6.14
7	17.77	57	15.14	107	11.06	157	6.06
8	17.74	58	15.07	108	10.96	158	5.98
9	17.70	59	15.00	109	10.87	159	5.91
10	17.67	60	14.93	110	10.77	160	5.83
11	17.63	61	14.86	111	10.67	161	5.76
12	17.59	62	14.79	112	10.58	162	5.69
13	17.55	63	14.72	113	10.48	163	5.62
14	17.51	64	14.65	114	10.38	164	5.55
15	17.47	65	14.58	115	10.28	165	5.49
16	17.43	66	14.50	116	10.18	166	5.42
17	17.38	67	14.43	117	10.08	167	5.35
18	17.34	68	14.36	118	9.98	168	5.29
19	17.30	69	14.28	119	9.88	169	5.23
20	17.25	70	14.21	120	9.78	170	5.17
21	17.21	71	14.13	121	9.68	171	5.11
22	17.16	72	14.06	122	9.57	172	5.05
23	17.12	73	13.98	123	9.47	173	4.99
24	17.07	74	13.90	124	9.36	174	4.93
25	17.02	75	13.82	125	9.26	175	4.88
26	16.97	76	13.75	126	9.15	176	4.82
27	16.92	77	13.67	127	9.05	177	4.77
28	16.87	78	13.59	128	8.94	178	4.71
29	16.82	79	13.51	129	8.83	179	4.66
30	16.77	80	13.43	130	8.73	180	4.61
31	16.72	81	13.35	131	8.62	181	4.56
32	16.66	82	13.26	132	8.51	182	4.51
33	16.61	83	13.18	133	8.40	183	4.46
34	16.56	84	13.10	134	8.29	184	4.41
35	16.50	85	13.02	135	8.18	185	4.36
36	16.45	86	12.93	136	8.07	186	4.32
37	16.39	87	12.85	137	7.95	187	4.27
38	16.33	88	12.77	138	7.84	188	4.23
39	16.28	89	12.68	139	7.73	189	4.18
40	16.22	90	12.59	140	7.62	190	4.14
41	16.16	91	12.51	141	7.51	191	4.09
42	16.10	92	12.42	142	7.41	192	4.05
43	16.04	93	12.33	143	7.30	193	4.01
44	15.98	94	12.25	144	7.20	194	3.97
45	15.92	95	12.16	145	7.10	195	3.93
46	15.86	96	12.07	146	7.01	196	3.89
47	15.80	97	11.98	147	6.91	197	3.85
48	15.73	98	11.89	148	6.82	198	3.81
49	15.67	99	11.80	149	6.73	199	3.77
50	16.65	100	11.71	150	6.64	200	3.73

ALLOWABLE AXIAL STRESS

For Compression Members with F_y=32 ksi (MT1010 "as-welded" tube)

F_y=32 ksi		F_y=32 ksi		F_y=32 ksi		F_y=32 ksi	
Kl/r	F_a, ksi	Kl/r	F_a, ksi	Kl/r	F_a, ksi	Kl/r	F_a, ksi
1	19.17	51	16.46	101	12.07	151	6.55
2	19.13	52	16.39	102	11.96	152	6.46
3	19.10	53	16.31	103	11.86	153	6.38
4	19.06	54	16.24	104	11.75	154	6.30
5	19.03	55	16.17	105	11.65	155	6.22
6	18.99	56	16.09	106	11.54	156	6.14
7	18.95	57	16.01	107	11.44	157	6.06
8	18.91	58	15.94	108	11.33	158	5.98
9	18.87	59	15.86	109	11.22	159	5.91
10	18.83	60	15.78	110	11.11	160	5.83
11	18.79	61	15.70	111	11.00	161	5.76
12	18.75	62	15.62	112	10.90	162	5.69
13	18.70	63	15.54	113	10.79	163	5.62
14	18.66	64	15.46	114	10.67	164	5.55
15	18.61	65	15.38	115	10.56	165	5.49
16	18.57	66	15.30	116	10.45	166	5.42
17	18.52	67	15.22	117	10.34	167	5.35
18	18.47	68	15.14	118	10.22	168	5.29
19	18.42	69	15.05	119	10.11	169	5.23
20	18.37	70	14.97	120	10.00	170	5.17
21	18.32	71	14.88	121	9.88	171	5.11
22	18.27	72	14.80	122	9.76	172	5.05
23	18.22	73	14.71	123	9.65	173	4.99
24	18.17	74	14.63	124	9.53	174	4.93
25	18.11	75	14.54	125	9.41	175	4.88
26	18.06	76	14.45	126	9.29	176	4.82
27	18.00	77	14.36	127	9.17	177	4.77
28	17.95	78	14.27	128	9.05	178	4.71
29	17.89	79	14.18	129	8.93	179	4.66
30	17.83	80	14.09	130	8.81	180	4.61
31	17.77	81	14.00	131	8.69	181	4.56
32	17.72	82	13.91	132	8.56	182	4.51
33	17.66	83	13.82	133	8.44	183	4.46
34	17.59	84	13.73	134	8.32	184	4.41
35	17.53	85	13.64	135	8.19	185	4.36
36	17.47	86	13.54	136	8.07	186	4.32
37	17.41	87	13.45	137	7.96	187	4.27
38	17.35	88	13.35	138	7.84	188	4.23
39	17.28	89	13.26	139	7.73	189	4.18
40	17.22	90	13.16	140	7.62	190	4.14
41	17.15	91	13.06	141	7.51	191	4.09
42	17.09	92	12.97	142	7.41	192	4.05
43	17.02	93	12.87	143	7.30	193	4.01
44	16.95	94	12.77	144	7.20	194	3.97
45	16.88	95	12.67	145	7.10	195	3.93
46	16.81	96	12.57	146	7.01	196	3.89
47	16.75	97	12.47	147	6.91	197	3.85
48	16.67	98	12.37	148	6.82	198	3.81
49	16.60	99	12.27	149	6.73	199	3.77
50	16.53	100	12.17	150	6.64	200	3.73

ALLOWABLE AXIAL STRESS

For Compression Members with $F_y=36$ ksi (Angle, Channel, I-beams, black pipe)

$F_y=36$ ksi		$F_y=36$ ksi		$F_y=36$ ksi		$F_y=36$ ksi	
Kl/r	F_a, ksi	Kl/r	F_a, ksi	Kl/r	F_a, ksi	Kl/r	F_a, ksi
1	21.56	51	18.26	101	12.85	151	6.55
2	21.52	52	18.17	102	12.72	152	6.46
3	21.48	53	18.08	103	12.59	153	6.38
4	21.44	54	17.99	104	12.47	154	6.30
5	21.39	55	17.90	105	12.33	155	6.22
6	21.35	56	17.81	106	12.20	156	6.14
7	21.30	57	17.71	107	12.07	157	6.06
8	21.25	58	17.62	108	11.94	158	5.98
9	21.21	59	17.53	109	11.81	159	5.91
10	21.16	60	17.43	110	11.67	160	5.83
11	21.10	61	17.33	111	11.54	161	5.76
12	21.05	62	17.24	112	11.40	162	5.69
13	21.00	63	17.14	113	11.26	163	5.62
14	20.95	64	17.04	114	11.13	164	5.55
15	20.89	65	16.94	115	10.99	165	5.49
16	20.83	66	16.84	116	10.85	166	5.42
17	20.78	67	16.74	117	10.71	167	5.35
18	20.72	68	16.64	118	10.57	168	5.29
19	20.66	69	16.53	119	10.43	169	5.23
20	20.60	70	16.43	120	10.28	170	5.17
21	20.54	71	16.33	121	10.14	171	5.11
22	20.48	72	16.22	122	9.99	172	5.05
23	20.41	73	16.12	123	9.85	173	4.99
24	20.35	74	16.01	124	9.70	174	4.93
25	20.28	75	15.90	125	9.55	175	4.88
26	20.22	76	15.79	126	9.41	176	4.82
27	20.15	77	15.69	127	9.26	177	4.77
28	20.08	78	15.58	128	9.11	178	4.71
29	20.01	79	15.47	129	8.97	179	4.66
30	19.94	80	15.36	130	8.84	180	4.61
31	19.87	81	15.24	131	8.70	181	4.56
32	19.80	82	15.13	132	8.57	182	4.51
33	19.73	83	15.02	133	8.44	183	4.46
34	19.65	84	14.90	134	8.32	184	4.41
35	19.58	85	14.79	135	8.19	185	4.36
36	19.50	86	14.67	136	8.07	186	4.32
37	19.42	87	14.56	137	7.96	187	4.27
38	19.35	88	14.44	138	7.84	188	4.23
39	19.27	89	14.32	139	7.73	189	4.18
40	19.19	90	14.20	140	7.62	190	4.14
41	19.11	91	14.09	141	7.51	191	4.09
42	19.03	92	13.97	142	7.41	192	4.05
43	18.95	93	13.84	143	7.30	193	4.01
44	18.86	94	13.72	144	7.20	194	3.97
45	18.78	95	13.60	145	7.10	195	3.93
46	18.70	96	13.48	146	7.01	196	3.89
47	18.61	97	13.35	147	6.91	197	3.85
48	18.53	98	13.23	148	6.82	198	3.81
49	18.44	99	13.10	149	6.73	199	3.77
50	18.35	100	12.98	150	6.64	200	3.73

ALLOWABLE AXIAL STRESS

For Compression Members with F_y=38 ksi (MT1020 "as-welded" tube)

F_y=38 ksi		F_y=38 ksi		F_y=38 ksi		F_y=38 ksi	
Kl/r	F_a, ksi	Kl/r	F_a, ksi	Kl/r	F_a, ksi	Kl/r	F_a, ksi
1	22.76	51	19.14	101	13.19	151	6.55
2	22.71	52	19.05	102	13.05	152	6.46
3	22.67	53	18.95	103	12.91	153	6.38
4	22.62	54	18.85	104	12.76	154	6.30
5	22.57	55	18.75	105	12.62	155	6.22
6	22.53	56	18.65	106	12.48	156	6.14
7	22.47	57	18.54	107	12.33	157	6.06
8	22.42	58	18.44	108	12.18	158	5.98
9	22.37	59	18.34	109	12.04	159	5.91
10	22.32	60	18.23	110	11.89	160	5.83
11	22.26	61	18.12	111	11.74	161	5.76
12	22.20	62	18.02	112	11.59	162	5.69
13	22.15	63	17.91	113	11.44	163	5.62
14	22.09	64	17.80	114	11.28	164	5.55
15	22.03	65	17.69	115	11.13	165	5.49
16	21.97	66	17.58	116	10.98	166	5.42
17	21.90	67	17.47	117	10.82	167	5.35
18	21.84	68	17.36	118	10.67	168	5.29
19	21.77	69	17.25	119	10.51	169	5.23
20	21.71	70	17.13	120	10.35	170	5.17
21	21.64	71	17.02	121	10.19	171	5.11
22	21.57	72	16.90	122	10.03	172	5.05
23	21.50	73	16.79	123	9.87	173	4.99
24	21.43	74	16.67	124	9.71	174	4.93
25	21.36	75	16.55	125	9.56	175	4.88
26	21.29	76	16.43	126	9.41	176	4.82
27	21.22	77	16.31	127	9.26	177	4.77
28	21.14	78	16.19	128	9.11	178	4.71
29	21.06	79	16.07	129	8.97	179	4.66
30	20.99	80	15.95	130	8.84	180	4.61
31	20.91	81	15.83	131	8.70	181	4.56
32	20.83	82	15.70	132	8.57	182	4.51
33	20.75	83	15.58	133	8.44	183	4.46
34	20.67	84	15.45	134	8.32	184	4.41
35	20.59	85	15.33	135	8.19	185	4.36
36	20.50	86	15.20	136	8.07	186	4.32
37	20.42	87	15.07	137	7.96	187	4.27
38	20.34	88	14.94	138	7.84	188	4.23
39	20.25	89	14.81	139	7.73	189	4.18
40	20.16	90	14.68	140	7.62	190	4.14
41	20.08	91	14.55	141	7.51	191	4.09
42	19.99	92	14.42	142	7.41	192	4.05
43	19.90	93	14.29	143	7.30	193	4.01
44	19.81	94	14.15	144	7.20	194	3.97
45	19.71	95	14.02	145	7.10	195	3.93
46	19.62	96	13.88	146	7.01	196	3.89
47	19.53	97	13.74	147	6.91	197	3.85
48	19.43	98	13.61	148	6.82	198	3.81
49	19.34	99	13.47	149	6.73	199	3.77
50	19.24	100	13.33	150	6.64	200	3.73

ALLOWABLE AXIAL STRESS
For Compression Members with F_y=46 ksi (structural grade tube)

F_y=46 ksi		F_y=46 ksi		F_y=46 ksi		F_y=46 ksi	
Kl/r	F_a, ksi	Kl/r	F_a, ksi	Kl/r	F_a, ksi	Kl/r	F_a, ksi
1	27.54	51	22.56	101	14.19	151	6.55
2	27.48	52	22.42	102	13.99	152	6.46
3	27.42	53	22.28	103	13.79	153	6.38
4	27.36	54	22.14	104	13.58	154	6.30
5	27.30	55	22.00	105	13.38	155	6.22
6	27.23	56	21.86	106	13.17	156	6.14
7	27.16	57	21.72	107	12.96	157	6.06
8	27.09	58	21.57	108	12.75	158	5.98
9	27.02	59	21.43	109	12.54	159	5.91
10	26.95	60	21.28	110	12.33	160	5.83
11	26.87	61	21.13	111	12.12	161	5.76
12	26.79	62	20.98	112	11.90	162	5.69
13	26.72	63	20.83	113	11.69	163	5.62
14	26.63	64	20.68	114	11.49	164	5.55
15	26.55	65	20.53	115	11.29	165	5.49
16	26.47	66	20.37	116	11.10	166	5.42
17	26.38	67	20.22	117	10.91	167	5.35
18	26.29	68	20.06	118	10.72	168	5.29
19	26.21	69	19.90	119	10.55	169	5.23
20	26.11	70	19.74	120	10.37	170	5.17
21	26.02	71	19.58	121	10.20	171	5.11
22	25.93	72	19.42	122	10.03	172	5.05
23	25.83	73	19.26	123	9.87	173	4.99
24	25.73	74	19.10	124	9.71	174	4.93
25	25.64	75	18.93	125	9.56	175	4.88
26	25.54	76	18.76	126	9.41	176	4.82
27	25.43	77	18.60	127	9.26	177	4.77
28	25.33	78	18.43	128	9.11	178	4.71
29	25.23	79	18.26	129	8.97	179	4.66
30	25.12	80	18.08	130	8.84	180	4.61
31	25.01	81	17.91	131	8.70	181	4.56
32	24.90	82	17.74	132	8.57	182	4.51
33	24.79	83	17.56	133	8.44	183	4.46
34	24.68	84	17.39	134	8.32	184	4.41
35	24.56	85	17.21	135	8.19	185	4.36
36	24.45	86	17.03	136	8.07	186	4.32
37	24.33	87	16.85	137	7.96	187	4.27
38	24.21	88	16.67	138	7.84	188	4.23
39	24.10	89	16.48	139	7.73	189	4.18
40	23.97	90	16.30	140	7.62	190	4.14
41	23.85	91	16.12	141	7.51	191	4.09
42	23.73	92	15.93	142	7.41	192	4.05
43	23.60	93	15.74	143	7.30	193	4.01
44	23.48	94	15.55	144	7.20	194	3.97
45	23.35	95	15.36	145	7.10	195	3.93
46	23.22	96	15.17	146	7.01	196	3.89
47	23.09	97	14.97	147	6.91	197	3.85
48	22.96	98	14.78	148	6.82	198	3.81
49	22.83	99	14.58	149	6.73	199	3.77
50	22.69	100	14.39	150	6.64	200	3.73

PIPE
Dimensions and Properties

nom. diam. in	O.D. in	I.D. in	wall thickness (t) in	D/t	Area in²	Weight plf	Moment of Inertia, I in⁴	Section Modulus, S in³	radius of gyration, r in
Schedule 10									
1	1.315	1.097	0.109	12.1	0.413	1.40	0.076	0.115	0.428
1 1/4	1.660	1.442	0.109	15.2	0.531	1.81	0.160	0.193	0.550
1 1/2	1.900	1.682	0.109	17.4	0.613	2.08	0.247	0.260	0.634
2	2.375	2.157	0.109	21.8	0.776	2.64	0.499	0.420	0.802
Schedule 40 - Standard									
1/8	0.405	0.269	0.068	6.0	0.072	0.24	0.001	0.005	0.122
1/4	0.540	0.364	0.088	6.1	0.125	0.42	0.003	0.012	0.163
3/8	0.675	0.493	0.091	7.4	0.167	0.57	0.007	0.022	0.209
1/2	0.840	0.622	0.109	7.7	0.250	0.85	0.017	0.041	0.261
3/4	1.050	0.824	0.113	9.3	0.333	1.13	0.037	0.071	0.334
1	1.315	1.049	0.133	9.9	0.494	1.68	0.087	0.133	0.421
1 1/4	1.660	1.380	0.140	11.9	0.669	2.27	0.195	0.235	0.540
1 1/2	1.900	1.610	0.145	13.1	0.799	2.72	0.310	0.326	0.623
2	2.375	2.067	0.154	15.4	1.07	3.65	0.666	0.561	0.787
2 1/2	2.875	2.469	0.203	14.2	1.70	5.79	1.53	1.06	0.947
3	3.500	3.068	0.216	16.2	2.23	7.58	3.02	1.72	1.16
3 1/2	4.000	3.548	0.226	17.7	2.68	9.11	4.79	2.39	1.34
4	4.500	4.026	0.237	19.0	3.17	10.79	7.23	3.21	1.51
5	5.563	5.047	0.258	21.6	4.30	14.62	15.16	5.45	1.88
6	6.625	6.065	0.280	23.7	5.58	18.97	28.14	8.50	2.25
8	8.625	7.981	0.322	26.8	8.40	28.55	72.49	16.81	2.94
10	10.750	10.020	0.365	29.5	11.91	40.48	160.7	29.90	3.67
12	12.750	12.000	0.375	34.0	14.58	49.56	279.3	43.82	4.38
14	14.000	13.250	0.375	37.3	16.05	54.57	372.8	53.25	4.82
16	16.000	15.250	0.375	42.7	18.41	62.58	562.1	70.26	5.53
Schedule 80 - Extra Strong									
1/4	0.540	0.302	0.119	4.5	0.157	0.54	0.004	0.014	0.155
3/8	0.675	0.423	0.126	5.4	0.217	0.74	0.009	0.026	0.199
1/2	0.840	0.546	0.147	5.7	0.320	1.09	0.020	0.048	0.250
3/4	1.050	0.742	0.154	6.8	0.433	1.47	0.045	0.085	0.321
1	1.315	0.957	0.179	7.3	0.639	2.17	0.106	0.161	0.407
1 1/4	1.660	1.278	0.191	8.7	0.881	3.00	0.242	0.291	0.524
1 1/2	1.900	1.500	0.200	9.5	1.07	3.63	0.391	0.412	0.605
2	2.375	1.939	0.218	10.9	1.48	5.02	0.868	0.731	0.766
2 1/2	2.875	2.323	0.276	10.4	2.25	7.66	1.92	1.339	0.924
3	3.500	2.900	0.300	11.7	3.02	10.25	3.89	2.225	1.14
3 1/2	4.000	3.364	0.318	12.6	3.68	12.51	6.28	3.140	1.31
4	4.500	3.826	0.337	13.4	4.41	14.98	9.61	4.271	1.48
5	5.563	4.813	0.375	14.8	6.11	20.78	20.67	7.431	1.84
6	6.625	5.761	0.432	15.3	8.40	28.57	40.49	12.22	2.19
8	8.625	7.625	0.500	17.3	12.76	43.39	105.7	24.51	2.88
10	10.750	9.750	0.500	21.5	16.10	54.74	212.0	39.43	3.63
12	12.750	11.750	0.500	25.5	19.24	65.42	361.5	56.71	4.33
14	14.000	13.000	0.500	28.0	21.21	72.09	483.8	69.11	4.78
16	16.000	15.000	0.500	32.0	24.35	82.77	731.9	91.49	5.48
Double - Extra Strong									
2	2.375	1.503	0.436	5.4	2.656	9.03	1.31	1.10	0.70
2 1/2	2.875	1.771	0.552	5.2	4.028	13.70	2.87	2.00	0.84
3	3.500	2.300	0.600	5.8	5.466	18.58	5.99	3.42	1.05
4	4.500	3.152	0.674	6.7	8.101	27.54	15.28	6.79	1.37
5	5.563	4.063	0.750	7.4	11.34	38.55	33.63	12.09	1.72
6	6.625	4.897	0.864	7.7	15.64	53.16	66.33	20.02	2.06
8	8.625	6.875	0.875	9.9	21.30	72.42	162.0	37.56	2.76

ROUND MECHANICAL TUBE
Dimensions and Properties

Dimensions		wall	Geometric Properties					
O.D.	I.D.	thickness		Area	Weight	I	S	r
in	in	(t) in	D/t	in^2	plf	in^4	in^3	in
0.500	0.430	0.035	14.3	0.0511	0.174	0.0014	0.0056	0.1649
0.500	0.402	0.049	10.2	0.0694	0.236	0.0018	0.0071	0.1604
0.500	0.370	0.065	7.7	0.0888	0.302	0.0021	0.0086	0.1555
0.625	0.555	0.035	17.9	0.0649	0.221	0.0028	0.0091	0.2090
0.625	0.527	0.049	12.8	0.0887	0.301	0.0037	0.0119	0.2044
0.625	0.495	0.065	9.6	0.1144	0.389	0.0045	0.0145	0.1993
0.625	0.459	0.083	7.5	0.1413	0.480	0.0053	0.0170	0.1939
0.750	0.680	0.035	21.4	0.0786	0.267	0.0050	0.0134	0.2531
0.750	0.652	0.049	15.3	0.1079	0.367	0.0067	0.0178	0.2484
0.750	0.620	0.065	11.5	0.1399	0.476	0.0083	0.0221	0.2433
0.750	0.584	0.083	9.0	0.1739	0.591	0.0098	0.0262	0.2376
0.750	0.532	0.109	6.9	0.2195	0.746	0.0116	0.0309	0.2299
0.875	0.805	0.035	25.0	0.0924	0.314	0.0082	0.0187	0.2972
0.875	0.777	0.049	17.9	0.1272	0.432	0.0109	0.0249	0.2925
0.875	0.745	0.065	13.5	0.1654	0.562	0.0137	0.0312	0.2873
0.875	0.709	0.083	10.5	0.2065	0.702	0.0164	0.0374	0.2815
0.875	0.657	0.109	8.0	0.2623	0.892	0.0196	0.0449	0.2736
1.000	0.930	0.035	28.6	0.1061	0.361	0.0124	0.0247	0.3414
1.000	0.902	0.049	20.4	0.1464	0.498	0.0166	0.0332	0.3367
1.000	0.870	0.065	15.4	0.1909	0.649	0.0210	0.0419	0.3314
1.000	0.834	0.083	12.0	0.2391	0.813	0.0253	0.0507	0.3255
1.000	0.782	0.109	9.2	0.3051	1.04	0.0307	0.0615	0.3174
1.000	0.732	0.134	7.5	0.3646	1.24	0.0350	0.0700	0.3098
1.125	1.055	0.035	32.1	0.1199	0.407	0.0178	0.0317	0.3856
1.125	1.027	0.049	23.0	0.1656	0.563	0.0240	0.0427	0.3808
1.125	0.995	0.065	17.3	0.2165	0.736	0.0305	0.0542	0.3755
1.125	0.959	0.083	13.6	0.2717	0.924	0.0371	0.0660	0.3696
1.125	0.907	0.109	10.3	0.3479	1.18	0.0454	0.0807	0.3613
1.125	0.857	0.134	8.4	0.4172	1.42	0.0522	0.0927	0.3536
1.250	1.180	0.035	35.7	0.1336	0.454	0.0247	0.0395	0.4297
1.250	1.152	0.049	25.5	0.1849	0.629	0.0334	0.0534	0.4250
1.250	1.120	0.065	19.2	0.2420	0.823	0.0426	0.0682	0.4196
1.250	1.084	0.083	15.1	0.3043	1.03	0.0521	0.0833	0.4136
1.250	1.032	0.109	11.5	0.3907	1.33	0.0642	0.1027	0.4052
1.250	0.982	0.134	9.3	0.4698	1.60	0.0742	0.1187	0.3974
1.375	1.305	0.035	39.3	0.1473	0.501	0.0331	0.0481	0.4739
1.375	1.277	0.049	28.1	0.2041	0.694	0.0449	0.0653	0.4691
1.375	1.245	0.065	21.2	0.2675	0.909	0.0575	0.0837	0.4637
1.375	1.209	0.083	16.6	0.3369	1.15	0.0706	0.1027	0.4577
1.375	1.157	0.109	12.6	0.4335	1.47	0.0875	0.1273	0.4493
1.375	1.107	0.134	10.3	0.5224	1.78	0.1017	0.1480	0.4413

ROUND MECHANICAL TUBE, continued
Dimensions and Properties

Dimensions		wall	Geometric Properties					
O.D.	I.D.	thickness		Area	Weight	I	S	r
in	in	(t) in	D/t	in²	plf	in⁴	in³	in
1.500	1.430	0.035	42.9	0.1611	0.548	0.0432	0.0577	0.5181
1.500	1.402	0.049	30.6	0.2234	0.759	0.0589	0.0785	0.5133
1.500	1.370	0.065	23.1	0.2930	0.996	0.0756	0.1008	0.5079
1.500	1.334	0.083	18.1	0.3695	1.26	0.0931	0.1241	0.5018
1.500	1.282	0.109	13.8	0.4763	1.62	0.1159	0.1545	0.4933
1.500	1.232	0.134	11.2	0.5750	1.95	0.1354	0.1806	0.4853
1.500	1.170	0.165	9.1	0.6920	2.35	0.1565	0.2087	0.4756
1.625	1.555	0.035	46.4	0.1748	0.594	0.0553	0.0680	0.5623
1.625	1.527	0.049	33.2	0.2426	0.825	0.0754	0.0928	0.5575
1.625	1.495	0.065	25.0	0.3186	1.08	0.0971	0.1195	0.5520
1.625	1.459	0.083	19.6	0.4021	1.37	0.1199	0.1475	0.5460
1.625	1.407	0.109	14.9	0.5191	1.76	0.1499	0.1845	0.5374
1.625	1.357	0.134	12.1	0.6277	2.13	0.1758	0.2164	0.5293
1.625	1.295	0.165	9.8	0.7568	2.57	0.2042	0.2514	0.5195
1.750	1.680	0.035	50.0	0.1886	0.641	0.0694	0.0793	0.6065
1.750	1.652	0.049	35.7	0.2618	0.890	0.0948	0.1083	0.6016
1.750	1.620	0.065	26.9	0.3441	1.17	0.1223	0.1398	0.5962
1.750	1.584	0.083	21.1	0.4347	1.48	0.1514	0.1730	0.5901
1.750	1.532	0.109	16.1	0.5619	1.91	0.1900	0.2171	0.5815
1.750	1.482	0.134	13.1	0.6803	2.31	0.2236	0.2555	0.5733
1.750	1.420	0.165	10.6	0.8216	2.79	0.2608	0.2981	0.5634
1.875	1.805	0.035	53.6	0.2023	0.688	0.0857	0.0914	0.6507
1.875	1.777	0.049	38.3	0.2811	0.956	0.1172	0.1251	0.6458
1.875	1.745	0.065	28.8	0.3696	1.26	0.1516	0.1617	0.6403
1.875	1.709	0.083	22.6	0.4673	1.59	0.1880	0.2005	0.6342
1.875	1.657	0.109	17.2	0.6047	2.06	0.2367	0.2524	0.6256
1.875	1.607	0.134	14.0	0.7329	2.49	0.2793	0.2980	0.6174
1.875	1.545	0.165	11.4	0.8864	3.01	0.3270	0.3488	0.6074
2.000	1.930	0.035	57.1	0.2161	0.735	0.1043	0.1043	0.6948
2.000	1.902	0.049	40.8	0.3003	1.02	0.1430	0.1430	0.6900
2.000	1.870	0.065	30.8	0.3951	1.34	0.1851	0.1851	0.6845
2.000	1.834	0.083	24.1	0.4999	1.70	0.2300	0.2300	0.6784
2.000	1.782	0.109	18.3	0.6475	2.20	0.2904	0.2904	0.6697
2.000	1.732	0.134	14.9	0.7855	2.67	0.3437	0.3437	0.6614
2.000	1.670	0.165	12.1	0.9512	3.23	0.4036	0.4036	0.6514
2.000	1.626	0.187	10.7	1.0651	3.62	0.4423	0.4423	0.6444
2.125	2.055	0.035	60.7	0.2298	0.781	0.1255	0.1181	0.7390
2.125	2.027	0.049	43.4	0.3196	1.09	0.1723	0.1621	0.7342
2.125	1.995	0.065	32.7	0.4207	1.43	0.2234	0.2102	0.7287
2.125	1.959	0.083	25.6	0.5325	1.81	0.2780	0.2616	0.7226
2.125	1.907	0.109	19.5	0.6903	2.35	0.3517	0.3311	0.7138
2.125	1.857	0.134	15.9	0.8382	2.85	0.4172	0.3927	0.7055
2.125	1.795	0.165	12.9	1.0160	3.45	0.4913	0.4624	0.6954
2.125	1.751	0.187	11.4	1.1385	3.87	0.5395	0.5078	0.6884

ROUND MECHANICAL TUBE, continued
Dimensions and Properties

Dimensions		wall	Geometric Properties					
O.D.	I.D.	thickness		Area	Weight	I	S	r
in	in	(t) in	D/t	in^2	plf	in^4	in^3	in
2.250	2.180	0.035	64.3	0.2436	0.828	0.1494	0.1328	0.7832
2.250	2.152	0.049	45.9	0.3388	1.15	0.2053	0.1825	0.7784
2.250	2.120	0.065	34.6	0.4462	1.52	0.2665	0.2369	0.7729
2.250	2.084	0.083	27.1	0.5650	1.92	0.3322	0.2953	0.7667
2.250	2.032	0.109	20.6	0.7332	2.49	0.4212	0.3744	0.7579
2.250	1.982	0.134	16.8	0.8908	3.03	0.5006	0.4449	0.7496
2.250	1.920	0.165	13.6	1.0808	3.67	0.5910	0.5253	0.7395
2.250	1.876	0.187	12.0	1.2120	4.12	0.6501	0.5778	0.7324
2.500	2.430	0.035	71.4	0.2710	0.921	0.2059	0.1647	0.8716
2.500	2.402	0.049	51.0	0.3773	1.28	0.2834	0.2268	0.8667
2.500	2.370	0.065	38.5	0.4972	1.69	0.3688	0.2950	0.8612
2.500	2.334	0.083	30.1	0.6302	2.14	0.4608	0.3686	0.8550
2.500	2.282	0.109	22.9	0.8188	2.78	0.5863	0.4690	0.8462
2.500	2.232	0.134	18.7	0.9960	3.39	0.6992	0.5594	0.8378
2.500	2.170	0.165	15.2	1.2104	4.11	0.8290	0.6632	0.8276
2.500	2.126	0.187	13.4	1.3588	4.62	0.9147	0.7317	0.8204
2.750	2.652	0.049	56.1	0.4158	1.41	0.3793	0.2758	0.9551
2.750	2.620	0.065	42.3	0.5483	1.86	0.4944	0.3595	0.9496
2.750	2.584	0.083	33.1	0.6954	2.36	0.6189	0.4501	0.9434
2.750	2.532	0.109	25.2	0.9044	3.07	0.7898	0.5744	0.9345
2.750	2.482	0.134	20.5	1.1013	3.74	0.9445	0.6869	0.9261
2.750	2.420	0.165	16.7	1.3400	4.56	1.1238	0.8173	0.9158
2.750	2.376	0.187	14.7	1.5057	5.12	1.2429	0.9040	0.9086
2.750	2.250	0.250	11.0	1.9635	6.68	1.5493	1.1268	0.8883
3.000	2.902	0.049	61.2	0.4543	1.54	0.4946	0.3298	1.0435
3.000	2.870	0.065	46.2	0.5993	2.04	0.6457	0.4304	1.0379
3.000	2.834	0.083	36.1	0.7606	2.59	0.8097	0.5398	1.0317
3.000	2.782	0.109	27.5	0.9900	3.37	1.0357	0.6905	1.0228
3.000	2.732	0.134	22.4	1.2065	4.10	1.2415	0.8277	1.0144
3.000	2.670	0.165	18.2	1.4696	5.00	1.4814	0.9876	1.0040
3.000	2.626	0.187	16.0	1.6526	5.62	1.6418	1.0945	0.9967
3.000	2.500	0.250	12.0	2.1598	7.34	2.0586	1.3724	0.9763
3.250	3.152	0.049	66.3	0.4928	1.68	0.6313	0.3885	1.1319
3.250	3.120	0.065	50.0	0.6504	2.21	0.8251	0.5077	1.1263
3.250	3.084	0.083	39.2	0.8258	2.81	1.0360	0.6376	1.1201
3.250	3.032	0.109	29.8	1.0756	3.66	1.3280	0.8173	1.1112
3.250	2.982	0.134	24.3	1.3118	4.46	1.5950	0.9815	1.1027
3.250	2.920	0.165	19.7	1.5991	5.44	1.9079	1.1741	1.0923
3.250	2.876	0.187	17.4	1.7994	6.12	2.1182	1.3035	1.0850
3.250	2.750	0.250	13.0	2.3562	8.01	2.6691	1.6425	1.0643
3.500	3.402	0.049	71.4	0.5312	1.81	0.7910	0.4520	1.2202
3.500	3.370	0.065	53.8	0.7014	2.38	1.0349	0.5914	1.2147
3.500	3.334	0.083	42.2	0.8910	3.03	1.3012	0.7435	1.2084
3.500	3.282	0.109	32.1	1.1612	3.95	1.6708	0.9547	1.1995
3.500	3.232	0.134	26.1	1.4170	4.82	2.0100	1.1486	1.1910

ROUND MECHANICAL TUBE, continued
Dimensions and Properties

Dimensions		wall		Geometric Properties				
O.D.	I.D.	thickness		Area	Weight	I	S	r
in	in	(t) in	D/t	in^2	plf	in^4	in^3	in
3.500	3.170	0.165	21.2	1.7287	5.88	2.4093	1.3767	1.1805
3.500	3.126	0.187	18.7	1.9463	6.62	2.6788	1.5308	1.1732
3.500	3.000	0.250	14.0	2.5525	8.68	3.3901	1.9372	1.1524
3.500	2.750	0.375	9.3	3.6816	12.5	4.5588	2.6050	1.1128
3.750	3.652	0.049	76.5	0.5697	1.94	0.9756	0.5203	1.3086
3.750	3.620	0.065	57.7	0.7525	2.56	1.2777	0.6814	1.3030
3.750	3.584	0.083	45.2	0.9562	3.25	1.6080	0.8576	1.2968
3.750	3.532	0.109	34.4	1.2468	4.24	2.0679	1.1029	1.2879
3.750	3.482	0.134	28.0	1.5222	5.18	2.4914	1.3288	1.2793
3.750	3.420	0.165	22.7	1.8583	6.32	2.9918	1.5956	1.2688
3.750	3.376	0.187	20.1	2.0932	7.12	3.3308	1.7764	1.2614
3.750	3.250	0.250	15.0	2.7489	9.35	4.2307	2.2564	1.2406
3.750	3.000	0.375	10.0	3.9761	13.5	5.7311	3.0566	1.2006
4.000	3.902	0.049	81.6	0.6082	2.07	1.1870	0.5935	1.3970
4.000	3.870	0.065	61.5	0.8035	2.73	1.5557	0.7778	1.3914
4.000	3.834	0.083	48.2	1.0214	3.47	1.9597	0.9799	1.3852
4.000	3.782	0.109	36.7	1.3324	4.53	2.5235	1.2618	1.3762
4.000	3.732	0.134	29.9	1.6275	5.53	3.0442	1.5221	1.3677
4.000	3.670	0.165	24.2	1.9879	6.76	3.6614	1.8307	1.3571
4.000	3.626	0.187	21.4	2.2401	7.62	4.0808	2.0404	1.3497
4.000	3.500	0.250	16.0	2.9452	10.0	5.2002	2.6001	1.3288
4.000	3.250	0.375	10.7	4.2706	14.5	7.0899	3.5449	1.2885
4.500	4.370	0.065	69.2	0.9056	3.08	2.2271	0.9898	1.5682
4.500	4.334	0.083	54.2	1.1517	3.92	2.8098	1.2488	1.5619
4.500	4.282	0.109	41.3	1.5036	5.11	3.6261	1.6116	1.5529
4.500	4.232	0.134	33.6	1.8380	6.25	4.3835	1.9482	1.5443
4.500	4.170	0.165	27.3	2.2471	7.64	5.2862	2.3494	1.5338
4.500	4.126	0.187	24.1	2.5338	8.61	5.9028	2.6234	1.5263
4.500	4.000	0.250	18.0	3.3379	11.3	7.5625	3.3611	1.5052
4.500	3.750	0.375	12.0	4.8596	16.5	10.4217	4.6319	1.4644
4.500	3.624	0.438	10.3	5.5894	19.0	11.6620	5.1831	1.4445
4.500	3.500	0.500	9.0	6.2832	21.4	12.7627	5.6723	1.4252
5.000	4.902	0.049	102.0	0.7621	2.59	2.3355	0.9342	1.7505
5.000	4.870	0.065	76.9	1.0077	3.43	3.0684	1.2274	1.7449
5.000	4.834	0.083	60.2	1.2821	4.36	3.8758	1.5503	1.7387
5.000	4.782	0.109	45.9	1.6748	5.69	5.0107	2.0043	1.7297
5.000	4.732	0.134	37.3	2.0485	6.96	6.0675	2.4270	1.7210
5.000	4.670	0.165	30.3	2.5063	8.52	7.3323	2.9329	1.7104
5.000	4.626	0.187	26.7	2.8275	9.61	8.1998	3.2799	1.7029
5.000	4.500	0.250	20.0	3.7306	12.7	10.5507	4.2203	1.6817
5.000	4.250	0.375	13.3	5.4487	18.5	14.6647	5.8659	1.6406
5.000	4.124	0.438	11.4	6.2774	21.3	16.4810	6.5924	1.6203
5.000	4.000	0.500	10.0	7.0686	24.0	18.1132	7.2453	1.6008

ROUND MECHANICAL TUBE, continued
Dimensions and Properties

Dimensions		wall	Geometric Properties					
O.D.	I.D.	thickness		Area	Weight	I	S	r
in	in	(t) in	D/t	in^2	plf	in^4	in^3	in
5.500	5.370	0.065	84.6	1.1098	3.77	4.0986	1.4904	1.9217
5.500	5.334	0.083	66.3	1.4125	4.80	5.1822	1.8844	1.9154
5.500	5.282	0.109	50.5	1.8461	6.28	6.7092	2.4397	1.9064
5.500	5.232	0.134	41.0	2.2589	7.68	8.1356	2.9584	1.8978
5.500	5.170	0.165	33.3	2.7655	9.40	9.8483	3.5812	1.8871
5.500	5.126	0.187	29.4	3.1213	10.6	11.0270	4.0098	1.8796
5.500	5.000	0.250	22.0	4.1233	14.0	14.2384	5.1776	1.8583
5.500	4.750	0.375	14.7	6.0377	20.5	19.9293	7.2470	1.8168
5.500	4.624	0.438	12.6	6.9654	23.7	22.4771	8.1735	1.7964
5.500	4.500	0.500	11.0	7.8540	26.7	24.7891	9.0142	1.7766
5.500	4.250	0.625	8.8	9.5720	32.5	28.9030	10.5102	1.7377
6.000	5.870	0.065	92.3	1.2119	4.12	5.3369	1.7790	2.0985
6.000	5.834	0.083	72.3	1.5429	5.25	6.7535	2.2512	2.0922
6.000	5.782	0.109	55.0	2.0173	6.86	8.7539	2.9180	2.0831
6.000	5.732	0.134	44.8	2.4694	8.40	10.6272	3.5424	2.0745
6.000	5.670	0.165	36.4	3.0246	10.3	12.8829	4.2943	2.0638
6.000	5.626	0.187	32.1	3.4150	11.6	14.4395	4.8132	2.0563
6.000	5.500	0.250	24.0	4.5160	15.4	18.6992	6.2331	2.0349
6.000	5.250	0.375	16.0	6.6268	22.5	26.3260	8.7753	1.9932
6.000	5.124	0.438	13.7	7.6534	26.0	29.7791	9.9264	1.9726
6.000	5.000	0.500	12.0	8.6394	29.4	32.9376	10.9792	1.9526
6.000	4.750	0.625	9.6	10.554	35.9	38.6285	12.8762	1.9132
6.625	6.295	0.165	40.2	3.3486	11.4	17.4793	5.2768	2.2847
6.625	6.251	0.187	35.4	3.7822	12.9	19.6119	5.9206	2.2771
6.625	6.125	0.250	26.5	5.0069	17.0	25.4746	7.6904	2.2556
6.625	5.875	0.375	17.7	7.3631	25.0	36.0821	10.8927	2.2137
6.625	5.749	0.438	15.1	8.5134	28.9	40.9397	12.3592	2.1929
6.625	5.625	0.500	13.3	9.6211	32.7	45.4184	13.7112	2.1727
6.625	5.375	0.625	10.6	11.781	40.1	53.5896	16.1780	2.1328
7.000	6.834	0.083	84.3	1.8036	6.13	10.7883	3.0824	2.4457
7.000	6.782	0.109	64.2	2.3597	8.02	14.0101	4.0029	2.4366
7.000	6.732	0.134	52.2	2.8904	9.83	17.0389	4.8683	2.4280
7.000	6.670	0.165	42.4	3.5430	12.0	20.7020	5.9149	2.4172
7.000	6.626	0.187	37.4	4.0025	13.6	23.2404	6.6401	2.4097
7.000	6.500	0.250	28.0	5.3014	18.0	30.2347	8.6385	2.3881
7.500	7.000	0.250	30.0	5.6941	19.4	37.4567	9.9885	2.5648
7.500	6.750	0.375	20.0	8.3939	28.5	53.4130	14.2435	2.5226
7.500	6.624	0.438	17.1	9.7174	33.0	60.8113	16.2163	2.5016
7.500	6.500	0.500	15.0	10.996	37.4	67.6915	18.0511	2.4812
7.500	6.250	0.625	12.0	13.499	45.9	80.4141	21.4438	2.4407
8.000	7.834	0.083	96.4	2.0644	7.02	16.1759	4.0440	2.7992
8.000	7.782	0.109	73.4	2.7021	9.19	21.0361	5.2590	2.7902
8.000	7.732	0.134	59.7	3.3114	11.3	25.6184	6.4046	2.7815
8.000	7.670	0.165	48.5	4.0614	13.8	31.1784	7.7946	2.7707
8.000	7.626	0.187	42.8	4.5900	15.6	35.0432	8.7608	2.7631
8.000	7.500	0.250	32.0	6.0868	20.7	45.7464	11.4366	2.7415

SQUARE MECHANICAL TUBE
Dimensions and Properties

Dimensions		wall	Geometric Properties					
Outside	Inside	thickness	Area	Wt		I	S	r
in	in	(t) in	in²	plf	b/t	in⁴	in³	in
0.375	0.305	0.035	0.0458	0.16	10.7	0.0009	0.0046	0.1378
0.375	0.277	0.049	0.0607	0.21	7.7	0.0011	0.0056	0.1321
0.375	0.245	0.065	0.0746	0.25	5.8	0.0012	0.0062	0.1253
0.500	0.430	0.035	0.0633	0.22	14.3	0.0023	0.0090	0.1887
0.500	0.402	0.049	0.0852	0.29	10.2	0.0029	0.0114	0.1829
0.500	0.370	0.065	0.1071	0.36	7.7	0.0033	0.0133	0.1760
0.500	0.334	0.083	0.1299	0.44	6.0	0.0037	0.0149	0.1692
0.625	0.555	0.035	0.0808	0.27	17.9	0.0046	0.0149	0.2397
0.625	0.527	0.049	0.1097	0.37	12.8	0.0060	0.0192	0.2339
0.625	0.495	0.065	0.1396	0.47	9.6	0.0072	0.0230	0.2269
0.625	0.459	0.083	0.1714	0.58	7.5	0.0083	0.0265	0.2199
0.750	0.680	0.035	0.0983	0.33	21.4	0.0083	0.0222	0.2907
0.750	0.652	0.049	0.1342	0.46	15.3	0.0109	0.0290	0.2848
0.750	0.620	0.065	0.1721	0.59	11.5	0.0133	0.0354	0.2778
0.750	0.584	0.083	0.2129	0.72	9.0	0.0156	0.0416	0.2707
0.750	0.532	0.109	0.2590	0.88	6.9	0.0172	0.0458	0.2577
0.875	0.805	0.035	0.1158	0.39	25.0	0.0135	0.0309	0.3418
0.875	0.777	0.049	0.1587	0.54	17.9	0.0179	0.0409	0.3358
0.875	0.745	0.065	0.2046	0.70	13.5	0.0221	0.0506	0.3288
0.875	0.709	0.083	0.2544	0.86	10.5	0.0263	0.0601	0.3215
0.875	0.657	0.109	0.3135	1.07	8.0	0.0298	0.0682	0.3086
1.000	0.930	0.035	0.1333	0.45	28.6	0.0206	0.0411	0.3928
1.000	0.902	0.049	0.1832	0.62	20.4	0.0274	0.0548	0.3868
1.000	0.870	0.065	0.2371	0.81	15.4	0.0342	0.0684	0.3797
1.000	0.834	0.083	0.2959	1.01	12.0	0.0410	0.0821	0.3725
1.000	0.782	0.109	0.3680	1.25	9.2	0.0476	0.0951	0.3595
1.125	1.055	0.035	0.1508	0.51	32.1	0.0297	0.0528	0.4438
1.125	1.027	0.049	0.2077	0.71	23.0	0.0398	0.0708	0.4378
1.125	0.995	0.065	0.2696	0.92	17.3	0.0500	0.0889	0.4307
1.125	0.959	0.083	0.3374	1.15	13.6	0.0605	0.1075	0.4234
1.125	0.907	0.109	0.4225	1.44	10.3	0.0712	0.1265	0.4105
1.125	0.857	0.134	0.4963	1.69	8.4	0.0787	0.1398	0.3981
1.250	1.180	0.035	0.1683	0.57	35.7	0.0412	0.0659	0.4948
1.250	1.152	0.049	0.2322	0.79	25.5	0.0555	0.0888	0.4888
1.250	1.120	0.065	0.3021	1.03	19.2	0.0701	0.1122	0.4817
1.250	1.084	0.083	0.3789	1.29	15.1	0.0853	0.1364	0.4744
1.250	1.032	0.109	0.4770	1.62	11.5	0.1016	0.1625	0.4615
1.250	0.982	0.134	0.5633	1.91	9.3	0.1136	0.1818	0.4491
1.375	1.305	0.035	0.1858	0.63	39.3	0.0554	0.0805	0.5458
1.375	1.277	0.049	0.2567	0.87	28.1	0.0748	0.1088	0.5398
1.375	1.245	0.065	0.3346	1.14	21.2	0.0950	0.1381	0.5327
1.375	1.209	0.083	0.4204	1.43	16.6	0.1160	0.1688	0.5253
1.375	1.157	0.109	0.5315	1.81	12.6	0.1396	0.2030	0.5124
1.375	1.107	0.134	0.6303	2.14	10.3	0.1577	0.2293	0.5002

SQUARE MECHANICAL TUBE, continued
Dimensions and Properties

Dimensions		wall	Geometric Properties					
Outside	Inside	thickness	Area	Wt		I	S	r
in	in	(t) in	in^2	plf	b/t	in^4	in^3	in
1.500	1.430	0.035	0.2033	0.69	42.9	0.0724	0.0966	0.5969
1.500	1.402	0.049	0.2812	0.96	30.6	0.0982	0.1309	0.5908
1.500	1.370	0.065	0.3671	1.25	23.1	0.1251	0.1668	0.5837
1.500	1.334	0.083	0.4619	1.57	18.1	0.1534	0.2046	0.5763
1.500	1.282	0.109	0.5860	1.99	13.8	0.1860	0.2480	0.5634
1.500	1.232	0.134	0.6973	2.37	11.2	0.2118	0.2824	0.5512
1.500	1.170	0.165	0.7982	2.71	9.1	0.2226	0.2967	0.5280
1.625	1.555	0.035	0.2208	0.75	46.4	0.0927	0.1141	0.6479
1.625	1.527	0.049	0.3057	1.04	33.2	0.1259	0.1550	0.6419
1.625	1.495	0.065	0.3996	1.36	25.0	0.1610	0.1982	0.6347
1.625	1.459	0.083	0.5034	1.71	19.6	0.1981	0.2438	0.6273
1.625	1.407	0.109	0.6405	2.18	14.9	0.2418	0.2976	0.6144
1.625	1.357	0.134	0.7643	2.60	12.1	0.2772	0.3411	0.6022
1.625	1.295	0.165	0.8807	2.99	9.8	0.2957	0.3640	0.5794
1.750	1.680	0.035	0.2383	0.81	50.0	0.1164	0.1331	0.6989
1.750	1.652	0.049	0.3302	1.12	35.7	0.1585	0.1812	0.6929
1.750	1.620	0.065	0.4321	1.47	26.9	0.2032	0.2323	0.6858
1.750	1.584	0.083	0.5449	1.85	21.1	0.2507	0.2865	0.6783
1.750	1.532	0.109	0.6950	2.36	16.1	0.3077	0.3517	0.6654
1.750	1.482	0.134	0.8313	2.83	13.1	0.3547	0.4054	0.6532
1.750	1.420	0.165	0.9632	3.27	10.6	0.3833	0.4380	0.6308
1.875	1.805	0.035	0.2558	0.87	53.6	0.1439	0.1535	0.7499
1.875	1.777	0.049	0.3547	1.21	38.3	0.1963	0.2094	0.7439
1.875	1.745	0.065	0.4646	1.58	28.8	0.2522	0.2690	0.7368
1.875	1.709	0.083	0.5864	1.99	22.6	0.3119	0.3327	0.7293
1.875	1.657	0.109	0.7495	2.55	17.2	0.3847	0.4104	0.7165
1.875	1.607	0.134	0.8983	3.05	14.0	0.4455	0.4752	0.7042
1.875	1.545	0.165	1.0457	3.55	11.4	0.4866	0.5190	0.6821
2.000	1.902	0.049	0.3792	1.29	40.8	0.2396	0.2396	0.7949
2.000	1.870	0.065	0.4971	1.69	30.8	0.3085	0.3085	0.7878
2.000	1.834	0.083	0.6279	2.13	24.1	0.3823	0.3823	0.7803
2.000	1.782	0.109	0.8040	2.73	18.3	0.4735	0.4735	0.7675
2.000	1.732	0.134	0.9653	3.28	14.9	0.5506	0.5506	0.7553
2.000	1.670	0.165	1.1282	3.84	12.1	0.6068	0.6068	0.7334
2.000	1.626	0.187	1.2657	4.30	10.7	0.6670	0.6670	0.7259
2.125	2.027	0.049	0.4037	1.37	43.4	0.2889	0.2719	0.8460
2.125	1.995	0.065	0.5296	1.80	32.7	0.3727	0.3507	0.8388
2.125	1.959	0.083	0.6694	2.28	25.6	0.4626	0.4354	0.8313
2.125	1.907	0.109	0.8585	2.92	19.5	0.5751	0.5413	0.8185
2.125	1.857	0.134	1.0323	3.51	15.9	0.6711	0.6316	0.8063
2.125	1.795	0.165	1.2107	4.12	12.9	0.7453	0.7015	0.7846

SQUARE MECHANICAL TUBE, continued
Dimensions and Properties

Dimensions		wall	Geometric Properties					
Outside	Inside	thickness	Area	Wt		I	S	r
in	in	(t) in	in^2	plf	b/t	in^4	in^3	in
2.250	2.152	0.049	0.4282	1.46	45.9	0.3445	0.3062	0.8970
2.250	2.120	0.065	0.5621	1.91	34.6	0.4451	0.3957	0.8898
2.250	2.084	0.083	0.7109	2.42	27.1	0.5534	0.4920	0.8823
2.250	2.032	0.109	0.9130	3.10	20.6	0.6902	0.6135	0.8695
2.250	1.982	0.134	1.0993	3.74	16.8	0.8079	0.7182	0.8573
2.250	1.920	0.165	1.2932	4.40	13.6	0.9034	0.8030	0.8358
2.500	2.402	0.049	0.4772	1.62	51.0	0.4763	0.3810	0.9990
2.500	2.370	0.065	0.6271	2.13	38.5	0.6170	0.4936	0.9919
2.500	2.334	0.083	0.7939	2.70	30.1	0.7693	0.6154	0.9844
2.500	2.282	0.109	1.0220	3.47	22.9	0.9646	0.7717	0.9715
2.500	2.232	0.134	1.2333	4.19	18.7	1.1351	0.9081	0.9594
2.500	2.170	0.165	1.4582	4.96	15.2	1.2835	1.0268	0.9382
2.500	2.126	0.187	1.6397	5.57	13.4	1.4197	1.1357	0.9305
2.500	2.000	0.250	2.0890	7.10	10.0	1.6899	1.3519	0.8994
3.000	2.902	0.049	0.5752	1.96	61.2	0.8326	0.5551	1.2031
3.000	2.870	0.065	0.7571	2.57	46.2	1.0830	0.7220	1.1960
3.000	2.834	0.083	0.9599	3.26	36.1	1.3558	0.9038	1.1885
3.000	2.782	0.109	1.2400	4.22	27.5	1.7137	1.1425	1.1756
3.000	2.732	0.134	1.5013	5.10	22.4	2.0322	1.3548	1.1635
3.000	2.670	0.165	1.7882	6.08	18.2	2.3351	1.5567	1.1427
3.000	2.626	0.187	2.0137	6.85	16.0	2.5936	1.7291	1.1349
3.000	2.500	0.250	2.5890	8.80	12.0	3.1559	2.1039	1.1041
3.500	3.370	0.065	0.8871	3.02	53.8	1.7390	0.9937	1.4001
3.500	3.334	0.083	1.1047	3.76	42.2	2.1184	1.2105	1.3848
3.500	3.282	0.109	1.4419	4.90	32.1	2.7265	1.5580	1.3751
3.500	3.232	0.134	1.7441	5.93	26.1	3.2322	1.8469	1.3613
3.500	3.170	0.165	2.1182	7.20	21.2	3.8441	2.1966	1.3471
3.500	3.126	0.187	2.3877	8.12	18.7	4.2822	2.4470	1.3392
3.500	3.000	0.250	3.0890	10.50	14.0	5.2893	3.0225	1.3085
4.000	3.870	0.065	1.0171	3.46	61.5	2.6176	1.3088	1.6042
4.000	3.834	0.083	1.2707	4.32	48.2	3.2086	1.6043	1.5890
4.000	3.782	0.109	1.6599	5.64	36.7	4.1402	2.0701	1.5793
4.000	3.732	0.134	2.0121	6.84	29.9	4.9321	2.4660	1.5656
4.000	3.670	0.165	2.4482	8.32	24.2	5.8930	2.9465	1.5515
4.000	3.626	0.187	2.7617	9.39	21.4	6.5791	3.2896	1.5434
4.000	3.500	0.250	3.5890	12.20	16.0	8.2151	4.1076	1.5129
5.000	4.670	0.165	3.1082	10.57	30.3	11.9406	4.7762	1.9600
5.000	4.626	0.187	3.5097	11.93	26.7	13.3716	5.3486	1.9519
5.000	4.500	0.250	4.5890	15.60	20.0	16.9439	6.7776	1.9215
6.000	5.670	0.165	3.7682	12.81	36.4	21.1378	7.0459	2.3684
6.000	5.626	0.187	4.2577	14.47	32.1	23.7190	7.9063	2.3603
6.000	5.500	0.250	5.5890	19.00	24.0	30.3422	10.1141	2.3300

RECTANGULAR MECHANICAL TUBE
Dimensions and Properties

Dimensions						Major Axis (x-x)			Minor Axis (y-y)		
side x	side	t	Area	Wt		$I_{x\text{-}x}$	$S_{x\text{-}x}$	$r_{x\text{-}x}$	$I_{y\text{-}y}$	$S_{y\text{-}y}$	$r_{y\text{-}y}$
in	in	in	in^2	plf	b/t	in^4	in^3	in	in^4	in^3	in
0.375	0.625	0.035	0.0633	0.22	17.9	0.0031	0.0100	0.2223	0.0014	0.0074	0.1485
0.375	0.625	0.049	0.0852	0.29	12.8	0.0040	0.0128	0.2163	0.0018	0.0094	0.1439
0.375	0.625	0.065	0.1071	0.36	9.6	0.0047	0.0150	0.2089	0.0021	0.0110	0.1389
0.375	0.625	0.083	0.1299	0.44	7.5	0.0053	0.0169	0.2019	0.0024	0.1260	0.1347
0.375	0.75	0.035	0.0721	0.25	21.4	0.0050	0.0132	0.2624	0.0017	0.0088	0.1515
0.375	0.75	0.049	0.0974	0.33	15.3	0.0064	0.0170	0.2560	0.0021	0.0112	0.1469
0.375	0.75	0.065	0.1234	0.42	11.5	0.0076	0.0203	0.2481	0.0025	0.0133	0.1421
0.375	1.0	0.035	0.0896	0.30	28.6	0.0104	0.0208	0.3405	0.0022	0.0116	0.1557
0.375	1.0	0.049	0.1219	0.41	20.4	0.0136	0.0271	0.3336	0.0028	0.0148	0.1511
0.375	1.0	0.065	0.1559	0.53	15.4	0.0165	0.0329	0.3249	0.0033	0.0178	0.1464
0.375	1.0	0.083	0.1921	0.65	12.0	0.0193	0.0385	0.3166	0.0039	0.0208	0.1425
0.375	1.125	0.035	0.0983	0.33	32.1	0.0141	0.0251	0.3789	0.0024	0.0130	0.1572
0.375	1.125	0.049	0.1342	0.46	23.0	0.0185	0.0330	0.3718	0.0031	0.0167	0.1526
0.375	1.125	0.065	0.1721	0.59	17.3	0.0226	0.0403	0.3627	0.0038	0.0201	0.1479
0.375	1.125	0.083	0.2129	0.72	13.6	0.0267	0.0475	0.3541	0.0044	0.0235	0.1440
0.375	1.5	0.035	0.1246	0.42	42.9	0.0302	0.0402	0.4922	0.0032	0.0171	0.1604
0.375	1.5	0.049	0.1709	0.58	30.6	0.0401	0.0535	0.4846	0.0041	0.0221	0.1557
0.375	1.5	0.065	0.2209	0.75	23.1	0.0498	0.0664	0.4748	0.0050	0.0269	0.1511
0.375	1.5	0.083	0.2751	0.94	18.1	0.0596	0.0795	0.4656	0.0060	0.0318	0.1471
0.375	1.5	0.109	0.3407	1.16	13.8	0.0672	0.0896	0.4441	0.0069	0.0368	0.1424
0.375	2.625	0.035	0.2033	0.69	75.0	0.1383	0.1054	0.8248	0.0055	0.0295	0.1649
0.375	2.625	0.049	0.2812	0.96	53.6	0.1874	0.1428	0.8163	0.0072	0.0384	0.1601
0.375	2.625	0.065	0.3671	1.25	40.4	0.2382	0.1815	0.8054	0.0089	0.0473	0.1554
0.375	2.625	0.083	0.4619	1.57	31.6	0.2921	0.2225	0.7952	0.0106	0.0564	0.1513
0.375	2.625	0.109	0.5860	1.99	24.1	0.3489	0.2658	0.7716	0.0127	0.0677	0.1472
0.375	2.625	0.134	0.6973	2.37	19.6	0.3910	0.2979	0.7488	0.0148	0.0791	0.1458
0.50	0.75	0.035	0.0808	0.27	21.4	0.0061	0.0162	0.2744	0.0032	0.0129	0.1998
0.50	0.75	0.049	0.1097	0.37	15.3	0.0079	0.0211	0.2685	0.0042	0.0167	0.1948
0.50	0.75	0.065	0.1396	0.47	11.5	0.0095	0.0254	0.2613	0.0050	0.0200	0.1892
0.50	0.75	0.083	0.1714	0.58	9.0	0.0111	0.0296	0.2545	0.0058	0.0232	0.1841
0.50	1.0	0.035	0.0983	0.33	28.6	0.0124	0.0249	0.3556	0.0042	0.0167	0.2063
0.50	1.0	0.049	0.1342	0.46	20.4	0.0164	0.0357	0.3491	0.0054	0.0218	0.2013
0.50	1.0	0.065	0.1721	0.59	15.4	0.0200	0.0401	0.3412	0.0066	0.0264	0.1959
0.50	1.0	0.083	0.2129	0.72	12.0	0.0237	0.0474	0.3336	0.0078	0.0310	0.1908
0.50	1.0	0.109	0.2590	0.88	9.2	0.0260	0.0520	0.3169	0.0086	0.0346	0.1828
0.50	1.25	0.035	0.1158	0.39	35.7	0.0218	0.0350	0.4343	0.0051	0.0206	0.2107
0.50	1.25	0.049	0.1587	0.54	25.5	0.0290	0.0464	0.4275	0.0067	0.0269	0.2057
0.50	1.25	0.065	0.2046	0.70	19.2	0.0359	0.0575	0.4190	0.0082	0.0329	0.2003
0.50	1.25	0.083	0.2544	0.86	15.1	0.0429	0.0687	0.4108	0.0097	0.0388	0.1953
0.50	1.25	0.109	0.3135	1.07	11.5	0.0484	0.0774	0.3928	0.0111	0.0442	0.1878
0.50	1.5	0.035	0.1333	0.45	42.9	0.0349	0.0465	0.5115	0.0061	0.0244	0.2139
0.50	1.5	0.049	0.1832	0.62	30.6	0.0466	0.0621	0.5044	0.0080	0.0320	0.2088
0.50	1.5	0.065	0.2371	0.81	23.1	0.0582	0.0776	0.4954	0.0098	0.0393	0.2035
0.50	1.5	0.083	0.2959	1.01	18.1	0.0701	0.0935	0.4869	0.0116	0.0466	0.1984
0.50	1.5	0.109	0.3680	1.25	13.8	0.0805	0.1074	0.4678	0.0135	0.0539	0.1913
0.50	2.0	0.035	0.1683	0.57	57.1	0.0740	0.0740	0.6630	0.0080	0.0320	0.2182
0.50	2.0	0.049	0.2322	0.79	40.8	0.0997	0.0997	0.6554	0.0105	0.0422	0.2130
0.50	2.0	0.065	0.3021	1.03	30.8	0.1260	0.1260	0.6458	0.0130	0.0521	0.2077
0.50	2.0	0.083	0.3789	1.29	24.1	0.1536	0.1536	0.6366	0.0155	0.0622	0.2025
0.625	1.0	0.035	0.1071	0.36	28.6	0.0289	0.0289	0.3677	0.0070	0.0223	0.2550
0.625	1.0	0.049	0.1464	0.50	20.4	0.0383	0.0383	0.3615	0.0091	0.0292	0.2498
0.625	1.0	0.065	0.1884	0.64	15.4	0.0473	0.0473	0.3541	0.0112	0.0359	0.2440
0.625	1.0	0.083	0.2336	0.79	12.0	0.0562	0.0562	0.3470	0.0133	0.0425	0.2383
0.625	1.0	0.109	0.2862	0.97	9.2	0.0631	0.0631	0.3321	0.0150	0.0480	0.2289
0.625	1.5	0.035	0.1421	0.48	42.9	0.0396	0.0528	0.5278	0.0100	0.0321	0.2657
0.625	1.5	0.049	0.1954	0.66	30.6	0.0531	0.0708	0.5211	0.0133	0.0424	0.2605
0.625	1.5	0.065	0.2534	0.86	23.1	0.0666	0.0888	0.5127	0.0165	0.0526	0.2548
0.625	1.5	0.083	0.3166	1.08	18.1	0.0806	0.1075	0.5046	0.0197	0.0629	0.2491
0.625	1.5	0.109	0.3952	1.34	13.8	0.0939	0.1252	0.4874	0.0229	0.0733	0.2407
0.625	1.5	0.134	0.4628	1.57	11.2	0.1025	0.1366	0.4705	0.0252	0.0807	0.2334

RECTANGULAR MECHANICAL TUBE, continued
Dimensions and Properties

Dimensions			Area	Wt		Major Axis (x-x)			Minor Axis (y-y)		
side x	side	t				$I_{x \text{-} x}$	$S_{x \text{-} x}$	$r_{x \text{-} x}$	$I_{y \text{-} y}$	$S_{y \text{-} y}$	$r_{y \text{-} y}$
in	in	in	in^2	plf	b/t	in^4	in^3	in	in^4	in^3	in
0.625	2.0	0.035	0.1771	0.60	57.1	0.0825	0.0825	0.6824	0.0131	0.0419	0.2720
0.625	2.0	0.049	0.2444	0.83	40.8	0.1114	0.1114	0.6751	0.0174	0.0556	0.2667
0.625	2.0	0.065	0.3184	1.08	30.8	0.1413	0.1413	0.6661	0.0217	0.0694	0.2610
0.625	2.0	0.083	0.3996	1.36	24.1	0.1727	0.1727	0.6574	0.0260	0.0833	0.2552
0.625	2.0	0.109	0.5042	1.71	18.3	0.2056	0.2056	0.6386	0.0308	0.0986	0.2471
0.625	2.0	0.134	0.5968	2.03	14.9	0.2297	0.2297	0.6204	0.0345	0.1104	0.2404
0.75	1.0	0.035	0.1158	0.39	28.6	0.0165	0.0330	0.3776	0.0106	0.0282	0.3023
0.75	1.0	0.049	0.1587	0.54	20.4	0.0219	0.0439	0.3717	0.0140	0.0373	0.2969
0.75	1.0	0.065	0.2046	0.70	15.4	0.0272	0.0544	0.3647	0.0173	0.0461	0.2907
0.75	1.0	0.083	0.2544	0.86	12.0	0.0326	0.0651	0.3578	0.0206	0.0550	0.2847
0.75	1.25	0.035	0.1333	0.45	35.7	0.0283	0.0453	0.4608	0.0128	0.0342	0.3102
0.75	1.25	0.049	0.1832	0.62	25.5	0.0379	0.0606	0.4546	0.0170	0.0454	0.3049
0.75	1.25	0.065	0.2371	0.81	19.2	0.0474	0.0758	0.4471	0.0212	0.0565	0.2989
0.75	1.5	0.035	0.1508	0.51	42.9	0.0443	0.0590	0.5418	0.0151	0.0402	0.3162
0.75	1.5	0.049	0.2077	0.71	30.6	0.0595	0.0794	0.5354	0.0201	0.0535	0.3108
0.75	1.5	0.065	0.2696	0.92	23.1	0.0750	0.1000	0.5274	0.0251	0.0668	0.3049
0.75	1.5	0.083	0.3374	1.15	18.1	0.0911	0.1215	0.5197	0.0301	0.0804	0.2989
0.75	1.5	0.109	0.4225	1.44	13.8	0.1072	0.1430	0.5038	0.0354	0.0944	0.2895
0.75	1.5	0.134	0.4923	1.69	11.2	0.1184	0.1578	0.4884	0.0392	0.1046	0.2812
0.75	2.0	0.035	0.1858	0.63	57.1	0.0909	0.0909	0.6994	0.0196	0.0522	0.3245
0.75	2.0	0.049	0.2567	0.87	40.8	0.1231	0.1231	0.6925	0.0261	0.0697	0.3191
0.75	2.0	0.065	0.3346	1.14	30.8	0.1565	0.1565	0.6839	0.0328	0.0875	0.3132
0.75	2.0	0.083	0.4204	1.43	24.1	0.1918	0.1918	0.6755	0.0396	0.1057	0.3071
0.75	2.0	0.109	0.5315	1.81	18.3	0.2301	0.2301	0.6580	0.0473	0.1260	0.2982
0.875	1.0	0.065	0.2209	0.75	15.4	0.0308	0.0616	0.3734	0.0250	0.0571	0.3363
1.0	1.25	0.035	0.1508	0.51	35.7	0.0348	0.0557	0.4802	0.0247	0.0494	0.4046
1.0	1.25	0.049	0.2077	0.71	25.5	0.0467	0.0748	0.4743	0.0331	0.0661	0.3990
1.0	1.25	0.065	0.2696	0.92	19.2	0.0589	0.0942	0.4673	0.0416	0.0831	0.3926
1.0	1.25	0.083	0.3374	1.15	15.1	0.0715	0.1144	0.4603	0.0503	0.1006	0.3861
1.0	1.25	0.109	0.4225	1.44	11.5	0.0845	0.1352	0.4472	0.0594	0.1188	0.3750
1.0	1.25	0.134	0.4963	1.69	9.3	0.0938	0.1501	0.4347	0.0660	0.1320	0.3647
1.0	1.5	0.035	0.1683	0.57	42.9	0.0537	0.0716	0.5647	0.0288	0.0575	0.4134
1.0	1.5	0.049	0.2322	0.79	30.6	0.0725	0.0966	0.5586	0.0386	0.0773	0.4079
1.0	1.5	0.065	0.3021	1.03	23.1	0.0918	0.1224	0.5512	0.0487	0.0975	0.4016
1.0	1.5	0.083	0.3789	1.29	18.1	0.1121	0.1494	0.5439	0.0592	0.1183	0.3951
1.0	1.5	0.109	0.4770	1.62	13.8	0.1339	0.1786	0.5299	0.0706	0.1411	0.3846
1.0	1.5	0.134	0.5633	1.91	11.2	0.1502	0.2003	0.5165	0.0792	0.1583	0.3749
1.0	2.0	0.035	0.2033	0.69	57.1	0.1078	0.1078	0.7282	0.0369	0.0739	0.4262
1.0	2.0	0.049	0.2812	0.96	40.8	0.1464	0.1464	0.7216	0.0498	0.0995	0.4207
1.0	2.0	0.065	0.3671	1.25	30.8	0.1870	0.1870	0.7137	0.0631	0.1261	0.4145
1.0	2.0	0.083	0.4619	1.57	24.1	0.2301	0.2301	0.7058	0.0769	0.1538	0.4080
1.0	2.0	0.109	0.5860	1.99	18.3	0.2792	0.2792	0.6902	0.0928	0.1857	0.3981
1.0	2.0	0.134	0.6973	2.37	14.9	0.3180	0.3180	0.6754	0.1055	0.2110	0.3890
1.0	2.5	0.035	0.2383	0.81	71.4	0.1874	0.1499	0.8866	0.0451	0.0902	0.4351
1.0	2.5	0.049	0.3302	1.12	51.0	0.2556	0.2045	0.8798	0.0609	0.1218	0.4295
1.0	2.5	0.065	0.4321	1.47	38.5	0.3281	0.2625	0.8713	0.0774	0.1548	0.4233
1.0	2.5	0.083	0.5449	1.85	30.1	0.4058	0.3247	0.8630	0.0946	0.1893	0.4167
1.0	2.5	0.109	0.6950	2.36	22.9	0.4977	0.3981	0.8462	0.1151	0.2303	0.4070
1.0	2.5	0.134	0.8313	2.83	18.7	0.5730	0.4584	0.8303	0.1318	0.2637	0.3982
1.0	2.5	0.165	0.9632	3.27	15.2	0.6086	0.4869	0.7949	0.1422	0.2844	0.3842
1.0	3.0	0.049	0.3792	1.29	61.2	0.4060	0.2706	1.0347	0.0720	0.1441	0.4359
1.0	3.0	0.065	0.4971	1.69	46.2	0.5232	0.3488	1.0258	0.0918	0.1835	0.4296
1.0	3.0	0.083	0.6279	2.13	36.1	0.6497	0.4331	1.0172	0.1124	0.2247	0.4230
1.0	3.0	0.109	0.8040	2.73	27.5	0.8030	0.5354	0.9994	0.1374	0.2748	0.4134
1.0	3.0	0.134	0.9653	3.28	22.4	0.9316	0.6212	0.9826	0.1582	0.3163	0.4048
1.0	3.0	0.165	1.1282	3.84	18.2	1.0083	0.6722	0.9454	0.1732	0.3464	0.3918
1.0	3.5	0.049	0.4282	1.46	71.4	0.6038	0.3450	1.1875	0.0832	0.1664	0.4408
1.0	3.5	0.065	0.5621	1.91	53.8	0.7804	0.4460	1.1783	0.1061	0.2122	0.4344
1.0	3.5	0.083	0.7109	2.42	42.2	0.9721	0.5555	1.1694	0.1301	0.2602	0.4278
1.0	3.5	0.109	0.9130	3.10	32.1	1.2089	0.6908	1.1507	0.1597	0.3194	0.4182
1.0	3.5	0.134	1.0993	3.74	26.1	1.4114	0.8065	1.1331	0.1845	0.3690	0.4097
1.0	3.5	0.165	1.2932	4.40	21.2	1.5492	0.8852	1.0945	0.2042	0.4084	0.3974

RECTANGULAR MECHANICAL TUBE, continued
Dimensions and Properties

Dimensions			Area	Wt		Major Axis (x-x)			Minor Axis (y-y)		
side x	side	t				I_{x-x}	S_{x-x}	r_{x-x}	I_{y-y}	S_{y-y}	r_{y-y}
in	in	in	in^2	plf	b/t	in^4	in^3	in	in^4	in^3	in
1.25	2.5	0.049	0.3547	1.21	51.0	0.2924	0.2339	0.9079	0.0999	0.1599	0.5307
1.25	2.5	0.065	0.4646	1.58	38.5	0.3763	0.3011	0.9000	0.1277	0.2044	0.5244
1.25	2.5	0.083	0.5864	1.99	30.1	0.4666	0.3733	0.8920	0.1571	0.2514	0.5176
1.25	2.5	0.109	0.7495	2.55	22.9	0.5759	0.4607	0.8766	0.1929	0.3086	0.5073
1.25	2.5	0.134	0.8983	3.05	18.7	0.6674	0.5339	0.8620	0.2226	0.3561	0.4978
1.25	2.5	0.165	1.0457	3.55	15.2	0.7221	0.5777	0.8310	0.2432	0.3891	0.4822
1.5	2.0	0.049	0.3302	1.12	40.8	0.1931	0.1931	0.7648	0.1242	0.1655	0.6132
1.5	2.0	0.065	0.4321	1.47	30.8	0.2480	0.2480	0.7575	0.1590	0.2120	0.6066
1.5	2.0	0.083	0.5449	1.85	24.1	0.3066	0.3066	0.7502	0.1960	0.2613	0.5997
1.5	2.0	0.109	0.6950	2.36	18.3	0.3773	0.3773	0.7368	0.2407	0.3209	0.5885
1.5	2.0	0.134	0.8313	2.83	14.9	0.4359	0.4359	0.7241	0.2777	0.3702	0.5780
1.5	2.0	0.165	0.9632	3.27	12.1	0.4703	0.4703	0.6988	0.3011	0.4015	0.5591
1.5	2.5	0.049	0.3792	1.29	51.0	0.3292	0.2634	0.9318	0.1500	0.2000	0.6289
1.5	2.5	0.065	0.4971	1.69	38.5	0.4246	0.3396	0.9241	0.1926	0.2568	0.6224
1.5	2.5	0.083	0.6279	2.13	30.1	0.5274	0.4219	0.9165	0.2379	0.3172	0.6156
1.5	2.5	0.109	0.8040	2.73	22.9	0.6541	0.5233	0.9020	0.2940	0.3920	0.6048
1.5	2.5	0.134	0.9653	3.28	18.7	0.7617	0.6094	0.8883	0.3414	0.4552	0.5947
1.5	2.5	0.165	1.1282	3.84	15.2	0.8357	0.6686	0.8607	0.3769	0.5025	0.5780
1.5	3.0	0.049	0.4282	1.46	61.2	0.5127	0.3418	1.0942	0.1759	0.2345	0.6408
1.5	3.0	0.065	0.5621	1.91	46.2	0.6633	0.4422	1.0862	0.2262	0.3016	0.6343
1.5	3.0	0.083	0.7109	2.42	36.1	0.8266	0.5510	1.0783	0.2799	0.3732	0.6275
1.5	3.0	0.109	0.9130	3.10	27.5	1.0314	0.6876	1.0629	0.3474	0.4632	0.6169
1.5	3.0	0.134	1.0993	3.74	22.4	1.2082	0.8055	1.0484	0.4051	0.5401	0.6071
1.5	3.0	0.165	1.2932	4.40	18.2	1.3421	0.8948	1.0187	0.4527	0.6035	0.5916
1.5	3.0	0.187	1.4527	4.94	16.0	1.4862	0.9908	1.0115	0.4977	0.6636	0.5853
1.5	3.5	0.065	0.6271	2.13	53.8	0.9723	0.5556	1.2451	0.2598	0.3464	0.6436
1.5	3.5	0.083	0.7939	2.70	42.2	1.2146	0.6941	1.2369	0.3218	0.4291	0.6367
1.5	3.5	0.109	1.0220	3.47	32.1	1.5229	0.8702	1.2207	0.4008	0.5344	0.6262
1.5	3.5	0.134	1.2333	4.19	26.1	1.7921	1.0241	1.2055	0.4688	0.6251	0.6166
1.5	3.5	0.165	1.4582	4.96	21.2	2.0102	1.1487	1.1741	0.5284	0.7046	0.6020
1.5	3.5	0.187	1.6397	5.57	18.7	2.2316	1.2752	1.1666	0.5816	0.7754	0.5955
1.5	4.0	0.065	0.6921	2.35	61.5	1.3597	0.6898	1.4016	0.2934	0.3912	0.6511
1.5	4.0	0.083	0.8769	2.98	48.2	1.7019	0.8510	1.3932	0.3638	0.4850	0.6441
1.5	4.0	0.109	1.1310	3.84	36.7	2.1421	1.0710	1.3762	0.4542	0.6055	0.6337
1.5	4.0	0.134	1.3673	4.65	29.9	2.5302	1.2651	1.3604	0.5325	0.7100	0.6241
1.5	4.0	0.165	1.6232	5.52	24.2	2.8605	1.4303	1.3275	0.6042	0.8056	0.6101
1.5	4.0	0.187	1.8267	6.21	21.4	3.1820	1.5910	1.3198	0.6654	0.8872	0.6035
1.5	4.0	0.250	2.3390	7.95	16.0	3.8206	1.9103	1.2780	0.7938	1.0584	0.5825
2.0	3.0	0.065	0.6271	2.13	46.2	0.8034	0.5356	1.1318	0.4309	0.4309	0.8289
2.0	3.0	0.083	0.7939	2.70	36.1	1.0034	0.6689	1.1242	0.5363	0.5363	0.8219
2.0	3.0	0.109	1.0220	3.47	27.5	1.2598	0.8399	1.1103	0.6715	0.6715	0.8106
2.0	3.0	0.134	1.2333	4.19	22.4	1.4846	0.9897	1.0972	0.7894	0.7894	0.8001
2.0	3.0	0.165	1.4582	4.96	18.2	1.6759	1.1173	1.0720	0.8938	0.8938	0.7829
2.0	3.0	0.187	1.6397	5.57	16.0	1.8594	1.2396	1.0649	0.9876	0.9876	0.7761
2.0	3.5	0.065	0.6921	2.35	53.8	1.1642	0.6632	1.2969	0.4919	0.4919	0.8430
2.0	3.5	0.083	0.8769	2.98	42.2	1.4572	0.8327	1.2891	0.6128	0.6128	0.8360
2.0	3.5	0.109	1.1310	3.84	32.1	1.8369	1.0496	1.2744	0.7696	0.7696	0.8249
2.0	3.5	0.134	1.3673	4.65	26.1	2.1729	1.2417	1.2607	0.9073	0.9073	0.8146
2.0	3.5	0.165	1.6232	5.52	21.2	2.4712	1.4121	1.2339	1.0349	1.0349	0.7985
2.0	3.5	0.187	1.8267	6.21	18.7	2.7480	1.5703	1.2265	1.1446	1.1446	0.7916
2.0	3.5	0.250	2.3390	7.95	14.0	3.3180	1.8960	1.1910	1.3769	1.3769	0.7672
2.0	4.0	0.065	0.7571	2.57	61.5	1.6114	0.8057	1.4589	0.5529	0.5529	0.8545
2.0	4.0	0.083	0.9599	3.26	48.2	2.0206	1.0103	1.4509	0.6893	0.6893	0.8474
2.0	4.0	0.109	1.2400	4.22	36.7	2.5553	1.2776	1.4355	0.8677	0.8677	0.8365
2.0	4.0	0.134	1.5013	5.10	29.9	3.0321	1.5160	1.4212	1.0251	1.0251	0.8263
2.0	4.0	0.165	1.7882	6.08	24.2	3.4695	1.7347	1.3929	1.1761	1.1761	0.8110
2.0	4.0	0.187	2.0137	6.85	21.4	3.8650	1.9325	1.3854	1.3015	1.3015	0.8039
2.0	5.0	0.065	0.8871	3.02	76.9	2.7980	1.1192	1.7759	0.6748	0.6748	0.8722
2.0	5.0	0.083	1.1047	3.76	60.2	3.3852	1.3541	1.7505	0.8211	0.8211	0.8621
2.0	5.0	0.109	1.4419	4.90	45.9	4.3705	1.7482	1.7410	1.0478	1.0478	0.8525
2.0	5.0	0.134	1.7441	5.93	37.3	5.1727	2.0691	1.7222	1.2354	1.2354	0.8416
2.0	5.0	0.165	2.1182	7.20	30.3	6.1571	2.4629	1.7049	1.4583	1.4583	0.8297

RECTANGULAR MECHANICAL TUBE, continued
Dimensions and Properties

side x	side	t	Area	Wt		$I_{x\text{-}x}$	$S_{x\text{-}x}$	$r_{x\text{-}x}$	$I_{y\text{-}y}$	$S_{y\text{-}y}$	$r_{y\text{-}y}$
in	in	in	in^2	plf	b/t	in^4	in^3	in	in^4	in^3	in
2.0	6.0	0.083	1.2707	4.32	72.3	5.3870	1.7957	2.0590	0.9742	0.9742	0.8756
2.0	6.0	0.109	1.6599	5.64	55.0	6.9708	2.3236	2.0493	1.2440	1.2440	0.8657
2.0	6.0	0.134	2.0121	6.84	44.8	8.2863	2.7621	2.0293	1.4711	1.4711	0.8551
2.0	6.0	0.165	2.4482	8.32	36.4	9.9039	3.3013	2.0113	1.7406	1.7406	0.8432
2.0	6.0	0.187	2.7617	9.39	32.1	11.0837	3.6946	2.0033	1.9293	1.9293	0.8358
2.0	6.0	0.250	3.5890	12.20	24.0	13.8135	4.6045	1.9618	2.3730	2.3730	0.8131
2.5	3.0	0.065	0.6921	2.35	46.2	0.9435	0.6290	1.1676	0.7140	0.5712	1.0157
2.5	3.0	0.083	0.8769	2.98	36.1	1.1802	0.7868	1.1602	0.8919	0.7135	1.0085
2.5	3.0	0.109	1.1310	3.84	27.5	1.4882	0.9922	1.1471	1.1234	0.8987	0.9966
2.5	3.0	0.134	1.3673	4.65	22.4	1.7610	1.1740	1.1349	1.3279	1.0624	0.9855
2.5	3.0	0.165	1.6232	5.52	18.2	2.0097	1.3398	1.1127	1.5172	1.2137	0.9668
2.5	3.0	0.187	1.8267	6.21	16.0	2.2326	1.4884	1.1055	1.6826	1.3461	0.9597
2.5	4.0	0.065	0.8221	2.79	61.5	1.8632	0.9316	1.5054	0.9070	0.7256	1.0503
2.5	4.0	0.083	1.0429	3.55	48.2	2.3392	1.1696	1.4977	1.1349	0.9079	1.0432
2.5	4.0	0.109	1.3329	4.53	36.7	2.9044	1.4522	1.4761	1.4112	1.1290	1.0290
2.5	4.0	0.134	1.6101	5.47	29.9	3.4331	1.7165	1.4602	1.6658	1.3326	1.0172
2.5	4.0	0.165	1.9532	6.64	24.2	4.0784	2.0392	1.4450	1.9715	1.5772	1.0047
2.5	4.0	0.187	2.2007	7.48	21.4	4.5479	2.2740	1.4375	2.1893	1.7515	0.9974
2.5	4.0	0.250	2.8390	9.65	16.0	5.5940	2.7970	1.4037	2.6820	2.1456	0.9720
2.5	5.0	0.065	0.9521	3.24	76.9	3.1939	1.2776	1.8315	1.1000	0.8800	1.0748
2.5	5.0	0.083	1.1877	4.04	60.2	3.8871	1.5548	1.8091	1.3446	1.0757	1.0640
2.5	5.0	0.109	1.5509	5.27	45.9	5.0230	2.0092	1.7997	1.7241	1.3793	1.0544
2.5	5.0	0.134	1.8781	6.38	37.3	5.9671	2.3869	1.7825	2.0433	1.6347	1.0431
2.5	5.0	0.165	2.2832	7.76	30.3	7.1237	2.8495	1.7663	2.4258	1.9406	1.0307
2.5	5.0	0.187	2.5747	8.75	26.7	7.9636	3.1854	1.7587	2.6961	2.1569	1.0233
2.5	5.0	0.250	3.3390	11.35	20.0	9.9061	3.9624	1.7224	3.3305	2.6644	0.9987
3.0	4.0	0.065	0.8871	3.02	61.5	2.1149	1.0575	1.5440	1.3639	0.9093	1.2399
3.0	4.0	0.083	1.1047	3.76	48.2	2.5730	1.2865	1.5261	1.6630	1.1086	1.2269
3.0	4.0	0.109	1.4419	4.90	36.7	3.3176	1.6588	1.5169	2.1374	1.4249	1.2175
3.0	4.0	0.134	1.7441	5.93	29.9	3.9350	1.9675	1.5021	2.5332	1.6888	1.2052
3.0	4.0	0.165	2.1182	7.20	24.2	4.6873	2.3436	1.4876	3.0110	2.0074	1.1923
3.0	4.0	0.187	2.3877	8.12	21.4	5.2309	2.6155	1.4801	3.3522	2.2348	1.1849
3.0	4.0	0.250	3.0890	10.50	16.0	6.4800	3.2404	1.4484	4.1429	2.7619	1.1581
3.0	5.0	0.065	1.0171	3.46	76.9	3.5898	1.4359	1.8786	1.6441	1.0961	1.2714
3.0	5.0	0.083	1.2707	4.32	60.2	4.3891	1.7556	1.8585	2.0167	1.3444	1.2598
3.0	5.0	0.109	1.6599	5.64	45.9	5.6755	2.2702	1.8491	2.5942	1.7294	1.2501
3.0	5.0	0.134	2.0121	6.84	37.3	6.7615	2.7046	1.8331	3.0860	2.0573	1.2384
3.0	5.0	0.165	2.4482	8.32	30.3	8.0902	3.2361	1.8178	3.6786	2.4524	1.2258
3.0	5.0	0.187	2.7617	9.39	26.7	9.0498	3.6199	1.8102	4.0986	2.7324	1.2182
3.0	5.0	0.250	3.5890	12.20	20.0	11.3241	4.5296	1.7763	5.1038	3.4025	1.1925
3.0	6.0	0.065	1.1471	3.90	92.3	5.5733	1.8578	2.2042	1.9244	1.2829	1.2952
3.0	6.0	0.083	1.4367	4.88	72.3	6.8405	2.2802	2.1820	2.3704	1.5802	1.2845
3.0	6.0	0.109	1.8779	6.38	55.0	8.8635	2.9545	2.1725	3.0510	2.0340	1.2746
3.0	6.0	0.134	2.2801	7.75	44.8	10.5942	3.5314	2.1555	3.6387	2.4258	1.2633
3.0	6.0	0.165	2.7782	9.44	36.4	12.7173	4.2391	2.1395	4.3462	2.8974	1.2508
3.0	6.0	0.187	3.1357	10.66	32.1	14.2497	4.7499	2.1317	4.8450	3.2300	1.2430
3.0	6.0	0.250	4.0890	13.90	24.0	17.9619	5.9873	2.0959	6.0648	4.0432	1.2179
4.0	5.0	0.065	1.1471	3.90	76.9	4.3816	1.7526	1.9544	3.1220	1.5610	1.6497
4.0	5.0	0.083	1.4367	4.88	60.2	5.3930	2.1572	1.9374	3.8476	1.9238	1.6365
4.0	5.0	0.109	1.8779	6.38	45.9	6.9806	2.7922	1.9280	4.9704	2.4852	1.6269
4.0	5.0	0.134	2.2801	7.75	37.3	8.3504	3.3402	1.9137	5.9426	2.9713	1.6144
4.0	5.0	0.165	2.7782	9.44	30.3	10.0234	4.0093	1.8994	7.1230	3.5615	1.6012
4.0	5.0	0.187	3.1357	10.66	26.7	11.2223	4.4889	1.8918	7.9628	3.9814	1.5935
4.0	5.0	0.250	4.0890	13.90	20.0	14.1600	5.6640	1.8609	10.0276	5.0138	1.5660
4.0	6.0	0.165	3.1082	10.57	36.4	15.5307	5.1769	2.2353	8.3408	4.1704	1.6381
4.0	6.0	0.187	3.5097	11.93	32.1	17.4156	5.8052	2.2276	9.3287	4.6643	1.6303
4 0	6.0	0.250	4.5890	15.60	24.0	22.1104	7.3701	2.1950	11.8011	5.9005	1.6036
4.0	8.0	0.165	3.7682	12.81	48.5	31.3727	7.8432	2.8854	10.7765	5.3883	1.6911
4.0	8.0	0.187	4.2577	14.47	42.8	35.2540	8 8135	2.8775	12.0606	6.0303	1.6830
4.0	8.0	0.250	5.5890	19.00	32.0	45.1447	11.2862	2.8421	15.3479	7.6740	1.6571

SQUARE STRUCTURAL TUBE
Dimensions and Properties

Dimensions			Geometric Properties					
b	nom. t	act. t	A	Wt		I	S	r
in	in	in	in^2	plf	b/t	in^4	in^3	in
1.25	1/8	0.116	0.49	1.78	10.8	0.101	0.162	0.454
1.25	3/16	0.174	0.67	2.40	7.2	0.121	0.194	0.425
1.50	1/8	0.116	0.61	2.20	12.9	0.188	0.251	0.556
1.50	3/16	0.174	0.84	3.04	8.6	0.235	0.314	0.528
1.625	1/8	0.116	0.67	2.42	14.0	0.246	0.302	0.608
1.625	3/16	0.174	0.93	3.36	9.3	0.312	0.384	0.579
1.75	3/16	0.174	1.02	3.68	10.1	0.405	0.462	0.630
2.00	1/8	0.116	0.84	3.05	17.2	0.486	0.486	0.761
2.00	3/16	0.174	1.19	4.32	11.5	0.640	0.640	0.732
2.00	1/4	0.233	1.51	5.41	8.6	0.745	0.745	0.703
2.25	1/8	0.116	0.96	3.48	19.4	0.712	0.633	0.863
2.25	3/16	0.174	1.37	4.96	12.9	0.952	0.847	0.835
2.25	1/4	0.233	1.74	6.26	9.7	1.130	1.00	0.805
2.50	1/8	0.116	1.07	3.90	21.6	0.998	0.798	0.965
2.50	3/16	0.174	1.54	5.59	14.4	1.350	1.08	0.937
2.50	1/4	0.233	1.97	7.11	10.7	1.630	1.30	0.908
2.50	5/16	0.291	2.35	8.45	8.6	1.820	1.45	0.879
3.00	1/8	0.116	1.30	4.75	25.9	1.78	1.19	1.17
3.00	3/16	0.174	1.89	6.87	17.2	2.46	1.64	1.14
3.00	1/4	0.233	2.44	8.81	12.9	3.02	2.01	1.11
3.00	5/16	0.291	2.94	10.6	10.3	3.45	2.30	1.08
3.00	3/8	0.349	3.39	12.2	8.6	3.77	2.51	1.05
3.50	1/8	0.116	1.54	5.61	30.2	2.90	1.66	1.37
3.50	3/16	0.174	2.24	8.15	20.1	4.05	2.31	1.35
3.50	1/4	0.233	2.91	10.5	15.0	5.04	2.88	1.32
3.50	5/16	0.291	3.52	12.7	12.0	5.84	3.34	1.29
3.50	3/8	0.349	4.09	14.7	10.0	6.48	3.70	1.26
4.00	1/8	0.116	1.77	6.46	34.5	4.40	2.20	1.58
4.00	3/16	0.174	2.58	9.42	23.0	6.21	3.10	1.55
4.00	1/4	0.233	3.37	12.2	17.2	7.80	3.90	1.52
4.00	5/16	0.291	4.10	17.8	13.7	9.14	4.57	1.49
4.00	3/8	0.349	4.78	17.3	11.5	10.3	5.13	1.46
4.00	1/2	0.465	6.02	21.6	8.6	11.9	5.95	1.41
4.50	1/8	0.116	2.00	7.31	38.8	6.35	2.82	1.78
4.50	3/16	0.174	2.93	10.70	25.9	9.02	4.01	1.75
4.50	1/4	0.233	3.84	13.91	19.3	11.4	5.08	1.73
4.50	5/16	0.291	4.68	16.96	15.5	13.5	5.99	1.70
4.50	3/8	0.349	5.48	19.82	12.9	15.3	6.78	1.67
4.50	1/2	0.465	6.95	25.03	9.7	18.0	8.02	1.61
5.00	1/8	0.116	2.23	8.16	43.1	8.80	3.52	1.99
5.00	3/16	0.174	3.28	11.97	28.7	12.6	5.03	1.96
5.00	1/4	0.233	4.30	15.62	21.5	16.0	6.41	1.93
5.00	5/16	0.291	5.26	19.08	17.2	19.0	7.61	1.90
5.00	3/8	0.349	6.18	22.37	14.3	21.7	8.67	1.87
5.00	1/2	0.465	7.88	28.43	10.8	26.0	10.4	1.82

RECTANGULAR STRUCTURAL TUBE
Dimensions and Properties

Dimensions				A	Wt		Major Axis (x-x)			Minor Axis (y-y)		
bxd		nom.t	act. t				I_{x-x}	S_{x-x}	r_{x-x}	I_{y-y}	S_{y-y}	r_{y-y}
in		in	in	in^2	plf	b/t	in^4	in^3	in	in^4	in^3	in
2.0	1.0	1/8	0.116	0.61	2.2	17.2	0.280	0.280	0.679	0.092	0.184	0.389
2.0	1.0	3/16	0.174	0.84	3.0	11.5	0.349	0.349	0.645	0.112	0.223	0.364
2.0	1.5	1/8	0.116	0.72	2.6	17.2	0.383	0.383	0.727	0.244	0.325	0.580
2.0	1.5	3/16	0.174	1.02	3.7	11.5	0.494	0.494	0.697	0.312	0.416	0.553
2.5	1.5	1/8	0.116	0.84	3.1	21.6	0.668	0.535	0.892	0.299	0.399	0.597
2.5	1.5	3/16	0.174	1.19	4.3	14.4	0.881	0.705	0.859	0.389	0.519	0.571
2.5	1.5	1/4	0.233	1.51	5.4	10.7	1.03	0.820	0.825	0.447	0.596	0.544
3.0	1.0	1/8	0.116	0.84	3.1	25.9	0.82	0.545	0.987	0.138	0.275	0.405
3.0	1.0	3/16	0.174	1.19	4.3	17.2	1.07	0.713	0.947	0.172	0.344	0.380
3.0	1.5	1/8	0.116	0.96	3.5	25.9	1.06	0.706	1.05	0.355	0.474	0.610
3.0	1.5	3/16	0.174	1.37	5.0	17.2	1.42	0.945	1.02	0.466	0.621	0.584
3.0	1.5	1/4	0.233	1.74	6.3	12.9	1.68	1.12	0.982	0.541	0.722	0.558
3.0	2.0	1/8	0.116	1.07	3.9	25.9	1.30	0.866	1.10	0.692	0.692	0.804
3.0	2.0	3/16	0.174	1.54	5.6	17.2	1.76	1.17	1.07	0.931	0.931	0.777
3.0	2.0	1/4	0.233	1.97	7.2	12.9	2.12	1.41	1.04	1.11	1.11	0.750
3.0	2.0	5/16	0.291	2.35	8.5	10.3	2.38	1.59	1.01	1.23	1.23	0.724
3.0	2.5	1/8	0.116	1.19	4.3	25.9	1.54	1.03	1.14	1.16	0.93	0.990
3.0	2.5	3/16	0.174	1.71	6.2	17.2	2.11	1.41	1.11	1.59	1.27	0.962
3.0	2.5	1/4	0.233	2.21	8.0	12.9	2.57	1.71	1.08	1.93	1.54	0.935
3.0	2.5	5/16	0.291	2.64	9.5	10.3	2.91	1.94	1.05	2.17	1.74	0.907
3.5	2.5	1/8	0.116	1.30	4.7	30.2	2.23	1.28	1.31	1.33	1.06	1.01
3.5	2.5	3/16	0.174	1.89	6.9	20.1	3.09	1.76	1.28	1.82	1.46	0.983
3.5	2.5	1/4	0.233	2.44	8.9	15.0	3.79	2.17	1.25	2.23	1.78	0.956
3.5	2.5	5/16	0.291	2.94	10.6	12.0	4.34	2.48	1.21	2.53	2.03	0.929
3.5	2.5	3/8	0.349	3.39	12.2	10.0	4.74	2.71	1.18	2.75	2.20	0.902
4.0	2.0	1/8	0.116	1.30	4.7	34.5	2.65	1.32	1.43	0.898	0.898	0.830
4.0	2.0	3/16	0.174	1.89	6.9	23.0	3.66	1.83	1.39	1.22	1.22	0.804
4.0	2.0	1/4	0.233	2.44	8.8	17.2	4.49	2.25	1.36	1.48	1.48	0.778
4.0	2.0	5/16	0.291	2.94	10.6	13.7	5.12	2.56	1.32	1.66	1.66	0.752
4.0	2.0	3/8	0.349	3.39	12.2	11.5	5.59	2.80	1.28	1.79	1.79	0.727
4.0	2.5	3/16	0.116	2.06	7.5	34.5	4.30	2.15	1.44	2.06	1.65	0.999
4.0	2.5	1/4	0.174	2.67	9.7	23.0	5.32	2.66	1.41	2.53	2.02	0.973
4.0	2.5	5/16	0.233	3.23	11.6	17.2	6.13	3.06	1.38	2.89	2.31	0.946
4.0	3.0	1/8	0.116	1.54	5.6	34.5	3.52	1.76	1.51	2.27	1.51	1.21
4.0	3.0	3/16	0.174	2.24	8.2	23.0	4.93	2.47	1.49	3.16	2.10	1.19
4.0	3.0	1/4	0.233	2.91	10.5	17.2	6.15	3.07	1.45	3.91	2.61	1.16
4.0	3.0	5/16	0.291	3.52	12.7	13.7	7.13	3.57	1.42	4.52	3.01	1.13
4.0	3.0	3/8	0.349	4.09	14.7	11.5	7.92	3.96	1.39	5.00	3.33	1.11
5.0	2.0	1/8	0.116	1.54	5.6	43.1	4.65	1.86	1.74	1.10	1.10	0.848
5.0	2.0	3/16	0.174	2.24	8.2	28.7	6.50	2.60	1.70	1.51	1.51	0.822
5.0	2.0	1/4	0.233	2.91	10.5	21.5	8.08	3.23	1.67	1.84	1.84	0.796
5.0	2.0	5/16	0.291	3.52	12.7	17.2	9.34	3.74	1.63	2.09	2.09	0.771
5.0	2.0	3/8	0.349	4.09	14.7	14.3	10.3	4.14	1.59	2.27	2.27	0.746

RECTANGULAR STRUCTURAL TUBE, continued
Dimensions and Properties

Dimensions				A	Wt		Major Axis (x-x)			Minor Axis (y-y)		
bxd		*nom.t*	*act. t*				I_{x-x}	S_{x-x}	r_{x-x}	I_{y-y}	S_{y-y}	r_{y-y}
in		in	in	in²	plf	b/t	in⁴	in³	in	in⁴	in³	in
5.0	2.5	1/8	0.116	1.65	6.0	43.1	5.34	2.14	1.80	1.82	1.46	1.05
5.0	2.5	3/16	0.174	2.41	8.8	28.7	7.51	3.01	1.77	2.53	2.03	1.02
5.0	2.5	1/4	0.233	3.14	11.4	21.5	9.40	3.76	1.73	3.13	2.50	0.998
5.0	3.0	1/8	0.116	1.77	6.5	43.1	6.03	2.41	1.85	2.75	1.83	1.25
5.0	3.0	3/16	0.174	2.58	9.4	28.7	8.53	3.41	1.82	3.85	2.57	1.22
5.0	3.0	1/4	0.233	3.37	12.2	21.5	10.7	4.29	1.78	4.81	3.20	1.19
5.0	3.0	5/16	0.291	4.10	14.8	17.2	12.6	5.03	1.75	5.59	3.73	1.17
5.0	3.0	3/8	0.349	4.78	17.3	14.3	14.1	5.65	1.72	6.23	4.16	1.14
5.0	3.0	1/2	0.465	6.02	21.6	10.8	16.4	6.56	1.65	7.14	4.76	1.09
5.0	4.0	3/16	0.174	2.93	10.7	28.7	10.6	4.22	1.90	7.48	3.74	1.60
5.0	4.0	1/4	0.233	3.84	13.9	21.5	13.4	5.35	1.87	9.46	4.73	1.57
5.0	4.0	5/16	0.291	4.68	17.0	17.2	15.8	6.32	1.84	11.1	5.57	1.54
5.0	4.0	3/8	0.349	5.48	19.9	14.3	17.9	7.16	1.81	12.6	6.29	1.52
5.0	4.0	1/2	0.465	6.95	25.0	10.8	21.2	8.48	1.75	14.8	7.41	1.46
6.0	2.0	1/8	0.116	1.77	6.5	51.7	7.42	2.47	2.05	1.31	1.31	0.861
6.0	2.0	3/16	0.174	2.58	9.4	34.5	10.5	3.49	2.01	1.80	1.80	0.835
6.0	2.0	1/4	0.233	3.37	12.2	25.8	13.1	4.37	1.97	2.21	2.21	0.809
6.0	2.0	5/16	0.291	4.10	14.8	20.6	15.3	5.11	1.93	2.52	2.52	0.784
6.0	2.0	3/8	0.349	4.78	17.3	17.2	17.1	5.71	1.89	2.75	2.75	0.759
6.0	3.0	1/8	0.116	2.00	7.3	51.7	9.43	3.14	2.17	3.23	2.15	1.27
6.0	3.0	3/16	0.174	2.93	10.7	34.5	13.4	4.47	2.14	4.55	3.03	1.25
6.0	3.0	1/4	0.233	3.84	13.9	25.8	17.0	5.66	2.10	5.70	3.80	1.22
6.0	3.0	5/16	0.291	4.68	17.0	20.6	20.1	6.69	2.07	6.66	4.44	1.19
6.0	3.0	3/8	0.349	5.48	19.8	17.2	22.7	7.57	2.04	7.47	4.98	1.17
6.0	3.0	1/2	0.465	6.95	25.0	12.9	26.8	8.94	1.96	8.65	5.77	1.12
6.0	4.0	1/8	0.116	2.23	8.2	51.7	11.4	3.81	2.26	6.15	3.08	1.66
6.0	4.0	3/16	0.174	3.28	12.0	34.5	16.4	5.46	2.23	8.76	4.38	1.63
6.0	4.0	1/4	0.233	4.30	15.6	25.8	20.9	6.96	2.20	11.1	5.56	1.61
6.0	4.0	5/16	0.291	5.26	19.1	20.6	24.8	8.27	2.17	13.1	6.57	1.58
6.0	4.0	3/8	0.349	6.18	22.4	17.2	28.3	9.43	2.14	14.9	7.46	1.55
6.0	4.0	1/2	0.465	7.88	28.4	12.9	33.9	11.3	2.08	17.7	8.87	1.50
6.0	5.0	3/16	0.174	3.63	13.2	34.5	19.3	6.44	2.31	14.6	5.84	2.01
6.0	5.0	1/4	0.233	4.77	17.3	25.8	24.7	8.25	2.28	18.7	7.47	1.98
6.0	5.0	5/16	0.291	5.85	21.2	20.6	29.6	9.85	2.25	22.3	8.91	1.95
6.0	5.0	3/8	0.349	6.88	24.9	17.2	33.9	11.3	2.22	25.5	10.2	1.92
7.0	3.0	1/8	0.116	2.23	8.1	60.3	13.8	3.95	2.49	3.71	2.48	1.29
7.0	3.0	3/16	0.174	3.28	12.0	40.2	19.8	5.65	2.45	5.24	3.50	1.26
7.0	3.0	1/4	0.233	4.30	15.6	30.0	25.2	7.19	2.42	6.59	4.40	1.24
7.0	3.0	5/16	0.291	5.26	19.1	24.1	29.9	8.54	2.38	7.74	5.16	1.21
7.0	3.0	3/8	0.349	6.18	22.4	20.1	34.0	9.73	2.35	8.70	5.80	1.19
7.0	3.0	1/2	0.465	7.88	28.4	15.1	40.7	11.6	2.27	10.2	6.78	1.14
7.0	4.0	1/8	0.116	2.46	9.0	60.3	16.6	4.73	2.59	7.03	3.51	1.69
7.0	4.0	3/16	0.174	3.63	13.2	40.2	23.8	6.80	2.56	10.0	5.02	1.66
7.0	4 0	1/4	0 233	4.77	17.3	30.0	30.5	8.7	2.53	12.8	6.38	1.64
7.0	4.0	5/16	0.291	5.85	21.2	24.1	36.4	10.4	2.50	15.2	7.58	1.61
7 0	4.0	3/8	0.349	6.88	24.9	20.1	41.8	11.9	2.46	17.3	8.63	1.58
7.0	4.0	1/2	0.465	8.81	31.8	15.1	50.6	14.5	2.40	20.7	10.30	1.53

ANGLES
Properties for Designing

size and thickness			area	wt	Geometric Properties, x-x					Geometric Properties, y-y					z-z	Added Variables*		
leg 1	leg 2	t	in²	#/ft	I in⁴	S in³	r in	y in	V_{all} kips	I in⁴	S in³	r in	x in	V_{all} kips	r in	Q red. fac	C_c'	F_b ksi
9	4	5/8	7.73	26.3	64.9	11.5	2.90	3 36	58.76	8.32	2 65	1 04	0.858	24.27	0 847	0.95	129.1	20.60
9	4	9/16	7.00	23.8	59.1	10.4	2.91	3.33	52.94	7.63	2.41	1.04	0 834	21.92	0 850	0.91	132 1	19 68
9	4	1/2	6.25	21.3	53 2	9 34	2.92	3.31	47.32	6.92	2.17	1 05	0.810	19.58	0 854	0.86	136.2	18.52
8	8	1 1/8	16.7	56 9	98.0	17.5	2.42	2.41	90.32						1.56	1.00	126.1	23.76
8	8	1	15 0	51.0	89.0	15.8	2.44	2 37	80.87						1.56	1.00	126.1	23.76
8	8	7/8	13.2	45.0	79.6	14.0	2.45	2.32	71.06						1.57	1.00	126.1	23 76
8	8	3/4	11.4	38 9	69.7	12 2	2 47	2.28	61 35						1 58	1.00	126.1	23.76
8	8	5/8	9.61	32 7	59 4	10.3	2.49	2.23	51.38						1.58	1.00	126 3	21.53
8	8	9/16	8.68	29 6	54.1	9.34	2.50	2.21	46.48						1.59	0 96	128.8	20 70
8	8	1/2	7.75	26.4	48.6	8 36	2.50	2.19	41.46						1.59	0 91	132.1	19 68
8	6	1	13.0	44.2	80.8	15 1	2.49	2 65	81.30	38 8	8.92	1.73	1 65	59.05	1.28	1.00	126 1	23.76
8	6	7/8	11.5	39.1	72 3	13 4	2 51	2 61	71.67	34 9	7.94	1 74	1 61	52.15	1.28	1.00	126.1	23 76
8	6	3/4	9.94	33 8	63 4	11.7	2.53	2.56	61.70	30.7	6 92	1 76	1.56	44 85	1 29	1.00	126.1	23 76
8	6	5/8	8.36	28.5	54 1	9 87	2 54	2.52	51 88	26.3	5 88	1 77	1.52	37.74	1.29	1.00	126.3	21.53
8	6	9/16	7.56	25.7	49.3	8.95	2.55	2.5	46 94	24.0	5.34	1.78	1.50	34.13	1.30	0.96	128 8	20.70
8	6	1/2	6.75	23.0	44.3	8.02	2 56	2.47	41 72	21 7	4 79	1.79	1 47	30 45	1.30	0 91	132 1	19 68
8	6	7/16	5.93	20 2	39 2	7 07	2.57	2.45	36.65	19.3	4.23	1.80	1 45	26 85	1 31	0.85	136.8	18.35
8	4	1	11.0	37 4	69.6	14.1	2.52	3.05	81.81	11.6	3.94	1.03	1.05	38 39	0.846	1 00	126.1	23.76
8	4	3/4	8.44	28.7	54 9	10 9	2.55	2 95	62.00	9.36	3.07	1 05	0 953	0 852	0 852	1.00	126.1	23.76
8	4	9/16	6 43	21.9	42.8	8 35	2.58	2 88	47.02	7.43	2.38	1.07	0.882	22.01	0.861	0.96	128.8	20.70
8	4	1/2	5.75	19.6	38.5	7.49	2.59	2.86	41.97	6.74	2.15	1.08	0.859	19.68	0.865	0.91	132.1	19.68
7	4	1	37.8	26.2	37.8	8.42	2.22	2.51	54.00	9.05	3.03	1.09	1.01	29.15	0 860	1.00	126.1	23.76
7	4	5/8	32.4	22.1	32.4	7.14	2.24	2.46	45.27	7.84	2.58	1.10	0.963	24.48	0.865	1 00	126.1	21.60
7	4	1/2	26 7	17.9	26.7	5.81	2.25	2.42	36.66	6.53	2.12	1 11	0.917	19.79	0.872	0.96	128 4	20.83
7	4	3/8	20.6	13.6	20.6	4 44	2.27	2.37	27.68	5.10	1.63	1.13	0.870	14.99	0 880	0.84	137.6	18 13
6	6	1	11.0	37.4	35.5	8.57	1.80	1.86	59 65						1.17	1.00	126.1	23.76
6	6	7/8	9.73	33 1	31.9	7.63	1 81	1.82	52.58						1.17	1.00	126.1	23.76
6	6	3/4	8.44	28.7	28 2	6.66	1.83	1.78	45 61						1.17	1.00	126.1	23.76
6	6	5/8	7.11	24.2	24 2	5.66	1.84	1.73	38 23						1 18	1.00	126 1	23 76
6	6	9/16	6 43	21.9	22.1	5 14	1 85	1.71	34.58						1 18	1.00	126.1	23 76
6	6	1/2	5.75	19.6	19.9	4.61	1 86	1.68	30.71						1.18	1 00	126.1	21.60
6	6	7/16	5.06	17.2	17.7	4.08	1.87	1.66	27.06						1 19	0.97	127.9	21.00
6	6	3/8	4.36	14.9	15 4	3.53	1.88	1 64	23 33						1.19	0 91	132 1	19 68
6	6	5/16	3.65	12.4	13.0	2.97	1.89	1.62	19.52						1 20	0.83	138.8	17 82
6	4	7/8	7.98	27.2	27.7	7.15	1.86	2.12	52.99	9.75	3.39	1.11	1.12	33.85	0.857	1.00	126 1	23 76
6	4	3/4	6.94	23.6	24.5	6.25	1.88	2.08	45 92	8.68	2.97	1.12	1.08	29.32	0.860	1.00	126.1	23.76
6	4	5/8	5.86	20.0	21.1	5 31	1.90	2 03	38.56	7.52	2.54	1 13	1.03	24.55	0 864	1.00	126.1	23.76
6	4	9/16	5.31	18.1	19.3	4.83	1.90	2 01	34.91	6.91	2.31	1.14	1.01	22 26	0 866	1.00	126.1	23 76
6	4	1/2	4.75	16.2	17.4	4.33	1.91	1.99	31.16	6.27	2 08	1.15	0.987	19 89	0.870	1.00	126.1	21 60
6	4	7/16	4.18	14.3	15 5	3.83	1.92	1.96	27.35	5.60	1.85	1.16	0.964	17 50	0.873	0 97	127.9	21.00
6	4	3/8	3 61	12.3	13.5	3.32	1.93	1.94	23.59	4.9	1.60	1.17	0.941	15.08	0.877	0.91	132.1	19.68
6	4	5/16	3.03	10.3	11.4	2.79	1 94	1.92	19.72	4.18	1.35	1.17	0.918	12.67	0.882	0.83	138.8	17.82
6	3 1/2	1/2	4.5	15.3	16 6	4.24	1.92	2.08	31.11	4 25	1.59	0.972	0.833	17.21	0.759	1 00	126.1	21.60
6	3 1/2	3/8	3.42	11.7	12.9	3.24	1.94	2.04	23.69	3.34	1.23	0.988	0.787	13.07	0.767	0.91	132.1	19.68
6	3 1/2	5/16	2.87	9.80	10.9	2.73	1.95	2.01	19.72	2.85	1.04	0.996	0 763	10.96	0.772	0.83	138.8	17.82
5	5	7/8	7.98	27.2	17 8	5.17	1.49	1.57	43.57						0.973	1.00	126.1	23.76
5	5	3/4	6.94	23.6	15.7	4.53	1.51	1.52	37.34						0 975	1.00	126.1	23.76
5	5	5/8	5.86	20.0	13.6	3.86	1.52	1 48	31.61						0 978	1.00	126.1	23.76
5	5	1/2	4.75	16.2	11.3	3.16	1.54	1.43	25.53						0 983	1 00	126.1	23.76
5	5	7/16	4.18	14.3	10.0	2.79	1.55	1.41	22.35						0.986	1.00	126.1	21.60
5	5	3/8	3.61	12.3	8.74	2.42	1.56	1.39	19.31						0.990	0.98	127.2	21.22
5	5	5/16	3.03	10.3	7.42	2.04	1.57	1.37	16.22						0.994	0.91	132.1	19.68
5	3 1/2	3/4	5.81	19.8	13.9	4.28	1.55	1.75	37.90	5.55	2.22	0 977	0.996	25.49	0.748	1.00	126.1	23.76
5	3 1/2	5/8	4.92	16.8	12.0	3.65	1.56	1.70	31.74	4.83	1.90	0.991	0.951	21.41	0.751	1.00	126.1	23.76
5	3 1/2	1/2	4.00	13.6	9.99	2.99	1.58	1.66	25.79	4.05	1.56	1.01	0.906	17.33	0 755	1.00	126.1	23.76
5	3 1/2	7/16	3.53	12.0	8.90	2.64	1.59	1 63	22.57	3.63	1.39	1 01	0.883	15.26	0.758	1.00	126.1	21.60
5	3 1/2	3/8	3.05	10.4	7.78	2 29	1 60	1.61	19.50	3.18	1.21	1.02	0.861	13.15	0.762	0.98	127.2	21.22
5	3 1/2	5/16	2.56	8.70	6.60	1.94	1.61	1.59	16.35	2.72	1 02	1.03	0 838	11 05	0.766	0.91	132.1	19 68
5	3 1/2	1/4	2.06	7 00	5.39	1.57	1.62	1.56	13.12	2 23	0.830	1.04	0.814	8.90	0 770	0 80	140.7	17.36
5	3	5/8	4 61	15.7	11.4	3.55	1.57	1.80	32 06	3 06	1.390	0.815	0.796	18.14	0.644	1.00	126.1	23.76
5	3	1/2	3.75	12.8	9.45	2.91	1.59	1.75	25.77	2.58	1.150	0.829	0.750	14.68	0.648	1.00	126.1	23.76
5	3	7/16	3.31	11.3	8.43	2.58	1.60	1.73	22.71	2.32	1.020	0.837	0.727	12.93	0 651	1.00	126.1	21.60
5	3	3/8	2.86	9.80	7.37	2.24	1.61	1.70	19.49	2.04	0.888	0.845	0.704	11.14	0.654	0.98	127.2	21.22
5	3	5/16	2.40	8.20	6.26	1.89	1.61	1.68	16 36	1.75	0.753	0 853	0.681	9.37	0 658	0.91	132.1	19.68
5	3	1/4	1.94	6 60	5.11	1.53	1.62	1.66	13.19	1.44	0.614	0.861	0.657	7.55	0.663	0.80	140.7	17.36
4	4	3/4	5.44	18.5	7.67	2.81	1.19	1.27	29.64						0.778	1.00	126.1	23.76
4	4	5/8	4.61	15.7	6 66	2.40	1 20	1.23	25.00						0.779	1.00	126.1	23.76
4	4	1/2	3.75	12 8	5.56	1.97	1.22	1.18	20.14						0 782	1 00	126.1	23.76
4	4	7/16	3.31	11.3	4.97	1 75	1.23	1.16	17.75						0.785	1.00	126.1	23.76
4	4	3/8	2.86	9 80	4.36	1.52	1.23	1.14	15 35						0 788	1.00	126.1	23.76
4	4	5/16	2 4	8 20	3 71	1.29	1.24	1.12	12.88						0.791	1.00	126.3	21.53
4	4	1/4	1.94	6.60	3.04	1.05	1.25	1.09	10.34						0.795	0.91	132.1	19.68

ANGLES, continued
Properties for Designing

size and thickness			area	wt	Geometric Properties, x-x					Geometric Properties, y-y					z-z	Added Variables*		
leg 1	leg 2	t	in²	#/ft	I in⁴	S in³	r in	y in	V_{all} kips	I in⁴	S in³	r in	x in	V_{all} kips	r in	Q red. fac.	C_c'	F_b ksi
4	3 1/2	1/2	3.50	11.9	5.32	1.94	1.23	1.25	20.26	3.79	1.520	1.04	1.00	17.46	0.722	1.00	126.1	23.76
4	3 1/2	7/16	3.09	10.6	4.76	1.72	1.24	1.23	17.87	3.40	1.350	1 05	0.978	15.40	0.724	1.00	126.1	23.76
4	3 1/2	3/8	2.67	9.10	4.18	1.49	1.25	1.21	15.47	2.95	1.170	1.06	0.955	13.12	0.727	1.00	126.1	23.76
4	3 1/2	5/16	2.25	7.70	3.56	1.26	1.26	1.18	12.89	2.55	0.994	1.07	0 932	11.14	0.730	1.00	126.3	21.53
4	3 1/2	1/4	1.81	6.20	2.91	1.03	1.27	1.16	10.39	2.09	0.808	1.07	0.909	8.97	0.734	0.91	132.1	19.68
4	3	1/2	3.25	11.1	5.05	1.89	1.25	1.33	20.40	2.42	1.120	1.06	1.06	18.52	0.639	1.00	126.1	23.76
4	3	7/16	2.87	9.80	4.52	1.68	1.25	1.30	17.86	2.18	0.992	1.07	1.04	16.34	0.641	1.00	126.1	23.76
4	3	3/8	2.48	8.50	3.96	1.46	1.26	1.28	15.42	1.92	0.866	1.07	1.01	13.96	0.644	1.00	126.1	23.76
4	3	5/16	2.09	7.20	3.38	1 23	1.27	1.26	12 97	1.65	0.734	1.08	0.990	11.76	0.647	1.00	126.3	21.53
4	3	1/4	1.69	5.80	2 77	1.00	1.28	1.24	10.47	1.36	0.599	1.09	0.968	9.49	0.651	0.91	132.1	19 68
3 1/2	3 1/2	1/2	3.25	11.1	3.64	1.49	1 06	1.06	17.61						0 683	1.00	126.1	23 76
3 1/2	3 1/2	7/16	2.87	9.80	3.26	1.32	1.07	1.04	15.51						0.684	1.00	126.1	23 76
3 1/2	3 1/2	3/8	2 48	8.50	2 87	1.15	1.07	1.01	13.33						0.687	1.00	126 1	21 60
3 1/2	3 1/2	5/16	2.09	7.20	2.45	0.976	1.08	0.990	11.20						0.690	1.00	126 1	21 60
3 1/2	3 1/2	1/4	1.69	5 80	2.01	0.794	1.09	0 968	9.03						0.694	0 96	128.4	20 83
3 1/2	3	1/2	3.00	10.2	3.45	1.45	1.07	1.13	17.69	2.33	1.100	0.881	0.875	14.86	0.621	1.00	126.1	23.76
3 1/2	3	7/16	2.65	9.10	3.10	1.29	1.08	1.10	15.50	2.09	0.975	0.889	0.853	13.06	0.622	1.00	126.1	23.76
3 1/2	3	3/8	2.30	7.90	2.72	1.13	1 09	1.08	13.38	1.85	0.851	0.897	0.830	11.31	0.625	1.00	126.1	23.76
3 1/2	3	5/16	1.93	6 60	2.33	0.954	1.10	1 06	11.27	1.58	0.722	0.905	0.808	9.47	0.627	1.00	126.1	21.60
3 1/2	3	1/4	1.56	5 40	1.91	0.776	1 11	1.04	9.09	1.30	0 589	0.914	0.785	7.63	0.631	0.96	128 4	20.83
3 1/2	2 1/2	1/2	2.75	9.40	3.24	1.41	1 09	1.20	17.64	1.36	0.760	0 704	0.705	12.16	0.534	1.00	126.1	23.76
3 1/2	2 1/2	7/16	2.43	8 30	2 91	1.26	1.09	1.18	15.57	1.23	0.677	0 711	0.682	10.72	0.535	1.00	126.1	23.76
3 1/2	2 1/2	3/8	2.11	7.20	2.56	1.09	1.10	1.16	13.46	1.09	0.592	0.719	0.660	9.27	0.537	1.00	126.1	23.76
3 1/2	2 1/2	5/16	1.78	6.10	2.19	0.93	1.11	1.14	11.32	0.939	0.504	0.727	0.637	7.79	0.540	1.00	126.1	21.60
3 1/2	2 1/2	1/4	1.44	4.90	1.80	0.76	1.12	1.11	9.08	0.777	0.412	0.735	0.614	6.29	0.544	0.96	128.4	20 83
3	3	1/2	2.75	9.40	2.22	1.07	0.898	0.932	14.95						0.584	1 00	126.1	23.76
3	3	7/16	2.43	8.30	1.99	0 954	0.905	0.910	13.12						0.585	1.00	126.1	23.76
3	3	3/8	2.11	7.20	1.76	0.833	0.913	0.888	11.36						0.587	1.00	126.1	23.76
3	3	5/16	1.78	6.10	1.51	0.707	0.922	0.865	9.54						0.589	1.00	126.1	23.76
3	3	1/4	1.44	4.90	1.24	0.577	0.930	0.842	7.67						0.592	1.00	126.1	21 60
3	3	3/16	1.09	3 71	0 962	0 441	0.939	0.820	5.83						0.596	0.91	132.1	19 68
3	2 1/2	1/2	2.50	8.50	2.08	1.04	0.913	1.00	14.98	1.30	0.744	0.722	0.750	12.23	0.520	1.00	126 1	23.76
3	2 1/2	7/16	2.21	7.60	1.88	0.928	0 920	0.978	13.24	1.18	0 664	0.729	0.728	10.82	0.521	1.00	126.1	23.76
3	2 1/2	3/8	1.92	6.60	1 66	0.810	0.928	0.956	11.44	1.04	0.581	0.736	0 706	9.31	0.522	1.00	126.1	23.76
3	2 1/2	5/16	1.62	5.60	1 42	0.688	0 937	0.933	9.57	0.898	0.494	0.744	0.683	7.83	0.525	1 00	126.1	23.76
3	2 1/2	1/4	1.31	4.50	1.17	0.561	0.945	0 911	7.72	0.743	0.404	0.753	0.661	6 33	0.528	1.00	126.1	21.60
3	2 1/2	3/16	0.996	3.39	0.907	0.430	0.954	0.888	5.86	0.577	0.310	0.761	0.638	4.79	0.533	0.91	132.1	19.68
3	2	1/2	2.25	7.70	1.92	1.00	0.924	1.08	15.00	0.672	0.474	0.546	0.583	9.64	0.428	1.00	126.1	23.76
3	2	7/16	2.00	6.80	1.73	0.894	0.932	1.06	13.24	0.609	0.424	0.553	0.561	8.47	0.429	1.00	126.1	23.76
3	2	3/8	1.73	5.90	1.53	0.781	0.940	1.04	11.47	0.543	0.371	0.559	0.539	7 33	0.430	1.00	126.1	23.76
3	2	5/16	1.46	5.00	1.32	0.664	0.948	1 02	9.70	0.470	0.317	0.567	0.516	6.15	0.432	1 00	126.1	23 76
3	2	1/4	1.19	4.10	1.09	0.542	0.957	0.993	7.79	0.392	0.260	0.574	0.493	4.97	0.435	1.00	126.1	21.60
3	2	3/16	0.902	3.07	0.842	0.415	0.966	0.970	5.88	0.307	0.200	0.583	0.470	3.78	0.439	0.91	132.1	19.68
2 1/2	2 1/2	1/2	2.25	7.70	1.23	0.724	0.739	0.806	12.34						0.487	1.00	126.1	23.76
2 1/2	2 1/2	3/8	1.73	5.90	0.984	0.566	0.753	0.762	9.38						0.487	1.00	126.1	23.76
2 1/2	2 1/2	5/16	1.46	5.00	0.849	0.482	0 761	0.740	7.89						0.489	1.00	126.1	23.76
2 1/2	2 1/2	1/4	1.19	4.10	0.703	0.394	0.769	0.717	6.37						0.491	1.00	126.1	23.76
2 1/2	2 1/2	3/16	0.902	3 07	0.547	0.303	0.778	0.694	4.83						0.495	0.98	127.2	21.22
2 1/2	2	3/8	1.55	5.30	0.912	0 547	0.768	0.831	9.43	0.514	0.363	0.577	0.581	7.35	0.420	1.00	126.1	23.76
2 1/2	2	5/16	1.31	4.50	0.788	0.466	0.776	0.809	7.94	0.446	0.310	0.584	0.559	6.19	0.422	1.00	126.1	23.76
2 1/2	2	1/4	1.06	3.62	0.654	0.381	0.784	0.787	6.42	0.372	0.254	0.592	0.537	5.01	0.424	1.00	126.1	23.76
2 1/2	2	3/16	0.809	2.75	0.509	0 293	0.793	0.764	4.86	0.291	0.196	0.600	0.514	3.80	0.427	0.98	127.2	21.22
2	2	3/8	1.36	4.70	0.479	0.351	0.594	0.636	7.41						0.389	1 00	126.1	23.76
2	2	5/16	1.15	3.92	0.416	0.300	0.601	0.614	6.24						0.390	1.00	126.1	23.76
2	2	1/4	0.938	3.19	0.348	0.247	0.609	0.592	5.06						0 391	1.00	126.1	23.76
2	2	3/16	0.715	2.44	0.272	0.190	0.617	0.569	3.83						0.394	1.00	126.1	23.76
2	2	1/8	0.484	1.65	0.190	0.131	0.626	0.546	2.59						0.398	0.91	132.1	19.68
1 3/4	1 3/4	1/4	0 813	2.77	0 227	0.227	0.529	0.529	4.39						0.341	1.00	126.1	23.76
1 3/4	1 3/4	3/16	0 621	2.12	0.179	0.144	0.537	0.506	3.33						0.343	1.00	126.1	23.76
1 1/2	1 1/2	1/4	0.688	2.34	0.139	0.134	0.449	0.466	3.74						0.292	1.00		23.76
1 1/2	1 1/2	3/16	0.527	1.80	0.110	0.104	0.457	0.444	2.84						0.293	1.00	126.1	23.76
1 1/4	1 1/4	1/4	0 563	1.92	0.077	0.091	0 369	0.403	3.09						0.243	1.00	126.1	23 76
1 1/4	1 1/4	3/16	0.434	1.48	0.061	0.071	0.377	0.381	2.33						0.244	1.00	126.1	23.76
1 1/8	1 1/8	1/8	0.266	0.90	0.032	0.040	0.345	0.327	1.45						0.221	1.00	126.1	23.76
1	1	1/8	0.234	0.80	0.022	0.031	0.304	0.296	1.28						0.196	1.00	126.1	23.76

Additional Bar Sizes

size and thickness			wt	size and thickness			wt	size and thickness			wt	size and thickness			wt
leg 1	leg 2	t	#/ft	leg 1	leg 2	t	#/ft	leg 1	leg 2	t	#/ft	leg 1	leg 2	t	#/ft
2 1/2	1 1/2	5/16	3.92	2	1 1/4	1/4	2.55	1 1/2	1 1/4	3/16	1.64	1	3/4	1/8	0.70
2 1/2	1 1/2	1/4	3.19	2	1 1/4	3/16	1.96	1 3/8	7/8	3/16	1.32	1	5/8	1/8	0.64
2 1/2	1 1/2	3/16	2.44	1 3/4	1 3/4	1/8	1.44	1 3/8	7/8	1/8	0.91	7/8	7/8	1/8	0 70
2	1 1/2	1/4	2.77	1 3/4	1 1/4	1/4	2.34	1 1/4	1 1/4	1/8	1.01	3/4	3/4	1/8	0.59
2	1 1/2	3/16	2.12	1 3/4	1 1/4	3/16	1.80	1	1	1/4	1.49	5/8	5/8	1/8	0.48
2	1 1/2	1/8	1.44	1 3/4	1 1/4	1/8	1.23	1	1	3/16	1.16	1/2	1/2	1/8	0.38

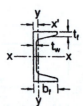

CHANNELS, AMERICAN STANDARD
Dimensions and Properties

| Designation | | Area | depth | web | flange | | x-x Axis | | | y-y Axis | | | | |
| nom | wt | A | d | t_w | width | avg t | I | S | r | I | S | r | x' | L_u |
ht	plf	in²	in	in	b_f (in)	t_f (in)	in⁴	in³	in	in⁴	in³	in	in	ft
C15 x 50		14 7	15 0	0 716	3 716	0 650	404	53 8	5 25	11 00	3 78	0 867	0 798	7 5
x 40		11 8	15 0	0 520	3 520	0 650	349	46 5	5 44	9 23	3 37	0 886	0 777	7 1
x 33 9		9 96	15 0	0 400	3 400	0 650	315	42 0	5 62	8 13	3 11	0 904	0 787	6 8
C12 x 30		8 82	12 0	0 510	3 170	0 501	162	27 0	4 29	5 14	2 06	0 763	0 674	6 1
x 25		7 35	12 0	0 387	3 047	0 501	144	24 1	4 43	4 47	1 88	0 780	0 674	5 9
x 20 7		6 09	12 0	0 282	2 942	0 501	129	21 5	4 61	3 88	1 73	0 799	0 698	5 7
C10 x 30		8 82	10 0	0 673	3 033	0 436	103	20 7	3 42	3 94	1 65	0 669	0 649	6 1
x 25		7 35	10 0	0 526	2 886	0 436	91 2	18 2	3 52	3 36	1 48	0 676	0 617	5 8
x 20		5 88	10 0	0 379	2 739	0 436	78 9	15 8	3 66	2 81	1 32	0 692	0 606	5 5
x 15 3		4 49	10 0	0 240	2 600	0 436	67 4	13 5	3 87	2 28	1 16	0 713	0 634	5 3
C9 x 20		5 88	9 0	0 448	2 648	0 413	60 9	13 5	3 22	2 42	1 17	0 642	0 583	5 6
x 15		4 41	9 0	0 285	2 485	0 413	51 0	11 3	3 40	1 93	1 01	0 661	0 586	5 3
x 13 4		3 94	9 0	0 233	2 433	0 413	47 9	10 6	3 48	1 76	0 962	0 669	0 601	5 2
C8 x 18 75		5 51	8 0	0 487	2 527	0 390	44 0	11 00	2 82	1 98	1 01	0 599	0 565	5 7
x 13 75		4 04	8 0	0 303	2 343	0 390	36 1	9 03	2 99	1 53	0 854	0 615	0 553	5 3
x 11 50		3 38	8 0	0 220	2 260	0 390	32 6	8 14	3 11	1 32	0 781	0 625	0 571	5 1
C7 x 14 75		4 33	7 0	0 419	2 299	0 366	27 2	7 78	2 51	1 38	0 779	0 564	0 532	5 6
x 12 25		3 60	7 0	0 314	2 194	0 366	24 2	6 93	2 60	1 17	0 703	0 571	0 525	5 3
x 9 80		2 87	7 0	0 210	2 090	0 366	21 3	6 08	2 72	0 968	0 625	0 581	0 540	5 1
C6 x 13		3 83	6 0	0 437	2 157	0 343	17 4	5 80	2 13	1 05	0 642	0 525	0 514	5 7
x 10 5		3 09	6 0	0 314	2 034	0 343	15 2	5 06	2 22	0 866	0 564	0 529	0 499	5 4
x 8 2		2 40	6 0	0 200	1 920	0 343	13 1	4 38	2 34	0 693	0 492	0 537	0 511	5 1
C5 x 9		2 64	5 0	0 325	1 885	0 320	8 90	3 56	1 83	0 632	0 450	0 489	0 478	5 6
x 6 7		1 97	5 0	0 190	1 750	0 320	7 49	3 00	1 95	0 479	0 378	0 493	0 484	5 2
C4 x 7 25		2 13	4 0	0 321	1 721	0 296	4 59	2 29	1 47	0 433	0 343	0 450	0 459	5 9
x 5 4		1 59	4 0	0 184	1 584	0 296	3 85	1 93	1 56	0 319	0 283	0 449	0 457	5 4
C3 x 6		1 76	3 0	0 356	1 596	0 273	2 07	1 38	1 08	0 305	0 268	0 416	0 455	6 7
x 5		1 47	3 0	0 258	1 498	0 273	1 85	1 24	1 12	0 247	0 233	0 410	0 438	6 3
x 4 1		1 21	3 0	0 170	1 410	0 273	1 66	1 10	1 17	0 197	0 202	0 404	0 436	6 0

Additional Bar Sizes

length	height	web t	wt plf	length		height	web t	wt plf
2 1/2 x 5/8		3/16	2 27	1 1/2	x	9/16	3/16	1 44
2 x 1		3/16	2 32	1 1/2	x	1/2	1/8	1 12
2 x 1		1/8	1 59	1 1/4	x	1/2	1/8	1 01
2 x 5/8		1/4	2 28	1 1/8	x	9/16	3/16	1 16
2 x 9/16		3/16	1 86	1	x	1/2	1/8	0 84
2 x 1/2		1/8	1 43	1	x	3/8	1/8	0 68
1 1/2 x 3/4		1/8	1 17	3/4	x	3/8	1/8	0 56

EULER CRITICAL BUCKLING STRESS, F_e'
$E = 2,900$ ksi
FOR COMBINED LOADING CALCULATIONS

Kl/r	F_e' ksi	Kl/r	F_e' ksi	Kl/r	F_e' ksi	Kl/r	F_e' ksi	Kl/r	F_e' ksi
1	149,331.41	41	88.83	81	22.76	121	10.20	161	5.76
2	37,332.85	42	84.65	82	22.21	122	10.03	162	5.69
3	16,592.38	43	80.76	83	21.68	123	9.87	163	5.62
4	9,333.21	44	77.13	84	21.16	124	9.71	164	5.55
5	5,973.26	45	73.74	85	20.67	125	9.56	165	5.49
6	4,148.09	46	70.57	86	20.19	126	9.41	166	5.42
7	3,047.58	47	67.60	87	19.73	127	9.26	167	5.35
8	2,333.30	48	64.81	88	19.28	128	9.11	168	5.29
9	1,843.60	49	62.20	89	18.85	129	8.97	169	5.23
10	1,493.31	50	59.73	90	18.44	130	8.84	170	5.17
11	1,234.14	51	57.41	91	18.03	131	8.70	171	5.11
12	1,037.02	52	55.23	92	17.64	132	8.57	172	5.05
13	883.62	53	53.16	93	17.27	133	8.44	173	4.99
14	761.89	54	51.21	94	16.90	134	8.32	174	4.93
15	663.70	55	49.37	95	16.55	135	8.19	175	4.88
16	583.33	56	47.62	96	16.20	136	8.07	176	4.82
17	516.72	57	45.96	97	15.87	137	7.96	177	4.77
18	460.90	58	44.39	98	15.55	138	7.84	178	4.71
19	413.66	59	42.90	99	15.24	139	7.73	179	4.66
20	373.33	60	41.48	100	14.93	140	7.62	180	4.61
21	338.62	61	40.13	101	14.64	141	7.51	181	4.56
22	308.54	62	38.85	102	14.35	142	7.41	182	4.51
23	282.29	63	37.62	103	14.08	143	7.30	183	4.46
24	259.26	64	36.46	104	13.81	144	7.20	184	4.41
25	238.93	65	35.34	105	13.54	145	7.10	185	4.36
26	220.90	66	34.28	106	13.29	146	7.01	186	4.32
27	204.84	67	33.27	107	13.04	147	6.91	187	4.27
28	190.47	68	32.29	108	12.80	148	6.82	188	4.23
29	177.56	69	31.37	109	12.57	149	6.73	189	4.18
30	165.92	70	30.48	110	12.34	150	6.64	190	4.14
31	155.39	71	29.62	111	12.12	151	6.55	191	4.09
32	145.83	72	28.81	112	11.90	152	6.46	192	4.05
33	137.13	73	28.02	113	11.69	153	6.38	193	4.01
34	129.18	74	27.27	114	11.49	154	6.30	194	3.97
35	121.90	75	26.55	115	11.29	155	6.22	195	3.93
36	115.22	76	25.85	116	11.10	156	6.14	196	3.89
37	109.08	77	25.19	117	10.91	157	6.06	197	3.85
38	103.42	78	24.54	118	10.72	158	5.98	198	3.81
39	98.18	79	23.93	119	10.55	159	5.91	199	3.77
40	93.33	80	23.33	120	10.37	160	5.83	200	3.73

Appendix F: Plywood Reference Values

The **APA** – *The Engineered Wood Association* has graciously allowed us to reprint the following tables from the *Plywood Design Specifications* and *PDS Supplement 3* (*Design and Fabrication of Plywood Stressed-Skin Panels*).

*Neither published nor approved by the APA.

1.4.2 Veneer Classifications

Veneer is divided into essentially five levels as follows: *(These veneer classifications are referred to as "veneer grades.")*

N and A – Highest grade level. No knots, restricted patches. *N is intended for natural finish while A is intended for a paintable surface. Check local suppliers for availability of N grade before specifying.*

B   – Solid surface – Small round knots. Patches and round plugs are allowed. *Most common use is faces for PLYFORM.*

C Plugged – Special improved C grade. Used in APA RATED STURD-I-FLOOR and UNDERLAYMENT.

C   – Small knots, knotholes, patches. Lowest grade allowed in Exterior-type plywood. *For sheathing faces, and inner plies in Exterior panels.*

D   – Larger knots, knotholes, some limited white pocket in sheathing grades. This grade not permitted in Exterior panels.

1.5 Wood Species

The woods which may be used to manufacture plywood under Voluntary Product Standard PS 1-95 are classified into five groups based on elastic modulus in bending, and important strength properties. Most woods listed in Table 1.5 are individual species but some are trade groups of related species commonly traded under a single name without further identification.

Design stresses for a group are determined from the clear wood group assignments developed using principles set forth in ASTM D-2555, ESTABLISHING CLEAR WOOD STRENGTH VALUES. Design stresses are published for groups 1 through 4. All woods within a group are assigned the same working stress.

The species grouping system is designed to simplify the design and identification that would otherwise be necessary for the seventy-some species and trade groups of wood from which construction plywood may be manufactured. Thus, the designer need only concern himself with four design stress groups rather than seventy.

The group classification of a plywood panel is usually determined by the face and back veneer with the inner veneers allowed to be of a different group. Certain grades such as MARINE and the STRUCTURAL I grades, however, are required to have all plies of Group 1 species.

TABLE 1.5 CLASSIFICATION OF SPECIES

Group 1	Group 2		Group 3	Group 4	Group 5[a]
Apitong[b][c]	Cedar, Port Orford	Maple, Black	Alder, Red	Aspen	Basswood
Beech, American	Cypress	Mengkulang[b]	Birch, Paper	Bigtooth	Poplar,
Birch	Douglas-Fir 2[d]	Meranti, Red[b][e]	Cedar, Alaska	Quaking	Balsam
Sweet	Fir	Mersawa[b]	Fir, Subalpine	Cativo	
Yellow	Balsam	Pine	Hemlock,	Cedar	
Douglas-Fir 1[d]	California Red	Pond	Eastern	Incense	
Kapur[b]	Grand	Red	Maple, Bigleaf	Western Red	
Keruing[b][c]	Noble	Virginia	Pine	Cottonwood	
Larch, Western	Pacific Silver	Western White	Jack	Eastern	
Maple, Sugar	White	Spruce	Lodgepole	Black (Western	
Pine	Hemlock, Western	Black	Ponderosa	Poplar)	
Caribbean	Lauan	Red	Spruce	Pine	
Ocote	Almon	Sitka	Redwood	Eastern White	
Pine, Southern	Bagtikan	Sweetgum	Spruce	Sugar	
Loblolly	Mayapis	Tamarack	Engelmann		
Longleaf	Red Lauan	Yellow-poplar	White		
Shortleaf	Tangile				
Slash	White Lauan				
Tanoak					

(a) Design stresses for Group 5 not assigned.

(b) Each of these names represents a trade group of woods consisting of a number of closely related species.

(c) Species from the genus Dipterocarpus are marketed collectively: Apitong if originating in the Philippines; Keruing if originating in Malaysia or Indonesia.

(d) Douglas-fir from trees grown in the states of Washington, Oregon, California, Idaho, Montana, Wyoming, and the Canadian Provinces of Alberta and British Columbia shall be classed as Douglas-fir No. 1. Douglas-fir from trees grown in the states of Nevada, Utah, Colorado, Arizona and New Mexico shall be classed as Douglas-fir No. 2.

(e) Red Meranti shall be limited to species having a specific gravity of 0.41 or more based on green volume and oven dry weight.

KEY TO SPAN RATING AND SPECIES GROUP

For panels with "Span Rating" as across top, and thickness as at left, use stress for species group given in table.

Thickness (in.)	Span Rating (APA RATED SHEATHING grade)							Span Rating (STURD-I-FLOOR grade)			
	12/0	16/0	20/0	24/0	32/16	40/20	48/24	16 oc	20 oc	24 oc	48 oc
5/16	4	3	1								
3/8			4	1							
15/32 & 1/2				4	1[1]						
19/32 & 5/8					4	1					
23/32 & 3/4						4	1				
7/8										3[2]	
1-1/8											1

(1) Thicknesses not applicable to APA RATED STURD-I-FLOOR.
(2) For APA RATED STURD-I-FLOOR 24 oc, use Group 4 stresses.

GUIDE TO USE OF ALLOWABLE STRESS AND SECTION PROPERTIES TABLES

INTERIOR OR PROTECTED APPLICATIONS

Plywood Grade	Description and Use	Typical Trademarks	Veneer Grade Face	Veneer Grade Back	Veneer Grade Inner	Common Thicknesses	Grade Stress Level (Table 3)	Species Group	Section Property Table
APA RATED SHEATHING EXP 1 or 2[3]	Unsanded sheathing grade for wall, roof, subflooring, and industrial applications such as pallets and for engineering design, with proper stresses. Manufactured with intermediate and exterior glue.(1) For permanent exposure to weather or moisture only Exterior type plywood is suitable.	APA THE ENGINEERED WOOD ASSOCIATION RATED SHEATHING 32/16 15/32 INCH SIZED FOR SPACING EXPOSURE 1 000 PS 1-95 C-D PRP-108	C	D	D	5/16, 3/8, 15/32, 1/2, 19/32, 5/8, 23/32, 3/4	S-3(1)	See "Key to Span Rating"	Table 1 (unsanded)
APA STRUCTURAL I RATED SHEATHING EXP 1[3]	Plywood grades to use where shear and cross-panel strength propelies are of maximum importance. Made with exterior glue only. Structural I is made from all Group 1 woods.	APA THE ENGINEERED WOOD ASSOCIATION RATED SHEATHING STRUCTURAL I 24/0 3/8 INCH SIZED FOR SPACING EXPOSURE 1 000 PS 1-95 C-D PRP-108	C	D	D	5/16, 3/8, 15/32, 1/2, 19/32, 5/8, 23/32, 3/4	S-2	Group 1	Table 2 (unsanded)
APA RATED STURD-I-FLOOR EXP 1 or 2[3]	For combination subfloor-underlayment. Provides smooth surface for application of carpet and pad. Possesses high concentrated and impact load resistance during construction and occupancy. Manufactured with intermediate and exterior glue. Touch-sanded.(4) Available with tongue-and-groove edges.(5)	APA THE ENGINEERED WOOD ASSOCIATION RATED STURD-I-FLOOR 20 OC 19/32 INCH SIZED FOR SPACING T&G NET WIDTH 47-1/2 EXPOSURE 1 000 PS 1-95 UNDERLAYMENT PRP-108	C plugged	D	C & D	19/32, 5/8, 23/32, 3/4, 1-1/8 (2-4-1)	S-3(1)	See "Key to Span Rating"	Table 1 (touch-sanded)

GUIDE TO USE OF ALLOWABLE STRESS AND SECTION PROPERTIES TABLES

INTERIOR OR PROTECTED APPLICATIONS, CONTINUED

Plywood Grade	Description and Use	Typical Trademarks	Veneer Grade Face	Veneer Grade Back	Veneer Grade Inner	Common Thicknesses	Grade Stress Level (Table 3)	Species Group	Section Property Table
APA UNDERLAYMENT EXP 1, 2 or INT	For underlayment under carpet and pad. Available with exterior glue. Touch-sanded. Available with tongue-and-groove edges.(5)	APA THE ENGINEERED WOOD ASSOCIATION UNDERLAYMENT GROUP 1 EXPOSURE 1 000 PS 1-95	C plugged	D	C & D	1/2, 19/32, 5/8, 23/32, 3/4	S-3(1)	As specified	Table 1 (touch-sanded)
APA C-D PLUGGED EXP 1, 2 or INT	For built-ins, wall and ceiling tile backing. Not for underlayment. Available with exterior glue. Touch-sanded.(5)	APA THE ENGINEERED WOOD ASSOCIATION C-D PLUGGED GROUP 2 EXPOSURE 1 000 PS 1-95	C plugged	D	D	1/2, 19/32, 5/8, 23/32, 3/4	S-3(1)	As Specified	Table 1 (touch-sanded)
APA APPEARANCE GRADES EXP 1, 2 or INT	Generally applied where a high quality surface is required. Includes APA N-N, N-A, N-B, N-D, A-A, A-B, A-D, B-B, and B-D INT grades.(5)	APA THE ENGINEERED WOOD ASSOCIATION A-D GROUP 1 EXPOSURE 1 000 PS 1-95	B or better	D or better	C & D	1/4, 11/32, 3/8, 15/32, 1/2, 19/32, 5/8, 23/32, 3/4	S-3(1)	As Specified	Table 1 (sanded)

(1) When exterior glue is specified, i.e. Exposure 1, stress level 2 (S-2) should be used.

(2) Check local suppliers for availability before specifying Plyform Class II grade, as it is rarely manufactured.

(3) Properties and stresses apply only to APA RATED STURD-I-FLOOR and APA RATED SHEATHING manufactured entirely with veneers.

(4) APA RATED STURD-I-FLOOR 2-4-1 may be produced unsanded.

(5) May be available as Structural I. For such designation use Group 1 stresses and Table 2 section properties.

(6) C face and back must be natural unrepaired; if repaired, use stress level 2 (S-2).

GUIDE TO USE OF ALLOWABLE STRESS AND SECTION PROPERTIES TABLES

EXTERIOR APPLICATIONS

Plywood Grade	Description and Use	Typical Trademarks	Veneer Grade Face	Back	Inner	Common Thicknesses	Grade Stress Level (Table 3)	Species Group	Section Property Table
APA RATED SHEATHING EXT[3]	Unsanded sheathing grade with waterproof glue bond for wall, roof, subfloor and industrial applications such as pallet bins.	APA THE ENGINEERED WOOD ASSOCIATION RATED SHEATHING 48/24 23/32 INCH SIZED FOR SPACING EXTERIOR 000 PS 1-95 C-C PRP-108	C	C	C	5/16, 3/8, 15/32, 1/2, 19/32, 5/8, 23/32, 3/4	S-1[6]	See "Key to Span Rating"	Table 1 (unsanded)
APA STRUCTURAL I RATED SHEATHING EXT[3]	"Structural" is a modifier for this unsanded sheathing grade. For engineered applications in construction and industry where full Exterior-type panels are required. Structural I is made from Group 1 woods only.	APA THE ENGINEERED WOOD ASSOCIATION RATED SHEATHING STRUCTURAL I 24/0 3/8 INCH SIZED FOR SPACING EXPOSURE 1 000 PS 1-95 C-D PRP-108	C	C	C	5/16, 3/8, 15/32, 1/2, 19/32, 5/8, 23/32, 3/4	S-1[6]	Group 1	Table 2 (unsanded)
APA RATED STURD-I-FLOOR EXT[3]	For combination subfloor-underlayment where severe moisture conditions may be present, as in balcony decks. Possesses high concentrated and impact load resistance during construction and occupancy. Touch-sanded.(4) Available with tongue-and-groove edges.(5)	APA THE ENGINEERED WOOD ASSOCIATION RATED STURD-I-FLOOR 20 OC 19/32 INCH SIZED FOR SPACING EXTERIOR 000 PS 1-95 C-C PLUGGED PRP-108	C plugged	C	C	19/32, 5/8, 23/32, 3/4	S-2	See "Key to Span Rating"	Table 1 (touch-sanded)
APA UNDERLAYMENT EXT and APA C-C-PLUGGED EXT	Underlayment for floor where severe moisture conditions may exist. Also for controlled atmosphere rooms and many industrial applications. Touch-sanded. Available with tongue-and-groove edges.(5)	APA THE ENGINEERED WOOD ASSOCIATION C-C PLUGGED GROUP 2 EXTERIOR 000 PS 1-95	C plugged	C	C	1/2, 19/32, 5/8, 23/32, 3/4	S-2	As Specified	Table 1 (touch-sanded)

GUIDE TO USE OF ALLOWABLE STRESS AND SECTION PROPERTIES TABLES

EXTERIOR APPLICATIONS, CONTINUED

Plywood Grade	Description and Use	Typical Trademarks	Veneer Grade Face	Veneer Grade Back	Veneer Grade Inner	Common Thicknesses	Grade Stress Level (Table 3)	Species Group	Section Property Table
APA B-B PLYFORM CLASS I or II[2]	Concrete-form grade with high reuse factor. Sanded both sides, mill-oiled unless otherwise specified. Available in HDO. For refined design information on this special-use panel see APA Design/Construction Guide: Concrete Forming, Form No. V345. Design using values from this specification will result in a conservative design.(5)	APA THE ENGINEERED WOOD ASSOCIATION / PLYFORM B-B CLASS 1 / EXTERIOR / 000 / PS 1-95	B	B	C	19/32, 5/8, 23/32, 3/4	S-2	Class I use Group 1; Class II use Group 3	Table 1 (sanded)
APA MARINE EXT	Superior Exterior-type plywood made only with Douglas-fir or Western Larch. Special solid-core construction. Available with MDO or HDO face. Ideal for boat hull construction.	MARINE • A-A • EXT / APA • 000 • PS 1-95	A or B	A or B	B	1/4, 3/8, 1/2, 5/8, 3/4	A face & back use S-1 B face or back use S-2	Group 1	Table 2 (sanded)
APA APPEARANCE GRADES EXT	Generally applied where a high quality surface is required. Includes APA A-A, A-B, A-C, B-B, B-C, HDO and MDO EXT.(5)	APA THE ENGINEERED WOOD ASSOCIATION / A-C GROUP 1 / EXTERIOR / 000 / PS 1-95	B or better	C or better	C	1/4, 11/32, 3/8, 15/32, 1/2, 19/32, 5/8, 23/32, 3/4	A or C face & back use S-1(6); B face or back use S-2	As Specified	Table 1 (sanded)

(1) When exterior glue is specified, i.e. Exposure 1, stress level 2 (S-2) should be used.

(2) Check local suppliers for availability before specifying Plyform Class II grade, as it is rarely manufactured.

(3) Properties and stresses apply only to APA RATED STURD-I-FLOOR and APA RATED SHEATHING manufactured entirely with veneers.

(4) APA RATED STURD-I-FLOOR 2-4-1 may be produced unsanded.

(5) May be available as Structural I. For such designation use Group 1 stresses and Table 2 section properties.

(6) C face and back must be natural unrepaired; if repaired, use stress level 2 (S-2).

EFFECTIVE SECTION PROPERTIES FOR PLYWOOD

TABLE 1: FACE PLIES OF DIFFERENT SPECIES GROUP FROM INNER PLIES
(INCLUDES ALL PRODUCT STANDARD GRADES EXCEPT THOSE NOTED IN TABLE 2.)

Nominal Thickness (in.)	Approximate Weight (psf)	t_s Effective Thickness For Shear (in.)	Stress Applied Parallel to Face Grain				Stress Applied Perpendicular to Face Grain			
			A Area (in.²/ft)	I Moment of Inertia (in.⁴/ft)	KS Effective Section Modulus (in.³/ft)	lb/Q Rolling Shear Constant (in.²/ft)	A Area (in.²/ft)	I Moment of Inertia (in.⁴/ft)	KS Effective Section Modulus (in.³/ft)	lb/Q Rolling Shear Constant (in.²/ft)
Unsanded Panels										
5/16-U	1.0	0.268	1.491	0.022	0.112	2.569	0.660	0.001	0.023	4.497
3/8-U	1.1	0.278	1.866	0.039	0.152	3.110	0.799	0.002	0.033	5.444
15/32- & 1/2-U	1.5	0.298	2.292	0.067	0.213	3.921	1.007	0.004	0.056	2.450
19/32- & 5/8-U	1.8	0.319	2.330	0.121	0.379	5.004	1.285	0.010	0.091	3.106
23/32- & 3/4-U	2.2	0.445	3.247	0.234	0.496	6.455	1.563	0.036	0.232	3.613
7/8-U	2.6	0.607	3.509	0.340	0.678	7.175	1.950	0.112	0.397	4.791
1-U	3.0	0.842	3.916	0.493	0.859	9.244	3.145	0.210	0.660	6.533
1-1/8-U	3.3	0.859	4.725	0.676	1.047	9.960	3.079	0.288	0.768	7.931
Sanded Panels										
1/4-S	0.8	0.267	0.996	0.008	0.059	2.010	0.348	0.001	0.009	2.019
11/32-S	1.0	0.284	0.996	0.019	0.093	2.765	0.417	0.001	0.016	2.589
3/8-S	1.1	0.288	1.307	0.027	0.125	3.088	0.626	0.002	0.023	3.510
15/32-S	1.4	0.421	1.947	0.066	0.214	4.113	1.204	0.006	0.067	2.434
1/2-S	1.5	0.425	1.947	0.077	0.236	4.466	1.240	0.009	0.087	2.752
19/32-S	1.7	0.546	2.423	0.115	0.315	5.471	1.389	0.021	0.137	2.861
5/8-S	1.8	0.550	2.475	0.129	0.339	5.824	1.528	0.027	0.164	3.119
23/32-S	2.1	0.563	2.822	0.179	0.389	6.581	1.737	0.050	0.231	3.818
3/4-S	2.2	0.568	2.884	0.197	0.412	6.762	2.081	0.063	0.285	4.079
7/8-S	2.6	0.586	2.942	0.278	0.515	8.050	2.651	0.104	0.394	5.078
1-S	3.0	0.817	3.721	0.423	0.664	8.882	3.163	0.185	0.591	7.031
1-1/8-S	3.3	0.836	3.854	0.548	0.820	9.883	3.180	0.271	0.744	8.428
Touch-Sanded Panels										
1/2-T	1.5	0.342	2.698	0.083	0.271	4.252	1.159	0.006	0.061	2.746
19/32- & 5/8-T	1.8	0.408	2.354	0.123	0.327	5.346	1.555	0.016	0.135	3.220
23/32- & 3/4-T	2.2	0.439	2.715	0.193	0.398	6.589	1.622	0.032	0.219	3.635
1-1/8-T	3.3	0.839	4.548	0.633	0.977	11.258	4.067	0.272	0.743	8.535

EFFECTIVE SECTION PROPERTIES FOR PLYWOOD

TABLE 2: STRUCTURAL I AND MARINE

Nominal Thickness (in.)	Approximate Weight (psf)	t_s Effective Thickness For Shear (in.)	Stress Applied Parallel to Face Grain				Stress Applied Perpendicular to Face Grain			
			A Area (in.²/ft)	I Moment of Inertia (in.⁴/ft)	KS Effective Section Modulus (in.³/ft)	lb/Q Rolling Shear Constant (in.²/ft)	A Area (in.²/ft)	I Moment of Inertia (in.⁴/ft)	KS Effective Section Modulus (in.³/ft)	lb/Q Rolling Shear Constant (in.²/ft)
Unsanded Panels										
5/16-U	1.0	0.356	1.619	0.022	0.126	2.567	1.188	0.002	0.029	6.037
3/8-U	1.1	0.371	2.226	0.041	0.195	3.107	1.438	0.003	0.043	7.307
15/32- & 1/2-U	1.5	0.535	2.719	0.074	0.279	4.157	2.175	0.012	0.116	2.408
19/32- & 5/8-U	1.8	0.707	3.464	0.154	0.437	5.685	2.742	0.045	0.240	3.072
23/32- & 3/4-U	2.2	0.739	4.219	0.236	0.549	6.148	2.813	0.064	0.299	3.540
7/8-U	2.6	0.776	4.388	0.346	0.690	6.948	3.510	0.131	0.457	4.722
1-U	3.0	1.088	5.200	0.529	0.922	8.512	5.661	0.270	0.781	6.435
1-1/8-U	3.3	1.118	6.654	0.751	1.164	9.061	5.542	0.408	0.999	7.833
Sanded Panels										
1/4-S	0.8	0.342	1.280	0.012	0.083	2.009	0.626	0.001	0.013	2.723
11/32-S	1.0	0.365	1.280	0.026	0.133	2.764	0.751	0.001	0.023	3.397
3/8-S	1.1	0.373	1.680	0.038	0.177	3.086	1.126	0.002	0.033	4.927
15/32-S	1.4	0.537	1.947	0.067	0.246	4.107	2.168	0.009	0.093	2.405
1/2-S	1.5	0.545	1.947	0.078	0.271	4.457	2.232	0.014	0.123	2.725
19/32-S	1.7	0.709	3.018	0.116	0.338	5.566	2.501	0.034	0.199	2.811
5/8-S	1.8	0.717	3.112	0.131	0.361	5.934	2.751	0.045	0.238	3.073
23/32-S	2.1	0.741	3.735	0.183	0.439	6.109	3.126	0.085	0.338	3.780
3/4-S	2.2	0.748	3.848	0.202	0.464	6.189	3.745	0.108	0.418	4.047
7/8-S	2.6	0.778	3.952	0.288	0.569	7.539	4.772	0.179	0.579	5.046
1-S	3.0	1.091	5.215	0.479	0.827	7.978	5.693	0.321	0.870	6.981
1-1/8-S	3.3	1.121	5.593	0.623	0.955	8.841	5.724	0.474	1.098	8.377
Touch-Sanded Panels										
1/2-T	1.5	0.543	2.698	0.084	0.282	4.511	2.486	0.020	0.162	2.720
19/32- & 5/8-T	1.8	0.707	3.127	0.124	0.349	5.500	2.799	0.050	0.259	3.183
23/32- & 3/4-T	2.2	0.739	4.059	0.201	0.469	6.592	3.625	0.078	0.350	3.596

ALLOWABLE STRESSES FOR PLYWOOD

TABLE 3: ALLOWABLE STRESSES FOR PLYWOOD (psi)

conforming to Voluntary Product Standard PS 1-95 for Construction and Industrial Plywood. Stresses are based on normal duration of load, and on common structural applications where panels are 24" or greater in width.

Type of Stress		Species Group of Face Ply	Grade Stress Level[1]				
			S-1		S-2		S-3
			Wet	Dry	Wet	Dry	Dry Only
EXTREME FIBER STRESS IN BENDING (F_b)	F_b & F_t	1	1430	2000	1190	1650	1650
TENSION IN PLANE OF PLIES (F_t)		2, 3	980	1400	820	1200	1200
Face Grain Parallel or Perpendicular to Span F_t (At 45° to Face Grain Use 1/6 F_t)		4	940	1330	780	1110	1110
COMPRESSION IN PLANE OF PLIES	F_c	1	970	1640	900	1540	1540
		2	730	1200	680	1100	1100
Parallel or Perpendicular to Face Grain		3	610	1060	580	990	990
(At 45° to Face Grain Use 1/3 F_c)		4	610	1000	580	950	950
SHEAR THROUGH THE THICKNESS[3]	F_v	1	155	190	155	190	160
Parallel or Perpendicular to Face Grain		2, 3	120	140	120	140	120
(At 45° to Face Grain Use 2 F_v)		4	110	130	110	130	115
ROLLING SHEAR (IN THE PLANE OF PLIES)	F_s	Marine & Structural I	63	75	63	75	—
Parallel or Perpendicular to Face Grain (At 45° to Face Grain Use 1-1/3 F_s)		All Other[2]	44	53	44	53	48
MODULUS OF RIGIDITY (OR SHEAR MODULUS)	G	1	70,000	90,000	70,000	90,000	82,000
		2	60,000	75,000	60,000	75,000	68,000
Shear in Plane Perpendicular to Plies		3	50,000	60,000	50,000	60,000	55,000
(through the thickness) (At 45° to Face Grain Use 4G)		4	45,000	50,000	45,000	50,000	45,000
BEARING (ON FACE)	$F_{c\perp}$	1	210	340	210	340	340
Perpendicular to Plane of Plies		2, 3	135	210	135	210	210
		4	105	160	105	160	160
MODULUS OF ELASTICITY IN BENDING IN PLANE OF PLIES	E	1	1,500,000	1,800,000	1,500,000	1,800,000	1,800,000
		2	1,300,000	1,500,000	1,300,000	1,500,000	1,500,000
		3	1,100,000	1,200,000	1,100,000	1,200,000	1,200,000
Face Grain Parallel or Perpendicular to Span		4	900,000	1,000,000	900,000	1,000,000	1,000,000

(1) See pages 380 through 383 for Guide.
To qualify for stress level S-1, gluelines must be exterior and only veneer grades N, A, and C (natural, not repaired) are allowed in either face or back.
For stress level S-2, gluelines must be exterior and veneer grade B, C-Plugged and D are allowed on the face or back. Stress level S-3 includes all panels with interior or intermediate (IMG) gluelines.

(2) Reduce stresses 25% for 3-layer (4- or 5-ply) panels over 5/8" thick. Such layups are possible under PS 1-95 for APA RATED SHEATHING, APA RATED STURD-I-FLOOR, UNDERLAYMENT, C-C Plugged and C-D Plugged grades over 5/8" through 3/4" thick.

(3) Shear-through-the-thickness stresses for MARINE and SPECIAL EXTERIOR grades may be increased 33%. See Section 3.8.1 for conditions under which stresses for other grades may be increased.

Table 3.6.2 A and y' for Computing Qs*

| Plywood Thickness (in.) | STRUCTURAL I Grades | | | | All Other Panels | | | |
| | Face Grain ‖ to Stringers | | Face Grain ⊥ to Stringers | | Face Grain ‖ to Stringers | | Face Grain ⊥ to Stringers | |
	Area (in.²)	y' (in.)	Area (in.²)	y' (in.)	Area (in.²)	y' (in.)	Area (in.²)	y' (in.)
Unsanded Panels								
5/16	3.22	0.0335	4.75	0.149	3.00	0.0375	2.64	0.149
3/8	4.46	0.0465	5.75	0.180	3.72	0.0465	3.19	0.180
15/32, 1/2	5.42	0.0565	8.70	0.227	4.60	0.0575	4.03	0.227
19/32, 5/8	9.22	0.176	11.0	0.305	4.64	0.0580	5.14	0.289
23/32, 3/4	11.2	0.176	11.3	0.352	5.57	0.0580	6.25	0.352
Sanded Panels								
1/4	2.54	0.0265	2.51	0.121	2.54	0.0265	1.39	0.121
11/32	2.54	0.0265	3.00	0.168	2.54	0.0265	1.67	0.168
3/8	3.36	0.0350	4.50	0.184	3.36	0.0350	2.50	0.184
15/32	3.89	0.0405	9.01	0.231	3.89	0.0405	5.00	0.231
1/2	3.89	0.0405	10.1	0.246	3.89	0.0405	5.64	0.246
19/32	8.69	0.193	10.0	0.293	6.32	0.156	5.56	0.293
5/8	9.07	0.207	11.0	0.309	6.53	0.151	6.11	0.309
23/32	11.6	0.262	12.5	0.356	7.92	0.220	6.95	0.356
3/4	12.1	0.278	15.1	0.371	8.19	0.233	8.32	0.371
Touch-Sanded Panels								
1/2	4.56	0.0475	9.95	0.226	4.56	0.0475	4.64	0.224
19/32, 5/8	7.92	0.174	11.2	0.279	4.38	0.0685	6.24	0.279
23/32, 3/4	10.4	0.177	14.5	0.345	5.06	0.0790	8.06	0.345
1-1/8 (2-4-1)	—	—	—	—	12.5	0.354	16.2	0.542

*Area based on 48"-wide panel. For other widths, use a proportionate area.

Table 3.2.2 Basic Spacing, b, For Various Plywood Thicknesses

Plywood Thickness (in.)	Basic Spacing, b (inches)*			
	Face Grain ‖ to Stringers		Face Grain ⊥ to Stringers	
	3, 4, 5-ply 3-layer	5, 6-ply 5-layer	3, 4, 5-ply 3-layer	5, 6-ply 5-layer
Unsanded Panels				
5/16	12	–	13	–
3/8	14	–	17	–
15/32, 1/2	18	22	21	27
19/32, 5/8	23	28	22	31
23/32, 3/4	31	32	29	31
Sanded Panels				
1/4	9	–	10	–
11/32	12	–	13	–
3/8	19	–	15	–
15/32	19	22	18	24
1/2	20	24	19	26
19/32	–	27	–	28
5/8	–	28	–	30
23/32	–	33	–	34
3/4	–	35	–	36
Touch-Sanded Panels				
1/2	19	24	21	27
19/32, 5/8	26	28	24	29
23/32, 3/4	32	34	28	36
1-1/8 (2-4-1)	–	55	–	55

*Use value in boldface for plywood thickness and orientation unless another layup is specified and available.

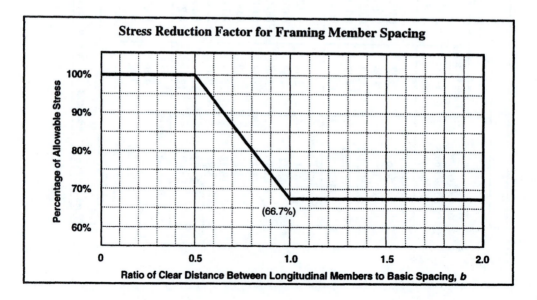

TABLE 5.6.1.2: BUTT JOINTS – TENSION OR FLEXURE

Plywood Thickness (inches)	Length of Splice Plate (inches)	Maximum Stress (psi)			
		All STRUC. I Grades	Group 1	Group 2 and Group 3	Group 4
1/4	6				
5/16	8				
11/32 &		1500	1200	1000	900
3/8 Sanded	10				
3/8 Unsanded	12				
15/32 & 1/2	14	1500	1000	950	900
19/32, 5/8 23/32 & 3/4	16	1200	800	750	700

5.6.1.2 Butt Joints – When backed with a glued plywood splice plate on one side having its grain perpendicular to the joint, of a grade and species group equal to the plywood spliced, and being no thinner than the panel itself, joints may be considered capable of transmitting tensile or flexural stresses as in Table 5.6.1.2 (normal duration of loading). Strength may be taken proportionately for shorter splice-plate lengths.

3.1.2 Butt joints in plywood skins shall be backed with plywood splice plates centered over the joint and glued over their full contact area. Splice plates shall be at least equal in thickness to the skin, except that minimum thickness shall be 15/32" if nail-glued. Minimum splice plate lengths, face grain parallel with that of the skin, shall be as follows (unless otherwise called for in the design):

Skin Thickness	Splice Plate Length
1/4"	6"
5/16"	8"
3/8" sanded	10"
3/8" unsanded	12"
15/32" & 1/2"	14"
19/32" - 3/4"	16"

3.3.2 Plywood skins shall be glued to framing members over their full contact area, using means that will provide close contact and substantially uniform pressure. Where clamping or other positive mechanical means are used, the pressure on the net framing area shall be sufficient to provide adequate contact and ensure good glue bond (100 to 150 psi on the net glued area is recommended), and shall be uniformly distributed by caul plates, beams, or other effective means. In place of mechanical pressure methods, nail-gluing may be used. Nail sizes and spacings shown in the following schedule are suggested as a guide:

Nails shall be at least 4d for plywood up to 3/8" thick, 6d for 1/2" to 7/8" plywood, 8d for 1" to 1-1/8" plywood. They shall be spaced not to exceed 3" along the framing members for plywood through 3/8", or 4" for plywood 15/32" and thicker, using one line for lumber 2" wide or less, and two lines for lumber more than 2" and up to 4" wide.

Application of pressure or nailing may start at any point, but shall progress to an end or ends. **In any case, it shall be the responsibility of the fabricator to produce a continuous glue bond which meets or exceeds applicable specifications.**

SAMPLE STRESSED SKIN PANELS

All of the following stressed-skin panels are 4' wide with a top skin of 5/8" Sturd-I-Floor (Exposure 1, 20" o.c.), a bottom skin of 3/8" Sheathing (20/0, Exposure 1), and 2x stringers on 1' centers. All allowable loads are given in psf.

Total panel height	span	w_Δ	$w_\Delta(ts)$	w_{bb}	w_{bt}	w_p	w_s	w_v
2.5"	4'	264	✓	223	246	150	**144**	162
	6'	87	✓	99	110	**67**	96	108
	8'	**38**	✓	56	62	**38**	72	81
3.5"	8'	89	✓	93	104	**64**	122	116
	10'	47	✓	60	67	**41**	97	93
	12'	**28**	✓	42	46	**28**	81	77
4.5"	4'	1020	✓	546	614	374	357	**299**
	8'	165	✓	137	154	**94**	178	149
	12'	52	✓	61	68	**42**	119	100
5.5"	8'	267	✓	185	209	**128**	242	181
	12'	85	✓	82	93	**57**	162	121
	16'	37	✓	46	52	**32**	121	90
6.5"	12'	128	✓	107	121	**74**	209	142
	16'	56	✓	60	68	**41**	157	106
7.5"	14'	118	✓	98	111	**68**	224	139
	16'	80	✓	75	85	**52**	196	122
	18'	57	✓	60	67	**41**	174	108
8.5"	16'	110	✓	92	104	**63**	238	137
	20'	57	✓	59	66	**40**	191	110
10.5"	16'	187	✓	130	146	**89**	335	168
	20'	98	✓	83	93	**57**	268	134

Notes:
- Stringers are Doug-Fir South, Construction grade.
- Splice plates are assumed to be in the center of the span.
- Limiting loads are in bold typeface.
- A ✓ character indicates that the top-skin deflection is adequate for the allowable load in bold typeface.
- Note that the total height is given; the stringers are 1" less than the total height.
- All spans are simple spans.

G

Appendix G: Useful Information

This Appendix contains the following tables from various sources:

BH is *The Backstage Handbook, 2nd Edition.*
UBC is the *Uniform Building Code.*
WRUM is the *Wire Rope User's Manual.*

AVERAGE WEIGHTS OF MATERIALS - Per Cubic Foot (lb/ft³)

Material	Lb/Ft^3	Material	Lb/Ft^3
Alcohol	50	Salt, common	48
Aluminum	169	Sand, dry	100
Asbestos	150	Sand, wet	125
Brick, common	112	Silver	650-657
Brick, fire	143	Slate	175
Brick, hard	125	Snow (see water)	
Brickwork, in mortar	100	Soapstone	168
Brickwork, in cement	112	Stainless steel	510
Cement, Portland (set)	193	Steel	489
Chalk	143	Stone, plain	144
Charcoal	25	Sulphur	125
Coal, anthracite	94	Tar	64-75
Coal, bituminous	81	Tile	112
Concrete (average density)	137	Tin	455
Copper	555	Turpentine	54
Cork	15	Vermiculite	25-60
Earth, dry	65-88	Water	62.5
Earth, moist	95-135	Ice	56
Emery	249	Snow, fresh	5-12
Gasoline	44	Snow, wet, compact	15-20
Glass, common	150-175	Zinc	443
Glass, flint	180-370		
Gold	1204		
Granite	165-172		
Gravel, damp,	82-125		
Gravel, dry	90-145	**Gases**	
Gypsum	145-150		
Ice	56	Acetylene	.0732
Iron, cast gray	439-445	Air	.0807
Iron, wrought	487-493	Ammonia	.04813
Iron slag	168	Butane, iso	.1669
Ivory	114-120	Carbon dioxide	.123
Kerosene	50	Carbon monoxide	.07806
Lead	687	Chlorine	.2006
Leather	59	Ether vapor	.2088
Lime	53-75	Ethylene	.07868
Limestone	162	Helium	.01114
Magnesium	109	Hydrogen	.00561
Marble	160-177	Mercury vapor	.56013
Masonry	150	Methane	.04475
Mica	175	Nitrogen	.07807
Mortar	94	Oxygen	.08921
Nickel	549	Propane	.1254
Paper	58	Sulfur dioxide	.1827
Paraffin	54-57	Water vapor	.05028
Phenolic plastic, cast	79-82		
Platinum	1334		
Plaster of Paris	112		
Plastic, styrene	66		
Plastic, vinyl	87		
Polyethylene	57		
Quartz	162		

AVERAGE WEIGHTS OF MATERIALS - Per Square Foot (lb/ft²)

Material	Lb./Ft.²
Concrete	
Reinforced (per 1" of thickness):	
stone	12.5
slag	11.5
light-weight	6-10
Plain (per 1" of thickness):	
stone	12
slag	11
light-weight	3-9
Glass	
Sheet:	
1/8"	1.60
1/4"	3.25
Wire: 1/4"	3.50
Steel	
Mild steel plates:	
3/16"	7.65
1/4"	10.21
5/16"	12.75
Walls and Partitions	
Brick (per 4" of thickness)	35
Concrete block:	
stone & gravel aggregate:	
4" thick	34
6" thick	50
8" thick	58
12" thick	90
light-weight aggregate:	
4" thick	22
6" thick	31
8" thick	38
12" thick	55
Glass block, 4" thick	18
Gypsum board, 1/2" thick	2
Metal lath	0.5
Metal studs, w/ lath & plaster	18
Plaster (per 1" of thickness):	
cement	10
gypsum	5
Plywood:	
1/8"	.42
1/4"	.80
1/2"	1.52
3/4"	2.25
1"	3.00

Material	Lb./Ft.²
Walls and Partitions (continued)	
Stone:	
granite, 4"	59
limestone, 6"	55
marble, 1"	13
sandstone, 4"	49
slate, 1"	14
Tile:	
ceramic mosaic, 1/4"	2.5
structural clay, 4"	18
6"	28
10"	40
Wood studs:	
2 x 4 w/ lath & plaster	16
Flooring	
Marble, 1"	13
Terrazzo, 1"	13
Tile, 3/4" ceramic or quarry	10
Wood:	
hardwood, 25/32"	4
softwood, 3/4"	2.5
woodblock, 3"	15
Vinyl tile, 1/8"	1.33
Ceilings	
Acoustical fiber tile, 3/4"	1
Acoustic plaster:	
on gypsum, lath base	10
Channel suspended system	1
Roofing	
Built-up (5-ply felt & gravel)	6
Corrugated iron (galvanized)	1.5
Fiberglass	0.5
Lead, 1/8"	8
Shingles:	
asphalt	3
asbestos cement	3
slate, 1/4"	10
wood	2
Tile:	
cement tile	16
clay tile	14

AVERAGE WEIGHTS OF SHEET MATERIALS

	-------Pounds per-------				-------Pounds per-------	
	Sq. Ft.	4' x 8' Sheet			Sq. Ft.	4' x 8' Sheet
Plywood				**Particle Board / Press Board**		
$^1/_8$"	.42	13		$^1/_4$"	.75	24
$^1/_4$"	.80	26		$^1/_2$"	1.94	62
$^1/_2$"	1.52	49		$^3/_4$"	2.99	96
$^3/_4$"	2.20	70				
1"	3.00	96		**Homosote / Soundboard**		
				$^1/_2$"	1.00	32
Masonite						
$^1/_8$"	.59	19		**Acrylic**		
$^1/_4$"	1.19	38		$^1/_8$"	.74	24
				$^3/_{16}$"	1.11	36
Gypsum				$^1/_4$"	1.48	48
$^3/_8$"	1.5	48		$^3/_8$"	2.22	71
$^1/_2$"	2	64		$^1/_2$"	2.96	95

AVERAGE WEIGHTS OF BOARD LUMBER

	Per 1' *	Per 8'	Per 12'	Per 16'
1 x 3, pine	0.326	2.60	3.91	5.21
1 x 6, pine	0.716	5.73	8.59	11.46
1 x 12, pine	1.465	11.72	17.58	23.44
$^5/_4$ x 3, pine	0.543	4.34	6.51	8.68
$^5/_4$ x 6, pine	1.194	9.55	14.32	19.10
$^5/_4$ x 12, pine	2.441	19.53	29.30	39.06
2 x 4, fir	0.911	7.29	10.94	14.58
4 x 4, fir	2.130	17.01	25.52	34.03

* At 25 lbs. per cubic foot (.1736 lbs. per cubic inch).

AVERAGE WEIGHTS OF LIGHTING INSTRUMENTS

Lighting Instruments		"Hanging weight" = 25 lbs.
6" fresnel	6 - 8 lbs	(Average weight per instrument, with cable,
8" fresnel	13 - 16 lbs	on a 60' batten.)
6" x 9" ERS	12 - 16 lbs	

AVERAGE WEIGHTS OF BEVERAGES

6-pack, cans	5 lbs	Note: The beer dispenser known as a "keg" is
6-pack, bottles	8.6 lbs	actually a "half-keg" and there are approx. 250
keg	140 lbs	glasses in a half-keg. There is also half size keg
		called a "quarter-keg."

Reproduced from the 3rd edition of *The Backstage Handbook* with permission of Broadway Press.

RECOMMENDED DESIGN LOADS, TABLES 23-A AND 23-B (ABRIDGED)

UNIFORM AND CONCENTRATED LOADS

Use or Occupancy		Minimum Design Loads	
Category	Description	uniform load, psf	concentrated load, plf
Access floor systems	Office use	50	2,000
	Computer use	100	2,000
Armories		150	0
Assembly areas[1] and auditoriums and balconies therewith	Fixed seating areas	50	0
	Movable seating and other areas	100	0
	Stage areas and enclosed platforms	125	0
Cornices and marquees and residential balconies		60	0
Garages	General storage and/or repair	100	
Hospitals	Wards and rooms	40	1,000
Offices		50	2,000
Residential[2]		40	0
Reviewing stands, grandstands and bleachers		100	0
Schools	Classrooms	40	1,000
Storage	Light	125	
	Heavy	250	

SPECIAL LOADS

Category	Description	Vertical load	Lateral load
Grandstands, reviewing stands and bleachers (live load)	Seats and footboards	120 plf	
Stage accessories (live load)	Gridirons and fly galleries	75 plf	
	Loft block wells [3]	250 plf	250 plf
	Head block wells and sheave beams [3]	250 plf	250 plf
Ceiling framing (live load)	Over stages	20 psf	
	All other uses	10 psf	
Balcony railings, guard rails, and handrails	Exit facilities serving an occupant load greater than 50		50 plf [4]
	Other		20 plf [4]

1. Assembly areas include such occupancies as dance halls, drill rooms, gymnasiums, playgrounds, plazas, terraces, and similar occupancies which are generally accessible to the public.
2. Residential occupancies include private dwellings, apartments, and hotel guest rooms.
3. Head block wells and sheave beams shall be designed for all loft block well loads tributary thereto. Sheave blocks shall be designed with a factor of safety of five.
4. A load per lineal foot to be applied horizontally at right angles to the top rail.

Reproduced from the 1997 edition of the *Uniform Building Code* with the permission of the publisher, the International Conference of Building Officials.

NOMINAL STRENGTHS OF WIRE ROPE

| Nominal Diameter | Approximate mass lbs per 100' | | Nominal Strength, lbs | | | |
| | 7x7 | 7x19 | Galvanized | | Corrosion Resistant | |
			7x7	7x19	7x7	7x19
1/32	0.16*		110*		110*	
3/64	0.42		270		270	
1/16	0.75	0.75	480	480	480	480
5/64	1.1		650		650	
3/32	1.6	1.7	920	1,000	920	920
7/64	2.2		1,260		1,260	
1/8	2.8	2.9	1,700	2,000	1,700	1,760
5/32	4.3	4.5	2,600	2,800	2,400	2,400
3/16	6.2	6.5	3,700	4,200	3,700	3,700
7/32	8.3	8.6	4,800	5,600	4,800	5,000
1/4	10.3	11.0	6,100	7,000	6,100	6,400
9/32	13.4	13.9	7,600	8,000	7,600	7,800
5/16	16.7	17.3	9,200	9,800	9,000	9,000
11/32	20.1	20.7	11,100	12,500	10,500	
3/8	23.6	24.3	13,100	14,400	12,000	12,000

*3x7 construction

Reproduced from the *Wire Rope Users Manual* with permission of the Wire Rope Technical Board.

H

Appendix H: Nomenclature

UNITS

in is inch(es)

ft is foot or feet

ft^2 is feet squared

in^2 is inches squared

in^3 is inches cubed

kip is a thousand pounds

ksi is kips per square inch

lb(s) is pound(s)

pli is pounds per lineal inch

plf is pounds per lineal foot

psf is pounds per square foot

psi is pounds per square inch

sf is square feet

GENERAL DESIGN VARIABLES

A is cross-sectional area of the member, in^2

b is the breadth of a beam or column or the thickness of a plane, in

c is the extreme fiber distance, in

d is the diameter (also D), in

d is the depth of a beam or column, in

Δ_{max} is the maximum allowable deflection, in

e is the total deformation, in

e is the eccentricity of a load, in

E is the modulus of Elasticity (Young's Modulus), psi or ksi

f is an actual stress, psi or ksi

F is an allowable stress, psi or ksi

F_b is the allowable bending stress, psi or ksi

f_b is the actual bending stress, psi or ksi

f_c is the actual compressive stress, psi or ksi

F_t is the allowable axial tensile stress, ksi or psi

f_t is the actual tensile stress, psi or ksi

F_v is the allowable shear stress, psi or ksi

f_v is the actual shear stress, psi or ksi

I is the moment of inertia, in^4

l/r is the slenderness ratio for column design

l is the length of a column or span, in or ft

M_{max} is the maximum bending moment, inlb, ftlb, or kip-ft

P is a point load, lb(s) or kips

r is the radius, in

r is the radius of gyration, in

R_1 is the leftmost reaction, lb(s) or kips

R_2 is the reaction to the right of R_1, lb(s) or kips

s is the strain, inches/inch

S is the section modulus of the appropriate axis, in^3

t is a thickness, in

V is the actual vertical shear, lb

V_{max} is the maximum vertical shear, lb(s)

w is a uniformly distributed load per unit of length, pli, plf, kli, klf

W is a total evenly distributed load, lb(s) or kips

z is a perpendicular distance, in

SAWN LUMBER DESIGN VARIABLES

a is the eccentricity of a load on a column, in

C_D is the load duration factor

C_F is the size factor

C_{fu} is the flat use factor

C_L is the beam stability factor

C_p is the column stability factor

C_r is the repetive member factor

d_n is the depth of the notched member, in

f_{bx} is the actual bending stress in the x-x axis, psi

f_{by} is the actual bending stress in the y-y axis, psi

F_b' is the adjusted allowable bending stress, psi

F_{bx}' is the adjusted allowable bending stress in the x-x axis, psi

F_{by}' is the adjusted allowable bending stress in the y-y axis, psi

F_b^* is an intermediate base allowable bending stress, psi

F_{bE} is the critical buckling design value for bending, psi

F_c is the base allowable compressive design value parallel to grain, psi

F_c^* is an intermediate allowable compressive design value, psi

F_c' is the adjusted allowable compressive design value, psi

F_{cE} is the critical buckling design value for compression, psi

F_{cr} is the maximum allowable compressive stress, psi

F_t' is the adjusted allowable tensile design value, psi

F_v is the base allowable design value for shear parallel to grain, psi

F_v' is the adjusted allowable shear design value, psi

K_{bE} is the Euler buckling coefficient for beams (0.438 for sawn lumber)

K_e is the buckling length coefficient

l_e is the effective buckling length, in

l_p is the vertical distance from the bracket to the farthest end of the column, in. $l=l_p$ for eccentric loads at the top of the column.

l/d is the slenderness ratio for sawn lumber columns (≤ 50)

P_{cr} is the critical buckling load, lbs

P_s is the assumed horizontal side load acting at the center of the column, lbs

Q is the statical moment of area above or below the plane at which the horizontal shear is being computed, in^3

STEEL DESIGN VARIABLES

F_a is the allowable axial compressive stress, ksi or psi

f_a is the actual axial compressive stress, ksi or psi

f_a/F_a is the amplication factor for steel columns with bending

F_e' is the Euler buckling stress in the plane of bending for the corresponding Kl/r, psi

F_u is the ultimate stress, ksi or psi

F_y is the minimum yield stress, ksi or psi

h is the clear distance between flanges of an I-beam or channel, in

Kl/r is the slenderness ratio for steel columns (≤ 200)

L_c is the maximum unbraced length of the compression flange of an I-beam at which the allowable bending stress may be taken at $0.66F_y$, ft

l_u is the unbraced length of a column, in or ft

L_u is the maximum unbraced length of the compression flange of an I-beam for which the allowable bending stress may be taken at $0.60F_y$, ft

M_r is the beam resisting moment of an I-beam, kip-ft, where $F_b = 0.66F_y$

Q is a reduction factor for single angles

S_b is the section modulus of the plane of bending, in^3

t_f is the flange thickness of an I-beam or channel, in

t_w is the web thickness of an I-beam or channel, in

PLYWOOD DESIGN VARIABLES

C is the deflection criteria for a stressed skin panel (240 or 360)

c is the appropriate extreme fiber distance to the neutral axis for deflection, in

Δ_{all} is the recommended allowable bending deflection, $l/240$, in

Δ_b is the actual bending deflection, in

Δ_{ts} is the actual deflection of the top skin in a stressed skin panel, in

d_s is the distance from the neutral axis to the center of the effective area outside of the critical plane, in

E_L is the adjusted modulus of elasticity for stressed skin calculations, psi

$E_L I_g$ is the gross stiffness factor, psi per 4' width

$E_L I_n$ is the net stiffness factor, psi per 4' width

F is the allowable tensile stress for the tension splice plate for a stressed-skin panel, psi

F_c' is the adjusted allowable compressive stress of the top skin for a stressed-skin panel, psi

F_s is the allowable rolling shear stress, psi

F_t' is the adjusted allowable tensile stress of the bottom skin for a stressed-skin panel, psi

G is the modulus of rigidity, psi

Ib/Q is the rolling shear constant, in²/ft

$I_\perp$ is the moment of inertia (stress applied perpendicular to face grain), in⁴

KS is the effective section modulus, in³/ft

l is the center to center distance between supports, in

L is the span length of a stressed-skin panel, ft

Q_s is the statical moment for rolling shear, in³ per 4' panel

Q_v is the statical moment of horizontal shear, in³ per 4' width

ΣF_{st} is the sum of the glue widths multiplied by the applicable rolling shear stress, inlb

t is the thickness of the stringers, in

w is an evenly distributed load, psi, psf, ksi, or ksf

w_b is the allowable load based on bending stress, psf

w_{bt} is the allowable load due to top skin bending for a stressed-skin panel, psf

w_{bb} is the allowable load due to bottom skin bending for a stressed-skin panel, psf

w_Δ is the allowable load based on deflection, psf

$w_{\Delta(ts)}$ is the allowable load due to top skin deflection of a stressed-skin panel, psf

w_p is the allowable load due to tension in the splice plate for a stressed-skin panel, psf

w_s is the allowable load based on shear stress, psf

w_s is the allowable load based on rolling shear stresses for a stressed-skin panel, psf

w_v is the allowable load based on horizontal shear for a stressed-skin panel, psf

y' is the distance from the edge of the plywood to the center of the effective area for stressed-skin panel, in

Appendix I: Answers to Even Numbered Problems

CHAPTER 2 ANSWERS

2.1.2 Magnitude is 75#, direction is vertical; sense is up, positive.

2.1.4 Horizontal component is –26#, to the left. Vertical component is +148#, up.

2.1.6

2.1.8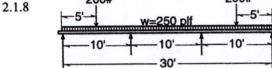

2.2.2 Magnitude is 360 ftlb; sense is counter-clockwise, negative.

2.2.4 Magnitude is 433 ftlb; sense is clockwise, positive.

2.2.6 Yes.

2.2.8 Yes.

2.3.2 $A_{req'd}$=0.2315 in²; 1"x1"x1/8" angle.

2.3.4 10,869.6 psi.

2.3.6 $A_{req'd}$=0.1395 in²; 3/8" Schedule 40 pipe.

2.3.8 1/4" rod: 1,413.6#; 5/16" rod: 2,208.8#; 3/8" rod: 3,180.8#.

2.4.2 E=10,000,000 psi; approximately three times stiffer

2.4.4 e=0.0884"; yes.

2.4.6 P=21,353#; no.

2.4.8 s=0.00303 in/in

CHAPTER 3 ANSWERS

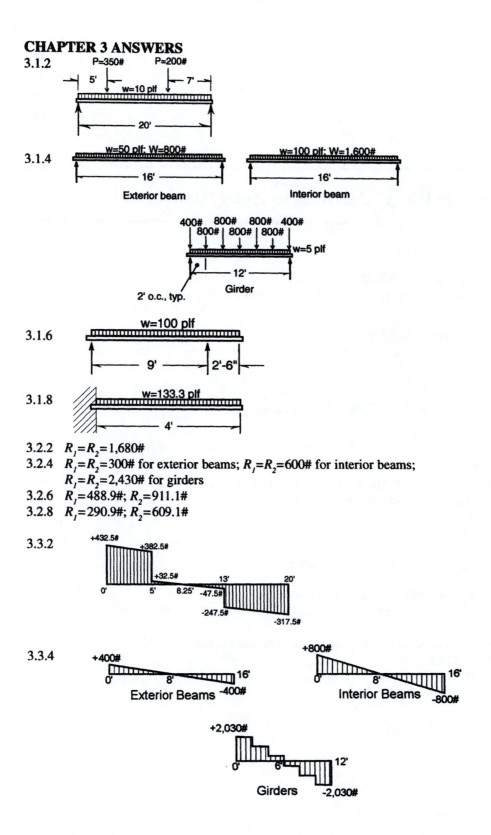

3.1.2

3.1.4

3.1.6

3.1.8

3.2.2 $R_1 = R_2 = 1,680\#$
3.2.4 $R_1 = R_2 = 300\#$ for exterior beams; $R_1 = R_2 = 600\#$ for interior beams;
       $R_1 = R_2 = 2,430\#$ for girders
3.2.6 $R_1 = 488.9\#$; $R_2 = 911.1\#$
3.2.8 $R_1 = 290.9\#$; $R_2 = 609.1\#$

3.3.2

3.3.4

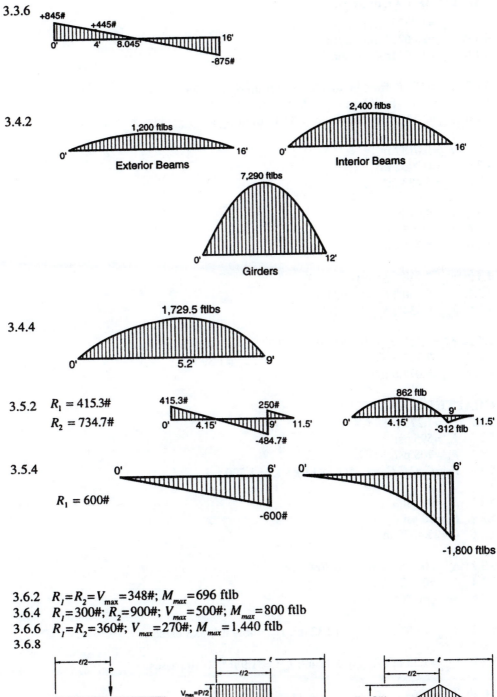

3.3.6

3.4.2

Exterior Beams

Interior Beams

Girders

3.4.4

3.5.2 $R_1 = 415.3\#$
        $R_2 = 734.7\#$

3.5.4

$R_1 = 600\#$

3.6.2 $R_1 = R_2 = V_{max} = 348\#;\ M_{max} = 696$ ftlb
3.6.4 $R_1 = 300\#;\ R_2 = 900\#;\ V_{max} = 500\#;\ M_{max} = 800$ ftlb
3.6.6 $R_1 = R_2 = 360\#;\ V_{max} = 270\#;\ M_{max} = 1{,}440$ ftlb
3.6.8

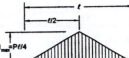

CHAPTER 4 ANSWERS

4.1.2 $c_{x-x}=1.4375"$ from top or bottom
4.1.4 $c_{y-y}=2.0625"$ from right
4.1.6 $c_{x-x}=1.92"$ from bottom

4.2.2 $c_{x-x}=2.007"$ from bottom; $c_{y-y}=2"$ from right or left
4.2.4 $c_{x-x}=1.64"$ from top; $c_{y-y}=1.55"$ from right
4.2.6 $c_{x-x}=3.32"$ from bottom; $c_{y-y}=3.51"$ from right

4.3.2 $I_{x-x}=0.0187$ in^4
4.3.4 $I_{x-x}=0.0952$ in^4
4.3.6 $I_{x-x}=5.483$ in^4

4.4.2 $I_{y-y}=8.97$ in^4
4.4.4 $I_{y-y}=151.5$ in^4
4.4.6 $I_{y-y}=4.995$ in^4

4.5.2 $r_{x-x}=0.236"$; $S_{x-x}=0.0386$ in^3
4.5.4 $r_{x-x}=0.360"$; $S_{x-x}=0.1904$ in^3
4.5.6 $r_{x-x}=0.834"$; $S_{x-x}=3.13$ in^3

4.6.2 $c_{x-x}=4.25"$; $I_{x-x}=215.62$ in^4; $r_{x-x}=3.23"$; $S_{x-x}=50.73$ in^3
        $c_{y-y}=2.75"$; $I_{y-y}=8.029$ in^4; $r_{y-y}=0.624"$; $S_{y-y}=1.89$ in^3
4.6.4 $M_R=9,075.6$ inlb

CHAPTER 5 ANSWERS

5.1.2 $F_b'=1,275$ psi
5.1.4 $F_b'=595$ psi
5.1.6 $F_b'=708$ psi
5.1.8 $F_b'=C_D C_f C_r C_{fu}=1.15(1.3)(1.0)(1.15)=1,590$ psi

5.2.2 $F_v'=90$ psi
5.2.4 $F_v'=80$ psi
5.2.6 $Q=25.4375$ in^3

5.3.2 $\Delta_{max}=0.255"+0.054"=0.309"$. Yes.
5.3.4 $\Delta_{max}=0.112"$. Yes.
5.3.6 $\approx\Delta_{max}=0.2066"$. Yes.

5.4.2 $S_{req'd}=17.99$ in^3; $A_{req'd}=12.32$ in^2; $I_{req'd}=46.9$ in^4; 3x8 passes.

5.5.2 $S_{req'd}=7.29$ in^3; $A_{req'd}=11.11$ in^2; $I_{req'd}=31.9$ in^4; 2x10 passes.

5.6.2 $V_{max}=296\#$
5.6.4   2" notch exceeds allowable depth of 1.8125"
5.6.6   Yes, beam selection does change.

5.7.2   7.56 pli=90.7 plf (bending failure rules).

CHAPTER 6 ANSWERS
6.1.2 d=3.84"; nominal dimension = 5x5 (4.5")
6.1.4 (a) F_{cE}=283.6 psi (b) F_{cE}=283.4 psi
6.1.6 F_{cE}=177 psi
6.1.8 F_{cE}=677 psi

6.2.2 7': P_{all}=7,592.8#; 14': P_{all}=2,166.2#
6.2.4 l/d=64, which exceeds maximum allowable slenderness ratio.

6.3.2 $A_{req'd}$=11.57 in²; 4x4 passes

6.4.2 P_{all}=3,526#
6.4.4 maximum l=38.49'; P_{all}=2,749.8#

CHAPTER 7 ANSWERS
7.1.2 3x3; interaction equation=0.706
7.1.4 2x8; interaction equation=0.993

7.2.2 2x4; interaction equation=0.648

7.3.2 2x4; interaction equation=0.512

7.4.2 3x8; interaction equation=0.842

CHAPTER 8 ANSWERS
8.1.2 C7x9.80; $I_{req'd}$=14.8 in⁴
8.1.4 (a) P_{all}=408.88#; (b) w_{all}=6.815 pli=81.8 plf

8.2.2 3"x4"x0.25", wt=10.5 plf; $S_{req'd}$=2.603 in³; $I_{req'd}$=6.203 in⁴

8.3.2 3"x0.49", wt=1.54 plf; $S_{req'd}$=0.194 in³; $I_{req'd}$=0.3898 in⁴

8.4.2 3"x2"x3/16", wt=3.07 plf; $I_{req'd}$=0.2632 in⁴;

8.5.2 S4x7.7, wt=7.7 plf; $S_{req'd}$=0.817 in³; $I_{req'd}$=3.343 in⁴

CHAPTER 9 ANSWERS
9.1.2 l=78.36"=6.53'
9.1.4 l=305.1"=29.175'
9.1.6 $F_{a,66}$=20.37 ksi
9.1.8 N.A.; kl/r=266.67

9.2.2 P_{all}=3,204#
9.2.4 P_{all}=20,261#
9.2.6 3"x3"x1/8" is lightest; 2.5"x2.5"x3/16" has least dimension; r_{min}=0.57"
9.2.8 0.875"x0.035"; r_{min}=0.18"

9.3.2 N.A.; *kl/r*=226.4
9.3.4 L4"x3-1/2"x1/4"; r_{min}=0.72"
9.3.6 L2-1/2"x2-1/2"x3/16"; r_{min}=0.48"

CHAPTER 10 ANSWERS

10.1.2 1-1/4" schedule 10; interaction equation=0.911
        1-1/4" schedule 40; interaction equation=0.750

10.2.2 3"x0.25"; interaction equation=0.97
10.2.4 W6x9; interaction equation=0.319

10.3.2 3"x3"x1/8"; interaction equation=0.611

10.4.2 2.5"x0.134"; interaction equation=0.9975

CHAPTER 11 ANSWERS

11.1.2 Compression AB=150#; Tension BC=212.1#
11.1.4 Compression AB=156.5#; Tension BC=234.8#
11.1.6 Compression BC=516#; Tension AB=420#

11.2.2 Compression AB=550#; Tension BC=641.7#
11.2.4 Compression AB=100#; Tension BC=133.33#
11.2.6 Compression AB=100#; Moment AB=75 ftlb; Tension BC=125#

11.3.2

Member	Stress	Member	Stress	Member	Stress
1-2; 8-9	2,929# c	2-4; 6-8	3,125# c	4-6	4,375# c
2-3; 7-8	1,953# t	3-4; 6-7	1,953# c	4-5; 5-6	0
1-3; 7-9	1,875# t	3-5; 5-7	4,375# t	R_1=R_2=2,250#	

11.4.2

Member	Stress	Member	Stress	Member	Stress
1-2	3,254# c	2-4	3,542# c	4-6	5,208# c
6-8	4,375# c	8-9	3,905# c	1-3	2,083# t
3-5	5,000# t	5-7	5,417# t	7-9	2,500# t
2-3	2,278# t	3-4	2,278# c	4-5	325# t
5-6	325# c	6-7	1,627# c	7-8	2,929# t

R_1=2,500# R_2=3,000#

11.5.2 Use 1"x0.065" square tube for all members; remember to bevel the internal diagonals at joints 2, 4, and 5 to achieve appropriate panel points.

11.6.2 T_{max}=T_{AC}=172#; T_{BC}=76#; S.F.=10; EFF=0.95; 1/8" cable
11.6.4 T_{max}=T_{AC}=200#; T_{BC}=134#; S.F.=10; EFF=0.8; 5/32" cable (7x7 construction)

11.7.2 T_{max}=160#; S.F.=10; EFF=0.95; 1/8" cable

CHAPTER 12 ANSWERS

12.1.2

				Stress Parallel	Stress Perpendicular
F_t, F_b	1,380 psi		A	2.354 in²/ft	1.555 in²/ft
F_c	1,265 psi		I	0.123 in⁴/ft	0.016 in⁴/ft
F_v	138 psi		KS	0.327 in³/ft	0.135 in³/ft
F_s	55.2 psi		Ib/Q	5.346 in²/ft	3.220 in²/ft
$F_{c\perp}$	210 psi				
E	1.5x10⁶ psi		$t_s = 0.408$ in		

12.1.4

				Stress Parallel	Stress Perpendicular
F_t, F_b	1,650 psi		A	2.226 in²/ft	1.438 in²/ft
F_c	1,540 psi		I	0.041 in⁴/ft	0.003 in⁴/ft
F_v	190 psi		KS	0.195 in³/ft	0.043 in³/ft
F_s	75 psi		Ib/Q	3.107 in²/ft	7.307 in²/ft
$F_{c\perp}$	340 psi				
E	1.8x10⁶ psi		$t_s = 0.371$ in		

12.2.2 16" span: w_b=89 psf; w_s=294 psf; w_Δ=**59 psf**
24" span: w_b=53 psf; w_s=196 psf; w_Δ=**18 psf**
48" span: w_b=13 psf; w_s=98 psf; w_Δ=**2 psf**

12.2.4 w_b=43 psf; w_s=157 psf; w_Δ=**19 psf**

12.3.2 $w_{\Delta(ts)}$=289 psf

12.6.2 w_p=82 psf

Works Cited

Ambrose, James. *Design of Building Trusses*. New York: John Wiley, 1994.

American Forest and Paper Association. *National Design Specification for Wood Construction, 1997 Edition*. Washington, D.C.: 1997.

- - -. *NDS Supplement for Wood Construction, 1997 Edition*. Washington, D.C.: 1997.

American Institute of Steel Construction. *Manual of Steel Construction, Allowable Stress Design*, 9th Edition. Chicago: 1989.

American Institute of Timber Construction. *Timber Construction Manual*, 4th Edition. New York: John Wiley, 1994.

American Society for Testing and Materials. *A53 - 97, Standard Specification for Pipe, Steel, Black and Hot-Dipped, Zinc-Coated, Welded and Seamless*. Philadelphia, PA: 1992.

- - -. *A500 - 93, Standard Specification for Cold-formed Welded and Seamless Carbon Steel Structural Tubing in Rounds and Shapes*. Philadelphia, PA: 1992.

- - -. *A513 - 92, Standard Specification for Electric-Resistance-Welded Carbon and Alloy Steel Mechanical Tubing*. Philadelphia, PA: 1992.

APA - The Engineered Wood Association. *Plywood Design Specification, January 1997*. Tacoma, WA: 1997.

- - -. *PDS Supplement 3, Design and Fabrication of Stressed Skin Panels*. Tacoma, WA: August 1990.

- - -. *Panel Handbook & Grade Glossary*. Tacoma, WA: March 1993.

Buck, William J. *Structural Design Workbook*. MFA Thesis of Yale University, 1984. New Haven, CT.

Carter, Paul. *Backstage Handbook*, 3rd Edition. Shelter Island, NY: Broadway Press, 1994.

Fitzgerald, Robert W. *Mechanics of Materials*, 2nd Edition. Reading, MA: Addison-Wesley, 1982.

Gillispie, Charles. *Dictionary of Scientific Biography, Volume XIV*. New York: Charles Scribner's Sons, 1976.

Hibbeler, Russell. *Structural Analysis*, 3rd Edition. Englewood Cliffs, NJ: Prentice Hall, 1995.

International Conference of Building Officials. *Uniform Building Code*. Whittier, CA: 1997.

Levy, Matthys and Mario Salvadori. *Why Buildings Fall Down*. New York: WW Norton, 1992.

McClintock, Robert D. *The Design of Scenic Wood Structures*. MFA Thesis of Yale University, 1982. New Haven, CT.

Oberg, Erik and F.D. Jones. *Machinery's Handbook*, 25th Edition. New York: The Industrial Press, 1992.

Parker, Harry and James Ambrose. *Simplified Engineering for Architects and Builders*, 8th Edition. New York: John Wiley, 1993.

Sperling, Abraham and Monroe Stuart, *Mathematics Made Simple*, 5th Edition. New York: Doubleday, 1991.

Steel Tube Institute of North America. *Handbook of Welded Carbon Steel Mechanical Tubing*. Mentor, OH: 1994.

Steel Tube Institute of North America. *Hollow Structural Sections, Dimensions and Section Properties*. Mentor, OH: 1997.

Wire Rope Technical Board. *Wire Rope Users Manual*, 3rd Edition. Woodstock, MD: 1993.

Index